Lexicon and Grammar: The English Syntacticon

For Jurgen –
how do the German are!
Joe.

D1717681

Studies in Generative Grammar 50

Editors

Henk van Riemsdijk
Harry van der Hulst
Jan Koster

Mouton de Gruyter
Berlin · New York

Lexicon and Grammar:
The English Syntacticon

by

Joseph E. Emonds

Mouton de Gruyter
Berlin · New York   2000

Mouton de Gruyter (formerly Mouton, The Hague)
is a Division of Walter de Gruyter GmbH & Co. KG, Berlin.

The series Studies in Generative Grammar was formerly published by
Foris Publications Holland.

Die Deutsche Bibliothek − Cataloging-in-Publication Data

Emonds, Joseph E.:
Lexicon and grammar : the English syntacticon / by Joseph E. Emonds. −
Berlin ; New York : Mouton de Gruyter, 2000
(Studies in generative grammar ; 50)
ISBN 3-11-016981-9 brosch.
ISBN 3-11-016689-5 Gb.

Printing: Werner Hildebrand, Berlin.
Binding: Lüderitz & Bauer GmbH, Berlin.

For Henk van Riemsdijk
Scientist, scholar, bon vivant,
research organizer and fellow-traveller

Preface

This book focuses on the urgent need for a *formal, constrained* and *empirically revealing* theory of a syntactic lexicon. To satisfy this need, it proposes new principles regulating subcategorization which determine how syntactic structures project from a language's lexicon. In the theory developed here, the trees projected by lexical subcategorization frames are not always copies of the frames themselves, as they are in the first classical proposals of Chomsky's (1965) *Aspects of the Theory of Syntax*. This study's highly restrictive sub-theories of grammatical categories and features, abstract case, derivational levels and economy principles have the consequence that sisterhood between a selecting and selected element is only subcategorization's "simplest case."

The data and paradigms here are for the most part drawn from English, but properties of Romance languages also form an essential part of the argumentation, and some points are discussed in terms of constructions from yet other languages, especially Japanese.

This study defends a strictly syntactic approach to the lexicon, i.e. it elaborates a theory of c-selection (subcategorization) and argues against the use of any thematic grids or lexical conceptual structures in grammatical computation. Constructions which have been widely invoked as necessarily involving semantic selection, such as the *spray/ load* alternation, propositional complements, light verbs and understood arguments are shown to be better analyzed without it (cf. especially Chapters 2, 6 and 9). A central organizing factor for this approach to the lexicon is a crucial distinction between an item's "cognitive syntactic" features F used in syntactic derivations and its "purely semantic" features *f* which are not (Chapter 1). The first use of the former (Chapter 2) sharpens the theory of c-selection by using these features in lexical frames (e.g., +___ANIMATE rather than +___DP and +___PATH rather than +___PP).

The principal innovation based on the F/*f* distinction is the proposal in Chapter 3 that the lexicon consists of two quite different components, a grammatical lexicon bereft of purely semantic features (the "Syntacticon") and a mental lexicon which consists of the open classes of the more specified contentful lexical items (the "Dictionary," which is the faculty of human linguistic memory and culture). There are only four categories in the Dictionary (N, V, A and P), what I term "nature's bottleneck" in a final discussion in Chapter 10. Dictionary items are always inserted at the outset of transformational computations on a domain, as in Chomsky (1965). The perennial question "why do transformations exist?" is answered as follows: to assemble sets of disparate open class items in structures which can be communicated at the Phonological Form interface (PF) and interpreted at the Logical Form interface (LF).

In contrast to the Dictionary, the Syntacticon is regulated by a theory of *multi-level lexical insertion*: the feature composition of a lexical item in the Syntacticon determines at which stage in a derivation it is inserted, i.e., satisfies its c-selection properties. I take it that sweeping statements about levels of lexical insertion are empty unless tied to predictions about particular items satisfying specific insertion contexts. Chapters 4 and 5 explore the predictive consequences of this study's theory of multi-level insertion for the Syntacticon's bound morphemes and Chapters 6 and 7 for its free morphemes. In the limiting case, entirely uninterpreted Syntacticon items are inserted at PF; in particular, the entire class of items traditionally called inflections are characterized as "late-inserted" in this way. Inflections which apparently contribute to meaning (past tense, noun plurals, etc.) in fact serve only to license empty nodes in other interpretable free morpheme positions (I, D).

While developing the theory of the Syntacticon and multi-level insertion, I argue not only against semantic selection but also against any autonomous "morphological component" with combinatorial properties, in the lexicon or elsewhere. I claim the only statements needed for morphology are those with phonological effects, possibly conditioned by syntactic factors. The entire content of morphology is thus akin to interface statements such as a rule of Classical Greek, "verbs and adjectives receive penultimate stress." Except for the effects of such statements, the combinatory principles of bound morphology are exactly the same as those governing the syntax of free morphemes, especially those of compounding (Chapter 3). Supposed differences between compounding and morphology in e.g. Romance languages are shown to be differences between free and bound morphemes.

The notion that some categories in trees are associated with lexical items in the course of derivations raises the question of how these categories act prior to such insertion. Many analyses in this book demonstrate that a category in a head position *does not act like a head until it is lexically filled.* This principle regulating underlying empty heads is introduced in Chapter 4 and used throughout the rest of the study. Since grammatical elements can be inserted at later derivational levels, the empirical properties of particular grammatical elements are typically due to (i) their delayed status as head of a construction and/ or (ii) whether they are interpreted in Logical Form. Simple and uniform lexical specifications leading to insertion of single morphemes at two or three derivational levels provide novel explanations for many previously poorly understood complex grammatical patterns, for example in both the passive and perfect periphrastic constructions of Germanic and Romance (Chapter 5).

In Chapter 6, Syntacticon entries of the form X, +___Y are shown to induce syntactic "flat structures" if both X and Y are the same category and X lacks purely semantic features f (i.e., is subject to late lexical insertion). This peculiar conjunction of properties provides analyses which solve many recalcitrant syntactic puzzles of especially the Romance languages. Causative, restructuring, linking and light verbs, which have all been treated differently in the literature, actually realize very similar structures. The explanations all crucially exploit the notion of "empty underlying head." Another area which demonstrates the explanatory power of syntactically empty heads is a range of PPs headed by grammatical P, including adjuncts as well as complements (Chapter 7).

Chapter 8 builds to what is in some way the intellectual climax of the book. It begins by extending case theory and refining certain formal properties of subcategorization in a way that fully defines, in conjunction with the category and feature theory of Chapter 1, the notion of "possible syntactic part of a lexical entry." *This chapter demonstrates that quite general and familiar classes of complements in the English lexicon instantiate all and only the structures predicted by the category and subcategorization theories of this book.* This reformalization of the notion "lexical entry," after twenty years of promissory notes in the ever novel coinages of theta theory, semantic selection, conceptual structures and the like, finally proposes limits imposed by Universal Grammar on the construct "possible lexical entry." This step removes the vagueness that has been associated with the lexicon for decades and enables us to embed the study of syntactic derivations in a fully generative system, in which all modules are formalized.

The last two chapters pursue another hypothesis that privileges syntax over any active role for the lexicon in language use. These chapters argue that all understood arguments are represented syntactically; a case is made against various notions of "unprojected arguments" which have appeared in the literature. In particular, Chapter 9 justifies unexceptional, purely syntactic representations for "null complement anaphora" and "null generic objects," and derives obligatory PRO as a by-product of subcategorization for a V-headed rather than I- or C-headed complement. Finally, Chapter 10 argues for a discourse-governed reference of optional PRO subjects, which turn out to have a broader distribution than usually envisioned and include subjects of imperatives and agent phrases in verbal passives. All understood arguments are thus syntactically present arguments.

A central theme in this book's approach to lexical theory is that contextual features in individual entries must be *formally simple, uniform in format*, and stated in terms of *psychologically accessible categories* – i.e., categories which classify the concrete words of PF, not the abstract phrases of LF; as real as these latter are, they are not present in the data used by the child. That is, the many detailed properties of complex constructions (e.g., participles, nominalizations, passives) must derive from syntactically combining extremely transparent lexical entries. These entries can contain no diacritics or purely formal features. The motivation for this is simply a classic Chomskyan argument from poverty of the stimulus. What individual children do in learning a specific language is acquire a hoard of lexical entries for "small" grammatical items, both bound and free. Now we observe that not only some but essentially *every one of these learned grammatical items differs syntactically* from its closest counterparts in closely related languages. For example, if there is a handful of grammatical free or bound English morphemes lexically specified as exact translations of French ones, they are exceptions which prove the rule (I have yet to encounter a single one). Given that pre-school or unschooled children learn hundreds of these language-particular grammatical items fast and well, their lexical representations must have a simple and uniform format, expressed in categories readily accessible in the linguistic data, i.e. subcategories of words.

On the other hand, the facts of rapid acquisition do not suggest that lexical insertion theory, presumably uniform across the species, has to itself be transparent, any more than transformational theory or phonological theory are transparent. The structure of the uniform lexical theory developed in this study is subject only to general considerations of parsimony, elegance and empirical coverage which we require of any scientific enterprise.

Curiously, most generative treatments of the lexicon, including those of Chomskyan inspiration, search for extreme simplicity just where it seems least likely to be found: areas of species-wide genetic predisposition which have taken eons to perfect are felt to be governed by simple statements such as "affect alpha." Yet in the area where poverty of the stimulus and rapid acquisition have some force, the largely non-genetic lexical lists, essentially any quasi-formalized linguistic or conceptual properties are attributed to individual items and no principles regulate either lexical form or the lexicon-syntax interface. I do not see how this combination of abstract principles operating on unconstrained lexicons contributes to explaining acquisition of actual languages. Worse, the unformalized nature of the lexicon renders largely untestable any empirical claims made for the derivational component of UG (which depends on "projection from the lexicon").

The literature under the rubric of Head Driven Phrase Structure Grammar, which human time limitations have prevented me from seriously investigating, does nonetheless seem to have a failing in this area as well, though one that is not so maddening as the hand-waving approach to the lexicon widely practiced in transformational syntax. While HPSG pays careful attention to formalizing the lexicon, it seems to care less about constraining it. Practitioners seem to be complacent and satisfied that if it works (i.e. can be computationally modeled), it's (relatively at least) good enough. In my tentative excursions into this literature, I sense little concern with trying to formulate a theory of lexical entries all and only of whose possible instantiations are realized in the lexicon of a language or some collection of languages.

A potentially controversial psychological implication of this study is that language can express only those combinatory meanings which simply "arise" from valid syntactic combinations. In the view developed here, syntax determines entirely any *propositions* we can formulate about our mental world and yet is largely independent of and provides very little insight into how we otherwise conceptualize it. Moreover, a little reflection shows (see in particular the concluding sections of each of the last three chapters) that our mental world and the form of natural language are almost entirely incommensurable, at least in terms of our ability to consciously reflect on them. So for example, while models of propositions are always discrete and almost invariably two-dimensional, our conceptualizations are obviously continuous and three or four dimensional: *The room slowly filled with smoke.*

Thus, even if thematic relations between a verb and its arguments are just "convenient mnemonics for particularly prominent configurations" in conceptual structures (Jackendoff 1987: 385), a given verb's lexical conceptual structure, while psychologically applicable to the world, is still linguistically opaque and unlikely to correspond to any structure in a grammatical phrase marker outside the verb. Consequently, any pieces of conceptual structure attached to lexical items remain unanalyzable and are hence next to useless as a guide to more general knowledge about the interface of conceptual structure with syntax.

Acknowledgments

This book was entirely researched and written in the atmosphere of Generative Linguistics in the Old Worlds of Europe and Japan. I am very grateful to the intellectuals, institutions, cooks, house mates, and surgeon (Mr. Gaynor of North Tyneside General Hospital) who have welcomed me as an emigrant or perhaps vagrant, and kept me respectively stimulated, comfortably paid, well fed, entertained and reasonably free of pain during this work.

Especially the following friends have been involved with this work for sustained periods of time, supported the intellectual ideas throughout and integrated them into their own work: Henk van Riemsdijk, Miori Kubo, Lida Veselovská, Andrew Caink and Mi-Jeung Jo. These intellectual companions have given me the sense that the ideas presented here are a basis for fruitful research in areas where I previously had very little conception of how they could be. This enthusiasm for my approach has been an indispensable aid in helping me to persevere. They also seem to share an approach to linguistic analysis which values working out consequences over a period of time and maintaining some fidelity to the insights and analyses of the past; theirs is therefore not only a valued companionship of ideas, but also an even more treasured companionship of method. I am especially grateful to Lida for the careful reading and many comments she has provided for the final version.

I have been particularly fortunate in this last decade to have benefited from generous fellowships and visiting professorships arranged by some of the most effective and tireless organizational supporters of the generative enterprise. As always, these times have proved the most fruitful in terms of developing the material in this study. For providing proper working conditions and research and writing time and for many unexpected professional extras, I am therefore deeply indebted especially to the following friends and colleagues:

To Prof. Henk van Riemsdijk who invited me both as visiting professor to Tilburg in 1992 and as Fellow to the Netherlands Institute for Advanced Study in 1997. The project of extending Alternative Realization to Romance clitics began during my lectures at Tilburg, which set me on the road to using it to encompass all of inflection; the linguistic community at Tilburg was a real source of initial inspiration for this study. The excellent research atmosphere Henk and Co-director Martin Everaert created in the SYNCOM project at NIAS enabled the writing of the book to get to the crucial halfway point. I very much benefited from the constant interchanges on syntax with my project colleagues there, Norbert Corver, Denis Delfitto, Sten Vikner and Martin. I am of course also indebted to the Institute and its Officers for the excellent conditions for collaborative research they provide.

I also wish to thank the doctoral students and colleagues in linguistics at the University of Durham, who over several years have developed a challenging and active research community. I especially appreciate the explicit and implicit encouragement of my research direction provided by my colleague Dr. Bonnie Schwartz and former supervisees Andrew Caink, Cécile de Cat, Dalina Kallulli and Roger Maylor. This linguistic community has been made possible by the efforts of Vice-Chancellor Evelyn Ebsworth, who gave the strongest possible support to our field during his tenure and encouraged me to take every opportunity to pursue this research both at Durham and when invited elsewhere. This support culminated with a Christopherson Research Fellowship for the academic year 1998-1999, which was indispensable in bringing the scholarship for this book to a timely conclusion.

The greatest part of this work was written and revised during my several invited stays in Japan since 1994. Consequently a major share of my gratitude goes to the figures of Japanese generative grammar who have provided a pattern of invitations and support for research and advanced teaching that I think are practically unparalleled in present-day linguistics. The first versions of some material were undertaken as revisions of the summer 1995 TEC lectures in Tokyo, given at the invitation of Professors K. Hasegawa, K. Inoue and M. Kajita, and the last revisions were made during my first semester at the new Kobe-Shoin Graduate School, organized by Dr. Taisuke Nishigauchi. Thus, this book began, came to maturity and has been completed in Japan, in settings very conducive to research.

The support of my long-time friend and wide-ranging intellectual model Prof. S.-Y. Kuroda has provided crucial links in several of these initiatives, and I earnestly thank him for his sustained efforts on my behalf.

Three chapters of this book were largely written while I was visiting professor at Kanda University of International Studies in Japan. The research atmosphere and facilities there were superb, and I am most grateful to its President, Prof. Kazuko Inoue, for integrating me into the scholarly community she has created. And not the least benefit of my three years at Kanda was the introduction it facilitated into the wider world of Japanese linguistics.

Three further chapters of this book were written while a Fellow of the Japanese Society for the Promotion of Science at Nanzan University. I am most grateful for this excellent arrangement, and especially to my host scientist Prof. Mamoru Saito at Nanzan. His successful efforts in obtaining this grant and his scientific consultation and encouragement during my stay were indispensable contributions.

During all these stays in Japan, Miori Kubo has provided me with feedback and commentary on several chapters and sections, as well as often being extremely helpful in technical matters.

I gratefully acknowledge permissions from Taishukan Press, Tokyo, to revise and reprint material from Emonds (1997) forming the bulk of Chapter 2 and from Kaitakusha Press (Tokyo) to revise and reprint material for Chapter 9 from my "Subcategorization as the Unique Source of Null Complements," in their 1999 volume *In Search of the Human Mind – a Festschrift for Prof. Kazuko Inoue*, M. Muraki and E. Iwamoto (eds.).

Finally, I am also grateful to Sean Burke, José Deulofeu, Shalom Lappin and Pat Waugh for their personal enthusiasm and collegial support, which have also sustained me at particular stages of this work.

In producing this book, stellar performances in absolutely central roles have been delivered by the series editor Henk van Riemsdijk, an anonymous referee for Mouton de Gruyter, the editor Ursula Kleinhenz, the technical editor Monika Wendland, and the tireless creator of the subject index, Lida Veselovská. Thanks to them, bringing this book to a physical incarnation has been a *relatively* painless project.

Author's academic biography

Born in 1940 in North Dakota; his father Joseph was a highway engineer for the Bureau of Indian Affairs in the American West, and his mother Margaret (Embley) was a primary school teacher. He attended high school in Milwaukee, Wisconsin, received a BA in mathematics from Loras College, Dubuque, Iowa (1962), and an MA in mathematics at the University of Kansas, Lawrence, Kansas (1964).

After a year of teaching at the U.S. Naval Academy, he studied for the PhD in linguistics at the Massachusetts Institute of Technology (1965–1970), including a final fellowship year at the newly inaugurated University of Illinois Center for Advanced Study.

An intermittent European career began at the Université de Paris VIII (Vincennes) in 1969–1970, after which he began his first permanent position at the University of California at Los Angeles (1970–1979). His son Peter was born in 1973. While still a novice at the joys of fatherhood, he lectured at Princeton University (1973–1974) and the Université de Paris VII (1976–1977), where a Guggenheim Fellowship permitted extending his stay. He also gave a summer school course at the International Christian University in Japan. The decade closed with a self-granted half-year respite from academia in London.

A second permanent position, including five years as chair, was at the University of Washington (1980–1991). Research and teaching leaves were spent at the Massachusetts Institute of Technology (1984), the Stanford Center for Advanced Study in the Behavioral Sciences (1985–1986), the Université de Provence (1987) and the Université de Paris VIII (1989). He was also co-director of the Dubrovnik summer school (1987) and made frequent academic visits to the Netherlands. The last four Seattle years coincided with experiencing high school a second and more exciting time.

Expatriation began in earnest with a teaching fellowship at Tilburg University (1992), followed by taking up the Chair of Linguistics and English Language at the University of Durham in 1992. During this period, he was active in H. van Riemsdijk's European Science Foundation Eurotyp Group 8 and visiting professor at Kanda University of International Studies from 1994 through 1996. After fellowships at the Netherlands Institute for Advanced Science in 1997 and at Nagoya's Nanzan University in 1998 (sponsored by the Japanese Society for the Promotion of Science), he accepted a professorship at Kobe Shoin University's new graduate school in 2000.

Table of Contents

Chapter 1
Categories and feature inventories of Universal Grammar

1.1 A theory and practice of well-formed lexical entries

1.1.1 Specifying the well-formed sentences

Generative grammar originally took and can still take as its goal, to formally specify all and only the grammatically well-formed strings of a language. "The fundamental aim in the linguistic analysis of a language L is to separate the *grammatical* sequences which are the sentences of L from the *ungrammatical* sequences which are not sentences of L and to study the structure of the grammatical sequences." Chomsky (1957, 13)[1] The earliest period focused on the form of phrase structure and transformational rules, which were independent of individual lexical items. Although the actual statements of many early generative rules in fact mentioned specific morphemes, their dependence on these items was accidental; the development of an appropriate formal theory was not concerned with lexical statements as such.

Subsequently, the "standard theory" period of generative grammar (from Chomsky's *Aspects of the Theory of Syntax* through his "Conditions on Transformations," 1965–1973) recognized the necessity of succinctly formalizing co-occurrence relations between lexical items and the word classes they appear with; e.g., some verbs are obligatorily transitive, others are optionally so, and still others are incompatible with object nouns. The burden of expressing these well-formedness conditions was placed on base rules and syntactic subcategorization, the latter much later renamed "c-

---

[1] "The grammar, then, is a device that (in particular) specifies the infinite set of well-formed sentences and assigns to each of these one or more structural descriptions. Perhaps we should call such a device a *generative grammar* to distinguish it from descriptive statements that merely present the inventory of elements that appear in structural descriptions, and their contextual variants." (Chomsky, 1964, 9).

There are well-formed strings not technically sentences, which should still be generated by the grammar: *Off the porch with you both! (*With you both off the porch!); Well, what a nice present! (*What a nice present, well!)* As observed in Banfield (1982, Ch. 1), these constructions are not generally embeddable. Perhaps for this reason, both traditional and generative grammar have concentrated on sentences. Nonetheless, the syntax of non-embeddable constructions is intriguing.

selection". Base rules constituted the "outer limit" on the complexity of lexical subcategorization.

In a later third period (say from "Conditions on Rules" through Mark Baker's *Incorporation*, 1974–1988), base rules were rightly replaced by universal conditions on category inventories and projections via a parsimonious bar notation. The residual content of such rules were to be expressed by a few parameters such as the head-initial/head-final parameter. This reduced role of base rules could have suggested expanding and refining the role of subcategorization. In fact, in studies of morphology and compounding, Lieber (1980, 1983) moved in this direction. With the demise of base rules, there also arose a (largely unacknowledged) need to limit the form of possible lexical entries.

Instead, in syntax proper, a disturbingly anti-theoretical option was suddenly almost universally embraced around 1980, one which tended to entirely discount any role for subcategorization. Most syntacticians abandoned work on the lexicon, but whether one worked on the lexicon or not, the field as a whole seemed to pin its hopes on a future theory of semantic selection or "s-selection". Additionally, any concern with the limits on "possible lexical entry" was deemed premature. It thus became widely accepted that deep structures (i.e., inputs to a syntactic derivation) were to be determined via s-selection and the projection principle. For example, this step is endorsed in Chomsky's *Lectures on Government and Binding* (1981) and *Barriers* (1986). That is, heads combine semantically with some complement(s) by "assigning theta roles" to them, somehow thereby projecting or "licensing" deep structures. A consensus that deep structures project from (unformalized, intuitive) lexical-semantic structures effectively replaced the previous formal syntactic theory; syntacticians focused their efforts on constraining possible steps in derivations and on finding well-formedness conditions on co-indexing in the outputs.

Oddly, mainstream syntax showed almost no interest in the very lexical semantic structure that was newly considered the basis of syntax; it found little use for articulated proposals, notably by Jackendoff (1987, 1990), for specifying well-formed semantic combinations of elements such as lexical heads and complements. Nor did later lexico-semantic formalizations of head-complement structure find much favor in analyses using the framework of *Lectures on Government and Binding*.[2] Nonetheless, a moment's

---

[2]   Theories developed to answer the need within government and binding theory for a formal mechanism to generate deep structures include Zubizarreta (1987) and Grimshaw (1990). Revealingly, one finds few references to precise aspects of such lexical formalisms in theoretical syntactic research.

reflection about a generative model in which all syntactic structures project from the lexicon reveals the key role of characterizing "possible lexical entry" – of exactly determining and formalizing lexical properties.

Instead of pursuing this goal, influential syntactic studies after 1980 have focused almost exclusively on how to relate steps and levels in a derivation. Though such studies often allude to combinatorial devices (s-selection, feature checking, well-formed objects at Logical Form), their lexical specifications for the most part remain undefined and underexemplified, and so fail to advance understanding of the lexical base of syntactic structures. In fact, research in government and binding and minimalism (the framework of Chomsky, 1995) seems to have abandoned a goal of working out some type of formalized lexicon to actually generate the syntactic structures which then undergo the carefully studied derivations. Perhaps this testifies to an unspoken realization that lexicalist s-selection for describing co-occurrence has simply failed to improve on earlier and more restrictive syntactic formulations in capturing co-occurrence generalizations.[3]

Inescapably, if formal syntax has little to say about how syntactic categories and specific lexical items combine, but concentrates only on transforming structures *assumed* to be lexically well-formed, it is not generative grammar in the original sense. One might object that the original goal was misformulated or too ambitious. However, if a particular framework actually revealingly approaches the original goal, such objections become a priori and irrelevant. This study's purpose is to develop a theory of subcategorization which accurately captures the patterns and structural generalizations projected from the English lexicon (i.e., a theory of c-selection). Additionally, it succeeds (in Chapter 8) in imposing a very strict limit on the notion "possible lexical entry" and argues that this limit nicely corresponds to the observed range of lexical complementation.

By incorporating many results of generative grammar's third period as well as more recent concepts such as Principles of Economy, I hope that this study's deliberately syntactic approach to the lexicon and its syntactic projections will help re-instate the generative ideal, which studies not only derivations but also characterizes the formal objects to which they apply.

---

[3] This is my argument in Emonds (1991b). What is at issue is not the priorities of particular researchers, but why syntactic researchers as a (large) group feel no need to address the flagrant weakness of an unformalized lexicon, which undermines any theory's claim to be a formal model of language.

1.1.2 Judging the well-formed sentences

It seems appropriate to explain at the outset how my grammatical argumentation treats data for which native speakers make conflicting acceptability judgments.

Sometimes, conflicting judgments are clear-cut enough to justify different rule systems, parameter settings or, in terms to be developed in this study, different syntactic entries in the lexicon. For example, while many Standard American speakers clearly accept patterns with post-verbal particles separating double objects as in (1.1), others simply do not.

(1.1)   Mary brought her kids out some clothes.
         Some students may send companies back their free samples.
         Write the customers up an order.

In constructions where comparative judgments are murkier, I follow a heuristic proposed by N. Chomsky in 1967 class lectures: if native speakers assess differently the acceptability of an example which has a clear meaning and presents no processing difficulty (such as center embedding, undue length, homonyms, ambiguity, etc.), *the example should be taken as ungrammatical.* The reason is that, by hypothesis, there is no reason for its partial rejection other than it being ungrammatical. In varying degrees, speakers obviously accept and process all sorts of ill-formed utterances (e.g., by children, foreigners, the speech-impaired, or speakers making performance errors) without the slightest consciousness of deviance. Thus, if no processing factors intervene, a reaction of acceptability cannot be trusted in the face of conflicting judgments, while one of unacceptability may be.[4] For this reason, the questionable sentences as in (1.2) should be analyzed as ungrammatical.

(1.2)   ?John believes that the earth the moon circles weekly.
         ?Mike probably considers some professors fools and Ann many knaves.
         What did other students { think that/ ?wonder whether } Mary bought?

---

[4] Perhaps facetiously, Chomsky also suggested that being more sensitive to unacceptability might be an evolutionary disadvantage, since not noticing it might enhance communication. Then, if awareness of ungrammaticality has negative survival value, any vestigial consciousness of it suggests an underlying mental reality.

Bill or { his brothers / ?they } Mary doesn't believe can win.
Which paints did Sue buy before { showing / ?her brother showed }
to Sam?

Consequently, in this study, among sentences easily understood and
processed, *only those universally judged as acceptable* are taken as grammatical. This simple heuristic conflicts with widespread justifications of
analyses which treat data accepted only by some speakers as grammatical,
a practice which more often than not undermines the most interesting and
contentful theoretical formulations.

1.2 Types of syntactic categories and features

1.2.1 Canonical matching of features and categories

Any framework purporting to characterize syntactic well-formedness requires an approximate inventory of the categories whose co-occurrence is
to be determined.[5] Since language clearly distinguishes four "open" or
"lexical" categories whose members number in the hundreds or thousands
(nouns, verbs, adjectives, and pre / post-positions: N, V, A, P), these categories must play a central role. Moreover, the great membership of these
lexical categories never fails to astonish; informal sampling today still confirms Jespersen's (1905, 227) observation: "People who had never been to
college, but, … were regular readers of books and periodicals, … reported
generally from 25,000 to 30,000 words …" That is, the combined membership of the four lexical categories X must typically be well over 20,000.
Outside of compounds in a well-formed syntactic structure, each of these
lexical categories X has a "maximal projection" XP which obligatorily
contains ("dominates") its structural head X as well as any modifiers and
complements which may modify X.

In addition to and in contrast to the open categories, a number of syntactic categories of limited membership modify and help extend the projections
of the lexical categories. Each of these non-lexical "closed" or "functional"

---

[5] An exact inventory of the categories in a theory cannot be required a priori, since
otherwise the theory would be fully specified before investigation begins. No scientist can
demand that an exact inventory of all distinctive features precede research in formal
phonology, that a full inventory of chemical elements precede experimentation based on
the periodic table, or that a complete inventory of elementary particles precede work in
atomic physics. In fact, one rationale for pursuing a science is to arrive at such inventories.

categories seems to contain at most twenty or so morphemes. The most prominent functional categories are the elements I making a verb phrase into a finite Fregean judgment and a class of quantificational and/or definite items D determining the referential properties of noun phrases. I and VP together form an "extended projection" IP of V, while D and NP together an extended projection DP of N.

For a number of other closed class elements which are characteristic modifiers of at least the four lexical categories X, I continue to use the early cover term specifier SPEC(XP) as in Chomsky (1970); in this study, specifiers can include both closed classes of grammatical elements and/or phrases. For example, there seems to be a single "slot" in which modifiers of English adjectives appear: certain degree words such as *very* and *so*, measure phrases (*two hours, ten feet*) and short adjective phrases (*less believably, somewhat tolerably*) are in complementary distribution:

(1.3)   *That lecture was { very two hours/ two hours very } long.
         *That { unbelievably too/ too unbelievably } optimistic estimate was foolish.
         *Be sure to install a { tolerably ten feet/ ten feet tolerably } deep pool.

I will consider all these elements to be in SPEC(AP) and do not commit myself to analyzing morphemes such as *very* as either a head or a phrase; but little if anything in my arguments hinges on this decision. Nonetheless, this use of SPEC does not conform to the practice of authors who reserve this symbol for phrasal positions.[6]

Syntactic categories thus fall into two separate classes, whose diverging nature can be derived from the following five properties of Universal Grammar:

a. UG provides a restricted set of morpheme categories {B}: lexical heads X, specifiers SPEC(XP), I, D and perhaps a few others.[7]

---

[6] It is not obvious that expletives such as *there* in the supposedly phrasal position SPEC(IP) or unmodifiable question and relative markers such as *whether, why,* French *dont* 'of which' or Dutch *wer* 'where' in SPEC(CP) are phrasal either, other than by assumption.

On the other hand, certain finer analyses of extended projections of A (Corver, 1997) and P (van Riemsdijk, 1998b) argue that head and phrasal positions can be kept distinct, in line with suggestions in Chomsky (1986).

[7] These include (i) coordinate conjunctions, (ii) the discourse particles or "delimiters" of several languages *even, only, also,* etc. which attach to any XP (Kuroda, 1965), and (iii)

b. UG matches a small range of *cognitive syntactic features* F (upper case) with each B whose combinations [B, $\pm$F] characterize up to a maximum of twenty or so members of B.[8]

c. The cognitive syntactic features F on B contribute *centrally* to meaning (that is, to "Logical Form") in all syntactic classes.

d. Finer distinctions of meaning in terms of purely semantic features f (lower case script) which play no role in syntax (Chomsky, 1965, Ch. 4) appear *only in the four open lexical classes N, A, V and P.*

e. All non-lexical categories are "closed" because they crucially lack these purely semantic features f, which apparently proliferate and recombine fairly freely. Hence, the closed categories have few members and disallow coining (Emonds, 1985, Ch. 4).

Some plausible examples of purely semantic features f: (i) I would imagine that color terms share a feature f_i, permitting for example unexceptional compound adjectives such as *dark pink* and *light magenta*, in contrast to (compounds) **dark smooth* or **light dirty*. (ii) Among verbs of say "harm" (which itself might be a semantic feature), some exclude further normal use of an object (*!He destroyed/ ruined/ totaled/ wrecked the bicycle and then rode away on it*) while others don't (*He damaged/ harmed/ messed up/ misused the bicycle and then rode away on it*). Plausibly, some feature f_j meaning roughly "usable for intended purpose" seems involved. It seems incontrovertible that elaboration of syntactic theory does not in general depend on such features f.

I now discuss the properties (a–e) in more detail. Properties (a–b) are reflected in the partial and tentative table (1.4), which may well be modified as research proceeds. Most of these matches are inherited from traditional grammar, with generative grammar providing a number of non-trivial modifications, as in note 8. Many features F have unique canonical positions in

---

the emphatic particles *too, so, either* which appear only with finite verbs. (ii) and (iii) seem to escape classification as specifiers precisely because they can occur with them. Aoyagi (1998) nonetheless considers the discourse particles to be specifiers which can further adjoin to otherwise maximal phrasal projections. The category of emphatic particles is uncertain; perhaps, as argued in Laka (1990), they constitute a separate class of functional heads.

[8] I do not identify all the features which traditional grammar associates with a lexical category as its features in UG; e.g. generative analyses of English, Kru languages (Koopman, 1984) and Chinese (Huang, 1990) have shown that TENSE is not a feature on V but rather a separate category. But neither do I assume a priori that every syntactic feature projects as a separate head.

which they are realized, such as PAST on I, but for some F, UG may provide more than one possible host. Thus, POTENTIAL is matched with I and A in English (*can, able*) but with V in French (*pouv-*), and the COMPARA-TIVE features can occur in several specifier positions (Bresnan, 1973: *more into Zen, more of a man*).

(1.4)   Examples of *probable* UG matches:

syntactic features F	categories B
tense and modal features	I
quantifier features	D or NUM
space-time co-ordinates	P
ACTIVITY	V
PERFECTIVE (aspect)	V
ANIMATE, COUNT	N
comparative features	SPEC(XP)

Certain features F may cross-classify the syntactic categories B. Thus, a [+N] feature subsumes N, D and A, while [-N] subsumes V, I and P.[9] The much discussed feature ±WH most plausibly occurs on the "specifier" (SPEC) of both the marked [+N] categories D and A in e.g. *which, what, how,* and so also does ±PROXIMATE; e.g. *{this / that} + {bread / tall}.*

A central tenet in this study's approach to the lexicon is thus a general condition on syntactic features (1.5), which expresses (b) and also (c) above.

(1.5)   *Canonical Realization. UG associates a few cognitive syntactic features F with each syntactic category B. These features F contribute to semantic interpretation (Logical Form) only in these "canonical positions" on B, and appear elsewhere only via language-particular lexical stipulation.*

Chapter 4 returns to examples of syntactic features which are *not* canonically realized and to mechanisms which severely limit the distribution of these uninterpreted features.

---

[9] Whether plus values of features can always correspond to marked values is discussed below; the feature +N unifying nouns and adjectives was historically adopted without regard to this issue. A little reflection shows, however, that -N (V and P) is a marked value; N is certainly the unmarked word class, while P is the least numerous and hence plausibly the most marked. We might think of case-marking of N and A (+N, accepts +*f*) by V, P, I and D as categories in a "higher energy" or marked state discharging this "energy" (markedness) onto the less active categories N and A.

Notice that properties (a–c) do *not* distinguish open from closed classes; the distinction follows rather from properties (d–e). These two properties which set off closed class categories can be formally linked as follows:

(1.6)   *Outside the lexical categories N, V, A and P, the only features allowed are the cognitive syntactic features F (and the small sets of morphemes they generate).*

Observe now that the lexical categories are defined as those whose features *may* extend beyond the inventory F; this possibility of additional semantic features *f* makes these classes "open." The question arises as to whether every N, V, A and P *must* have *f* distinct from F. In fact, there is no reason to assume this, i.e., Canonical Realization (1.5) can apply as its stands to the four lexical categories. Indeed, certain subclasses of N, V, A and P have properties characteristic of the non-lexical classes, such as post s-structure insertion and unique syntactic behavior (cf. Emonds, 1985, Ch. 4, and 1987). *The lexical categories are in this way like the others: each has a subset of say up to twenty or so elements fully characterized by cognitive syntactic features F and entirely lacking purely semantic features f.*

These closed subsets of open categories can be called "grammatical" N, V, A or P; in contrast, open class subsets which have purely semantic features will be called "lexical" N, V, A or P. English grammatical verbs include *be, have, do, get, go, come, let, make, say,* etc. Its grammatical nouns include *one, self, thing, stuff, people, other(s), place, time, way, reason.* A widely acknowledged distinction between grammatical and lexical or "contentful" prepositions also falls into place as a predicted subcase of a more general property of a theory of lexical categories: lexical P are specified with purely semantic *f* and grammatical P are not.[10]

(1.7)   *Definition. A closed grammatical class X (including N, V, A, P) is one whose members have no purely semantic features f, but only cognitive syntactic features F.*

In Chapter 3 of this work, I define the subpart of the lexicon which contains all and only the closed grammatical classes of elements as the

---

[10] Studies of types of aphasia invariably show that forms of the English copula group with closed class elements. But since such research is not examining any proposal to group morphemes except as members or non-members of the four lexical classes, it does not systematically investigate whether other grammatical members of these classes differ from open class items.

"Syntacticon" of a language, and show that it has properties quite distinct from an open class "Dictionary". In the first two chapters, however, this distinction will not yet play a central role. Nonetheless, it will be necessary to retain the definitions and proposals in this and the next subsections, for the explanatory accounts throughout this study will repeatedly utilize the distinctions between grammatical and lexical X and between features in canonical and non-canonical positions.

1.2.2 Marked feature values, including Absence of Content

This study takes no position as to whether lexical entries are specified for all their features, for marked feature values only, or in some other way. However, this study will carefully develop a conception whereby *marked syntactic features* on lexical items can appear in syntax outside their canonically matched base positions under very restricted syntactic conditions. Thus, to facilitate properly defining these conditions, it is important to have criteria for when a feature value is marked.

The canonical positions of syntactic features such as PLURAL, PERSON or DEFINITE are somewhere in the extended projections of nouns, most likely on D. Thus, when such features appear under V in e.g. an agreement morpheme or a Romance pronominal clitic, they are not in their canonically realized positions inside DP. How complex and stipulative such "alternative realizations" are should be calculated only in terms of marked features. Thus, PLURAL and DEFINITE are marked (and hence costly) features to realize under V, or in other words, the Romance pronominal clitic system is a lexically marked subsystem. But once a PLURAL clitic appears in Romance, it is probably not additionally more costly or stipulative if the clitic is further Masculine and 3rd Person, since these are unmarked feature values with PLURAL.

Use here of a plus value on a feature will usually reflect some previous or obvious argumentation that a certain feature is a marked option: e.g., +PLURAL number, 2nd Person,[11] Romance +FEMININE gender, +PAST tense, IRREALIS = +MODAL, the +SOURCE value of PATH, +NEGATIVE polarities of antonymous adjectives, etc. In other cases, it turns out that certain feature *combinations* are unmarked, such as possibly [ACCUSATIVE, -DEFINITE] and [NOMINATIVE, +DEFINITE]. Ideally, one

---

[11] Benveniste (1966) argues extensively that 3rd Person is the least marked of the Person features, and Banfield (1982) that 2nd Person is the most marked.

would like to equate plus values, marked values, and simple presence, and similarly identify minus values, unmarked values, and absence. But this is not possible if unmarked values of a feature such as ±DEFINITE vary according to syntactic context. When this situation arises, I will simply remark in the text that a minus value is the marked value.

An important but rarely remarked correlation within the open classes is that their more numerous syntactic subclasses have what one might call "more content." For example, the vast majority of verbs are activity verbs, that is, not +STATIVE; the vast majority of English nouns are countable, and a great majority of prepositions indicate spatial or temporal relations. It seems plausible that these more numerous and more contentful subclasses of X^0 are the cognitively primitive or unmarked ones, and that *the less numerous subclasses of less content are lexically marked* (stative verbs, mass nouns, logical or grammatical prepositions), that is, less expected by the language learner.

If so, the appropriate way to reflect these facts is to let certain cognitive syntactic features on N, V, A and P represent a *marked Absence of Content*. Thus, +STATIVE is the marked lexical value for V; there are fewer stative verbs and their defining property is *failing to* contribute certain typical content of V to interpretation. For instance, Chomsky's rule for determining agenthood of subjects (cf. Chapter 2) does not apply to (precisely) STATIVE verbs. From this point of view, then, the -STATIVE verb *do* is less marked than the +STATIVE verb *have*.

Similarly, the unmarked class of P have the feature +LOCATION. Those P which fail to specify spatial or temporal location (*of, despite,* most uses of *for* and *with*) are lexically marked for this feature and hence are not as finely subdivided for semantic nuances as are the locational P. In Chapter 2, we will see that certain classes of V also receive +LOCATION, but as a *marked* value, so as with ±DEFINITE above, there is no consistent ± notation meaning "marked for location": +LOCATION is lexically marked for V, while -LOCATION is marked for P. -LOCATION is an "Absence of Content," and so for P it is a "marked Absence of Content".

As we proceed, it will become evident that among the syntactic features F (the only features within closed classes), three subclasses are not interpreted in LF: (i) purely contextual features, (ii) copies of a feature F outside of F's canonical position(s), referred to subsequently as "alternatively realized F," and (iii) features which specify a marked absence of content. These three classes of syntactic F which are not used at LF will be called "purely syntactic" or uninterpreted. Other cognitive syntactic features which are used at LF, for instance those discussed above, will be called "cognitive syntactic" or simply cognitive or interpreted features notated in upper case. Lexical elements will turn out to have very different syntactic properties depending on which of these types of features they realize.

There are thus three main types of features on categories which interact differently with respect to lexical insertion, syntactic derivation and logical form ("LF"):

(i) Purely semantic features *f*, which are present *only* on the head categories X = N, V, A and P. They are not used in syntax and are not present on closed subclasses of grammatical X.

(ii) Cognitive syntactic features F in canonical positions, which can occur with all syntactic categories. They play a central role in both syntax and at Logical Form.

(iii) Purely syntactic features F, also occurring with all syntactic categories. They indicate contexts, realize the features in (ii) in non-canonical positions, or stipulate a marked lack of content (e.g, +STATIVE on V, -LOCATION on P). They are centrally used in syntax but play no role in Logical Form.

Summarizing, as stated earlier, both the types of features used in syntax, i.e. in (ii) and (iii), are uniformly notated with upper case F.

1.3 A theory of phrase structure as Extended Projections

1.3.1 Lexical Projections

The co-occurrence properties of the categories and features for which the preceding section gives a rough inventory must be accounted for by a universal theory of phrase structure and language-particular lexicons. So before turning in especially Chapters 2, 3 and 8 to the task of formalizing the notion "possible lexical entry," we need a general theory of how, independent of lexical specification, the categories of section 1.2 can combine.

Around 1986, generative grammar reached a seeming consensus that a restrictive and universal set of syntactic categories, called the "bar notation", was empirically adequate and cross-linguistically appropriate. Under this conception, any language contains at most the four lexical heads X, a very few functional heads such as D (associated with NP) and I (associated with VP), non-maximal or maximal projections of these six or so heads (respectively X' and XP), and specifier (SPEC) daughter nodes of XP. As argued in Speas (1990, section 2.2), non-maximal X' differ from maximal projections XP only in that the latter do not head some larger XP; i.e., adjoining @ to a phrase renders this phrase non-maximal. My own research has argued that an additional functional head C for introducing clauses ("complementizer") reduces to a class of grammatical P with sentence complements (Emonds, 1985, Ch. 7); this revision of the bar notation is adopted throughout this work.

Such a conception of syntax suggests strong restrictions on the category inventories available in Universal Grammar. Consequently, in that work's Introduction, I formulated two principles which are still tenable if, as just outlined, we are justified in postulating only a very small set of syntactic categories.

(1.8)   *Categorial Uniformity. The categories defined in terms of the bar notation, X^j and SPECIFIER(X), do not differ from language to language, but their subcategories which are realized in each language's syntax may vary.*

(1.9)   *Hierarchical Universality. The range of hierarchical combinations of syntactic categories does not vary from language to language at the level of deep structure.*

Although many analysts in intervening years have reanalyzed the syntactic features of the six or so lexical and functional heads as a greatly expanded set of functional heads and projections, I remain unconvinced of the fruitfulness of this line of research.[12] Rather, the earlier, more parsimonious theory retains its appeal and promise. I thus utilize a conservative category system, elaborated along the following lines:

   a. Lexical category heads X together with their complements and adjunct phrases constitute units of syntax, called *maximal projections* XP of these X.
   b. Finite verbs V and *all* their arguments are syntactic units, called clauses IPs.
   c. Analogously, nouns N including derived nominals and all their linguistic (as opposed to pragmatic) arguments are syntactic units, called DPs.

---

[12] Chomsky (1995, section 4.10) seems less enthusiastic about such analyses, e.g. about separate projections for agreement features. My skepticism about a greatly expanded set of functional categories does not preclude the possibility that the set widely recognized in the mid-eighties is too small.

Formally specifying how these heads combine with complements is the subject matter of succeeding chapters, which each modify or expand or limit the role of subcategorization. Chapter 7 also includes discussion of adjuncts, i.e. phrases which are both a sister and a daughter of the same type of phrase. Provided that CPs are special cases of PPs, one may impose a general syntactic restriction: *Adjuncts are always PPs or APs*.[13] APs are sometimes "adjectival" (they agree with a modified NP) and sometimes "adverbial" (they lack such agreement).

The divisions in (a-c) above suggest that a certain subclass of "external arguments" of V and N is generated outside VP and NP. The remainder of this chapter focuses not on the internal structure of XP, but rather on how XP containing all of X's complements and adjuncts combine into larger phrases with functional heads, namely IP and DP.

1.3.2 The Subject as a special phrase: I and IP

Within finite clauses, one argument NP/DP of the verb, a "subject phrase," is external to the VP. Indirect evidence for its special status is of many sorts: (i) the role of the subject – predicate pairing in Aristotle's logic and its wide and long-standing acceptance; (ii) its central role in Cartesian *grammaire générale* and the resulting "traditional grammar"; and (iii) the still valid descriptive value of Chomsky's (1957) original phrase structure rule, S → NP - VP. Many of the thirty odd properties examined in Keenan (1976) that "cluster" around subjecthood are prototypically exhibited by subjects of finite clauses.

Several direct, empirical syntactic arguments for the VP-external nature of the subject are provided by processes such as e.g. VP-fronting and VP-ellipsis in English and Japanese, English tag questions, widespread subject-verb agreement in languages lacking other agreement patterns, etc. Notably, these arguments all concern or work best with the subject phrase of *finite* clauses.

By the same arguments and others, the finite elements I are just as external to VP as the subject phrase is. This can be seen easily with English

---

[13] Finite adverbial clauses are invariably introduced by complementizers, and in turn, as mentioned above, CPs can be shown to be PPs. "Bare NP adverbials" as well as adjunct purpose clause infinitivals are argued to be PPs with empty heads in Emonds (1987). Present participles, which might be thought of as adjunct VPs or reduced IPs, are argued to have the structural form of APs is Emonds (1991a); Chapter 5 extends this idea to passive participles.

modals, which are prototypical instances of the finiteness category. Like subject phrases, modals don't front or ellipt with VPs and they appear in tag questions. They furthermore contract with the subject and with the negative (in the form *n't*) in ways that Vs do not.

(1.10)   *Deep structure finite clauses are of the form IP = DP - I - VP, where I is a grammatical "finiteness" head paired with V.*

For uniformity with the rest of the bar notation, we can assume that this DP is in SPEC(IP) and that the combination I + VP constitutes an I' (Chomsky, 1986).[14]

The structure in (1.10) differentiates a special argument called the subject from other "internal arguments" or complements, which is then defined by (1.11). In most cases, Keenan's special properties of a subject can be related to its VP-external status. A counterpart to such a definition is needed in any theory of grammatical relations which differentiates subjects and objects.

(1.11)   *Definition of Subject (tentative): The subject (or external argument) of a head V is a DP/NP which c-commands VP within the minimal IP containing V.*

1.3.3 The DP Hypothesis and a generalized definition of Subject

Chomsky (1970), Jackendoff (1977), George and Kornfilt (1981) and Abney (1987) all argue that the internal structure of noun phrases parallels that of sentences (IP), in that many classes of head nouns have a "subject", analogous to the subject of verbs, realized as a possessive noun phrase within a traditionally conceived larger noun phrase. Abney further proposes, following Brame (1984), that the noun phrases of the earlier generative literature contain two heads, where one is a grammatical "reference or quantification" head, say D (= Determiner), paired with N much as I is paired with V. This is Abney's DP-hypothesis. Under this conception, the earlier noun phrases

---

[14] CPs and PPs can appear to be subjects of English finite clauses. However, investigation of a range of embedded contexts reveals these non-DP subjects to be a root phenomenon akin to topicalization (See Emonds, 1976, Ch. 4 for CPs and Emonds, 1985, Ch. 7 for PPs). Moreover, Higgins (1973) shows that these topicalized CPs have their source only in DP positions: *That Mary would be late { *it didn't seem / few believed (*it) / we thought (*it) obvious }.*

have the form (1.12) analogous to finite clauses as in (1.10). This structure then defines an external argument for N, which again we call SPEC(DP).[15]

(1.12)   *Deep structure nominal phrases are of the form DP = (DP) - D - NP, where D is a grammatical "reference or quantification" head paired with N.*

The parentheses around the possessive DP in (1.12), in contrast to an IP subject's obligatory status in (1.10), reflects the fact that nouns, including derived nominalizations of verbs, often lack a linguistic subject within the larger DP (Wasow and Roeper, 1972). That is, their understood subject can only be pragmatically determined.

One argument for this is that a syntactically represented understood subject, a so-called "arbitrary PRO", must have animate reference at least in the positions SPEC(IP) and SPEC(DP), as shown in (1.13a-b). In contrast, the pragmatically understood subjects of derived nominals are often inanimate (1.13c).

(1.13)   a.   Inferred PRO must be animate; the following cannot refer to a volcanic eruption:
             To explode like that does a lot of harm.
             Exploding like that does a lot of harm.
                                   (inferred subject = +ANIMATE)
         b.   A V which cannot have an animate subject is incompatible with a PRO subject:
             *Few people like to unexpectedly occur.
             *Few people like unexpectedly occurring.
         c.   Noun-headed nominalizations may have a pragmatic subject or no subject:
             An explosion like that does a lot of harm.
                                   (inferred subject = ±ANIMATE)
             Few people like unexpected occurrences.

Serious questions remain as to exactly which morpheme classes realize the functional head D paired with N (= Determiner). Often without argument, the best candidates are assumed to be the definite demonstratives and

---

[15] The advent of the DP hypothesis has given rise to especially interesting work on Semitic languages focusing on the "construct state" of DPs which modify Ns: Borer (1984, 1989), Ritter (1988), Fassi-Fehri (1993) and Siloni (1997), among others.

articles. Nonetheless, Jackendoff's (1977, Ch. 4) detailed empirical work on English noun phrase specifiers isolates two distinct closed class or functional category positions which can occur in sequence, a definiteness / quantifier position and a numeral / quantifier position. Both are exemplified in the sequences *those many books, any three vertices, the little nitrogen remaining.*

On the face of it, both classes of morphemes might qualify for D, or there may be two rather than one functional projections matched with N. For example, Szabolcsi (1987) argues on the basis of extractions in Hungarian that a definiteness category D shares properties of C, while an additional functional head between D and N, analogous to I, assigns case to subjects. In other work in principle compatible with this analysis, Cardinaletti and Giusti (1991) and Giusti (1991) argue that both the definiteness and numeral positions should be functional heads.

On the other hand, these approaches seem to exclude a priori a possibility I retain, that closed classes of morphemes might be listed as SPEC(DP) or SPEC(NP). Lobeck (1995) explores parallelisms between English VP and NP ellipsis, both presumably licensed only if a functional head is present outside the ellipted phrase. Clearly, Jackendoff's second numeral / quantifier position may play this role and thus qualify as D, while his first position (for definite elements and certain quantifier morphemes) might conceivably be SPEC(DP).[16] In this work I will not try to definitively establish criteria for membership in D, nor determine whether two independent functional heads can appear above nouns in a DP.

Leaving aside the exact nature of D, let us proceed to formalize further parallels between NP and VP, besides the fact that each is the complement of a functional head. For these we need definitions.

(1.14) a. *N and the projections of N and D are "N-projections"; V and the projections of V and I are "V-projections."*
        b. *DPs and IPs are "extended projections" of N and V respectively.*
        c. *IP and DP are "cyclic domains" of V and N respectively.*

---

[16] Under this view (to which I am not committed), the ellipsis in *Your wine but not Sam's was tasty* would require a null functional head D. Such null heads might then be licensed by the possessive morpheme *'s* as an "alternative realization" of D on the SPEC(DP) sister of D', as in section 4.3.2.

A reviewer observes that if non-phrasal morphemes can be SPEC(XP), then they must still be specified as ± ___X', a head-like property. Thus, if *every* and *all* are SPEC(DP), *every* is +___D' and *all* is ± ___D'.

It is a natural step to extend the notion of "subject of V" in (1.11) so as to encompass "subject of N", including of nominalizations:

(1.15)   *Generalized Subjects: The subject or external argument of a head X is the lowest N-projection which c-commands a phrasal projection of X within its minimal cyclic domain.*[17]

(1.15) correctly requires that a *linguistic* subject of N (including nominalizations) must be inside DP. It further predicts that if a head noun has no such DP-internal subject, it can only have an unprojected, pragmatic subject (Wasow and Roeper, 1972). This generalized definition of subject will play an important and recurring role throughout this study.

The construction known as "subject small clauses" confirms the appropriateness of (1.15). Kubo (1993b, 103–107) provides evidence that such predications have both the internal structure and external distribution not of clauses but of DPs. In her structures (1.16), the brackets indicate the smallest cyclic DP domains containing italicized heads X of predicate phrases; the bold N or N' are the nominal projections which are the subjects of these X.

(1.16)   [**Young workers** *angry* over their pay] looks revolutionary.
          [**Children** *in* dangerous parks] is a scene used to convince women to quit jobs.
          [The **flags of many lands** *flying* over the plaza] is a good scene for a postcard.
          [**Paris** *and* its perfumes] fascinates American women.
          [**Sake** *and* tofu (together)] makes me sick.

By interpreting the predicate category as covering A, P, non-finite V and even co-ordinate conjunctions, Kubo shows that a definition similar to (1.15) correctly characterizes the (bold) nominal projections in (1.16) as the subjects of the italicized predicates. Her analysis makes no appeal to any clause-like structure not independently motivated as DP-internal.

---

[17] Generalized Subjects permits subjects of X to be within maximal projections of X but does not require them to be. It is thus neutral with respect to the issue of the "VP-internal subject hypothesis" (Zagona, 1982) and in fact allows for the possibility that in some constructions a subject is outside VP and in others within it.

1.3.4 The EPP: explaining the "strong D feature on Tense"

Let us now return to the discrepancy between (1.10) and (1.12): subjects of IPs are obligatory while those of DPs are optional. To maintain that, uniformly, only heads of projections and extended projections are obligatory and that argument positions are optional, we can revise (1.10) to IP = (DP) - I - VP, parallel to the formula for DP (1.12). The obligatory linguistic presence of the subject of a V under IP is then factored out as Chomsky's (1981) Extended Projection Principle, which can be expressed as (1.17).

(1.17)   *Extended Projection Principle. Every head verb present in Logical Form must have a structural subject phrase to which a semantic role may be assigned.*[18]

We will see in later chapters that the EPP plays an explanatory role well beyond allowing the IP projection (i) to parallel that of DP and (ii) to conform to the generalization that only heads are structurally obligatory.

The EPP and the formulation of Generalized Subjects (1.15) guarantee that the SPEC(IP) will always contain a structural DP subject for the highest V in IP. While this seems correct for English and many languages whose finite I obligatorily agrees with its subject, there is evidence that SPEC(IP) in a non-agreeing language such as Japanese can be absent, i.e. Japanese seems to directly reflect the optionality in the formula IP = (DP) - I - VP.

Sells (1996) contrasts two types of raising and obligatory control complements of Japanese verbs, both of which are uniformly IPs with past – non-past tense alternations. He shows how one type permits an overt (reflexive) subject DP presumably in SPEC(IP), while the other entirely lacks such a DP position. This latter type of IP, for which he constructs I believe incontrovertible arguments, Sells calls "sub-clausal" and observes that their understood subject appears in either subject or object position in the main clause. His arguments thus establish that Japanese robustly instantiates a subjectless (head-final) structure [VP - I]. In a somewhat more general and

---

[18] Impersonal verbs with so-called "theta-bar" subjects (like *seem* and French *falloir* 'be necessary') do not actually assign such roles in LF, but they still require a subject position. The EPP has come to be known in the Minimalist Program as the "strong D feature on Tense," i.e. the Tense projection (here IP) in many languages must have a DP in its Specifier position at Spell Out. As far as I can tell, this is simply stipulated and is moreover significantly less general than (1.17). For example, (1.17) will crucially explain why the lower lexical verbs in both verbal passives (Ch. 5) and Romance causatives (Ch. 6) must have (possibly understood) subjects, which are outside SPEC(IP).

theory-based treatment, Kuroda (1992, 321) reaches the same conclusion: SPEC(IP) "can be left vacant" in Japanese but not English.

These arguments, taken at face value, suggest that a Generalized Subject @ of a V need not always be present within the smallest finite IP; i.e., @ can be the lowest DP which c-commands VP within some domain *larger* (in Japanese) than its minimal IP.[19] We get this consequence if we include a condition – not stated in (1.14c) – that a cyclic domain of V must additionally contain *a potential subject,* i.e. a DP c-commanding a projection of V. Under this condition, SPEC(IP) can, like SPEC(DP), be entirely absent in certain instances. Nonetheless, cyclic domains for a VP do not under this conception extend upward in the tree without limit; the lowest IP containing a potential DP controller of VP will then be the latter's cyclic domain, and the EPP (1.17) guarantees that there must be such a DP.

This now raises the question: if the EPP doesn't force SPEC(IP) to contain DP, why must it do so in English and other agreeing languages? To account for this, I extract a part of a general hypothesis of Kuroda (1992, 325) that "English is a forced Agreement language." While he derives several contrasting properties of English and Japanese from the respective presence and absence of his generalized notion of agreement, I focus here on perhaps the morphologically most salient difference between the two languages:

(1.18)   *Number Filter. The functional heads (I and D) must be specified for number (±PLURAL) at PF in certain languages (e.g., English but not Japanese).*

Now, the cognitive syntactic feature PLURAL is canonically associated with D – at least for this discussion I mean D to be precisely the canonical locus of PLURAL as in (1.5). (1.18) then specifies the fairly uncontroversial property that the English but not the Japanese DP must express the ±PLUR distinction; for related discussion of (optional) Japanese noun classifiers, see Kubo (1996) and section 6.4.3 here.

But equally, PLURAL is *not* a canonical feature of I. Number can only surface on I and hence satisfy (1.18) when the latter agrees with some phrasal projection in its SPEC which *is* specified for ±PLUR, i.e. SPEC(IP) must be a DP in a "Number Filter" language. We thus derive not only the

---

[19] Neither Kuroda's nor Sells' framework can accept this conclusion because of commitments to other hypotheses (VP-internal subjects and argument structures respectively).

obligatory presence of a phrase in SPEC(IP) from a more general property of English but also the fact that its SPEC(IP) must be DP rather than just any XP.[20] In light of (1.18), the specifiers of both IP and DP can remain optional at the level of UG, as can all non-heads in the bar notation.

In conclusion, the combinations of the basic syntactic categories discussed in section 1.2 are the classic bar notation XP projections of the four lexical heads N, V, A and P and the extended projections given by the formula (1.19). Strictly speaking, these latter expansions are not rules, but simply definitions of the extended projections of N and V.

(1.19)   *Functional Projections. FP = (DP) - F - XP; when F is I, then X is V and when F is D, then X is N.*[21]

The subject positions of FP can be referred to as SPEC(IP) and SPEC(DP). The left to right order of the elements in these projections is related to general word order principles in section 3.1. Beyond projections $<$ wo of these six heads, I do not envision greatly expanding the inventory of possible phrases.

----

[20] If the XP in SPEC(IP) need not be DP in certain "V second" languages such as Icelandic and Yiddish, then number ageement on their I must be ensured differently than in English. This obviously holds independently of (1.18).

It is tempting to say that a null and caseless DP in SPEC(IP), though sufficiently specified for number for ensuring compliance with the Number Filter (1.18), is not a visible source at PF for any concrete morphemes which realize agreement on I. From this would follow the correct result that a null caseless subject in English implies a null I at s-structure. (The converse of course doesn't hold.)

[21] In my view, A and P do not have extended projections, at least in the sense that these extended projections *contain DP subjects of A and P.* For example in English, no movement of an AP or a PP which may happen to be adjacent to its subject, as in *We consider Bill stupid* or *We found John in the library,* ever includes that subject:

(i)   *What we considered was Bill stupid.
      *Bill stupid though she considered, she married him anyway.

(ii)   *It was John in the library that we found.
      *Whose father in the library did they find?
      Cf. How many feet behind the house was it placed?

I don't exclude the possibility that full APs and PPs include functional projections, but such projections, unlike those of N and V, don't contain subjects of A and P. My use of the term "extended projection" covers only functional projections which include subjects.

1.4 The interplay among derivations, the Lexicon, and Economy Principles

1.4.1 Transformational derivations

The descriptive and explanatory successes of transformational generative grammar have been based on a model which assembles choices from a lexicon, puts them together in trees (or phrase markers) in terms of a theory of phrase structure, and then subjects these underlying trees to a sequence of Chomskyan "transformational operations" which maps them into some sort of "well-formed surface structures" in which, possibly among other elements, overt morphemes appear in the order pronounced. Abstracting away from actual phonological processes (e.g. assimilations, epentheses, deletions, aspirations, etc.), we can, along with many syntacticians, still refer to the results of these transformational derivations as "Phonological Form" or "PF".

Chomsky (1976) and Chomsky and Lasnik (1977), building on a decade of "interpretivist semantics" on the relation of syntax to a range of generalizations about meaning, codified the notion that the basic locus of the interface of syntactic structure with the use and understanding of language was "late" in a transformational derivation, i.e. subsequent to most or all of the transformations that had been scrutinized up to that time. The transformationally derived syntactic structures which speakers use to interpret and understand language are widely called "Logical Form" or "LF", following Chomsky (1976).

A number of often rather abstract debates have surrounded the relation between LF and PF. The most usual positions are that a transformational derivation of PF "branches" to LF (or vice-versa, depending on one's point of view), and that subsequent to this branching, a number of invisible or "covert" transformational operations further rearrange syntactic structure before it reaches the LF interface with understanding and use. Many "minimalist" models postulate even more covert syntax than is observed in the overt part of derivations. At the other extreme, the "linear model" of van Riemsdijk and Williams (1981) and van Riemsdijk (1982) simply defines LF as a certain intermediate point in the derivation of PF; this model does not countenance covert movements. However these debates are eventually settled, cyclic domains (1.14) at the branch point (also called Spell Out) can be called s-structures, without claiming or denying that they exhibit interesting sets of properties. In all current competing derivational models (i.e. those which transformationally map combinations of lexical choices to PF), the derivational structures at the branch point, whether close or far from either LF or PF in terms of operations, are agreed to contain various types of empty categories (traces, "silent copies," empty pronouns, empty discourse anaphors, certain null morphs), as well as indices which link these empty categories (and other co-referring categories) to antecedents of various sorts. That is, any current derivational conceptions of s-structures are much more than structuralist-style trees, whose only function is to impose structure and classification on sequences of overt morphemes.

Throughout this work, I adhere to such a derivational model, in which transformations map sets of lexical choices combined in phrase structures into s-structures with empty categories and co-indexing and subsequently into LF and PF; hence I frequently employ the acronyms PF and LF. A transformational operation which precedes s-structure is said to occur "in syntax," while one which applies subsequent to s-structure in deriving PF is said to take place "on the way to PF" or "late" or even, somewhat misleadingly, "at PF." Since I am unconvinced that morphemes are actually reordered between s-structure and LF, my operations "on the way to LF" or "in LF" refer, unless explicit mention is made of movement, to either deletions as in Lasnik and Saito (1984) or to copyings. I tend to think of LF copying as applying to indices, which express identity of reference for projections of D and identity of sense for other constituents.

1.4.2 The Lexicon

Chomsky (1995) systematically refers to PF and LF as "interfaces" of syntax with respectively a perception/articulation system and an interpretation/use system. Although perception, articulation and use of language can common-sensically be thought of as part of the "real world," the systems or components to which Chomsky refers are clearly mental faculties. PF is then the interface with a mental faculty that allows us to produce and understand phonological material in terms of lexical items packaged in syntactic structures, while LF is the interface with a mental faculty which allows us to use lexical items packaged in syntactic structures to exchange linguistic information in the here and now (and/or plan, reflect on the past, reason things out, express emotion or art, etc.).

While I agree with this "minimalist" line of thought (and hope I have not grossly misrepresented it), there seems to be a missing element in many discussions of how syntax mediates between the PF and LF interfaces. The missing element is the nature of the lexicon, or at least that major part of the lexicon which is not purely syntactic. Along these lines, in fact, Chomsky

(1991, 46) assumes:

> "... that there are three 'fundamental' levels of representation: D-structure, PF, and LF. Each constitutes an 'interface' of the syntax (broadly construed) with other systems: D-structure is a projection of the lexicon, via the mechanisms of X-bar theory; PF is associated with articulation and perception, and LF with semantic interpretation."

At this point, I am not yet concerned with how a syntactic representation is built up from the lexicon,[22] but rather with maintaining that whatever the mechanisms for assembling lexical items, the mental location of these items (the lexicon) is just as much a system or mental faculty as are, broadly speaking, the phonology-articulation-perception and semantics-interpretation-use faculties. More precisely, the open class lexicon, perhaps together with principles for assembling its items into trees, *is a syntactic interface*, and what it interfaces with is the mental faculty of culture and human memory.

In fact, the structure of the mental lexicon, as we will see in this book, is eminently more knowable than various aspects of the other two faculties. This is because the elements of the lexicon leave so many syntactic signatures, and syntactic behavior is the area of language to which we have the most direct and extensive access. In contrast, though at relatively abstract levels we know quite a bit about PF and LF interface representations, *our knowledge of what they are interfacing with* is largely shrouded in mystery.

I am not sure if taking the lexicon as a mental interface in its own right really requires defense, but if so the following considerations may be offered. Basic aspects of linguistic perception (PF interface) and use (LF interface) are plausibly shared with primates.[23] Syntax itself is defined in terms of the cognitive categories of the lexicon and must additionally be largely designed to "fit" the LF and PF interfaces. Consequently, the lexicon presents itself as the best candidate for a *purely human* mental faculty.

---

[22] On this point I have always agreed with arguments given in class lectures by E. Klima (Emonds, 1985, Ch. 2) that lexical items should be inserted in trees from the bottom up, subsequent to transformational operations on their complements, rather than simultaneously at a single level of "deep structure."

[23] It may well be that an oral production faculty is not shared with primates, but it is harder to exclude the possibility that primates share in a non-oral or "signed" mode the perception/ production faculties with which human language interfaces.

(1.20)   a.   *Species-specific nature of the Lexicon. The open class lexicon is a fully independent faculty of "human knowledge."*

There is thus no close counterpart to an open class lexicon among even higher primates.[24]

When we think that the English mental lexicon probably fully characterizes various complex concepts such as *advantage, flaw, furniture, game, history, religion, vacation, vegetable, collect, intricate* and *outdoors*, it is not so clear that any other knowledge that is both systematic (rather than intuitive) and *effortlessly shared throughout a culture* (neither specialized nor consciously taught) still remains outside the lexicon. It thus seems reasonable to further conjecture:

(1.20)   b.   *The Lexicon as Knowledge. The open class lexicon is the systematic shared part of human memory.*

This formulation is fairly close to de Saussure's (1916) conception of "Langue", as articulated in his *Course on General Linguistics.*[25]

---

[24] The specifically human "design features" of natural language in Hockett (1960), provided certain of his definitions are clarified, are displacement, duality of patterning, and traditional (rather than genetic) transmission of a large lexicon.

Somewhat speculatively, it is plausible to trace everything specifically human here to the property of duality of patterning, whereby both (i) the smallest elements concatenated in the system (roughly, phonemes) are meaningless *and* (ii) the smallest meaningful elements (roughly, morphemes) again concatenate according to a system. Natural animal communication systems fail to *simultaneously* satisfy both conditions.

This duality is plausibly a necessary precondition for a large, human-like lexicon, which then is passed on through culture. There is no reason to assume that primates couldn't amass a large lexicon if they could divorce phonological units from meaning.

Most likely, really massive lexical transmission, in order to be successful, must additionally be divorced from the here and now, in that we can't learn our large lexicons (containing abstract nouns, illnesses, internal organs, virtues, verbs of mental activities, etc.) merely by pointing. That is, full lexical learning must involve displacement. Thus, displacement, as well as duality of patterning, may be a necessary condition for a large lexicon; in this case, the two design features together would be sufficient for the large lexicon and human language.

A final reduction would consist in showing that either a large lexicon or a division between phonology and syntax (duality) is sufficient to provide a user with a means of displacing thought away from the conceptual template of the here and now.

[25] I share the generative critique of de Saussure, that he simply omitted Universal Grammar from his object of study, identifying "Langue" with a store of signs, i.e., the lexicon. An earlier version of this criticism was that de Saussure omitted all of syntax. But a recent

Finally, as de Saussure also emphasized in the first chapters of the *Course,* while mature individuals may trivially add to or modify their "inventories of signs," they do not lose or even seriously modify the vast majority of their lexical entries over a lifetime. Upon reflection, it seems plausible that the very permanence of lexical entries (in contrast to the notoriously fleeting nature of individual sentences, almost immediately inaccessible to exact recall) may be the basis of Hockett's (1960) natural language "displacement," which is either unavailable to animals or present on a much reduced scale. In any case, its permanence and resistance to modification further support the lexicon's claim to being a mental faculty separate from syntactic computation.

(1.20)   c. *Permanence of the Lexicon. The entries of the lexicon, once acquired in youth, remain basically unchanged and unaffected by use throughout life.*

The three conditions (1.20) justify treating the lexicon as a separate mental faculty. The inventories of syntactic categories and features (section 1.2) and the theory of phrase structures as extended projections (section 1.3) then become interface conditions with this faculty. In particular, the fact that syntactic features and categories F are drawn entirely from the cognitive categories which organize the lexicon suggests that syntax in this respect at least is a "perfect system," in the sense discussed in Chomsky (1995). Less obvious is why precisely four of these categories should give rise to (extended) phrasal projections and be at the center of the system; I will not investigate this rather abstract question in this work, though it is a subtheme throughout Emonds (1985).

1.4.3 Economy Conditions

Under the conception that the lexicon is a mental faculty or system, a transformational derivation becomes a device which mediates between *three* syntactic interfaces, the Lexicon, PF, and LF.[26] This suggests that there may

---

generative tendency, which this work adheres to, tends to ascribe all language-particular syntax to the lexicon (cf. Chapters 3 and 4). Perhaps de Saussure also made this assumption, thereby including any syntax linked to a particular language's grammatical morphemes under "Langue." If so, he stands accused not of omitting all of syntax, but only its universal component from his object of study.

[26] Conditions on lexical insertion are, under this conception, properly called interface conditions.

also be three different types of what Chomsky (1991) terms "least effort" conditions on syntactic derivations, that is, some formal condition of economy may hold at each interface. As this work proceeds, we will see how two well-known conditions proposed in Chomsky (1995) govern the lexical interface and PF. Economy of Representation will play a central role throughout in determining exactly how lexical insertions satisfy the specifications of individual items and thus qualifies as the economy condition for the lexical interface. The particular version of Economy of Derivation used in this work, introduced in Chapter 4, minimizes the number of phonological words and is hence the economy condition for PF.

This study does not extensively use an economy condition for LF, but as the one interface where reference plays a role, some "Economy of Reference" may be a good candidate for such a condition. According to the analysis of free and bound pronouns in Emonds (1995), the only *linguistic* antecedents available in sentence grammar are those that c-command a pronoun, as in (1.21a); I then claim *that a pronoun and a linguistic antecedent together make only one reference to a universe of discourse.* In contrast, apparent antecedents in discourse grammar which do not c-command pronouns, as in (1.21b), actually require a separate reference by the pronoun to the universe of discourse.

(1.21)   a. I asked John$_i$ if Sue would ever fire him$_i$.
         b. We ignored John$_i$, because Sue would never fire him$_i$.

The contrast in (1.22) then follows from the fact that the quantifiers *each* and *every* are grammatically singular, as shown independently by subject agreements, but have plural reference in the universe of discourse.[27]

(1.22)   a. Mary warned every pupil$_i$ that the needle would hurt him$_i$.
         b. Mary warned every pupil$_i$, since the needle might scare { them$_i$/ *him$_i$ }.

Similarly, the contrast in (1.23) follows from the fact that a DP quantified by *no* is also grammatically singular but has no reference in the universe of discourse.

_____

[27] In informal speech today, *every N* can be the linguistic antecedent of a plural animate pronoun as well as a singular. But if c-command is lacking, the pronoun *must* be plural. This contrast corresponds to the difference in types of coreference at issue.

(1.23) a. Mary warned no pupil$_i$ that the needle would hurt him$_i$.
  b. *Mary warned no pupil$_i$, since the needle might scare { them$_i$/ him$_i$ }.

I argue in the work cited that this difference in how many independent references are involved in using a pronoun accounts for the above and certain other grammatical differences between the two types of pronouns, and conclude that these contrasting paradigms of pronominal co-reference are explained by condition (1.24).

(1.24) If they can, pronouns choose a linguistic antecedent rather than a pragmatic reference in the universe of discourse.

Now, let us make another plausible assumption, that non-pronominal, non-trace DPs, those with the possibility of independent reference, must involve pragmatic reference rather than linguistic co-reference. This suggests re-interpreting Chomsky's (1981) Principle C as a condition which prefers a DP$_i$ to be a pronoun or an anaphor rather than a referring expression in any position where a potential antecedent c-commands DP$_i$. That is, at least part of Principle C can be expressed as (1.25):[28]

(1.25) If two co-indexed DP$_i$ are in a c-command relation, prefer forms which allow them to be in a relation of linguistic rather than pragmatic co-reference.

It is plausible to assume that co-referential epithets, like other lexical expressions, always require reference to the universe of discourse. This correctly predicts that they can be chosen only if their antecedent does not c-command them:

(1.26) a. *I convinced John$_i$ that Sue would never fire the pest$_i$.
  b. We ignored John$_i$, because Sue would never fire the pest$_i$.

Under the formulation (1.25), pronouns or anaphors with linguistic antecedents should be chosen in preference to lexical referring expressions if either

---

[28] Not all Principle C violations can be treated in this way; in particular, those involving A-bar-bound traces cannot be. But such traces may by definition require their closest binder to be in an A-bar position.

choice leads to the same interpretation. Thus, both types of forms are more "economical" than any referring expression with which they are in competition.

The effects of (1.24) and (1.25) together can be expressed in a single statement:

(1.27)   *Economy of Reference at LF (Conjecture). Among representations with the same interpretations at LF, prefer the representation with the fewest pragmatic references to the universe of discourse.*

This unified principle then serves as the Economy Condition for the third (LF) interface. A transformational derivation thus mediates three interfaces, the lexical interface, PF and LF. The derivation is subject to an economy condition at each interface. Two of these, Economy of Representation (for the lexical interface) and Economy of Derivation (for PF), play central roles throughout this work.

1.5 An excursus into IP reference and economy at the LF Interface

LF Economy (1.27) contributes to the logic of this book only in developing the subcategorization frames for clausal complements in section 8.1.3. I set the stage for this use here, but the conclusions seem interesting in themselves.

Since (1.27) mentions reference in the universe of discourse, the issue arises as to which constituents carry reference. The motivation for establishing (1.27) involved only the reference of DPs, which might plausibly be the only constituents with reference; cf. also section 9.3 for further discussion.

Nonetheless, G. Frege's famous contribution to reference and sense claims that sentences also have reference, namely their truth. Assuming sentence reference is possible and that (1.27) which regulates it is a principle of sentence grammar (like everything in this study not explicitly formulated otherwise), LF Economy implies that *a sentence should only have one truth value*. That is, if two sentences have separate truth values, one should not be embedded in another.[29] This conclusion then partly explains why

---

[29] Many studies have shown that direct quotation (and certain styles of indirect speech not typically found in spoken English) involves two independent main clause sentences,

embedded clauses are not asserted (or if they are, the main clause is not) but rather at most presupposed. That is, the embeddings in (1.28b) are not synonymous with the main clause pairings in (1.28a):

(1.28)   a.   It is raining; I feel bad today.   It is raining and I feel bad today.
        b.   Because it is raining,   As it is raining, I feel bad today.
           I feel bad today.

To fully explain why a sentence has only one truth value, we should first locate which constituent carries it. The following non-embedded infinitives (1.29) and other non-embeddable root constructions in (1.30) lack an I with specified features in LF, or perhaps lack I entirely. It is clear that they also have no truth value:

(1.29)   a.   Maybe Sue and Ann were on time. Response: What? Them be
           on time!
        b.   (Do) Be more considerate!
        c.   Everybody be more considerate!
        d.   Oh, to be in Paris again!

Regarding (1.29d), Lobeck (1995, Ch. 6) argues that the English infinitival marker *to* is absent in LF. (I return to this point in connection with "obligatory control" in section 10.1.)

(1.30)   Into the street with that junk!
        A cup of coffee, please.
        Good for Harry! But screw you!

Truth value in English thus seems to be signaled by the lexical content in LF of the I node in the main clause; that is, [I, -MODAL] carries truth value (cf. also Emonds, 1986):

---

neither embedded in the other. Thus, the following two examples are essentially syntactically equivalent.

Mary said to me yesterday, "Gosh, just between us, I frankly don't have time."
Mary said this to me yesterday: "Gosh, just between us, I frankly don't have time."

Banfield (1982, Ch. 1) provides a review of relevant literature and arguments for this conclusion.

(1.31)   *Truth value. Certain lexical items in I in LF carry reference, i.e.*
         Frege's truth value.[30]

But we need not stipulate in (1.31) that only a single I within a sentence is
used to determine truth, because using more than one I would violate LF
Economy (1.27).

We still need to know why the main clause I and not some other I is used
to calculate truth value (reference). Again, we can determine this entirely on
the basis of main clause data, and then extrapolate to dependent clauses. It
is widely accepted that information and yes-no questions as in (1.32a) have
no truth value, and similarly other types of "inverted" clauses in which an
I raises to C, as in (1.32b), lack truth value as well.

(1.32)   a. Which person did you meet?
            Why would he do that?
            Can Mary swim?
         b. Ah, were Mary only here! Then I would be happy.
            Damn! Could you please finish that soon!
            May your family prosper for a thousand years!

Moreover, main clause constructions introduced by an overt C are wishes,
questions or suggestions in several languages, which again have no truth
value.

(1.33)   a. If only she would arrive early!
            How come your friend has no money?
            What if we went to bed early?
         b. French wishes introduced by *que* 'that' and the subjunctive
            mood:
            Que ce type ne m'emmerde plus!
            'May that guy never bother me again!'
         c. French suggestions introduced by *si* 'if' and the imperfect tense:
            Si nous allions tous au marché!
            'Suppose we all went to the market!'

---

[30] I suggest below that in Japanese, an additional condition on lexical I for expressing a
truth value is that these items be raised to C in LF. That is, particular languages may
specify not only which items in I carry truth value but where they must be in LF in order
to do so.

Overall, it appears that if SPEC(CP) contains a phrase lacking reference as in (1.32a) or no phrase at all, as in (1.32b) and (1.33), then an IP introduced by C has no truth value. These sets of main clause data together thus strongly suggest (1.34); as throughout, I take C to be a P lacking purely semantic features *f*.

(1.34)   *Truth Value Neutralization. A P (i.e., C) lacking semantic features f whose specifier lacks reference takes away the truth value of a clausal complement of P.*

In contrast, a CP whose SPEC contains a topicalized referring DP, as in German or Dutch verb-second declarative sentences, is exempt from (1.34). With Lasnik and Saito (1984), I assume that embedded topicalizations occur within IP, whose introductory C still neutralizes IP's truth value.

We have arrived at (1.34) without any reference to embedded clause data. Truth Value Neutralization thus permits a non-circular account for why dependent clause IPs are typically embedded in CPs in English and many similar languages.[31] If one finite IP were embedded in another without a CP, it would have its own reference to the universe of discourse (i.e., its own truth value), and so a single sentence would have two references and would violate LF Economy (1.27).[32]

---

[31] M. Saito pointed out to me that my theory of categories and case-marking, in Chapter 7, should require CP-housing over IPs in contexts where their DP counterparts do not need PPs for case. This observation led me to develop the notion of LF economy of reference in this section; Truth Value Neutralization (1.34) expresses the needed asymmetry between IP and DP. Recall that a CP is a special case of PP in this work (Emonds, 1985, Ch. 7). While DPs are housed in grammatical PPs for case assignment, IPs appear to be housed in these purely grammatical PPs to prevent them from having independent truth values (reference).

I don't attempt here to derive (1.34) from a deeper analysis of the nature of C/ P.

[32] English IP complements to a huge class of verbs such as *believe, convince, know, mean, persuade, promise, say,* etc. can appear, at least optionally, without an introductory *that*. The issue is, do such finite IP lack C, leading to a violation of (1.27)?

(i)   John promised everybody there (that) *the dinner would soon be ready.*
      We believe (that) *you were honest* now.
      He persuaded us (that) *Mary should quit her job.*

As soon as these complements are displaced so that they are no longer c-commanded by the verb which selects them, a complementizer is again obligatory, showing that English is not so different from other languages:

There is a way nonetheless for embedding an IP without a CP to house it. Recall that it is the lexical items in I rather than simply I which carry truth value (1.31). Hence, an I which dominates no lexical item in LF cannot violate Economy of Reference.

(1.35)   *Theorem of LF Economy. An IP may be embedded other than as a sister to C only if its I is Ø in LF, i.e. only if it is non-finite and hence without truth value.*

In other words, any *finite* embedded clause must be a sister to C, but infinitival IP need not be. This result will be extremely useful in discussing how embedded clauses are related to subcategorization features in Chapter 8.

Before leaving the topic, I should explain why (1.31) may require language-particular refinements. A range of different empirical studies has established that *embedded finite IPs need not be housed in CPs in Japanese.* A central conclusion of Murasugi's (1991, 1994) grammatical and language acquisition studies is that Japanese finite relative clauses are IPs but not CPs. Kubo's (1994, 226) survey of clausal complements of N observes that a rather mysterious purely grammatical higher verb -*iu* is required in order to embed certain instances of [$_{CP}$IP-*to*] inside Japanese noun phrases, yielding a sequence [$_{IP}$ [$_{CP}$ IP-*to*]-*iu*]-N. She concludes that "a clausal sister to a noun must be IP [rather than CP] in Japanese for an as yet unknown reason." The work of Sells (1996) discussed above in section 1.3.4 implies that certain Japanese IP complements of V are not CPs either.

This pattern of "bare" embedded finite IPs (without CPs) indicates that (1.35) doesn't hold for Japanese, which suggests in turn that its Is do not have truth value in isolation. In corroboration of this, Kubo (1994) argues that Japanese main clauses *have the force of judgments (potetntial truth values) only if they are CPs,* which are recognizable by virtue of permitting

---

(ii)   What John promised Mary was *(that) the dinner would soon be ready.
   *(That) the dinner would soon be ready was promised by John.
   *(That) you were honest { we believe/ is difficult to believe } now.
   He persuaded us, as everyone knows, *(that) Mary should quit her job.

This pattern suggests that the morpheme *that* in C has a special lexical property, call it "optionality," which allows it to alternate with a zero *if its CP projection remains in its base position throughout the syntactic derivation.* There are other such morphemes: the present tense copula in Malay can (and sometimes must) be absent in its base position, but surfaces if it precedes the subject, presumably by I to C movement (Kader, 1981, Ch. 6).

e.g. exhaustive listing *ga*-phrases, fronted VPs, and predications with the copula [$_C$ *da*]; in contrast, its bare root IPs with the copula [$_I$ *na*] are less forceful non-predicational commentaries indicating states of affairs.[33]

These patterns taken together indicate that something like (1.36) may be a proper refinement of (1.31):

(1.36)   *Truth value. In Japanese, lexical items in **I must raise to C** to carry reference **in LF** (i.e., truth value).*

LF Economy (1.27) consequently imposes no limits on the distribution of embedded IPs in Japanese. Furthermore, since a bare IP clearly has less structure than one housed in a CP, Economy of Representation then *prefers* bare IPs to CPs for Japanese dependent clauses. Economy of Reference of course places no limits on the distribution of its WH complementizer *-ka*, since question clause CPs have no truth value. However, Japanese CPs of the type that do express truth value should be subject to limited embedded distribution.

Interestingly, Kubo's (1994, Ch. 7) study of Japanese conditional clauses isolates two distinct types of embedding: double CPs of the form CP + [$_C$ *to* 'if' / *kara* 'because'], which she terms "empirical conditionals" because of their relation to factivity, and bare IPs terminating in *(r)eba*, termed "subjunctive" or "hypothetical conditionals." What is missing is an embedded IP with the familiar single C position. But an explanation for this gap now suggests itself. There is no ban on bare finite IPs in Japanese, as seen above. But an embedded CP with I raised to C in Japanese would express a truth value, by (1.36), and hence potentially violate Economy of Reference (1.27). The way to circumvent this potential violation is by again embedding this CP in a larger CP whose head lacks any purely semantic feature *f*, in accord with (1.34). This yields the double CP structure justified but not explained by Kubo's analysis.

Whatever the value of these tentative remarks on truth values and reference, Principle (1.27), which can be justified solely in terms of DP reference, nicely fills out an expectation that each of the three psychological

---

[33] Hence, in reporting a given situation, non-predicational, non-judgmental root IPs terminating in *na-no* are often, according to Kubo, considered more "feminine" while the predicational, judgmental versions terminating in *da* are more "masculine." Of course, in many situations the sexual styles are abandoned; e.g. anybody's exclamative comment on a scene of surprising natural beauty would be better described in a non-predicational form, anyone can moralize by using the judgmental form, etc.

interfaces with UG has an appropriate economy measure. In conjunction with a Fregean conjecture (1.31) about sentence reference as truth value, LF Economy (1.27) also makes accurate predictions about the distribution of finiteness in main clause constructions and, with the aid of an interpretive principle (1.34) for the category C, accounts for why CPs invariably house finite English dependent clause IPs, even when no other grammatical principle requires this "extra structure."

Chapter 2
Subcategorization: Syntax as the material basis
of semantics[1] > d. Maurice Gross / Harris ?

2.1 Advantages of classical subcategorization

This chapter investigates the lexical mechanisms which permit lexical heads X to combine with phrasal sisters, their "complements," in order to form X' projections. Following Stowell (1981), well-formed X' are licensed, not by phrase structure rules, but rather by lexical properties specified for each X^0. That is, the lexical entries of the heads X^0 determine which combinations of heads and complements are well-formed. The word order among them is set by both invariant and parameterized properties of Universal Grammar.[2]

As introduced in Chomsky (1965), contextual "subcategorization features" of the form +___YP are the central lexical formalism for indicating how different classes of verbs (subsequently, of any lexical heads) select complements. For example, leaving aside finer grained distinctions to which we return, the three verbs *seem, describe,* and *glance* are lexically listed for different complements as in (2.1). These contextual features then expressing the obligatory co-occurrences shown in (2.2). For more details and examples of this notation, such as the decision to lexically stipulate only plus values for these features, see Chomsky (1965, Ch. 2). Throughout, I utilize DP to notate full noun phrases.

---

[1] This material was first presented as a lecture with this title at the Conference on the Formation of Culture in Ljubljana in 1987; I am grateful to the organizer Rastko Mocnik. The version in this chapter is an expansion of Emonds (1997). I have benefited greatly from M. Kajita's careful reading of that essay. The first two sections rework subject matter also treated in the first sections of Emonds (1991b).

[2] As examples of invariant UG properties, I would include the set of syntactic categories (1.8) and dominance relations (1.9), Canonical Realization (1.5), the definition of subject (1.15), the Extended Projection Principle (1.17) and the three Economy Principles (Ch. 7).

As parameterized UG properties, I would include the head-initial/final parameter, some variation in Subjacency domains, and the possibility that some few semantic features f might be "syntacticized" (i.e. be cognitive syntactic features F) in some languages but not in others. For example, features which characterize closed classes of Classifier morphemes might be +F in "classifier" languages but not in "plural-forming" languages (cf. Kubo, 1996, for discussion of this dichotomy).

(2.1)   seem, V, +__AP   describe, V, +__DP   glance, V, +__PP

(2.2)   Mary { described/ *glanced/ *seemed } the task.
        Mary { *described/ glanced/ *seemed } toward the room.
        Mary { *described/ *glanced/ seemed } thirsty.
        Mary { *described/ *glanced/ *seemed } (that it was late).

Many verbs can take a second, usually optional complement, most simply represented in trees as their second phrasal sister. Such "oblique" complements are licensed by subcategorization features as in (2.3); parentheses
indicate optionality. Thus, *describe* and *seem*, but not *undertake* or *remain*,
may have indirect objects introduced by *to*. As we refine subcategorization,
we will see that such predictable grammatical P need not appear in frames
for individual verbs, but for now we retain Chomsky's original notation, in
which the introductory P is stipulated.

(2.3)   describe, V, +__DP (to^DP)   undertake, V, +__NP
        seem, V, +__AP (to^DP)   remain, V, +__AP

(2.4)   Mary { described/ *undertook } the task to the boss.
        Mary { seemed/ *remained } thirsty to the boss.

Authors since Bresnan (1970) have noted that subcategorization as originally formulated is inadequate. For example, consider a verb like *reside*
which like *glance* also requires a PP complement; the simple feature +___PP
accounts for neither the contrast among Ps in (2.5) nor the distinction between *reside* and *glance* in (2.6).

(2.5)   Mary { resided /glanced } { near/ by / outside / *of / *with /
        *for } the hall.

(2.6)   Mary { *resided / glanced } { down / { toward / into } a small
        apartment }.
        Mary { resided / *glanced } { within walking distance / at home }.

Examples of such inadequacies can easily be multiplied. Consequently,
many researchers have concluded that co-occurrence relations between
various head X and complements YP may be better captured through
"s(emantic)-selection," that is, by lexically specifying deeper semantic regularities directly. Grimshaw's (1979) study of co-occurrence patterns involv-

vs. c-selection

ing finite complements is typically considered initial evidence of how semantic selection provides more descriptively adequate accounts. Jackendoff (1990) is perhaps the most comprehensive attempt to derive syntactic co-occurrence from underlying semantic regularities.

Before evaluating the problems with classical subcategorization, however, it might be instructive to point out some paradigms which it handles well, and which would appear to defy description in any terms other than simple notational variants of a syntactic treatment.

First, the conclusions of Grimshaw's (1979) essay are more circumspect about syntactic selection than interpretations usually put on it. Much of her article is devoted to demonstrating the essential role of syntax in the selection of complement clause types by verbs. In particular, she argues for three points: (i) Selection of DP vs. selection of CP is irreducibly syntactic.(ii) Null, elliptic sentence complements are also determined by item-particular syntactic subcategorization (her sections 3 and 5, esp. pp. 296–297). (iii) Complement selection of indirect question vs. exclamatory complements is largely predictable on the basis of an *inherent* semantic feature of predicates rather than on the basis of selectional mechanisms (her Appendix). In light of these arguments *for* syntactic selection, two of which have not been subsequently addressed, the interpretation of her article as tolling the death knell for syntactic subcategorization is surprising. We return to these issues in section 2.3.[3]

---

[3] Pesetsky (1982) suggests replacing +___DP with a lexical property of "assigns case"; the field adopted this sweeping proposal to eliminate subcategorization with the same eagerness as Grimshaw's more modest proposal to supplement it. Nonetheless, replacing +___DP with "assigns case" succeeds only in obscuring issues and raising unanswered questions:

(i)   Do verbs with the features + __(DP) or +__{DP, CP} "assign case"? If they do so "optionally," then why should a passive morpheme be necessary to absorb case? That is, shouldn't NP Movement be able to derive two equivalent passives *French is {spoken/ speak(ing)}* from the entry *speak,* +___(DP), which would then contrast with a single passive allowed by +___DP, *French is {used/*use(ing)}*?

(ii)   If "assigns case" expresses a verb's transitivity, how is the transitivity of a derived nominal to be expressed? *Mary's quick making *(of the dinner) surprised us.*

(iii) In Grimshaw's framework, DP complements of verbs taking indirect questions can be interpreted as "concealed questions." Pesetsky's proposed extension therefore allows **The arrival time should have been wondered earlier,* alongside *The arrival time should have been wondered about earlier,* because in both examples, *wonder* does not assign case.

Second, consider the type of lexical generalization needed to describe the behavior of grammatical verbs such as *be* and *get*. These verbs must have a complement, but one *of any type*, i.e. their subcategorization frames contain +___XP. These two "grammatical V" (cf. Emonds, 1985, Ch. 4, and section 1.2.1 above) are related in that *get* is the inchoative (change of state) counterpart of *be* (Kimball, 1973). Another difference is that *be* doesn't assign accusative case (cf. note 3), so that its DP sister is a predicate nominal rather than a direct object (*Harry may be a doctor* vs. *Harry may get a doctor*).

To fix ideas, we will here examine only *get*.[4] If *get* is transitive, its DP object receives the semantic role "Theme" (the object moving); the Location role may then be assigned in either the subject or the PP complement position:

(2.7)   John (Location, optional Agent) got the letter (Theme).
        Seattle (Location, not a possible Agent) got a lot of rain (Theme).
        John (Agent, not Location) got the letter (Theme) to Victoria (Location).

If *get* is intransitive and its obligatory complement is a PP, the subject is the Theme, again optionally agentive if animate:

(2.8)   The storms (Theme, not a possible Agent) (*tried to) get to Seattle (Location).
        The tourists (Theme, optional Agent) (tried to) get to Seattle (Location).

(iv) How do we express that a linking verb such as *become* takes a DP, when such verbs don't assign accusative in many languages with morphological case? Linking verbs in fact show that lexical subcategorization is needed independently of "assigns case," precisely in order to characterize predicate nominals. Since abstract case is required on well-formed DPs in PF, lack of accusative or oblique case leads to a DP case assigned by a default agreement in PF (cf. Ch. 7 and 8), which is tantamount to interpretation as a predicate nominal.

If we wish to retain a predictive model, problematic consequences such as (i)–(iv) leave us with Grimshaw's conclusion (that syntactic selection cannot be eliminated), not Pesetsky's.

[4] The discussion is adapted from Emonds (1991b, 417–418). In the framework developed there, the interpretations of (2.7) and (2.8) follow from general principles of theta role assignment which apply to structures generated from item-particular syntactic subcategorizations. We summarize these principles in section 2.4.

In a lexical framework which treats assignment of theta roles as a primitive, such variation would require tortuous stipulations linking them with DP positions. Moreover, the obligatory nature of *get*'s complement remains mysterious in such a framework. *Get* does not "obligatorily assign case" – cf. (2.8) – nor is any role obligatory other than Theme, which may appear as a subject. Yet we have clear evidence that some complement to *get* inside V is necessary:

(2.9)   *Seattle sure did get during this winter.
          *Will the letter get over the weekend?

Consequently, the generalization about *get* concerns not its semantics, but its peculiar subcategorization frame, +___(DP)^XP.[5]

Third, a single syntactic frame can correctly encompass not only a range of theta role assignments, as with *get,* but also a range of more particular lexical meanings. Many verbs with multiple usages almost invariably require exactly the same syntactic frame. For example, grammatical verbs such as *have* and *put,* even though they appear in expressions with dozens of distinct senses, are respectively best described as +___DP and +___DP^[PP, PATH].[6] As is widely accepted, since English directional particles, whether idiomatic or literal, are "intransitive P" (Emonds, 1985, Ch. 6), they satisfy subcategorization for PP.

(2.10)   Varied senses of *have* and *put* in idioms:
          a. have { a cold, friends, a look, a heart of gold, fun, a go, pity, backbone, class, sense, the jitters, one's way, what it takes, (half) a mind to …, the nerve to … }
          b. put someone { to the test, on trial, in jeopardy, on hold, at risk, on drugs, onto something, out ("inconvenience"), off ("irritate"), on ("mislead"), up ("lodge"), down ("insult"), away ("imprison"), through ("connect") }
          c. put something { in limbo, in writing, on record, out of one's mind, to somebody, off ("delay"), by ("save"), together ("prepare") }

---

[5] The XP complement of *get* can be a controlled infinitival IP, but not a full CP: *We got (friends) { (*for their kids) to visit Seattle / {*that / *how} their kids visit Seattle}.* Chapter 10 discusses how this should be expressed in subcategorization.

[6] The exceptional combinations (*have at someone, have to do something, put into a harbor, put out*) are so few in number that they serve to underscore the lexical generalizations. Such combinations violating the general syntactic frames are more costly lexical entries, and hence rare.

Because idioms respect these verbs' subcategorization features (+___DP and +___DP^[PP, PATH]), entire classes of possible idioms which would violate a syntactic requirement are excluded *in principle:*[7]

(2.11)   Excluded *have* idioms lacking DP: have to the test, have on trial, have at risk, have in jeopardy, have out, have off, have on, have up, have down, have away, have in limbo, have out of one's mind, have to somebody, etc.
*Sadly, Sue had on trial. Consequently, she had out of her mind.
*If you have at risk or have out, then it's best to have away or have in limbo.

(2.12)   Excluded *put* idioms without a PP: put a cold, put friends, put a heart of gold, put a look, put fun, put a go, put the jitters, put pity, put one's way, put what it takes, etc.
*When feeling anti-social, I go around and put a cold.
*You shouldn't put the jitters; try to always put a go if you put what it takes.

Many authors writing on idioms have noted their high degree of syntactic conformity to basic lexical patterns. Any attempt to capture these regularities in semantic terms, e.g., to select *have* and *put* in terms of the content of their various complements in (2.10) without essentially building in syntactic subcategorization, would really appear to be a fool's quest.

Having now reviewed some positive aspects of classical subcategorization, we can turn to remedying some of its shortcomings.

2.2   Extending and restricting subcategorization to syntactic features

A classical subcategorization frame of a lexical item, @, X, +___YP, means that YP is a sister of [$_X$ @] after lexical insertion occurs. Brame (1984), Baltin (1987) and Emonds (1991a; 1993) argue that such frames should be reformulated rather as @, X, +___Y, *where Y⁰ is the head of a maximal*

---

[7]   The point about the examples in (2.11)–(2.12) is not just that they are not is current use; rather, such candidates for idioms sound radically deviant because they violate syntactic subcategorization.

projection which is a sister to X^0. Beyond arguments for this conclusion based on descriptive adequacy, which will be reviewed in appropriate sections, such a notation has the consequence of eliminating all mention of phrases in the lexicon. I therefore adopt this notation, so that, for example, +___D henceforth means the +___DP of previous usage.[8]

(2.13)   *Lexical Interface Principle. The lexicon uses only morpheme categories in its statements. It cannot mention phrases, nor distinguish between X and XP.*

The step of excluding phrases from the lexicon in fact allows us to characterize two levels of the "unconscious" of language. At a first level below consciousness, children learn words and build up a lexicon in terms of *non-phrasal cognitive categories* such as TENSE, N, ANIMATE, A, PATH, WH, etc., akin to say how an accomplished swimmer unconsciously refines various muscular activities appropriate to different styles, speeds, water conditions, etc. A swimmer cannot consciously provide scientifically accurate analyses of the acquired abilities, but if questioned (by a non-swimmer), (s)he can make up terms for body movements to describe common-sensically what constitutes good swimming, perhaps with a goal of teaching the skill to the uninitiated. Similarly, an intelligent native speaker may roughly verbalize about linguistic patterns de facto in terms of features such as PATH, WH, ANIMATE, etc. and can thereby teach vocabulary semi-systematically to a non-native speaker.

But at a deeper level, the swimmer's actual physical state (increased heart beat, adrenaline level, blood flow to the muscles) is totally beyond what the swimmer can conceptualize outside a class in scientific biology (e.g. a swimmer of 1,000 years ago). Similarly, according to (2.13), the *phrasal structures of syntax* and transformational operations involving phrase structure are more deeply unconscious and in this sense entirely inaccessible to a child's lexical learning.

Together with this limitation on the lexicon, I also endorse an extension. I claim that the inadequacies of classical subcategorization mentioned

---

[8] These modified subcategorization frames could be confused with the word-internal "morphological" frames introduced by Lieber (1980) for bound morphemes. Since left-right order between heads and phrases is clearly not a stipulated item-specific relation, the ordering reflected in classical subcategorization should be used rather for word-internal frames, while some order-free notation for phrasal frames should replace +___Y. I address this point in Chapter 3.

briefly in section 2.1 can be resolved if lexical frames can specify not only categories of heads of complements as in (2.13) but also closed class cognitive syntactic features on their heads (cf. section 1.2).[9] With this formal extension of subcategorization, I claim that *all* co-occurrence information in the lexicon is of the following syntactic form, where F are intrinsic cognitive syntactic features and f are intrinsic semantic features (cf. section 1.2) of a selecting head @ of category X. Lexical entries contain no phrasal categories, nor, as will be demonstrated in subsequent sections, do they involve any "theta grids" or other s-selection devices. [10]

(2.14)   @, X, F_i, f_j, +___F_k

Since lexical items are plausibly the only learned aspect of natural language, it is highly desirable to thus limit the inventory of categories and devices involved in acquiring a lexicon.

Various authors have claimed that co-occurrence necessitates adding more specific semantic f_n to syntactic co-occurrence frames +___F_k. If this is so, I claim that these f_n are always limited to inherent features of the items satisfying +___F_k, i.e. that no relational notions such as a theta role can

---

[9]   Some previous studies, beginning with Bresnan (1970), have explored extending subcategorization in this way.

   Chomsky (1965) reserves the term "selection" for co-occurrence statements involving features on heads. This term can be retained, provided it is understood (i) that the selection features under study are and contain only syntactic features in Chomsky's sense (1965, Ch. 2), and (ii) that the subcategorization and selection features investigated here are formally identical (respectively, +___D and +___ANIMATE), with exactly the same properties and impact upon well-formedness. As he suggests, however, they may have a different status in measuring degrees of deviance from well-formedness, which is not our concern.

[10]   The reviewer inquires how the lexicon lists idioms such as *kick the bucket* if it makes no use of phrasal categories. I don't pretend here to greatly elucidate our understanding of idioms, but I see advantages in non-phrasal listings such as (i), where a Subcategorized Features Convention (8.18) justified in Chapter 8 makes unnecessary any specification of concatenation within the contextual frame.

(i)   kick, V, F_i, semantic f_i for *die*, +___[N, bucket, DEF]

Idioms generally do *not* consist in entire VPs, as in DiSciullo and Williams (1987), but rather are formed from partial verb-complement combinations. Idiomatic combinations such as *put at risk* "endanger" and *spill the beans* "reveal the secret" respectively additionally require a direct object and allow an indirect object within the VP. To treat these freely combined complements in "idiomatic VPs" as internal to the idioms would only complicate matters. These considerations thus further support (2.13).

appear in (2.14). But I am doubtful that this area involves linguistic competence rather than language use. Typical contrasts cited in favor of semantic selection include *a herd of { horses / ?dogs }, diagonalize { matrices / ?floors }, the { airplane / ?minicab } taxied for an hour, the hero drank the { butter / ?carpet }*, etc. In my view, the questioned combinations are not the data of linguistic competence but are in the realm of language use, similar to knowledge that men don't get pregnant (though Freud has pointed out a brief stage of young boys insisting they will; presumably this isn't a problem with their grammar). For example, we can imagine animated films in which characters suddenly drink apparent solids as if they are liquids, or *a herd of dogs* could occur as a (stylistically hopeless) metaphor, etc. It is of some interest (J. Treasure, pers. comm.) that we cannot imagine **drinking sincerity* or **drinking an earthquake*, but it is precisely such combinations which *syntactic* frames such as +___CONCRETE suffice to exclude. (CONCRETE is the syntactic feature which allows mass nouns to have plurals denoting different kinds: *alcohols, skies, waters* vs. **admirations, *courages, *funs*.)

Let us return now to resolving the difficulties posed by differences among various locational prepositions as in (2.5) and the differences between *glance* and *reside* in (2.6). Various considerations indicate that cognitive syntactic features subdivide the class of P into several subclasses, in particular those which refer to space and time, which will be labeled +LOC(ATION), vs. those which do not. For example, the fact that only a spatial-temporal P accepts the intensifier *right* in SPEC(PP) justifies treating LOCATION as a syntactic feature:

(2.15) a. John spoke right to the director.
            The UFO flew right { by / through } (the forest).
            She remained right in the city.
            She finished right before three o'clock.
            He dashed right { upstairs / off}.
            My friend ate the sandwich right up.

        b. John spoke (*right) of the director.
            The agent arrived (*right) { by train / through his business connections}.
            John smeared the wall (*right) with the paint.
            She worked (*right) for another company.
            Mary knows (*right) about your activities.
            My friend began his speech (*right) thus.

Thus, even though most P which are +___(D) are +LOC, others such as *of, without, despite,* etc. are lexically specified instead for the marked Absence of Content feature -LOC (section 1.2.2). Similarly, *about, for* and *with* are -LOC in most uses.

Another syntactic use of +LOC is the fact that the French relative pronoun *où* 'where, when' can replace only PPs with this feature:

(2.16) a. Jean habite une maison où il y a peu de lumière.
            'John lives in a house where there is little light.'
        b. Jean est mort le jour où il a pardonné Marie.
            'John died   the day when he forgave Mary.'
        c. Jean possède une maison { dont/ *où } il n'a pas besoin.
            'John owns a house   of which   he has no need.'
        d. Jean a des vertues { sur lesquelles/ *où } l'on peut compter.
            'Jean has some virtues on which   one can count.'

A finer division of [P, +LOC] into spatial vs. temporal is necessary. Thus, a focus PP in a pseudo-cleft construction introduced by a *where*-clause must be [+LOC, +SPACE]:

(2.17) Where this ugly machine goes is { into the trunk, near the others, by the door, downstairs, outside, at the entrance, to the foreman, *of the director, *by train, *for another company, *about the sale, *without postage, *with the repressive atmosphere, *before three o'clock, *afterwards, *during lunch }.

Additionally, as established in Jackendoff (1983, Ch. 9), there are two kinds of locative PPs, one whose head indicates a static location or "place," and one whose head indicates a "path" (*to, toward, into, onto, from,* etc. and also post-verbal particles which can appear in V___DP). In English, most spatial P double in both functions; very few are restricted to the role of place, although in my speech two such P are *within* and the locution *at home*.

Since heads share features with their phrasal projections (the only sense of "feature percolation" I use here), placing such features in the lexical frame itself appropriately expresses limitations on sub-types of complements. In this way, verbs such as *glance* and *reside* can be respectively represented as +___ [P, LOC, SPACE, PATH] and +___[P, LOC, SPACE, PLACE]; the logic here does not depend on which feature values are marked. These features and lexical entries thereby account for data as in (2.5) and (2.6), repeated here.

(2.5)   Mary { resided / glanced } { near / by / *of / *with } the hall.

(2.6)   Mary { *resided / glanced } { down / { toward / into } a small apartment }.
Mary { resided / *glanced } { within walking distance / at home }.

Since the features PATH and PLACE are canonically matched with [P, LOC] (section 1.2.1), mentioning the latter categories in the subcategorization frames above is redundant. The following principle formalizes both using the (small) inventory of cognitive syntactic features in subcategorization and eliminating redundancy. In all the cases that will interest us, a complement is defined as a phrasal sister of an X^0.

(2.18)   *Extended Classical Subcategorization. @, X, +___Y is satisfied if and only if Y is a cognitive syntactic feature of a lexical head of a complement in XP.*

In these terms, *glance* becomes simply +___[SPACE, PATH] and *reside* becomes +___[SPACE, PLACE].[11]
Since only features F with an independent role in syntax are used in extended subcategorization, I continue to call this device syntactic, reserving the term "semantic selection" for features written with small script *f*, which play no role in regular syntactic processes. A simple frame such as ____D or +___A, without further feature specification, conforms to Extended Classical Subcategorization provided we trivially define a lexical head category X as a feature of itself.

While intransitive P ("particles") and P with DP objects are selected according to the features just discussed, other cognitive syntactic features play analogous roles in subcategorizing P with IP complements, i.e. in choosing among CP. The pioneering study of Bresnan (1970) established that indirect questions result from the subcategorization feature +___WH, and that other classes of CP complements should be licensed similarly. Thus the lexicon contains frames like the following:

(2.19)   wonder, V, +___WH   exclaim, V, +___(WH)^IP

---

[11] If we wish to further streamline the notation, it is probably safe to consider temporal P as the marked value for [P, LOC]. If so, spatial P may not require lexically marked feature specification beyond ±PATH.

Chomsky (1965, Ch. 2) exemplifies several subclasses of transitive verbs defined by co-occurrence with syntactic-feature-specified subclasses of DPs or PPs:

(2.20) amuse, V, +___ANIMATE   (This class is generally
                                        termed "psych verbs.")
        put, V, +___D^PATH   (See section 2.1)
        place, V, +__D^PLACE
        disperse, V, +___PLURAL

Disperse seems to be an "unaccusative" verb whose object DP can move to an unoccupied subject position; it thus parallels the French unaccusative verbs *monter* 'go up, take up' and *descendre* 'go down, take down'. Collective nouns also satisfy its selection feature as in (2.21); when such nouns appear as subjects, the plural agreement of British usage confirms that these nouns are indeed inherent plurals:

(2.21) The staff / team { are / *is } being dispersed by the emergency workers.

The American usage with singular verbs suggests that the lexical PLURAL feature on the N fails to be copied in D, and hence fails to cause agreement with the verb.

I have now exemplified that certain PP and DP are selected by cognitive syntactic features F matched with them, rather than simply by +___XP. We can further justify Extended Classical Subcategorization (2.18) with more instances of the same phenomenon with AP and IP.[12]

It is well-known that two Spanish copulas, *ser* and *estar,* contrast in the context ___AP. The first appears with predicate adjectives which are or can be interpreted as "inherent" properties (*grande* 'tall', *enfermo* 'sick' but not *muerto* 'dead') and the second with those specifying "non-inherent" properties (*muerto* 'dead', *enfermo* 'sick' but not *grande* 'tall'). Assuming that

---

[12] Because in most cases VP is a sister to I and NP to D (section 1.3), I have not included examples of lexical frames selecting VP (in addition to IP) and/or NP (in addition to DP) in terms of features matched with these categories.

In later chapters, I will argue that selecting "V-headedness" via +___V does not inevitably lead to the presence of a VP. In contrast the feature +___N, which I argue in section 8.1.2 characterizes predicate nominals, invariably generates a DP in English but not in several other languages (Kallulli, 1999).

±INHERENT is a cognitive syntactic feature matched with A (cf. section 1.2.1), we can list *ser* as +___+INHERENT and *estar* as +___-INHERENT. In other terminologies, +INHERENT = "individual level" or "characterizing" while -INHERENT = "stage-level" or "state descriptive."[13]

Less appreciated is the fact that inchoative counterparts to the copula exhibit the same contrast among some English linking verbs, and hence appear with the corresponding subcategorization features.

(2.22) a. get, V, +___-INHERENT   (like Spanish *estar* 'be';
                                           A = -INHERENT)
        become, V, +___+INHERENT (like Spanish *ser* 'be';
                                           A = +INHERENT)
        remain, V, +___A
    b. Mary got { thirsty/ warm/ sick/ *penniless/ *Canadian }.
        Mary became { *thirsty/ *warm/ sick/ penniless/ Canadian }.
        Mary remained { thirsty/ warm/ sick/ penniless/ Canadian }.

Thus, some but not all subcategorized AP are selected via a feature value on their lexical head, in accordance with Extended Classical Subcategorization (2.18).

The category IP is selected by C, or more generally by the class of subordinating conjunctions P. C is the grammatical subclass of P whose elements lack semantic features *f*. Various English C and P select finite I (*that, if, than, unless, because*, etc.) and others non-finite I (*for, so as*). It is a commonplace that in other languages some subordinating conjunctions P select indicative mood and others subjunctive (i.e., they select contrasting values of a syntactic feature canonically realized on the finiteness category I). For instance, French *si* 'if', *quand* 'when' and *puisque* 'since' select IP whose head I is indicative, while *quoique* 'although', *afin que* 'in order to' and *à moins que* 'unless' select IP whose head is subjunctive. Thus, some

---

[13] A little reflection shows that the restrictions imposed by syntactic features appearing in frames such as +___PLURAL, +___ANIMATE and +___INHERENT can be violated for rhetorical effect. Thus, the following violations of syntactic selection can be metaphorically interpreted.

Having the windows open during the party didn't amuse my cold.
Can't they disperse this wall of traffic?

Nonetheless, the frames still impose themselves as conditions on felicitous interpretation of their UG-matched lexical categories. Similarly, Spanish *enfermo* is interpreted as ±INHERENT depending on the copula chosen.

feature +__F, where F is a syntactic feature canonically matched with I by UG, is also a possible subcategorization frame. A likely candidate for the F that characterizes mood in some languages is TENSE; according to a convincing analysis of Picallo (1984), the head of a Catalan indicative clause is [I, +TENSE], while that of a subjunctive clause is [I, -TENSE]; a similar analysis seems appropriate for Modern French.[14] In languages where subjunctives exhibit a fuller range of tenses, they may rather be characterized as [I, -REALIS].

We have now seen cases where Extended Classical Subcategorization (2.18), which syntactically selects phrasal complements via features of their heads, is needed for selecting the extended projections (DP, IP, AP and PP) of all four lexical heads (N, V, A and P). This understanding of subcategorization will play a continuing and central role in the rest of this work.

2.3 Syntactic vs. semantic selection: sisterhood is powerful

Few would dispute Chomsky's early claim that head-complement co-occurrence patterns are at least as complex as those captured by syntactic selection and subcategorization, unified here under the notation +___F. The consensus of the field is rather that co-occurrence is *more* complex than this; that is, that many additional facts of co-occurrence are "meaning-based," in a sense that is difficult to formalize in an enlightening way. Once meaning-based co-occurrence is properly modeled, syntactic selection will supposedly fall out as a special and simple case.[15]

Co-occurrence is undeniably based on lexical properties which play a role in interpretation. Certainly, intrinsic features appearing inside contextual features (e.g., N, ANIMATE, PAST, INHERENT, PATH, etc.) will figure centrally in any eventual contentful theory of meaning or conceptual semantics. As a result, features such as V, +__ANIMATE, which specify one class of psychological predicates, could be terminologically declared to

---

[14] There may be structures in which V rather than I is directly selected by P (= C), but for our purposes here it suffices that *some* IP are chosen by virtue of syntactic features realized on I.

[15] In my view, this professional consensus about lexical co-occurrence is a disguised layman's intuition about language in general, to wit: "Language is difficult to formalize in an enlightening way, but once this communication system is properly modeled in terms of meaning, syntax will fall out as a special and simple case."

Apparently, some early students of modern chemistry similarly felt that the combinatorial properties they were discovering would eventually be derived from deeper, more meaningful, and yet to be discovered principles of alchemy.

be "meaning-based," and such contextual features themselves even have implications for interpretation (cf. note 13).

However, my point is different. Even if certain heads require selected complements to exhibit some semantic feature f (for example, the object of *drink* must be a liquid or interpreted as one), such a selection itself neither depends on nor imposes a semantic *relation* with the complement. That is, the interpreted syntactic features F or semantic features f required on well-formed complements are themselves simply *lexical properties of the selected items in isolation*, without independent combinatorial properties. A crucial point in my brief against "semantic selection devices" in (2.14) is that the only relational property needed in lexical entries for linking heads and complements and determining distribution is syntactic sisterhood.

In contrast to my view, numerous researchers feel that well-formed combinations of heads @ and complements B instantiate certain abstract semantic relations R that are features of neither @ nor B taken in isolation. Since these relations R are clearly not *intrinsic* to the complement, they are taken rather as properties which a head "assigns to," "associates with," or "links with" the complement. For example, predicates, not themselves exclamatory or goal-linked, are lexically stipulated to "select" exclamative clauses or goal DPs, even though no aspect of clausal complements is intrinsically "exclamative," nor in studies using thematic roles can any (non-idiomatic) class of DPs or NPs or Ns be classified as e.g. "intrinsic goals."

Introducing such relations, these researchers feel, better expresses various semantics-based combinatorial properties than classical co-occurrence features. In essence, such research sanctions contextual features @, +___B, where B is *not* an intrinsic feature of a complement but one that @ imposes on the complement in a context. The actual notation matters little, because all the devices in question utilize categories or relations that are not *lexical properties of the class of selected items*, and are therefore listed as lexical properties of the *selecting* items.[16]

---

[16] Ironically, studies whose lexical entries freely dispatch abstract semantic categories to phrases in their environment fail to use these same categories more restrictively as word-internal semantic features f on roots of denominal verbs. For example, the verbs *hammer, butter,* and *box* are formed from nouns which serve as, respectively, intrinsic instrument, theme, and goal. If theta roles are first sent out to complements which are then later "incorporated," simple-minded examples such as (i) become problems.

(i)   It's better to butter toast with slightly warm butter.
       Sue couldn't hammer down her tacks$_i$ *(with that hammer$_j$), so I lent her mine$_j$.
       Box all the art books in new *(boxes) which are strong.

I will now examine some well known types of analyses which describe co-occurrence with non-intrinsic semantic properties, to see if expanding the semantic vocabulary in this way actually clarifies or simplifies any distributional statements. I first discuss Grimshaw (1979), which is widely understood to contain telling arguments for independent semantic selection; she claims that at least finite CP complements are selected not only by syntactic features like +__WH but by semantic features as well. One of her arguments is based on "exclamatory complements" and another on "concealed questions." These issues are discussed in more detail in Emonds (1992); here I limit myself to summarizing the main lines of argument.

Sections 2.4 and 2.5 then take up the related question as to whether descriptive adequacy in devices of lexical selection requires that verbs select DPs in terms of semantic theta roles or analogous positions in conceptual structures.

2.3.1 Exclamatory complements

In Grimshaw's framework, the verb *realize* has a syntactic subcategorization +__WH. Additionally, (2.23a,b) result from her semantic selection feature +__E ("exclamation"), whereas the CP in (2.23a,c) result from +__Q ("question"). Since E clauses may not be infinitival and Q clauses may not be introduced by *what a*, (2.23d) is ill-formed.

(2.23)

Mary finally realized [$_{CP}$ {
a. what expensive cars we needed to buy
b. what an expensive car we needed to buy
c. what expensive cars to buy
d. *what an expensive car to buy
}].

While the verb *realize* selects E or Q, other verbs may not, as in (2.24)-(2.25):

(2.24)   *Mary finally asked what an expensive car we needed to buy.
Mary finally asked what expensive cars to buy.

(2.25)   Mary was amazed what an expensive car we needed to buy.
*Mary was amazed what expensive cars to buy.

But if instead the whole theta role assignment /incorporation schema is abandoned, the semantic doublings in (i) are unremarkable, since complement phrases are licensed independently of open class lexical detail.

Despite the distinctions in (2.23)–(2.25), several facts suggest that exclamatory clauses are not an independent complement type on which to base a theory of lexical selection. No predicates obligatorily select them; they do not occur in (non-extraposed) subject position (her note 18); no other elaborations of complementation theory are based on their properties; and Grimshaw herself concludes in the appendix: "... the distribution of exclamatory complements does seem to be predictable to a large extent." (318)

In fact, this distribution is *entirely* predictable on the basis of two factors, as suggested to me by M. Kubo. First, *only factive verbs can take exclamatives*, a generalization credited to Elliott (1971, 1974) and whose basis in interpretive semantics Grimshaw in fact nicely elaborates. And since "Exclamatory and interrogative complements ... do not differ in syntactic form in any systematic way; both are derived by Wh Fronting, ... all the available evidence indicates that the two complement types are derived by the same rules" (283), the second necessary condition for exclamatory complements seems to be *selection by the syntactic feature +__WH or +__(WH)^IP*. Together, these two conditions then suffice for permitting an (optional) exclamatory clause.[17] Grimshaw points out that certain factive verbs (*count, be sufficient, make sense*) do not take exclamatory subject clauses (2.26), but the reason is that such predicates are incompatible with WH-clauses of any form (2.27):

(2.26) *It doesn't count what a small salary John earns.
        *It's sufficient what a lot of money John earns.

(2.27) *Who fixes the machines doesn't count.
        *How to visit your relatives may not count.
        *Which story John told is sufficient.
        *Whether Harry should like her is sufficient.

The predictability of exclamatory distribution is thus greater than that (almost) conceded in Grimshaw's appendix. In spite of many possible com-

---

[17] In Grimshaw's framework, such WH clauses are inexplicably never obligatory: *Mary exclaimed that it was late.*

Grimshaw claims that *concede*, which takes indirect questions but not exclamatory complements, is factive. But it is not:

The spokesperson {conceded / *admitted} her candidate had lost, but he hadn't.
Jim rashly {concedes / *admits} he is guilty when he isn't.

binations in her notation for selecting WH, Q, and E independently, each being in principle absent, optional, or obligatory, she exemplifies only a handful of complement classes. The two classes exemplified by *wonder* and *inquire*, resulting from +__Q and -__E, and *ask* as in (2.24), resulting from +__(Q) and -__E, are fully accounted for by these verbs being +__WH but not factive.[18]

The only remaining class of verbs which apparently distinguishes Q and E includes *surprised, exclaim,* and in negative polarity *believe,* which are -__Q and +__(E); cf. (2.25). These verbs all fall in the class of "psychological predicates" which require animate "experiencers" as either subjects or objects. A salient fact about all such predicates, whichever the syntactic position of the experiencer DP, is (2.28), exemplified in (2.29).

(2.28)   Psychological predicates do not accept indirect question arguments.

(2.29)   *He fears { how soon Ann can lose her job / what to do next }.
         *Many people like {whether it's raining / who to talk to when lonely }.
         *{ Which men worked hard / Who to arrest } really amused her.
         *{Whether it's raining / How to fix this } is bothersome.

One might loosely claim that (2.28) is an aspect of complement selection that is independent of syntax, but crucially for my general claim, such "selection" *is not a fact about individual lexical items.* Rather, classes of predicates are subject to certain *general* interpretive principles; for example, all psychological predicates can (and many must) be used as stative predicates. Far from arguing against such principles, I formulate a number of them in Emonds (1991b) and review them in the next section; what I oppose is a conception of the lexicon in which *item-particular* combinatorial properties can be semantic. Thus, a general property such as being a psychological predicate or a verb of motion may well be incompatible with a certain interpretation (e.g., since inanimate subjects can't be agents, we need not lexically stipulate that *elapse* fails to select an agent). My claim is that a combinatorial semantic property like (2.28), or whatever interpretive principle it follows from, is always statable as an exceptionless generalization over classes of structures and that any residual item-particular selection is purely syntactic.

---

[18] The rather contrived interpretation of "obligatory" WH selection used to distinguish *wonder* and *inquire* from *discover* and *realize* in Emonds (1992, 221–222) is consequently unnecessary.

Thus, the class of predicates defined by -__Q and +__(E) are just psychological predicates with a lexical argument licensed by +___WH.[19] Arguments of such predicates are exempt from a general rule for indirect questions, which, according to Grimshaw, assigns WH-marked Determiners certain values of "indeterminateness." But this is a fact about an interpretive rule, perhaps explainable on more general grounds or perhaps not. It is not a fact about item-particular selectional properties.[20] Complements of exclamatory form, therefore, provide no evidence for item-particular selection by any feature other than the syntactic feature +__WH.

2.3.2 Concealed questions

A second construction used by Grimshaw to argue for semantics-based selection of complements is the Concealed Question. The following abbreviated version of Emonds (1992, 216–218) indicates why I think the properties of this construction argue rather *against* semantic selection.

Concealed questions are DPs which are interpreted as indirect questions, as in *John found out the arrival time* and *Mary told us the cars she had bought.* Grimshaw observes that such concealed question DPs "occur in legitimate NP positions, ... only with verbs that are subcategorized for NP complements" (303) and simultaneously for indirect questions. Therefore, concealed questions occur neither with verbs like *wonder* and *inquire* (which lack the frame +___D), nor with verbs like *believe* and *deny*, which cannot take indirect questions. (**John believed the arrival time* and **Mary denied the cars she had bought*.) Thus, only a verb which allows both the frames +___D and +___WH may occur with a concealed question.

Now, according to Grimshaw: "The Concealed Question Rule interprets noun phrases as interrogative – it assigns to them representations of the same form as those assigned to *wh*-questions." (300; this informal statement upon which the argument depends is not subsequently formalized.) Thus, a CQ rule optionally modifies a DP argument, imposing a feature crucially

---

[19] As in Chomsky (1965, Ch. 2), it appears that subjects are not subcategorized, although features on subjects may be. I do not investigate here how such restrictions on subjects might be best notated.

[20] If the feature PSYCHOLOGICAL were used only to exempt a verb's complement from indirect question interpretation, it would be tantamount to semantic selection. But the feature is used elsewhere; for example, PSYCH verbs with experiencer objects always form derived adjectives, as observed in Chomsky (1957): *very amusing, very amused; how pleasing, how pleased; so troubling, so troubled;* etc. PSYCH verbs may also have empty deep subjects, as argued in Belletti and Rizzi (1988).

involved in the form of *wh*-questions. Presumably, a feature which has "the same form as those assigned to *wh*-questions" involves WH itself; that is, CQ optionally imposes WH ... on a DP. Recalling that all CQ verbs are +___WH, we may partially formalize the interpretation of concealed questions as follows.

(2.30)   *CQ: D* ===> *WH ..., where DP is selected by V, +___{ D, WH }*[21]

This view of CQ yields an immediate empirical prediction: no verb which doesn't take indirect questions (i.e., which lacks the frame +___WH) can have a concealed question DP complement. And precisely as observed in Grimshaw's note 33: "Predicates like this do not seem to exist" even though in her theory of independent semantic selection there could be "a predicate which took concealed questions or exclamations but not the *wh* kind (it would be subcategorized for NP only, and select Q and E.)"

Grimshaw claims that this same problem arises in "the syntactic theory," because a predicate could select both WH and NP but not CP. But this is impossible unless "the syntactic theory" is modified by stipulation to include the very weakness of the semantic theory, namely that selecting phrases and features on heads is independent. Without such stipulation, a syntactic framework permits WH, classically a feature on the head C of CP, to be selected only when CP is present. Thus, the syntactic counterpart WH of Grimshaw's Q cannot in principle be selected by a predicate which takes DPs but not indirect questions. In other words, the absence of concealed questions with verbs which lack +___WH furnishes evidence *for* selecting indirect questions via feature annotations on heads of subcategorized arguments as in (2.14), and *against* autonomous semantic selection.

As the basis of an additional observation, we may compare CQ with what would be Grimshaw's counterpart: *D* ===> *WH ..., where DP is selected by V, + __Q.* As she indicates, there also exist Concealed Exclamations, so that either the semantically based framework needs another rule or else E has to be added to her version of CQ.

(2.31)   Concealed Clauses: D ===> WH ..., where DP is selected by V,
          +___{ Q or E }

---

[21] Although the use of such a rule is part of Grimshaw's argument, not mine, I take it to mean that the surface form of *John found out the arrival time* would be interpreted in Logical Form as *John found out which arrival time*. I have changed my earlier formulation to make it consistent with the notation here.

A generalization is clearly being missed. In contrast, CQ (2.30) requires no revision; since it must modify Logical Form representations of Determiners prior to rules which interpret WH-marked Determiners in clauses of any type, it need not build in references to the two distinct interpretations of these forms.

The considerations of these two subsections leave no reason to think clausal complement selection involves any device other than the subcategorization permitted in (2.14), i.e. selection of complements by +__F, where the F are inherent cognitive syntactic features on the head C of a complement CP.

2.4 Determining Theta Roles by interpretive principles

In the first decade of generative grammar, Chomsky (1965, 161–163) recognized the poor match between deep structures and semantic properties of the sort exemplified in pairs such as those in (2.32). In each pair, the DP in bold seems to bear the same semantic relation to the verb, despite standing in different grammatical relations to the verb in each column. (The italics will be explained shortly.)

(2.32)   *The girls* regard **John** as pompous.   **John** strikes *the girls* as pompous.

               The girls liked **the play**.   **The play** pleased *the girls*.

Similarly in (2.33) and (2.34), the bold DPs bear the same relation to synonymous verbs, often the *same* verb, despite their different syntactic positions.

(2.33)   A driver moved **the truck** to *the west*.   **The truck** moved to *the west*.

               The host passed **the main dish**.   **The main dish** passed (*the guest of honor*).

               Sue tasted **the fish**.   **The fish** tasted salty to *Sue*.

               We got **the letter** to *Seattle*.   **The letter** got to *Seattle*.

               John knows (about) **Bill**.   **Bill** worries *John*.

(2.34)   John smeared **paint** on *the wall*.   John smeared *the wall* with **paint**.

               Beavers can strip **any bark** off *trees*.   Beavers can strip *trees* of **any bark**.

               We discussed **Japan**.   We spoke about **Japan**.

               John fears **Bill**   *John* worries about **Bill**.

To put the problem another way, direct objects in the left column seem to bear the same semantic relations to the verbs as do corresponding right column subjects in (2.32)–(2.33) and objects of prepositions in (2.34).

Subsequent studies of Gruber (1976), Jackendoff (1972 and several later works), Talmy (1975, 1978) and others have treated the relation between the verbs and the bolded left column objects in (2.32)–(2.34) by associating these objects with a sememe or semantic role, often called a theta role, of "Theme" or "Figure"; the bolded DPs in the right column supposedly have the same role. A different theta role, subsumed for convenience under a single label called "Location" (Talmy's label is "Ground"), then holds of DPs indicating physical or psychological locations of the action or state expressed by the Verb + Theme. These Location DPs are in italics in (2.32)–(2.34). The examples show that under appropriate conditions, each type of theta role can be realized in subject, direct object or object-of-P position. In the studies cited, individual lexical entries of verbs are designed to appropriately assign or link theta roles to direct object and other argument positions. Something like these theta roles, which are non-intrinsic semantic properties imposed on lexically selected phrases, are then taken to adequately express relations between the pairs in (2.32)–(2.34), and in particular, to lay a better basis for explaining co-occurrence patterns.

Under this conception, each DP argument of a verb must stand in some relation to the selecting predicate; this can be expressed by (2.35):

(2.35)   *Full Interpretation.*[22] *Every DP argument of Y^0 is assigned at least one out of a specified list of semantic roles, unless its grammatical position is lexically specified by Y^0 as semantically empty, and each role is assigned to at most one argument.*

Semantically empty or "theta-bar" positions include, e.g., subjects of verbs like *seem* and French *falloir* 'be necessary' and also expletive object positions in idioms such as *catch it, make it, get with it.*

In my view, Full Interpretation (2.35) should be satisfied by general interpretive principles which are *independent of individual verbs*. The issue here is thus not whether the semantic roles of DPs exist, but *whether they play any part in the mechanisms of lexical selection*. That is, does using theta roles or equivalent linking devices, for example in "theta grids" or "lexical conceptual structures," capture distributional generalizations better

---

[22] Chomsky (1986, section 3.3.3.3.2) discusses this general requirement on interpretation. My formulation here focuses only on DPs.

than lexical entries of the restricted form (2.14)? Recall from the Introduction that the cognitive syntactic F and semantic f are *intrinsic*, not relational, features of the selecting head.

(2.14)   @, X, F_i, f_j, +___F_k

To fix ideas, let us consider some verbal paradigms that exemplify a range of thematic roles in different syntactic positions. In each paradigm, we hold constant a theta role assigned by the V to each lexical noun; let A = agent, T = theme, and L = location.

(2.36)   The singer [A] filled the stadium [L] (with fans [T]).
         *The singer [A] filled (the fans [T] (into the stadium [L])).
         The stadium [L] filled (with fans [T]).
         *The stadium [L] filled the fans [T].
         The fans [T, optional A] filled (*into) the stadium [L].
         *The fans [T] filled.

The linked lexical "theta grid" for *fill*, prior to any attempt to generalize, would be (2.37), while its the subcategorization frame would be (2.38):

(2.37)   < **location** [→ subj or obj], **(theme)** [→ subj or *with*___], **(agent)**
         [→ subj] >

(2.38)   fill, V, +___(D)^(P)

Certain notations, such as Williams's (1981) proposal to specially mark the external theta role, lead not to clarification but to further stipulations. The theta grid (2.37) stipulates but offers no insight into the selectional fact that a PP complement of *fill* is -LOCATION, i.e. that the Location role may not be in a PP. Nor does the idea that *fill* "optionally assigns case" in any way clarify the asymmetries in (2.36).

There is, however, an interpretive principle of a somewhat different sort which is independent of individual lexical entries and which starts to make sense of the distributional pattern in e.g. (2.36). As is well-known, agent *by*-phrases occur as adjuncts only in certain complex syntactic structures such as passives and causatives (cf. Chapters 5 and 6). But we must still ask why no lexical entries ever sanction agent interpretations in *complement* phrases. That is, why can agent phrases never appear as objects of P or V *inside* V¹?[23]

---

[23] That is, why could the meanings in the left column sentences never be expressed by the

Chomsky (1972, 75) has answered this with a statement that can serve as a second principle of interpretation. His principle, which he suggests is universal, describes almost entirely the distribution of agent phrases not only in (2.36) but in active sentences in general; that is, it is the *only source* of agent phrases in active sentences:

(2.39)   *Agent Specification. "Thus one rule (probably universal) will stipulate that for verbs of action, the animate subject may be interpreted as the agent."*[24]

Full Interpretation (2.35) and Agent Specification (2.39) together explain why the Agent Role becomes obligatory when there are three arguments; since there are but three roles to distribute, (2.35) requires that each role be assigned to a different DP. Then, if the Agent is attributed only to a subject, the subject *must* take that role.

Given this clarification, one still needs the following linking information to accurately express the paradigm in (2.36):

(2.40)   When *fill* is intransitive, its subject is Location rather than Theme or Agent.

(2.41)   When *fill* is transitive, its direct object is Location rather than Theme.

From (2.40) and (2.41) it follows that an optional PP complement of *fill* cannot have a Location role; it may only be a Theme (expressed via a *with*-phrase), the completive *up,* or part of an idiom such as *in, out (fill in / out the permission slip).*

---

corresponding right column strings? (Italics indicate Agent interpretation.)

The UFO moved the train.	*The train moved by *the UFO.*
The UFO passed the message.	*The message passed *the UFO.*
Sue tasted the fish.	*The fish tasted to *Sue.*
We got the letter to Seattle.	*The letter got of *us* to Seattle.
John smeared paint on the wall.	*Paint smeared on the wall by *John.*
Beavers can strip trees of bark.	*Bark can strip trees by *beavers.*
We discussed Japan.	*Japan discussed *us.*

[24] Apparently, if a verb of action *obligatorily* takes an animate subject (e.g. *swim, buy, read,* etc.), then this subject *must* be interpreted as agent. With this proviso, Chomsky's rule seems accurate and eliminates not only "linking" agents to subjects but also any need to ever mention agenthood in lexical entries.

I first discuss (2.40). Clearly, (2.40) is not information about the *distribution* of complements, but rather suggests that a given semantic role (Location) is essential to the meaning or conceptual structure of *fill*. Since the subject of a verb is usually non-null, it is natural enough that it expresses a semantically indispensable argument. In the same way, semantic or conceptual structures of hundreds of typical one-place adjectival predicates specify how their sole argument (i.e., their subject) relates to the adjective's meaning or conceptual structure. In this way the Location subject of intransitive *fill* resembles that of its cognate adjective *full*.[25]

The theta grid (2.37) expresses the content of (2.40) by the lack of parentheses around Location. But this kind of information can in fact be completely factored out of both subcategorization and theta grids as follows.

(2.42)   *Principal Argument Role. A predicate @ of category V or A typically specifies in its lexical entry that some particular theta role f must be assigned to a subject or an object. This can be notated formally by listing the role f in the entry of @.*

I have just discussed a verb (*fill*) which requires a Location among its arguments, but many verbs require rather a Theme.

PAR (2.42) neither specifies nor implies any "linking" of semantic content or relations with syntactic positions by particular lexical items; the position where an obligatory theta role occurs must be logically deduced from subcategorization possibilities. For example, if a verb or adjective is intransitive, then an obligatory theta role is naturally found on the subject; if a verb irregularly requires a null syntactic subject (French *falloir* 'be necessary'), then the principal role is found in direct object position.[26]

Given the principles (2.39) and (2.42), the only remaining function of the theta grid (2.37) is to express (2.41), i.e., to account for **The stadium filled the fans*. But before deciding whether to retain theta grids for this purpose, let us leave (2.41) as a "semantic residue" for the moment, and examine a slightly different verb *pack*.

(2.43)   The singer [A] packed the stadium [L] (with fans [T]).
         *The singer [A] packed (the fans [T]).

---

[25] *Fill's* intransitive antonym *empty* similarly requires a Location subject (**The water emptied*), but a related concept *drain* allows either Location or Theme: *The {sink/ water} drained.*

The singer [A] packed (his music [T]). With the sense: consolidate belongings
The singer [A] packed the fans [T] into the stadium [L].
*The stadium [L] packed (with fans [T]).
*The stadium [L] packed the fans [T].
The fans [T, A] packed (*into) the stadium [L].
*The fans [T] packed.

Neither the theta grid nor the subcategorization of *pack* expresses the semantic fact that *pack* can also have a special sense ("consolidate belongings"). Assuming that this specialized sense is part of the same basic lexical entry, *pack* is not obligatorily transitive. Thus, its subcategorization is the same as for that of *fill:* +__(D)^(P).

However, the theta grid of *pack* (2.44) differs from that of *fill* (2.37); for example, *pack* requires an Agent:

(2.44)   < **(location)** [→ obj or P__], **(theme)** [→ subj or *with*__], **agent** [→ subj] >

So the question again is, what work is the relatively complex statement (2.44) actually doing? The counterpart to the semantic residue of *fill* (2.40)– (2.41) for *pack* is (2.45):

(2.45)   a.   One of the arguments of *pack* must be Agent.
         b.   When *pack* is transitive, its direct object is either Location or Theme.

Like (2.40), (2.45a) says nothing about distribution of complements; it is simply an expected effect of PAR (2.42) when Agent is listed as a semantic feature *f* in the lexical entry of *pack*. The only real linking statement needed for *pack* is (2.45b), the analog to the semantic residue of *fill* (2.41).[27]

---

[26] Or consider *reach*, whose principal argument is Goal. This verb syntactically requires a complement with the feature +__{ PATH, D }, but the XP expressing the Goal may be either a PP itself or a DP. Thus, *The wind reached ((into) the hollow)*. Section 2.5 deals with why the direct object of *reach* may not be a Theme.
[27] In order to reduce the amount of lexically stipulated linking between his Lexical Conceptual Structures and syntactic positions, Jackendoff (1990, 252) suggests that aspects of these LCS may carry a "marker of argumenthood notated as a subscript A." As M. Kajita has pointed out to me, my PAR (2.42) is a version of this device, since PAR permits a single salient aspect of a predicate's lexical meaning (whose internal structure may well

(2.41)   When *fill* is transitive, its direct object is Location rather than Theme.

Thus, in addition to subcategorization and the general interpretive principles (2.35) and (2.39), theta grids such as (2.37) and (2.44) are needed only to tell us whether a direct object must be a Theme (*get, fear, know, like, move, regard, taste, like* ; cf. the left column of (2.32)–(2.34)), a Location (*fill, approach, reach, please, strike, worry*) or can be either (*pack, pass, smear, strip*). The issue at hand thus reduces to this: is a separate lexical selectional device entirely distinct in form and content from subcategorization (2.14) really needed for such an apparently simple dichotomy?

2.5 Indeterminacy of object roles: the LOCATION feature on V

Since a negative answer to this question will allow us to maintain the very restricted notation of lexical selection (2.14), I pursue this tack. Recall two syntactic features of P adduced in section 2.2: ±LOCATION and ±PATH. The P of PATH are further divided into those of approach, +GOAL (*to, on, toward, into,* etc.) and those of source, -GOAL (*from, off, out of,* etc.). Unsurprisingly, a survey of the objects of P in (2.33)–(2.34) shows that the objects of Ps marked for Absence of Content as -LOCATION (*about, of, with*) are indeed Themes, while objects of unmarked Ps (which are +LOCATION: *to, off, on*) have Locational roles.

That is, the theta roles of the DP objects of P are just names which reflect the basic syntactic cognitive features of the Ps which govern these constituents.[28] If theta roles associated with physical location and motion (as well

---

be otherwise linguistically opaque) to be "named" by some (unlinked) DP argument of that predicate. However, Jackendoff's argument subscripts are more powerful (less constrained), since they can be attached to several elements in an LCS, and his system must still separately specify the obligatory vs. optional expression of arguments.

[28] Specifying features on P and specifying complement theta roles are not, however, notational variants. First, syntactic justifications for the features (co-occurrence with *right*, selection by verbs of motion, etc.) hold as well when the P are intransitive.

Second, examples like the following show that theta roles cannot predict the presence or choice of P, though the choice of P usually suffices to predict the theta role of its object.

John learned {of/ about/ *with /*Ø} your trip (from Sue).
John learned ({about/ *of/ *with}) how to calculate (from Sue).
John taught {about/ *of/ *with /*Ø} Paris (to tourists).

as with emotion, knowledge and ownership) were expressed only in PPs carrying such features, researchers could be content with simply identifying the theta roles of Location with features of the P introducing them, according to the following equivalences:

(2.46)   a. DP, Static Location =   [P, +LOC, -PATH] ___
         DP, Goal   =   [P, +LOC, +PATH, +GOAL] ___
         DP, Source   =   [P, +LOC, +PATH, -GOAL] ___
         DP, Experiencer =   [P, +LOC, +PATH, (GOAL)] ___,
                               where V has the feature
                               f = PSYCHOLOGICAL
         b. DP, Theme   =   [P, -LOC] ___

As discussed in Emonds (1991b), this purely interpretive and entirely general algorithm for assigning theta roles to objects of P can in fact be fruitfully extended from P to V. Moreover, since complements of N and A always appear within PP structures (Emonds, 1985, section 1.8), such an extension to V automatically and trivially encompasses *all* values of X (N, V, A and P). Consequently, I proposed that Universal Grammar can match the features LOCATION, PATH and GOAL with all values of X, not just with P. When X is V, the marked value is +LOCATION, unlike with P, for which -LOCATION is marked.

It then follows that features on Vs and Ps determine the syntactic positions of Location theta roles (= Talmy's Ground), according to (2.47). Marking Vs like Ps in this way then predicts the only facts captured by theta grids which remained unaccounted for at the end of the previous section, e.g., (2.41) and (2.45b).

(2.47)   *Ground Specification. An object DP of Y^0 (Y = V, P, N, A) is a Ground if and only if Y^0 is +LOCATION. Subcases of Ground (Location, Goal, etc.) are determined by the features co-specified with +LOCATION.*

———— ————————

John acquainted Sue {with/ *about/ *of /*Ø} Paris.
John informed Sue {*with/ about/ of /*Ø} your trip.

On such matters, Chomsky (1965, 29) strikes me as still accurate: "The rules involving contextual features, in other words, may be partially independent of semantic properties. Such examples must be borne in mind if any attempt is made to give some substance to the widely voiced (but, for the moment, totally empty) claim that semantic considerations somehow determine syntactic structure or distributional properties."

While Chomsky's Agent Specification (2.39) links agenthood to the subject position via a one-way implication, other interpretive theta role assignments are not generally linked to syntactic positions; for example, Ground Specification links DP interpretation not to position but to proximity of certain features on the governing V or P. And interpretation as a Theme (= Talmy's Figure) is syntactically free, under the stricture that the Figure and Ground are distinct (Talmy, 1978).[29]

(2.48) *Figure Specification. Exactly one Figure DP, distinct from the Ground, may be present among the arguments of Y^0.*[30]

A little reflection reveals that if lexical entries of V specify (i) their transitivity, (ii) whether they are ±LOC, and (iii) which types of PPs they occur with, *then the general interpretive principles (2.35), (2.39), (2.47), and (2.48) entirely determine the distribution of theta roles on DPs.* No item-particular theta grids or semantic specifications for complements are necessary. Here the principles which pair DPs and theta roles in various configurations have been presented in skeletal form with only a few remarks; cf. Emonds (1991b) for fuller illustrations of their interactions.

But to be concrete, let us apply these four interpretive principles to (2.32)–(2.34).

(2.32) *The girls* regard **John** as pompous.   **John** strikes *the girls* as pompous.
        The girls liked **the play**.   **The play** pleased *the girls*.

(2.33) A driver moved **the truck** to   **The truck** moved to *the west*.
        the west.
        The host passed **the main dish**. **The main dish** passed (*the guest of honor*).
        Sue tasted **the fish**.   **The fish** tasted salty to *Sue*.
        We got **the letter** to *Seattle*.   **The letter** got to *Seattle*.
        John knows (about) **Bill**.   **Bill** worries *John*.

---

[29] This disjointness no doubt reflects a cognitive dichotomy in higher animals, independent of syntax, as Talmy implies.

[30] It is of interest that a Theme (Figure) may never appear in adjunct position, unless accompanied by another role such as Agent (Emonds, 1976, Ch. 3).

> The room was entered by { the thief / *the gas }.
> The lake was crossed by { the sailboat / *the wind }.
> The closet was slipped into by { some guest / *some soap }.

(2.34)   John smeared **paint** on *the wall*. John smeared *the wall* with **paint**.
Beavers can strip **any bark**   Beavers can strip *trees* of **any**
off *trees*.   **bark**.
We discussed **Japan**.   We spoke about **Japan**.
John fears **Bill.**   *John* worries about **Bill**.

The left column verbs are unmarked (i.e. they have the minus value) for LOCATION, and so by (2.47) their objects are Themes. The right column verbs are marked as +LOC, so any direct objects in that column have the Locational theta roles of (2.46). Finally, other verbs such as *pass, smear* and *strip* are lexically specified as optionally (LOC), with the consequence that they appear transitively in both the left and right columns of (2.32)–(2.34).[31]

Other languages provide morphological evidence for the presence of the feature LOCATION on V. For example, German exhibits a semi-productive class of transitive lexical pairs of the form V and *be*+V. Maylor (1999) observes that the simple form has a Theme direct object, while the direct object of the prefixed form systematically has a Locational theta role. Four of his examples:

(2.49)   Er klebte Plakate an die Wand.
         'He stuck posters on the wall'
         Er trat auf den Rasen.
         'He stepped onto the grass'

(2.50)   Er beklebte die Wand mit Plakaten.
         'He be-stuck the wall with posters'
         Er betrat den Rasen.
         'He be-stepped (went onto) the grass'

Using Lieber's (1983) Percolation Conventions, Maylor proposes that the feature LOCATION on the left branch in (2.51) percolates to the immediately dominating V:

---

[31] Emonds (1991b, 387) provides lexical entries for many verbs including those in (2.32)–(2.34).

(2.51)

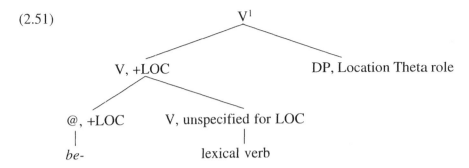

Maylor's analysis thus provides the direct objects of German verbs prefixed by *be-* with their Locational semantic roles according to Ground Specification (2.47). The only lexical information needed is that *be-* is a verbal prefix which at least in most uses is specified as +LOC. If an unmarked transitive verb such as *kleben* 'stick' or *treten* 'step' allows *be-* prefixation, no further lexical specification is needed to account for the alternations such as (2.49)–(2.50).

In languages which have applicative affixes, the sharing of the feature LOCATION by P and V can be quite transparent. Baker (1988, section 5.1.2) focuses discussion on the "productive and regular locative applicative constructions" of Kinyarwanda, as described by Kimenyi (1980). Baker shows how these constructions, which typically involve alternations between a Theme DP and a PP of Location, concern only argument and not adjunct PPs.[32] Four examples of Kimenyi's:

(2.52) a. Umwaana y-a-taa-ye   igitabo mu maazi.
            child   AGR-PAST-throw-ASP book in water
            'The child has thrown the book into the water.'
        b. Umwaana y-a-taa-ye-mo   amaazi   igitabo.
            child   AGR-PAST-throw-ASP-APPL water   book
            'The child has thrown the book into the water.'

(2.53) a. Umugore y-oohere-je umubooyi kw'-iisoko.
            woman AGR-send-ASP   cook to   market
            'The woman sent the cook to the market.'
        b. Umugore y-oohere-je-ho   isoko umubooyi.
            woman AGR-send-ASP-APPL market cook
            'The woman sent the cook to the market.'

---

[32] Nothing in the analysis here requires applicatives to be productive.

The Kinyarwandan verbal "applicative" suffixes *-ho* and *-mo*, which are historically reduced forms of the Ps *ku* 'on' and *mu* 'in' respectively, are uncontroversially +LOC. In conformity with Lieber's (1980, 1983) right hand head rule within X^0, this feature percolates from the suffixal head to the derived V in (2.52b) and (2.53b). In turn, [V, +LOC] then assigns a Locational theta role to the direct objects.[33] In the absence of the applicative suffixes in (2.52a) and (2.53a), the verbs in question, like all verbs unmarked for this feature, are -LOC. Hence by (2.47) and (2.48), the direct objects of the unmarked verbs in these examples must be Themes, while Locations are expressed in a PP.

In conclusion, examples such as (2.32)–(2.34) first led researchers to conclude that the theta roles of subjects and objects cannot be predicted from (motivated) syntactic structures. True enough, there is no evidence that given syntactic positions uniformly express particular semantic roles, nor that the identical thematic relations between DPs and Vs in the pairs of (2.32)–(2.34), (2.49)–(2.50), or (2.52)–(2.53) should imply their identical deep structural relationships.[34] But the supposed indeterminacy of the thematic relation of a DP in a given syntactic position *for a given verb class* has been overestimated; by combining lexical entries of the form (2.14) which are properly specified for ±LOC and ±PATH with the general principles of Full Interpretation (2.35), Agent Specification (2.39), Ground Specification (2.47) and Figure Specification (2.48), we can fully predict the semantic roles of object DPs.

---

[33] There seems to be no doubt that in applicative constructions, the non-Theme DP is the direct object; Baker (1988, section 5.3.1) summarizes the importance of Marantz's (1984) arguments in establishing this general point.

[34] Of course, in many well-studied cases in generative grammar, i.e., in cases where transformational relationships are fully justified, identical thematic relations are indeed explained by identical deep structural relationships. But inverting this result so that identical thematic relations become the basis for postulating identical deep structures is a giant leap of reasoning by the converse.

Generative grammar has twice witnessed this great leap sideways, once in generative semantics and a second time in Baker's (1988, 46) much cited "Uniformity of Theta Assignment Hypothesis (UTAH)". As that study shows, convincing syntactic argumentation can co-exist with this canon of semantically based grammar, but to my mind it gains nothing from the co-habitation.

2.6 Indeterminacy of subject roles: variation in principal role

As discussed in the preceding section, Chomsky (1965, 162) points out the inadequacy of motivated deep structures for uniquely determining the semantic roles of noun phrase arguments of pairs of verbs such as *please / like* and *strike / regard*. We have seen how proper assignment of the features LOCATION and PATH to the category V remedies this. But Chomsky also indicates that a pair of verbs (*buy, sell*) whose objects share a Theme reading can still have subjects with different semantic roles; other similar pairs are easily found:

(2.54)   John bought *War and Peace* from Bill.
         The prisoners got a reprieve from the positive report.
         The children learned Arabic from Fatima.

(2.55)   Bill sold *War and Peace* to John.
         The positive report gave the prisoners a reprieve.
         Fatima taught Arabic to the children.

Rather simplistically, we may say that the subject combines the roles of Goal + Agent in (2.54) and of Source + Agent in (2.55).[35] The key to accounting for the contrasting semantic roles on these subject DPs seems to be PAR (2.42), which acknowledges that different verbal meanings may highlight (e.g. require expression of) different theta roles, even though such meanings are not linked to the actual syntactic structure surrounding the verb. This possibility has been foreseen above with the semantic roles of Agent (for *pack*), Theme (for *move*) and Location (for *fill*).

(2.42)   *Principal Argument Role. A predicate @ of category V or A typically specifies in its lexical entry that some particular theta role f **must** be assigned to a subject or an object. This can be notated formally by listing the role f in the entry of @.*

For *sell, give* and *teach*, Source is the semantic role obligatorily expressed as a subject or object. But additionally, since these verbs have the unmarked lexical value -LOC, their direct object must be a Theme. Conse-

---

[35] In syntactically reinterpreting some devices in Jackendoff's (1987, 1989) lexical conceptual structures, Emonds (1991b) represents these pairs of roles with pairs of obligatorily co-indexed arguments. However, in light of the discussion in the text, such indexing now seems superfluous.

quently, PAR predicts that the only possible position where Source can surface is in their subject DP.

(2.56)   Mary sold Bill *War and Peace* (*from John).
The official gave the prisoners a reprieve (*from the positive report).
The language director taught the children Arabic (*from Fatima).

We can however dissociate the pairs of roles on the subject DPs of *buy* and *get*, but not of *learn* in (2.54): [36]

(2.57)   Mary bought John *War and Peace* (from Bill).
The official got the prisoners a reprieve (from the positive report).
The language director learned (*the children) Arabic (from Fatima).

Learn thus has a principal argument feature Goal. Since it like *teach* is -LOC, this theta role must appear on its subject.

Like this section's other verbs, *buy* also has the unmarked value -LOC, which means that its object is a Theme. Accordingly, *buy* and *get* permit a Goal to appear either in subject or indirect object position. If the latter is missing, then the subject may be *optionally* interpreted as a Goal, as indeed subjects may also be in *John fixed a drink, Bill baked a cake,* etc. But subjects of *buy* and *get* are not *obligatorily* Goals in the absence of indirect objects, as can be seen in (2.58).

(2.58)   This money won't buy much.
Our Treasurer has to buy all our company's computer equipment.

The parallelism of *buy* and *sell* has been slightly overestimated; a buyer does not necessarily become an owner (hence there are professional "buyers"), but a seller never retains ownership after the act. [37]

---

[36] The parenthesized *from*-phrases in (2.57) sound odd combined with an indirect object. If the indirect objects are replaced with a PP, these PPs are fully acceptable.

?John bought Mary *War and Peace* from Bill.
John bought *War and Peace* from Bill for Mary.

[37] Of further interest is the fact that the refinement for Agent Specification (2.39) proposed in note 24 holds for these verbs: *Buy, learn* and *sell* require animate subjects (except in very colloquial style), and these are always interpreted as agents. But since *get, give* and *teach* do not require animate subjects, their animate subjects need not be agents:

In sum, the interpretive system elaborated here successfully assigns theta roles to all classes of DP arguments without using any relational or linking device for lexical selection other than the features of classic syntactic subcategorization.

2.7 A *Gedanken Experiment* for learning lexical entries

linking: 64   *s,s q*   *63*

If principles of theta role interpretation such as Agent (2.39), Ground (2.47), and Figure (2.48) Specification can be maintained in their general form, we can conclude that descriptive adequacy in the lexicon does not require that verbs select DP arguments in terms of theta roles or positions in conceptual structures. Consequently, neither theta grids nor item-particular linking specifications should be allowed in lexical entries.

In fact, the term "argument" itself is not innocent in the debate between syntactic and semantic selection. Not accidentally, the term is most common both in the generative semantic literature and in formal syntax after 1980 when "s-selection" was embraced. In semantically based selection, argument is a primitive notion in the lexicon, which must then be grafted onto syntax. The usage of the term is itself subject to wide fluctuation, and "arguments" have few if any syntactic correlates, though they are often counterposed rhetorically to "adjuncts." At one extreme, Baker (1988, Ch. 5) argues that benefactive and instrumental PPs are not adjuncts but complements. At the other, some authors consider all optional phrases as adjuncts (i.e., not as arguments), even if they are selected, while others even consider some obligatory PPs to be adjuncts (e.g. *The garden swarmed *(with bees);* Jackendoff, 1990, 178). Sometimes all PPs are called adjuncts, but then one wonders what "argument" adds to the traditional term "direct object."

Under a syntactic approach, essentially any DP in an underlying (pre-movement) position is an argument of some X^0, and hence "argument" and "internal argument" are entirely derivative concepts.[38] So-called adjunct

---

John got a traffic ticket.

Mary gave us cause for concern.

The little girl and her pet taught us the meaning of devotion.

[38] Some subcategorized DPs fail to be in a position where they can receive a case in LF. This then allows them to agree with a c-commanding DP in the same clause and be interpreted as predicate nominals: *Mary became a doctor; Mary made John her slave.* Cf. section 8.3 for this analysis.

DPs are actually "arguments" (i.e., objects) of various Ps, even when these P are null in the syntax. Thus in syntactic terms, the until now unresolved issue of how to generate adjuncts concerns licensing PPs rather than DPs (see section 7.4).[39] True enough, both PPs and DP complements inside PPs subcategorized by a V behave in certain ways like objects of that V (Chomsky, 1965, Ch. 2; Emonds, 1985, Ch. 7), but this is due to their presumed structural position inside V^1. Calling them arguments sheds no light on such properties.

The elimination of relational semantic information (argument, theta grid, lexical conceptual structure, etc.) from lexical entries is welcome, since otherwise children would have to first learn such an "argument structure" from a simultaneous holistic pairing of the structure and the pragmatic context of *a sentence whose meaning is understood even though its most central words are not*. Such a process seems almost fantastically implausible.[40]

The following *conte morale* illustrates competing scenarios of how a child might learn a lexical entry for a verb such as *steal*. In the first, the child must learn (or grow) its "lexico-semantic argument structure"; in the second, the child must learn that *steal* is a type of *taking* that is *bad*, with optional complements headed by D and [P, SOURCE].

Mom, Pop and Baby are watching a gripping TV police serial about life in the city. On the screen, the feminist hippie-style third floor renter, known to be short of cash, knocks on the kindly old landlady's door. Upon it being opened, she shoves the old lady aside with a sneer, reaches into a previously carelessly revealed cash box, grabs back last month's rent and a few more bills besides, and rushes out the door. As Pop has momentarily bent over to tie his shoe, he asks, *"What happened?"* Mom conveniently answers, *"The hippie stole her money from the old lady."*

Scenario #1: Acquiring the theta grid/ lexico-semantic structure of *steal*. By hypothesis, Baby (only) understands Mom as saying, *The hippie*

---

[39] The licensing and interpretation of the null P of time, place and manner in "bare NP adverbials" is discussed in Emonds (1987). "Datives of interest" as in *His car broke down on John at the worst moment* exhibit an overt P, except in situations of cliticization or overt oblique morphological case. Since these latter constructions are also best analyzed as containing grammatical P (Emonds, 1993, and Ch. 7 here), datives of interest are complements of these P, while the PPs are in turn adjuncts in the VP.

In sum, adjuncts are invariably PPs or APs and not bare DPs; cf. section 7.4.

[40] One influential though to my mind purely abstract account of this process is elaborated in Pinker (1989, Ch. 6). Under this account, the child must also either inherit or develop a wealth of other lexical devices listed by Pinker (each gets a section in the cited chapter).

[s-t-o-l] her money from the old lady, with brackets indicating mere phonet-ics, since it has up to now been too young to use *steal.* Baby nonetheless (i) fully understands what has just transpired in the TV program (by analyzing and classifying the crime according to its "event structure," a crucial con-struct in this account), (ii) has a ready-made and furthermore accessible lexico-semantic argument structure for *steal,* including a feature indicating the action is "bad," and (iii) decides that this is a good time to consider (i) as instantiating (ii). For a kid that can't say *steal,* this is pretty impressive. Baby sits quietly by, files *[s-t-o-l]* with (ii), and thus acquires the word *steal.*

Hopefully, in a moment of laconic humor, Mom hasn't said *acquired, appropriated, expropriated, grabbed, needed, nicked, (re-)obtained, pock-eted, repossessed, scooped up, snatched, took back,* etc. since then Baby will learn the *wrong meaning* for that word – recall, Baby has conjured up an argument structure that fits both the pragmatic event structure and the sentence, and is lying in wait for the word meaning *steal.* If Mom says the wrong thing, poor Baby will, *for the rest of its life* (since negative evidence can't undo the damage) be misunderstood when using the word it has wrongly acquired in the place of *steal.*

Scenario #2: Acquiring the subcategorization of *steal.* The same situa-tion obtains. Alerted by the parental interchange, Baby decides to learn the new word that will allow participation in the exciting world on the screen, and so appropriately deduces from the principal caregiver's just presented positive evidence that the unfamiliar [s-t-o-l] must be in fact, V, +___D, +___[P, SOURCE]. (Presumably, Baby already knows a few similar words like *take.*) Sadly lacking linking rules conflation class definitions, both broad and narrow range lexical rules and lexico-semantic structures (see note 40), to say nothing of theta grids, this somewhat less endowed Baby is moved to ask, "*Mommy, what does **stole** mean?*" (In Scenario #1, the ques-tion would be just to confirm what is already known, or grown.) Mommy, insouciant of argument structures and theta grids, answers "*take something when you're not supposed to,*" from which Baby infers +ACTIVITY, +"bad", thereby completing its (childish) lexical entry.[41]

---

[41] The subcategorization scenario does *not require* a verbal interchange. Baby is learning the word for the activity 'stole', and +ACTIVITY is unmarked for verbs. Thus, the context need only furnish Baby with the marked feature +bad, which is not an intrinsic part of the definition of any of the other verbs listed (*acquire, appropriate, ...*). If Mom had moralized in linguistic or gestural terms Baby could interpret, e.g., "The {nasty/ naughty} hippie stole her money," Baby could get the message with no questions asked.

Past tense aside, the child now knows the word *steal* without benefit of innate argument structure, magical matching of argument structure and situation, or possibility (or necessity?) of lifelong error. For under scenario #2, and this is the evidence in the thought experiment, if Mom had said e.g. *snatched,* her answer to, *"What does **snatch** mean?"* would be something like, *"take real quick,"* and the child could learn that word correctly instead of *steal.*

I perhaps reveal a hopeless predilection for the uncomplicated, but lexical acquisition which depends only on positive evidence in the input and a few simple-minded indications of semantic features *f* such as "bad" by competent speakers strikes me as the more plausible scenario by far, in particular for the open class lexicon. Scenario #1 on the other hand seems not only far-fetched but wrong – children don't mislearn vocabulary (e.g. say *snatch* all their life when they mean *steal*) because their parents say unexpected and occasionally clever things.[42]

Independently of the ultimate worth of this thought experiment, the fact remains that most work developing semantic theories of head-complement co-occurrence, including work of otherwise entirely Chomskyan inspiration, pays almost no attention to the tremendous amount of lexical stipulation they postulate. Perhaps the only exception to this trend is one of its leading proponents. At the outset of a *final* chapter, Jackendoff (1990, 245) turns to "a glaring deficiency in my formulation of lexical correspondence rules; the fact that the correspondence of conceptual arguments to syntactic positions is completely stipulated." Consequently, he devotes a chapter to developing a theory of linking, and considers the feasibility of a "minimalist approach" (250) which would "eliminate the stipulation of coindexing between conceptual arguments and syntactic arguments. The question is, How far can we go in simplifying lexical entries?" (249) Then, in evaluating efforts in this direction (250–256), he observes "there still remain some residual cases where syntactic subcategorization is necessary." (256)

In this chapter I have argued that if we maintain and refine subcategorization (in particular, by proper use of head features) as the sole mechanism

---

[42] The fatal weakness of Scenario #1 is that certain potential "learning events" are somehow supposed to lead to acquiring lexical items. But any event or situation, perfectly or imperfectly perceived and/or analyzed, can have infinitely many true descriptions, and any description can apply to infinitely many events or situations. Therefore, any lexical learning strategy which suggests that argument structures can be inferred from understood events is a hopeless muddle.

which expresses head-complement co-occurrence, we can indeed achieve Jackendoff's minimalist goal, that is, we can eliminate *all* lexical co-indexing or linking between syntactic arguments of a lexical head and aspects of the conceptual structure which defines that head. The main components of this approach have been non-trivial principles of Agent, Ground, and Figure Specification, the possible presence of an unlinked "principal role" in a lexical entry (2.42), and extending the feature ±LOCATION to the category V.

The descriptive adequacy achieved by using subcategorization for all lexical co-occurrence, its parsimony, and the generality of the interpretive principles for determining semantic roles on DPs all lead me to claim, as indicated in section 2.3, that it is entirely unnecessary to enrich lexical entries by having them assign non-intrinsic semantic properties of complements. I therefore propose that argument structures, theta grids, linked conceptual structures and the like are simply unavailable as lexical mechanisms.

This reaffirms the conclusion of Emonds (1991b) that autonomous semantic selection by *individual lexical items* doesn't exist; purely semantic (= syntax-independent) well-formedness conditions on predicates and their complements are not needed. Lexical subcategorization features as in (2.14) fully suffice to determine head-complement combinations. Any item-particular semantic or conceptual conditions such as those conforming to PAR (2.42) are unlinked to any syntactic position. Conversely, any semantic interpretive conditions which *are* syntactically linked (as is Agent Specification) are not item-particular. This invariant property of the lexicon is referred to in Emonds (1991b) as Semantic Atomism.

Chapter 3
Subcategorization inside words: Morphology as grammatical compounding

This chapter extends the notions "head" and "subcategorization" to the X^0 domain of morphology and compounding, incorporating Lieber's (1980, 1983) important and innovative proposals whereby X^0-internal subcategorization forms words around "right-hand heads". These extensions necessitate clarifying principles of left to right order. Sections 3.1 and 3.2 compare some principles for ordering heads within X^0 domains (morphology) and XP domains (syntax). Although heads are widely presumed to be final in English morphology but initial in English syntax, these sections will show that domain size is not the factor that determines direction of headedness, nor are the two directly correlated. Sections 3.3 and 3.4 will go on to argue for completely conflating the notions of "head of a word" and "head of a phrase" and claim that "generalized subcategorization" inside and outside words is basically the same device.

Any discussion of the grammar of X^0 domains necessarily raises the question: How do compounding and morphology differ? I argue below that the difference between bound and free morphemes is not relevant to the question. (Of course, the Lieber-type subcategorizations can characterize bound forms of either type.) What turns out to be more important is a morpheme's lexical content in terms of the three types of features $\{ f, F, F' \}$ of section 1.2.[1] Sections 3.5 and 3.6 argue that bound morphology reduces in fact to an easily characterized sub-case of compounding; namely, morphology is simply the phonological form taken by compounding when a bound form lacks purely semantic features f. Nothing then remains of any separate monostratal or "autonomous" morphological domain except a small residue of morphological phonology dependent on the absence of semantic features.

The presence or absence of semantic features f in a lexical entry has a number of important consequences. Section 3.7 will introduce and amply justify a bifurcated model of the lexicon in which both bound and free morphemes have a wide range of differing properties according to the types

---

[1] Recall from that section that F are cognitive syntactic features interpreted in LF, while F' are uninterpreted syntactic features.

of features they spell out. That part of the lexicon which excludes purely semantic *f* will be labeled the "Syntacticon" while open class items with such *f* comprise the "Dictionary". In subsequent chapters, the subcategorization properties of the Syntacticon items, their formal simplicity and their ability interact in non-trivial ways with e.g., principles of Case and Economy, will permit me to defend extremely strong claims both about the English lexicon and about Universal Grammar.

To avoid misunderstanding, I want to emphasize that the lexicon here in no way encompasses "everything within a word," i.e. everything in X^0 domains. This study takes as established that syntactic theory must account for the regular and often fully productive grammatical patterns of morphology and compounding which operate both within and across X^0 domain boundaries. Although syntacticians who long to theorize about something supposedly "less messy" never seem to tire of idealizing away from practically the entire domain of traditional grammar, more studies than can be listed – perhaps the most brilliant being Baker's (1988) *Incorporation* – have forcefully established that a lexicon does not and will not account for regular grammatical dependencies that link structure inside X^0 with phrasal syntax.[2] Following Bloomfield (1933), the lexicon is more usefully defined as the totality of grammatical items and sequences of items stored in memory.

3.1 Marked and unmarked headedness: English vs. Japanese

3.1.1 Phrasal domains

The uniform category inventory and dominance relations imposed across languages by a universal bar notation (Chapter 1) contrast with variations in how grammatical elements are ordered left to right. At one extreme, (3.1) holds uniformly for morphology, compounding and syntax:

---

[2] Examples of novel, non-stored structures brimming with X^0-internal syntactic dependencies are as easy to construct and understand as are novel combinations of phrases:

(i) Our [$_A$ appointment free] [$_N$ cafe frequenting] during that [$_N$ four day work respite] [$_V$ [$_A$ bright] ened] our spirits and [$_V$ re [$_V$ set]] our priorities (*straight).

Characterizing and explaining such dependencies is central to any grammar that claims to be generative. Moreover, it is not just a question of including fully productive X^0-internal patterns in syntax; even patterns exemplified in stored items make use of, and hence can shed light on, the same syntactic principles:

(ii) Our [$_A$ trouble free] [$_N$ house cleaning] during the [$_N$ three week Christmas vacation] [$_V$ [$_A$ stabil] ized] our marriage and [$_V$ [$_A$ intens] ified] our sex life.

(3.1)   In Japanese, X^j is head-final.[3]

Obvious syntactic contrasts between languages like English and Japanese have led many researchers to describe the former as simply "head-initial" rather than "head-final." However, while English heads X^0 precede *full phrases*, some syntactic projections of lexical categories in English exhibit non-initial heads above the level of the word. In (3.2), well-formed pre-head modifiers are in bold:

(3.2)   Non-initial Noun heads:
the [$_A$ **other ten**] boys
boys [$_{AP}$ other than him]
[$_{AP}$ **very proud** (*of their team)] boys
boys [$_{AP}$ very proud of their team]
that **(crooked) three mile** path
*that three miles path
some (*very) **mere** boys
*that three mile crooked path

(3.3)   Non-initial Adjective heads:
five times more exciting
forty boring miles long
more surprisingly (*for an oldest child) spoiled

(3.4)   Non-initial Verb heads:
Aetna [$_{VP}$ { **never/ still/ seldom** } erupts].
*Fuji more seldom than Aetna erupts.
Mary [$_{VP}$ **angrily** (*at authority) spoke].
Mary [$_{VP}$ { **then/** *for hours } spoke].

(3.5)   Non-initial Preposition heads:
a few feet down the street
three additional feet behind the garage
right down into the street
*right a few feet down the street

This asymmetry between head-initial and head-final languages necessitates a more circumspect statement for English, rather than a full reversal of

---

[3]   Japanese does have a right dislocation which permits one XP to the right of a final verb in root contexts. A movement from underlying head-final constructions is involved, since constraints on extraction block right dislocation of XPs which are too deeply embedded. I believe the first treatment is an unpublished mid-seventies paper by S. Haraguchi.

(3.1). The above patterns suggest that even English syntax marginally re-flects an ordering specified in Universal Grammar (Emonds 1985, Ch. 2). In fact, Greenberg's (1963) initial and in many ways still most revealing study of cross-linguistic word order documents that while many languages are strictly head-final, so-called head-initial systems typically exhibit some non-initial heads. Languages are thus not entirely symmetrical with respect to head-complement order, but tend to take head-final as the norm and to depart from it in specific ways (or not at all).

(3.6)   *Universal Right Headedness. In the absence of language-particu-lar properties (whether of syntax or morphology), heads are al-ways on the right.*

A language such as Japanese conforms to (3.6) not only in its syntax but in its morphology; both its phrasal and word domains directly exhibit this universal tendency.

But a head-initial language is subject to some additional syntax-internal condition. To state such a condition for English, I will use the definition (3.7):

(3.7)   *Complete Projection. A maximal projection of a lexical category which cannot be further extended is its* **complete** *projection. All other projections are termed* **incomplete.**

As argued in section 1.3, complete projections in English are (only) IP, DP, AP and PP.

A clue to what actually determines English word order is now provided by the fact that several acceptable bold pre-head modifiers in the patterns in (3.2)–(3.5) are arguably not maximal projections; they are either in (possi-bly branching) X^0 or not grouped into larger constituents at all.[4] Thus, the only constituents which seem to follow heads are both phrases and at the same time *outside all X^0*:

---

[4] Demonstrating this in each case would take us too far afield. The grammaticality contrasts presented suggest some lines of argument. The ordering of AP adjuncts with respect to an English noun is related to whether or not they exhibit internal recursion; for discussion, see Emonds (1985, sections 3.4–3.5). These English pre-head adjectives seem not to be maximal projections and hence may result from adjunction to X^0, essentially making them subject to the universal (3.6) rather than (3.8).

(3.8)   *English Word Order. In any incomplete phrasal projection X^1, the head precedes its phrasal Y^j sisters.*[5]

The English measure phrase paradigms noted in Jackendoff (1977, Ch. 5) fall into place as a consequence of (3.8) and the theory of extended projections of Chapter 1. Measure phrases follow a V they modify because VP is incomplete; they precede A and P because they are immediately dominated by the latter's complete projections (i.e., AP and PP cannot have internal subjects; cf. section 1.3.4). Measure phrases precede N, but their otherwise inexplicable lack of plural marking and post-adjectival position, seen in (3.2), show that they are incorporated into an N^0 compounding structure and hence escape (3.8).

Note that not only the patterns in (3.2)–(3.5) but also *complete projections* are not subject to (3.8); they conform rather to the universal (3.6). Thus, any subject DPs in SPEC(IP) or SPEC(DP) are to the left of the heads I' and D', and the same holds for measure phrases in the Specifiers immediately dominated by maximal APs and PPs. But otherwise, any phrasal projection follows the head of an English phrase; this includes complements, adjuncts, and the X^{max} complements of functional categories such as I and D.[6]

3.1.2 Word domains

The linear position of heads is often claimed to be a central property which differentiates word-internal syntax from phrasal syntax. In this vein, heads are thought to precede phrasal complements in English but to follow word-internal sisters. However, closer scrutiny of English syntax has just revealed that the head position in phrasal domains is not entirely uniform, with both

---

[5]   I make no claim that (3.8) is a primitive condition that cannot be derived from something else. For example, English deep head-complement order might conform to (3.6) and be derived by raising of lexical heads to initial functional heads. This would explain why a head is not initial in a complete projection – there is no higher functional head to raise to.

[6]   The relation between the universal (3.6) and a language-specific principle (3.8) is the familiar Elsewhere Principle of the Sanskritist Panini formulated in generative grammar by S. Anderson and P. Kiparsky: a more specific principle, when applicable, overrides the more general.

    A reviewer suggests that null phrases, provided it makes sense to speak of their left to right order, might well be subject to the universal (3.6) rather than to a language-particular statement. If so, a PRO subject would always be to the left of its predicate.

Universal Grammar (3.6) and a principle of English syntax (3.8) playing roles.

Let us now consider left to right order and headedness within X^0 domains. Ever since Lieber's (1980, 1983) pioneer studies on the syntax of morphology and compounds, it has been widely accepted that in English and similar languages the right-hand elements within X^0 domains are their heads, at least in the regular patterns of compounds and derivational morphology.[7] That is, the bold elements in (3.9)–(3.11) are head X^0 whose categories percolate and determine the categories and properties of the larger X^0 structures, independently of any category on a left branch.

(3.9) Noun heads:

$[_N [_V$ develop$] [_N$ **ment**$]]$ $[_N [_N$ execution$] [_N$ **er**$]]$ $[_N [_A$ rapid$] [_N$ **ity**$]]$

$[_N [_V$ think$] [_N$ **tank** $]]$ $[_N [_?$ cran$] [_N$ **berry**$]]$ $[_N [_A$ sour$] [_N$ **cream**$]]$

(3.10) Adjective heads:

$[_A [_V$ present$] [_A$ **able**$]]$ $[_A [_N$ stress$] [_A$ **ful**$]]$ $[_A [_A$ blue$] [_A$ **ish**$]]$

$[_A [_?$ un$] [_A$ **free**$]]$ $[_A [_A$ dark$] [_A$ **green**$]]$ $[_A [_?$ double$] [_A$ **fresh**$]]$

(3.11) Verb heads:

$[_V [_?$ rect$] [_V$ **ify**$]]$ $[_V [_N$ length$] [_V$ **en**$]]$ $[_V [_A$ sterile$] [_V$ **ize**$]]$

$[_V [_?$ re$] [_V$ **develop**$]]$[8] $[_V [_N$ vacuum$] [_V$ **pack**$]]$ $[_V [_A$ dry$] [_V$ **clean**$]]$

---

[7] Walinska de Hackbeil (1985) argues, to my mind convincingly, that certain structures claimed in Lieber (1980) to have left-hand heads within English X^0 have empty but otherwise regular right-hand heads, and thus exemplify the phenomenon of "conversion." Thus *imprison* is right headed: *[$_V$ [$_{P'}$ [$_P$ in] [$_N$ prison]] [$_{V, +ACTIVITY}$ Ø]],* etc.

[8] We can sometimes develop an argument for the category of a non-head morpheme on a left branch even if the morpheme never appears as a free form. For example, the complementary distribution between post-verbal particles (widely agreed to be "intransitive P") and the English verbal prefix *re-* (noted by Keyser and Roeper, 1992) suggests that the latter is also a P incorporated into the verb:

(i) John shipped (off) his prizes.   John reshipped (*off) his prizes.
Let's build (up) our defenses   Let's rebuild (*up) our defenses.
You should write (down) the response. You should rewrite (*down) the response.
It's time to count (out) the money.   It's time to recount (*out) the money.

If *re-* is a P, the data in (i) follow from the fact that only one particle P can occur with one V:

(ii) *Please put down the cat out.   *We should bring on the cheese in.

These structures are supported by the fact that a suffix's properties, unlike those of a prefix, largely determine those of a word. For example, according to tests such as preceding a modified noun or modification by SPEC(AP), we know that all the items in (3.12a) are adjectives. Then by the same tests the compounds in (3.12b) and the derivational formations in (3.12c) are all adjectives.[9]

(3.12)   a.   free, happy, shy, sick, resistant, able, full, crowded, kind, lucky, sure
         b.   { appointment / furniture / insect / obstacle / responsibility }-*free*
              trigger-*happy*, gun-*shy*, home*sick*, germ-*resistant*
         c.   appoint*able*, deriv*able*, refund*able*, stack*able*
              content*ful*, deceit*ful*, delight*ful*, event*ful*
              un*crowded*, un*kind*, un*lucky*, un*sure*

A right-hand head analysis explains why the larger units test out to have the same adjectival behavior as their right-hand consituents.

Turning the logic around, we also analyze the italicized suffixes in (3.13) as adjectival heads, because various tests for adjectival status confirm that the larger formations are A:

(3.13)   a.   a { two-hand*ed*, strong-heart*ed*, talent*ed*, stunt*ed* } primate
         b.   to seem { rather, too, less } { Fascist*ic*, athlet*ic*, bas*ic*, poet*ic* }

Right-hand headed structures are also useful in analyzing, for example, grammatical gender in French and German nouns. The gender of a complex noun, whether formed by compounding or suffixation, is determined by the gender of its head. Thus, the German bound form diminutives -*chen* and -*lein* are simply neuter nouns in the lexicon (akin to a neuter free form such as *Weib* 'woman'). Hence it follows that *Maedchen* 'maiden' is also neuter, the grammatical gender of the non-head stem being irrelevant.[10]

Similarly, noun-forming bound suffixes in French are simply nouns and as expected have a grammatical gender. -*age* is masculine; -*erie* is feminine;

---

[9]   Throughout the chapter, many examples are taken from Selkirk's (1982) comprehensive study of X^0-internal formations.

[10]   From this point of view, the Spanish diminutive suffix -*ito* / *ita* is atypical in having no inherent gender. Alternatively, the diminutive suffix is -*it*- and the lexical gender of a Spanish noun is a second suffix.

the animate pair expressing agents *-eur/ -rice* follows natural gender (as do most animate nouns); *-heur* and the instrument noun suffix *-eur* are masculine; and the abstract noun suffix *-eur* is feminine. Hence, the genders of all the nouns in (3.14) are correctly predicted by the right-hand head hypothesis; genders of unsuffixed but phonologically similar nouns such as *page* 'page' (feminine), *coeur* 'heart' (masculine) and *fleur* 'flower' (feminine) are irrelevant:

(3.14)   le garage, le recyclage, un collage, une parfumerie, une connerie, un instituteur, une institutrice, le bonheur, un moteur, la candeur, la pâleur, la pudeur, la senteur, la torpeur

It has often been asserted that right headedness within English words, which contrasts with the left headedness of its phrasal syntax, necessitates some morphology-particular principle for English. But right headedness is clearly more parsimoniously characterized by appeal to the earlier *universal unmarked condition (3.6)*, which entirely conflates morphological (X^0) and syntactic (XP) domains.

(3.6)   *Universal Right Headedness. In the absence of language-particular properties (whether of syntax or morphology), heads are always on the right.*

The right headedness of English compounds and morphological structures, proposed by Lieber (1980, 1983), Williams (1981) and Selkirk (1982), follows from (3.6). The only language-particular statements needed are those which contravene and by the Elsewhere Condition override (3.6), such as the English head-complement ordering (3.8).[11] From this perspective, no morphology-specific "word headedness principle" regulates English word formation; its compounds and derivational morphology both conform perfectly to (and in fact reveal) the universal expectation of grammatical theory.

While we have good evidence that the right-hand elements of both English compounds and derivational morphology are heads, we have not yet

---

[11] L.-Y. Huang (1990) claims that in Chinese, all and only YP sisters follow X^0, for X = V and P ([-N]); otherwise, Chinese is head-final. Accordingly, Chinese simply has a more restricted version of the English (3.8).

If the *underlying* word order of all languages is uniform, it seems more likely that it conforms to (3.6), since right-headedness seems to be the "elsewhere" case.

spelled out the internal structure of these formations. While some have proposed further bar notation levels (e.g. negative superscripts) to distinguish various levels inside X^0, many researchers use simple combinations of zero-level categories for both types of combinations, as in (3.15):

(3.15)   a.   b.

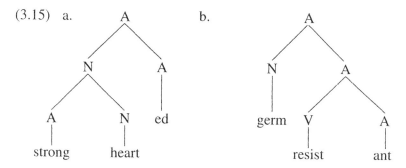

It is often remarked that a structure like (3.15b) exhibits a "bracketing paradox" in that lexical dependencies require it (e.g., non-productive *-ant* combines with *resist* but not *subsist: *subsistant, *germ-subsistant*), even though it conflicts with the semantics of the compound, roughly *"have the property [v resist germ]."*

This problem may have been exaggerated. Some statement of interpreting, i.e., often simply erasing, derivational morphemes is required for LF in any case. In Chapters 4 and 5 I will use the syntax of derived nominals and passive adjectives in order to propose such a principle:

(4.48)   *Transparent Derivational Heads. If a lexical suffix @ on X at Spell Out selects no complements, then (i) the lowest argument c-commanding @ and (ii) any lower arguments may be interpreted as the corresponding arguments of X.*

Since *-ant* does not itself take complements (most derivational morphemes don't, though there are cases like *-ful* in (3.25a) below), the lowest potential argument c-commanding the adjective headed by *-ant* in (3.15b) is its sister *[N germ]*. Then by (4.48) *[N germ]* may be interpreted as the argument of *[v resist]*, i.e., as its direct object. It doesn't seem like any real paradox remains.

Section 3.5 will return to specifying more precisely a general relation between morphology and compounds which justifies conflating their syntactic structures as in (3.15).

3.2 The indepdendence of head directionality and domain size: French word order

French has initial heads in a different range of structures than does English. In phrasal projections, clitic realizations of complements and adjuncts, which are by definition bound morphemes, can precede the head, which is an impossible order for an English phrasal complement or adjunct. Clitic orderings as in (3.16) exemplify bound Y^j which precede a head V or P:

(3.16)   le voir 'it-see'   les y mettre 'them-there-put'
         là-dessus 'there-upon'   ci-joint 'here-attached'

In these French configurations phrases precede heads, i.e. universal right headedness emerges even within incomplete phrasal projections.

On the other hand, the head can be initial inside French word level projections, under the condition that both the head and the non-head are *free morphemes*.

(3.17)   *French Word Order. In any incomplete projection (whether X^1 or X^0), a free head precedes its free Y^j sisters.*[12]

Consequently, in various word level projections in which English shows a head-final configuration in accord with Universal Right Headedness (3.6), near synonymous compounds of French free morphemes conform rather to (3.17), with initial heads. As expected, these initial heads *invariably* determine the compound's grammatical gender.

(3.18)   English: French:[13]
         ten storey building   bâtiment à/de dix étages
         apple pie   tarte aux pommes
         bedroom suburb   ville dortoir
         vacuum pack   emballage à vide
         restaurant ticket   ticket restaurant
         tanker truck   camion citerne
         video cassette   cassette vidéo
         dark green   vert foncé
         self love   amour propre

---

[12] One exception to (3.17) in French, in fact common to both phrasal syntax and compounding, is that adjectives sometimes precede head nouns: *gentilhomme* 'gentleman', *grand-mère* 'grandmother', *grande fille* 'tall girl', *long discours* 'long speech'.

[13] I am grateful to S. Pourcel for contributions and verification here.

dry cleaning	nettoyage à sec
railroad	chemin de fer
steamboat	bâteau à vapeur
paper tissue	mouchoir (en) papier
milk tooth	dent de lait
sleeping car	wagon lit
miracle solution	solution miracle
Lincoln Avenue	Avenue Jean Jaurès
New York City	Ville de Paris
Rocky Mountains	Montagnes Rocheuses
Macy's Store	Magasin Printemps

In spite of this pervasive pattern, a hasty conclusion that French compounds are uniformly left-headed is quite inaccurate. If *either* element of a compound is a bound morpheme (bold below), French exhibits the universal default right headedness of (3.6). Again, this right-hand head determines the gender of a compound noun.

(3.19)   French:[14]   Translations, often structurally identical:

contre-exemple	**counter**example
franco-allemand	French-German
mi-Janvier	**mid**-January
minijupe	**mini**-skirt
motocyclette	motorcycle
pluridisciplinaire	**multi**-disciplinary
russophobie	Russian phobia
téléjournal	television news
klepto+mane	**klepto**maniac
sino+phile	**sino+phile**
homéo+pathie	**homeo+pathy**
phallo+crate	??
bureau**crate**	bureau**crat**
mal**heur**	**mis**fortune

Thus, the "break" between head-initial and head-final order in French does not fall where it does in English. The specifically English headedness principle (3.8) affects only a subpart of what can be called phrasal syntax

[14] My bold plus + in some of these words indicates a boundary between two bound morphemes; this is not reflected in spelling. Interestingly, French spelling consistently shows whether a compound morpheme is bound (via no spacing or hyphenation) or free, as seen in (3.18–3.19).

(i.e., syntax outside X^0), while the French headedness principle (3.17) cuts across the division between X^0 (words) and X^1 (phrases).

I thus conclude that the linear order of heads correlates neither with domain size nor with different "components" of syntax and morphology. Rather, the ordering of heads is determined enitrely by *syntactic* constructs (defined in terms of the bar notation) and *lexical* concepts such as "bound morpheme" and applies to compounds as well as to bound morphology. No morphology-specific categories or principles are needed. English and French syntax each depart in their own way from the Universal Right Headedness tendency (3.6), but neither has any special property that refers to a special construct "morphological head."

3.3 Combining word-internal and phrasal trees

Since the principles determining the position of heads do not coincide with the domains of X^0 and X^1 in either English or French (or for that matter Japanese), I see no reason to maintain that heads of words differ in character from heads of phrases. I thus conflate the notions "head of a word" and "head of a phrase," rendering the relation of headedness transitive: if **x** is a head of (a word) **y** and **y** is a head of (a phrase) **z**, then **x** is a head of **z**. The heads of NP are exemplified in bold in (3.20).

(3.20)

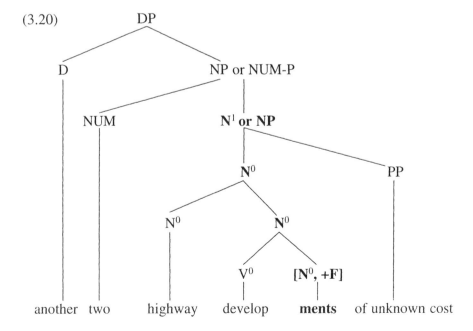

In (3.20), the N -*ments* is head of the word *developments* as well as morpheme head of the compound N^0, the intermediate N^1, the NP and finally the extended projection DP of N. In addition, *developments* is the head word of these nominal projections, and *developments of unknown cost* is a phrasal head of both the maximal NP and the DP. My claim is therefore:

(3.21)   *Unified headedness. Heads of words are also heads of phrases.*

Without special principles of headedness for morphology, there is little motivation for claiming that syntactic principles should be formulated differently within "minimal words," a term sometimes used to characterize a separate domain of "autonomous morphology." Other motivations offered for this separation are observations that (i) left-to-right morpheme ordering inside words admits of almost no variation and that (ii) native speaker judgments about violations of such ordering are psychologically of a stronger and different nature than judgments concerning syntactic deviance. Thus, *ing-read, ness-ish-fool, apply-re*, etc. are so ungrammatical as to be essentially unrecognizable, in contrast to ungrammatical permutations among phrasal sisters.

But the fact is that these observations hold equally well of morphology and compounding: languages generally forbid variations in ordering in compounds, and unless some odd "meaning" can be ascribed to misordered compound structures, their deviance is equally strong: *crat-demo, centric-theo, size-man, mare-night, berry-straw*, etc. Hence, these observations indicate not that morphology is autonomous, but rather the opposite, that morphology and compounding fully share the internal syntax of X^0 domains.[15]

An additional confirmation of assimilating morphology and compounding is provided by the fact that both types of formation rarely countenance the category P as a right-hand head. The only remotely possible English candidate for a suffix of category P might be the adverb forming -*ly* on adjectival stems.[16] In languages with "inflected prepositions" such as Welsh, the inflections are more like clitics on P than heads of P. Nor do there seem

---

[15] These observations do strongly support the notion that X^0 (word domains) and X^1 (phrasal domains) are separate mental constructs, a point sometimes denied in enthusiastic endorsements of "bare phrase structure."

[16] However, Artiagoitia (1992) argues for Basque and Kubo (1994) for Japanese that the inflectional suffixes of certain active non-finite forms seem to be of category P.

The fairly productive class of English V+P (*breakthrough, fly over, gadabout, go between, lean to, set up, tie in, walk on*, etc.) are nouns of a special sort and hence *not headed* by the right-hand P.

to be compound prepositions of the form V+P, A+P, or N+P; the few English compound P that exist take only grammatical elements as their left-hand member: *without, throughout, henceforth, heretofore, therein,* etc.

3.4 Conflating syntactic and morphological subcategorization

In light of the cross-linguistic properties of headedness just considered, I have suggested that morphology and syntax are less distinct than commonly thought. In particular, morphology and compounding, in fact often subsumed under a single rubric of word formation in traditional grammar, appear to be subject to the same combinatorial syntax. In Chapter 2, I argued that subcategorization is the sole *item-particular* device for licensing phrasal complements. I will now argue that the same holds for word formation, and furthermore that word-internal and phrasal subcategorization are cut from the same formal cloth.

Using Williams's proposal that derivational suffixes are heads, Lieber (1980) proposes that adjective-forming suffixes such as *-ive (expressive, invasive, supportive)* and *-less (defenseless, heartless, penniless)* can be simply listed as A that subcategorize within a larger A^0 domain for V and N respectively. Hence they appear in the lexicon as *-ive*, A, +V___ and *-less*, A, +N___. Along the same lines, the lexical entry for a prefix contains a frame of the form +___X: thus, *multi*, A, PLUR, +___N (*multi-family, multi-purpose, multi-use*). This device straightforwardly distinguishes pairs such as the verbal prefix of "reversal," *un-*, NEG, +___V and the adjectival negation prefix *un-*, NEG, +___A. The generalizations in X^0 domains expressible by these frames for affixes provide evidence that subcategorization is not limited to selecting phrases. This independently confirms a conclusion (2.13) of section 2.2: *Lexical mechanisms can and should be stated without reference to phrasal categories.*

On the other hand, the lexical entries of bound derivational affixes require the left-right ordering specified in the original subcategorization notation. In order to facilitate comparison of order-free co-occurrence in an X^1 domain and ordered co-occurrence in an X^0 domain, I will use the symbols "<...>" in writing subcategorization frames. (3.22) exemplifies this notation for suffixes:

(3.22) *Ordered subcategorization. The entry "@, X, +< F___>" means that @ has a left-hand sister immediately dominated by X^0 whose lexical head has a feature F.*

I now propose to unify Lieber's morphological subcategorization with the "order-free" subcategorization of syntax. As has been realized at least since Stowell (1981), if left-to-right ordering of heads and phrasal complements is due to general parameters holding throughout a language, such as universal (3.6), (3.8) for English and (3.17) for French, then the item-particular ordering stipulated in Chomsky's original subcategorization notation is redundant. The lexical notation @, +___F was devised to mean "@ precedes F," but it would be preferable to specify only that "@ occurs with F."[17] The same notation could of course be given a different meaning, but since co-occurrence within an X^0 domain indeed requires left-to-right stipulation, it is best to express co-occurrence in the X^1 domain with some order-free notation. Using the terms of Extended Classical Subcategorization (2.18):

(3.23)   *Order-free subcategorization. The entry "@, X, +< F >" means that @ has a complement immediately dominated by X^1 whose lexical head has a feature F.*

In terms of (3.23), the lexical entries (2.19)–(2.20) are rewritten as follows:

(2.19)   wonder, V, +< WH >   exclaim, V, +< (WH) I > or +<{ WH, I }>[18]
(2.20)   amuse, V, +< ANIMATE >   disperse, V, +< PLURAL >
         put, V, +< D, PATH >   place, V, +< D, PLACE >

In chapters focusing on relating syntax to morphology, I adhere to the above notation, but in some later chapters where only phrasal syntax is at issue, I occasionally use the more familiar classical notation (with features replacing phrases) +___D rather than +< D >.

Section 2.2 has argued that phrases must be selected on the basis of features of their heads. Consequently, as comparing (3.22) with (3.23) shows, it is now possible to express phrasal and morphological subcategorization almost identically. I therefore claim that the lexicon contains only one combinatorial device. Consequently, I combine (3.22) and (3.23), which will then be the proper basis for further developing lexical theory.

---

[17] Originally, +___F^G also means that F precedes G. But Stowell (1981) demonstrates that patterns where such precedence holds are due to more general factors e.g. Case Theory. No language permits individual heads to specify item-particular ordering among complements.
[18] A WH complementizer independently selects an IP sister.

(3.24)   *Unified Classical Subcategorization. The frames $+< F >$,*
$+< F__> or +<__F > in a lexical entry @, X are satisfied if and
only if F is a cognitive syntactic feature of a lexical head of a sister
to X^0.

In the combined principle (3.24), word-internal subcategorization is involved if left-right order is specified via a "blank"; otherwise, F is a feature
on the head of a maximal phrase whose linear order with respect to X is
determined not by lexical entries but by general principles such as (3.6),
Case Theory and language-particular orderings like (3.8) and (3.17).

If certain subcategorizations are partially reflected both within and outside of X^0, the formal similarity between (3.22) and (3.23) can be exploited,
for example by parenthesizing the context symbol ___ in lexical entries.
Clearly, any generalizations thus expressed lend support to my proposal that
subcategorization is the single universal mechanism for stating item-
particular co-occurrence. And empirically, some quite disparate phenomena such as (i)–(v) indicate that the notations of (3.22) and (3.23) are indeed
two sides of the same coin:

(i) English adjectival compounds. Words containing the right-hand head
suffixes *-ful, -free* and *-like* on nouns seem to paraphrase full adjective
phrases:

(3.25)   a.   contentful, deceitful, delightful, eventful
full of content, full of deceit, full of delight, full of events
b.   { appointment / furniture / insect / obstacle / responsibil-
ity }-free
free of { appointments / furniture / insects / obstacles / respon-
sibilities }
c.   { child / city / park / vacation / war }-like
like a { child / city / park / vacation / war }

Chapter 7 will show that the *of* in (3.25a-b), while required by principles
of abstract case, is irrelevant for the adjective's lexical frame, which is A,
$+< D >$ (i.e., $+\_\_\_DP$ in classical notation). Under the plausible assumption
that D and N share features, say [+N, -V] or [+N, -AD],[19] only a frame (3.26)

---

[19] These features express the fact that DP and NP form a natural class, which was notated
N^j prior to general acceptance of Brame's (1984) DP hypothesis. My term +AD unites A
and P, recalling adjective, adverb, adjunct. Thus, N, D, V and I constitute a natural class

conflating syntax and morphology captures the similarity of the phrasal frame +___DP and the morphological frame +N___ for *ful(l), free* and *like*.

(3.26) ful(l), A, +< [+N, -AD] (___) >
        free, A, +< [+N, -AD] (___) >
        like, A, +< [+N, -AD] (___) >

In contrast to *free* and *like,* the bound morpheme *-ful* does not productively combine; I assume that this non-productive morpheme is part of the Dictionary information of each stem it combines with: *deceit(ful)* and *meaning(ful)* but not *conceit(*ful)* or *cunning(*ful).*[20]

(3.26) illustrates how productive compounding and non-productive morphological structures inside X^0 share the same syntax, a point stressed earlier in this chapter. Not only do these items share the same subcategorizations, but this subcategorization affects both the word and phrasal domains.

(ii) Causative affixes for secondary predicates. The unified notation of (3.24) helps reveal the similarity between a causative verb as in *(We will* **make** *this city modern)* and a causative affix *(We will* **modernize** *this city).*

-AD. (3.26) doesn't mention the restriction that D cannot appear inside X^0, since this holds in general.

Some might prefer to specify nouns with -V, since for many researchers V and A form a class +V. But there are no reasons outside logic-inspired systems to adopt ±V; syntactic facts favor Jackendoff's (1977) grouping of A and P. AP and PP often coordinate and they are the canonical realizations of adjunct phrases. Neither combines with overt phrase-internal subjects or richer arrays of functional category modifiers (i.e., neither forms extended projections in the sense of Chapter 1), and both share similar systems of pre-head measure phrases in English. Finally, if A and P share a marked feature +AD, it is correctly predicted that each constitutes a less numerous class than their unmarked N and V counterparts.

[20] This is interestingly the practice of commercial dictionaries; the combinatory possibilities of a non-productive derivational affix, whether suffix or prefix, are listed only indirectly in the entries of its stems. Full lists do not appear with the entry of the affix itself, as can be quite frustrating for the second-language learner (this practice could easily be changed with computational tools). These dictionary traditions may unwittingly reveal the "balance of power" between the open class items of the Dictionary, which encompass more information, and the more sparse grammatical closed class items.

On the other hand, a list of items which a non-productive morpheme can combine with is essentially phonological rather than syntactic or semantic information, and hence is compatible with claiming that closed class lexical entries are associated with very little semantic or syntactic information.

The formal difference between the two lexical entries is minimized, thus capturing the common properties of the two forms:

(3.27)   make, V, +CAUS, +< D, A >   -ize, V, +CAUS, +< D, A___>

We will see in Chapter 4 that a *productive* causative V morpheme (unlike *-ize*) is absent in a deep structure and that in such a situation, projections of V are treated as projections of a lexically specified sister of V. Consequently, Generalized Subjects (1.15) correctly captures the fact that the DP is the subject of A in both deep structures (3.28a) and (3.28b), even though they are superficially very different. The two As and the projections of these As relevant for (1.15) are in bold.

(1.15)   *Generalized Subjects: The subject or external argument of a head X is the lowest N-projection which c-commands a phrasal projection of X within its minimal cyclic domain.*

(3.28)   a.

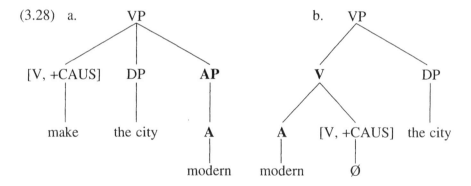

(iii) Japanese passives. It is widely recognized that Japanese passives embrace two different constructions. Both use a verbal suffix *-(r)are* whose morphology shows it is a V; hence all its passive verbs have the surface form [$_V$ V-V] with *-rare* as a right-hand head. Like all lexical head verbs, the EPP (1.17) requires that this suffixal V have a subject DP.

Kubo (1994) argues that the Japanese passives should be divided as follows. In a "gapped passive" the characteristic suffix *-(r)are* prevents its non-head sister V within V^0 from assigning a theta role to an external argument in SPEC(IP). This lack of interpretation for the clausal subject position thereby induces NP-movement from any base position (the gap) so as to satisfy Full Interpretation (2.35). Thus in (3.29), any of three DPs can move to subject position and leave a trace t_i as indicated.[21]

(3.29) a. Direct object:[$_{DP}$ Taro-no yuuki-ga]$_i$ ookuno hito-ni t_i tatae-rare-ta.
Taro-GEN courage-NOM   many people-by t_i praise-PASS-PAST
'Taro's courage was praised by many people.'

   b. Indirect object: [$_{DP}$Taro-ga]$_i$ Jiro-ni t_i Hanako-o shookais-are-ta.
Taro-NOM Jiro-by t_i Hanako-ACC introduce-PASS-PAST
'Taro was introduced Hanako by Jiro.'

   c. Possessive DP: [$_{DP}$ Hanako-ga]$_i$ (dorobou-ni) [$_{DP}$ t_i yubiwa-o] tor-are-ta
Hanako-NOM (thief-by) [$_{DP}$ t_i ring-ACC] steal-PASS-PAST
'Hanako had a thief steal her ring on her.'

Kubo proposes that in the second type, a "gapless passive," *-(r)are* is a main verb with both its own interpreted subject in SPEC(IP) and an underlying VP complement, bracketed in (3.30), whose head incorporates into a surface complex V headed by *-(r)are*.

(3.30) [$_{SPEC(IP)}$ Taro-ga] [$_{VP}$ Hanako-ni Jiro-to kekkons]-[$_V$ are]-[$_I$ ta].
Taro-NOM   Hanako-DAT Jiro-with marry-PASS-PAST
'Taro had Hanako marry Jiro on him.'

She then argues that grammatical principles predict all further differences between the two passive types. Her final lexical entry for *-rare* (i) optionally assigns a malefactive theta role and crucially (ii) *contains a single frame* +[V^k]___ unifying +V___ (for gapped passives) and +VP___ (for gapless passives).

---

[21] Most analyses of Japanese passives treat (3.29a) as "direct" while (3.29c) and (3.30) are "indirect." Kubo provides several arguments that (3.29b-c), as well as other passives formed by moving even more deeply embedded DPs, pattern with (3.29a) rather than with (3.30).

  The child language evidence in Harada and Furuta (1999, 416), though its import is somewhat obscured by discussion of several alternative (unsupported) analyses, confirms that (only) Kubo's division of passive types is reflected in the stages of acquisition: "In sum, the results … all point to the same tendency that direct and possessive passives which include NP-movement are acquired earlier than those which do not include NP movement …"

According to the Lexical Interface Principle (2.13), this unified lexical entry must be recast without bar levels, but Unified Classical Subcategorization (3.24) still permits it to be written as a single frame:

(3.31)   Japanese passive: -(r)are, V, +< V(___) >, (assign "malefactive" role)[22]

The fact that a single parenthesized entry accounts not only for similarities but also for differences between the two Japanese passive constructions justifies the conflated subcategorization notation which permits both YP and Y to be read off a single frame.

(iv) English adjective-verb compounds. Consider the following compound adjective pattern, formed from A+V combinations.

(3.32)   a.   weak-tasting, strong-smelling, happy-looking, loud-sounding
         b.   *sad-seeming, *sick-remaining, *cold-turning, *old-becoming

A necessary but not a sufficient condition for such compounds is that the right-hand head V be *syntactically* subcategorized for A-headed complements. That is, we never find analogous compounds as in (3.33) if the head V are not +___ AP.

(3.33)   *weak-testing, *sick-suffering, *happy-exuding, *loud-working

The linking verbs of perception *taste, smell, look,* and *sound* are apparently listed with a single frame as V, +< A(__ [$_A$ *ing*]) >, which conflates

---

[22] This analysis does not crucially depend on how the subject DP of a gapless passive receives its malefactive role. I conjecture that, since agenthood is unavailable for a stative verb, a benefactive/ malefactive interpretation may be a universal "default theta role" for any *non-complement animate DP.* Since the Japanese passive morpheme is indeed stative (the progressive passive V+*(r)arete iru* is ill-formed*),* its subject cannot be agentive by (2.39). Thus, its malefactive theta role assignment could result from general principles rather than from the individual item -*(r)are.*

The malefactive theta role of the gapless passive subject is reminiscent of the datives of interest of traditional grammar, which Authier and Reed (1992) show are adjuncts. Whether such a dative is necessarily malefactive seems to be parameterized; e.g., the English dative of interest in *She washed the doors on me* is malefactive whatever the discourse pragmatics, while its Spanish counterpart *Ella me a lavado las puertas* is neutral.

the older +___ AP and +A___ *ing*. Without a notation unifying morphological and syntactic subcategorization, the fact that the verbs in (3.32a) are a
proper subset of those which take AP complements would be accidental.[23]

(v) Simultaneous phrasal and word-internal frames. Randall (1988)
shows that certain deverbal endings such as adjectival -*able* and nominal -*er*
are incompatible with PPs:

(3.34)   That plane is flyable ({ *by experts/ *into the wind/ *to Paris/
         *by computer }).
         We all admired the arranger of this furniture ({ *with no assistant/
         *in a novel way/ *by telephoning the maid/ *for Bill }).

She contrasts these with other suffixes such as -*ing* and passive -*en,*
which are compatible with PP:

(3.35)   The flying of that plane ({ by experts/ into the wind/ to Paris/ by
         computer }) caused little comment.
         John's schedule seemed arranged ({ with no assistant/ in a novel
         way/ by telephoning the maid }).

Crucially, -*er* and -*able* are compatible with any complements resulting
from subcategorizations for DP, even though these complements are realized within PPs for purposes of case assignment (cf. Chapter 7).

(3.36)   The bill is payable to me.
         Readers of such stories to children need a lot of patience.
         The loaders of the next truck should talk to the foreman.
         Any climbers of this mountain know caution is needed.

Thus, word-internal frames for these suffixes must also mention their
phrasal (in)compatibilities, roughly as in (3.37), even though their V hosts
must provide the content for assigning theta roles to complements.

(3.37)   -er, N, Agent, +< V___, (D), (D) >

---

[23] Section 4.7 will propose that the morpheme -*ing* can be inserted during a derivation into
a head position which is empty. In particular, the structural head A of these syntactic
compounds is empty at the point when V selects its left sister.

As expected under a subcategorization account, the same derived nominals with the same thematic roles realized in PPs with lexical heads are excluded:[24]

(3.38)   *The loaders (of books) into the next truck should talk to the fore-man.
　　　　*Any climbers up this mountain know caution is needed.

We have now reviewed a series of constructions which support unifying heads in both X^0 and X^1 domains by virtue of the fact that their sub-categorizations in the two domains share properties. Nonetheless, conflating morphological and syntactic heads as in (3.20) raises a serious question as to how far to extend this idea into the traditional domain of morphology. As Lapointe (1980) and Lieber (1980) emphasize, pervasive phonological lan-guage-particular generalizations unite the traditional sub-types of deriva-tional and inflectional morphology across languages. But if we extend some-thing like the right headedness of derivational morphology to suffixal inflection and yet claim that morphology and syntax form a single compo-nent, we run into problems about the nature of a syntactic head. For instance, is the verb or its finite suffixal inflection the syntactic head of a VP in languages like English? If the latter, how can one maintain that it is the head of a phrase which subcategorizes for and determines the case of comple-ment phrases?

These sorts of questions can be answered by a (non-trivial) theory of how to insert closed class lexical items into derivations, which is developed in the next chapter. This theory will maintain the idea that a lexical V rather than its inflection heads VP in the syntactic component, while inflection becomes its (right-hand) head in PF. Such a theory will moreover be seen to provide simple and explanatory accounts of several previously recalci-trant and seemingly unrelated syntactic problems.

In the rest of this chapter, however, we will restrict our focus to the relation of morphology to the syntax of X^0 domains (compounding) and to the nature of lexical entries.

---

[24] The fact that Randall (1988) discusses the complements of these suffixed forms in terms of "thematic inheritance" doesn't change the fact that the lexical generalization covering her data is syntactic (selection of DP vs. selection of PP). It cuts across any supposed s-selection, as the contrast between (3.36) and (3.38) shows.

3.5 Where it's at: Morphology as a special case of compounding

If morphology is to be subsumed under syntax, we still need to delineate what counts as bound morphology (both derivational and inflectional) from what counts as syntactic compounding. The line does *not* seem to lie between bound and free forms. Many morphemes of no special grammatical significance appear only in combination, as for instance in semi-productive learned compounds of Classical Greek stems (*theocentric, technocrat, pan-African, rheostat, neophilia*) or in formations such as *counter-example, mega-store, multi-purpose, email, workaholic, tri-lingual, healthwise, Franco-German, chock-full, mish-mash, tex-mex,* etc. Individual morphemes in these compounds generally have quite specific semantic content and thus must have their own lexical entries. It thus seems obvious that no line in the Dictionary between "appears in isolation" and "must be combined" is significant; for instance, the stem *tele* appears alone in British but not American English.

For English at least, independent word stress suggests a more significant division between compounding and morphology. The difference between secondary stress and no stress in English words is well-known, and can be heard for example in the second element of *postman* (delivers mail, possible with no stress) and *post man* (a possible basketball coinage, secondary stress required). Thus:

(3.39) The right-hand heads of morphological formations do not carry their own stress in English, while those of compounds carry at least secondary stress.

From this point of view, the fact that English stress rules applying in a single word may cause primary or secondary stress to fall on a syllable in a suffix is irrelevant: *authenticity, enunciation* and *Japanese* are morphological formations unrelated to compounding patterns. On the other hand, a few traditionally classed suffixes (*-esque, -hood, -ship*) may be more properly analyzed as heads of compound formations, as they seem to carry their own stress.

Using the criterion (3.39), we can refer to English affixes which have no inherent word stress as *dependent forms*, using the term of Kato (1985). Dependent forms cannot occur in isolation in English, i.e., they are bound morphemes. However, the converse doesn't hold: examples like *chock-, mega-, pan-, theo-, -centric, -crat, -mex, -philia,* etc. must be combined and yet are among the many non-dependent (stressable) forms. On the other hand, unstressable Slavic and Germanic pronouns, Cardinaletti and Starke's (1999) "weak pronouns," appear to be bona fide dependent forms even though they lack morphological subcategorization frames.

So the question now is, what kind of English bound forms are dependent (i.e., inherently stressless)? The answer appears to be that all such dependent forms, i.e. forms traditionally considered as bound morphology, *lack purely semantic features f*. This conclusion is supported by the fact that even the most semantically specific (-*able, -ism, -ize, -man*) of the inherently stressless English affixes surveyed in Selkirk (1982, 80–86) do not carry more meaning than commonly recognized cognitive syntactic features F such as POTENTIAL, MASS, ABSTRACT, CAUSATIVE, ANIMATE, HUMAN. Of course, semantically specified stems can combine with these suffixes to form more complex open class items, but this is simply akin to the fact that even open class idioms contain particular grammatical words and not others: *walk the (*a) plank, rock the (*a) boat, take a (*the) powder, get a (*the) life,* etc.

Hence, in contrast to the bound forms in compounds, *all dependent morphemes lack purely semantic features f.*[25]

In addition to this property, Selkirk's affix lists reveal other facets of English morphology: all clear cases of its dependent forms consist of at most one phonological foot, and none have an initial consonant cluster. From this perspective, the entire "morphological component" of English reduces to a single phonological or "phono-semantic" condition on compounding (3.40):

---

[25] It is interesting to examine the dependent forms whose features might be thought of as purely semantic. Invariably, whatever sets them apart from other forms turns out to be needed in syntax, no matter how narrowly conceived.

For example, numerals with the ordinal suffix -*th* have a different syntax than cardinals without it:

I have several pairs but the four (*ones) I bought in Italy are the best.
I have several pairs but the fourth *(ones) I bought in Italy are the best.

Quite possibly, -*th* is simply a member of the category A while cardinals are not:

In the photo, your horse seemed { fifth / *five }.
Chomsky's birthday would make a good tenth holiday.
Chomsky's and Halle's birthdays would make { two good/ *good two } holidays.

Whatever the exact analysis, the feature characterizing -*th* must have syntactic status.

(3.40) *English Morphology. If the head of a compound lacks purely semantic features f, then it contains at most one inherently stressless
foot with a one-segment onset.*[26]

Condition (3.40) permits us to entirely identify structures whose right-
hand heads are dependent suffixes with compound structures, as already
suggested by the combinations in (3.15):

(3.15)

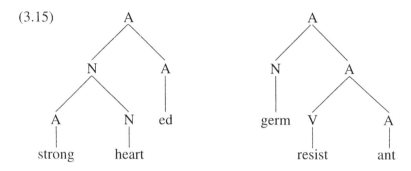

The relation between purely grammatical heads of compounds and phonological weakening may differ across languages; (3.40) is only the English
version. These different relations are simply definitions of different morphologies. For example the weak pronouns and other second position forms
of German also appear to lack purely semantic features *f* and contain at most
one inherently stressless foot with a one-segment onset. German weak forms
are thus defined like those of English, but their distribution is wider than in
English, where they occur almost exclusively as bound forms satisfying X^0-
internal subcategorizations. Another different possibility is furnished by

---

[26] This statement has no effect on prefixes: and indeed in each pair like *re-clean, dry
clean, misread, speed-read, outswim, free swim, counterspy, German spy, ex-friend, sex
friend, unsuited, red-suited,* one observes the same (English compound) stress patterns:
non-contrastive stress usually falls on the non-head left-hand element. It then comes as
no surprise that traditional analyses ascribe "prefixal" rather than "compound" status to
an English bound form on a left branch just when the element seems to have grammatical
rather than lexical meaning.
   The category P is exempt from (3.40): e.g., *herewith* and *thereby* have compound stress.
As in traditional treatments, English bound morphology may be limited to nouns, verbs
and adjectives.

Japanese, whose bound suffixes apparently have the option of inherent lexical stress, unlike those of English.[27]

In a limiting case, a language which "lacks morphology," as is often said of Chinese, may lack rather only a statement of phonological weakening like (3.40). In such a language, highly grammaticalized compounding would appear to the traditional linguist to "usurp" or "replace" morphology. But under the view developed here, such typological differences among morphological systems, which loomed large in historical disputes between e.g. Humboldt and Sapir, reduce to simple phonological conditions, or possibly their absence in an "isolating" or "analytic" language. The supposed genius of a language, expressed by its morphological type, can be entirely captured by somewhat less gripping statements such as (3.40), a conception closer to Sapir than to Humboldt.

I would like to draw a final inference from both the inherent stresslessness of heads in English morphology (3.40) and the typically secondary stress on heads of its compounds. This lesser stress on heads conforms to a general structural tendency, one which I think provides a novel argument for the innateness of Universal Grammar. Since Universal Grammar decrees that heads are obligatory, they are the *expected* constituents within a given domain, both for language learners and language users. Consequently (if UG is innate), language is better designed if heads are less salient than arguments, because the presence of the latter is not predictable on general grounds.

Inside X^0 in English, we have just seen that heads are indeed less salient: less stressed in compounds and not stressed at all if morphological. If users or learners had no access to UG, the structurally central elements should be more, not less salient. In fact, within compounds structurally obligatory heads may even be silent, while arguments may not be.[28] This latter claim will be presented in context in section 9.2:

---

[27] Kubo (1993a) proposes to characterize the four recognized types of Japanese derivational and inflectional suffixes by (i) whether the suffix's syntactic category is lexical or functional and (ii) a stress-related condition on overall word accent, whose effects depend on whether a suffix is inherently lexically stressed or not. Certain Japanese suffixes may thus have stress in the lexicon.

[28] According to Walinska de Hackbeil (1985), English nouns which double as verbs, widely termed conversion, can be best analyzed as resulting from empty right-hand heads. Thus, examples such as *butter the toast, ice the beer,* and *air the clothes* mean roughly, "do the toast with butter", "do the beer with ice", "do the clothes with air."

$[_V [_N$ butter $] [_{V, \text{ACTIVITY}} \emptyset]]$
$[_V [_N$ ice $] [_{V, \text{ACTIVITY}} \emptyset]]$

It thus seems likely that *heads of words* may be zero morphemes.

(9.23)   *Any linguistically represented arguments of the head within X^0 must be overt.*

Since non-head almost by definition implies optional, "non-pronounced" non-heads should in principle mean absent rather than structurally empty.

Turning to the phrasal syntax of X^1 domains, the intonation contours of English head-initial phrasal projections generated by (3.8) have primary stress on the right, i.e., not on the head (Chomsky and Halle, 1968, Ch. 2).[29] Grammatical heads such as copulas (V), articles (D), complementizers (C), grammatical prepositions (P), so-called "auxiliaries" (I), and the pro-noun *one* are often completely stressless or even omitted from speech. Overall then, the last thing to expect is a correlation between head status and phonological prominence; optional constitutents in a string will require the stronger PF indications of their presence.[30] English compounding, morphology and phrasal syntax all conform to this.

3.6 Relating morphological typology to free form properties

Throughout this chapter, the often presupposed differences between morphology and phrasal syntax have been under attack; the tactic has been to show that morphology is a minor variant on compounding defined by a correlation between an item's lexical semantics (i.e. a bound morpheme's lack of purely semantic features f) and its phonological form. That is, I claim that bound morphology has no special syntax.

For example, sections 3.1 and 3.2 proposed that the ordering of heads is either the same in syntax and morphology, as in Japanese, or dependent on factors which do not coincide with any syntax-morphology border, as in English and French. Section 3.3 also pointed out that firmer native speaker intuitions about left-right ordering violations are the same for any X^0 domain, whether of morphology or of (productive) syntactic compounding.

In Chapter 4, the difference between derivation and inflection, another supposed special property of morphology, will be explained in terms of early vs. late lexical insertion into syntactic derivations; this distinction is then shown in the rest of the book to play an equally crucial role in explain-

---

[29] The fact the French stress is so resolutely rightmost in *any* domain may account for the left-headedness of French free form compounds.

[30] Clausal subjects are often null, under a range of structural conditions, precisely because they are obligatory and hence "expected."

ing properties of constructions built around free as well as bound grammatical morphemes. That is, the differences between derivational and inflectional morphology are better accounted for in terms of differences between syntactic and PF insertion, and this latter distinction extends to all grammatical items, free as well as bound, which lack purely semantic features f.

A final area where the categories of traditional grammar might suggest the existence of an autonomous morphological domain concerns supposed "language typologies," for instance between inflecting and agglutinating languages. The focus on morphology-based typology traces back to W. von Humboldt, who argued for the superiority of the "inflecting" Classical language Sanskrit over "agglutinating" Malay, and continued through Sapir (1921), who forcefully and convincingly argued that Humboldt's conceptions were simplistic in the extreme.[31]

One of Sapir's main clarifications was that "types" of languages differ in the degree of phonetic fusion between their stems and affixes independently of syntax. This is of course at bottom a phonological property and might well be related to language-particular morphology-defining statements such as (3.40) or less general phonological processes of internal sandhi.

According to Sapir, what remains for typology after phonological fusion is factored out is two properties: (i) the length of the bound morpheme sequences permissably concatenated within single words in a language, and (ii) the internal complexity of grammatical feature bundles expressed by individual affixes in a language. The former dimension seems to vary without significant breaking points; thus French allows, rather uninterestingly, at least eleven sequentially ordered morphemes in a word, with all but two in the following example pronounced. The plus signs in the single bold word indicate proclisis: *Ces boussoles, **elle-s+ne+se+re-de-magnét-ise-er-ai-ent** pas* 'These compasses, [$_V$ [NOM, FEM, III]-PLUR-NEG-REFL-ADV-NEG-magnet-CAUS-FUT-ASP-[III,PLUR]] not', i.e. "These compasses would not again get demagnetized."

For Humboldt, what constituted true inflection was property (ii). An inflecting language allowed single affixal morphemes to express multiple grammatical ideas ("features" in present terms). With the help of phonological fusions, the true inflections of Classical languages permitted many ideas

---

[31] Sapir showed that according to the best typology he could (somewhat skeptically) devise, Latin and Greek were very mixed systems and closely related to certain American Indian languages with which he was quite familiar. The implicit political critique of Humboldt is obvious.

to be expressed "compactly," i.e. close to a root morpheme. By this criterion, the world's many "agglutinative languages" from Malay to Navajo to
Greenlandic to Turkish fare poorly, as in fact does the French word above
as well.

Whether or not one would prefer a language to have this "compact" property (or any other), the question that remains about property (ii) is whether
the bound morphemes of some languages permit simultaneous expression of
more syntactic features. A related question, more pertinent to the issue of
whether bound morphology has any properties other than phonological, is:
(iii) do the bound morphemes of a given language permit simultaneous expression of syntactic features any differently than do that language's free
grammatical morphemes? Here I think the answer is clearly no.

First, the feature complexes of the true inflections of for example Latin
never seem more complex than something like [+PLUR, +FEM, +CASE],
and the language's free pronouns express these same combinations (*eas*
'them', a feminine accusative plural). Second, languages that are typically
classed as agglutinative do have bound morphemes that qualify as Hum-
boldtian inflections; for example, the Japanese suffix *-ra* is [+ANIM,
+PLUR], and the final suffix in a Greenlandic agglutinated verb sequence
spells out both Person and Number. And third, as expected, such languages
have free morphemes expressing these same combinations, e.g., Japanese
mure 'group' is simultaneously plural and animate. Thus, it seems that a
language's bound and free grammatical morphemes express essentially the
same range of feature combinations, and moreover languages do not seem
to greatly differ in what kinds of feature combinations are associated with
either type of morpheme.[32]

Consequently, there remain no clear "typological" properties of language characteristic of bound morphology, other than possibly those related
to phonology (both general weakening of affixes lacking semantic f and
internal sandhi/ phonetic fusion) or to the number of morphemes allowed
per word. The latter property, if it has any reality at all, seems mainly
quantitative and without interest for the theory of syntax. It is akin to a
propety defined in terms of whether the open class morphemes of a language
are long or short.

In sum, motivations for some autonomous principles of bound morphology seem to have evaporated.

---

[32] Languages do of course differ according to which cognitive syntactic features its
inflections *must* express; cf. section 1.3.4 for Kuroda's contrast between Japanese and
English. Many so-called agglutinative languages exhibit, like English, his "forced Agreement." But this is not at issue here.

3.7 Dictionary and Syntacticon: a new slant on lexical research

Section 1.2 introduced purely semantic features f by observing that, while they give rise to open (large) lexical classes, they are limited to the four lexical categories; section 1.4.2 then related the open class items so defined to human memory and culture, as opposed to grammatical items without semantic f, which lack such relations. The possibility of dividing bound morphology from compounding in terms of the absence of these same features, as exemplified for English with (3.40), suggests that even more properties may be correlated with whether an item is specified for purely semantic features.

To develop this approach, I set up the following preliminary table of lexical correlations with semantic f. Just to recall that all items under discussion potentially contribute to well-formed LF, the table starts with two lexical properties from section 1.2 which are independent of f. Line e is simply (3.40).

(3.45)	Items with f	Items lacking f
a. Items have cognitive syntactic features F:	yes	yes
b. Cognitive features F canonically realized on UG-defined hosts:	yes	yes
c. Grammatical categories in the inventory:	N,V,A,P	ALL
d. Open classes; coining and neologisms for adult speakers:	YES	NO
e. Bound forms have inherent stress and head true compounds:	YES	NO
f. Interface with non-linguistic memory and culture:	YES	NO
g. Full suppletion inside paradigms (Emonds, 1985, Ch. 4):	NO	YES

Line g is from the cited source, which defines and discusses suppletive groupings such as *good, better, best; go, went, gone; is, are, were;* French *va, aller* 'go', the Spanish copula *ser, era, fui*; and the Latin causative verb *ferre, tuli, latus*. Traditional treatments clearly distinguish suppletion from less restricted simple morphological irregularities.

In fact, the list in (3.45) is easy to augment. Even prior to the era of empty categories, structuralist analyses postulated null morphs in many grammatical paradigms, null copulas, null pronouns, etc. Sections 4.2 and 9.4.2 will try to systematize some of their characteristics. But certainly one of them is that null morphs are not postulated as members of open lexical classes with highly specific semantic content; translations for elements like *horse, believe* or *rough* cannot be empty X^0 in any language.

Another property of items lacking semantic f is relative phonological simplicity. Hannahs (1995) has explored differences, especially in terms of phonological distinctions, between two types of lexical entries in languages: those in a core native vocabulary and those whose history is rooted in wholesale borrowings from another language. Hannahs cites several examples of such "lexical segregation," with the Romance / Latinate vocabulary of English and its special stress patterns being perhaps only the best known; others include the borrowed Sanskrit vocabulary in Malayalam, the Slavic vocabulary in Rumanian and the Spanish vocabulary in Nahuatl. In my view, further instances include the huge Japanese vocabulary borrowed from Chinese (the basic source of morpheme-final nasals in the language) and the sizable vocabulary of modern Turkish borrowed several hundred years ago from French and still exempt from native Turkish vowel harmony.

A borrowed vocabulary in many ways assimilates to the synchronic grammar of the language and its special historical status has no reality for the native speaker, yet it continues to maintain lexical forms and phonological patterns separate from the core vocabulary. Even so, individual words can pass from the secondary into the primary vocabulary over time, e.g. the two verbs *promise* and *offer* and the adjectival modifer *very*, all borrowed from French, have the completely unstressed non-initial syllables as well as syntactic behavior characteristic of English core or primary vocabulary.[33]

In discussions, Hannahs and I agree that those elements which I claim lack purely semantic features f, in particular every item outside the four lexical categories, are members of this English core or primary vocabulary. Among other things, such items exhibit the Old English stress pattern: their only stress is on non-prefixal initial syllables.

It is rare that a class of linguistic items with so many coincident properties as those in (3.45) does without a name – in fact, many popular grammatical coinings hardly extend to two properties, let alone a half dozen. But terms from traditional or generative linguistics do not spring to mind for the class of items which lack purely semantic features f. The word Dictionary corresponds to both common sense and technical linguistic usage for the inventory of open class words, those with the properties of column 1 in (3.45). Since the word Lexicon is needed as a cover term for all the morphemes in a language, it seems that we must invent a term for the inventory of morphemes, bound or free, which have the properties of column 2.

A term which has invented itself so to speak, out of some mix of the unconscious, memory and culture, is the Syntacticon. This label for the

---

[33] In a sketchy preliminary treatment focusing more on syntax, Emonds (1980) refers to the core native vocabulary as "primary" and the borrowed vocabulary as "secondary."

inventory of items lacking purely semantic features f permits us to rearrange and supplement the table (3.45) as follows:

(3.46)

	SYNTACTICON	
	DICTIONARY	↓
a. Items have cognitive syntactic features F:	yes	yes
b. Cognitive features F canonically realized on UG-defined hosts:	yes	yes
c. Grammatical categories in the inventory:	N, V, A, P	ALL
d. Items have purely semantic features f:	YES	NO
e. Open classes; coining and neologisms for adult speakers:	YES	NO
f. Bound forms have inherent stress and head true compounds:	YES	NO
g. Interface with non-linguistic memory and culture:	YES	NO
h. Full suppletion inside paradigms:	NO	YES
i. Certain phonetically zero morphemes (with restrictions):	NO	YES
j. Items must conform to core or primary vocabulary phonology:	NO	YES

The Syntacticon is thus a component of grammatical items *each of which is set off from all the others by cognitive features which play a role in syntax.* Consequently, each item has its own characteristic and in principle unique syntactic behavior.[34] Largely as a result of this, the Syntacticon is the repository par excellence of the language-particular.

This idea of a Syntacticon naturally extends the line of research initiated by Borer (1984) and Manzini and Wexler (1987) and fruitfully pursued in Ouhalla (1991). The latter author aptly sums up the justification for a special syntactic lexicon; emphases are mine:

> ... Borer's approach to parametric variation ... *associates parameters with individual lexical items, as part of the information included in their lexical entries,* rather than with the principles of UG.
> ... the nature of the lexical information which determines parametric variation [is] nothing other than *the usual type of information relating to selection and grammatical features,* ... it is not information which is available over and above the familiar type of lexical properties; rather, these properties themselves determine paramet-

---

[34] This implies a strong empirical claim. If two lexical items @ and @' are characterized with only syntactic features F, which are defined as those which play a role in syntactic rules and principles (Chomsky, 1965, Ch. 2), then @ will differ from @' by some feature F'. Hence @ and @' will not share whatever syntactic behavior depends on the value of F'. Therefore, we expect every item in the Syntacticon to exhibit "Unique Syntactic Behavior" (Emonds, 1985, Ch. 4 and 5). Two such items in the same language can have the same behavior only if rules using F' are accidentally inoperative in that language.

ric variation.

One can hypothesise ... that possibly functional categories and substantives belong to two separate modules of the mind/ brain. More precisely, one can assume, as suggested in Tsimpli and Ouhalla (1990), that there should in principle be a distinction between two notions of the lexicon, *a grammatical lexicon which contains functional categories and which belongs to the domain of UG*, in the sense that its categories are determined by UG, and *a mental lexicon which contains substantives and which exists independently of UG, that is an autonomous module of the mind/brain* (the conceptual system).

(Ouhalla, 1991, 7–10)

Tsimpli's and Ouhalla's grammatical lexicon I call the Syntacticon and the independent mental lexicon I call the Dictionary, as described in section 1.4.2.

In light of this bifurcated lexical model, it seems clear that suffixal morphology is the Syntacticon's counterpart of the Dictionary's compounding. When an element X^0 is chosen as the head of a compound structure from the Syntacticon, it receives no independent stress (it is dependent) and bound morphology results.

(3.47) *Morphology, in particular affixation, results from using a bound form in the Syntacticon for compounding.*

Thus, bound forms in the Dictionary with a frame +< X___> or +< X (___) > result in right-headed compound structures (*airborne, eastbound, nationhood, neophilia, polyglot, sleepwise, stress-free, technocrat, ten o'clock, warlike, workaholic,* etc.). Elements in the Syntacticon (e.g., *-ing, -able, -ic, -ed, -y*) with similar frames receive no word stress (in English), but otherwise appear in exactly the same type of structure: *readable, historic, painted, watery, (germ)-resistant,* etc.[35] In other words, if a lexical item under a right-hand X^0 is from the Syntacticon, (3.15) instantiates bound morphology, while if X^0 is from the Dictionary *the same syntactic structure (in English) is a compound.*

In light of this complementary distribution, parsimony demands that the two different components of the Lexicon utilize a single syntactic structure.

---

[35] Chapter 4 will argue that if the dependent form is inserted in the syntax it is called "derivational," while if inserted in phonology it is called "inflectional."

Interestingly, research focusing on both these areas (Lieber, 1980 and 1983; Selkirk, 1982) does not indicate that structurally differentiating morphology and compounding would lead to any gain in understanding; regular instances of both formations are adequately described as X^0 structures dominating X^0 right-hand heads.

A novel prediction of (3.47) is that Syntacticon items enter into what are traditionally recognized as compounds only by virtue of secondary use in the open class Dictionary, akin to the use of grammatical items in lexicalized idioms: *down-time, the get-go, a have not, a no go, one-way, self-made, a do-gooder, a go-getter,* etc. Indeed, Dictionary compounds containing only grammatical X^0 often don't conform to right-headedness and have a curiously strong idiomatic flavor beyond what might be implied by the literal combinations. This latter fact suggests that they are defined by the Dictionary's purely semantic features *f*.

In the realm of productive compounding, the Syntacticon cannot furnish its free morphemes with their own word stress as right-hand heads. Nonce compounds as in (3.48) (indicated with left-hand compound stress for clarity) are impossible, even though one can well imagine possible meanings. To underscore the real pattern in terms of *productive* compounding, I overstate the case slightly by also choosing left-hand elements from the Syntacticon.

(3.48)   Productive compounding of two free elements from the Syntacticon:[36]

N-N:	*time-place, *self-people, *stuff-thing, *way-man, *reason-self
A-N:	*óther-thing, *bád-self, *múch-time, *féw-bunch, *wéll-place
P-N:	*in-man, *up-stuff, *off-place, *on-way, *with-one
V-N:	*dó-stuff, *gét-one, *háve-fact, *gó-place, *bé-reason
N-A:	*people-good, *bunch-many, *way-other, *reason-worse
A-A:	*other-good, *worse-many, * bad-much, *well-much, *few-such
N-V-er:	*stuff-doer, *thing-getter, *fact-haver, *place-goer, *self-be-er
N-V-ing:	*way-going, *time-having, *stuff-getting, *self-making

These examples show productive English compounding of pairs of free grammatical X^0 morphemes is rather the province of the open classes of the Dictionary.

I terminate with two remarks on linguistic subfields that might perhaps profit from taking the lexical bifurcation as elaborated in (3.46) into careful

---

[36] The logic here doesn't require that each free morpheme in these examples be in the English Syntacticon, but there is some reason to think so for each morpheme chosen. If a certain one is not, then that example is simply irrelevant.

account. A little reflection shows that the Syntacticon, even though it has had no name, is the subject matter of most of the theory-oriented technical literatures on first and second language acquisition and aphasia. The division of the Lexicon argued for here may thus be able to help properly focus research design in these areas.

If there is a "critical period" roughly coinciding with childhood in which most people can learn a language's syntax qualitatively more easily than in later years, then certainly a large part of the issue is how easily and well items in the Syntacticon can be learned. Several language acquisition studies have concentrated on verb morphology or clitic pronouns, but studies on acquiring derivational morphology, expletives, adjectival intensifiers, and especially grammatical verbs and prepositions are equally well in order, and may show that these items have more in common with inflections than with open class vocabulary.

Similarly, studies on different types of aphasia contrast the loss of what is often loosely termed grammatical detail and function words with the loss of open class content words. The division of the Lexicon into clearly separate parts, as in (3.46), suggests that the usual dichotomy in such studies between the classes N, V, A and P and the "functional" categories may be misdrawing the line to look for. As proposed in section 1.2 and thoroughly justified in Chapters 4 through 6, the Syntacticon contains a good number of lexical items often loosely thought of as open class, namely grammatical verbs such as *go, come, get, let* and grammatical nouns such as *one, thing, place, stuff,* etc. I would expect the retention or loss of such items to correlate with that of others stored in the same mental inventory (the Syntacticon), rather than with that of other differently stored items of the same categories.[37]

Whatever the value of these observations on related fields, the bifurcated lexical organization of (3.46) is the basis for Chapter 4, which develops a theory of multi-level lexical insertion for the Syntacticon's grammatical inventory, while preserving classical lexical insertion at the outset of derivations for open class items.[38] According to this proposal, a syntactic theory

---

[37] Although this study shares many methodological and theoretical assumptions with Ouhalla (1991), there is a difference here. If I understand correctly, Ouhalla (1991, 4) excludes the lexical entries of what I consider to be grammatical N, V, A and P from language-particular syntax.

[38] In fact, I claim that transformational derivations are motivated as the means by which unconnected arrays of content items map into well-formed and interpretable LF structures.

which properly relates (i) feature compositon of lexical items, (ii) generalized subcategorization and (iii) levels of insertion can predict *the grammatical aspects of morphology from syntactic principles alone.* Among other things, it can predict the general differences between derivation and inflection so often enumerated in morphological treatises.

Chapter 4
Multi-level lexical insertion: Explaining Inflection and Derivation

4.1 The bifurcated lexical model: Dictionary and Syntacticon

Principally on the basis of English and French, the preceding chapter has motivated a basic division of the Lexicon of a generative grammar into two inventories with quite distinct properties. The division is based on what kinds of features appear in lexical entries. The cognitive syntactic features F needed to characterize items of closed grammatical classes appear to be just those which (i) suffice to characterize the elements of bound morphologies and (ii) are used in computations deriving Logical Forms from underlying syntactic structures. The quite limited numbers of lexical items *which use only such features* have special characteristics: they seem to be detached from non-linguistic memory and cultural constructs, and speakers cannot coin new elements of this type. I have called this latter inventory the Syntacticon. For the inventory of open class items in the four lexical categories, whose features include these F but also the purely semantic features *f,* I retain the term Dictionary.[1]

As argued in Chapter 3, the division between Syntacticon and Dictionary cuts across that between bound and free morphemes, which turn out to not be of such different syntactic character. Among Dictionary entries, bound morphemes (e.g., *cran-, phono-, -hood, -phile*) are those with the accidental property of occurring only in compounds. More interestingly, the Syntacticon's bound morphemes coincide almost exactly with those whose properties constitute the subject matter of traditional morphology. But other than status as free vs. bound (the latter including specification of a host), a productive bound morpheme such as the French future-conditional suffix *-r-* can have the same syntax as a free morpheme such as the English future-conditional *will / would*. What turns out to be more important for lexical theory is an item's feature composition, in terms of the three classes of section 1.2: cognitive syntactic features F, purely syntactic F' (those F not

---

[1] Of course, it would be pointless to give a new name to a lexical assemblage unless the name reflects a set of (ultimately combinatorial) common properties which previously have either not been recognized, or not recognized as correlated. This set of properties, to be enlarged in this chapter, appears as a list in (3.46).

used in LF) and purely semantic *f*. In the model of lexical insertion to be presented in this chapter and developed in the rest of this study, the nature of a morpheme's lexical features, regardless of whether it is bound or free, determines the level at which it enters derivations.

The important differences between the two lexical modules which have been discussed up to this point have been summarized as (3.46), repeated here. In this chapter, three further important and independent properties will be added to this list.

(3.46)

	DICTIONARY	SYNTACTICON ↓
a. Items have cognitive syntactic features F:	yes	yes
b. Cognitive features F canonically realized on UG-defined hosts:	yes	yes
c. Grammatical categories in the inventory:	N, V, A, P	ALL
d. Items have purely semantic features *f*:	YES	NO
e. Open classes; coining and neologisms for adult speakers:	YES	NO
f. Bound forms have inherent stress and head true compounds:	YES	NO
g. Interface with non-linguistic memory and culture:	YES	NO
h. Full suppletion inside paradigms:	NO	YES
i. Certain phonetically zero morphemes (with restrictions):	NO	YES
j. Items must conform to core or primary vocabulary phonology:	NO	YES

If these two lexical modules were related in the same way to a grammatical derivation, their contributions to constructing trees could be schematized simply as in (4.1).

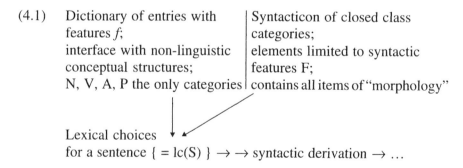

(4.1)   Dictionary of entries with features *f*; interface with non-linguistic conceptual structures; N, V, A, P the only categories | Syntacticon of closed class categories; elements limited to syntactic features F; contains all items of "morphology"

Lexical choices
for a sentence { = lc(S) } → → syntactic derivation → ...

However, I wish to establish in this chapter that the relations of the Syntacticon and the Dictionary to grammatical derivations are *not* the same. Even so, there will be no total surprises, except perhaps for the degree of lexical systematization and predictability. Combinatorial properties of open class Dictionary entries (e.g. verb transitivity) have always motivated a deep or pre-transformational generative level and will continue to do so here. At the same time, generative analyses have generally treated at least some grammatical elements as resulting from "late rules" or "post-transformational rules"; *do*-support, *of*-insertion and *there*-insertion are some frequently mentioned instances. Such constructions will here fall into place as expected rather than sporadic instances of closed class lexical insertions during the course of derivations.

The general development in this chapter is as follows. Section 4.2 modifies a previous generative conception of a unitary lexicon by schematically proposing a multi-level insertion model of the Syntacticon.[2] Section 4.3 explains how the two different kinds of traditional morphology, derivation and inflection, arise in this model. Section 4.4 introduces the key concepts of Phonological Lexicalization and Alternative Realization, illustrates empirical advantages and predictions of the late insertion model for many inflectional constructions of English and suggests extensions for some well-known inflectional patterns of other languages. Section 4.5 is a short excursus to demonstrate that Alternative Realization has explanatory force outside the domain of bound morphology. Finally, section 4.6 shows how derived morphology also finds its place within the multi-level insertion model, with section 4.7 demonstrating how this theory can fully explain recalcitrant problems in the rich system of English nominalizations.

4.2 Levels of lexical insertion

Before specifically relating lexical insertion to the Dictionary and the Syntacticon, it is appropriate to clarify the general relation between the lexicon and syntactic derivations assumed in this study. In current broadly Chomskyan syntactic analyses, (4.2) seems to embody an emerging consensus as to how syntactic derivations relate to universal grammatical representations.

(4.2)   *Each (unambiguous) sentence has a universal representation formed by a syntactic derivation. We call this the Logical Form of the sentence.*

---

[2] A few previous researchers have proposed that non-trivial properties set off a closed class lexicon from an open class dictionary. The "second lexical pass" of Stockwell, Schachter and Partee (1973) is a notable early move in this direction. Walinska de Hackbeil (1986) pursues a similar line of research. More recently, Ouhalla's (1991) parameterization theory is based on clearly distinguishing lexical properties of open class items from those in functional categories; he in fact suggests that the latter form a separate grammatical lexicon.

That is, Logical Forms (LF) of synonymous sentences are the same across languages; they are the endpoints of syntactic derivations. Of course, nothing requires that each language consist of the same set of LFs, a point established in Keenan (1975) on the basis of differing cross-linguistic possibilities for relativization. Moreover, the idea that languages share LFs does not in itself advance the work of determining what these LFs actually are, without evidence as to their proper form drawn from work on particular languages.

An extremely restrictive hypothesis in this perspective, first formulated I believe in Borer (1984, 29), is that all syntactic differences among languages result from how the purely grammatical morphemes of each language are lexically specified. That is, the inputs to derivations differ across languages, but their LF outputs, if well-formed, do not. Thus, counter to pedagogical and descriptive linguistic traditions which attribute "grammars" to particular languages, many generative grammarians now adhere at least in practice to (4.3):

(4.3)   *Language-particular syntax resides entirely in lexical specifications, namely the inherent and contextual feature combinations associated with closed class items.*[3]

Chomsky (1995, 26) voices a similar sentiment, referring to "language-particular parameters" rather than to lexical specifications of closed class items:

(4.4)   "The parametric options appear to be … restricted to two cases: (i) properties of the lexicon, or (2) the point in the derivation … at which structures are mapped to PF."

Although there seems to have been no real attempt at formally specifying the class of such parameters (outside of Borer's proposal), I claim that lexical specifications in the Syntacticon, whose form this study proposes to

---

[3]   Borer's proposal probably should be interpreted as more restrictive than (4.3), since she claims that language-particular syntax can be reduced to inflections. This formulation seems too restrictive to me, since I claim that many almost corresponding free morphemes have different syntax in different languages, e.g. the English complementizer *that* vs. its French counterpart *que*. However, I am not sure how narrowly she construes "inflection" in the light of later work on covert movement.

characterize, constitute the elusive class of language-particular parameters.[4] In this sense, (4.3) is more restrictive than (4.4), since it limits parameters to a certain form: that of lexical entries without purely semantic features f.

In the light of (4.2) and (4.3) and under the assumption of an undifferentiated lexicon, the syntactic derivation of a sentence S_i is nothing else but combining a set of choices from a language-particular dictionary according to language-independent well-formedness conditions and transformational operations so as to yield an LF for S_i. These choices, conditions and operations then together constitute what is called Universal Syntax or Universal Grammar. They are schematized according to the arrows in (4.5):

(4.5)

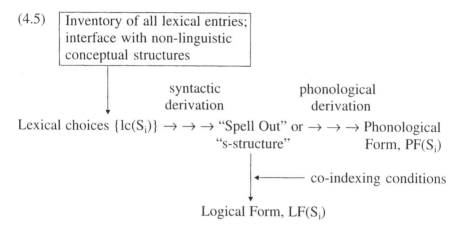

The theory of the lexicon that I propose modifies the general schema in (4.5) in terms of certain hypotheses concerning relations between the form

---

[4] One might object that this constitutes "too large a number of parameters," but this is a terminological issue in the absence of any serious arguments as to the form of lexical entries. Future work on the grammatical lexicon may or may not reveal that grammatical elements of different particular languages have exactly the same specifications. However, in the twenty years of the Principles and Parameters model, I cannot think of a single English grammatical morpheme that plausibly should be assigned the same lexical specification as its closest counterparts in French or Japanese.

Our understanding of syntax would indeed be greatly advanced if some ardent believer in "few parameters" would demonstrate how even one such parameter can explain away what appears to be the highly language-specific nature of individual grammatical morphemes. While awaiting this demonstration, I know of no arguments that could support a claim that closed class items across languages exactly share lexical specifications. The single plausibly general parameter so far discovered, the head-initial/ head-final parameter, sheds no light on how to specify *any* closed class items.

of lexical entries and the derivational level at which they are inserted. These hypotheses presuppose principles of lexical theory established earlier (2.13) and (3.24), and crucially utilize the three types of lexical features distinguished in section 1.2 and motivating a separate Syntacticon in Chapter 3.

(2.13) *Lexical Interface Principle. The lexicon uses only morpheme categories in its statements. It cannot mention phrases, nor distinguish between X and XP.*

(3.24) *Unified Classical Subcategorization. The frames* $+< F >$, $+< F\_\_\_ >$ *or* $+<\_\_\_F >$ *in a lexical entry* @, X *are satisfied if and only if F is a cognitive syntactic feature of a lexical head of a sister to* X^0.

(4.6)   Three types of features which appear in a lexical entry:
   a. Purely semantic features *f* present only on the categories X = N, V, A, P. They are not used in syntax and moreover closed subclasses of grammatical X don't use them.
   b. Cognitive syntactic features F with all syntactic categories. They are centrally used in syntax, PF and LF.
   c. Purely syntactic features F' with all syntactic categories. They are used in syntax and PF, but play no role in LF.

The last class includes contextual features $+<Y(\_\_\_)>$ as in (3.24), marked Absence of Content features (e.g, STATIVE on V, -LOCATION on P) and "Alternatively Realized" features, to be introduced in section 4.4.

Recall now from Chapter 3 that the Dictionary, which contains all and only information connected with the purely semantic features *f*, is the cognitive interface between our linguistic memory and a syntactic derivation.[5] From this conception of insertion from the Dictionary, hypothesis (4.7) is almost a logical consequence. Though lexical insertion at deep structure was a commonplace in early studies of the generative lexicon, it will here take on non-trivial content as we proceed.

---

[5] One might get the impression from Chomsky (1993) that there is no interface with memory, but only with cognitive components of sound and appropriate language use. But each use of language crucially employs lexical morpheme/concept pairings whose existence in our memory is independent of grammar, sound, or situation. Cf. section 1.4.

(4.7)   *Deep Lexicalization (DL). Items associated with non-syntactic,*
         purely semantic features f must satisfy lexical insertion conditions
         (just) before syntactic processing of the smallest cyclic domains
         containing them. Such f occur only on N, V, A and P.

The other lexical component, the Syntacticon, contains entries which are specified only for the two types of syntactic features in (4.6b-c), all uniformly notated with upper case F. As seen in section 1.2, all Syntacticon categories are closed classes, each with twenty or so members at most. These categories include closed classes of grammatical N, V, A and P. This chapter and Chapters 5 through 7 argue that significant improvements in our understanding the combinatorial properties of natural language result from the following hypothesis, which is schematically indicated by the three higher arrows in (4.9).

(4.8)   *Multi-Level Lexical Insertion. Lexical Items from the Syntacticon,*
         in accord with their feature content, can be inserted at different
         stages of a derivation, via the Dictionary ("deep structure"), dur-
         ing a syntactic derivation, and during a phonological derivation.[6]

(4.9)

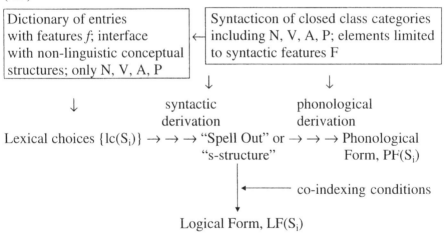

---

[6]   A. Caink suggested this revision of my earlier "two-levels" of lexical insertion. Caink (1998) justifies multi-level lexical insertion in a study of South Slavic clitic systems.

The accessibility of the Syntacticon at different levels of the derivation suggests a similarity to Borer's (1991) "Parallel Morphology." But I do not see why the word

Hypothesis (4.8) provides three basic types of insertion for grammatical or closed class items, corresponding to the three arrows from the Syntacticon in (4.9): The leftward arrow represents the situation when, at the start of a derivation or deep structure, a closed class item either doubles as or is associated with an open class item. For example a Syntacticon item can occur in some morphological formation with a lexicalized meaning or in an idiom. Moreover, a grammatical X^0 may simply take on an additional open class meaning via some feature *f,* as in *the self, stuff* 'illegal drugs', *come* 'experience orgasm' and combinations like Modal + *do* 'suffice' (*this won't do; that might do in a pinch*), *do (one's) thing, come to* 'recover from fainting', *have at NP, so-so, be into NP,* etc.[7] In such cases, items from the Syntacticon enter the syntactic derivation at an underlying level like open class items by virtue of their being linked to items and/or features *f* in the open class Dictionary.

A second type of insertion occurs "during the syntax," in particular, after certain deep structure properties are expressed, but prior to what is called s-structure or Spell Out. This is represented by the center downward arrow in (4.9); advantages of distinguishing syntactic from deep insertion of grammatical V are examined in detail in Chapter 6. Explanations provided by dual levels of insertion for pronouns appear in Emonds (1994) and for other X^0 categories in Emonds (2000) and Veselovská (2000). Among bound morphemes syntactic insertion is exemplified by what is traditionally termed "productive derivational morphology," which will be investigated here in section 4.7.

A third type of insertion, invisible at Logical Form, occurs in the phonological component or "at PF," as indicated by the rightmost downward arrow in (4.9). A number of earlier publications (Emonds 1991a, 1995, 1999) have examined consequences of at least the distinction between PF and deep insertion; this chapter and Chapter 7 summarize these analyses, and refine them in terms of the further distinction between syntactic and PF

"parallel" should be used, if no second derivation besides the syntactic one is implied. And as indicated here repeatedly, the Syntacticon is not limited to bound morphemes or "morphology."

[7] Section 2.1 presented lists of many idioms constructed around the closed class verbs *have* and *put,* showing that idioms generally satisfy the subcategorization frames of the heads they contain. Nonetheless, idioms such as *put down* 'denigrate' or *have a go at* 'try out' must occur in the Dictionary, where open class semantic features are available for specifying their meanings. This study doesn't claim to further the study of lexical representation of idioms, beyond claiming that they consist of sequences of X^0 categories which respect subcategorization frames, at least in the (unmarked) vast majority of cases.

insertion.[8] Other advantages of a three-way distinction in insertion levels are explored here for the first time; in particular, with respect to the passive construction in Ch. 5.

A final remark about the model (4.9) is in order. Counter to what I have proposed in some earlier formulations, I take it that an unindexed empty node in LF cannot be interpreted and that a filled node must be.

(4.10)   *LF Visibility Condition. A node is interpreted at LF if and only if it is either realized as a lexical morpheme, or is co-indexed with an interpreted structure of the same category.*[9]

Hence, an item to be interpreted must be inserted either at the start of the derivation or in the syntax prior to Spell Out, and an uninterpreted item must be inserted at PF. The rest of this study will repeatedly use this dichotomy to explain contrasting properties of closely related constructions based on the same morpheme.

A reviewer asks whether the lexical morphemes in (4.10) must be overt. In fact, they need not always be. As will be seen in several sections, phonetically zero morphemes are sometimes possible; see in particular section 9.4. Some transparent examples include (i) the English null operators which can introduce e.g. infinitival relative clauses, (ii) the English present tense morpheme outside the third singular, which accounts for the difference of interpretation between *I hear { the boys / they } swim* and *I hear { the boys / them } swim*; and (iii) the English past participle morpheme with certain irregular verbs, as in *They have put the books away*.[10] Obviously, it is an important task for lexical theory to specify limits on "possible empty morphemes." In fact, an important first step toward this end uses the dichotomy between the Syntacticon and the Dictionary:

---

[8]   Section 4.4 gives a resumé of PF insertion of bound forms, while Chapter 7 systematizes the treatment of and motivation for PF insertion of free forms.

[9]   My earlier formulations of late lexical insertion permitted an empty node in LF with cognitive syntactic features to be interpreted. However, restructuring verbs (section 6.5) convince me that the formulation (4.10) is superior, as well as more in line with general ideas about LF. Thus, the only empty constituents @ allowed at LF result from co-indexing with another interpreted @ (Wasow, 1972).

[10]   The "semi-auxiliaries" *come* and *go* are not compatible with verbal inflections: *they come put the books away* vs. **he come(s) put(s) the books away*. The null past participle morpheme blocks semi-auxiliaries just like its overt counterparts: **they have come put the books away*.

(4.11)   *The Syntacticon but not the Dictionary tolerates phonetically zero morphemes, which tend to occur as least marked members of paradigms.*

4.3 Defining and dividing morphology

We saw in Chapter 3 that "bound morphology" differs from compounding precisely in that the lexical entries of the former contain no purely semantic features *f*. They contrast with morphemes which are bound in that they appear only in compounds but nonetheless carry semantically specific features *f*. Thus, the features needed to characterize e.g., English suffixes such as the causative/ inchoatives *-en/ -ize/ -ify*, nominalizers such as *-ing, -(a)tion, -al, -age, -ment*, and adjective-forming elements such as *-less, -ly, -ive, -ory*, etc. do not go outside the inventory of features which are in any case used in syntactic computations. The inherent contribution of such affixes to formations they are part of will always be limited to some set of syntactic features F. Hence, such affixes are members of the Syntacticon.

Such syntactic features additionally divide into two types, (i) those which are central in LF (4.6b), and (ii) those which play no role in LF interpretation (4.6c). But if the affixes of derivational morphology are fully characterized by syntactic features F, are they of type (i) or (ii)? A review of Selkirk's (1982, 80–86) exhaustive lists of English derivational processes shows that morphemes of this type all play irreducible roles in interpretation. Even derivations which don't induce category change (*hand/ handful; acre/ acreage; green/ greenish; deep/ deeply*) clearly modify meaning. The LF Visibility Condition (4.10) therefore predicts that all bound morphemes typically taken as derivational (e.g., according to Selkirk's classifications) contain cognitive syntactic features F and, by (4.9), are inserted prior to Spell Out (= s-structure). Section 4.7 will illustrate the sharply contrasting behavior of derivational morphemes with those of inflection by studying examples where a single suffix exhibits both.

According then to whether an item is bound or not and according to the level(s) of its being inserted into a derivation (4.9), there are six types of closed classes in the Syntacticon whose elements are fully characterized by syntactic features F, as shown in (4.12). The next several chapters are devoted to showing how all these different possibilities provide interesting explanations for recalcitrant paradigms in an extremely wide range of cases.

(4.12)   Types of insertion from the Syntacticon:

INSERTION LEVEL	FREE MORPHEMES	BOUND MORPHEMES
Prior to syntactic computation ("deep structure")	closed class X with specialized meanings, and parts of idioms	non-productive derivational morphology with specialized lexical meanings[11]
During syntactic computation, prior to Spell Out	closed class grammatical words with LF syntactic features; cf. Chapter 6	productive derivational morphology; cf. sections 4.6, 4.7.2, 4.7.3 and Chapter 5
During PF computation, after Spell Out	closed class grammatical words which are "place-holders"; cf. Chapter 7	inflectional morphology; sections 4.4, 4.7.1 and Chapter 5

I do not try to incorporate every traditional claim about classifying in-flection and derivation (some being contradictory), but most of what seems linguistically interesting about distinguishing derivation from inflection can be shown to follow from the model now to be explored. In competing conceptions where morphology is an autonomous component, properties distinguishing the two types of bound morphemes are necessarily described either atheoretically or via ad hoc constraints. But this and the next chapter will show how the contrasting properties of derivational and inflec-tional morphology are unstipulated predictions of the bifurcated diction-ary / syntacticon model (4.9).

---

[11] I take the frequently used terms "semi-productive" and "partially productive" to be equivocations that obscure actual patterns. Either some affix occurs in a formally stateable context with all but a finite list of exceptions (e.g., the English past tense *-ed* suffix), in which case it is productive, or it occurs in a formally stateable context *only if* the context contains members of a finite list (e.g., the set of English causativizing adjectival suffixes *-en, -ize, -ify* and Ø), in which case it is not productive. It is often the case that linguists have not yet discovered the formally stateable context but suspect there is one; in such cases terms such as "semi-productive" tend to crop up, though they have no formal status.

4.4 Inflectional morphology as late insertion

4.4.1 Lexical insertion in PF

Careful generative study of a given grammatical formative @, whether free or bound, has typically led to formulating a "late transformation" specifying a unique insertion context for @ in terms of outputs of Move Alpha. Chomsky's (1957) *do*-support rule, Borer's (1984) analysis of Hebrew *šel*-insertion, and English *of*-insertion and *there*-insertion exemplify this practice. The "doubly-filled COMP filter" and other conditions on specific morphemes ascribed to filters in earlier work can easily be reformulated as more late transformations of this sort.

Such analyses taken together justify a hypothesis that the entire contribution to grammar of many closed class items is nothing other than these late transformations, reformulated as post s-structure (= PF) insertion contexts in their lexical specifications. But we are not yet sure of which formal characteristics of these lexical specifications actually *predict* PF insertion. To determine this, let us inspect some typical lexical entries for inserting some free contentless English closed class items. I use the order-free subcategorization from Chapter 3 for phrasal complements.

(4.13) *Of*-insertion: of, P, -LOCATION, +< [+N, -V] >[12]

The feature value -LOCATION is a marked Absence of Content feature for the category P and hence is not used at LF, as discussed in section 1.2.2. Although it is obvious that *of*-phrases don't satisfy frames calling for locational prepositions, for full justification of the presence of -LOCATION in the entry for *of*, see section 2.5 and also Emonds (1991b). Thus, *of*-insertion involves only an Absence of Content feature and a contextual feature.

(4.14) *That*-insertion: that, P, -WH, -LOCATION, +< I, FINITE >

Although (4.14) glosses over problems such as the exact restrictions on *that* in English relative clauses, different paradigms suggest that "complementizers" are best treated as PF-inserted instances of P with IP comple-

---

[12] I have indicated in Chapter 3 why the notation of a marked feature such as +AD is superior to -V, but retain ±V for familiarity. Since lexical entries don't recognize bar notation levels (2.13), (4.13) provides for inserting *of* in front of any projection of N or D; considerations of economy exclude superfluous insertions.

ments. Among other things, the empty status of P during the syntax contributes to explaining why extractions out of subordinate clauses introduced by
lexical P such as *because, before, since, unless*, etc. are worse than those out
of clauses headed by complementizers, even in adjunct positions (Emonds,
1985, Ch. 7). In any case, the entry (4.14) seems to contain only Absence
of Content features such as -WH and a contextual feature. (The frame +<I>
may itself imply that P can only be -LOCATION.)

(4.15) ***Do so*** and ***do*-support**: do, V, $\left\{\begin{array}{c}\{ +<D > / +<so > \} (<to^{\wedge}ANIM >) \\ < \underline{\quad} [I, -MODAL] > \end{array}\right\}$

The first line states that *do* is a grammatical V without purely semantic
f and occurs in frames such as *do something (to someone)* and *do so (to
someone)*. The feature ACTIVITY is unmarked for the category V and so
accompanies *do* in its canonically realized position as a head of VP without
lexical stipulation. Since ACTIVITY is used in LF, the insertions of *do* as
head of VP, resulting from the first line of (4.15), take place in the syntax
prior to Spell Out.

In contrast, the second line uses a context feature to specify that *do* can
be inserted internal to I under the condition that no modal is present. Since
ACTIVITY is neither an unmarked feature on I nor stipulated in (4.15), this
type of insertion involves no interpretable feature and takes place in PF.
Thus is represented the classical "late rule" of *do*-support of Chomsky
(1957).[13] The incompatibility of *do*-support with affix movement, here as in
much other current work, is due to Economy of Derivation; cf. section 4.4.4.

Jo's (1996) study of the Korean grammatical verb *ha* 'do', which characterizes it as [V, ACTIVITY], reveals a similar dichotomous distribution.
First, *ha* is a light verb which heads VPs and in this position exhibits a
typical non-stative present tense inflection -*n*. But second, *ha* can also occur
under INFL, where its feature ACTIVITY ceases to have any effect:

> "The inserted verbs *ha* in a construction like a Long Form Negation
> Construction and in the Obligation Modal Complex are semanti-
> cally empty. In our analysis, this is predicted by its not being in the
> head position of a VP; the syntactic feature of *ha* [ACTIVITY] is
> prevented from being discharged for an interpretation … As a mem-

---

[13] Thus, *do* under I is indifferent to ±STATIVE, while *do so* under VP is compatible only
with an ACTIVITY verb: *Bill { needs/ owns/ prefers } a motorcycle, and Mary does
(*so) too.*

ber of the closed subclass of verbs, the verb *ha* is qualified to occur as a constituent of an INFL element such as the modal complex [of] obligation-*eya ha*. The syntactic position of the verb *ha* in the OMC can adequately account for (i) the selection of the present tense morpheme [i.e., Ø, JE] ... and (iii) its nonoccurrence in a VP/AP complement and a nominalized VP/AP." (Jo, 1996, 1196)

(4.16)   ***There*-insertion:** there, D, -REFERENCE, -SPECIFIC

Expletives are widely understood to not contribute to LF and to be a PF phenomenon; I include one here to exemplify how the lexical formalism of the Syntacticon expresses this. Without a subcategorization frame +<N>, a D will not have an NP sister. A discussion in section 9.4.1 justifies classifying expletives as non-specific forms lacking reference. Since these are both Absence of Content features, i.e, not used at LF, the lexical entry (4.16) suggests insertion only at PF.

The entries (4.13)–(4.16) contain no purely semantic features *f* but only syntactic features F; according to the table (3.46) they are then in the Syntacticon. Besides specifying the morpheme's category, the features F in these entries are limited to two sub-classes called *purely syntactic* in section 1.2: (i) contextual features with no role in LF, and (ii) features marking an *absence* of semantic content (-LOCATION, -REFERENCE, -SPECIFIC, -WH).

The common property of all features F of late-inserted items is thus *playing no role in LF interpretation*. In this sense, late-inserted items are simply "place-holders" – they fill unidentified syntactic positions which may not be zero, but they do not themselves contribute to determining LF. In order to characterize this place-holding property of late-inserted items, we can now tentatively specify exactly the condition under which closed class items, i.e., items from the Syntacticon, are inserted in PF rather than the syntax.

(4.17)   Phonological Lexicalization (tentative). Items specified solely in terms of purely syntactic uninterpreted features F (contextual and "lack of content" features) are inserted subsequent to any operation contributing to Logical Form.

The place-holding entries in (4.13–4.16) are typical of the items subject to (4.17); their late insertion is indicated in the model (4.9) by the rightmost downward arrow.

Phonological Lexicalization (4.17) formalizes a possibility in any grammatical model with two syntactic levels: "This formulation allows later insertion of functional items that are vacuous for LF-interpretation, e.g., the *do* of *do*-support or the *of* of *of*-insertion." (Chomsky, 1992, note 22) Up until now, it is used only sporadically as a basis for syntactic explanation, but we will see in what follows that the phenomenon is entirely systematic.

4.4.2 Classical inflection as Alternative Realization

A cursory glance at a range of grammatical inflection suggests that much of it may have the same status as the PF-inserted free forms just discussed. Grammatical agreements and at least the basic morphological cases do not seem to contribute to LF.[14] Rather, they appear to "redundantly" realize syntactic features F which do contribute to LF, but by virtue of these F occurring elsewhere in a tree (in fact, close by) in their canonical positions (section 1.2.1).

For example, the phi-feature agreements on some I, verb or adjective are copies of these features in their canonical, LF-interpreted positions on some D or N head of DP:

(4.18) $[_{DP, III, SING}$ The boy $]$ $[_{I, III, SING}$ is $]$ pitching well.

(4.19) $[_{DP, III, SING}$ The boy $]$ $[_V$ $[_V$ pitch$]$ $[_{?, III, SING}$ es $]$ $]$ well.

Emonds (1987), called this phenomenon "Alternative Realization" of syntactic features; the following version is partly due to H. Kolb.

(4.20)   *Alternative Realization ("AR"). A syntactic feature F canonically associated in UG with category B can be alternatively realized in a closed class grammatical morpheme under X^0, provided X^0 is the lexical head of a sister of B^j.*

In (4.18–4.19), D is the canonical host of the person and number phi-features, and B^j = DP. In (4.18), I' is the sister of DP; in (4.19) in the absence of an I, V serves as the head of I' (we return to this just below).

---

[14] It is well-known that nominative and accusative cases are not linked to interpretations, and genitive case, which typically subsumes nominative and accusative in the nominal system, is even less so. In systems with up to five or six (non-vocative) cases, even oblique cases such as the Classical Greek, German or Icelandic dative or Latin ablative provide next to no information specific enough to contribute to an LF interpretation of a DP. Rather, they seem to indicate at most that the DP in question appears in what would be a PP position in a language without morphological case.

Alternatively realized features are thus a subclass of purely syntactic features F which don't contribute to LF, resulting from language-particular entries of bound morphemes of the Syntacticon. Since non-interpretability is the hallmark of insertion after Spell Out, alternatively realized features should be included among those which permit Phonological Lexicalization.

(4.21)   *Phonological Lexicalization (PL). Items specified solely in terms of purely syntactic, uninterpreted features F (contextual, alternatively realized and "lack of content" features) are inserted subsequent to any operation contributing to Logical Form.*

The question we can now ask is, should only rather transparently uninterpretable inflections be subject to PF insertion, or can this approach be fruitfully extended to other aspects of what has been classically treated as inflections? Consider for example English comparative (and similarly, superlative) inflections. One might say, these morphemes obviously contribute to meaning.

But in fact, we can only be sure that the *syntactic features* realized by the morphemes contribute to meaning. And in the context of co-occurrence restrictions between inflected comparatives and degree words (4.22), Bresnan (1973) suggests that the locus of comparative interpretation is not on A but rather on the AP modifier position in SPEC(AP):

(4.22)   *very fonder of sweets, *how fonder of sweets, *less fondest of sweets, etc.

(4.23)   er, A, COMPARATIVE, +<A ___ >

(4.24)

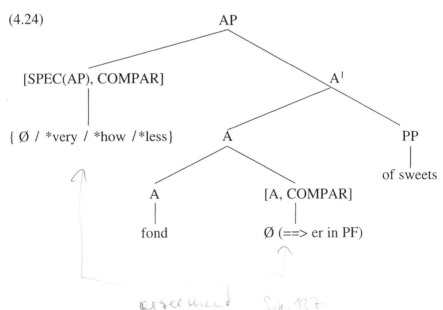

It seems thus preferable to identify the SPEC(AP) position as the uniform canonical locus of LF interpretation for the degree of an AP, and to consider the comparative/ superlative inflections in English as a kind of "PF agreement" with this position, i.e., an alternative realization of [SPEC(AP), +COMPAR]. While we must still address the difference between a "zeroing" of a canonical position as in (4.24) and the redundant "agreement" seen in (4.18)–(4.19), we can nonetheless assimilate at least the "meaningful" comparative inflections to PF-insertion (4.21).

An important advantage of treating inflection by AR is that it permits unifying the structures of both inflection and derivation. Morphological studies of internal phonological word structure (Lapointe, 1980; Lieber 1980) present strong evidence that inflection and derivation typically share language-particular properties; consequently, inflection should have the same structure as derivational morphology.[15] In particular, the inflection -*er* in (4.24), which alternatively realizes a feature of SPEC(AP), should be analyzed as a right-hand head of an A, akin to English right-hand heads in derivational morphology. That is, this inflection is an X^0 of the *same category* as its open class stem sister. But if AR can always realize closed class modifiers of some X as right-hand suffixal heads of category X, AR looks capable of characterizing all of classic inflectional morphology, whose very definition is often given as "affixation which doesn't change the category of a stem."

Let us turn to further examples of how this works. AR can for example subsume classic English affix movement and eliminate any need for either a lowering transformation or for abstract "LF raising" of verbs to I. First observe that competing accounts of English tense placement cannot avoid some minimal word-internal specification for -*ed* such as (4.25):

(4.25)   ed, V, PAST, +<V__ >

But now, the AR account affix placement shows itself superior, because it turns out to require no further statement. The tree structure (4.26) licensed by (4.25) constitutes a complete analysis. In this instance of AR, F = PAST, B = I, and X = V. The alternatively realized morpheme [V, PAST] in (4.26) is not interpreted in LF, while the canonically associated feature complex [I, PAST] is. All that remains is to account for why I in this tree *must be* null, a topic dealt with in terms of economy in subsection 4.4.4.

---

[15] Some particular properties shared by English derivation and inflection were brought out in section 3.5.

(4.26)   Context for PF insertion of *-ed*:

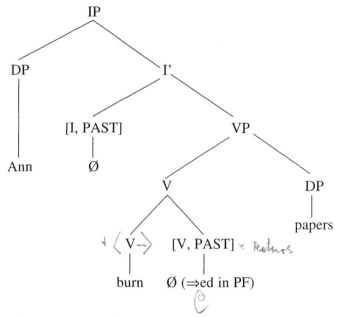

I propose to define more carefully what counts as the lexical head of VPs as in (4.26), during the syntactic derivation prior to s-structure. Since the features of *-ed* in (4.25) are purely syntactic (one alternatively realized and one context feature), Phonological Lexicalization (4.21) insures that *-ed* is inserted only in PF. At the same time, the role of being the syntactic head of VP, of being the element which selects complements and assigns accusative case, must clearly be reserved for the highest *lexically filled* V in the syntax, here the open class, transitive [$_V$ *burn*]. The following definition of lexical head serves to clarify the notion of lexical head for all levels at which a PF suffixal head V is empty:

(4.27)   *Lexical Head/Projection. Let Y^0 be the highest lexically filled head in Z^j. Then Y^0 is the lexical head of Z^j, and Z^j is a lexical projection of Y^0.*

Thus in (4.26), *burn* is the head of VP and in fact of I' in the syntax, while *-ed* is the head of both in PF. This now explains a point left unresolved above, namely why subject agreement can occur on V if and only if I is empty. Since V is the lexical head of the I' sister of DP in these cases, features of D can be alternatively realized on V.

I now revise Unified Classical Subcategorization (3.24) to incorporate the effects of (4.27).[16] To do this, I generalize the sisterhood relation so as to ignore intervening empty heads:

(4.28)   *Extended Sisterhood. If Z^0 and XP are sisters and if Z^1 is the small-est phrase (besides structural projections of Y) whose lexical head is Y^0, then Y^0 and XP are extended sisters.*

(4.29)   *Revised Classical Subcategorization. @, Y, $+<(\_\_\_)X(\_\_\_)>$ is satisfied if and only if X is a cognitive syntactic feature of the lexical head of an (extended) sister of $Y^0 = @$.*

At this point, the "lexical head of ZP" is no longer always synonymous with the structural head Z^0 which is highest in ZP. In (4.26), only at the PF level is [$_V$ *-ed*] the lexical head of the VP *burned the papers*. But this is exactly as desired, since the PF head *-ed* has no effect on complement selection or case assignment. Rather the open class V and its object DP are extended sisters at all levels other than PF.

The structures (4.24) and (4.26) suggest how AR, in conjunction with minimal lexical entries for closed class items, can account elegantly for a variety of language-specific and item-specific inflectional patterns. The proper generalizations about the distribution of bound forms thus neither require transformational apparatus nor interfere with the status of an open class host as lexical head of its phrase in the syntax. Simple subcategorization frames in the lexical entries for bound morphemes as in (4.23) and (4.25) do all the language-particular work; transformations are not involved.

More generally, inflectional morphology on a lexical head X^0 works as follows. Syntacticon entries for morphemes bound to X^0 express UG feature sets which in other languages appear in free morphemes under some func-tional category such as I, D, P or SPEC(XP) which is a sister of a lexical projection of X. Such morphology is an area where the closed class inven-tories of languages vary greatly. AR expresses exactly what is general in all this (differing morphological paradigms clustering around open class heads), while the Syntacticon entries subject to PF insertion (4.21) express the language-particular variation.

---

[16] For ease of comparison, the earlier formulation (3.24) is as follows:

(3.24)   Unified Classical Subcategorization. The frames $+< F >$, $+< F\_\_\_>$ or $+<\_\_\_F >$ in a lexical entry @, X are satisfied if and only if F is a cognitive syntactic feature of a lexical head of a sister to X^0.

Although of course detailed work in many areas remains to be done, the perspective at this point is that essentially every kind of familiar inflection is amenable to treatment as an instance of Alternative Realization (4.20). We have already seen examples involving person-number agreements and adjectival comparison. I conclude the subsection with a list of other types of inflections which I expect can be accounted for in a similar way, covering most of what is traditionally included under this topic.

(i) Verbal inflections whose source is higher than VP. The type of account of affix movement just discussed should extend to any inflections on V which spell out I and SPEC(VP) features such as tense, aspect and modality features (potential, future, conditional), as well as inflectional negation.

(ii) Verbal inflections whose source is in the VP. Section 6.5 and the Appendix to that chapter will summarize the detailed treatment of Romance clitics in Emonds (1999), which argues that the "clitic-climbing" so often alluded to in the literature is epiphenomenal, and evidence rather for certain "flat structures" of multiple Vs. Under this analysis, Romance clitics simply alternatively realize under a V^0 in the same VP the basic syntactic features of a range of complements and adjuncts. The constituents in the canonical DP and PP positions for these clitics are sometimes null and sometimes "double" the clitics. I call this analysis the Phrase Mate Hypothesis for Romance clitics and subsume it here under AR.

AR also subsumes the much studied verbal applicative suffixes found in Bantu languages (Baker, 1988), Indonesian (Chung, 1976) and other languages, whereby features F of a complement P are realized as an affix on a V; cf. the Bantu examples (2.52b) and (2.53b). In these cases, P plays the role of B and V of X in (4.20). AR can similarly account for grammatical features of complement DPs spelled out on V as object agreement morphemes in many, especially Bantu languages.[17] Moreover, it *explains* the conditions under which particular lexicons may have PF-inserted morphemes expressing agreements; for example, it explains why a V cannot agree with (nor host a clitic for) the object of a lexical P.

---

[17] Researchers often debate whether a clitic should be re-analyzed as an agreement marker or vice-versa. While both configurations are amenable to treatment via AR, my suggestion is that the notion "head" can sort out the analyses: agreement morphemes bound to a host are heads within X^0, but clitics are not.

(iii) Inflections involving P and the D head of its complement. Oblique morphological case inflections on D (or N in the absence of D) alternatively realize canonical cognitive syntactic features of P such as $\pm$LOCATION, $\pm$PATH and $\pm$SOURCE. Some simpler case morphologies are analyzed in Emonds (1985, Ch. 5). More complex systems specify additional PATH distinctions on DPs, such as 'toward' vs. 'up to' vs. 'into' (cross-classified by $\pm$SOURCE so as to also yield 'out from within' vs. 'out from on' vs. 'away from'). These alternatively realized features are frequently thought of as "inherent cases" of DPs, but such DPs usually share a lot of PP distribution and other PP behavior such as prohibiting floating quantifiers. Van Riemsdijk and Huijbregts (1999) analyzes in detail one of the most complicated of these systems.

Other sorts of morphemes under D can alternatively realize P features; French *au(x)* and *du, des* seem to be articles with alternatively realized features [LOC, $\pm$SOURCE]:

(4.30) a. Anne a mis les pains [$_{PP}$ [$_{DP}$ [$_{D, LOC, -SOURCE}$ au] four]].
         Anne has put the loaves   [$_{D}$ into-the] oven
     b. On a sorti les bagages [$_{PP}$ [$_{DP}$ [$_{D, LOC, +SOURCE}$ des] armoires]].
         We have taken-out the luggage   [$_{D}$ from-the] closets

In the other direction, affixation on P can alternatively realize features of its D-headed complement; cases in point are the Dutch "R pronoun" prefixes on P (van Riemsdijk, 1978), German P-D Contraction (Beerman, 1990; van Riemsdijk, 1998a) and Welsh inflected prepositions (cf. section 4.4.4 below).[18]

(iv) Inflections involving C (that is, P) and the I head of its complement. I features can be alternatively realized in PF on the C which takes IP as a complement. For example, the subject number agreement feature on I in West Flemish can be copied onto the complementizer (Haegeman, 1992, section 2.2.1):

---

[18] The productive Dutch R pronouns have the form of "locatives" analogous to atrophied English forms such as *therein, herein, wherein*. Plausibly, the category DP has an unmarked interpretation of REFERENCE. The "locative" forms of D may then be just those which surface when either D has a marked Absence of Content feature -REFERENCE or when D's features are alternatively realized outside DP.

(4.31) a. ... [$_{C, -PLUR}$ da] [$_{IP}$ den inspektur da boek gelezen [$_{I, -PLUR}$ eet]]
        ... [that, -PLUR] the inspector that book read [has, -PLUR]
    b. ... [$_{C, +PLUR}$ dan] [$_{IP}$ d'inspekturs da boek gelezen [$_{I, +PLUR}$ een]]
        ... [that, +PLUR] the inspectors that book read [have, +PLUR]

The most restrictive way to view this phenomenon is to try to relate it to a principle of "Free Rider" inflection, tentatively formulated just below.

(v) Inflections involving D, A and N within the DP. Inflections on N can spell out the features of definiteness and number from higher heads within its extended projection DP, as many Germanic and Slavic inflectional patterns show. At the same time lexical gender, convincingly argued in Ritter (1993) to be a syntactic feature of N, can also appear on D and sometimes even on low numerals (Veselovská, 2000). Additionally, all these features can in varying ways appear on attributive adjectives within the extended DP projection; for example, the definite prefix appears on both the Hebrew noun and adjective (Siloni, 1995):

(4.32) ha-'ish *(ha-)yafe
      the-man the-beautiful
      'the beautiful man'

The complex Germanic and Slavic systems of agreement within the DP seem to suggest that AR (4.20) not only can license canonical syntactic cognitive features of B on lexical heads of sisters of B, but also, at least in inflectional systems, may further "spread" features already alternatively realized. Thus in the Czech example (4.33), the bold case feature on D and the bold PLUR feature on N are already alternative rather than canonical realizations, and yet they additionally occur on intervening adjectives, essentially under the structural condition set by AR.[19] Since the adjective is distinctively marked as plural and instrumental, all these feature markings are overt:

(4.33) ... s(e) [$_{A, PL, INST}$ všemi] [$_{D, PL, \mathbf{INST}}$ těmi] [$_{A, PL, INST}$ krásnými]
      with   all   those   beautiful
      [$_{N, \mathbf{PL}, INST}$ děvčaty]
         girls

---

[19] The present framework contains no mechanism of SPEC-head agreement for morphology which is independent of Alternative Realization.

As formulated, AR (4.20) only displaces features *in their canonical positions* to the next lexical head, upward or downward in a tree. We do not want to weaken AR by allowing it to "apply to its own output" in order to derive paradigms typified by (4.33). Rather, we need to allow certain alternatively realized features which co-occur with canonical features to "piggyback" on the latter's alternative realizations, similar to the way in which formal features, called free riders, move with interpreted ones in Chomsky (1995, 270). The following tentative and perhaps not sufficiently restrictive statement of this idea characterizes what are typically called inflectional (as opposed to agglutinative) morphemes.

(4.34)   *Free Riders. If a morpheme @ alternatively realizes (on X^0) a feature F canonically associated with a category B, and some F' is also spelled out under B, then @ can also spell out F' on X^0.*

Thus, if an attributive adjective inflection @ alternatively realizes say the lexical gender feature of an N, and CASE and NUMBER are also spelled out under N (as alternative realizations), then the adjectival inflection @ can also spell out CASE and NUMBER.

(vi) Conjunctive inflections. Co-ordinate conjunctions can be spelled out as suffixes within XP conjuncts (e.g., Latin *-que*). In these cases a conjunction plays the role of B in AR, and the alternatively realized feature of the conjunction occurs on the head of the sister of the conjunction, namely the head of the conjunct.

   This list (i)–(vi) covers then a wide range of various types of language-particular inflections which AR (4.20) promises to explain in a uniform and simple way.

4.4.3 The distinctions between inflectional and derivational morphology

The application of the theory of multi-level lexical insertion (4.8) to bound morphology and the sharpened notion of lexical head at a level (4.27) predict the classic if atheoretical descriptive generalizations contrasting derivational with inflectional morphology.

   (i) "Inflection is productive while Derivation need not be." In the model (4.9), the Dictionary is the locus of any non-productive lists of open class stems which combine with given dependent forms, and hence such combinations are inserted prior to syntax (e.g. idiomatic English derivational causative formations such as V +*ize*). All subsequent insertions are from the

Syntacticon and result from productive elsewhere conditions. Since inflection results from a subcase of the latter, namely Phonological Lexicalization (4.21), it must be productive in this sense.[20]

(ii) "Inflection appears outside of Derivation." When inflection is suffixal as in English, the claim is that inflectional suffixes appear to the right of derivational ones under some Z^0. Since each English bound suffix @ in the model (4.9) is inserted into a position where it is (momentarily) a right-hand lexical head, only as yet unfilled empty Y^0 can follow @ under Z^0. Therefore @' is to the right of @ under Z^0 if and only if @' is inserted after @. Since derivational morphemes are inserted before s-structure and inflectional morphemes after, the latter are necessarily to the right of the former.

(iii) "Inflection generally obeys Baker's (1985) Mirror Principle." I assume that both Phonological and Deep Lexicalization proceed in bottom-up fashion in any given cyclic domain, and that in both cases, increasingly larger domains are looked at in turn for operations that apply on them. If some inflection @ is to the right of another @', i.e. further from an open class root, by (ii) @ is inserted after @'. Consequently, the syntactic domain which must be checked for the proper insertion of @ is at least as large as the domain checked for insertion of @'. This is the content of the Mirror Principle.

(iv) "Inflection doesn't change a stem's category, but Derivation may." In fact, the claim is too broad and imprecise. Participial suffixes which change a stem's category from say X to Y, exemplified below in section 4.7.1, actually give the impression of changing an "internal" XP to an "external" YP. For instance, the gerund formed from the completely productive English *-ing* appears to be an "internal" VP but an "external" NP. In traditional thinking, this category-changing inflection "preserves" the internal structure of the phrase XP and its head remains an X. But a more accurate rendering, to be examined in detail below, is that although participial inflection doesn't change the internal syntax of a phrase, it *does change the category* of the stem. Hence, inflection doesn't change a stem's *syntactic role in phrase-internal syntax*, but derivation may.

---

[20] This raises the question of irregular inflection. Exceptions to a productive process (e.g., the hundreds of English irregular past forms) are most likely listed in the Dictionary as composite X^0 with specified affixes, such as for example $[_V [_V bough] [_{V, PAST} t]]$ or $[_V shook] [_{V, PAST} \emptyset]]$. When these items are inserted with this kind of analysis (e.g. in adult but probably not young children's grammars), some sort of word-internal economy "blocks" (Aronoff, 1976) adding the productive affixes (*boughted, *shooked*), which would otherwise be inserted from the Syntacticon.

In summary, much diverse, language-particular inflectional morphology clearly falls under the single restrictive AR principle (4.20). The twin hypotheses of Alternative Realization and PF insertion of closed class items lacking LF-interpretable features permit the best of two worlds: Inflections can be structurally represented exactly like derivational morphology, permitting expression of their common properties; yet with the definition of Lexical Head (4.27), both the inflection and the lexical head are associated with head positions at the levels needed to explain their co-occurrence relations with other categories in their syntactic environment.

4.4.4 Why inflection exists: invisible categories and Economy

It appears that when Alternative Realization of the features F of some category B is "complete," then B can be licensed as empty by (4.35), discussed in more detail in Emonds (1987).

(4.35)   *Invisible Category Principle (ICP). If all marked canonical features F on B are alternatively realized by AR (4.20), except perhaps B itself, then B may be empty.*

For example, in conjunction with AR, the ICP licenses an empty SPEC(AP) with the comparative inflection in (4.24) and an empty I with a past tense V in (4.26).

However, the ICP doesn't itself require that B *must* be empty. The *obligatory* zeroing of e.g. I in (4.26) is performed by a separate principle which has effects outside of the area of Alternative Realization:

(4.36)   *Economy of Derivation: Two deep structures which differ only by empty categories not interpretable at LF count as equivalent. Of equivalent deep structures, prefer the derivation with the fewest insertions of free morphemes.*

Working in tandem, AR, the ICP and Economy of Derivation together exclude sequences such as (4.37–4.39).[21]

---

[21] The examples in (4.37–4.38) are taken to lack contrastive stress. I take such stress to be a syntactic feature which cannot be alternatively realized. Hence, if a contrastive stress is available in a given position and provided Case Theory and other principles of grammar are respected, an overt element can sometimes replace the null categories otherwise expected from the ICP and Economy of Derivation.

(4.37) *Ann did burn(ed) the papers.

(4.38) *Jim seems more tall(er) that he was.

(4.39) *Marie a vu lui au cinéma. (French accusative free form *lui* 'him')
        Marie l'a vu au cinéma.   (French accusative pre-verbal bound
                                    clitic *le* 'him')
        'Marie has seen him at the movies.'

The same combination of AR, the ICP and Derivational Economy excludes unstressed pronoun subjects in the more highly inflected "pro-drop" languages in favor of null subjects (Emonds, 1994). From this perspective, pro-drop phenomena result from the interplay of the following four factors:

a. A lexicon for a language contains entries for finite I with D features ("subject-verb agreement"). Since these agreement morphemes express only alternatively realized features, they are inserted in PF.

b. If these entries productively spell out *all* the features of subjects, they bring the ICP (4.35) into play, which *allows* the DP subjects to be null.

c. By Economy of Derivation (4.36), derivations with null subjects are more economical than derivations with non-null subjects expressing the same features (i.e. unstressed but free form pronouns).

d. Since contrastive stress can never be alternatively realized, contrastively stressed or so-called "strong pronouns" subjects are still permitted.

Since the pro-drop phenomenon depends on a Syntacticon's array of agreement entries, we can expect that particular lexical configurations with pro-drop may be limited to only certain tenses or persons; in fact, Italian dialects have such systems. Thus, there is no general "parameter setting" for pro-drop, just differing arrays of closed class agreement items in the Syntacticon, perhaps arranged in paradigms. Pro-drop is therefore another complex morphological phenomenon which AR (4.20), the ICP (4.35), and Economy of Derivation (4.36) taken together reduce to simple and uniform lexical statements.[22]

A final observation concerning two distinct behaviors of Alternatively Realized features of inflections is in order. Y. Ueda (pers. comm.) points out that Economy of Derivation as above explains zeroing only if we distin-

---

[22] Emonds (1994) contains more details on which aspects of Pro-drop reduce to AR and which require other principles.

guish bound morphemes *which occur only if the ICP also induces zeroing* such as the English TENSE affix on V and the COMPARATIVE affix on A (4.40a), from those *which occur whenever they can,* such as English PLURAL on N and agreement on V (4.40b):

(4.40)   a.   John (*would) burned the papers.
John is (*less) taller than Mary.

b.   Those three boys are tall.   *These three boy are tall.
John sings very well.   *John sing very well.

The fact is that a given morpheme may behave differently in dialects as well as in child vs. adult language. Thus, forms such as "more weaker" and "we bought a dozen egg" are found in varieties of English other than the present day standard.

The so-called inflecting prepositions of Welsh clearly exemplify the distinction between AR dependent on zeroing and AR in the presence of copying:

(4.41)   wrth-a (i)   wrth-yn (nhw)
to-I+SING (me)   to-III+PLUR (them)
'to me'   'to them'

Both versions of each example in (4.41) have an inflected enclitic on P which alternatively realizes its object DP. The parenthesized following free pronouns are omitted in literary Welsh, but obligatory in the colloquial language (M. Tallerman, pers. comm.) Thus, literary Welsh exemplifies AR dependent on zeroing, while colloquial Welsh exemplifies the "AR when possible" or doubling variant.

This general distinction may require lexical stipulation if no predictive factor can be found. Provisionally, I take it that alternatively realized morphemes which occur whenever their subcategorizations are satisfied, as in (4.40b), are lexically marked. Thus:

(4.42)   *Unmarked AR morphemes. A bound morpheme alternatively realizing F_i with no marked notation in the Syntacticon appears only when it zeroes the canonical position of F_i.*

Under this convention, unmarked adult usage is that which always aids Economy (4.36), although unmarked child usage at an early stage may rather be that AR is used whenever it can be, as in (4.40b). If so, unmarked child usage becomes marked (i.e. the usage changes) when Economy of Derivation matures.

It can thus be concluded that the *raison d'être* of inflectional morphology is Economy. The inflections of a language are preferred because they allow given Logical Forms to be derived with fewer insertions of free morphemes from the Syntacticon. In themselves, inflections contribute to PF (centrally), but their role in LF is entirely indirect: they allow for interpretation of phonetically unrealized complexes of canonically associated features such as [I, PAST}, [SPEC(AP), COMPAR], [P, LOC, $\pm$SOURCE], etc.

4.5 Alternative Realization on free morphemes

Alternative Realization (4.20) is not defined as a property of only bound morphemes. Yet because of the central role I assign to it in the analysis of inflections (section 4.4.2) and Romance clitics (section 6.5), one might wonder if it has any role in analyses of closed class *free* morphemes.

The "bare NP adverbs" analyzed in Larson (1985) are one construction where I claim that AR plays such a role. In Emonds (1987) I argue that the closed class of grammatical head nouns (*day, time, year, place, way*) in such adverbial expressions are lexically specified with the prepositional feature LOCATION; this feature percolates up to such an N's extended projection DP. Hence, via the Invisible Category Principle (4.35), these free morphemes with an alternatively realized feature permit the P sister of this DP to be empty. In my proposal, this P can also unexceptionally assign oblique abstract case to its sister, which I claim is less stipulative than a special case-assigning mechanism invoked by Larson.

English inflected auxiliaries (e.g., *is, was, has,* etc.) under I can also be elegantly analyzed in terms of Alternative Realization. This analysis allows us to dispense with a highly-stipulative and item-specific verb-raising rule in English.[23] Consider first a plausible and very general Syntacticon entry for the (non-finite) verb *be:*

(4.43)   be, V, STATIVE, +< X$_{-CASE}$ >

The category X means simply that the copula must have a caseless complement at the level it is inserted. The head of that complement may be D (a

---

[23] Emonds (1994) shows that *be*-raising alone in English involves five ad hoc properties; *have*-raising, which is analyzed differently in Chapter 7, is even more problematic.

predicate nominal), A (a predicate adjective), P (a locational PP) or V (a progressive; here *be* acts like other verbs of temporal aspect.[24] (4.43) further stipulates that *be* cannot assign case, but, as we will see just below, this may follow from its level of insertion.

Section 4.4.2 summarized the conditions for Phonological Lexicalization (4.21): items like (4.43) which are specified with only context and Absence of Content features must be inserted at PF. As discussed in Chapter 1, a canonical, expected, unmarked feature value of V is +ACTIVITY, equivalently -STATIVE, so STATIVE is a marked Absence of Content feature, implying that *be* is PF-inserted.[25]

This conclusion in turn suggests that Universal Grammar is equipped to interpret at LF the following s-structures, where V is Ø except in PF. (I omit intermediate projections.)

(4.44)

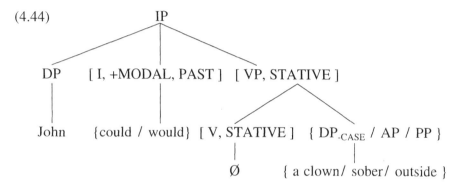

The empty V is legitimate since it can be filled in PF by late insertion of *be*, but it does not contribute to LF, by (4.10). Under the further plausible assumption that a V must be lexicalized (or properly co-indexed) at s-structure in order to assign case, we perhaps can simpify the entry for *be* even further by dropping the -CASE stipulation in (4.43).

Since the copular V in (4.44) has no role except at PF, the question arises as to whether it can ever fail to be inserted. Its feature +STATIVE, canoncially matched in UG with the category V, has a marked value, and so is a candidate for alternative realization under I according to (4.20). And now the reasoning based on economy for inflections in section 4.4.4 holds

---

[24] Chapter 5 will provide an analysis of passive structures with auxiliary *be*.

[25] Linguistic analysis, probably under the influence of logic and philosophy, typically concludes that *be* is somehow the unmarked verb. It is rather the uninterpreted verb; the unmarked verb is the more basic activity verb *do*. It is precisely *be*'s simple, uninterpreted but still marked status that allows the copula to be alternatively realized in I.

for free morphemes as well: if STATIVE, the *only* marked feature on V, is alternatively realized, the ICP (4.35) will allow V to be zero in PF. English permits this if I is -MODAL.

This then suggests that the Syntacticon entries for the finite copulas are just alternative realizations of the feature STATIVE (in any case uninterpretable) under an I unmarked for MODAL:

(4.45)   were, I, -MODAL, PAST, PLURAL, STATIVE
          was, I, -MODAL, PAST, STATIVE
          am, I, -MODAL, I PERSON, STATIVE
          ...[26]

Since this alternatively realized feature STATIVE is not marked in (4.45) to allow for doubling, the condition on unmarked AR morphemes (4.42) permits only zero in the canonical V position of STATIVE: *John was (*be) in the room.*

There are thus two morphological strings that spell out the structure in (4.44) when I is specified as -MODAL (and is -CONTRASTIVE): the unexceptional *John did be a clown* and the use of (4.45) for *John was [$_V$ Ø] a clown.* As expected, Economy of Derivation (4.36) selects the latter as well-formed, since it contains fewer free morphemes. We thus see that a very simple use of AR on the free morphemes *was, am,* etc. eliminates the whole troublesome mechanism of English *be*-raising, with its five ad hoc properties (cf. note 23).

At the same time, we can conclude that AR (4.20) has uses in all areas of the Syntacticon, not just with the bound morphemes which are the focus of this chapter.

4.6 Derivational morphology: the arguments of lexically derived forms

As a preliminary to analyzing derivational morphology in terms of multi-level lexical insertion, I wish to factor out the issue of how derived nouns and adjectives come to be associated with the DP arguments of their stems. To see why this is not obvious, let us recall the definition of lexical head of a phrase, which sanctions "passing over" empty Z^0 in determining the semantic and syntactic relations between a head and its complements:

---

[26] There are interesting issues about how paradigms, i.e. sets of morphemes with common features, are to be economically represented in the Syntacticon. These issues extend to many types of constructions and are orthogonal to the reasoning here.

(4.27) *Lexical Head/Projection. Let Y^0 be the highest lexically filled head in Z^j. Then Y^0 is the lexical head of Z^j, and Z^j is a lexical projection of Y^0.*

According to the syntacticon model (4.9), non-productive derivational morphemes are inserted at the beginning of syntactic derivations. Hence, in the following schematic but nonetheless representative trees, the suffixes *and not the open class items* are the lexical heads *at every derivational level.*

(4.46)

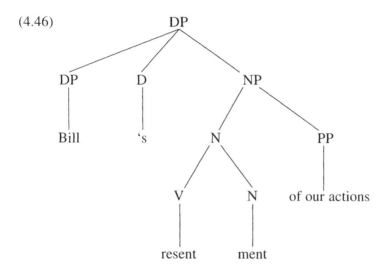

(4.47)

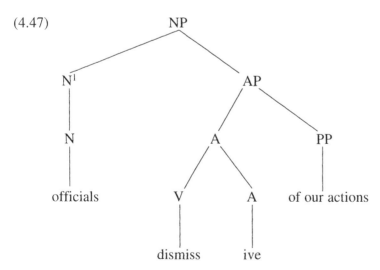

Even though *Bill* and *officials* are clearly selected and interpreted as the subjects of *resent* and *dismiss* respectively, Generalized Subjects (1.15) does not pick them out as the structural subjects of these V at any derivational level, since at no level are these V the lexical heads of NP in (4.46) or AP in (4.47). Nor, for that matter, can *our actions* be the structural objects of these V, for the same reason. *Bill* in (4.46) and *officials* in (4.47) are rather the respective subjects of the lexical heads *-ment* and *-ive*.[27]

The arguments of these V can be correctly interpreted only if we introduce a principle whose validity extends beyond any single type of derivational formation.[28]

(4.48)   *Transparent Derivational Heads. If a lexical suffix @ on X at Spell Out selects no complements, then (i) the lowest argument c-commanding @ and (ii) any lower arguments may be interpreted as the corresponding arguments of X.*[29]

Some examples of how (4.48) functions: If @ is a nominalizing suffix, a possessive DP is typically the only DP which can c-command @, so this DP and any others it c-commands may be the (italicized) arguments of a V stem such as *resent, arrive* or *insist* in (4.49–4.51). If @ is adjectival, A is c-commanded by its subject DP, so that DP, as well as any complements within AP, may act as arguments of a V stem such as *dismiss* in (4.52).

(4.49)   [DP *Bill's* resentment of *our actions*] was unexpected.

---

[27] This mismatch between heads and arguments doesn't arise with inflections, since late insertion guarantees that inflections are lexical heads only in PF.

[28] Although the mechanics of LF head-argument interpretation certainly require further work, a competence model of interpretive principles plausibly relates heads to arguments (e.g., assigns theta roles as in Chapter 2) in bottom-up fashion. This would seem to mean that once a head @ and an argument YP have been interpreted as standing in a relation R(@, YP), no head @' interpreted previous to @ can *subsequently* be determined to stand in some relation R'(@', YP'). By this reasoning, interpretation of a derivational suffix @, a right-hand head, must follow that of its stem @'.

Plausibly, interpreting an affix @ includes making any DP c-commanding @ within XP into an argument of its stem @' and erasing @. But bottom-up sequencing of head-argument interpretations then implies that the stem @' can be related to no argument higher than this DP. This reasoning thus derives (4.48) as a global effect of an LF algorithm for determining head-argument structures.

[29] (4.48) is consistent with the claims of Chapter 2 because it entails no item-specific mention of semantic roles in any entry of either the Dictionary or the Syntacticon.

(4.50) The fans awaited [$_{DP}$ *the train's* arrival *in Rome*].

(4.51) Mary disapproved of [$_{DP}$ *your* insistence *on an answer*].

(4.52) *The officials* were [$_{AP}$ dismissive of *our actions*].

Transparent Derivational Heads (4.48) restricts the access of a derivational head's X^0 host to surrounding syntactic structure in LF. For example, it disallows relations between V^0 and DP other than interpretation of DP as a productively generated argument. Thus, while the verbs in (4.53) can appear in idiomatic combinations, (4.48) correctly blocks parallel combinations of derived nominals and adjectives in (4.54).[30]

(4.53) During the trial, John has maintained silence.
His paying { bribes/ attention } to minor officials was foolish.
This show is pleasing local kids no end.

(4.54) *During the trial, all were impressed by John's maintenance of silence.
His payment of { bribes/ *attention } to minor officials was foolish.
*This show seems pleasing to local kids no end.

These paradigms again underscore the fact that idioms are first and foremost syntactic combinations rather than special interpretations assigned to semantic combinations. Thus, the syntactic categories in the idioms [$_V$ *maintain*] [$_N$ *silence*], [$_V$ *pay*] [$_N$ *attention*] and [$_V$ *please*] *no end* play a crucial role. Even a general interpretive mechanism such as (4.48) cannot define or extend an idiomatic meaning over a natural semantic domain (a head and its arguments); idioms are defined in terms of syntax.

In Chapter 3, I glossed over the need for the mechanism (4.48) because its effects perhaps seem obvious, but it clearly has predictive power. In the next chapter it will play a crucial role in explaining certain properties that distinguish adjectival from verbal passives.[31]

---

[30] That is, Transparent Derivational Heads (4.48) captures this general empirical difference between inflectional and derivational morphology, for which a-syntactic approaches of "autonomous morphology" provide no natural account.

[31] I take the empirical properties by which Wasow (1977) distinguishes verbal from adjectival passives as established but standing in need of explanation.

4.7 English nominalizations: confirming the Syntacticon model

Section 4.4.3 has proposed that classic generalizations counterposing derivation and inflection, as well as their other distributional and interpretive
properties, are captured by inserting these two types of grammatical elements at different derivational levels. Grammatical (derivational) elements
with features playing a role in LF are inserted prior to s-structure. Inflections, which play only an indirect role (via licensing empty categories and
fulfilling place-holding functions), are inserted in phonology according to
(4.21).

(4.21)   *Phonological Lexicalization (PL). Items specified solely in terms of
         purely syntactic, uninterpreted features F (contextual, alternatively
         realized and "lack of content" features) are inserted subsequent to
         any operation contributing to Logical Form.*

For the types of bound morphemes discussed so far, the level of insertion, prior or subsequent to s-structure (Spell Out), is determined uniquely
by the types of features present in their lexical entries. For example, a past
tense suffix spells out only an alternatively realized feature of I and so must
be inserted by (4.21), while a causative suffix presumably realizes at least
the cognitive feature ACTIVITY in its canonical position on V and so must
be inserted earlier in order to be present at LF.

Sometimes, however, a particular bound morpheme may be inserted at
more than one level. If its lexical entry contains a cognitive feature which
is parenthesized and thus comes into play "optionally" at LF, the morpheme
may have two or three apparently different "uses" with strikingly different
superficial properties.[32] Among such morphemes are the English participial
and gerund suffix *-ing,* discussed just below, and the English passive suffix
-en, to be discussed in Chapter 5. As will now be seen, different complexes
of properties are entirely predictable from simply formatted lexical entries
which give rise to insertion at different derivational levels. A careful theory
of lexical form will thus explain generalizations about morpheme distribution that have previously appeared accidental.

---

[32] Another possibility is that a disjunctive contextual feature, as with *do* in (4.15), permits
canonically realizing a feature (e.g. ACTIVITY) in one context, leading to insertion in the
syntax, but not in another, leading to insertion in PF.

4.7.1 PF lexical insertion in gerunds and present participles

The English suffix *-ing* gives rise to several distinct constructions: present participles, gerunds, derived nominals and classes of lexical adjectives. Emonds (1991a) develops the basic idea of accounting for the many contrasting paradigms of these different constructions by inserting the item *-ing* at different levels and critiques some competing attempts to treat *-ing* in unitary fashion.[33]

That study proposes a simple and succinct lexical entry (4.55) encompassing all the uses of this versatile morpheme. As is customary, +N refers to the class of nouns and adjectives. Additionally, nouns are -AD ("not adjuncts") and adjectives are +AD.

(4.55)   ing, [+N], +<V___>, ($\begin{cases} \text{-AD: } V = \text{+ACTIVITY, ...} \\ \text{+AD: } V = \text{+PSYCH, or ...} \end{cases}$)

The parenthesized material (the logic doesn't require that it be completely specified) represents information for LF interpretation; hence using this material forces insertion in the syntax. On the other hand, if this material is skipped, the entry has no interpretable features and so is subject to PF insertion. There are thus four possibilities: *-ing* is ±AD and the material in parentheses can be chosen or ignored.

(i) Derived and "mixed" nominals of Chomsky (1970). Using the parenthesized material in the first line of (4.55) to form a noun [+N, -AD] from an activity V leads to insertion prior to s-structure. These options yield the derived and mixed nominals of Chomsky (1970). As can be seen in (4.56), such nominalizations require activity verb stems:

---

[33] The terminology of that work and this one differ, but the formal analysis is basically unchanged. The equivalences are as follows:

Present work:	Emonds (1991a)
DP	NP
Lexical head (4.27)	Functional head
feature used at LF	semantic feature
insertion in the syntactic component	deep structure insertion
insertion in the phonological component	s-structure insertion

Note 15 of that work makes clear that "s-structure insertion" there means "in a context defined by s-structure"; that is, the *output* of late insertion, there as here, is *in phonology.*

(4.56)   We heard about some { shooting/ *fearing } of the hunters.
          Thorough { learning/ *knowing } of the model would help the
          students.
          The { making/ *liking } of money seems to define the social fabric.

This limitation to verbs with the feature ACTIVITY may be a primitive
characteristic of these nominals, or it may result from the optional presence
of some cognitive syntactic feature F on [$_N$ -*ing*] itself, which ensures their
being interpreted as events or results (cf. section 4.7.2). In either case, the
well-formedness of these nominals depends on a feature used in LF and
hence such -*ing* must be present in the syntax. The well-known nominal
syntactic properties of these derived nominals (Chomsky, 1970) then all
follow from their lexical head (as defined in 4.27) being an N both in the
syntax and at LF.

(ii) Psychological adjectives of Chomsky (1957). Similarly, using the parenthesized material in the second line of (4.55) to form adjectives [+N,
+AD] from certain classes of V prior to s-structure yields phrases whose
syntactic properties are adjectival: their specifiers are adjectival, complements appear in oblique case in PPs, etc.

(4.57)   How striking those baseball stars are!
          That story has a subtlety { very/ *right } pleasing to children.
          The spinal treatments were too frightening { to/ for } my friends.
          *The spinal treatments were too frightening my friends.

Only certain verb classes such as "psychological predicates" freely combine with [$_A$ -*ing*] to form this kind of adjective:

(4.58)   *How hitting those baseball stars are!
          *That story has a subtlety very escaping to children.
          *The spinal treatments were too hurting { to/ for } my friends.

There may be in fact be no default interpretation for these derived adjectives
defined in terms of syntactic features. Their well-formedness may always
depend on which classes and/ or lists of verbs defined in the open class
Dictionary accept them. But whether these conditions are syntactic or semantic or a combination, the well-formedness of these adjectives clearly
depends on LF-sensitive material, which is parenthesized in the second line
of the entry (4.55). Consequently, the syntacticon model (4.9) predicts that

their head [$_A$ -*ing*] is filled in syntax, which in turn predicts their phrase-internal adjectival properties.

Two quite different uses of -*ing* are generated by *ignoring* the parenthesized material in (4.55). The resulting pair of bound morphemes ([+N, ±AD]) is fully characterized by a single contextual feature +V__. Since they lack any feature used in LF, these uses of -*ing* are subject to Phonological Lexicalization (4.21).

(iii) The gerundive nominals of Chomsky (1970). The feature complex "[+N, -AD], +<V__>" in (4.55) yields the *ing*-inflected head of the classic gerundive DPs (4.59), whose internal structure is well-known to mimic that of VPs.

(4.59)   Does that justify [$_{DP}$ ({ our/ *some }) { shooting/ fearing } the hunters]?
[$_{DP}$ Thoroughly { learning/ knowing } (*of) the model] will guarantee a job.
[$_{DP}$ { Us/ *The } making money] is more troublesome than
[$_{DP}$ { us/ *the } liking it].

Chomsky (1970) enumerates many properties that distinguish lexically V-headed gerunds (4.59) from the lexically N-headed derived nominals (4.56); it would be tedious to go over this well-trod material in detail here. Like verbs, gerunds exhibit adverbial rather than adjectival modifiers (4.60a-b), aspectual auxiliaries (4.60b), prepositionless direct and indirect objects (4.60b), and they also exclude various types of D-modifications (quantification, WH, plurals, etc.), as in (4.60c).

(4.60)   a.   [{Deliberately/ *Deliberate} assigning novices tough problems] is a bad idea.
b.   She regrets [[having already written/ *the hasty writing } John a letter].
c.   [{Which shootings of hunters/ *Which shootings the hunters}] did he hear?

(iv) The present participle in all structural AP positions. Finally, the feature complex "[+N, +AD], +<V__>" in (4.55) yields present participles, which have exactly the external distribution of adverbial and adjectival phrases, as established in some detail in Emonds (1985, Ch. 2). Like gerunds, however, their internal behavior is that of a V-headed constituent: participles don't tolerate adjectival specifiers, their direct objects appear without a dummy P, etc.

(4.61)   They stumbled off the stage [$_{AP}$ ({ *more/ *too }) { striking/ hitting } their fans].
Subtleties [$_{AP}$ (*very) { pleasing/ escaping } children] rarely appear in his books.
The spinal treatments kept [$_{AP}$ frightening ({ *to/ *for }) my friends].
We see students [$_{AP}$ { relaxing less/ *less relaxing } than before].

The head *-ing* is absent except in PF in both gerundive nominals and participles, since both are formed without using any LF-interpretable features of *-ing*. The definition of lexical head (4.27) therefore determines that, *throughout the derivation from deep structure to LF*, V is the lexical head of both gerundive nominal NPs (4.59)–(4.60) and participial APs (4.61). As evidenced in (4.59)–(4.61), this head V can then assign accusative case and select whichever modifiers are permitted in SPEC(VP) or as adjuncts to verbs. Moreover in gerunds, these lexical head V require structurally represented subjects (possibly PRO) in their minimal cyclic DP domain, by Generalized Subjects (1.15) and the EPP (1.17). Since NPs project to DPs, the subject of a gerund is correctly predicted to be structurally represented within this DP; but since APs have no extended projection containing a subject (cf. Chapter 1), the subject of a present participle is correctly predicted to appear external to AP.

Although exact details deserve more careful formulation, I briefly indicate how the presence vs. absence of a lexicalized N head at s-structure can also account for two less studied differences between the gerunds and derived nominals exemplified above.

(a) Certain nominal modifiers (*other, same, different* and many choices of D) apparently require their containing phrase to be N-headed *throughout a derivation of LF*, while certain verbal modifiers (*yet, ever, already,* etc.) require their containing phrase to be V-headed throughout. Hence, V-headed gerunds and participles (4.59)–(4.61) permit verbal modifiers, but the derived nominals and adjectives (4.56)–(4.58) do not.

(b) Attributive APs inside NPs can acquire phi-features, which give them adjectival rather than adverbial form, only from a head N with such features. Therefore, both ordinary lexical Ns and derived nominals are modifiable by (different sets of) adjectives, but gerunds and participles are not since their N heads are empty and lack feature specification in the syntax.

In summary, late insertion of *-ing* as the PF head N of an NP predicts all the VP properties of gerunds examined in Chomsky (1970). There is no need for a special transformational or lexical rule to form gerundive nominals from VPs or IPs in DP positions, since naturally phrases projected from an N will occur where DPs do. For participles, I take it that APs and PPs are canonical structures for adjunct positions (cf. section 7.4). The analysis of present participles as headed by A in PF then correctly predicts that these structural APs are freely allowed in adjunct positions.[34]

The dual insertion level hypothesis thus allows direct expression of the following previously obscured generalizations. (i) All four uses of *-ing* result from a single entry in the Syntacticon: the insertion frame (4.55). (ii) The innovative NP gerund of Early Modern English was a natural and nearly immediate lexical extension of the Late Middle English conflation *-ing(e)* of Old English suffixes for the present participle ([$_A$ *-ende*]) and the derived nominal ([$_N$ *-ung*]).[35] (iii) The dichotomous behavior of gerunds, by which they are "externally NPs and internally VPs," and parallel facts about present participles ("externally APs and internally VPs") turn out to be consequences of UG definitions and principles. (iv) The characteristics of productive *-ing* as the first learned of English inflections and the one most uniform across dialects are due to its extremely simple lexical entry (4.55).

The possibility of empty, inert structural heads (whether overt or covert in PF) was introduced in Emonds (1991a) to account for the dual syntactic behavior of dependent *-ing* in gerunds and present participles. Throughout this work, such empty structural heads play a central role. In the case of bound morphemes, the notion of filled vs. empty right-hand head *in syntax* has additional explanatory power: the distinction separates derivation from inflection. Strikingly, the puzzling complex of syntactic properties shared by gerunds and present participles, namely the way their "internal V behavior" combines with "exterior distribution" as respectively DPs and APs, is fully predicted by their lexical insertion in PF (4.21). Gerunds and participles therefore require no other category-changing rules, principles or feature conventions. All their special properties result from an AP or DP

---

[34] We return in sections 7.5–7.6 to how the subcategorization feature +<V> can, under appropriate conditions, select either gerunds or present participles as arguments.

[35] In Chaucer's English, the parentheses in the entry (4.55) didn't yet include the first line, so there was no productive gerund matching the productive participle inherited from Old English. Emonds (1991a) briefly discusses the historical scenario.

having *a verbal lexical head throughout a syntactic derivation of LF, in-cluding at s-structure.*

4.7.2 Two levels of insertion in the syntax: derived nominals

According to the lexical model (4.9), however, dependent morphemes from the Syntacticon should be insertable not only at two levels but at three. Not only can they for example be inserted at PF (yielding inflection), but also at two distinct levels prior to Spell Out, once at deep structure and once during the syntactic derivation.

Two such constructions based on derivational morphemes are nicely illustrated in English by the distinction between what Grimshaw (1990, Ch. 3) calls complex event nominals, which derive from verbs and are "argument taking," and other homophonous nouns which "have no argument structure."[36]

Some italicized event nominals (several examples are hers) are given in (4.62).

(4.62)   a.   The frequent *expression* of one's feelings is desirable.
              We are forced to observe the constant *felling* of redwoods.
         b.   The *shooting* of rabbits is illegal.
              The *assignment* of unsolvable problems to novices is to be avoided.
         c.   I watched the instructor's deliberate *examination* of the papers.
              The *construction* of a parking garage to attract investment has backfired.

Grimshaw outlines several properties which differentiate these complex event nominals from other nouns, also observing that, "apart from a few lexicalized cases ..., nominals [formed with -*ing*] pattern perfectly as complex event nominals." (1990, 56) While uncertain about some of her diagnostics, I agree that complex event nominals (4.62) are like the verbs they are related to, in that:

---

[36] As Grimshaw shows, event nouns such as *race, trip, exam* and *event,* which semantically resemble the complex event nominals, behave rather like simple nouns. Thus, the interesting distinction is not in terms of an intuitive semantic classification ("event nominal"), but in terms of syntactic category and co-occurrence.

In some previous works by other authors, her complex event nominals are variously called mixed nominals or activity nominals.

(4.63)   a. A complement is (often) obligatory if obligatory with the corre-
sponding verb.
*The frequent expression is desirable.
*My children refuse to watch any felling.

b. Complex event nominals don't refer to concrete objects.
*That loud shooting of rabbits is illegal.
*The five-page assignment of tough problems to novices is to be
avoided.

c. Unlike many nouns, complex event nominals accept adjectives
with the sense of time, duration and frequency adverbs (4.62a).

d. Complex event nominals may indicate voluntary activities and
hence accept modifiers such as *deliberate, intentional* and
infinitival purpose clauses (4.62c).

e. They do not pluralize and can't be modified by numerals or
adjectives referring to physical objects.
*The constant shootings of rabbits are illegal.
*We were disturbed by other criminal fellings of old redwoods.
*I watched the instructor's hand-written examination of the pa-
pers.
*The dusty construction of a parking garage to attract invest-
ment has backfired.

f. Their counterparts in Spanish occur with passive agent *por*-
phrases which do not otherwise occur with nouns.[37]
El libro fue escrito por Chomsky.
'The book was written by Chomsky'
La destrucción de la ciudad por el ejercito
'The destruction of the city by the army'
Un libro { de/ *por } Chomsky
'A book by Chomsky',
'Chomsky's book'

---

[37] Grimshaw credits this observation to E. Torrego.

To exemplify how complex event nominals differ from other DPs, we may take ambiguous phrases such as *the writing* and *the city's development* and expand them as normal DPs as in (4.64) or as complex event nominals as in (4.65).

(4.64) The week's smudged ink writings are indecipherable.
We protest the city's three { high-rise/ treeless } developments with no schools.

(4.65) The quick { writing/ penning } of a letter to John Monday took only seconds.
We protest the city's constant development into the hills to attract industry.

By mixing the permitted expansions along each dimension, we can construct ungrammatical combinations (4.66).

(4.66) Those (*quick) ink writings (*to John) (*Monday) are indecipherable.
The (*week's) (*ink) penning(*s) of urgent correspondence took only minutes.
We protest the city's three (*constant) developments (*into the hills).
We protest { quick/ *high-rise/ *treeless } development to attract industry.

Because all the clear examples of complex event nominals seem to be derivationally constructed from verbal roots, these ambiguities can be expressed by hypothesizing the following contrasting deep structures.[38] (I am not concerned here with intermediate projections nor with exact placement of numerals with respect to the functional head structure above N.)

---

[38] Many nominalizations are not ambiguous. As Grimshaw notes, most gerundive nominals in *-ing* and others such as *expansion* and *arrival* have only event readings.

(4.67) Result or other non-productive nominalizations; *-ing, -ment,* etc. present at deep structure.

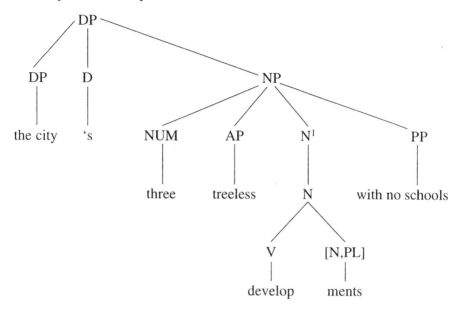

(4.68) Complex event nominals; *-ing, -ment,* etc. replace Ø during the syntax:

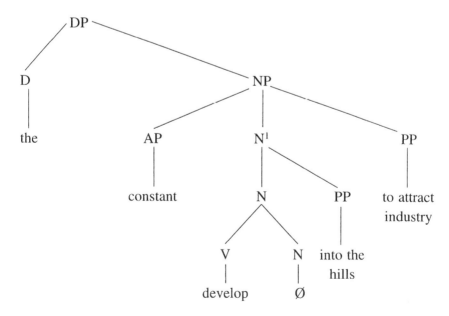

In a complex event nominal (4.68), the actual lexical head which selects at deep structure is the verbal root; the empty N is inert at this level.[39]

The properties of complex event nominals (4.63a-f) are precisely what we expect if the head of the construction is a verb and not a noun, as the reader may verify. Conversely, the negations of these properties are expected in, or at least consistent with, a phrase whose head is a noun. Thus, the contrasting trees (4.67)–(4.68) provided by the Syntacticon model (4.9), whereby a bound derivational morpheme can be inserted at different levels, *both of which precede s-structure*, provide a full and simple syntactic explanation for the six independent properties of complex event nominals listed in (4.63).

Grimshaw's treatment of complex event nominals attributes the empirical differences between (4.64) and (4.65) not to syntax but to lexical semantics. But such terminology actually masks what is going on.[40] For instance, she claims that "only the complex event nominals have the internal aspectual structure needed to license aspectual modifiers" (59). But the straightforward statement that V but not N heads license (verbal) aspect is simpler and more general.

For another example, why should noun heads having "argument structure" be somehow linked to the extreme restrictions on determiners in complex event nominals which she observes? Within her system, this correlation is an accident. But in terms of (4.67)–(4.68), an empirical claim that a V-headed phrase allows *only* a definite article or no determiner at all is natural enough; Spanish DPs with the internal form of infinitival VPs, studied in Plann (1981), are subject to exactly the same restriction. Similarly, it is not an "argument taking" property which distinguishes complex event nominals (i.e., whose lexical heads are verbs) from simple event nominals such as *John's gift of money to little children*. What characterizes complex

---

[39] This way of exploiting a possibility in the framework developed here was first suggested to me by A. van Hout. Using different terminology, earlier authors (Fraser, 1970; Ross, 1973; Walinska de Hackbeil, 1984) have claimed that V is the selecting head in complex event nominals.

[40] Grimshaw proposes that complex event nominals but not other nouns have "argument structure," an additional level of structure "constructed in accordance with the thematic hierarchy,... determined by universal principles based on the semantic properties of the arguments" (1990,7), even though "the details [of the thematic hierarchy] are obscure and/ or controversial in some places, especially with respect to the relationship between Theme and the Goal/ Source/ Location group and with respect to relationships within that group." (1990, 176) But obscure and controversial details then encompass four of the six theta roles in the hierarchy. The syntactic account here rests on no such equivocations.

event nominals is not whether arguments appear with them but rather which category "takes" the arguments: V or N.

Faced then with compelling evidence that the properties of complex event nominals stem from the fact that a V functions as their deep structure head, we must again conclude that the "lexical head of an XP" is not always rotely X^0, as an a priori approach to phrasal projections might suggest. Rather, the empty structural head in complex event nominals (4.68) is entirely inert prior to the derivational moment which associates it with a lexical item. This is expressed by (4.27), repeated here for convenience, which clearly distinguishes the *structural* head of XP (always X^0) from the *lexical* head.

(4.27)   *Lexical Head/Projection. Let Y^0 be the highest lexically filled head in Z^j. Then Y^0 is the lexical head of Z^j, and Z^j is a lexical projection of Y^0.*

For example, while the N -*ments* is the deep structure lexical head in (4.67), the deep structure lexical head of the DP in (4.68) is the verb *develop*. At any subsequent insertion levels including PF, -*ment* is the lexical head of DP in both structures.

According to the Syntacticon model, dependent forms such as -*ing* and -*ment* present at s-structure satisfy the Visibility Condition on LF (4.10) and hence realize some cognitive syntactic (interpretable) feature F. One possibility is that the suffix -*ing* carries some additional feature F_i not mentioned in (4.55) – possibly the category EV ("event") proposed by Grimshaw (1990, 64–68). Some interpretive principle more general than a single lexical entry might then link $V+F_i$ to LF "Events" and thus derive rather than stipulate that complex event nominalizations are formed only from ACTIVITY verb stems. If so, perhaps the lexical entry (4.55) should be recast into something like (4.69):

(4.55)   ing, [+N], +<V____>, ($\left\{ \begin{array}{l} \text{-AD: } V = \text{+ACTIVITY, ...} \\ \text{+AD: } V = \text{+PSYCH, or ...} \end{array} \right\}$)

(4.69)   ing, [+N], +<V____>, ({ [-AD, EVENT] / [+AD, ...] })

Another possibility is that the interpreted cognitive syntactic feature of -*ment, -ing,* etc. is N itself; i.e., that complex event nominals are indeed interpreted as *nouns*, i.e., according to whatever is the most general interpretable property of N (excluding the uninterpreted N of gerunds, which is inserted only in PF). If so, EVENT in (4.69) would be superfluous. I do not try to decide between these alternatives.

In the light of this analysis of complex event nominals, it is interesting to recall the few sentences devoted to the V-headed (or complex event) nominals based on *-ing* at the end of Chomsky's classic study of English nominalizations:

> "The discussion ... barely touched on a third category with some peculiar properties ...
> a. John's refusing of the offer
> b. John's proving of the theorem
> c. the growing of tomatoes
> These forms are curious in a number of respects, ... these forms, like derived nominals, appear to have the internal structure of noun phrases; ... On the other hand, adjective insertion seems quite unnatural in this construction. In fact, there is an artificiality to the whole construction that makes it quite resistant to systematic investigation."(Chomsky, 1970, 58)

It is now clear that the source of the "peculiar properties" resides in Chomsky's term for them: his "mixed forms" (a-c) are noun phrases whose lexical heads are verbs in deep structure but nouns in s-structure. This combination, i.e. resulting from lexical insertion neither at deep structure nor in PF but rather in the syntax, gives rise to the peculiar properties and explains them.

We have now seen how nominalization morphemes used both for complex event nominals and result nominals exemplify the differing consequences of pre-transformational insertion and insertion during the syntactic derivation, two possibilities furnished by Multi-Level Lexical Insertion (4.8) and the lexical model (4.9).

4.7.3 Two levels of insertion in the syntax: agentive nominals

A second and similar illustration of how a dependent morpheme may be inserted prior to s-structure at two different levels is provided by English animate agentive nominalizations in *-er*. A few examples suffice, since the reasoning is entirely similar to that for complex event nominals.

Certain agentive nominals formed with *-er* have highly specific meanings in the Dictionary; in such cases, *-er* is their deep structure head.

(4.70) That company employs four clever union *dispatchers* in four six-hour shifts.
I met several well-dressed local *interpreters*.

On the other hand, one can also fairly productively innovate with agentive nominals to mimic verb-headed structures within the nominal syntactic pattern of DPs:

(4.71) In your new role, you will be a frequent *dispatcher* of important packages to every corner of New York.
They need a fast *interpreter* from Italian into Slovenian.
A nervous student was selected as *introducer* of the panelists to the president.
An *opener* of mail for such a busy executive needs a lot of judgment.

As before, I propose that these productive agentive nominals in (4.71) have the deep structure form $[_N [_V \text{ } introduce] [_N \text{ } \emptyset \text{ }] \text{ }]$. The agentive suffix *-er* is then inserted not in deep structure, but during the syntactic derivation according to the Syntacticon entry (4.72).

(4.72) er, N, +< [V, ACTIVITY]___>, ANIMATE

In such cases, as with complex event nominals, various pre-head modifications which a deep structure noun would allow are unacceptable:

(4.73) The group included (*four) frequent (*union) dispatchers of important packages to large airports.
They need (*several young) interpreters from Italian into Slovenian.
We weren't impressed by that (*nervous) (*student) introducer of the panelists.
(*Extra) (*union) openers of mail for such a busy executive should be well paid.

Parallel to the complex event nominals, such nominal modifiers would require an N head *throughout* the syntactic derivation. But since the lexical head of these constructions doesn't become an N according to (4.27) until *-er* is inserted in the syntax, the noun modifiers in (4.73) are ill-formed.
A note of caution is required on how a derivation proceeds when the category of a constituent's lexical head changes. For example, it is clear that

a DP$_i$ such as *a dispatcher of important packages to large airports* is selected in a larger domain as an argument with an animate N head. Recall
from Chapter 1 that the cyclic domains are IP and DP; suppose now that DP$_i$
is to be selected by some predicate X. From what has been said the lexical
head of DP$_i$ at the start of the cycle on DP$_i$ is V, and at the end of this cycle
it is N. This is no difficulty if we adopt the technical revision of lexical
insertion first suggested in 1966 class lectures of E. Klima.

(4.74)   *Cyclic Lexical Insertion: A lexical head X imposes restrictions on
         its arguments ... only after the transformational cycle is terminated
         in all the cyclic domains properly contained inside X^{max}* (Emonds,
         1985, 98).[41]

In terms of this bottom-up procedure, the verb *dispatch* in DP$_i$ is the lexical,
argument-selecting head as the cycle on DP$_i$ begins, but by the end of this
cycle, the animate suffixal noun *-er* has been inserted and is thus the head
which determines how DP$_i$ will be selected as a constituent in a larger
structure.

We have now seen that both abstract derived nominals in *-ing, -ment,
-tion,* etc. and agentive nominals in *-er* occur in two separate patterns, as
expected in the Syntacticon model (4.9). In the lexicalized pattern listed in
Dictionary entries, the nominalizing suffixes are deep structure right-hand
head N and the nominals behave entirely like N-headed phrases. In a second, productive pattern (which is often stylistically rather stilted), the suffixes are not present at deep structure but are inserted in the syntax before
Spell Out. The V-headed deep structure of such nominals is illustrated in
(4.68). In both types of derived nominals and agentive nominals, the lexical
head at s-structure and LF is the N.

4.8   Expanded list of differences between the Dictionary and
       the Syntacticon

We have now constructed and justified in some detail a bifurcated lexical
theory (4.9) permitting insertion of bound and other grammaticalized morphemes at different levels of a syntactic derivation. Within this theory the
co-occurrence properties of these closed class items appear in a minimal and

---

[41] The proposed sequencing for the operation Merge in Chomsky (1995, section 4.3) also
has this effect.

uniform subcategorization format. Such a format easily expresses generalizations that unite derivational and inflectional morphology, such as those observed in Lapointe (1980) and Lieber (1980).

Within this framework, inflections systematically represent alternatively realized features and are inserted only in Phonological Form. The absence of inflections prior to this level permits a definition of "lexical head" (4.27) which prevents inflections from interfering with the syntax of head-complement combinations. And as section 4.7 has shown, we can use multi-level insertion based on an extremely simple Syntacticon entry to derive whole complexes of mystifying syntactic properties of particular affixes, such as those of the participial-gerund-nominalizing (category-changing) suffix *-ing*.

The following three points summarize how bound dependent morphemes, those lacking purely semantic features *f*, are inserted from the Syntacticon with different effects at three derivational levels:

(i) Deep Lexicalization. Most suffixes classically treated as derivational morphology, including those which combine with only selected lists of open class stems, can satisfy insertion contexts defined at the beginning of a transformational derivation. The meanings of their combinations with open class stems involve semantic specificity. They are lexical heads of their phrases at every stage of a syntactic derivation.

(ii) Syntactic Lexicalization. Certain more productive formations of derivational morphology, especially those which confound traditional category distinctions, are formed by inserting dependent forms during the deep to s-structure derivation. Such items are absent when the derivation begins but are both present in larger syntactic domains and interpreted at LF.

(iii) Phonological Lexicalization (4.21). Inflectional morphemes, including Romance clitics and the completely productive "phrase-changing" participial and gerundive morphemes, are inserted after Spell Out. Section 4.4.2 lists the types of inflection subsumed under PF insertion.

In contrast, open class elements from the Dictionary, whether singly or in idiomatic or productive patterns of combination, are always subject to Deep Lexicalization (4.7).

As a summary, the table below counterposes in upper case the differences between the basic items of the Dictionary and the Syntacticon introduced and justified in this and the preceding chapter.

(4.75)

SYNTACTICON
DICTIONARY   ↓

a. Items with both cognitive and purely syntactic features F:	yes	yes
b. Cognitive features F canonically realized on UG-defined hosts:	yes	yes
c. Insertion possible at the beginning of a syntactic derivation:	yes	yes
d. Grammatical categories in the inventory:	**N, V, A, P**	**ALL**
e. Items have purely semantic features _f_:	**YES**	**NO**
f. Open classes; coining and neologisms for adult speakers:	YES	NO
g. Bound forms have inherent stress and head true compounds:	YES	NO
h. Interface with non-linguistic memory and culture:	YES	NO
i. Full suppletion inside paradigms (Emonds, 1985, Ch. 4):	NO	YES
j. Certain phonetically zero morphemes (4.11):	**NO**	**YES**
k. Items must conform to core or primary vocabulary phonology:	NO	YES
l. Items with alternatively realized features (subject to 4.20)	**NO**	**YES**
m. Insertion also possible during syntax and at PF:	**NO**	**YES**

In particular, the five differences in bold in the table have been and will continue to be crucially used in the syntactic analyses of both bound and free morphemes in the chapters that follow.

Chapter 5
Passive syntactic structures

5.1 The common syntax of Verbal and Adjectival passives

An instructive example of a bound morpheme inserted at different derivational levels and exhibiting multiple syntactic behavior is the passive participle suffix *-en*. Since this morpheme interacts with so many different
points of the lexical theory developed in Chapter 4, a full analysis of passive
constructions of the type found in English requires its own chapter. I first
argue that generally accepted ideas about the contrast between verbal and
adjectival passives fail to capture their similarities, which have been obscured by so-called lexical accounts of the latter. I then propose an analysis
based on the uniform character of the bound participial suffix *-en.*

   In sections 5.2–5.4, I return to the well known differences between passive adjectives and passive verbs, and derive them from inserting the participial suffix at different derivational levels. Section 5.5 examines some
variations on the participial ("periphrastic") passive in other, particularly
Germanic languages. The entire analysis is confirmed in a final section by
the ease with which it accommodates the puzzling cross-linguistic properties of a morphologically homonymous perfect active construction.

5.1.1 The uniform Adjectival category of *-en*

The passive built around the participial morpheme notated *-en* is perhaps the
most studied inflectional construction. It is uncontroversial to claim that
typical Indo-European passive participles arc all in some sense adjectival.
Moreover, in most Germanic and Romance languages, the very same morpheme also forms an active "perfect" participle. In a research program
which reduces language-particular grammar to properties of inflections
(Borer, 1984), a lexical entry for *-en* carries the full burden of somehow
encompassing all the peculiarities of these formations in such languages.[1]

---

[1] In my view, this research program is feasible only if Borer's class of inflections is
extended to all closed class items, since roughly corresponding closed class elements of
fairly similar languages almost always differ syntactically, e.g. English vs. French: *that /
que; him / lui; will / -r-; -ed / -ai- to / à; of / de; for / pour; do / faire; have / avoir; much /
beaucoup; all / tout; there / là;* to a few hundred pairs. As we understand at most a handful

To this end, generative authors have attributed to *-en* sometimes elegant but still quite extraordinary, sui generis properties. Even as they leave aside the homonymous adjectival passives and perfect participles, Chomsky (1981, Ch. 1) and Jaeggli (1986) propose that the suffix *-en* is a "neutralized category" which "suppresses external theta roles" and/ or "absorbs case,"[2] while other authors following Baker, Johnson and Roberts (1989) pursue the notion that this suffix is itself "an argument" even though it is not nominal.

In contrast to such analyses, critically reviewed below, I would counter that the passive participle's lexical properties and those of other inflectional morphemes should be *formally similar*. Since, as seen in Chapter 4, inflectional morphemes are generally *alternative realizations*, a minimal theory of a periphrastic passive *-en* should really only have to answer one question about *-en:* what does it alternatively realize?

While the categorial status (A) of *-en* is unexceptional in many Indo-European languages, I will argue that its specificity is alternatively realizing the phi-features of an object DP. Moreover, the fact that multi-level lexical insertion of a single, simple Syntacticon entry for *-ing* successfully unifies so many superficially diverse structures (section 4.7) suggests extending this approach as well to the different participles formed from *-en*. Thus, Alternative Realization and Phonological Lexicalization are each fundamental in explaining properties of both passive and perfect constructions. While the many empirical consequences of a compact lexical statement are not easy to state briefly, we will nonetheless arrive at a final simple entry for *-en* which conforms to the restrictive lexical format (2.14).

The statement of AR (4.20) requires that any alternatively realized phi-features of $[_A en]$ must have their canonical origin on a DP sister of some A^i, i.e., that the V stem of *-en* is transitive, as in English. Moreover, such

---

of such differences, each closed class item in each language (= all entries in Syntacticons) in fact constitutes a still to be formalized language-specific parameter.

From this perspective, it can be appreciated how little we have progressed toward characterizing individual languages (i.e. what children learn). The fact that each child has several hundred "parameters to set" (i.e., closed class items to specify in its Syntacticon) provides an answer to Lasnik's (1991) "new troubling question": "How is it that a child's acquisition of language is so slow?" Until the nature of this task is better appreciated, linguists may progress even more slowly than children.

[2] In Indo-European languages whose productive morphology realizes abstract case, adjectives and participles often agree with DPs in case. Hence, passive participles are typically nominative in form. Therefore any terminology by which passives are said to "absorb" the (accusative) case of an object is unrelated to any case properties for which there is evidence.

features are unmarked *only if their canonical position is empty,* in accord with condition (4.42) on alternative realization.[3] Unmarked AR thus guarantees that the V appears with an empty object DP (or that of a stranded preposition), a fundamental property of English passives.[4] Inserting this -*en* in syntax, either at deep structure or during a derivation, then gives rise to two types of so-called "adjectival passives" (section 5.3); this term is natural enough, since the lexical head in both types is an adjective at every level. When the same morpheme is inserted rather in PF, the lexical head (4.27) remains a verb throughout the syntax and so "verbal passives" result (section 5.4).

Prior to examining the generally well known differences among passive constructions, I first justify three possibly more controversial hypotheses which unify all three subtypes of English passives: (i) the passive morpheme -*en* is always *fully adjectival,* (ii) *all passive structures involve phrasal movement in the same way,* and (iii) the lexical specification of participial -*en* indirectly causes the uniform movement.[5]

(i) Both adjectival and verbal passive participles inflect like adjectives. The adjectival properties in *both* types of passives contrast, for example, with an entirely verbal Latin finite synthetic passive (lost in Modern Romance) and the Japanese passive form -*(r)are,* which has none of that language's adjectival properties (Hasegawa, 1988; Kubo, 1992).[6] Thus, the Latin finite synthetic passive suffixes bold in (5.1) are incompatible with an auxiliary, inflecting for person (while adjectives do not) and *not inflecting*

---

[3]   The English case is unmarked; *marked* alternatively realized phi-features which allow a doubling constituent give rise to so-called transitive passives. Language-particular variations also result if these features are marked as optional; cf. section 5.5.3.

[4]   This work will not be concerned with the fact that English and Scandinavian passives permit prepositions to be stranded, i.e., that prepositions in the context V___DP appear to optionally "detach" themselves from their complement, in a way essentially unattested in the rest of the world's languages (van Riemsdijk, 1978).

[5]   My analysis of the passive here shares much with that in Ouhalla (1991, 100). In his analysis, however, passive movement results directly from his construction-specific stipulation: "Coindex PASS [-*en*] with the direct object of the verb." In my framework, this coindexation follows from alternative realization, a lexical device of considerable generality.

[6]   Thus, Japanese verbal inflections shared with -*(r)are* are -*u* 'present' and -*ta* 'past', while adjectival inflections are -*i* 'present' and -*katta* 'past'; productive verbal suffixes such as the causative -*(s)ase,* -*hajime* 'begin' etc. can follow both verbs and -*(r)are* but not adjectives; and accusatives *DP+o* can occur with verbs and -*(r)are* but not with A. My thanks to S. Ayano for clarifying these tests.

for gender or case (while adjectives do). I am grateful to V. Watts for consultation on these examples.

(5.1)   Duces boni ab uxoribus suis semper lauda**ntur** (*sunt).
Leaders good by wives their always praise-[PASS-III-PLUR] (are)
'Good leaders are always praised by their wives'

Illae mulieres in libris multis lauda**bantur** (*erant).
Those women in books many praise-[PASS-III-PLUR] (were)
'Those women were praised in many books'

Nos milites ab Caesare post bella sua lauda**mur** (*sumus).
We soldiers by Caesar after wars his praise-[PASS-I-PLUR] (are)
'We soldiers are praised by Caesar after his wars'

In notable contrast to the Latin synthetic passive, an Indo-European passive participle must inflect for number *and gender* (but not for person) in whatever constructions that language's adjectives so inflect.[7] This correlation holds equally well for the adjectival (5.2a) and verbal (5.2b) passives. In contrast, an active participle in a "composed" or "perfect" tense does not so agree (5.2c). The subject DPs of these French examples all have feminine gender.

(5.2)   a. A mon arrivée, cette porte semblait déjà repeinte.
          'At my arrival, that door seemed already repainted-FEM'
       b. Cette porte était vite   repeinte   par le locataire
          'That door was quickly   repainted-FEM by the renter
          pendant que je regardais.
          while I watched'
       c. Cette artiste a tout de même peint(*e)   seulement par nécessité.
          'That artist has all the same painted -(*FEM) only by necessity'

(ii) Both adjectival and verbal passive participles are selected by V, +___AP. In terms of external phrasal distribution, verbal passives occur as complements only to *be* and *get*, which indeed independently take AP complements. And as their name indicates, passive adjectives have an even more thoroughly adjectival distribution. Like other AP, they can be comple-

---

[7] Both German adjectives and passive participles agree with modified nouns in prenominal position but not in predicative positions. In French and Spanish, both forms agree with a modified DP in either type position.

ments of almost every intransitive V which is +___AP (+<A>), i.e., *act, appear, be, become, feel, look, remain, seem, smell, sound, stay, taste* as in (5.3a) and can serve as secondary predicates in the frame +___DP^AP (+<D (A) >) as in (5.3b).

(5.3)   a. The dish seemed too overprepared.
        Arthur remained unconvinced.
      b. Her decision made some of us very irritated.
        I often prefer vegetables uncooked.

(iii) Both types of passives have AP distribution in adjunct and other positions. Thus, they occur with the prepositional copula as in (5.4a), as adjuncts of verb phrases (5.4b) and as attributive modifiers of nouns (5.4c).

(5.4)   a. We all described him as { intelligent/ young/ unprepared/ well-trained }.
        He struck us as { quick/ pompous/ experienced/ overgrown }.
      b. Desolate and unwanted, the child spent its youth hungry and uncared for.
        Preceded by a stiff drink, chicken sushi is quite tasty taken with sake.
      c. Church bells { silent/ rung } at noon reflect the status of the church.
        Duties avoided today often come back to haunt us.

Given these adjectival properties, the right-hand headedness of English morphology (Chapter 3) dictates a partial entry for *-en* in the Syntacticon such as (5.5) and a corresponding syntactic structure (5.6) for adjectival passive participles:

(5.5)   Passive participles (partial entry): en, A, +<V___>, ...

(5.6)   Passive adjectives in syntax:
        (seem) [$_A$ [$_V$ *know*] [$_A$ *n*]] ; [$_A$ *un* [$_A$ [$_V$ *paint*] [$_A$ *ed*]]]

In accordance with the possibilities afforded by multi-level lexical insertion from the Syntacticon, (5.5) may in principle apply at three derivational levels. If its unspecified part contains some interpretable cognitive syntactic feature F, the insertion levels will be prior to Spell Out, which indeed will correspond to the two kinds of adjectival passives treated in section 5.3.

On the other hand, insertion of *-en* by Phonological Lexicalization (4.21) will yield verbal passives whose lexical heads at s-structure are V as in (5.7):

(5.7)   Passive verbs in syntax:
         (get) [$_A$ [$_V$ *know*] [$_A$ $\emptyset$]] ; [$_A$ [$_V$ *paint*] [$_A$ $\emptyset$]]

This analysis of the verbal passive in terms of PF insertion of *-en* will turn out to be a formal analog of the consensus among grammarians that a verbal passive is an inflection, while they treat adjectival passives under derivational morphology. We return to how the s-structures (5.7) predict certain properties peculiar to verbal passives in section 5.4.

5.1.2 The uniform NP Movement in all passives

I next show how transformational movement plays the same role in adjectival passives as in verbal passives: namely, it moves DPs in object positions to a subject position. Within generative syntax, it has become almost a matter of faith that adjectival passives are not derived in this way. Curiously, the burden of proof seems to be on proposing that their properties follow from syntactic principles and *don't* require theta grids or special lexical processes such as "externalization," "redundancy rules" or "theta role suppression." Nonetheless, the empirical findings of Levin and Rappaport (1986) clear the way for a straightforward syntactic treatment. Wherever the sociological burden of proof may lie, the intellectual one is then squarely on claiming that something more is needed.[8]

---

[8]   Failure to think about passive adjectives in syntactic terms might suggest that their Dictionary idiosyncrasies somehow interfere with deriving their subjects from deep objects, but it does not; Chomsky (1970) is the classic generative treatise distinguishing derivation from inflection, and yet it resolutely analyzes (possessive) subjects in derived nominals like *the tower's construction took months* as transforms of deep objects.

Incidentally, I do not claim that the same mechanism triggers passive movement and movement to possessive position. The well known different conditions on these movements have never been related to non-syntactic factors in any but the vaguest terms (the so-called "aboutness" property, undefined and meaningless to my mind).

(i)   a publication of { that issue/ last month }
       {that issue's/ last month's } publication
       We published { that issue/ last month }.
       { That issue/ *Last month } was published.

(ii)   obedience to the law, vs. *the law's obedience
        We obeyed the law, vs. The law was obeyed.

Levin and Rappaport (1986, section 2 and 3) lay to rest any idea that anything other than the deep structure direct object can correspond to the subject of a passive adjective. They show that, provided that Prepositionless Dative constructions (V-DP-DP) are transformationally derived (Emonds, 1993, is one such analysis) and that unaccusative constructions are derived from deep transitive verbs (654), an English passive adjective is built around a transitive verb whose *deep direct object DP is absent and whose subcategorization frame is otherwise respected*:

(5.8)   verb: They stuffed the feathers *(into the pillow).
         adjective: The feathers stayed stuffed *(in the pillow).

(5.9)   verb: We place our company records *(where they belong).
         adjective: Our company records are placed *(where they belong).

(5.10)   The trees { are being stripped/ look stripped } { of/ *with } bark.
         The bark { is being stripped/ remains unstripped } { from/ *on } those trees.

In stating this first generalization, the authors systematically avoid reference to syntactic structure; the closest they come, as far as I can determine, is first stating a "more basic insight: the properties of an AP headed by an adjectival passive participle are determined by the complement structure of the base verb." (637)[9]

The above contrasts do not exhaust the differences: English passives can induce stranded Ps, but possessive movement cannot; abstract nouns are often incompatible with possessive movement, as in e.g., *[the king of England's] arrest* vs. *[the destruction of London's] description*. Hence, possessive movements are not instances of the passive.

[9] Their section 4.1 explains their reticence about a syntactic account, though my view is that Chomsky (1981) finally endorsed a view he had until then been reticent about. "In accordance with the program initiated in Chomsky (1981), we eschew the explicit use of subcategorization frames in lexical entries as a representation of the complement structure of verbs." Consequently, after establishing their empirical results for adjectival passives, the second half of their essay (section 4) rephrases their result in terms of theta grids, using (or taking issue with) various competing semantic formulations. Their choice of lexical framework has made it impossible to express their main result in a natural way, namely, that adjectival passives lack exactly that overt DP licensed by a frame +___DP.

In a footnote to this passage, Stowell (1981) is said to "derive the subcategorization properties of predicates" from theta grids. More accurately, he reformulates *some* aspects of NP subcategorization in terms of theta grids. But an elementary fact such as *load* but not *spray* being obligatorily transitive is not expressed in, nor derived from, theta grids.

The authors continue that "… the theta-role assigned to the direct argument internal to the VP headed by the verb is assigned external to the AP headed by the related adjectival passive participle …" (643). Abstracting away from the semantic overlay, the syntactic import of their conclusion is straightforward: *the semantic role of a verb's deep direct object DP is assigned to the subject of the related passive adjective.* These two quotes together constitute a paraphrase of a passive relation between a direct object and a subject, and point to the presence of a DP trace in adjectival passives. Moreover, the usual motivation for what forces "NP movement" to subject position, namely the inability of an A to assign case to a DP sister, works perfectly here.[10]

I therefore conclude that passive adjectives, and not only passive verbs, are based on the presence of an empty direct object DP. With passive adjectives, this must be a *deep structure direct object,* which corresponds to the fact that -*en* is already present in the syntax as illustrated in (5.6). In accord with a well-known difference between passive verbs and passive adjectives described in Wasow (1977), the empty surface DP in a verbal passive can on the other hand correspond to any *surface* accusative, which dovetails with the proposed level of PF-insertion of -*en* in verbal passives shown in (5.7).

5.1.3 The Syntacticon entry for -*en* and NP trace

In order to offer a full analysis of English passive movement, we now need to know two things:

(5.11)   Why does the insertion of passive [$_A$ V + *en*] require an empty sister DP (which qualifies as an object of V at the level of inserting -*en*)?

(5.12)   Why must this object DP be a trace of movement to a subject position?

To answer these, I undertake to complete the partial Syntacticon entry (5.5) for -*en*.

---

[10] For passive *verbs,* the case-based analysis doesn't work, nor does it need to. Section 5.4 will analyze verbal passives as having a lexical head V capable of assigning case at s-structure. Movement in passives will be shown to have a motivation other than lack of case. Case theory then explains rather why the subject of a passive adjective always corresponds to a deep accusative, while that of a passive verb need not.

(i) Forcing a DP sister of [$_A$ V + *en*] to be empty. The entry for *-en* does not yet characterize *-en* as "passive" in any special way, and (5.11)–(5.12) are nothing more nor less than two facets of the question: what makes [$_A$ V + *en*] a passive? To account for the presence of the DP gap, I again call upon the basic principle which accounts for inflection throughout this work:

(4.20) *Alternative Realization. A syntactic feature F canonically associated in UG with category B can be alternatively realized in a closed class grammatical morpheme under X⁰, provided X⁰ is the lexical head of a sister of B^j.*

AR allows a morpheme under a head X⁰ to spell out features of one of the head's complements; accusative Romance clitics are a pertinent example. They alternatively realize a direct object's +DEF and phi-features on a morpheme bound to a verbal stem and thus by the ICP (4.35) license an empty object DP (see section 6.5 for a fuller discussion).

Along these lines, I propose that the passive inflection *-en* alternatively realizes features of an empty object DP. In particular, the most basic features of a direct object are the canonical phi-features of D (Person, Number, Gender), which I notate as ØF. Although *-en* cannot alternatively realize D itself (otherwise it would be a pronominal clitic rather than an adjectival inflectional head), it can be lexically specified for phi-features ØF as follows:[11]

(5.13) Passive participles: en, A, +<V___>, ØF, ...

Now by AR, these phi-features ØF must appear canonically on a sister of some projection of *-en*, i.e., on some DP object of [$_A$ V + *en*] marked with ØF. Moreover, the Invisible Category Principle (4.35), the companion principle to AR, licenses this DP as empty if all its features save D are alternatively realized. These principles thus predict that a DP object of a passive form *may* be empty. Finally according to (4.42), unmarked instances of AR *must* occur with some empty category, which indeed appears to hold for English *-en* .[12] These considerations together thus answer (5.11): the alternatively realized phi-features ØF in the lexical entry of *-en* ensure that a passive participle has an empty DP sister.

---

[11] A further specification in (5.13) will be necessary to prevent completely free generation of passive adjectives; some such feature is indispensable in any analysis which reflects the uncontroversial fact that they are not productive; the only fully productive English passive construction is verbal.

[12] Section 5.5 will treat language-particular variants of (5.13) which permit overt objects of some passive participles.

My approach to the licensing of passive gaps in terms of AR reflects ideas of McA'Nulty (1983), Lefebvre (1988) and Ouhalla (1991). According to Lefebvre's (2a): "agreement morphology on the past participle spells out the features of the trace of the NP governed by the past participle."[13] Ouhalla's rule for co-indexing *-en* with the verb's direct object achieves a similar effect. All three analyses account for many of the same paradigms and restrictions as my own, since all set up a structural link between a passive participle and its object. In my view however, neither McA'Nulty's feature copying nor Ouhalla's object co-indexing nor Lefebvre's Co-Case marking afford sufficient theoretical generalization. The former two rules remain construction-specific copying statements, exactly the kind of structural description which AR is designed to eliminate. Lefebvre's (1988, 238) Co-Case procedure, which marks "elements moved out of their projections with the projections they are moved out of," is explicitly limited to maximal projections which bear Case. As a mechanism for licensing empty categories, AR is vastly more general, as is shown for example by the many processes listed in section 4.4.2 which fall under its scope.

A reviewer observes that the empty category t_i in the subject position of an infinitival complement to a passivized verb as in (5.14) does not satisfy the strict sisterhood with the participle required in the formulation (4.20) of AR.

(5.14)   [$_{DP}$ That boy]$_i$ was expected [$_{IP}$ t_i to kiss her in Paris].

However, it is doubtful that there is any problem here. Consider first what counts as the lexical head of the infinitival IP in (5.14) according to the definition (4.27).

(4.27)   *Lexical Head/Projection. Let Y^0 be the highest lexically filled head in Z^j. Then Y^0 is the lexical head of Z^j, and Z^j is a lexical projection of Y^0.*

Recall that section 1.5 justifies inserting *to* under I only at PF. Hence the structure of the IP complement in (5.14) prior to movement of the lower subject is as follows:

---

[13] Lefebvre continues, "Agreement morphology may be viewed as a Case marker on the past participle thus reflecting the Case assigning properties of the past participle." Perhaps, but I don't relate movement in verbal passives to any case-assigning property of V. Note that if any "case-absorbing" morpheme were necessary for NP-movement, there would be no unaccusative or subject-raising movement.

(5.15)

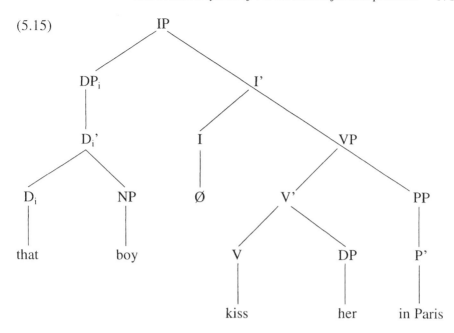

Perhaps surprisingly, but in fact exactly as needed for allowing DP$_i$ to become a passive gap, the D$_i$ *that* is the lexical head of this IP in the syntax (its own structural head is Ø).

If we now generalize AR (4.20), projections of the lexical head D of IP and *expected* in (5.14) qualify as sisters prior to movement.

(5.16) *Generalized Alternative Realization. A syntactic feature F canonically associated in UG with category B can be alternatively realized in a closed class grammatical morpheme under X^0, provided X^0 and B^0 are each the lexical heads of two sister constituents.*

Since the [$_A$ -*en*] suffix of *expected* in (5.14) is the lexical head of a sister of a lexical projection of D$_i$, it may alternatively realize the phi-features of D$_i$.

More generally, it appears that an overt subject furnishes a non-finite IP with the latter's lexical head.[14] As a result, an overt subject of an infinitive becomes available for generalized AR relations with sisters of that clause. Though this extension of AR is suggestive and doesn't bring to mind any immediate problems, I will not use it further without specific mention.

---

[14] What counts as the complement in LF is not its lexical head, but the phrasal configuration itself (here IP). Since the lexicon does not use phrases (by the Lexical Interface Principle 2.13), the whole purpose of constructing them in the syntactic computation is to make them available in LF.

(ii) Why the empty DP sister of [$_A$ V + *en*] is a trace. I turn now to answering (5.12), why the empty object DP in both types of passives must be a trace of movement to subject.[15] Co-indexing between DPs is normally a necessary condition for phi-feature agreement, so it seems plausible to assume that the lexical entry (5.13) for passive participles implies co-indexing between the participle and the direct object.

But now, the *category* of passive participles has an important consequence that has basically played no role in prior generative accounts: the participle's adjectival status brings about a *second co-indexing* between it and the subject DP, like any other adjective in the Romance and Germanic systems under consideration. That is, in s-structure, an A and its AP (as a special case, a passive participle) are co-indexed with its subject DP as follows:

(5.17)

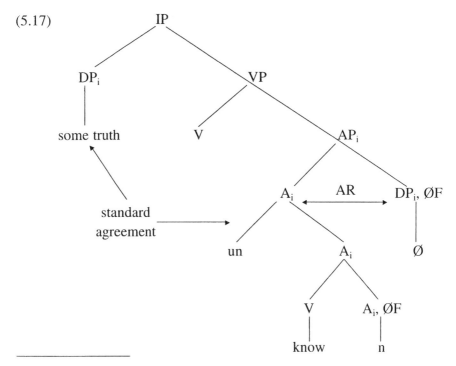

---

[15] Here, as in McA'Nulty's and Lefebvre's accounts, NP traces have phi-features. Romance floating quantifers clearly agree with traces of NP:

French: Les filles me semblaient   avoir déjà toutes [FEM, PLUR] perdu leur argent.
Italian: Le ragazze mi sono sembrata aver giá tutte [FEM, PLUR] perduto il loro denaro.
         'The girls seemed to me   to have already all   lost   their money.'

But now the participle – object co-indexation induced by the lexical entry (5.13), together with transitivity of co-indexing, *derives* the obligatory subject – object co-indexing of passive structures.[16] That is, this characteristic co-indexing of all passive transforms is guaranteed by the lexical entry for -*en* itself, which links the category A (co-indexed with the subject) with explicit alternatively realized phi-features (co-indexed with the object). Moreover, the entry (5.13) for -*en* specifies nothing other than this – i.e., it is a minimal and elegant representation of the passive property.

The final step in answering (5.12) is provided by Chomsky's (1981) Binding Theory: an empty object co-indexed with the subject of its clause must be the trace of that subject; alternatively, it must be in the same chain as that subject (Brody, 1995).[17]

We have now seen that adjectival and verbal passives both involve an identical adjectival suffix -*en* and that both involve "NP movement" from object to subject position. In the next section, we will see that the differences between the two constructions follow from the level of insertion of -*en;* adjectival passives result from the presence of -*en* in syntax and verbal passives from its absence.

In the present analysis, the only stipulation concerning passives in English – or any similar system with adjectival passive participles – is that -*en*

The presence of canonical phi-features on DP traces is thus a welcome consequence of analyzing passive participles as alternatively realizing such features.

[16] The object trace in a participle-based passive cannot arise independently of a co-indexed participle. That is, the trace is not the cause of the co-indexed chain, but rather vice-versa. This suggests that any landing site of "A-movement" must be preliminarily marked as an already co-indexed site, akin to the scope markers of "A-bar landing sites" in theories developed by H. van Riemsdijk and E. Williams. Such analyses automatically solve a rarely addressed problem: how movement manages to create a pair of indices from a single one in the input.

All this may suggest that co-indexing in chains is determined independently of movement, thus impressionistically supporting Brody's (1995) non-movement chain theory.

[17] One does not need all the classical Binding Theory to derive this result; in particular, Principle A can be circumvented. Principles B and C combined imply (i), where lexical anaphors, however they are to be analyzed, provide the only exceptions:

(i)   If @ binds ß and if @ and ß are assigned separate theta roles, then @ is outside the governing category of ß, i.e., @ c-commands the lowest subject binding ß.

Now suppose that ß is an object whose phi-features are realized by -*en*, and let @ be the subject of -*en*. This violates the consequent of (i) so either @ does not bind ß, or @ and ß are assigned a single theta role. But with @ and ß chosen as above @ must bind ß, so they must be assigned a single theta role, i.e., ß is the trace of @.

is the unique suffix of category A in the Syntacticon which alternatively realizes phi-features.[18] In every other respect, *-en* is a full-fledged adjectival right-hand head, requiring no mention of any further semantic or syntactic property related to theta roles, case or argument structures.

5.2 Differences between Verbal and Adjectival passives

I will contend here that the insertion levels of the Syntacticon entry for *-en* (5.13) account for the differences between the adjectival and verbal passives documented for example in Wasow (1977).

(i) A defining difference: ongoing vs. completed activity. A special interpretive property distinguishes between the two passives and somewhat limits the productivity of passive adjectives. Traditional as well as generative grammarians have long observed that the adjectives have a sense of completed action not shared with passive verbs, as in (5.18):

(5.18)   The door { remained/ was } closed during the noon hour.
                                        (Adj: door closed by noon)
         The door { got/ was } closed during the noon hour.
                                        (V: door can be open at noon)
         John { seems/ is } (*being) very (un)satisfied.
                                        (Adj: satisfaction already obtained)
         John is { getting/ being } (*very) (*un)satisfied.
                                        (V: satisfaction still on the way)
         The door looked (un)painted.   (Adj: painting complete)
         The door is being (*un)painted.   (V: painting incomplete)

Certain verbs of manner are incompatible with this completive sense and hence do not appear in adjectival passives. These verbs thus become diagnostics for verbal passives just as most linking verbs (*seem, remain,* etc.) are diagnostics for adjectival passives:[19]

---

[18] The definition of Alternative Realization (4.20) guarantees the phi-features in the entry (5.13) are those of a direct object. Although any A agrees in phi-features with its subject *in PF*, such features (±FEM,±PLUR) are still canonical features of D not of A. Hence they can appear on A at s-structure only by virtue of Alternative Realization.

[19] Reflection on these examples shows that the restriction in (5.19) does not depend on the theta roles of the surface subjects. In any case, Levin and Rappaport (1986) demonstrate that the well-formedness of adjectival passives is independent of this latter factor.

(5.19) *New York seems (very much) { *approached / left* } in the tourist season.

*That good dinner felt { *preceded / followed* } by too much drink.

*Many polluted cities remain { *(un)avoided / escaped* } during the summer.

*The clay looked { *handed* to the customers / *pressed* into a bowl }.

*The basketball sounded { *dribbled* across the floor / *thrown* against the wall }.

This sense of completed action seems to be nothing other than a general sense of "having a property," which is a sort of minimal and undifferentiated interpretation for an adjectival construction.[20] That is, A itself seems to be the cognitive syntactic feature in the entry (5.13) which contributes to LF interpretation of passive adjectives but not passive verbs.

In the general case, most affixes of derivational morphology do not "double" in this way as inflections not interpreted in LF. This suggests that a *marked* property of a morpheme in the Syntacticon can be a sort of "cancellation" of its most basic categorial interpretation. Another instance of this is probably the marked Absence of Content feature -LOCATION which has been earlier assigned to P such as *of*. In this way, *-en* can be assigned an Absence of Content feature -PROPERTY, where the relation between A and PROPERTY is the same as between P and LOCATION. The unmarked interpretation of A at LF is thus +PROPERTY, while the Absence of Content feature -PROPERTY leads to PF insertion.[21]

(5.20) Passive participle entry: en, A, +<V___>, ØF, (-PROPERTY)

A formally more interesting and restrictive notation would be to list categories which can be deprived of their usual interpretive contribution as

---

[20] Two subcases of adjectival properties, the stage level and the individual level, while lexical in English, seem linked to different structures in Japanese (Kubo, 1994, Ch. 8). She argues that these more specific "constructional meanings" of adjectives result in LF from A syntactically incorporating into other categories such as I and C.

[21] A question arises as to whether the PF insertion of *-ing* in section 4.7.1 requires a marked Absence of Content feature. I tentatively conclude no, based on the fact that *-ing* is associated only with a feature +N rather than a fully specified category.

Recall here also the general condition determining when nodes are interpretable:

(4.10) LF Visibility Condition. A node is interpreted at LF if and only if it is either realized as a lexical morpheme, or is co-indexed with an interpreted structure of the same category.

"optional," as in (5.21). Of course, this would mean that the category is optionally interpreted in LF, not that it is absent. I will not pursue this possibility here, however.

(5.21)   Alternative passive participle entry: en, (A), +<V___>, ØF

The full Syntacticon entry (5.20) or (5.21) now explains not only the different interpretations of passives but also has the following structural consequence (5.22).

(5.22)   In adjectival passives, the head [$_A$ -*en*] *is present in LF and at Spell Out*. In verbal passives, -*en* is absent in the syntactic derivation and LF, *being present only at PF*.

This insertion-level distinction is the basis of my account of all the syntactic differences between adjectival and verbal passives, which I now take up in turn.

(ii) Various SPEC(AP) freely modify only adjectival passives. Most adjectival modifiers require that a lexical A be present throughout a derivation, which matches the fact that certain nominal modifiers have a parallel requirement for a lexical N (section 4.7.1). As predicted by (5.22), these SPEC(AP) can't appear in verbal passives.

(5.23)   The garden seemed too overplanted.
         The garden is being (*too) overplanted.

(5.24)   New York remains more affected by strikes than other cities.
         *New York is more avoided by tourists than other cities.

(5.25)   too irritated, how oppressed, very satisfied, so scared, etc.
         *too approached, *how followed, *very avoided, *so dribbled, etc.

(iii) Only adjectival passives accept the adjectival prefix *un-*. This observation is from Siegel (1973). As *un-* clearly contributes to LF, it must be inserted in the context +___A prior to Spell Out, where A is lexicalized. By (5.22), it can't appear in verbal passives.

(5.26)   uncut, unknown, unpainted, unrewarded, unsatisfied

(5.27)   *unleft, *unpreceded, *unavoided, *unhanded, *undribbled

(iv) Only verbal passives have the full internal structure of VPs. A verbal passive VP is just like an active VP except that the passive VP contains one trace replacing a "passivized" DP (5.28); the presence of other (italicized) DP complements is irrelevant. But adjectival passive VPs tolerate no overt internal DP (5.29).

(5.28)   Peter was (being) forgiven *his sins.*
         Peter's sins were (being) forgiven *him.*
         Those workers were (being) allowed *a lot of vacation.*
         He was (being) charged *a lot of money.*
         Ann was given *the letter.*
         That letter { was/ got } sent *all the candidates.*
         Who got taken *such unfair advantage* of?
         How much unfair advantage was taken of *Bill?*

(5.29)   *Peter felt forgiven *his sins.*
         *Peter's sins stayed forgiven *him.*
         *Those workers seemed allowed *a lot of vacation.*
         *He felt charged *a lot of money.*
         *Ann seemed given *the letter.*
         *That letter remained unsent *all the candidates.*
         *Who acted taken *such unfair advantage* of?
         *How much unfair advantage looked taken of *Bill?*

Since the V in a verbal passive is the lexical head of the VP, it can assign case within the VP. However, the V in an adjectival passive is not the lexical head, as is clear in (5.22), and so no DP complement in this construction can receive case from V. This striking distinction between the two types of passives has been glossed over repeatedly in proposals for attributing passive movement to the Case Filter.[22]

---

[22] Government and Binding attempts to motivate passive NP-movement by lack of case imprecisely invoke the adjectival character of passive participles. But what Chomsky (1981, 50) proposes formally for passive verbs is a special "neutralized" category *between* adjectives and verbs, "unspecified for ±N," which ends up not assigning case only by stipulation. Recall that [-N] is the general case assigner and that [+N] doesn't assign case, so the question is, does "unspecified for ±N" assign case or not? Chomsky (1981, 50) proposes that passive participles are [+V, unspecified for N] and *don't* assign case, whereas on p. 51, it is suggested that *of* is [-V, unspecified for N] and *does*. Hence, the ad hoc "neutralized category" (unspecified for N), encompassing only *of* and *-en*, fails to yield a natural class of case assigners (one somehow related to [-N]).

(v) Idiomatic object nouns occur freely only in verbal passives. Transparent Derivational Heads (4.48) from section 4.6 combines with (5.22) to account for this property of passive adjectives.

(4.48)   *Transparent Derivational Heads. If a lexical suffix @ on X at Spell Out selects no complements, then (i) the lowest argument c-commanding @ and (ii) any lower arguments may be interpreted as the corresponding arguments of X.*

Though any *-en* can alternatively realize the phi-features of nouns in idiomatic non-argument complements (e.g. in *a great deal was made of* and *advantage was taken of)*, (4.48) implicitly disallows any LF relation other than argumenthood between a DP and a derived V in a passive adjective. That is, an intervening *-en* prevents any relation between a verb stem and other elements specified in Dictionary idioms. Therefore, while a (PF-inflected) verbal passive may occur in an idiom, a (derived) adjectival passive may not:

(5.30)   A great deal { was (being) made/ got made/ *sounded made } of your resignation.
          No attention { is being paid/ gets paid/ *seems paid } to minor officials.
          Some advantage may finally { be/ *feel } taken of our new wealth.
          Was justice done in that war?
          *How done was justice in that war?

This theoretical account in terms of multi-level lexical insertion has now explained the properties of adjectival passives treated in Wasow (1977): their regular AP distribution (section 5.1), their completive interpretation (i), their potential modifiers (ii)–(iii), and their incompatibility with a range of structures which occur within VP (iv)–(v).

(vi) Only verbal passives have an overt or understood structural subject. A final characteristic of adjectival passives observed in Wasow (1977) also follows from the above analysis: the absence of even an understood subject for the verb stem in adjectival passives. There are two ways a DP might be interpreted as such a subject : either by the structural definition of subject (1.15) in Chapter 1 or by the mediation of Transparent Derivational Heads (4.48). The verbal stems of passive adjectives fail to have subjects by either route.

(a) Structurally, the adjectival passive participles have the form (5.6) at s-structure, i.e. their A head -en is already lexicalized, and so the V they contain *does not satisfy the definition of a lexical head* (4.27) at s-structure.

(5.6)   Passive adjectives in syntax:
   (seem) [$_A$ [$_V$ *know*] [$_A$ *n*]] ; [$_A$ *un* [$_A$ [$_V$ *paint*] [$_A$ *ed*]]]

Since Generalized Subjects (1.15) and the Extended Projection Principle (1.17) apply only to *head* V rather than to V in general, they simply don't apply inside X^0 to the V in passive adjectives. That is, since the V stem inside a passive adjective is not a head at any level, it lacks a purely structural subject. Instead, it resembles the subjectless Vs in compounds and derived morphology, as in ***meeting** place, **think** tank, **go** cart, **infestation, bereavement***, etc.

(b) Given the proposed levels of insertion of -en, Transparent Derivational Heads as formulated in (4.48) will apply to all (and only) adjectival passives where -en is present at Spell Out. In a passive AP, the lowest DP argument c-commanding @ = -en is the trace in object position, which is then correctly interpreted as the direct object of that V. But by implication, (4.48) simultaneously *suppresses any possible argument relation between V and a higher external argument*, whether it be an overt *by*-phrase or covert PRO. We thus have a complete account for why adjectival passives lack any type of external argument.

This section has provided a full syntactic account of passive adjectives of the form [$_A$V-*en*]. The DP sister of A alternatively realized by -en is the direct object of its verbal base; since this object must be empty and co-indexed with A and hence with A's subject, it necessarily exemplifies the "Move NP" subcase of transformational movement. The fact that the -en of a passive adjective is present at s-structure and hence LF sets up a kind of partial immunity between its verbal base and the surrounding syntactic structure (thereby excluding understood subjects and idiomatic combinations). This immunity was formulated in the previous chapter as Transparent Derivational Heads (4.48).

A contrasting late insertion of -en explains why verbal passives, even though they exhibit adjectival morphology and some distributional characteristics of adjectives, fail the adjectival tests in (i)–(iii). However, we still need to account for certain special properties of passive verbs which have been overlooked in the literature. I return to using PF insertion of -en to explain them in section 5.4.

5.3 Two insertion levels in syntax: two types of passive Adjectives

Some passive adjectives are full-fledged open class A with purely semantic features *f* in their Dictionary entry. These features relate them to, and sometimes differentiate them from corresponding verbs. Consider for example adjectives such as *(un)attracted to* and *tired of.* The lack of productive correspondences in (5.31)–(5.32) strongly suggests that they can be derived from the verbs *attract* and *tire* only through further dictionary specification.

(5.31)   Last year, cultural events attracted { Sam/ new investment } (to large cities).
　　　　*Last year, Sam appeared attracted.
　　　　*Last year, new investment appeared attracted to large cities.
　　　　Last year, Sam appeared attracted to large cities.

While the open class base verb *attract* requires neither an animate object nor an obligatory indirect object, it seems that the passive adjective formed from it does. These particularities are to be stated in the Dictionary as deep structure lexical insertion contexts of this adjective.

(5.32)   Long speeches tire me (*of this kind of meeting).
　　　　I feel { very/ rather } tired (of this kind of meeting).

The open class verb *tire* does not subcategorize for an *of*-phrase, but its derived passive adjective *tired* does. In this way, *tired* can select two complements, one an Animate DP inherited from its base verb and the second an *of*-phrase of its own.

　　As expected in the lexical model (4.9), the Dictionary can use any form in the Syntacticon, here *-en*, to further elaborate open class entries. The passive adjectives *attracted* and *tired* can therefore be listed in the Dictionary along with their base verbs @, ß in the formats (5.33)–(5.34). We can assume that derived forms, unless lexically marked to the contrary, inherit the features of the base form in each entry. Consequently, since the category of *-en* is A and right-hand headedness within X^0 is predictable, these are not stipulated separately in every Dictionary entry.

(5.33)   Basic Dictionary entry @ for V: attract, V, +<D>, +(<to^D>), +*f*, …
　　　　Related derived entry:　　　　　(un)+@+en, +<ANIM>, <to^D>

(5.34)   Basic Dictionary entry ß for V: tire, V, +PSYCH, +LOC,
                                            +<ANIM>, +*f*, ...
         Related derived entry: ß + en, +(<of^D>)

Recall from Chapter 2 that any V such as *tire* whose object is a Ground (i.e.
an "Experiencer" with psychological predicates) has a +LOC feature. Except for the uninvestigated purely semantic features *f*, the format of these
dictionary entries is sparse and succinct, with no ad hoc symbols or tell tale
repetitions forced by inadequate theorization.

Additionally, note that these particular passive adjectives allow a range
of SPEC(AP), which confirms that the lexical head of the construction is A
throughout the syntactic derivation.

(5.35)   Sam appeared { very/ too/ less } { attracted to/ tired of } large
         cities last year.
         How unattracted to large cities did he sound?
         I feel rather tired of this kind of meeting.
         As tired of this kind of meeting as she looks, she always signs up
         for more.

A third example of a passive adjective in the Dictionary is provided by
strewn. In my speech, the base verb *strew* requires that its direct object must
be a Figure rather than a Ground, even though both roles must be present
(5.36). These restrictions are peculiarly reversed for the passive adjective
strewn (5.37).[23]

(5.36)   *The children were strewing daisies.
         *They were strewing the path (with daisies).
         The children were strewing daisies across the path.

(5.37)   *The path looks strewn.
         The path looks strewn with daisies.
         *The daisies look strewn across the path.

---

[23] The examples in (5.36–5.37) show that both the base and derived forms *strew(n)* share
subcategorization for obligatory PP, independently of where theta roles are located.

By the theory and terminology of Chapters 2 and 3, this type of transitive V is subcategorized for a PP via +<P> and carries the unmarked V value -LOCATION, which causes its object to be interpreted as Figure. In contrast, the dictionary entry for the derived passive adjective has a marked inherent feature value +LOCATION; the interpretive principles of sections 2.4 and 2.5 then properly locate the theta roles.

(5.38) Basic Dictionary entry @ for V: strew, V, +<D>, +<P>, +*f*, ...
        Related derived entry: @ + en, +LOCATION

In contrast to dictionary adjectives such as *attracted, tired* and *strewn*, other passive adjectives seem formed productively from certain verb classes; exactly which subclasses of verbs allow this requires further study. In such cases, the passive adjectives share the same range of complements as their verbal bases.

(5.39) That light seems switched off.
        Mary remains persuaded to take the risk.
        The books look loaded onto the truck.

And at the same time, these more productively formed passive adjectives do not accept a range of SPEC(AP) modifiers.

(5.40) That light seems { *very/ *rather/ *more } switched off.
        Mary remains { *so/ *less/ *too } persuaded to take the·risk.
        The books look { *so/ *very/ *too } loaded onto the truck.

The restriction in (5.40) suggests that the categorial status of the lexical head changes during the syntactic derivation, as with the complex event (in *-ing*) and agentive nominals (in *-er*) of section 4.7. Consequently, these passive adjectives are compatible with neither SPEC(AP) nor SPEC(VP) modifiers. They are thus distinguishable from fully lexicalized passive A by virtue of the fact that their s-structure head [$_A$ -*en*] is inserted during the syntactic derivation. Prior to this at deep structure, the lexical head (4.27) of the passive forms in (5.39) is V, and hence these forms select complements like their corresponding verbal base.

We here see a third instance of a bound morpheme inserted in two different ways prior to s-structure in accordance with the lexical model (4.9). The keystone of these accounts is the claim (4.27) that the *lexical head* of a Z^i at a given level is not always Z^0, but can rather be some X^0 other than

Z^0, provided X^0 is the highest lexically filled zero-level category in ZP. Empirical properties divide passive adjectives into two such types, one in which their suffix *-en* is a right-hand adjectival head in deep structure (5.35)–(5.37), and a second one (5.39) in which the same *-en* is inserted under an empty structural right-hand head in the syntax. It is these empirical differences, like those between two types of derived and agentive nominals, which confirm the appropriateness of postulating not just two, but three insertion levels in the Syntacticon model (4.9).

5.4 The Verbal (inflectional) passive

5.4.1 Explaining the Verbal passive with PF insertion

In sections 5.1 and 5.2, I argued that the English Syntacticon specifies the passive participle by (5.20) and that inserting *-en* interpreted as a PROPERTY (i.e. by ignoring the parenthesized, marked Absence of Content feature) accounts for all syntactic and interpretive properties of adjectival passives.

(5.20) Passive participles: en, A, +<V___>, ØF, (-PROPERTY)

The phi-features ØF on the A headed by *-en* alternatively realize features whose canonical position is on a DP sister of this A, i.e. the stem verb's direct object.

The contrasting verb vs. adjective interpretations in section 5.2 also showed that the category A over *-en* plays no role in the LF of verbal passives, which lack a "completive sense." This then leads to the conclusion that verbal passives result from Phonological Lexicalization of (5.20), i.e., from ignoring the interpretative feature PROPERTY. Thus, in deriving verbal passives, *-en* is not present under A in the syntax, as exemplified in (5.42).

(5.41) Mary will { be/ get } shown many letters.

(5.42)   Verbal passive structure; $\emptyset F_i = [\pm FEM, \pm PLUR]_i$, omitting irrelevant X' nodes:

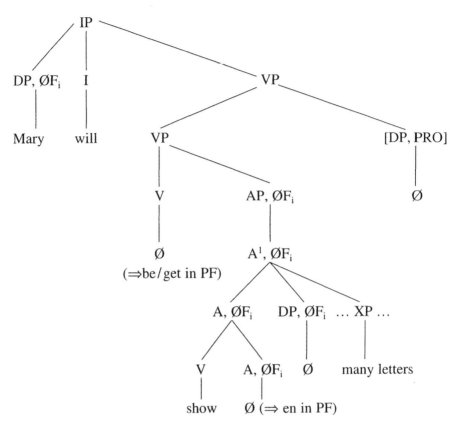

I can now show how the PF insertion option of (5.20), in conjunction with
independently justified principles of grammar, completely explains seven
syntactic properties of the English verbal passive. The properties recalled in
(i)–(iii) have already been mentioned in the discussion of adjectival passives.

(i) Verbal passives have adjectival morphology. The phi-features $\emptyset F$ on
the adjective *-en* are co-indexed with and hence agree with the adjective's
subject, as is morphologically signaled in Romance languages. Since these
$\emptyset F$ are D features which are alternatively realized, a morpheme which spells
them out appears only in PF.

(ii) Verbal passives lack adjectival Specifiers. Lexical specifiers in e.g.,
SPEC(XP) require that X be lexically filled throughout a derivation (section

4.7.1). The absence of -en in the position of A at syntactic levels therefore explains why verbal passives do not tolerate adjectival prefixes such as -un or specifiers such as *very, too,* etc.

(iii) Verbal passives tolerate idioms. Since the lexical head of the verbal passive is V at every syntactic level, by (4.27), it is natural that verb-object idioms such as *make a big deal of* and *take advantage of* occur freely in verbal passives.

(iv) Obligatory expressed or understood agent. Since V in (5.42) is a lexical head (4.27), the Extended Projection Principle (1.17) requires that it have a structural external argument. But because the direct object in all passives must be a co-indexed trace of NP-movement (cf. section 5.1.3), SPEC(IP) is its antecedent and hence unavailable as a separate argument of the V. The required external argument must therefore be realized as covert PRO or "less economically" in a PP as an overt *by*-phrase. The reasoning here is similar to that of Ouhalla (1991, 101). Section 10.4 develops this in more detail.

(v) Internal structure of verbal passives. One might well ask, why do verbal passives have this name, if their head is adjectival? They can only be called verbal because they head phrases which *have the internal structure of VPs.*[24] It is a commonplace that a verbal passive is identical to an active VP except that a passive contains one trace of a "passivized" DP. In fact, in contrast to adjectival passives, different DP complements can be candidates for NP-movement in a verbal passive, with any DPs which don't move remaining overtly realized inside VP. A variety of verbal passives containing overt DPs have been exemplified above in (5.28).

The present analysis easily accounts for such active-passive parallels because in thc verbal (as opposed to the adjectival) passive, *the selecting lexical head in the derivation from deep structure through LF is a full-fledged V and hence can assign case.* This difference between passive verbs and passive adjectives, unavailable in government and binding accounts which deny that passive verbs can assign case, is precisely what accounts for contrasts in double object constructions in (5.28)–(5.29), repeated here for convenience.

---

[24] In fact, Fassi-Fehri (1993) reserves the term verbal passive for Arabic constructions more akin to the Latin synthetic passive, and refers to the Arabic counterpart of an English "verbal passive" as an adjectival passive, precisely because it is internally verbal but externally adjectival.

(5.28)   Peter was (being) forgiven *his sins*.
Peter's sins were (being) forgiven *him*.
Those workers were (being) allowed *a lot of vacation*.
He was (being) charged *a lot of money*.
Ann was given *the letter*.
That letter { was/ got } sent *all the candidates*.
Who got taken *such unfair advantage* of?
How much unfair advantage was taken of *Bill*?

(5.29)   *Peter felt forgiven *his sins*.
*Peter's sins stayed forgiven *him*.
*Those workers seemed allowed *a lot of vacation*.
*He felt charged *a lot of money*.
*Ann seemed given *the letter*.
*That letter remained unsent *all the candidates*.
*Who acted taken *such unfair advantage* of?
*How much unfair advantage looked taken of *Bill*?

It follows that complement structures inside verbal passives and correspond-ing active verb phrases are identical, modulo the fact that one DP comple-ment in the former is a trace. The suggestion in Chomsky (1981) that a second overt object in passive verb phrases (5.28) receives some kind of "inherent case" in fact comes down to having (only) passive verbs assign case, since the related passive adjectives in (5.29) clearly cannot.

More generally, structural cases should always be assigned *optionally*, along lines detailed in Emonds (1985, Ch. 1); then when an object DP doesn't receive case from V and an appropriate landing site is available, DP may move to get case. The guarantee that a V-headed passive phrase con-tains an empty object DP is therefore not related to case. It is rather the obligatory presence in English of unmarked *alternatively realized phi-fea-tures* on [$_A$-*en*], which force the Invisible Category Principle (4.35) to license an empty DP.[25]

(vi) Verbal passives lack VP distribution. Although the category of a verbal passive in traditional English and Romance grammars is "participle," which typically refers to adjectival distribution, generative grammar seems to have overlooked the fact that verbal passives don't share the external distribution of verb phrases.

---

[25] Section 5.5 provides an account of impersonal passives with overt objects or no objects found in different Germanic languages (cf. Vikner, 1995, Ch. 6).

(5.43)   The boy will [$_{VP}$ { take/ *taken } the letter].
         He hoped to [$_{VP}$ { give/ *given } lots of presents].
         Mary went on [$_{VP}$ { speaking/ *spoken to } in French].
         For children to [$_{VP}$ { study/ *examined } often] is important.
         We let John [$_{VP}$ { examine us for stress/ *examined for stress by a
         nurse }].

The analysis here explains this lack of VP distribution straightforwardly;
because verbal passives are APs, they cannot appear in the characteristic VP
positions in (5.43).

(vii) Verbal passives allow only two auxiliaries. A related limitation on
verbal passives, which research seems to have ignored, concerns this *extremely restricted external distribution*. The problem to be solved is why
only two grammatical V *be* and *get* and no other predicates can select
passive verbs as complements. The problem divides into two questions:

(5.44)   How do these two grammatical V select verbal passives?

(5.45)   How is it that no other V or P do so?

Assuming that lexical insertion proceeds upwards in a tree, once *-en* is
inserted under A in PF, the resulting structure can then be selected by *a verb
which is itself inserted in PF and moreover subcategorized by the feature
+<A>* (+__AP). Now a consequence of Phonological Lexicalization (4.21)
is that verbs with semantic content cannot be inserted in PF; the next
chapter will furnish more empirical support for this. In fact, *be* and *get* are
the only verbs with the frame +<A> which additionally appear to lack
interpretable features.[26] Hence *be* and *get* are lexicalized subsequent to PF-

---

[26] It is unproblematic that *be* has no LF features and so undergoes Phonological
Lexicalization (4.21); see section 4.5 for arguments to this effect.

One might conclude that *get* has an interpretable feature, since some verbs which lack
passive adjectives (cf. 5.19) do not appear in "*get*-passives" (i), although others do (ii):

(i)   *The mountains got {reached /avoided } during the night.
      *Some storms are getting predicted on the news.
      *Few prisoners got thought to be dangerous.
      *New York gets { approached / left } in the tourist season.
      *A good dinner might get { accompanied / followed } by too much drink.
      *Many polluted cities get { avoided / escaped } during the summer.

insertion of *-en* and can take any AP complements headed by *-en*; this answers (5.44). Moreover, verbs inserted in PF cannot assign semantic roles (in government and binding terms, their subjects are "theta-free positions"), so the subject DPs of *be* and *get* can serve as landing sites for NP-movement, i.e., bind an object trace.

This answer to (5.44) implies that a verbal passive structure results only from PF selection of *an A which is filled after Spell Out*. Question (5.45) about the restricted distribution of verbal passives can therefore be rephrased as a more general one about empty A:

(5.46)   Why is the verbal passive configuration [$_A$ lexical V + [$_{A, \varnothing F}\varnothing$]] an unselectable complement structure (at all levels)?

That is, why do no predicates (other than the PF-inserted "passive auxiliaries" just discussed) take verbal passive complements? The answer is provided by a principle (5.47) to be developed in Chapter 7, which more fully specifies the role of empty structural heads in selection.[27]

(5.47)   *Condition on Selection. If a subcategorization frame +<[X, F$_i$]> is satisfied by ZP, any features in ZP not licensed by the lexical head X must be stipulated among the F$_i$.*

This condition can explain why a verbal passive is never selected prior to PF, where its lexical head becomes [$_A$ *-en*]. In order for the configuration in (5.46) with an empty A and phi-features to be a complement, (5.47)

(ii)   The clay got {handed to the customers / pressed into the cup }.
        The basketball got {dribbled across the floor/ thrown against the wall }.

But it would be wrong to conclude that a grammatical element (i.e. *get*) whose presence is conditioned by a semantically interpretable (LF) feature must itself be the locus of this interpretation. A little reflection shows that phi-feature agreements on adjectives, the dependence of *many* and *much* on the count/ mass distinction, and the choice of *than* or *as* for introducing English comparative clauses do not imply that these secondary agreements are themselves meaningful. These grammatical distinctions depend on the presence of some interpreted cognitive syntactic feature F, but are not meaningful in themselves. Thus, the fact that the passive auxiliary *get* is incompatible with certain passive verbs does not imply that *get* itself is interpreted in LF.

[27] I indicate here one other justification of (5.47). An indirect object with the deep form [$_{PP}$[$_{P, PATH}\varnothing$] DP] is typically selected by the features +<[D, PATH]>. But we don't want an empty P thus selected to be able to spell out any feature (e.g. SOURCE) other than the one specified in the frame itself.

requires that it be selected by a contextual frame +<[V, ØF]>; it is un-surprising that lexical entries typically don't use such a complex selection feature, i.e. a complement headed by a verb with phi-features. In fact, phi-features such as Person and Gender rarely enter even into selection of DPs, which are their canonical hosts. Consequently, predicates do not select a passive V until -*en* is *actually present in the tree in PF*. Since -*en* in the verbal passive is inserted late, so must be any V (*be* and *get*) which select them.

This analysis of verbal passives in terms of PF Lexicalization (4.21) thus succeeds in explaining why *only* PF-inserted *be* and *get* are passive "aux-iliaries." In earlier accounts, they must have had an ad hoc property such as selecting a special passive-type phrase. Restricting landing sites to "theta-free" positions has previously provided no principled reason why *seem, appear, become,* etc. are not possible additional "auxiliaries" for the verbal passive. In the present account this follows from the simple fact that these verbs have features used in LF and hence are present prior to Spell Out, while *be* and *get* are not.

Summarizing, we have now seen how English and Romance passive morphemes can be inserted either pre-transformationally or during the syn-tactic derivation (yielding the two types of passive adjectives analyzed in section 5.3) or during the phonological derivation (yielding verbal passives).

(5.20)   Passive participle entry: en, A, +<V___>, ØF, (-PROPERTY)

Ignoring the parenthesized Absence of Content feature leads to insertion prior to Spell Out and an LF "property interpretation" of passive adjectives. In the PF-inserted option, the category A is not interpreted as a property, and V is the lexical head of the construction at every syntactic level. This gives rise to all the just enumerated properties (i)–(vii) of the verbal passive construction. As throughout, PF insertion again corresponds to what more traditional approaches call an inflection.[28]

---

[28] As the Syntacticon entry (5.20) shows, the passive morpheme -*en,* like -*ing,* is uni-formly a category-changing suffix; it changes V to A. So, as discussed in section 4.4.3, we cannot say "inflections never change the category of the stem." Rather, this traditional statement was revised as follows: *Inflections never affect the phrase-internal properties of the lexical head.* This statement, fully predicted by the theory of PF Lexicalization, accurately encompasses the behavior of both -*ing* and the passive inflection: when -*en* is inserted in PF, the lexical head of the passive construction remains V from deep structure through LF, resulting in the many phrase-internal properties characteristic of a VP: V-modifying adverbials, possible agent-phrase, verbal idioms, case-marking of more than one complement DP, and exclusion of both SPEC(AP) and the adjectival prefix *un-*.

5.4.2 An influential alternative analysis

A number of authors, perhaps the first being Sobin (1985), have come to the conclusion that "the essential property of the passive phenomenon is that the subject position of a passive clause is theta-free and thus becomes a possible landing site for NP movement" (Åfarli, 1989, 102).

For any passive based on a participle, i.e., an adjectival head, I agree entirely with this statement. Moreover, I derive this "essential property of the passive" from the presence on *-en* of phi-features ØF, required by syntacticon entries such as (5.20) in all the periphrastic passives under discussion. *These alternatively realized ØF on A ensure co-indexing of an object with the participle*, in turn co-indexed with its subject like any other adjective. These co-indexed subject and object positions in a single clause cannot then be separate theta-positions, since no lexical anaphor is involved.[29] That is, they must form a single chain. This chain, whether a movement or expletive chain, receives its theta role in its lower position, that of the object (cf. the Main Thematic Condition of Brody, 1995). It follows that the subject position of a passive clause is theta-free.

Åfarli (1989) and Baker, Johnson and Roberts (1989), however, pursue a different logic. They attribute the theta-free property of the passive subject position to a direct stipulation that the morpheme *-en* itself receives a passive verb's external theta role, which then pre-empts it being assigned to a DP. This proposal, while startlingly original, nonetheless associates an inflection with properties we typically expect to be associated with maximal projections. Ouhalla (1991, 91–93) presents four theory-internal and two empirical arguments against their approach, with which I concur.

Advocates of "*-en* as external argument" also fail to mention its centrally *adjectival* character (section 5.1) and so deftly sidestep the somewhat obvious fact that adjectival elements never otherwise receive theta roles or carry reference. Baker, Johnson and Roberts (1989) go so far as to claim that *-en* is an I (not an A), essentially because as "implicit external argument" in a verbal passive, it should be high enough in a tree to play certain roles with respect to Principle C.[30] But I seems an even less likely categorial

---

[29] Since unmarked alternatively realized features (the English case for *-en*) require that their canonical position be empty, the object position cannot be a lexical anaphor.

[30] Section 10.4.2 will show that Åfarli's (1989) "essential property of the passive," the co-indexing of standard subject and object positions, forces an explicit external argument in verbal passives to be less economically realized, namely in a PP. Since this argument is external to VP, it is high enough to display the binding properties observed in Baker, Johnson and Roberts (1989).

candidate than A for receiving a theta role or carrying nominal reference. Moreover, the authors make no attempt to account for the extremely limited distribution of such IPs.

Baker, Johnson and Roberts elaborate on their statement that *-en* is an argument by comparing it to a Romance clitic with "properties similar to arbitrary PRO," suggesting that its relation to an overt agent phrase "resembles clitic-doubling." These unexamined similarities turn out rather to be the opposite: phrases which clitics double can often appear without a clitic but an agent phrase requires *-en*; clitics are typically definite and thereby unlike PRO; Romance versions of *-en* neither climb like a clitic nor occur as proclitics; Romance clitics generally don't appear on passive participles; and clitics but not *-en* are distinctly specified for person.

A final and additional defect of treating *-en* as an argument emerges from considering adjectival passives. Once these structures are re-integrated into the domain of syntax proper, as justified in section 5.1, the proposal that *-en* carries an external argument is completely untenable. For a central property of passive adjectives, formed with *-en* just as passive verbs are, is the entire *absence* of such an argument.[31]

The properties of *-en* then do not suit it for receiving reference or a theta role; i.e., it is not an argument. Rather, its co-indexing properties play a central part in guaranteeing the "essential property" that passive constructions have in common, namely that "the subject position of a passive clause is theta-free." As explained in section 5.1.3, a lexical entry for *-en* (5.20) juxtaposing A (co-indexing with its subject) and ØF (co-indexing with its object) accomplishes precisely this and nothing more.

5.5 Cross-linguistic variation in impersonal passives

5.5.1 The range of variation

Other Germanic languages present variations on the English participle-based passive (Åfarli, 1989 and 1992; Baker, Johnson and Roberts, 1989), and according to Sobin (1985) and Lappin and Shlonsky (1993), these variations and further combinations can be observed in Slavic and Semitic languages as well. In these variations, the clausal subject position in a verbal

---

[31] The levels at which *-en* is inserted explain why verbal passives must have an overt or covert external argument while adjectival passives may not; neither option is stated directly in the lexical entry for *-en* (section 5.2).

passive is empty or contains an expletive, i.e., they are "impersonal passives" which are not possible in English.[32] The following summarizes Lappin and Shlonsky (1993, 15), using examples from the above cited authors.

The first variation concerns "in situ transitive passives," wherein no object DP of a transitive verb moves to subject position. (Norwegian, Ukrainian, and Hebrew):

(5.48) a. Det   vart gitt   den såra soldaten   ein medalje.
                                                                    (Norwegian)
            *{ It/ There } was given the wounded soldier a medal.
        b. Cerkv-u   bul-o zbudova-n-o   v 1640 roc'i.
           church-ACC/FEM   was-IMP built-PASS-IMP in 1640
                                                                    (Ukrainian)
           *{ It/ There } was built this church in 1640.
        c. Nixtevu   harbe ma?amarim ¢al nose   ze. (Hebrew)
           write-PASS-PLUR many articles   on subject this
           *{ It/ There } was written many articles on this subject.

The second variation involves "intransitive impersonal passives" in which there is no object DP (German, Norwegian, Arabic):

(5.49) a.   Es wurde bis spät   in die Nacht getrunken. (German)
             it was   until late in the night drunk
             *{ It/ There } was drunk until late in the night.
        b.   Det   vart gestikulert. (Norwegian)
             *{ It/ There } was gesticulated.
        c.   Siira   ?ila l-madrasat-i   kull-a   yawm-in.
             walked-PASS-3MS to the-school-GEN every-ACC day-GEN
             *{ It/ There } was walked to school every day.   (Arabic)

_____

[32] The expletive subject *it* in English is possible only with clausal or PP extraposition. It occurs in two forms independently of whether the predicate is passive.
Clausal arguments which must be in extraposition:

It { appeared to us/ was reasoned } that the conclusion was false.
*That the conclusion was false { appeared to us/ was reasoned }.

Optional extraposition of clauses or PP subjects:

It { disappointed us/ was widely believed } that the conclusion was false.
It was warm inside the house.
That the conclusion was false { disappointed us/ was widely believed }.
Inside the house was warm.

The authors cited propose to account for these variants in (5.48–5.49) by parameters which restrict case marking to varying degrees and which sometimes assign a theta role to *-en* and sometimes do not. But section 5.4.1 has argued that case-marking is available in all verbal passives, and section 5.4.2 has argued against the device of assigning theta roles to adjectival suffixes, so such parameters are unavailable in my framework. But there is little to lose here, since the particular parameters proposed in the cited studies are ad hoc in form, that is, fit into no general theory of lexical or syntactic variation. I will replace these parameters by proposing variations on my participial syntacticon entry (5.20) for *-en*, variations whose forms are independently attested, and indicate how these lexical entries account for at least the differing Indo-European systems exemplified in (5.48–5.49).

I will treat impersonal passives only to the extent that they impinge on the focus of interest here, namely the form of the basic lexical entry for a passive participle in a periphrastic construction. Hence reflexive passives or the synthetic passives of Semitic are not investigated. Before moving to my proposals for the different impersonal passives, I need to comment briefly on expletives in general.

5.5.2 A note on expletives and phi-features

In general, DP expletives and the arguments they replace, exemplified by the italicized pairs in (5.50), must somehow be marked as related at some point in a syntactic derivation.

(5.50)   *There* could have occurred *a riot.*
         It was believed by many *that the election was fraudulent.*
         It convinced no one *that the son had rented a mansion.* (ambiguous)

If such pairs were not singled out as "co-indexed" or "co-marked" in some sense, there would be no basis for distinguishing (5.50) from corresponding examples in (5.51).

(5.51)   *Anything could have occurred a riot.
         *Something else was believed by many that the election was fraudulent.
         That convinced no one that the son had rented a mansion. (unambiguous)

For purposes of discussing impersonal passives, whatever elements associate DP expletives and corresponding complements (e.g. in the expletive chains of Brody, 1995) can simply be called "identification co-indices." That is, the italicized pairs of (5.50) share such indices.[33]

Expletives need not co-occur with a complement, and in such cases probably simply lack any identification index. But when an expletive is paired with some argument as in (5.50), a question arises as to which features accompany the co-identification indices of two [+N] elements (projections of N, A, and D), as for example in *There $_i$ could have occurred a riot$_i$.* While an expletive typically does not exhibit morphologically overt phi-features, co-indexed expletives nonetheless seem to covertly include as least a number feature, as the following considerations show.

Verbal number agreement on the English or French copula does not generally depend on the grammatical number of a following predicate nominative:

(5.52)   English: The students { were/ *was } an angry mob.
              That couple { is/ *are } my parents.

(5.53)   French: Mes parents { sont/ *est } un phénomène intérréssant.
              'My parents are an interesting phenomenon'

Number agreement should thus depend solely on the basis of properties of a subject DP. But then, since the predicate nominatives in (5.54–5.55) do influence number agreement, their identificationally co-indexed expletive subjects must be at least be optionally marked for the same number:

(5.54)   English: There { was/ remains/ *were / *remain } an angry mob
              outside.
              There { was/ remains/ were/ remain } lots of students
              outside.

(5.55)   French: { C'est/ Ce sont } mes parents qu'on voit là-bas.
              '{ It is/ It are } my parents which one sees over there'

Paradigms like these suggest that identification indices for [+N] elements, including co-indexed DP expletives, may be accompanied by a set of phi-features ØF. In the rest of this chapter I will assume this: *Expletives*

---

[33] Since expletives are a type of pronoun which c-commands its antecedent in a local domain, they are in complementary distribution with other pronouns. Consequently, we can almost certainly conflate their identification indices with other syntactic co-indexing.

have the same phi-features as any [+N] phrase they are co-indexed with. Even so, the evidence for this is only indirect, as in (5.54–5.55), for in at least the Germanic and Romance languages under discussion, ØF is not morphologically spelled out on an expletive or on any A which agrees with an expletive in an extraposition construction.[34]

5.5.3 Parenthesis and underline notations for Alternative Realization

Let us return to the Indo-European passive participle paradigms treated by other authors. I propose to correlate them with the formal possibilities of Alternative Realization as follows: (5.56) = English; (5.57) = Norwegian, Ukrainian; (5.58) = German, Norwegian.

(5.56)   *-en* alternatively realizes phi-features ØF which by AR (4.20) are those of an object DP; as an unmarked use of AR, this DP must be an empty category.

(5.57)   *-en* alternatively realizes phi-features ØF which by AR (4.20) are those of an object DP; as a marked use of AR, this DP can be filled. In the latter case, the subject is then an expletive.

(5.58)   *-en* has the option of alternatively realizing no phi-features ØF when there is no object DP. The subject DP is then an expletive.

I proposed in (4.42) that *lexically unmarked* alternatively realized features are to be interpreted as requiring that their nearby source is empty. For *-en*, this means that the object sister of A with which the ØF are canonically associated is empty. The lexical entry (5.20) as it stands thus accounts for the unmarked system (5.56), where ØF represents the alternatively realized phi-features of an object. (Alternatively, ØF is the "identification index" of an object, in case one claims that phi-features don't suffice to define an expletive chain; cf. note 34.)

---

[34] If one wishes to claim that identification indices on [+N] are somehow crucially *distinct* from phi-features in syntax and PF, then my claim is that these same indices, not simply phi-features, appear in the lexical entries for passive participles such as (5.20). That is, such readers should mentally replace what I continue to notate as ØF with whatever broader syntactic interpretation they wish to give it, keeping in mind that they have assumed a burden of proof for replacing the more transparent interpretation of ØF in (5.20) as a phi-feature set.

(5.20)   Passive participle entry: en, A, +<V___>, ØF, (-PROPERTY)

Let us next turn to Indo-European systems which include transitive in situ passives such as Norwegian and Ukrainian (5.57). According to (4.22), alternatively realized features which can co-occur with (or "double") an overt source are marked; we can express this by a lexical notation of underlining. Standard English noun plurals provide a simple example of doubling, though benefactive clitics in certain Romance languages would do as well:

(5.59)   English plural: s, N, +<N_>, <u>PLUR</u>

The interpretation of <u>PLUR</u> is that whenever PLUR is present on a sister of a projection of N, that is, whenever a D or NUM sister of some N^j is PLUR, then the plural suffix on N *must* appear, whether or not the canonical position for PLUR on its D or NUM source is empty.

Using this notation, a passive participle which can occur with an overt direct object such as those in Ukrainian (5.48b) is notated as (5.60):

(5.60)   Ukrainian: en, A, +<V___>, (-PROPERTY), <u>ØF</u>

If the source object DP for the alternatively realized ØF is empty, the results are as in English; this DP must be co-indexed, via *-en,* with the subject DP and hence is its trace.

But now suppose the object DP which agrees with *-en* is overt, as (5.60) permits. It must still be co-indexed with the subject, since A remains a predicate adjective which must agree with the subject it modifies. The resultant subject-object co-indexing via the passive participle implies one of two things: either the object is a lexical anaphor or the subject is an expletive.[35] The first case, a passive with a bound anaphor in object position, can be excluded by Economy of Representation.[36] The second case correctly

---

[35] I don't pretend that this statement is a theory of expletives, but in light of the argument of the previous subsection, it must be a consequence of any adequate treatment.

[36] To see this, suppose the entry in (5.60) licenses a (translated) counterpart to the following string at Spell Out, yielding the string *They will be written themselves letters*:

They$_i$ will [$_V$ Ø] write+[$_A$ Ø]$_i$ themselves$_i$ letters.

The empty categories here contribute nothing to LF, nor do they satisfy any requirements of the lexical categories that do so contribute. Hence the structure it contains beyond that in the active *They will write themselves letters* is superfluous, and so must be ruled out by both Economy of Representation and of Derivation.

yields the Norwegian and Ukrainian in situ impersonal transitive passives of (5.48) in addition to standard passives.

Finally, we consider the intransitive impersonal passives of (5.49). For such systems, I propose to modify (5.20) and (5.60) by parenthesizing ØF, yielding respectively (5.61a) for German and (5.61b) for Norwegian.

(5.61)   a. German: en, A, +<V____>, (-PROPERTY), (ØF)
            b. Norwegian: en, A, +<V____>, (-PROPERTY), (<u>ØF</u>)

The notation used in (5.61), which specifies alternatively realized features as optional, has not been previously defined. Since AR features can't exist without being present in their canonical position as well, a plausible interpretation is that *parentheses around AR features indicate that both they and their canonically located source features, taken together, are optionally absent*. This interpretation in effect disallows specifying AR (typically, inflectional) features as optional whenever their canonical source is present. Such an exclusion in fact corresponds to a widely understood empirical generalization that inflection is typically obligatory if present at all.

I therefore adopt this interpretation for parenthesized alternatively realized features. Under this lexical formalism, German (5.61a) then reproduces the English system of (5.20) with the addition that it sanctions passive intransitive participles with no phi-features. Norwegian similarly extends the Ukrainian system.

But now the absence of ØF on a passive participle in (5.61) means that this adjective fails to agree, i.e., has no identification index. But since adjectives must agree with the DP they modify, it follows that the DP subject of a passive intransitive lacks an identification index entirely, i.e. this DP must be an expletive and the verb impersonal, exactly as in (5.49). Of course, since all passive verbs (but not passive adjectives) require a subject by the Extended Projection Principle (1.17), this subject in passive intransitives must then be realized elsewhere, namely as a *by*-phrase or a PRO counterpart, just as with personal passives.

This completes the analysis of the Indo-European passive participles which permit impersonal transitive and intransitive passives. The different systems of English, Ukrainian, German, and Norwegian result from lexical items of minimally different formats, respectively (5.20), (5.60), (5.61a) and (5.61b).

5.6 The strange Case of perfect participles

I turn now to the last participial inflection that must be linked to the passive. A great number of Germanic and Romance languages exhibit a composed or "periphrastic" past tense, consisting of a purely syntactic grammatical or "auxiliary" verb followed by a participle inflected with *-en.* The English perfect with *have (John has taken the exam)* and the French composed past with *avoir* or *être* are typical examples. For convenience, I will refer to all such past periphrastics as "perfectives" and the auxiliary verb as the "perfective auxiliary." The syntactic similarity among the perfective pasts in so many languages and the fact that it *but no other active form* utilizes the passive participle morpheme suggest an intimate connection between the two types of periphrasis. Yet no analysis I know of formally captures this striking relationship as a natural combination.

In light of the certain close relation between passives and perfectives, the entry (5.20) for *-en* should also be the basis for its perfective use. We have in fact already accounted for why an active *-en* participle appears (in many languages) only with a late-inserted grammatical verb, since the Condition on Selection (5.47) explains why no open class verb can select an *-en* form.[37]

Let us now consider the distinction between the grammatical verbs *have /avoir* and *be / être* in their regular uses. We can express their complementary distribution by assigning them the related lexical entries (5.62)–(5.63), where X means a head D, I, A or P of any maximal extended projection, and ACC abbreviates ACCUSATIVE.

(5.62)   have/ avoir, V, STATIVE, $+< X_{ACC} >$

(5.63)   be/ être, V, STATIVE, $+< X >$

In terms of the Syntacticon model (4.9), since *have / avoir* and *be / être* have no interpretable features (their features are contextual or indicate Absence of Content), they are subject to Phonological Lexicalization (4.21). The fact that the perfective *have / avoir* lacks its lexical meaning, e.g. possession in

---

[37] Recapitulating, since *-en* realizes phi-features independent of (not licensed by) its verbal host, then by (5.47) any frame selecting V+*en* would have to stipulate selection of not only V but also these features.

English and French or motion in Catalan, constitutes further evidence for inserting this item in PF.[38]

Following Mateos (1996), I consider Romance adjectival agreement a mechanism for assigning case to AP in PF. Because a syntactic derivation operates in bottom up fashion, lexically unmarked AP complements to V are thus caseless when a copula (5.62)–(5.63) is chosen, since they will receive case only later via phi-feature agreement with their subject. Hence regular AP, including passive structures, appear with *be / être* rather than *have / avoir*.

But questions still arise: why is *have / avoir* the (usual) perfective auxiliary rather than some other grammatical verb?[39] And why does the Romance perfective participle formed on the basis of [$_A$ *-en*] never agree with its surface subject, in most unadjectival fashion?

Particularly suggestive in this regard is the fact that the same French grammatical verb *avoir* occurs with other non-agreeing complement A in rather marked lexical expressions such as (5.64). These expressions contrast with normal adjectives following a linking verb, which agree in gender and number with their subject.

(5.64)   Nous   avons   moins   { chaud/ *chauds } maintenant.
         We   have   less   hot [no agreement] now
         'We feel less warm now'
         Marie aura   { beau/ *belle }   répéter ces arguments.
         Mary will have beautiful [no agreement] repeat those arguments
         'Mary will repeat those arguments in vain'

Avoir is by no means the only transitive verb in French to take non-

---

[38] Perhaps the essay on composed pasts in Benveniste (1966) is the most valiant attempt to find some kind of deep or vestigially historic "possession" lurking in the cross-linguistic use of *have* in perfectives. But there is no independent notion of possession that can be defined to support the otherwise question-begging argument.

At most the perfect tense conveys that the past act remains a property of the subject, the so-called "present relevance" of the present perfect. Thus, *Princeton has been lived in by Einstein* indicates that Princeton still has this property, while **Einstein has lived in Princeton* is strange precisely because such a property is not attributed to the deceased; similarly, **Atlantis has been visited by Plato*.

[39] French *avoir* 'have' is subject to further language-particular restrictions, since *être* 'be' is used for the perfect periphrastic with "unaccusative" verbs of pure motion and with *any* reflexive clitics, including indirect objects, inherent reflexives or datives of interest. I exclude here questions relating to past participle behavior that involve auxiliary choice.

agreeing adjectival complements; i.e. structures as in (5.64) are idiomatic but are nonetheless of some currency.[40]

(5.65)   Elle pèse lourd. 'She weighs heavy'
Elle voit grand. 'She sees big' i.e, 'she has big plans'
Elle { risque/ perd } gros. 'She { risks/ loses } heavy'
Elle chante faux. 'She sings false'
Elle sent bon. 'She smells good'
Elle vise haut. 'She aims high'
Elle mange léger. 'She eats light'
Elle écrit penché. 'She writes slanted'
Elle tient bon. 'She holds steady'

The adjectives in (5.64) shouldn't be listed in the Dictionary with two special characteristics, namely lack of agreement *and* a special copula. If the A in the expressions *avoir chaud, avoir beau, péser lourd, voir grand,* etc. are lexically listed with an inherently marked "quirky" accusative case, they are automatically exempt from PF agreement, since the latter is at bottom a case-assigning mechanism (Mateos, 1996; cf. section 8.3 here).[41] Such adjectives may be listed as combining with special verbs (*péser, voir,* etc.), but the fact that the default case is *avoir* rather than *être* is predicted by (5.62–5.63).

Have/ avoir is then inserted, as (5.62) is formulated, not only with structurally case-marked DP objects but also with any XP complement lexically marked for accusative. Consequently, the device of linking one meaning of exceptional adjectives such as French *chaud* and *beau* with a quirky lexical case accounts at one stroke not only for their lack of agreement but also for their occurrence with *avoir.*[42]

---

[40] I thank M. Fender for furnishing me with these transitive verbs whose complements are non-agreeing adjectives. It is irrelevant how they are translated into English. The point is that they are adjectival not adverbial in form, that they are complements of transitive verbs rather than adjuncts, and that they do not agree.

[41] While specific case features do not directly contribute to interpretation, I will argue in Chapter 8 that predicate nominals are precisely those DPs which enter LF case-less, and of course they thus differ from direct objects. Consequently, having case and being case-less are linked to differences in interpretation. As a plausible special instance of this idea, the idiomatic French form [$_{+LF\,CASE}$ *chaud*] in *avoir chaud* 'feel hot' indeed has a different interpretation than the regular [$_{-LF\,CASE}$ *chaud*] in *être chaud(e)(s)* 'be hot (to the touch)'.

[42] The English locutions *had { better/ best } do something* can be analyzed in a similar way. *Better/ best* are grammatical adjectives, as shown by their suppletive alternation with *good*; like all +N categories, they need case. They are then listed as appearing with

Now lack of agreement and occurrence with *avoir* are exactly the two properties of the Romance perfect participle. So it seems plausible that perfective -*en* should also be marked for quirky case in the Syntacticon:

(5.66)   Perfective participle entry (tentative):   en, A, +<V___>, ACC

In conjunction with (5.62), this entry ensures that *have / avoir* will be the perfect auxiliary in English/ French.

We need to determine the level that the item (5.66) enters derivations. If perfective -*en* were inserted at either deep structure or during the syntax, the internal structure of its phrase would be adjectival, akin to a passive adjective. Then verbal specifiers, overt direct objects, double objects, verb-object idioms and other structures incompatible with an adjectival lexical head would be excluded, but they are not: *We have already taken { the prisoners food/ advantage of the new regime }*. Perfective -*en* must therefore be inserted subsequent to Spell Out by Phonological Lexicalization (4.21). -*En* is thus a right-hand head in PF, but as we have seen for other participial inflections, this in no way interferes with its verbal host being a lexical head in the syntax. As expected with a PF-inserted head, a perfective VP is internally structured exactly like a simple VP.

Moreover, if the adjectival head of a perfect participle were present in the syntax, linking verbs such as *act* or *seem* or *become* could select it, but this is also impossible: **John { acted/ seemed/ looked } taken the exam*. Other than forcing selection of the grammatical verb *have / avoir*, the accusative feature on -*en* does not interact or interfere with syntactic environments, unlike alternatively realized phi-features of a direct object. Hence the perfective construction is a transparent example of inflection, and such empirical considerations overwhelmingly point to (5.66) being a PF insertion. The full specification of the perfective entry should thus be (5.67), where the role of -PROPERTY is to cancel the adjectival interpretation associated with the category A:

(5.67)   Perfective participle entry: en, A, +<V___>, ACC, -PROPERTY

If -*en* is a PF insertion, then the quirky feature ACC in (5.67) shouldn't contribute to LF interpretation. More generally, we have good reason to believe that specific case features of even regularly assigned abstract case

---

quirky accusative case in the syntactic context [I, PAST]___V, which forces insertion of *have* rather than *be*: *Mary had best not leave the house; Bill had better not [VP Ø] either.*

do not directly contribute to LF. Emonds (1985, Ch. 1) argues that such all case features are actually just feature copies on DPs of their case-assigning sisters, and feature copying on sisters is nothing but alternative realization. In particular then, ACC, NOM, DAT and GEN alternatively realize V, I, P and D respectively. In light of this, it seems obvious that specific irregular lexical cases contribute even less to LF; for example, *help* takes an irregular dative in German but a regular accusative in French, and yet this reflects no difference in LF-interpretation. Thus, whatever the ultimate form of case theory, the following restriction serves as a workable hypothesis:

(5.68)   *Case Corollary of Alternative Realization. Since specific case features, whatever their provenance, are alternative realizations. they do not contribute to interpretation at LF.*[43]

On the other hand, the presence of an AP in the LF of the perfective appears to be crucial for interpretation. The LF form of a representative perfective verb phrase *have shaken some rugs* is (5.69):

(5.69)

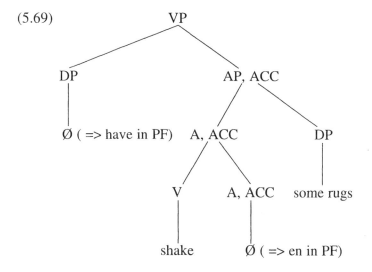

The difference in LF between a simple VP and a perfective VP thus comes down to this: both are phrases with a lexical head V, but a perfective structure like (5.69) consists of a *V-headed phrase housed in an AP*, whereas

---

[43] This accords with Chomsky's (1993) proposal that Case Features are uninterpretable. However, it seems to me that he stipulates rather than derives this.

a non-perfective or simple VP is not.[44] The following seems to be a plausible candidate for a universal characterization of perfect tense:

(5.70)   *Perfect Tense in LF. An AP whose lexical head is a V is taken as a property of the subject, i.e., it constitutes a V-headed phrase with "present relevance" (to the subject).*

It is hence no accident that the present perfect periphrastic with *have* expresses present relevance while the purely verbal past tense does not, rather than vice-versa. Most theories of aspect fail to take into account the adjectival syntax of the perfect and thereby fail to predict this correlation (cf. note 38).

Let us now combine the passive participle (5.20) and perfective participle (5.67) entries for *-en* in the Syntacticon into a single entry (5.71) for languages such as e.g. English and Modern Spanish.

(5.20)   Passive participle entry: en, A, +<V___>, ØF, (-PROPERTY)

(5.67)   Perfective participle entry: en, A, +<V___>, ACC, -PROPERTY

(5.71)   Combined participle entry #1:
         en, A, +<V___>, { ØF/ -PROPERTY { ØF/ ACC } }

The entry (5.71) describes a system wherein (i) *-en* is co-indexed with a trace [DP, ØF] in object position and also co-indexed with the subject (the

---

[44] Further study of the role of the AP in the LF structure (5.69) is needed for specifying the strangely variable cross-linguistic meanings of the composed pasts formed with it. The precise nuance of temporal meaning of the "perfective" varies even among dialects of the same language, e.g. Peninsular and Latin American Spanish. A French "composed past" need convey no perfective sense; it is the standard past tense of conversation. The English periphrastic past is necessarily "perfective" only when *have* is finite, assuming inability to occur with past adverbs characterizes the present perfect.

(i)   *Bill has shaken some rugs yesterday.
      *Sue has then received that prize.
      *He has left last week.

(ii) Bill should have shaken some rugs yesterday.
      For Sue to have then received that prize would amaze me.
      We believe him to have left last week.

On the basis of examples like (i)–(ii), Emonds (1974) proposes that verbal periphrasis with *have* has two types of interpretation, with the choice being determined post-transformationally, in present terms at LF.

two types of passives), or alternatively (ii) *-en* carries a special accusative feature in a PF-inserted variant. In the latter case, the perfective form *never* shows agreement with either the subject or any other DP (e.g. the perfect in Modern Spanish and, vacuously, in Modern English).[45]

A confirming argument for this chapter's approach to participles is that a slight modification in (5.71) provides a simple and natural account for one of the most intriguing variations of Romance syntax. Suppose now that *-en* may spell out the quirky ACC *together with* phi-features, rather than realizing only one or the other. At least at first glance, this can be achieved by slightly varying the entry (5.71):

(5.72)   Combined participle entry #2:
en, A, +<V___>, { ØF/ -PROPERTY { (ØF), (ACC) } }[46]

All the options in (5.71) are also available in (5.72), but the formal combination of ACCUSATIVE *together with* phi-features is novel.

Let us investigate the consequences when *-en* represents the maximal combination insertable in PF, @ = [$_{ACC, ØF}$ -en]. As throughout, choosing features on *-en* which alternatively realize an object DP's canonical features ØF forces that DP to be empty, since unmarked AR (4.42) allows only zeroing but not overt doubling. Therefore @ occurs with an empty DP object, as exemplified in (5.73) with the French participle *écrites* 'written'.

(5.73)

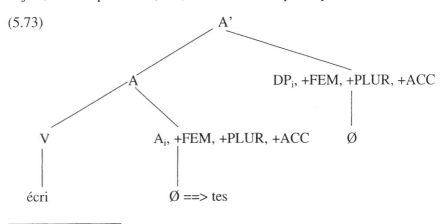

---

[45] As suggested to me by A. Mateos, [$_A$-*en*] satisfies the Case Filter either by agreeing in PF with its surface subject like any other inflected A or by its quirky lexical accusative case feature.

[46] As is standard, the notation { A / B } means exactly one of A and B is to be chosen. I take the notation { (A), (B) } to mean that *at least* one of A and B is to be chosen. Such a notation seems widely needed, but is not in such general use.

Now, as seen earlier, an A marked with its own quirky accusative, here
-tes '-en', does not need to agree with its subject to get case and so is not
co-indexed with it. Therefore, the necessarily empty object DP$_i$ co-indexed
with @$_i$ can't agree with the subject either; hence *the empty object in (5.73)*
cannot be a trace of the subject, but must be licensed in some other way. In
Romance, the remaining possible empty objects are traces of "A-bar" movements to a non-argument position such as WH-fronting or Old Spanish
Object Shift, or empty objects identified by a clitic on V.

In most striking fashion, exactly this situation obtains in Romance languages such as French, Italian and Old Spanish. The active perfective participle can exhibit phi-feature agreement with empty direct objects resulting
either from cliticization or movement to non-argument position, as for example in French:

(5.74) [Quelles lettres]$_i$ aurait   écrites
        Which letters [+FEM, +PL]   would-have   written [+FEM, +PL]
        [$_{DP}$ Ø]$_i$ un tel homme?
        [$_{DP}$ Ø] such a man
        'Which letters would such a man have written?'
        J'ai vu [ces lettres]$_j$.   Je ne les$_j$ aurais
        I saw those letters [+FEM, +PL]. I not them would-have
        pas écrites   [$_{DP}$ Ø]$_j$.
        not written [FEM,+PL] [$_{DP}$ Ø]
        'I saw those letters. I would not have written them.'

For these varieties of Romance, then, (5.72) replaces the Spanish (5.71).[47]

An apparent problem is the parentheses around the phi-features in (5.72).
They suggest that agreement of an active perfect participle and an empty
object is optional, since quirky ACC (the defining feature of the active
perfect) can apparently always be chosen alone. In a description based
solely on a corpus where present day school grammar is not a factor in
intuitions, e.g. Old French as treated in Foulet (1930,100-105), it turns out

---

[47] The lexical entry for *être* (5.63) predicts that if *être* appears, the participle can get its
abstract case only via agreement with *the subject*. (Object agreement is possible only with
avoir.) Hence, the presence of *être* with unaccusative verbs guarantees agreement with a
subject DP, even when that DP is e.g. an expletive. This accounts for the much discussed
failure of object agreement in (i); cf. for example Lefebvre (1988, section 4.1).

(i)   Combien de filles est-il arrivé(*es) t ?
      How many girls is-there arrived (FEM, PLUR)?

that object agreement of the type seen in (5.74) is indeed optional. Thus (5.72) is correct at least for Old French.

However, more traditional descriptions of standard French claim that past participle agreements with null objects as in (5.74) are obligatory.[48] Such dialects might therefore justify an additional stylistic statement permitting a different interpretation for a lexical combination of syntactic features F+(F'), as seen in (5.72).

(5.75)   *Strict Style ("Style Soutenu"). Optional inflectional features F' linked to a syntactic feature F must be chosen if they are available.*

It should be kept in mind that the stylistic variant (5.75) applies only to parenthesized *purely syntactic* (i.e., PF) features; I do not propose that any lexical information interpretable at LF can be manipulated in this way.

These diverse lexical characterizations of passive/ perfective participle morphemes in terms of Alternative Realization of an object's phi-features provide simple and predictive solutions for a whole gamut of participle-object agreements in Romance. The much debated paradigms of different languages, dialects and styles of Romance have occasioned many an ad hoc treatment. But several of the systems studied now follow without further stipulation from formally compact and unified entries such as (5.71) and (5.72) in the Syntacticon and the principles of Alternative Realization (4.20) and Phonological Lexicalization (4.21) developed and justified throughout this work.

Finally, there are also Slavic systems and historical and child grammars of Romance languages in which participles in perfective tenses also agree with *overt* direct objects, in some cases obligatorily. These situations correspond to marked versions of alternatively realized features which tolerate copying (doubling) as well as zeroing, akin to English plural noun and subject agreement inflections and to the transitive impersonal passives of Norwegian and Ukrainian (section 5.5). By the notation introduced in section 5.5.3 for such doubling, ØF should be underlined in the Syntacticon entry for such systems. However, without both more study of the paradigms in these languages and dialects and more refinement in the parentheses and brace notations for lexical entries, it is premature to hazard proposals for exact Syntacticon entries for their participles. But even short of such devel-

---

[48] The French Academy in recent years has tended to consider the object agreement described here as optional, but this might stem from sociolinguistic competition between non-agreeing and obligatorily agreeing dialects.

opments, the Syntacticon entries presented above nicely succeed in conflating passive participles with the better studied cases of Romance perfective participle agreement. The variations allowed in the systems just examined seem to conform to what is predicted by the multi-level lexical insertion of Chapter 4.

More generally, working out lexical specifications for both the agreeing passive and non-agreeing past participle morphemes in light of the theory of the Syntacticon (4.9) has not only led to relatively complete analyses of each of the constructions separately. It also provides a novel understanding of why exactly these two superficially very distinct constructions occur in tandem in so many grammatical systems.

Chapter 6
The genesis of flat structures:
Linking verbs, "light" verbs and "restructuring"

6.1 Surprising consequences of higher empty heads

Chapter 4 and 5 have characterized both derivational and inflectional forms of bound morphology as lexical items which have only cognitive or purely syntactic features F. Bound morphemes (affixes) are precisely those items which enter into compound structures but lack the purely semantic features f characteristic of open class items.[1] That is, these items are the compounding elements of the Syntacticon. When at least some of an affix's cognitive features are interpreted at Logical Form, the item is inserted either prior to transformations or during the syntax and is "derivational." If none of an affix's features are interpretable, in particular if it spells out *only* "alternatively realized" features, it is inserted in the Phonological Component and is traditionally termed "inflectional" (section 4.4). In a number of complex cases, a suffix can be inserted at two or three levels, depending on whether interpretable features are chosen or ignored (sections 4.7, 5.3 and 5.4).

The pivotal formal construct in these insertion-level based explanations of morphological contrasts such as result nominals vs. event nominals vs. gerundive nominals and adjectival vs. verbal passives has been an underlying "empty right hand head" Z in word-internal structures $[_Z Y - [_Z \emptyset]]$. The definitions of lexical head and of extended sisterhood (repeated below) render these empty suffixal heads crucially invisible at the point when subcategorization licenses complements of Y. That is, prior to an affix's insertion under such a Z, its host Y^0 is the lexical head of any larger structure Z^j, and hence this Y^0 determines the complements which are daughters of Z^1.

---

[1] Bound morphemes have always caught linguists' attention because most languages subject these purely grammatical elements to some condition of "phonological impoverishment," such as the Condition (3.40) on English suffixes. This special phonological status superficially seems to mark off a self-contained domain, which theories of "autonomous morphology" treat as a cause rather than an effect.

However, the grammatical importance of suffixes derives from which level they function as heads *inside a syntactic system*; their phonological behavior is a consequence of their syntactic status (they lack open class features f) rather than the reverse. This central conceptual error has introduced an apartheid between syntax and morphology that deprives each domain taken separately of much of its interest.

(4.27) *Lexical Head/Projection. Let Y^0 be the highest lexically filled head in Z^j. Then Y^0 is the lexical head of Z^j, and Z^j is a lexical projection of Y^0.*

Now nothing in this definition applies only to heads which happen to be bound morphemes. Nor does anything in the lexical feature theory in Chapter 1 suggest that correlations between feature types and level of insertion should somehow be limited to bound morphemes. Indeed, in a language poor in inflection such as English, most closed class morphemes appear to be free (separate words). The framework being developed here therefore creates three explicit expectations about late-inserted independent "grammatical words" in the Z^0 positions of (4.27).[2]

(i) Expected selection relations between non-sisters. One expectation of the Syntacticon model (4.9) is that words lacking purely semantic features f, and hence not in a tree when a transformational derivation begins, can nonetheless be inserted prior to Spell Out and interpreted in LF. In this situation (as well as for insertion in PF), derivations will contain deep empty heads Z^0. The definition (4.27) will then dictate that in the underlying structure (6.1), *the lexical head of ZP is X^0 and/ or Y^0.*

(6.1)

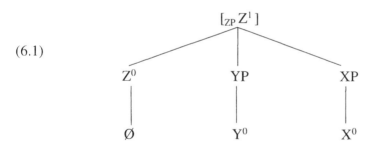

A head-initial condition on word order under Z^1, e.g. (3.8) for English or (3.17) for French, disambiguates the choice between X and Y as the lexical head in (6.1). In such a system the leftmost zero-level element, here Y^0, must be the lexical head which governs selection of its non-sister XP within ZP. Constructions such as (6.1) where XP is a non-sister complement of Y^0 are the focus of this chapter.

---

[2] Since this chapter focuses on phrasal syntax, its analyses don't use Lieber's word-internal subcategorization frames.

(ii) Expected dual (or tripartite) behavior of grammatical items. Like the bound forms of derivational morphology, most closed class words of category Z^0 spell out interpretable syntactic features F. They may then be inserted at two different levels, either prior to a transformational derivation (deep insertion) or in the syntax, and this may well give rise to "dual grammatical behavior." If insertion is pre-transformational, we expcct the word's behavior to be indistinguishable from that of open class items, those which *must* undergo Deep Lexicalization (4.7).

But a word inserted "in syntax" actually comes to fill an underlying null position Z^0 as in (6.1), which brings into play not only (4.27), but also (4.28) and (4.29).

(4.28)   *Extended Sisterhood. If Z^0 and XP are sisters and if Z^1 is the smallest phrase (besides structural projections of Y) whose lexical head is Y^0, then Y^0 and XP are extended sisters.*

(4.29)   *Revised Classical Subcategorization. @, Y, +< X > is satisfied if and only if X is a cognitive syntactic feature of the lexical head of an (extended) sister of Y^0= @.*

Let us scrutinize in more detail what happens concretely when selection involves non-sisters, as permitted for Y^0 and XP in (6.1). For concreteness, take Z in (6.1) to be V; that is, we focus on closed class or "grammatical verbs" which seem to be fully characterized by interpretable syntactic cognitive features F. Since such verbs lack purely semantic features f, they can be inserted in principle either in deep structure or later in the syntax, under Vs which are empty when a derivation starts.

Candidates for grammatical verbs to play the role of deep empty heads Z in (4.27) include *be, have, do, get, go, come, let, make, say*. For explicitness, consider some simple structures for a linking verb *get* subcategorized as +<A> and a transitive verb *make* subcategorized as +<D>. If *get* and *make* are inserted at deep structure, then unexceptionally, the lexical projections of their complements *angry* and *claim* are respectively AP and DP as in (6.2); that is, the latter open class items license their own subcategorized complements within these phrasal domains. (Arrows represent insertions at a non-underlying level; for simplicity of exposition, I omit intermediate projections.)

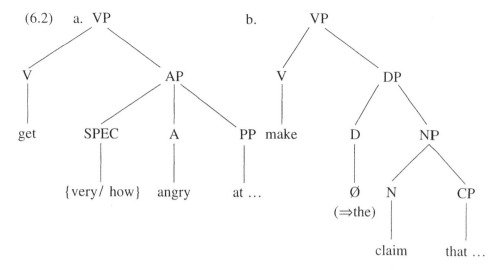

However, if the grammatical verbs *get* and *make* are instead inserted later in the syntax, the situation is different. By the definition of lexical head (4.27), the *top VPs* can now count as the underlying lexical projections of *angry* and *claim*, and so extended sisterhood (4.28) permits their sub-categorized complements to be sisters either of the selecting elements them-selves *(angry* and *claim),* again as in (6.2), *or of the higher empty Vs as in* (6.3).

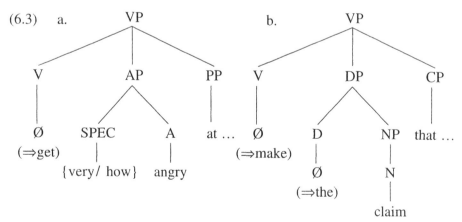

The definition of lexical projection (4.27) thus *predicts dual complement structures* for grammatical linking and transitive verbs. A head of a comple-ment of a higher grammatical V (e.g. *get* or *make*), which can be empty at deep structure, can realize its own complements either in its own maximal projections as in (6.2) *or alternatively* in "flatter" structures (6.3). In the latter case, the "complements of the complements" are generated higher, as sisters to the grammatical verbs themselves.[3] Sections 6.2 and 6.3 will discuss further implications of these alternative phrasal architectures, e.g. for predicting extraction patterns. The flatter structures predicted here by the theory of dual level lexical insertion have already occasioned much grammatical discussion, but previous accounts have not found a way to generalize across different constructions.

(iii) Expected dummy or "place-holding" syntactic words. The grammatical literature sometimes calls words which seem to have no semantic function dummy elements or place-holders. According to the theory of the lexicon in Chapter 4, if the features F of some closed class morpheme make no contribution to LF but rather are simply contextual and/ or indicate a marked absence of semantic content (e.g. like +STATIVE on a non-activity verb), then that morpheme can be inserted *only* in a PF-defined context, by (4.21):

(4.21)   *Phonological Lexicalization (PL). Items specified solely in terms of purely syntactic features (contextual, alternatively realized, and "lack of content" features) are inserted subsequent to any operation contributing to Logical Form.*

As reviewed extensively in the previous two chapters, PL characterizes the bound morphemes which traditional grammar calls inflections. But PL equally well applies to free morphemes, i.e., to semantically empty words, as illustrated in the brief introductory discussion of this topic (section 4.4.1). As a more structured example of how PF-insertion of such "grammatical words" explains their properties, I terminate this section by scrutinizing more closely some special properties of copula verbs.

Traditional and generative grammarians alike recognize the auxiliary verbs *have* and *be* (French *avoir/ être*, Italian *avere/ essere* and Spanish *haber/ ser*) as having no inherent content and differing from each other only by contextual features. For English, as discussed in section 5.6, *have* is the empty stative V which occurs with accusative XPs (DPs and quirky case-marked As), while *be* is the copula elsewhere. In the lexical model (4.9) these copulas, which have the Syntacticon entries (5.62) and (5.63), are excellent candidates for free morphemes which enter a derivation only in PF.

---

[3]   The situation is slightly different when X and Y are both V, i.e., when a grammatical V appears with a frame +<V>. This is the subject matter of section 6.5 and the Appendix.

(5.62)   have, V, STATIVE, +< X_{ACC} >[4]

(5.63)   be, V, STATIVE, +< X > (elsewhere)

The question now arises, are there aspects of grammatical behavior specific to semantically empty *be* and *have* which can plausibly be predicted by the hypothesis of their Phonological Lexicalization (4.21)? Although I do not fully understand all the paradigms that typify these place-holders, at least four of their properties (a)–(d) which set them off from all other English verbs seem attributable to their absence in the syntactic component.

a. *Unlike interpreted V,* **be** *comes under the scope of Economy of Derivation (4.36).*[5] This principle implies that free morphemes are not inserted at all unless they contribute to LF interpretation or fill otherwise unlicensed obligatory structural positions. In this vein, Emonds (1994) claims that   X
finite English copulas *(am, is, are, was, were)* are not V but actually morphemes of category I which license an empty head in their VP sister. Economy of Derivation then ensures that semantically empty *be* cannot appear under a V which follows these copulas or, for that matter, in certain other non-finite contexts as yet not fully understood, e.g. as heads in many reduced restrictive relatives: *They broke a suitcase (*being) newer than mine; the books (*being) contained in the box were old.*

b. *Only a place-holding V can select the passive/perfective participle.* Because *be* and *have* are inserted in PF, they can select some X^0 which is itself inserted only in PF. Notably, they can select the PF-inserted category-changing participial suffix *-en* of category A. This unique co-occurrence property of late-inserted verbs was introduced and explained in some detail in sections 5.4 (verbal passives) and 5.6 (perfect participles).

c. *A place-holding V is unavailable for copying in LF.* A vast literature on English VP-ellipsis (some representative works are Wasow, 1972; Williams, 1977; Reinhart, 1983; Lappin, 1991) supports the idea that a principle of interpretation copies a VP linguistically specified at LF into the position of an ellipted one. I italicize the copied VP and represent the ellipted VP as e_i.

---

[4]   The notation accords with Revised Classical Subcategorization (4.29) repeated just above. Section 7.2.4 has more discussion of the grammatical verb *have;* we concentrate here on *be.*

[5]   *(4.36) Economy of Derivation: Two deep structures which differ only by empty categories not interpretable at LF count as equivalent. Of equivalent deep structures, prefer the derivation with the fewest insertions of free morphemes.*

(6.4)   a.   I make Mary *get examined often* even though her brother refuses
to e$_i'$.
After their vacation, Bill will *continue representing our inter-
ests,* and I see no reason why Mary shouldn't e$_i$ as well.
For us to *send cash* is more dangerous than for you to e$_i$.
b.   I make Mary be *examined often* even though her brother refuses
to be e$_i$.
Since in the past you have *represented us well,* I'm sure you
must have e$_i$ yesterday.
For us to have been *sent cash* is more shocking than for Ann to
have been e$_i$.

In the examples (6.4b), the left contexts of the copied VP and the ellipted
VP are identical empty V: *be, have* and *have been* respectively. This might
suggest that these verbs also could be ellipted under identity, but they cannot be:

(6.5)   *I make Mary *be examined often* even though her brother refuses
to e$_i$.
*Since in the past you *have represented us well,* I'm sure you must
e$_i$ yesterday.
*For us to *have been sent cash* is more shocking than for Ann to e$_i$.
*For us to *have been sent cash* is more shocking than for Ann to
have e$_i$.

Hence, a necessary condition for copying of a projection of V in LF appears
to be the natural one that V itself be lexicalized. The auxiliary VP heads *be*
and *have* are invisible for LF copying because, as determined by (4.21), they
are absent except at PF.

  d. A place-holding V is unavailable for focusing via VP-preposing.
Whatever the exact mechanism which licenses focusing at LF, the same
empty PF-inserted auxiliary verbs which are not visible for copying in LF
in (6.5) fail to satisfy a similar need for an LF-interpreted head of a proposed
VP in (6.6a). That is, focusing also requires VP to be a lexical projection of
a syntactically present V (6.6b):

(6.6)   a.   *They said it should be checked daily, and be checked daily it
will.
*I wanted him to have represented us, and have represented us
he must.
*No one hoped we would be sent cash, and yet have been sent
cash we may.

b. They said it should be checked daily, and checked daily it'll be.
   I wanted him to have represented us, and represented us he must have.
   No one hoped we would be sent cash, and yet sent cash we may have been.

There thus seems to be solid justification for proceeding on the basis that Phonological Lexicalization widely applies to free morphemes without semantic content such as copulas. We will encounter many further interesting confirmations of this in Chapter 7, concerning other grammatical free forms such as *of, to, as, do, for, with,* etc.

6.2 Flatter lexical projections for predicate adjectives and participles

I now turn to constructions which exemplify selection relations between non-sisters, as previewed in the brief discussion of the structure (6.3).

Traditional grammars call intransitive verbs which take predicate adjectives "linking verbs" and usually attempt to enumerate such verbs, which suggests they are a closed class. E.g., English *be, become, get, seem, stay,* some sense verbs (*feel, look*) and a few more.[6] Most linking verbs have unique grammatical behavior which suggests that they are characterized by a small set of syntactic features F_k and hence should be analyzed as grammatical V.[7] Since these features differentiate linking verbs in LF, they are inserted in the syntax although absent at the underlying level. As seen earlier, this option yields a choice between the structures in (6.2a) and (6.3a) for realizing the complements of predicate adjectives.

(6.2)   a.

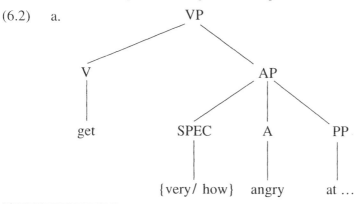

---

[6] Some combinations seem idiomatic: *turn { serious/ sour/ cold },* but **turn { tired/ drunk/ silly }.*

(6.3)   a.

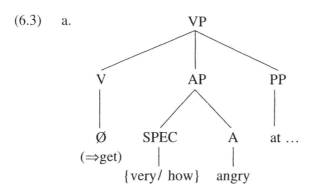

The following three arguments show that these dual structures predicted by the definition of lexical projection (4.27) are precisely what is needed to explain the syntactic behavior of predicate adjectives and their complements.

(i) English AP questions. Hendrick (1978) argues for precisely the two positions of complements to predicate adjectives in (6.2a-6.3a).[8] In support of dual structures, he observes that when an English AP is fronted, a complement to the A can either prepose or stay in situ, exactly as expected if it has these two structural realizations.

(6.7)   a. AP fronting, with a complement to A inside AP as in (6.2a):
                How ready to go is Sue?
                How satisfied with his work does he feel?
                How angry at Bill will John get?
                Mary asked how mad at John the supervisors seemed.

---

[7] Grammatical differences among linking verbs establish that each has the unique behavior expected of Syntacticon elements: *Become* and *get* are distinguished by the same feature that distinguishes the Spanish copulas *ser* and *estar* (section 2.2), while *be* conflates the two. *Seem* has the widest range of frames. Neither *become* nor *grow* take locational PP complements, and *grow* does not take predicate nominals (**You will soon grow a frequent flyer*), etc.

[8] Hendrick (1978) argues that "... adjectives have no posthead complements in the base" (297) and that "... the Adjectival Complement originates as a sister to V" (262). I propose that complements to at least predicate adjectives with grammatical linking verbs may be projected *either* inside or outside AP.

   b. AP fronting, with a complement to A outside AP as in (6.3a):[9]
      How ready is Sue to go?
      How satisfied does he feel with his work?
      How angry will John get at Bill?
      Mary asked how mad the supervisors seemed at John.

A reviewer observes that certain idiomatic PPs with linking verbs have the same behavior as predicate APs, i.e., the complement to the head of an idiomatic expression can front with the PP as in (6.7a) or it can stay in post-verbal position, as in (6.7b): *How much out of favor with the British people was he?* vs. *How much out of favor was he with the British people?*

(ii) Romance clitic "climbing" with Adjectives. Romance clitic behavior provides two more arguments for flatter predicate adjective structures. One is based on predicate adjectives and another on auxiliary and participle constructions.

   Kayne (1975, 71) observes that French verbal clitics can correspond to PP complements of predicate adjectives introduced by *à* 'to' and *de* 'of'.

(6.8)   a. Jean leur restera fidèle (à toutes les deux).
           Jean them-stay-will faithful (to all two)
           'Jean will stay faithful to them (both).'
        b. Elle m'en paraît capable.
           She me-thereof-appears capable
           'She appears to me capable of it.'
        c. La situation y semble lieé.
           The situation thereto-seems related
           'The situation seems related to that.'

----

[9] Some linking verbs (*grow, remain, sound, taste*) may be open class verbs with semantic features *f*. If so, they should be ungrammatical in the paradigm (6.7b). Although the following judgments seem murky, their marginal status, by the reasoning in section 1.1.2, may well indicate ungrammaticality. That is, these verbs possibly exclude the flatter structure (6.3a).

?How much taller did your brother grow than Mary?
?Somebody asked me how fond Mary remained of Bill.
?You forget how irritated the boss sounded at your decision.

Many analyses of Romance clitics have taken this paradigm to indicate that clitics must "climb" out of adjective phrases. However, these and other cases of putative clitic climbing are each, in my view, better analyzed as instances of cliticizing complements to an initial head V in essentially flat structures.[10] A more complete study (Emonds, 1999) claims that there are no exceptions to the descriptive generalization (6.9).

(6.9)   *Phrase Mate Hypothesis. Romance clitics on V_i are associated only with XP sisters to some V_i^k, where XP = DP, IP, PP, NP, AP, VP.*

As a little reflection shows, the Phrase Mate Hypothesis conforms to and is in fact an archetypal instance of Alternative Realization (4.20).

Now, since (6.9) doesn't permit clitics to be related to DPs embedded inside APs in an articulated structure (6.10a), then French clitics as in (6.8) which correspond to DP complements of predicate adjectives must have their source in the flatter structures like (6.10b) predicted by (4.27).

(6.10)   a.

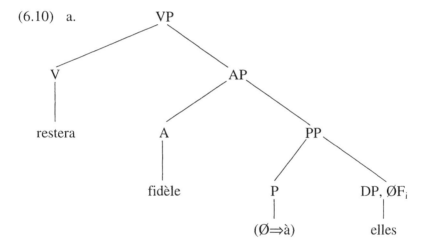

---

[10] There are five standard cases of Romance clitic climbing discussed in the literature. This section briefly discusses two of them. Section 6.5 and the Appendix to this chapter review in some detail an account of two further cases of climbing with restructuring and causative verbs. For a summary of my analysis of the fifth case, that of French *en* (Italian *ne*), see note 11 of Chapter 9.

(6.10) b.

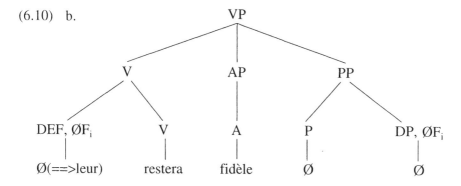

Of course, if clitic constructions in (6.8) realize only flatter s-structures like (6.10b), one can legitimately ask what excludes structure (6.10a) for a predicate adjective construction.[11] The answer seems to be that the two structures in (6.10), both well-formed in structures without pronouns, are equivalent for the first clause of Economy of Derivation (4.36). Its second clause can then be used to decide between them.

(4.36)   *Economy of Derivation: Two deep structures which differ only by empty categories not interpretable at LF count as equivalent. Of equivalent deep structures, prefer the derivation with the fewest insertions of free morphemes.*

Since the pronoun in (6.10b) is a bound proclitic, it is more economical than the (non-contrastively stressed) free form pronoun in (6.10a). On the other hand, if the DP in (6.10a) is contrastively stressed, the trees differ by an interpretable feature and are hence not equivalent; in this case (6.10a) survives as well-formed.

---

[11] Kayne reports that the cliticizations in (6.8) are obligatory. Although I think that the uncliticized (i) may be acceptable with a stressed pronoun, I accept his claim that an unstressed pronoun is ungrammatical.

(i)   ?Jean restera fidèle à elles.
      Jean will stay faithful to them

In any case, the argumentation favoring the Phrase Mate Hypothesis for Romance clitics is not compromised by the need to account for the sometimes obligatory nature of cliticization. Any unacceptability of (i) suggests if anything that the structure (6.10a) with more embedding, which we would independently expect to represent (i), is for some reason not freely available. This in turn supports an alternative flatter structure (6.10b) and hence actually reinforces the Phrase Mate Hypothesis (6.9).

The source for cliticized complements of Romance predicate adjectives should thus be flat structures like (6.10b), induced by linking verbs which are inserted in the syntax rather than pre-transformationally at the outset of derivations. Such flat structures exemplify the selection restriction between non-sisters predicted by the definition of lexical projection (4.27), which crucially permits subcategorization features to ignore empty deep structure heads.

(iii) Romance clitic "climbing" with auxiliary verbs. As outlined in section 6.1, certain semantically empty place-holding verbs such as the auxiliaries with passive and past participles (English *be* and *have*; French *être* and *avoir*) are inserted only in PF. According to sections 5.4 and 5.6, these participles formed by *-en* are both As: passive *-en* alternatively realizes an object's phi-features ØF and perfective *-en* carries lexical ("quirky") accusative case. The tree (6.11) illustrates the syntax of combining these periphrastics, without using the alternative flatter structures permitted by (4.27). I omit intermediate projections and the feature ACC on the past participle *-en*.

(6.11)   Prisoners may have been taken food.

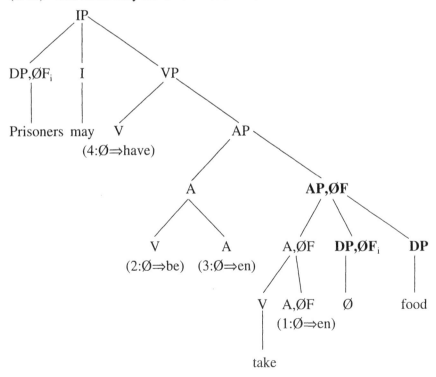

The integers in (6.11) indicate bottom-up ordering of PF insertions: each head of an XP is inserted only after the head of its complement (thus 2 selects 1, and 4 selects 3), while items inserted as heads within words must be their rightmost filled element (thus 3 follows 2). In this tree, all XP complements are sisters to the heads which select them, like the PP complements in conventional articulated structures such as (6.2) and (6.10a).

In fact, descriptive adequacy for English *requires* this articulated structure, as a basis for explaining the patterns of well-formed VP ellipsis in (6.4b) and VP fronting in (6.6b). In any flatter structure, the fronted and ellipted sequences would not be constituents.

However, as explained in the preceding section, *any* of the three lower XP complements bolded in (6.11) can equally well be generated higher in the structure, since they each satisfy subcategorization *before* insertion of higher empty heads spelled out in PF as *have* and *been*. As a result, any of these complement XPs positioned higher, for example as daughters of VP, count as extended sisters (4.28) of the heads which select them. In these positions they still satisfy Revised Classical Subcategorization (4.29), just like the complements of predicate adjectives in the earlier flatter structures (6.3a) and (6.10b).

Such a flat structure variant on (6.11) is illustrated for French in tree (6.12); for simpler exposition we can ignore the effect of French finite verb raising to I.[12]

The flatter structure (6.12) explains why Romance clitics appear to "climb" over passive and past participles and surface on a preceding auxiliary, as in *Des repas **leur** ont été apportés* 'Meals them-have been brought'. Such clitics are simply satisfying the Phrase Mate Hypothesis (6.9): e.g., the bold XP *aux prisonniers* which the clitic *leur* replaces is a sister of the latter's verbal host *ont*, as in (6.12). There is no climbing here, any more than in the examples (6.8) in which clitics replace complements of lexical adjectives. So-called clitic climbing is thus explained by the Phrase Mate Hypothesis in conjunction with the alternative flatter structures made possible by late insertion of grammatical verbs.

---

[12] The illustrative trees (6.11) and (6.12) are equally possible options in both English and French. It is of interest to note that the empirical argument for an articulated variant (6.11) involves paradigms of English participles (6.4) and (6.6), while the argument for the flatter alternative (6.12) is based on Romance clitics. But neither argument *excludes* the co-existence of the other structure in either language under consideration.

(6.12)   Des repas ont été apportés aux prisonniers.
         'Meals have been brought to the prisoners'

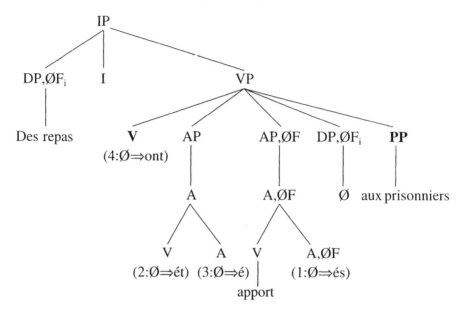

It is well known that Romance clitics not only may appear on the first auxiliaries but in fact are generally obligatory in this position. So just as with the complements of predicate adjectives, questions arise: why can't un-cliticized pronouns appear in situ in a less flat structure like (6.11)? And why can't the clitics appear on the past and passive participles rather than on the finite verb?

The answers are as follows. Just as with the French predicate adjectives discussed earlier, in situ pronouns are blocked by Economy of Derivation: clitic pronouns reduce the number of free morphemes inserted in a derivation. The reason that clitics do not appear on the passive and past participles themselves is simply that Romance clitics are bound morphemes lexically specified for verbal and not adjectival hosts.[13]

We have thus seen three independent arguments, one from English question formation and two from Romance cliticization, which confirm that grammatical verbs subcategorized with the frame +<A> have the dual syntactic structures and consequent dual behavior predicted by the Syntacticon model (4.9).

---

[13] This restriction is sometimes relaxed in Italian if no finite verb is present.

6.3 Flatter lexical projections induced by "light" verbs

The alternative possibilities in (6.7) for AP fronting in questions recall English "light verb" paradigms, that is, verbs of somewhat vague semantic content whose objects are nominalized lexical verbs. The combination "light verb plus nominalized object" is a near paraphrase of the lexical verb alone: *take a walk = walk; have a look = look; make complaints = complain.* When the nominalized object of a light verb is questioned or passivized, its complement can prepose with the noun as in (6.13a) and (6.14a), or stay in situ as in (6.13b) and (6.14b) (Ross, 1967). (6.13) is the same option as seen earlier in (6.7) with complements of predicate adjectives.

(6.13)   a.   What complaints about the food did they make?
         How long a walk into the forest should Mary take?
         How serious a look at that painting did you have?
      b.   What complaints did they make about the food?
         How long a walk should Mary take into the forest?
         How serious a look did you have at that painting?

(6.14)   a.   Some complaints about the food were made (by the guests).
         A long walk into the forest should be taken (by Mary).
      b.   Some complaints were made about the food (by the guests).
         A long walk should be taken into the forest (by Mary).

When verbs with the same objects are not themselves "light," question formation (6.15a) and passive movement (6.15b) cannot separate the objects from their complements, as conventional articulated constituent structures correctly predict. The contrasts between (6.13b-6.14b) and (6.15) observed in Ross (1967) are fairly striking.

(6.15)   a.   *What complaints did they ridicule about the food?
         *How long a walk should Mary avoid into the forest?
         *How serious a look did you recommend at that painting?
      b.   *Some complaints were ridiculed about the food (by the hosts).
         *A long walk should be avoided into the forest (by Mary).

Rather, complements of the objects of open class verbs form a phrase with the object, as expected:

(6.16)   a.   What complaints about the food did they ridicule?
         How long a walk into the forest should Mary avoid?
         How serious a look at that painting did you recommend?

b. Some complaints about the food were ridiculed (by the hosts).
A long walk into the forest should be avoided (by Mary).

Grimshaw and Mester (1988) discuss Japanese light verbs in terms of whether and how they and their object nouns assign theta roles to complements. However, such an approach cannot assimilate the paradigms in (6.13)–(6.14) to those in (6.7), since a linking verb and its predicate adjective are not related by theta role assignment.[14]

Countering their analysis, Kajihara (1991) argues that light verbs should be taken as transitive grammatical V (lacking purely semantic features *f*) which are empty in deep structure. She then proposes that in either English or Japanese, a daughter of the VP such as the PP in (6.17) *can be interpreted as a complement to N* at any level which precedes insertion of the grammatical V. (At the same time, a more familiar tree in which these PP complements are sisters to N can also be generated.)

(6.17)

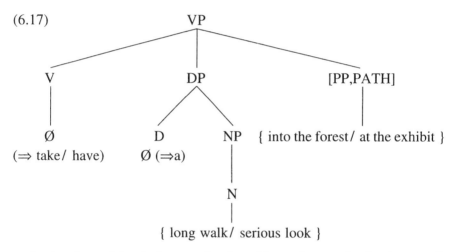

In the almost identical terms developed here, the nominalizations *walk* or *look* in (6.17) can be lexical heads of light verb VPs at deep structure, since insertion of the grammatical verbs *take* and *have* optionally takes place later, in the syntax. When insertion is delayed in this way, the PP

---

[14] Moreover, I claim to have demonstrated in Emonds (1991b) and in Chapter 2 here that individual verbs do not assign theta roles in any case. Rather, they select complements via subcategorization, and theta role assignment to complements then proceeds via interpretive principles which use the verbs' inherent features. If this is correct, theta role assignments are invariably consequences of syntactic structure, and can never be used to predict it.

complements in (6.17) are deep structure extended sisters of the nominalizations *walk* and *look* and thus satisfy the subcategorization frame +<PATH> which they inherit from their base verbs.

Structures like (6.17) with higher empty heads are the basis of the split constructions in (6.13b) and (6.14b); they are excluded with open class lexical verbs, as in (6.15). These correct results require no stipulations; they are consequences of the present model by virtue of the simple fact that the lexical entries of "light verbs" such as *take* and *have* are precisely those with no purely semantic feature f (unlike e.g. *avoid* and *ridicule*). No alternative analysis can avoid stipulating this minimal lexical difference between the two types of verbs, and *the present model requires nothing beyond this*. In the Syntacticon model (4.9), the mere absence of semantic f leads to possible late insertion and dual structures, and late syntactic insertion freely permits the structure (6.17).

Light verbs thus reduce to a special case of closed class grammatical verbs which lexicalize either pre-transformationally or in syntax. Lexicalization theory itself thus fully predicts the syntactic alternations of "light verbs" as the transitive subcase of grammatical verbs. The phenomenon therefore requires no special lexical treatment; it merely serves to illustrate interesting consequences of late (i.e., non-deep) syntactic insertion.

6.4 Theoretical limits on possible flat structures

6.4.1 The exclusion of P from extended sisterhood

We have just analyzed cases of extended sisterhood (4.28) which exemplify the structural possibility of higher empty heads in tree (6.1). In the two constructions examined so far, with Z a higher V which is empty in deep structure, Y is A (with linking verbs) and Y is N (with light verbs).

(6.1)

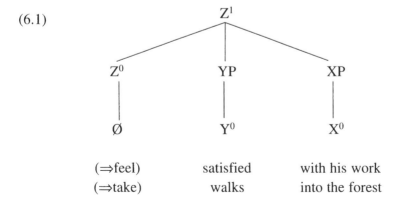

It is to be remarked that P never seems to play the roles of either Y or Z in such configurations. First, Y cannot be P, since phrasal complements of P do not "split upwards" away from P like the complements of A such as *satisfied* in (6.7) and *walk* in (6.13)–(6.14).[15] Second, Z cannot be P since "complements of complements" of P don't surface as sisters of P rather than of the lower head.

This more restricted behavior of P is perhaps related to its status as the most marked of the Dictionary's four head of phrase categories (among other things, it is the least numerous; cf. note 9 of Ch. 1). In general, I take nouns to be the least marked categorial head: the marked value -N unites V and P, and the marked value +AD unites A and P (cf. note 19 of Ch. 3). According to this analysis, P has more than one marked categorial feature, which allows us to distinguish its behavior indirectly rather than by stipulation.

(6.18)   *In the definition of Extended Sisterhood (4.28), Z and Y can each have at most one marked categorial feature.*[16]

In particular, a lexical category X^j complement of P cannot be an extended sister of P; it must be a X^j sister of P in the classical sense.

It is of some interest to note that the phonology of compounds and of morphology presented in Chomsky and Halle (1968) does not include P with its lexical categories N, V and A. Research in the intervening thirty years has shown that P should be included in the basic inventory of heads in syntax, even though much of this work has, as argued in Chapters 4 and 5, wrongly segregated phrasal and word-internal syntax. But when we re-

---

[15] A referee is curious as to whether P-stranding might be accounted for as this kind of split. However, P-stranding is not limited to complements of grammatical V, as the theory here would require. Second, the principles which give rise here to dual complement structures for grammatical verbs are proposed as part of UG – and indeed are largely justified throughout this chapter on the basis of languages other than English. But P-stranding is of extremely limited distribution in the world's languages (van Riemsdijk, 1978); its full form seems limited to North Germanic (and the influence of Old Norse on Early Modern English).

[16] One might conjecture that any sister of P must be *phrasal*, i.e. that P cannot be the right-hand head of a compound nor a suffixal head in derivational or inflectional morphology. I am skeptical on all three counts. (i) English *hereby, therein, therefore,* etc. may be D-P compounds. (ii) *-ing* may be a derivational P head in *concerning, including, excepting,* etc. (iii) Artiagoitia (1992) and Kubo (1994) respectively analyze participial suffixes *-te* in Basque and *-te* in Japanese (accidental homonyms) as word-internal right hand P heads.

integrate syntax and morphology, we find that the category P does not completely "fit" with N, V and A; it does not have their freedom of occurrence but, somewhat like its grammatical cousins I and D, must directly combine with sisters as expressed in (6.18). In this sense, the doubly marked category P behaves more like a functional category than a more flexible (singly marked) lexical category.[17]

The restriction (6.18) imposes rather strong limits on the distribution of "flat structures." The rest of this chapter can be thought of as demonstrating the following thesis: within the limits set by (6.18), grammars exemplify exactly the predicted range of flat structures (6.19).

(6.19)

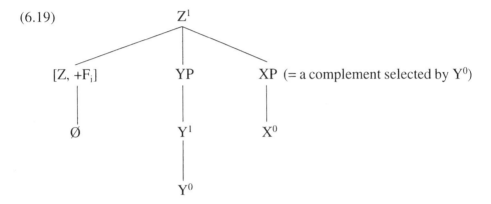

We have just seen in (6.18) that neither Z nor Y in (6.19) can have the value P. There thus remain precisely nine possibilities of extended sisterhood to investigate, since Z and Y can be any of N, A or V.

However, six of these are immediately ruled out by a restriction on complement structure described in Emonds (1985, Ch. 1). In English and many similar systems any complement phrases of an N or A head must be further embedded in a PP (or a CP, a special case of PP). In Chapter 7, the paradigms which exemplify this restriction are used to justify a "Deep Case

---

[17] M. Kubo suggests that all the members of P, like those of I and D, may be characterizable by cognitive syntactic features F, without recourse to purely semantic features *f*. The category P has been widely understood in generative grammar to be too large a class for such a treatment. However, many intransitive English P such as *aside, downstairs, overboard, uptown,* etc. are possibly [P - N] compound *nouns* whose first element's features, via alternative realization (section 4.4.2), can license an empty head P in contexts requiring PPs. Such analyses would greatly reduce the number of lexical P, essentially back to the grammatical prepositions, particles, and subordinating conjunctions of traditional grammar.

Filter," which is a formal construct with this consequence.[18] The Deep Case Filter (7.40) thus implies that if Z is an N or A in (6.19), then some PP other than Z^1 is a smaller phrase whose lexical head is Y^0, and so extended sisterhood (4.28) cannot come into play. Hence Z can only have the value V in (6.19).

Consequently, the only subcases of structures (6.19) permitted by Universal Grammar are those in which Z is V and Y = N, A or V. But section 6.2 has already treated the combination of Z = V and Y = A (linking verbs with predicate adjectives), while section 6.3 has analyzed the combination of Z = V and Y = N (so-called light verbs). It remains only to investigate when Z and Y in (6.19) are both V. We turn now to the possibility of such flat V-V structures.

6.4.2 Flat structures for grammatical V and N

The discussion of extended projections of V and N in section 1.3 did not fully take up the much debated question of whether non-finite V always project to VP and IP. Chapters 4 and 5 have argued that both present and passive/ past participles with underlying V heads are structural APs rather than VPs, so for participial V I have given a negative answer. The question that remains is whether bare infinitival V and English infinitival V with *to* invariably head their own VPs and IPs.

Fairly well-supported hypotheses of Longobardi (1994) and Kallulli (1999) indicate that NPs, under rather restricted circumstances, need not project to DPs, so we might expect, by parallelism, that some limited set of infinitives are not IPs. On the other hand, Koster and May's (1982) classic overview of the properties of English infinitives strongly suggests that at least those marked by *to* do project to IP, with *to* directly signaling the presence of I.

The answer that will emerge here as to which infinitives project is not based on any of the verbal dichotomies previously discussed in the grammatical literature. The crucial issue of whether and which infinitives project to VP and IP is based rather on the difference between open class and closed class (grammatical) verbs. I will show that in the framework (4.9) of the

---

[18] There appear to be languages in which DP sisters of N can be assigned structural case; construct states in Semitic probably exemplify this. Other such structural cases may include non-nominative in Swedish (Platzack, 1982) and genitive in Czech (Veselovská, 1998). It is beyond this study's scope to determine whether the structure (6.19) with Z as N and Y as N or D is appropriate for these systems.

Syntacticon, infinitival complements of open class verbs must be IPs, while those of closed class verbs need not project even to VP.[19]

Syntactic category theory (e.g. the bar notation) requires that any non-maximal X^j (not internal to some Y^0) must further project to X^k.[20] However, this statement does not guarantee the *uniqueness* of X^j under X^k, but we may be able to derive a uniqueness condition on heads of phrases from other principles rather than stipulating it. If uniqueness of heads turns out to not be absolute, then (head-initial) flat structures (6.20) may co-exist with the more classically conceived phrasal complements in (6.21).

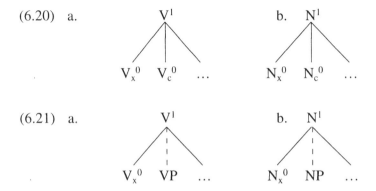

(6.20)   a. V^1 b. N^1

  V_x^0 V_c^0 ... N_x^0 N_c^0 ...

(6.21)   a. V^1 b. N^1

  V_x^0 VP   ... N_x^0 NP   ...

The flat structures in (6.20), which seem to have "two heads," might plausibly be licensed by subcategorization of lexical items V_x or by some other rule of LF interpretation which takes flat X^0 - X^0 structures as input. To see how the first possibility works, I will now show that the lexical theory of Chapter 4 predicts that a flat structure (6.20a) can formally satisfy a lexical subcategorization frame of the form @, V_x, +<V>, but only *under the condition that V_x is a closed class (grammatical) verb.*[21]

To begin, since V_x and V_c are in the same phrase, the left-headedness of phrases in English and Romance requires that *V_c be lexicalized first* (or else

---

[19] A reader who wishes to see only empirical support for this conclusion but not its formal justification may wish to skip to the illustrative tree (6.22) at the end of this subsection.
[20] Recall from Chapter 1 that the symbol XP throughout this work conforms to a theoretical simplification proposed and justified in Speas (1990, section 2.2): XP is not formally distinct from X^1. Rather, *XP is only a notation for a topmost X^1 which is not itself a phrasal head* of a higher X^1. (That is, [$_{XP}$ XP - @] is not defined.)
[21] Such entirely flat options for the V-A and V-N combinations in (6.3) are unavailable, because in such cases A^0 or N^0 would be daughters of V^1, which are prohibited dominance relations.

it will not be leftmost under V^1 when it becomes a lexical head). There are then two possibilities: V_c is lexicalized pre-transformationally (at deep structure) or it is not. If V_c is not lexicalized pre-transformationally then clearly V_x is not lexicalized pre-transformationally either, i.e. V_x is a closed class item, as is to be shown.[22]

Suppose alternatively that V_c is lexicalized pre-transformationally, i.e. it is itself an open class item. In Chomsky's (1965) earliest work on the transformational cycle, lexical insertion takes place just prior to the transformational derivation. Moreover, since his insertion of heads is always in terms of the properties of already lexicalized arguments, lexical insertion itself constitutes a sort of preliminary bottom-up cycle. Klima's suggestion of Cyclic Lexical Insertion (4.74) – interspersing merge and move, in current minimalist terms – simply replaces these two cycles by one.[23]

From this perspective, Chomsky's original idea that the cycle applies right after deep lexical insertion amounts to requiring that transformations apply on a cyclic domain (that is, the lowest IP dominating a V) no later than when that domain acquires a lexical head. In fact, my formulation of Deep Lexicalization (4.7) has included this condition.

(4.7)   *Deep Lexicalization (DL). Items associated with non-syntactic, purely semantic features f satisfy lexical insertion conditions (just) before processing of the smallest cyclic domains containing them. Such f occur only on N, V, A and P.*

That is, the transformational cycle on the lowest IP containing a pre-transformationally lexicalized V_c must begin prior to insertion of V_x. In other words, V_x in (6.20) cannot be inserted pre-transformationally. So again the only option is that V_x in (6.20) is inserted in syntax or at PF, i.e., it is a closed class item.

That is, it follows as a theorem from DL that *the only V which can take "bare V" complements as in (6.20) are grammatical verbs lacking purely semantic features f.*

Let me review. According to multi-level lexical insertion (4.8), a grammatical verb $[V_x, F_i]$ lacking purely semantic features f can be inserted

---

[22] Open class items are always subject to Deep Lexicalization (4.7).

[23] For convenience, (4.74) is repeated from Chapter 4:

Cyclic Lexical Insertion: A lexical head X imposes restrictions on its arguments only after the transformational cycle is terminated in all the cyclic domains properly contained inside X^{max}.

either at deep structure or later in a derivation. If such a V_x specified with the frame +<V> is inserted in deep structure, it appears in (6.21a) just as would an open class verb. But if V_x is inserted later, in the syntax, it can indeed license the structure (6.20a) as the technical discussion has just shown. The definitions of Lexical Projection (4.27) and Extended Sisterhood (4.28) then permit the complements YP of the second verb V_c to be realized in a flat structure, effectively turning the complements of V_c into sisters of V_x. The latter configuration, similar to those attested for linking verbs in (6.3a) and for transitive light verbs in (6.3b), is represented in (6.22).

(6.22)

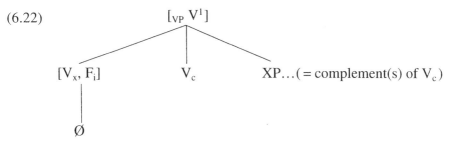

(lexicalized in syntax or PF)

Finally, since the flat structures in (6.20) are well-formed at Spell Out, a fairly uncontroversial formulation of Chomsky's (1991) idea of Economy of Representation rules out the articulated trees (6.21) at that level, though not as deep structures:

(6.23)   *Economy of Representation. Structural requirements such as subcategorization frames are to be satisfied at a level of derivation with as few phrasal nodes as possible.*

I thus conclude that flat V_x-V_c structures (6.22) are permitted if and only if grammatical verbs are post-transformationally inserted in V_x. The same verbs inserted at deep structure have the conventional complement structure in (6.21).

All the above reasoning applies equally well to the DP system. The only head N_x which can have "bare N_c complements" are grammatical nouns lacking purely semantic features f, and these nouns must be inserted in the syntax or in PF. These important consequences of the lexical theory of the Syntacticon (4.9) are amply confirmed by the empirical studies cited in the following sections. I will first discuss briefly the flat structures (6.20b) containing N heads, and then complete the chapter with more extensive treatment of those with V heads (6.20a).

6.4.3 Flat structures for pseudo-partitives

Nothing in the reasoning of the preceding subsection is confined to the category V; under the DP hypothesis, formal relations among V, VP, I and IP are mirrored by those among N, NP, D and DP. Although we do not ordinarily think of some class of grammatical N taking "N-headed sisters," the theory of multi-level insertion for closed classes of elements in the Syntacticon predicts the existence of such a configuration, i.e. (6.20b).

In fact, Kubo (1996) proposes just this kind of flat structure for the pseudo-partitive construction in Japanese, contrasting it with an embedded phrasal structure [$_{NP}$ DP - [N_x, F_i]] needed to properly represent Japanese true partitives. I cite two of her contrasting examples (CL = the italicized nominal classifier construct required for explicit counting):

(6.24) a. Pseudo-partitive:
  Chikako-wa   kinou   takai CD   *go-mai-o*   katta.
  Chikako-TOP yesterday   expensive CD five-CL-ACC bought
  'Chikako bought five instances of expensive CDs yesterday.'
  b. True Partitive:
  Chikako-wa   kinou   katta   takai CD-no
  Chikako-TOP yesterday   bought expensive CD-GEN
  go-mai-o   sudeni kiita.
  five-CL-ACC already listened
  'Chikako has already listened to five of the expensive CDs she bought yesterday.'

Kubo claims that the closed class of Japanese classifiers N_x obligatorily present in such counting constructions are grammatical nouns with alternative lexical frames +<N> and +<D>. She proposes the structures (6.25) for these constructions, where N_n stands for a numeral, N_c is an open class lexical noun quantified over, and YP are any complements or adjuncts of N_c. The PP over DP is necessary to provide case.

(6.25)   a. Pseudo-partitive with N, +<N>: NP

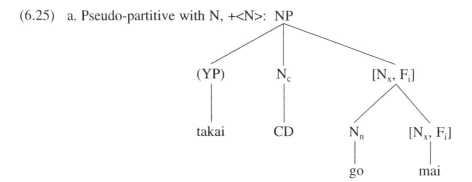

b. True Partitive with N, +<D>:

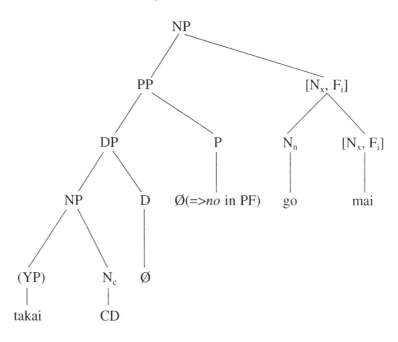

She supports this structural difference with five arguments based on Japanese. Some of them show that sequences YP + N_c are constituents (only) in true partitives. Others demonstrate that two independent references are available for N_c and N_x in true partitives (6.25b) but not in (6.25a), again indicating that only the latter contain an embedded DP, i.e., the locus of reference in terms of the DP Hypothesis. Subsequently, she shows that an analysis of the English constructions parallel to that proposed for Japanese accounts for all Selkirk's (1977) English-based empirical arguments for distinguishing the two constructions.[24]

Kubo's pseudo-partitive tree (6.25a) is exactly (6.20b) with reversal of left-right order (reflecting the head-final phrase structures of Japanese) and provision made for the "numeral-classifier cluster," which she does not further analyze.

Given these clarifications as to the genesis and extent of flat structures and independent justification for them inside N/D projections, we are ready to empirically confirm the theoretically predicted "flat structures" (6.20a) in the V/I system as well.

6.5 Differing lexical projections induced by restructuring verbs

6.5.1 Rizzi's compelling evidence for flat structures

Section 6.4.2 has outlined how the lexical theory of Chapter 4 predicts that closed class (grammatical) verbs V_x listed in the Syntacticon as @, V, +<V> can give rise to flat structures as in (6.22). The complements XP of the selected V_c then appear as sisters to V_x rather than inside a separate VP headed by V_c.

(6.22)

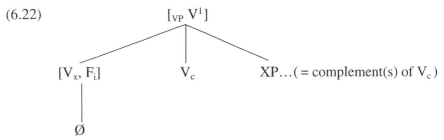

$[_{VP} V^1]$

$[V_x, F_i]$ V_c XP...(= complement(s) of V_c)

Ø

(lexicalized in syntax or PF)

At the same time, nothing prevents a grammatical verb V_x with the frame +<V> from appearing with infinitival IP complements *in deep structure*. Moreover, the same subcategorization frame +<V> of typical open class

---

[24] As observed by a referee, an adjective modifying a head noun in an English pseudo-partitive flat structure can be attributed to either noun: *John bought a { tasty/ green } bottle of wine*, whereas in the articulated partitive structure, the attribution is restricted to the higher noun: *John bought three { green/ *tasty } bottles of this wine.*

verbs yields *only* IP complements, as shown in the same section. In this section, we will see that these formal possibilities explain some of the most intriguing lexical alternations of Romance syntax.

In a richly empirical and tightly argued study, Rizzi (1978) demonstrates that non-finite complement structures of about a dozen Italian verbs systematically exhibit a kind of dual syntactic behavior. This subsection reviews Rizzi's argumentation in some detail, since generative analyses rarely find so many independent grammatical properties which all point to the same solution. All these "restructuring verbs" V_x are a subset of so-called "raising" or "control" verbs, in that their overt surface subject is the same as the understood subject of their complement verb V_c. Burzio (1986, 324) associates such restructuring behavior with Italian *andare* 'go', *venire* 'come', *sembrare* 'seem', *stare* 'stay', *continuare* 'go on', *cominciare* 'begin', *sapere* 'know', *volere* 'want', *dovere* 'should', and *potere* 'can'. Aissen (1974) and Aissen and Perlmutter (1976) analyze a similar Spanish phenomenon in terms of the "clause union" of Relational Grammar, providing a similar, slightly larger list of V_x for Spanish. The meanings of these verbs are among the most basic, and their translations tend to serve as auxiliaries or "semi-auxiliaries" in various languages.

Although speakers vary as to exactly which verbs trigger restructuring (Rizzi, 1978, note 6), there is always a pattern of "semantically more impoverished verbs allowing restructuring more readily" (Burzio, 1986, 220). *In previous accounts the limitation to "semantically impoverished verbs" has been treated as accidental.* But in the present account, a lack of purely semantic features f is precisely the formal property of grammatical verbs, as seen in the previous section, which can license a flat structure (6.22).[25]

Schematically, restructuring verbs appear in italicized sequences as in (6.26), where YP is a complement or adjunct of V_c. Throughout this section, I use Rizzi's examples.

---

[25] Rizzi (1978, note 6) mentions that some verbs meaning 'try' are marginally acceptable as restructuring verbs. The present framework can account for variability in the triggering classes (even in a single speaker's speech) as follows. Suppose some verb with a purely semantic feature f, which consequently requires DL (4.7), is lexically listed as @, V, F (syntactic features), f, +<V>. Now, some speakers may modify this entry by parenthesizing the feature f, yielding @, V, F, (f), +<V>. A single speaker might link these parentheses to various stylistic factors. When a derivation containing $[_V$ @ $]$ does not include f, then late insertion of @ is a possibility. Although the full meaning of @ which includes f might be pragmatically associated with such a derivation, one could say that restructuring stylistically suggests a less specific meaning than a verb actually has. I believe this corresponds to the "feel" of restructuring, if such can be said to exist.

(6.26)   V$_x$ (restructuring verb) + V$_c$ (non-finite complement) + YP . . .

    a.   Questi argomenti, dei quali *verrò a parlarti*   al piu presto,...
       These topics, of which come-will to talk-you   at most soon,...
       'These topics, about which I will come to talk to you as soon as
       possible...'
    b.   *Ho cominciato a discuterne*   con Mario da Gianni.
       Have begun   to discuss-thereof with Mario at Gianni's
       'I have begun at Gianni's house to discuss (of) it with Mario.'

Rizzi adduces no less than nine contrasts to show that the verb complements and adjuncts YP in (6.26) appear in trees in two distinct but not
overlapping ways.[26] He claims, and I concur, that in one type of structure
(6.27), the sequence V$_c$ + YP . . . acts like an ordinary non-finite clausal
constituent (when infinitival, plausibly an IP with a null subject). In another
"restructured" version (6.28), essentially (6.22), *YP complements or YP'
adjuncts of V$_c$ act like surface daughters of some projection of the initial
verb V$_x$.*

(6.27)   Ordinary non-finite complementation:

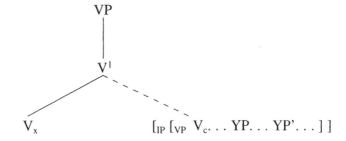

(6.28)   Restructured VP; cf. Rizzi's tree (138):[27]

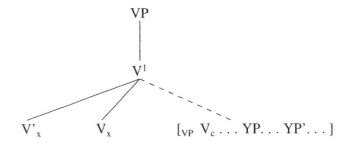

---

[26] Although Rizzi introduces his study by exemplifying "clitic climbing" with these

My only disagreement with Rizzi's analysis concerns not the existence of these two structures, but rather what gives rise to them. That is, we need not postulate a rule or indeed any kind of stipulated "restructuring" process to account for the alternation (6.27)–(6.28); it suffices to lexically associate the single subcategorization frame +<V> *with a grammatical verb*. The two alternative structures needed to account for the complex syntax of closed class verbs are then unstipulated consequences of the definition of lexical projection (4.27) and dual-level insertion from the Syntacticon.[28] This then avoids what Rizzi acknowledges as the "many nontrivial formal problems created by the existence of a fully productive reanalysis rule."

Let us now review his arguments for his dual structures (6.27)–(6.28).

(i) Uniform clitic climbing under restructuring. In accordance with a general property of Romance which I have termed the Phrase Mate Hypothesis (6.9), the Italian enclitics on V_c in (6.26) (*ti, ne*) replace complement YPs of which they are "clause mates" (Rizzi, 1978, 115). In this sense, the examples in (6.26) are infinitival complements with the ordinary embedded structure (6.27). But Italian (and Spanish) restructuring verbs V_x themselves can also host the clitics corresponding to complements and adjuncts of the lower V_c, as the italicized sequences in (6.29) show:

---

verbs, this phenomenon is logically on a par with all the other properties he studies, and so has no special status in logic of his or this discussion.

[27] Rizzi's "slight evidence" for grouping V_x and V_c into a single verbal complex depends on there being a special verb movement rule for causative constructions. Emonds (1999) and the Appendix below analyze Romance causatives without the ad hoc verb movement which serves as its only justification; Zagona (1988) argues against such verbal complexes in general.

The possibility of an adverb and an atrophied introductory morpheme between the two verbs, both italicized in (i), might suggest that a phrasal node (*which excludes YP*) appears over V_c in (6.28); nothing in this section depends on this issue.

(i)   [Gli stessi errori]$_i$ si continuano *stupidamente a* commettere e$_i$.
       'The same errors PRO continues stupidly to do'.

But since bare adverbials are generally allowed as left sisters to V in otherwise head-initial VPs, no lower verb phrase is really needed in (6.28) to group them with V_c as a constituent.

[28] The sharply different syntax of closed and open class verbs (exemplified by restructuring) and its explanation in terms of dual level lexical insertion reveal a fundamental inadequacy of any theory in which lexical insertion all takes place at one level or in one component. Conceptualizations in which a derivation manipulates only unlexicalized "abstract objects" fare no better than Chomsky's (1965) original model in this respect. The fact is, all generative theories of lexical insertion deal with "abstract objects," but they differ in how well they account for the paradigms of natural language.

(6.29) a. Questi argomenti, dei quali *ti verrò*   a parlare al più presto,…
            These topics,   of which you-come-will to talk at most soon,…
            'These topics, of which I will come to talk to you as soon as
            possible…'
        b. *Ne ho*   *cominciato* a discutere con Mario da Gianni.
            Thereof-have begun   to discuss with Mario at Gianni's
            'I have begun at Gianni's house to discuss (of) it with Mario.'

By using a flat structure (6.28) for the finite verb phrases in (6.29), the
YP complements of the second verb V_c surface as clitics on V_x, exactly as
(6.9) predicts.

(6.9)   *Phrase Mate Hypothesis. Romance clitics on V_i are associated only*
         with XP sisters to some V_i^k, where XP = DP, IP, PP, NP, AP, VP.

The appearance of clitics on restructuring verbs is the third instance of
"climbing" we have seen in Romance, whereby a clitic's host is not the same
verb which lexically licenses the phrase corresponding to the clitic. As with
the apparent climbing of clitic complements of adjectives and participles
analyzed in section 6.2, the independently justified structure (6.28) eliminates a whole class of putative exceptions to the Phrase Mate Hypothesis.[29]

As often noted (Contreras, 1979; Bok-Bennema, 1981), all Romance
clitics corresponding to complements and adjuncts of a single V_c must
surface on a single verbal host, *either* V_c *or* V_x; no "mixing" of hosts is
allowed. That is, "climbing" to a higher verb is not an optional process, but
proceeds uniformly on the basis of *either* the ordinary structure (6.27) or the
restructured (6.28). In both structures, *clitics uniformly attach to the left-
hand head V of the lowest VP dominating the phrases they correspond to.*

(ii) Non-finite VP preposing in non-restrictive relatives. The enclitic *-ti*
'you' on V_c in (6.30a) indicates an ordinarily structured preposable VP
complement (6.27). But a sequence with a proclitic *ti* on the governing V_x
verrò is evidence of restructuring. As is then predicted, no internal VP
dominates only the sequence V_c + YP. Consequently the sequence *parlare
dei quali* is not a constituent and so cannot be preposed in (6.30b):

---

[29] Napoli (1981) and other authors have applied Rizzi's arguments to Romance passive
and past auxiliaries, treating them as obligatory restructuring contexts. The analysis of
these auxiliaries in section 6.2 here also uniformly attributes both types of climbing to a
single cause: late lexical insertion of V_x.

(6.30)   a. Questi argomenti, [$_{VP}$ a *parlarti* dei quali] verrò al più presto, ...
       b. *Questi argomenti, a parlare dei quali *ti verrò* al più presto, ...

(iii) Non-finite VP as focus of a cleft sentence. By the same reasoning, an enclitic -*ne* on V$_c$ indicates an familiarly structured VP complement (6.27) which can be focused in a cleft sentence as in (6.31a). In contrast to this, the proclitic *ne* on the V$_x$ *dovresti* in (6.31b) indicates a restructured sequence (6.28) which lacks such an internal VP. Since in this case the sequence V$_c$ + YP *discutere con Mario* is not a constituent, it cannot be moved to focus position:

(6.31)   a. E [$_{VP}$ *discuterne* con Mario] che dovresti.
         'It is discuss-thereof with Mario that you should have.'
       b. *E discutere con Mario che *ne dovresti.*
         'It is discuss with Mario that you thereof should have.'

(iv) "Heavy Constituent Shift" of VP over a PP. Rizzi's argument for this construction is parallel to his argument from focus movement. When an enclitic is on the V$_c$ *discutere*, there is an internal VP which can move rightwards over a PP (6.32a). But the appearance of the same clitic on V$_x$ *ho cominciato* (6.32b) indicates restructuring, which means that there is no VP candidate for rightward movement.

(6.32)   a. Ho cominciato [$_{PP}$ da Gianni] [$_{VP}$ a *discuterene* con Mario].
       b. *Ne ho cominciato* [$_{PP}$ da Gianni] a discutere con Mario.

(v) "Right-Node Raising" of VP. Rizzi's argument and examples are exactly parallel to the ones for Heavy Constituent Shift. If a clitic appears on V$_c$, the VP which it heads can "right-node raise" in a conjoined sentence. However, if the same clitic appears on V$_x$, there is no internal VP headed by V$_c$ available for movement.

(vi) Attachment of the Italian enclitic *loro* to V$_x$ or V$_c$. The syntax of the disyllabic clitic *loro* 'to them' is different from that of other Italian clitics. It can only be enclitic, and it may *attach to any verbal form in its VP*. For example, unlike the other clitics, *loro* can attach to a passive or past participle as well as to finite and infinitival V. When an open class verb such as *pensar* 'think' has an infinitival complement (6.33a), the latter's indirect object *loro* naturally enough obeys the Phrase Mate Hypothesis and so cannot attach to the higher verb in (6.33b):

(6.33)   a.   Pensavo di [$_{VP}$ consegnare loro i soldi].
          'I thought to give them the money.'
         b.   *Pensavo loro di consegnare il soldi.

But with a restructuring verb, *loro* predictably can appear on either V_c or V_x since the flat structure alternative (6.27) allows V_x to be in the same VP as *loro* in its base position:

(6.34)   a.   Dovrai parlare loro al più presto di questa storia.
         b.   Dovrai loro parlare al più presto di questa storia.
              Both: 'I should talk to them as soon as possible about this story.'

The alternation again shows that a V_x - V_c sequence can realize a flat structure, provided that V_x is a grammatical or closed class V.

(vii) Blocked extractions of null operators in Italian. The Italian counterpart to the English "*easy to please* construction" doesn't permit extraction of a DP out of even a simple infinitival complement of an open class verb such as *promettere* 'promise', as seen in (6.35).

(6.35)   *[Questo lavoro]$_i$ è facile [$_{VP}$ da promettere [$_{VP}$ di finire e$_i$ per domani]].
          'That work is easy to promise to finish by tomorrow.'

However, a restructuring verb such as *cominciare* 'begin' permits a flat structure sequence of infinitives without any internal VP as in (6.36). Consequently, in contrast to (6.35), a "clausemate" extraction of a null operator O_i can apply:

(6.36)   [Questa canzone]$_i$ è facile O$_i$ [$_{VP}$ da cominciare a cantare e$_i$].
          'That song is easy to begin to sing.'

(viii) Italian object NP-preposing over *si* + V. Like null operator extraction, this object to subject movement, justified in some detail in Rizzi's section 2, can affect only clausemates. An ordinary embedded phrasal complement of an open class verb like *promettere* blocks this movement:

(6.37)   *[Le nuove case popolari]$_i$ si sono promesse di [$_{VP}$ costruire e$_i$ entro un anno].
          'The new council houses themselves have promised to build in a year.'

But complements of restructuring verbs can appear without such an embedded VP, and so an object can prepose to a subject position over a sequence of V. As expected then, NP-preposing is compatible with clitics placed on V_x, since both clitic "climbing" and object preposing can occur only with restructuring, i.e. in a flat structure.

(6.38) Queste case (gli) si vogliono vendere a caro prezzo.
          'These houses (to him) themselves want to sell at a high price.'

(6.38) thus contrasts crucially with (6.37), in which the embedded VP blocks this kind of preposing.

If one tried to replace the restructuring tree (6.28) with some kind of "transparent" or "small" VP over V_c and YP, which somehow allowed (but didn't force) both clitic raising and NP-preposing, then a clitic optionally placed lower on V_c in such a VP should have no effect on NP-preposing. But a clitic on V_c such as *gli* 'to them' blocks NP-preposing over *si* + V:

(6.39) *Queste case si vogliono vendergli a caro prezzo.

This again shows that a clitic on V_c implies that the structure simply is not flat, in sharp contrast to clitics on V_x which always unequivocally indicate a flat structure.

(ix) Auxiliary alternation in the V_x position. At the end of section 6.2, we saw how Romance auxiliaries, such as Italian *avere* 'have' and *essere* 'be', appear as additional V'_x at the left edge of flat structure VPs. With restructuring verbs V_x, this means they appear in the two following structures; YP is a complement to V_c and YP' is an adjunct.

(6.40) Ordinary complementation:

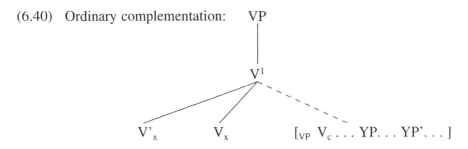

(6.41)   Restructured VP:

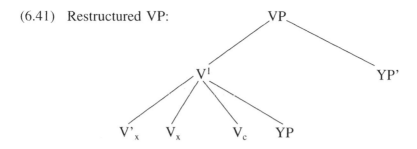

In this discussion, we can ignore the fact that V_x occurs with a participial A inflection. The important point is that a complement verb V_c of the participle can appear both inside its own VP in (6.40) and in a flat structure (6.41).

The literature on Italian has made clear that the choice of auxiliary V'_x in composed tenses depends on the class of the main verb. Burzio (1986) proposes that the formal choice of *essere* over the more general *avere* depends on subject-object co-indexing, since *essere* is required by reflexive, unaccusative and passive verbs, all of which involve a surface object co-indexed with the subject. More exactly, if YP in e.g. (6.41) is a *null* DP co-indexed with the subject, the first auxiliary V'_x is *essere*. From this point of view, the open class verb V_c doesn't trigger auxiliary selection directly; it rather contributes to determining whether YP must or can be an empty DP corresponding to a reflexive clitic or a trace of NP-movement.

In sequences of restructuring verbs, Rizzi (1978, 137) gives a rule for determining the choice of auxiliary: "In short, only the last verb of the verbal complex created by Restructuring can trigger *avere* → *essere* of the first Restructuring verb, no matter which other Restructuring verbs . . . are in the middle." Although the data he presents in support of this generalization are complex, the result is simple enough: the rightmost V which is a (restructured) *sister* to V'_x determines whether V'_x is *avere* or *essere*. Thus, whatever the contributions of V_c itself or a null DP in choosing V'_x, the flat structure of (6.41) clearly succeeds in transparently relating the paired constituents V'_x and YP as respectively head and DP complement *in the same VP*.

We have now reviewed Rizzi's nine arguments in favor of an optional "flat structure" representation (6.28) for (sequences of) restructuring verbs. As his more complex examples show, the diagnostics for flat structures *reinforce each other*; flat structures are associated with one set of patterns and articulated structures with another. It is unusual to find so many mutually converging reasons for the same hypothesis. Hence, we can be confident of his main conclusion, which is crucial for the argumentation here: restructuring verbs head two distinct structures, one like typical non-finite complement clauses (6.27) and a second (6.28) in which *the complements selected by V_c are sisters of V_x*.

Rizzi (1978, 148–150) convincingly argues that any dual lexical sub-categorization of V_x would fail to adequately express the *thoroughly op-tional* restructuring alternation. Dual subcategorizations typically correlate with different senses of a verb and other syntactic differences within the complement, which these alternations lack. He correctly concludes that a *single lexical specification* of V_x must somehow yield two distinct but syn-onymous surface configurations. That is, *descriptive and explanatory ad-equacy demand a lexical theory which allows the subcategorization feature +<V> of (only) a closed class of verbs to be satisfied by both a non-finite IP and a flat structure V alternative to VP/IP*.

Yet, without some ad hoc rule or other process in the transformational component, neither the unrevised subcategorization of Chomsky (1965) nor any plausible semantic-based system of "s-selection" can achieve this needed effect. In contrast, in terms of the multi-level Syntacticon (4.9), *the dual structures (6.27)–(6.28) and derivations for closed class verbs are characteristic and unstipulated consequences of the single subcatego-rization frame +<V> for any grammatical verb V_x*, since (only) such a V_x can optionally be left empty at deep structure. When V_x is left empty, the definition of Lexical Projection (4.27) determines that V_c is the deep lexical head of the VP in (6.28). Insertion of V_x during the syntax then results in flat structures. These structures in turn explain all effects of restructuring.

We come now to a surprising result, namely a general insertion condition for those grammatical elements (such as restructuring verbs) specified for *interpretable* syntactic features F but for no purely semantic features f. By inspecting Deep Lexicalization (4.7) and Phonological Lexicalization (4.21), we see that *restructuring verbs are subject to neither principle*. It therefore follows without stipulation:

(6.42) *Corollary. Grammatical N, V, A and P whose features are inter-pretable at LF may be inserted either at the Dictionary interface ("deep structure") or in the syntax.*

The corollary of course does not apply to the grammatical verbs *be* and *have* or their Romance counterparts, because they have no interpretable features and are hence inserted only at PF. When a restructuring verb V_x is inserted at deep structure, its infinitival complement V_c heads a VP and probably an IP, like that of any open class verb (cf. section 6.4.2 for formal justification). When a restructuring verb V_x is inserted in the syntax, its complement V_c appears as its sister.

6.5.2 The location of the lower subject in flat structures

Throughout the twenty years since Rizzi's study, syntacticians using a "T model" of derivations proposed in Chomsky and Lasnik (1977) have always assumed that each verb interpreted in Logical Form must have a separate subject at that level, here expressed as (1.17) in Chapter 1.

(1.17)   *Extended Projection Principle. Every head verb present in LF must have a structural subject phrase to which a semantic role may be assigned.*

There is no problem in satisfying the EPP for verbal heads in the ordinarily structured non-finite complements (6.27) of restructuring verbs. Since the latter are all either "control" or "raising" verbs, selected by a feature +<V>, the embedded subjects must be empty. This empty DP subject of V_c is realized in (6.27) exactly as for other control and raising verbs, either in SPEC(IP) or in the SPEC of the lower VP.

However, the EPP raises a difficult question for Rizzi's restructuring analysis, one that he neither poses nor answers: *In a flat structure, where is the subject of V_c in LF?* A quite elegant answer is within easy reach, once we abandon the notion that restructuring is a process *within* the syntactic component.

Observe first that certain consequences of restructured or "clause union" VPs, which the *output* of his reanalysis is meant to explain, must *precede* the most central transformational operations. For example, Null Operator movement in his seventh paradigm, (vii) above, is a main case of A-bar movement, and NP-preposing over *si* in his eighth paradigm, (viii) above, centrally represents A-movement. Hence the two different complement structures for restructuring verbs (6.27) and (6.28) must *already be distinct prior to the application of Move Alpha.* What then happens during a derivation to the underlying null subject of V_c in Rizzi's pre-restructuring tree, his (16)? There is no place for it except somehow "internal" to the restructured V_x - V_c sequence. It can no longer be an "external" argument of V_c at Spell Out or at LF since a VP headed by V_c no longer exists.[30]

---

[30] Even if one countenances "reconstruction" in LF, there is no internal VP for the subject of V_c to move back to, if restructuring is taken as transformational.

The fact that the "restructured" VPs (6.28) contain no separate subject position for the second verb between the two verbs has posed a severe barrier for accepting an unmodified version of Rizzi's analysis, as convincing as it otherwise is. In the phrasing of Burzio (1986, 337): "Subject deletion is therefore not compatible with the theoretical framework assumed here, in which the semantic component has no access to D-structure." He supplements this passage with arguments against subject deletion, which lead him to summarize: "On the basis of these arguments we will conclude that in restructured complexes the embedded subject is present at S-structure." (340)

As will now be seen, it is not difficult to locate the subject of V_c once a flat structure (6.28) is accepted as representing restructuring throughout a derivation. To independently motivate the analysis, let us consider for a moment languages which do *not* have restructuring.

It is well-known that languages not so different from Italian and Spanish, such as Modern French and English, do not permit restructuring. For example, French translations of restructuring sequences never permit clitics corresponding to complements of the second verb V_c to appear on the first V_x.

(6.43)   French translations of the "clitic climbing" in Italian (6.29):
   *Ces sujets, desquels je *te* viendrai parler aussitôt que possible ...
   *J'*en* ai commencé à discuter avec Mario chez Gianni.

At the same time, simple clauses in Italian and Spanish, but not in Modern French or English, exhibit freely postposed (overt) subject DPs, widely taken to be adjoined to some phrasal verbal projection and co-indexed with an empty DP in SPEC(IP). I propose that two co-occurring patterns, (i) restructuring of $V_x + V_c$ and (ii) the existence of freely postposed subjects *follow from a single property*. This single structural property from which (i) and (ii) follow seems to be that "primary" subject positions in SPEC(IP) and "secondary" ones adjoined to VP *can be freely co-indexed in Italian and Spanish, but not in French and English*.

I thus propose that the EPP (1.17) is satisfied in Italian and Spanish flat structures (6.28) as in (6.44), where a covert postposed subject is in the same position as overt postposed subjects in these languages. Recall that restructuring verbs are a subset of control and raising verbs, whose subjects must be co-indexed in LF with the subjects of their complements. Since Italian and Spanish allow co-indexing between SPEC(IP) and DPs adjoined to VP, *each verb in a restructured sequence has its own subject*.

(6.44)

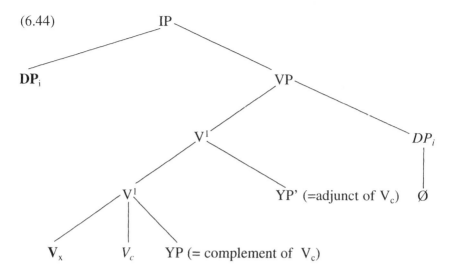

French and English are prevented from having such *co-indexed* subject positions, so a restructured VP in French or English would fail to satisfy the EPP requirement in (1.17).

To see how (6.44) satsifies the EPP, let us examine the definition of Generalized Subjects (1.15) used throughout this work:

(1.15)   *Generalized Subjects: The subject or external argument of a head X is the lowest N-projection which c-commands a phrasal projection of X within its minimal cyclic domain.*

As can be seen, each V in (6.44) has a separate DP subject which c-commands one of its phrasal projections. The exact subject-verb pairing in (6.44) has no importance for restructuring, since V_x is always a control or raising verb whose null subject is co-indexed with that of the matrix verb.[31]

I note in conclusion that one cannot wed this simple answer as to the whereabouts of the subject of V_c in (6.28), nor the accompanying explanation as to why French and English lack restructuring, to any analysis which transformationally derives a flat structure from an ordinary complement

---

[31] However, section A.3 of the Appendix will show that in e.g., (6.44), V_c must have a "closer" subject than V_x. Under this conception, the fonts in (6.44) show how subjects pair with verbs. This pairing will be derived from the fact that the phrases V' and VP are no longer projections of V_c at LF, except when V_x is an uninterpreted vacuous auxiliary *be* or *have*.

structure (6.27). To do so would necessitate a second, ad hoc "subject postposing" lowering transformation.[32] In contrast, the base-generated postpositioned subject of the complement verb V_c, as in the present analysis, further motivates attributing the flat structures (6.28) needed for restructuring paradigms not to the transformational or reanalysis component but to a theory of multi-level lexical insertion.

Although this section has concentrated on reconceptualizing long familiar alternations in Romance syntax, verbal flat structures are by no means limited to this language group. Jo (1996, 1199–1200) concludes, after basically agreeing with Lee's (1993) analysis of grammaticalized serial verb constructions in Korean:

> "… the doubly headed VP and Incorporation of V1 and V2 within a VP seems to be a device which turns the open [class] verbs (i.e., V2) into virtual grammatical verbs within the structure of a VP; as the result of the operation, they are in the nonhead position within a VP at s-structure. Their semantic contribution, though limited, is still substantial, … This is the second property different from the grammatical verb *ha* ['do'] in a construction like Long Form Negation which has no semantic content at all. The notion of an auxiliary verb in the literature, which vacillates between a non-primary semantic content and semantic vacuity, is incapable of capturing the different structural distributions existing between the 'grammaticalized' open [class] verbs and the grammatical verb *ha* …"[33]

We have now seen that the predictions of section 6.1 concerning complementation in flat structures are borne out. Namely, governing or selecting heads V can be empty (and ignored) in deep structure but filled in the syntactic component prior to Spell Out. Different sections have empirically motivated this theoretical conclusion by explaining paradigms in three previously unrelated constructions: "linking verbs" with A-headed complements (section 6.2), "light verbs" with N-headed complements (section

---

[32] Approaches wedded to the deeply ingrained (but as I claim throughout, unmotivated) view that subjects are invariably sisters of their predicates as well as daughters of some clause-like node (a kind of filiaque doctrine) are inexorably caught in this two rule trap.

[33] Thus, a small subset of open class verbs with semantic *f* lose their semantic specificity in Korean double-headed VPs, as Lee's analysis shows in detail. Their remaining cognitive syntactic features F still make a limited ('non-primary') contribution to LF; in contrast, the late-inserted purely grammatical *ha* is PF-inserted and so has a different distribution.

6.3), and "restructuring verbs" with V-headed complements (section 6.5). In all three constructions, the "YP complements of the complements" of the governing grammatical verb V_i are optionally projected as sisters to V_i rather than within a phrasal sister to V_i. Throughout, such configurations have been called "flat structures."

The difference between a restructuring sequence [$_{V'}$ V-V-YP] and the other two sequences ([$_{V'}$ V-AP-YP] and [$_{V'}$ V-NP-YP]) follows from the fact that V' can immediately dominate V in the bar notation, but cannot immediately dominate a non-maximal A or N. Thus, the complements to linking and light verbs are each in a "small phrase," which I have called flatter structures to contrast them with the entirely flat structures (6.41) of restructuring sequences.

An appendix to this chapter discusses at some length another instantiation of flat structure sequences of V, namely Romance causatives. In this construction, the governing verbs are not subject control or raising verbs, but rather transitive verbs.

6.6 The excess content of integrating syntax and morphology

Let me now review how this chapter on structures within a VP is related to the preceding chapters on the syntax of word-internal inflections. In Chapter 3, I formally identified derivational morphology as a sub-type of compounding, i.e., within the compound structures of English and many languages, a right-hand head lacking purely semantic features f has no independent stress and hence is descriptively termed a suffix. It then follows that derivational suffixes are "heads" of words (and phrases), since compounds of the same type are right-headed in these languages.[34]

Then, to accommodate the argumentation of Lapointe (1980) and Lieber (1980) that inflection and derivation typically share language-particular properties, Chapter 4 extended the right-hand headedness of compounding and derivational morphology to inflection. But since head-complement selection and other head-dependent syntactic processes such as case-mark-

---

[34] Recall from section 3.2 that a Romance compound, *unless* both its members are free forms, is right-headed. More French examples beyond those given there, for the benefit of the skeptical: *aéroport, antisemite, autocollant, bi-sexuel, bonheur, demi-sec, francophonie, hypermarché, malfaiteur, mi-temps, pétomane, stupéfait, surdoué,* etc. Thus, the head status of Romance derivational suffixes, as in English, follows from the rightheadedness of compounds containing bound forms.

ing ignore inflection, I had to treat right-hand inflectional heads as inert or "empty" in the syntax. This suggested the hypothesis that inflectional heads are lexically filled only in PF, as independently argued for in section 4.4.

In taking this step, I was in effect treating right-hand headedness as a part of an "unfalsifiable core" of a "research program" *which unifies phrasal and word-internal syntax*. (Quoted terms are drawn from Lakatos, 1978.) That is, on grounds of parsimony, I could not analyze inflections as heads of words without simultaneously and automatically analyzing them as heads of phrases as well. Naturally enough then, since the bold inflections in *blamed the accident on John* and *three times fonder of John than you might think* are not the obvious heads of these phrases, I proposed, following Lakatos's terminology, an "auxiliary hypothesis": Namely, the definition of Lexical Projection (4.27) allows such inflectional heads to be ignored in the syntactic component, at levels where they are empty X^0. Schematically, *a unified syntax-morphology ignores empty heads.*

According to Lakatos's philosophy of science, whether a research program is "productive" or "degenerate" depends entirely on whether auxiliary hypotheses for an unfalsifiable core shed light on and explain previous anomalous phenomena, beyond those for which they are initially proposed. If so, the auxiliary hypotheses are said to have "excess content," which is the crucial test for evaluating a research program. If auxiliary hypotheses, however cleverly formulated in theory-internal terms, serve essentially only to name the phenomena for which they are devised, they lack "excess content" and the research program is deemed degenerate. That is, these additional hypotheses fail to provide new explanations for previously unexplained anomalies.

In the present case, the auxiliary hypothesis of Chapter 4 is that of ignoring higher empty heads (which surface as bound inflections) when satisfying subcategorization and throughout the syntax. This has considerable excess content. If certain empty heads in syntax are late-inserted bound morphemes, the null hypothesis suggests that syntax also permits late-inserted empty heads which are free morphemes.

It then turns out that late-inserted higher empty heads lead naturally to the dual syntactic complement structures that descriptive adequacy demands be associated with (i) predicate adjectives, (ii) English and Japanese light verbs, (iii) English and Japanese pseudo-partitives, (iv) Romance restructuring verbs and (v) Romance causatives. It is no exaggeration to say that the generative literature has treated (i)–(v), most particularly Romance restructuring and causative verbs, as anomalies for twenty years, ever since abandonment of construction specific rules at the end of its "second period" (cf.

section 1.1.1). The many competing previous auxiliary hypotheses for each of the phenomena (i)–(v), completely separate from each other among other things, have little if any independent justification. But *all five constructions fall into place as subcases of multi-level lexical insertion* (4.8), once grammatical empty V and N heads are taken as invisible in the syntax. Apparently, a research program that unifies syntax and morphology delineates a fruitful path toward the elusive but nonetheless indispensable excess content which generative syntax badly needs.

Chapter 7 proposes more evidence for the hypothesis that "empty heads" are structurally present but invisible when lexical selection uses subcategorization features. While the preceding chapter has focused on higher, or at least selecting, empty heads, the next will investigate empty heads *between* the selecting and selected items. Through the explanations achieved, the chapter will further demonstrate the explanatory value of multi-level lexical insertion and of retaining syntactic subcategorization as the unique natural language mechanism for combining lexical items.

Appendix to chapter 6
Causative and perception verb "clause union"

A.1 Burzio's parallels between causatives and restructuring

Section 6.5 has discussed a closed class of *intransitive* "restructuring" verbs in Italian and Spanish whose infinitival complements occur in two distinct structural configurations: a "clitic climbing" or "clause union" pattern analyzed as a flat structure and a separate VP pattern of a familiar sort.

In these Romance languages and in French as well, non-finite complements of a small number of *transitive* causative and perception verbs also occur in distinct syntactic patterns, giving rise to different clitic configurations reminiscent of the restructuring alternations. In (6.45)–(6.46), V_x is the causative/ perception verb, V_c is the non-finite complement, and WP and WP' are the complement and adjunct positions respectively of V_c. Clitics with verbal hosts typically replace or sometimes double these WP and WP'.[35]

(6.45) Climbing pattern: $[_V$ clitics $+ V_x] - V_c \ldots$ WP $\ldots$ WP' $\ldots$

(6.46) Separate VPs pattern: V_x - DP subject of V_c - $[_V$ clitics $+ V_c] \ldots$ WP $\ldots$ WP' $\ldots$

In the climbing pattern (6.45), clitics appear on V_x only if any lower subject DP of V_c is located among its complements and adjuncts (in ways to be specified as we proceed). (6.47) exemplifies this pattern, with lower subjects italicized.

(6.47) a. French causative *laisser* 'let':
          Marie les   a laissés   laver à *Anne*.
          Marie them-has let   wash to Anne
          'Marie has let Anne wash them.'
        b. Italian causative *fare* 'make':
          La ho fatta   riparare a *Giovanni*.
          It+[FEM]-I've made+[FEM] repair to John
          'I have made John repair it.'

---

[35] Non-imperative French verbs and finite Spanish and Italian verbs always have proclitics; non-finite Italian or Spanish verbs take enclitics.

    c. Spanish causative *dejar* 'let':

        Los hermanos la han   dejado preparar a *Ana*.

        The brothers it+[FEM]-have   let   prepare to Ana

        'The brothers have let Ana prepare it.'

In fact, non-reflexive object clitics may not occur on V_c when the lower subject follows it:[36]

(6.48)   *Marie a laissé les laver à *Anne*.   (with the sense of 6.47a)

        *Ho fatto ripararla a *Giovanni*.   (with the sense of 6.47b)

        *Los hermanos han dejado prepararla a *Ana*.

                                         (with the sense of 6.47c)

In the lower clitic pattern (6.46), the italicized lower subject is between the two verbs, and this is exemplified in (6.49a-c).[37] English causative expressions also have this structure, as the translations show.

(6.49) a. French *laisser*:   Marie laisse *Anne* les leur distribuer.

                          Marie lets Anne them-to-them-distribute

                          'Marie lets Anne distribute them to them.'

      b. Italian perception Ho visto *Giovanni* ripararla.

        verb *vedere* 'see':   I've seen John   repair-it

                          'I've seen John repair it.'

      c. Spanish *dejar*:

               Los hermanos dejan a *Ana* prepararsela algunas veces.

               The brothers   let   to Ana prepare-them-it sometimes

               'The brothers let Ana prepare it for them sometimes.'

      d. *Marie les leur laisse *Anne* distribuer.

        *La ho vista *Giovanni* riparare.

        *Los hermanos se la dejan a *Ana* preparar algunas veces.

---

[36] Rouveret and Vergnaud (1980, sections 2 and 3) show that the French reflexive clitic *se* and adverbial clitics *y* and *en* can occur on V_c in the climbing pattern (with postposed lower subjects). This does not violate the Phrase Mate Hypothesis (6.9), which only requires clitics and their corresponding phrases to be in the same VP. Their paradigms suggest rather that either (i) clitics bound to V are always related to lexical heads but that some clitics appear in derivations before lexicalization of V_x or (ii) that clitics bound to Vs sometimes attach to empty structural heads rather than lexical heads.

[37] It is often concluded that French *faire* can't occur at all in the lower clitic pattern (6.46), but Abeillé, Godard and Miller (1997) show that it often can.

    These and other authors attribute different interpretations to the different structural positions of the lower subject. Such variation suggests that each causative construction has an LF structure peculiar to it, as is the case in the analysis here.

(6.49d) demonstrates the correlation between climbing and a postposed lower subject; when the italicized lower subject precedes V_c, then object clitics cannot appear on V_x.

As with restructuring verbs, several empirical correlates of the causative climbing pattern (6.45) provide arguments that any constituent containing V_c and WP also contains V_x – i.e., that V_x *and* V_c *in climbing causatives are in the same VP*. Since this point has been so amply documented in the Romance causative literature, I restrict myself for the most part to citing sources for relevant paradigms.

(i) The single accusative. Only one accusative case is available in a single VP. In the climbing pattern, therefore, a lower subject DP cannot co-occur as an accusative with a direct object DP of V_c (for Italian examples, see Burzio, 1986, 234–235). Notice that this argument for a single VP is not available for restructuring verbs, since the lower subject in the latter is always null.

(ii) Past participle agreement in Italian. In only the clitic climbing pattern, the "past participle [of the causative] agrees with the antecedent to the direct object of the embedded verb, from which we conclude ... dependents of the embedded verb are reanalyzed as dependents of the matrix verb ..." (Burzio, 1986, 344)[38] The simplest account of Burzio's paradigm is to consider that a direct object WP in the climbing pattern (6.45) is a sister to V_x. This analysis is entirely analogous to Rizzi's conclusion for direct objects of restructuring verbs.

(iii) Similarities with Italian restructuring. While some of these similarities discussed by Burzio involve complexities of Italian NP Movement, others can be easily summarized. For example, Longobardi (1980) observes that sequences of Italian infinitives are well-formed *only* in restructuring and causative sequences.

(iv) Lack of independent negation and aspect. Zagona (1982, 20) gives examples that in both the restructuring and causative clitic climbing Spanish patterns, the complement verbs V_c lack independent negation and aspect: "... there is a marked absence of complex structure in the complement itself.

---

[38] *Active* past participles in Modern Spanish never show agreement with their direct objects; only a small class of French active past participles show phonetic agreement, and this agreement doesn't seem to participate in Burzio's paradigm (cf. section 5.6).

This pattern extends to the [causative and restructuring] verbs in those paradigms in which clitics appear on the matrix verb." Kayne (1975, 230) observes the same lack of lower negation in French causatives when clitics appear on the higher verb.

(v) Clefting of VPs in focus position. A lower subject of a transitive verb in the climbing pattern (6.45) is cliticized as a dative, while a lower subject in the separate VP pattern is always accusative. Consequently, because the Italian causative *fare* appears freely only in the climbing pattern, a lower subject with *fare* must often be dative (6.50):

(6.50)   E che   { gli/ *lo }   faccio   leggere il libro.
         It's that him[DAT]-I'll make   read the book
         'It's that I'll make him read the book.'

Since Italian infinitives can become the focus in a cleft sentence, Burzio's dative subject causative data in (6.51a), parallel to restructuring data as in (6.51b), suggest the lack of any embedded VP in the climbing pattern. A form of the auxiliary *essere* in (6.51b) simply confirms the presence of a flat structure.

(6.51)   a. *E proprio   [leggere il libro]   che gli faccio.
            It's exactly read the book   that I will make him
         b. *E proprio   [andare a casa]   che sarei voluto.
            It's exactly to go home   that I would have wanted

We saw earlier in (6.31) that trying to focus V_c and its complements in a flat (climbing) structure causes the same ill-formedness with restructuring verbs.

(vi) Clausemate restrictions. Like restructuring, causatives interact with certain other constructions which exhibit clausemate restrictions. For example, objects of infinitives following adjectives like *facile* 'easy' can become the surface subject of the adjective (6.52a). But as pointed out by Abeillé, Godard and Miller (1997), French does not permit an object inside a lower VP to become a subject in this way (6.52b):

(6.52)   a. Ce manteau   est difficile à porter.
            'That coat   is   difficult to wear.'
         b. *Ce manteau   est difficile à persuader Paul de porter.
            That coat   is   difficult to persuade Paul to wear

They go on to show that when this type of adjective's complement is a causative sequence, the object of V_c can become a subject (only) in the climbing pattern, suggesting the absence of any lower VP. As expected, the contrasting separate VP pattern excludes this object-to-subject relation. Thus in (6.53), the lower dative subject associated with climbing allows the raising relation, while an accusative lower subject indicates the separate VP pattern and blocks the relation.

(6.53)   Cette chanson est difficile à { leur/ *les } faire   apprendre.
         That song   is difficult to {them [DAT]/ them[ACC]}-make
         learn
         'That song is difficult to make them learn.'

These six syntactic tests, most from Burzio (1986, section 5.4), establish the structural identity of restructuring and causative "clitic climbing" constructions. One seems forced to concur with his conclusion that "… all differences between causative and restructuring constructions are due to the fact that main and embedded subjects are coindexed in restructuring cases, … but not in causative cases." (1986, 325) That is, the sole difference between the two constructions is the relation between the subjects of the two verbs, co-indexed in restructuring sequences and disjoint in reference in causative sequences.

A.2 Kayne's three patterns of Romance causatives

To account for the parallels between restructuring and causative climbing complements, Zagona (1982) analyses both as non-maximal projections V'.[39] I propose to go a step further – these non-finite V_c complements are uniformly V^0 sisters to V_x.[40] The lack of independent negation and aspect which Zagona attributes to the absence of a maximal projection is predicted a fortiori if the climbing constructions have neither an embedded V' nor VP. That is, the arguments of Burzio's just reviewed equally well support a flat

---

[39] Zagona's analysis crucially distinguishes V' and VP as different categorial constructs. This is not an option in the framework of Speas's (1990) bare phrase structure; cf. note 20.
[40] My proposals for Romance causative structures have been influenced by the analyses and data in Rouveret and Vergnaud (1980) and Milner (1982). The structures I propose are similar to those argued for in Aissen (1974), Miller (1992), and Abeillé, Godard and Miller (1997).

structure hypothesis. In this way, causative/ perception ("c/p") verbs are just transitive counterparts to intransitive restructuring verbs.

Moreover, since Modern French lacks restructuring only because it does not tolerate co-indexing of postposed and sentence-initial subjects (section 6.5.2), the fact that causative verbs are independently incompatible with "like-subjects" correctly predicts that French as well as Italian and Spanish will have causative structures.

According to the Syntacticon model (4.9), flat complement structures automatically result for any Romance c/p verbs which have the selection feature +<V> and are fully characterized by basic cognitive syntactic features F, i.e. which lack semantic features f. Such an analysis seems appropriate because the c/p verbs V_x which tolerate the climbing pattern (6.45) are indeed few in number and further have only the most basic cognitive content.[41] Like other closed class verbs with interpretable syntactic features F, these V_x may be inserted prior to Move Alpha or in the syntax. As seen in section 6.4.2, using the frame V, +<V> at deep structure gives rise to standard embedded VP complements (6.46), while using it in the syntax provides flat structures appropriate for (apparent) clitic climbing (6.45).

While restructuring verbs are intransitive, c/p verbs are subcategorized not only as +<V> but at least optionally as +<D>.[42] Moreover, the transitive c/p verbs in simplex sentences vary as to whether they permit indirect

---

[41] Open class "semantically causative" verbs completely exclude the climbing pattern (6.45) and the attendant syntax of lower subjects, e.g., French *amener* 'lead', *autoriser* 'authorize', *convaincre* 'convince', *encourager* 'encourage', *engager* 'hire', *forcer* 'force', *obliger* 'oblige', *permettre* 'permit', *persuader* 'persuade', etc. The grammatical properties of causatives derive not from the semantic notion "causative" but rather from a syntactic complex: "*closed class* verbs with both a direct object and a non-finite verbal complement."

The fact that perception verbs share this syntax but are in no way causative reinforces this "anti-semantic" conclusion. Moreover, like causatives, only basic grammatical perception verbs occur in flat structures. Verbs of more specific semantic content such as *écouter* 'listen' and *regarder* 'watch' don't permit climbing paradigms (Abeillé, Godard and Miller, 1997).

[42] When an infinitive is sole complement to a causative verb, the infinitive's understood subject PRO is projected as a postposed adjunct (like an understood logical subject of a passive), and is necessarily disjoint in reference from the subject of the causative. Existing subcategorization theory does not readily capture this basic difference between causative and restructuring complements: obligatory disjointness of subjects vs. their obligatory co-indexing. Perhaps the indexing device in Jackendoff's (1987) conceptual structures which requires (or forbids) a given complement of X from being predicated of X's subject should be used in subcategorization frames as well.

objects, and this difference carries over to their use in the causative construction. For example, non-causative uses of the French verb *laisser* 'let' allow a direct and an optional indirect object, and accordingly its causative complement may appear with a DP marked as direct or indirect object. On the other hand, *entendre* 'hear, understand' and other French perception verbs "require a direct but prohibit an indirect object in simplex sentences ... The complex sentences [i.e., containing causative and perception verbs, JE] of all the verbs correspond to their simplex sentences." (Herschensohn, 1981, note 47)

We can thus specify the subcategorization frames for two typical French causative / perception verbs *laisser* 'let' and *entendre* 'hear, understand' as follows; for exposition, I retain here the blanks of older subcategorization notation.

(6.54) a. laisser, V, +F, +____{ D, V }, ((PATH)^D)[43]
        b. entendre, V, +F, +____{ D (V), V }[44]

The c/p complement subcases of (6.54) are generated by the frames +___V and +___D^V (equivalent to +___V^D). Since left-right order of complements is determined independently of lexical statements, these frames actually permit three linear combinations:

(6.55) V_x - DP - V_c ...

(6.56) V_x - V_c ... DP...

(6.57) V_x - V_c ...

As with restructuring verbs, either a V or a VP sister can satisfy the frame +___V for a grammatical verb like *laisser*. Its frames +___V (D) therefore

---

[43] The need for a case-assigner for the second DP forces the combination +___D^D to include the intermediate category PATH. Our interest here is rather the frame +___V((PATH)^D). Economy of Representation excludes +___V^PATH^D if there is no LF interpretation for PATH and P is not needed for case assignment.

[44] In (6.54b), we would like to be able to simply write: *entendre* takes at least one of D and V. Perhaps refinements in lexical notation have been slow in coming due to the widespread faith in the (ever-receding) future theory of "semantic selection."

Since this frame has no PATH feature, *entendre* prohibits any type of surface dative complement: *J'ai entendu { la radio/ ouvrir la radio } (*à mes enfants)* 'I heard { the radio/ turn on the radio } (to my children)'.

yield six structures in total. In the illustrative trees below, WP represents a complement of V_c, WP' represents an adjunct of V_c, and the subcategorized DP is a possible subject of V_c.

(6.55) V_x - DP - V_c ...

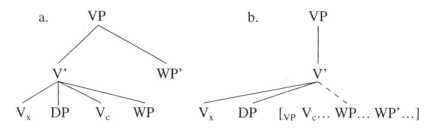

(6.56) V_x - V_c ... DP ...

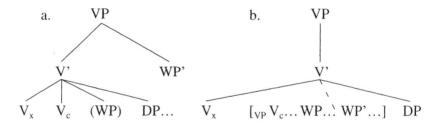

(6.57) V_x - V_c ...

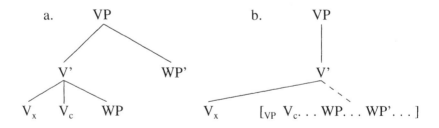

As we will now see, other grammatical factors exclude three of the above six structures as ill-formed. The remaining three each correspond to exactly one of three well-defined structural types of Romance causatives delineated in Kayne (1975).

(i) The separate VP causative. The DP in (6.55a) prevents V_c from being head-initial at any point in a derivation, making it impossible to lexicalize. This violation of head-initiality therefore excludes (6.55a) and leaves us with (6.55b).

The layered VP structure (6.55b) is the well-known causative "separate VP" pattern (6.46). It results from deep insertion in the frame V, +___D^V; as seen in section 6.5 on restructuring, deep insertion always gives rise to phrasal complements. Kayne (1975, section 4.1) observes that whenever an embedded infinitive follows its DP subject, clitics for phrases in the lower VP don't climb; cf. (6.49d). The Phrase Mate Hypothesis (6.9) correctly predicts that clitics for complements or adjuncts of V_c occur only on V_c in (6.55b), while any clitic replacing the lower subject DP appears on V_x. Unlike Kayne, therefore, I attribute the lower positioning of clitics in the separate VP structure to the Phrase Mate Hypothesis and make no appeal to the presence of a subject between the verbs to block climbing.[45]

As in standard government and binding analyses of object controlled infinitives, the lower VP in (6.55b) projects to an IP with a null subject, which is co-indexed with the object DP in the main clause.

(ii) The *faire* ... *à* construction. (6.56b) is excluded by the lack of a case-assigner for the object DP. Even if a dummy PP provided a case-assigner, (6.56b) would still realize the frame +___D^V less economically than the just discussed (6.55b), so (6.56b) cannot be salvaged.[46]

(6.56a) is a second structure licensed by the frame +___D^V, and results from inserting a grammatical verb during the syntactic derivation. It represents the right structure for the complex clitic climbing pattern with c/p verbs (6.45). Its trademark is that *the DP subject of the lower V_c is located among the internal arguments of V_c.* This flat structure (6.56a) is then my proposal for the famous *faire* ... *à* construction of Kayne (1975, Ch. 3). We

---

[45] Burzio (1986, 333) provides an independent argument which shows that the subject status of the intervening DP is irrelevant for blocking climbing in (6.55b).The same blocking is also caused by the deep object of an unaccusative restructuring verb such as *venire* 'come'. That is, any overt *non-subject* DP in its base position between two verbs also blocks the possibility of a flat structure, i.e., clitics may not climb. The non-subject status of the blocking DP is exactly the point of Burzio's unaccusative analysis of *venire*.
[46] This reasoning is not particular to syntactic causatives; Economy of Representation (6.23) also prevents open class verbs like *persuade* from realizing their direct objects in PPs as in **persuade to go away { of/ to } John.*

return in section A.5 to the role of the "internal argument subject" in (6.56a) in blocking cliticization of certain complements WP.[47]

(iii) The *faire ... par* construction. Neither version of (6.57) can be well-formed unless V_c has a separate subject DP, as required by the Extended Projection Principle (1.17). In (6.57b) this subject of V_c must be a PRO in the SPEC of an IP obligatorily projected above the embedded VP, as in a standard government and binding treatment of object control. By hypothesis, however, there is no object outside IP in (6.57b) to control this PRO, unlike in (6.55b). Since V_c and V_x cannot both be predicated of the single higher subject, the only remaining structural candidate for a separate controller of V_c would be a postposed DP adjunct outside the higher V'. Yet Economy of Representation (6.23) always rules out such control (see note 46: *Bill { forced/ encouraged/ persuaded } to change the schedule by Mary*). Thus, either the EPP or Economy of Representation rules out (6.57b).

(6.57a) is the well-formed result of post-transformational insertion into the frame V, +___V. It yields a causative complement V_c whose own subject appears in the position of an adjunct WP' as in (6.58), as either covert PRO or an overt agent phrase, provided a language-particular Syntacticon contains appropriate grammatical P such as French *par* and *de*, Italian *da* and Spanish *por*.

(6.58)

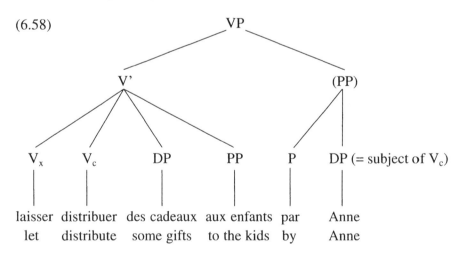

---

[47] Section 6.4.2 has established that a flat structure such as (6.56a) arises only when V_x is empty in deep structure and inserted later in a syntactic derivation. A framework of multi-level lexical insertion thus explains why clitic climbing is invariably restricted to

The structure (6.57a) is thus appropriate for the *faire ... par* construction of Kayne (1975, sections 3.5 and 3.6), who shows this construction is closely related to the passive. This relation is transparent in the present analysis, since (6.58) with an explicit agent replicates the passive verb phrase structure with *être* 'be' (cf. section 6.2). I consider postposed agent phrases in the passive and *faire ... par* constructions true subjects because they do indeed receive theta roles of external arguments and fulfill the definition of Generalized Subjects (1.15) and the version of the EPP (1.17) utilized throughout this study.[48] The only difference between the two kinds of postposed agents is that a passive grammatical verb V_x requires a "theta role free" higher DP subject outside VP, while c/p grammatical verbs V_x have a syntactic feature ACTIVITY which assigns an agent interpretation to their VP-external subject, thus precluding any movement into this position.

Kayne (1975, 327–329), Herschensohn (1981, 238–240) and Burzio (1986, 257–258) all observe that the lower subject *par*-phrases in the WP' position of (6.57a) *never block free cliticization onto V_x*, e.g. in (6.58), of the

---

a few grammatical verbs V_x and never generalizes to all non-finite complements. This cross-linguistic pattern, an apparent universal failure of speakers to generalize the grammatical patterns of "frequent" verbs, is entirely mysterious in accounts which fail to crucially distinguish grammatical from lexical verbs. Cf. the discussion of Kayne (1975, 206–207).

[48] Nonetheless, the situation is complex and not yet fully formalized. Burzio (1986, section 4.4) nicely puts together several arguments of his own and from Kayne (1975) to establish the following broad descriptive generalization: unlike the postposed subject in a *faire ... à* causative, a postposed DP introduced by *par* 'by' *does not function as a subject in the role of an (agreeing and c-commanding) antecedent* for floating quantifiers, possessives, reflexives and various VP-idioms. This generalization suggests that agentive *par / da / por / by* are already inserted in syntax rather than in PF. Their object then fails to c-command various expressions in their predicate and so fails as an antecedent, in both LF and PF. Confirmation that these prepositions are present in LF could be interaction with theta role assignment; they are incompatible with a "pure theme" (Emonds, 1976, Ch. 3):

(i) *That road was crossed by the forest fire.
    The closet was slipped into by the { thief/ *soap }.
    *Our apartment was entered by some noxious gas.

I propose the following account for these seemingly incompatible aspects of postposed agents. As with productive derivational morphology, interpretation of grammatical agent marking morphemes consists of deleting them *after* certain LF procedures, such as finding antecedents for reflexives. At this late point then, their DP objects *do* finally act as external c-commanding arguments which satisfy the EPP and can receive agent and ground theta roles.

PP *aux enfants* by the proclitic *leur*. That is, the Phrase Mate Hypothesis correctly predicts that the clitics corresponding to either complements WP or adjuncts WP' in the *faire ... par* passive-like construction (6.57a) systematically and entirely freely appear on the first verb of the sequence V_x.[49]

The lexical theory of tri-level insertion (4.9) of Chapter 4 has thus predicted that transitive grammatical verbs with simple subcategorization frames as in (6.54), to wit causative and perception verbs, will appear in three distinct syntactic configurations: one is a standard articulated nonfinite clausal complement (6.55b); a second flat structure (6.56a) has the lower subject among the lower verb's complements – this is Kayne's *faire ... à* construction; and a third flat structure (6.57a) has the lower subject realized as a postposed adjunct – this is Kayne's *faire ... par* construction.

These exact structural predictions are natural consequences of the lexical theory of Chapter 4 and have required no construction-specific "causative-raising," "V-raising," "clitic-climbing" or "clause union rules." Nor have we called upon any "Restructuring Rule," "Reanalysis" or "S-bar (CP) deletion" to generate the needed special structures for causatives. The predictions result simply from drawing a full range of conclusions from a lexical theory which allows a wider range of insertion possibilities for (only) that closed subclass of verbs which lack specialized semantic features f; the predictions are amply confirmed by the descriptive and explanatorily adequate accounts they provide.

---

[49] The flat structures of the *faire ... à* causative (6.56a) and the *faire ... par* causative (6.57a) both result from insertion of c/p verbs during a syntactic derivation. Since these insertions apply at the same level, they compete to satisfy Economy of Representation (6.23). A lower subject of the complement verb V_c must therefore be realized if possible as a DP rather than with the extra structure of a PP, if the latter's only function is to provide abstract case.

(i)   Marie fait danser (*{ à/ par }) Jean.
       Mary makes dance ({ to/ by }) John
       'Mary makes John dance.'

This solves a puzzle noted by Burzio (1986, 253): why does *faire ... par* in French and Italian not accept deep intransitive V_c if the *par*-phrase is overt?

In systems such as Spanish where subjects of intransitive V_c appear both with and without a P, it usually is acknowledged that this P not only assigns case but also contributes to interpretation. Since "dative causatives" and "accusative causatives" then differ in LF, Economy of Representation doesn't compare them.

A.3 Implications of a generalized definition of subject

The explanatory conclusions of the previous section collide head on with an essentially fetishistic insistence of most generative syntactic research: that subjects and predicates exhaustively form clausal units. The subject positions associated with the dependent verbs V_c in (6.55)–(6.57) break completely with this thirty year legacy of generative semantics.

Since LF is now widely understood as the (only) level of derivation relevant for interpretation, LF is in fact the only level where subjects really need to be defined. We need only be concerned that subjects are correctly paired with predicates for interpretation at this level. Along these lines, the analysis of agent phrases in the *faire ... par* causatives (6.57a) and in passives in section 10.4 as subjects of V is fully consistent with the view that subjecthood contributes to interpretation only at LF.[50]

Throughout this work, a carefully formulated definition accomplishes the crucial task of structurally locating subjects in syntax and Logical Form:

(1.15)   *Generalized Subjects: The subject or external argument of a head X is the lowest N-projection which c-commands a phrasal projection of X within its minimal cyclic domain (IP or DP).*

The wording of (1.15), as explained in Chapter 1, covers predicates of categories other than V and subjects which are not full DPs (e.g., participles, nominal projections within DPs which count as subjects of adjectives, etc.). For clarity in discussing causatives, let's exclude these cases and "particularize" (1.15) to the cases at hand:

---

[50] If any aspect of a postposed agent's interpretation ever crucially depended on having "moved through" a canonical subject position, e.g. via raising from a lower position of theta role assignment, then defining only its final LF position as a subject would not suffice for interpretation.

For example, suppose a raising verb could be passivized, further transforming *John seemed to Mary to have been examined* into **Mary was seemed to by John to have been examined*. Then part of the interpretation of *John* would derive from being the object of *examine*, and it would not suffice to simply define *John* as LF subject of *seem*. But such cases never arise, since raising verbs never passivize.

The earliest generative accounts of the passive suggest linking agentive interpretation to a deep position as daughter of S or IP, but defining a postposed agent phrase as a structural subject at LF makes this unnecessary. Agenthood is a possible interpretation of (only) subjects and is not linked in any special way to SPEC(IP), as derived nominals independently show.

(6.59)   *Verbal Subjects: The subject of a V is the lowest DP which c-commands some phrasal projection of V within a minimal IP.*

This generalized definition of subject accounts for a wide range of structures which express the subject-predicate relation (Emonds, 1985, Ch. 2). For example, incorporating the results of the analysis of present participles in section 4.7.1, (6.59) correctly and uniquely associates each participial lexical projection in (6.60) with its subject DP, as indicated by the matching fonts.[51]

(6.60)   [$_{DP}$ **She**] [$_{VP}$ [$_{V'}$ heard [$_{DP}$ *the hours*] [$_{AP}$ *ticking away*]]] [$_{AP}$ **drinking tea**]]

If the participles are structurally exchanged as in (6.61a), their selection features for subjects together with (6.59) exclude the result. (6.61b) shows that it is structure rather than some surface nesting condition which excludes (6.61a).

(6.61)   a. *She heard the hours drinking tea ticking away.
          b. *The hours* **she** heard *ticking away* **drinking tea** were many.

Let us now apply Verbal Subjects (6.59) to the structures for causative and restructuring verbs. A glance at the articulated causative structure (6.55b) shows that (6.59) correctly locates the DP subject of the lower verb V_c. However, in the flat structure VPs which I propose for "clitic climbing" causative and restructuring sequences, (6.56a), (6.57a) and (6.44), it is unclear what constitutes "some phrasal projection" of the complement V_c for (6.59), since V_x rather than V_c is the lexically filled LF head of all the phrasal projections V^i in all three trees.

To see why this is so, I repeat for convenience both a flat structure (6.56a) and the definition of lexical head.

---

[51] As in Chapter 4, the *-ing* inflections in the head positions of these participles are inserted in PF. Consequently, during the syntactic derivation and at LF, the participial APs are lexical projections of the verbs. By (6.59), the subject of each V_i is then the lowest DP which c-commands the AP containing V_i.

(6.56a) Structure for the *faire ... à* construction, where DP should be the subject of V_c:

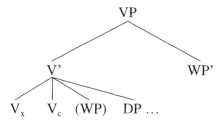

(4.27) *Lexical Head/Projection. Let X^0 be the highest lexically filled head in Z^j. Then X^0 is the lexical head of Z^j, and Z^j is a lexical projection of X^0.*

Keeping in mind that Romance phrases are head-iniital, both V' and VP in this tree are projections of V_x in LF, since V_x is filled prior to Spell Out.[52]

As established in section 6.4.2, flat structures such as (6.56a) can arise only if V_x is inserted post-transformationally, i.e. is a closed-class grammatical verb, and so V_c is their lexical head in deep structure. In the causative and restructuring structures, the lexical choice of V_x is needed for interpretation and so must be inserted in the syntax rather than PF. These points taken together imply that *the lexical head of a flat VP (and V') changes from V_c at deep structure to V_x at Spell Out and LF.* That is, there is no verbal projection distinct from V_c in LF whose head is V_c; the open class V_c seems to lack an LF subject!

Nonetheless, an almost trivial extension of the notion "phrasal projection" correctly pairs V_x and V_c with their LF subjects:

(6.62) *Definition. A phrasal projection of a lexical head X^0 consists of any of its lexical projections Z^1, as defined by (4.27). If X^0 is a daughter but not the head of Z^1, it counts as its own phrasal projection.*[53]

As just seen, the second verb V_c in a flat structure heads no projection distinct from itself at LF. Hence by (6.62) *these V_c are their own phrasal*

---

[52] In a flat surface structure, both V are sisters and neither is "higher." Since verb phrases in Romance languages are systematically head-initial, I take it that if X' immediately dominates two or more lexically filled X^0, then only the initial X^0 is a head.

[53] If X^0 is a daughter of Z^1, then the bar notation ensures that X = Z. Recall that formally, ZP is only a mnemonic for those Z^1 which do not further project.

projection in LF (though not in deep structure). Verbal Subjects (6.59) thus allows a DP sister of V_c to be its LF subject in the *faire ... à* causative (6.56a). Similarly, a post-verbal adjunct DP which c-commands V_c in the *faire ... par* causative can be its LF subject. In both configurations, these DPs are the lowest ones available, as Verbal Subjects requires.

A related question concerns the location of the subject of the c/p verb itself in a flat structure. At first glance, nothing seems more natural than that the subject of the initial causative/ perception V_x head of a VP should be the subject DP external to VP. However, in flat structures of the *faire ... par* causative type in (6.58), the *lowest* DP which c-commands a phrasal projection of V_x is instead the postposed adjunct DP, i.e. the actual subject of V_c. Verbal Subjects thus seems to produce a wrong result.

However, a more careful discussion shows there is no problem. We at least know that the two Vs in a flat structure cannot share a single subject. In this study, this restriction has been expressed as a version of Chomsky's (1981) Extended Projection Principle.[54]

(1.17)   *Extended Projection Principle. Every head verb present in LF must have a structural subject phrase to which a semantic role may be assigned.*

So the problem is how to determine the proper subject – predicate pairings e.g., as indicated by the fonts in the following French example:

(6.63)   *Jean laisse* **distribuer**   des cadeaux aux enfants par **Anne**.
          'John lets   distribute   some gifts   to the children by Anne'

Verbal Subjects (6.59) straightforwardly forbids taking *Jean* as the subject of *distribuer;* because *Anne* is lower in the tree, *Jean* is not the *lowest* DP c-commanding the only phrasal projection of that verb in LF, namely by (6.62) that verb itself. Our theoretical statements thus properly exclude the pairing *(Jean, **distribuer**; **Anne**, laisse)*. We can however take *Jean* as the subject of *laisse* because it is the lowest DP c-commanding "some projection" of *laisse* at LF, namely the maximal VP. And since *Anne* is the lowest

---

[54] The EPP used here is a special case of a Revised Theta Criterion justified in Emonds (1985, Ch. 2). A consequence of that principle is that two X^0 can share an argument only if they are not themselves in a head-argument relation. Since in all cases considered in this chapter, one verb is taking another as its complement, the EPP (1.17) can here always replace the Revised Theta Criterion. Section 7.6 goes into more detail.

DP c-commanding *distribuer,* the correct pairing *(Jean, laisse; **Anne,** distribuer)* conforms to both (6.59) and (1.17).[55]

We thus see that Verbal Subjects, a special case of Generalized Subjects (1.15), is fully adequate for specifying the subject-predicate pairings in both the layered, bi-clausal causative structure (6.55b) and in the mono-clausal flat structures (6.56a) and (6.57a). It also assigns separate structural subjects to both Vs in restructuring sequences such as (6.44). Generalized Subjects thus provides a non-trivial account of why, even though flat and articulated structures are quite distinct, the predications involved are exactly the same.

A.4 The syntax of internal arguments which are LF Subjects

I have proposed that the DP subject of the complement verb V_c in the *faire* ... *à* construction is structurally an internal argument licensed by the subcategorization frames (6.54) of causative or perception verbs V_x. This DP serves as an LF subject by virtue of Generalized Subjects. This unusual configuration, in which a verb's sister is simultaneously its subject, is due to the fact that in LF, a V_c in a flat structure is not a head of any phrase containing it and so constitutes "its own phrasal projection" by (6.62).

Reviewing, if V_c is has no direct object, Economy of Representation (6.23) requires that its DP subject be realized with minimal embedding as a sister to V_c. (All examples in this section are French.)

(6.64)   Marie fait danser ({ *à/ *par }) Pierre avec les convives.
        Mary makes dance ({ to/ by }) Peter with the guests
        'Mary makes Peter dance with the guests.'

On the other hand, if V_c is transitive, its object receives the only accusative case available in a flat VP. An overt DP subject of V_c can then only receive case inside a PP. If V_x is subcategorized to take indirect objects, as causative but not perception verbs typically are, a PF-inserted grammatical P for indirect objects can assign case to this subject of V_c (bold in 6.65a). In addition, a subject of V_c can always receive case in a PP adjunct outside V' as in (6.65b).

---

[55] The direct object *des cadeaux* in (6.63) also c-commands the vacuous projection of *distribuer* at LF (i.e., V itself). This DP is excluded from consideration because no DP can simultaneously be both a verb's object and its subject.

(6.65) a. Marie fait laver   toute la vaisselle à **Pierre** sans eau chaude.
        Mary makes wash all the dishes   to Peter without hot water
        'Mary makes Peter wash all the dishes without hot water.'
        b. Marie fait mettre toute la vaisselle dans le placard par **Pierre**.
        Mary makes put   all the dishes   into the cabinet by Peter
        'Mary makes Peter put all the dishes into the cabinet.'

In contrast to this type of analysis, generative studies of the *faire ... à* construction influenced by Kayne (1975, Ch. 3 and 4) have assumed that these lower subjects of V_c in (6.64)–(6.65) originate, not as complements in a single VP, but rather inside some deep clausal projection @ of V_c as in (6.66). Then, to maintain some correspondence with syntactic data, some ad hoc "causative formation" must later transformationally extract V_c from this propositional node to get V_x and V_c into the same VP:

(6.66) a. Marie fait danser$_i$ [@ **Pierre** t$_i$ avec les convives].
        b. Marie fait laver$_i$ toute la vaisselle [@ à **Pierre** t$_i$ ... sans eau chaude].

That is, Kayne and his successors have tried to elaborate natural language syntax in terms of a kind of "propositional logic," whereby ß is a predicate of γ only if γ-ß form a propositional unit @ at some level. In spite of the many problems introduced by this empirically pointless assumption, decades have passed and the approach still predominates.[56] Indeed, the grip that non-empirical structures invented by logicians have had on 20th century syntax would be worthy of a chapter in the history of ideas.

---

[56] Some studies arguing for moving V_c from within a putative lower clause @ are Kayne (1975, Ch. 3 and 4), Quicoli (1980), Rouveret and Vergnaud (1980), Herschensohn (1981), Aoun (1985) and Burzio (1986). In all these, a construction-specific and language-specific rule moves either a sequence of constituents or a (crucially) intermediate bar projection V^k of V_c, defined ad hoc. Some versions of this V^k exclude subcategorized and even obligatory indirect objects.

Variations on the causative rule crucially use context predicates to specify landing sites and have to stipulate left-right order of terms. Since the constituent(s) moved don't involve functional categories, the rule cannot be a language-particular late insertion, inflectional or checking operation of the type allowed in current models. In view of the premium on a universal syntactic component, what can be retained from such studies are descriptive generalizations, but not their dependence on language-specific and construction-specific rules and conditions.

This intruding propositional category @, whose existence I deny, has confused subject-based explanations of prohibited cliticizations. Any such @, besides necessitating an ad hoc movement rule, conflicts with the following six grammatical properties of the *faire ... à* construction which each independently confirm that *the lower subject DP is syntactically an internal argument*.

(i) Clausal @ conflicts with subcategorization. As discussed in section A.2, whether or not the lower DP subject of V_c may occur in an *à*-phrase is entirely determined by the subcategorization frames of the causative / perception verbs V_x. (Herschensohn, 1981, her note 47, and note 44 above). The presence of a clausal @ over DP completely obscures this regularity, since a DP within a lower clause is inaccessible to a subcategorization frame of V_x.

(ii) Clausal @ obscures complementary distribution. Kayne (1975, Ch. 4) argues that many dative clitics in French causatives must result from a subcategorization frame not of V_c, but of causative verbs like *faire*.

(6.67) a. On lui fera   mourir son chien.
            One him-make-FUT   die his dog
            'We'll make his dog die'
        b. Le soleil lui a   fait   rougir la peau.
            The sun him-has made redden the skin
            'The sun made his skin redden.'

These clitics, uncontroversially indirect objects of the governing verb V_x, are in complementary distribution with *à*-phrases interpreted as subjects of V_c. The present analysis licenses both types by the subcategorization of V_x and hence predicts this complementarity, which is a mystery under the hypothesis of the clausal node @.

(iii) Clausal @ predicts the wrong word orders. A lower DP subject of V_c without a P (and cliticizable with an accusative clitic) *precedes* any oblique complements of V_c (6.64). If a DP subject is dative (with the preposition *à*), it *follows* a direct object of V_c (6.65a). Moreover, a dative subject can be optionally ordered with respect to other PP complements of V_c (Miller, 1992). These are precisely the expected word orders of an internal argument DP, but as Kayne acknowledges, they require ad hoc reorderings if DP is underlyingly a subject within some clausal @. For wherever this lower subject would be positioned within @, we would not expect it to be *between* the direct and the indirect objects of V_c.

Speakers apparently vary as to whether they accept sentences where both the subject and indirect object of V_c appear in *à*-phrases (6.68). But several authors report that in the somewhat acceptable variants the lower subject *must be* the second *à*-phrase.

(6.68)   Jean fait porter une lettre à Marie à Paul.
   John makes take a letter to Mary to Paul
   'John makes Paul take a letter to Mary.'

Since the *à*-phrase form of the lower subject results from selection by V_x, as just seen under point (i), it seems obvious that both verbs in (6.68) are simply selecting a phrase of the same form. The usual nesting provided by a phrase structure system predicts the correct order. The only confusion (i.e., again, "the wrong order") is introduced by hypothesizing an embedded clausal node @.

(iv) Clausal @ forces movements of non-constituents. Kayne (1975, 217–219) argues that V_x and V_c do not together form a constituent; yet elsewhere (his section 6.4) he admits that his causative verb movement must apply to sequences. (V-V-NP) Why? Because if the rule moved only one V_c, unacceptable word orders are predicted by the underlying position of a DP subject of V_c inside a clausal @. For instance, suppose that in his (6.69) the verb *sauter* undergoes causative formation leaving the trace t_j; if a second application of causative formation only moved one V, the ungrammatical (6.69) would result.

(6.69)   *Jean fera faire$_i$ [@ son fils [$_V$ Ø]$_i$ sauter$_j$ [@ le pont t_j]].
   John will-make make his son   blow up the bridge

In order to get the correct word order (6.70), successive extractions from @ by the causative rule must re-create anew the base order sequence "V – object – other constituents," that is, the unstipulated and expected order in a flat structure with a single underlying VP.

(6.70)   Jean fera faire sauter le pont à son fils.
   John will-make make blow up the bridge to his son
   'John will make his son blow up the bridge.'

(v) Clausal @ renders incomprehensible Kayne's own generalization.
Through examples like (6.71), Kayne (1975, 254–261) establishes a secondary hypothesis that the lower DP subject of V_c is never the landing site of "raising to subject."

(6.71)   *Son expression peinée fait { sembler Jean souffrir / paraître Jean être en colère }.
His expression pained makes { seem John suffer / appear John to be in anger }

His examples (6.72) show additionally that this restriction is not due to combining a causative and stative, which can be well-formed.

(6.72)   Son nouveau régime lui fera péser dix kilos de moins d'ici un mois.
His new diet him-will-make weigh ten kilos of less from here one month
'His new diet will make him weigh ten kilos less in one month.'
Cet éclairage te fait ressembler à ton frère.
That lighting you-makes resemble to your brother
'That lighting makes you resemble your brother.'

But in all well-studied cases of "NP Movement," it is precisely internal rather than external arguments which cannot serve as landing sites for NP movement. Thus, Kayne's secondary hypothesis supports an *internal argument* position for the lower subject in a causative, contra his own proposal to locate it as a subject of VP inside some clausal @.

(vi) Clausal @ blocks too many clitic placements. Kayne attempts to explain how a lower subject DP of V_c can block cliticization of certain complements of V_c by analyzing DP as a "specified subject" inside the clausal node @. However, he must postulate construction-specific devices to explain why Chomsky's Specified Subject Condition fails to affect clitics for both a direct object and adjuncts of V_c. The final section discusses this issue in detail.

These six considerations each independently demonstrate the superiority of a mono-clausal representation of the *faire ... à* construction (6.56a) to any proposal using an embedded clause @ as a basis for explaining the clitic climbing paradigms of causative / perception verbs.

A.5 Revising the SSC and Principle A: Local Binding in LF

In order to discuss whether and how certain cliticizations can be blocked by a DP which is interpreted as subject of V_c by Verbal Subjects (6.59), I first structurally situate the various constituents in the flat structure proposed for the (French) *faire ... à* construction, adding a complement PP to the tree (6.56a):

(6.56a) The *faire ... à* structure:

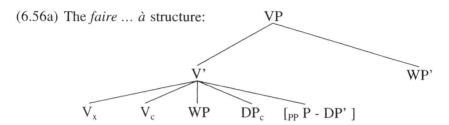

The DP_c in (6.56a), with or without a case-assigning P *à,* is interpreted as the subject of V_c. Kayne (1975, Ch. 4) claims that this lower subject has another property which can be attributed to its subjecthood: it can stop some clitics in this construction from appearing on the first verb V_x. One succinct summary of these restrictions has been formulated in Aoun (1985, 128); bracketed material and italics are mine:

(6.73) "... neither the direct object [if WP = DP in (6.56a)] ... nor the circumstantial complements [WP'] are subject to the SSC [i.e., they can cliticize on V_x]. The only complements that remain subject to the SSC [i.e., they *cannot* cliticize on V_x] are ... *the subcategorized nondirect objects* [i.e., DP' in (6.56a)] ..."[57]

The literature has repeatedly contested whether these restrictions in the *faire ... à* construction are systematic. If they are not, there is nothing further to discuss: the flat structure (6.56a) can allow cliticization on V_x freely in

---

[57] Aoun (1985) recognizes that Chomsky's Binding Theory can't express the apparent "local binding" in (6.73), because a clitic binder is not in an argument position, and yet Binding Theory requires local binders to be argument DPs. In order to subsume clitic binding under some broader mechanism, Aoun sets up "clitic binding" as an A-bar analog to A(rgument) binding. Since Aoun's theory of binding presupposes a movement approach to clitics, it relates the locality of clitic-binding to that of phrasal A-bar movements.

In the present framework, this locality is expressed by Alternative Realization, of which the Phrase Mate Hypothesis (6.9) is a special case.

accord with the Phrase Mate Hypothesis (6.9), subject perhaps to some processing or pragmatic factors. But if the combined observations (6.73) of Kayne (1975), Rouveret and Vergnaud (1980) and others are indeed correct, these restrictions should be explained without assuming that the lower subject in a causative climbing pattern originates in an embedded clause, so as to avoid the problems (i)–(vi) in section A.4.

Kayne (1975, Ch. 4) proposes to explain the patterns of (6.73) in terms of Chomsky's (1973) Specified Subject Condition ("SSC"), which blocks a relation between elements which are separated by an embedded clause subject. However, this attempt inevitably encounters the problem of finding a principled reason for why certain constituents of this embedded clause, namely a direct object of V_c and the adjuncts WP' in the *faire ... à* construction, can cliticize onto V_x, as observed in point (vi) just above. This stumbling block underlies many of the ad hoc properties in the Kayne-inspired treatments of causatives listed in note 56.

The structure (6.56a) for the *faire ... à* construction, which lacks the embedded clausal node @ over the lower subject in Kayne's structure (6.66), provides for a more revealing theoretical account of Aoun's descriptive generalization. I maintain Kayne's idea that a subject (in LF) can block certain binding relations involving clitics, but as throughout this study, my reformulation of the SSC neither stipulates nor requires that any propositional category @ uniquely encompasses a subject-predicate pair.[58] For a start, the first five difficulties with @ listed as (i)–(v) in section A.4 disappear.

Turning now to (vi): subsequent to Kayne's proposal, Chomsky (1981, Ch. 3) has reformulated the SSC as Principle A of his binding theory. The essence of this principle of "local binding" is that two elements X and Z cannot stand in an antecedent-anaphor relation if there is an intervening subject phrase Y in a category @ containing Z but not X. The mention of @ in defining a domain for this locality condition has in effect guaranteed two things. First, the external category X c-commands the intervening subject phrase Y.[59] Second, Y asymmetrically c-commands Z, since any subject of a domain @ asymmetrically c-commands any other anaphor inside @.

---

[58] Kayne's use of the SSC blocks certain *movements*. But since the Government and Binding descendent of the SSC is Principle A of Chomsky's (1981) Binding Theory, Kayne's role for embedded subjects should be built into an appropriate revision of Principle A.

[59] Here is why: Principle A has always applied to anaphors Z, whose antecedents X must c-command Z. Hence X must c-command any category @ containing Z but not X, and consequently must c-command any subject within @.

If we eliminate the troublesome and in fact inessential mention of a clausal @, we obtain a simpler relation of "Local Binding" among three rather than four elements in terms of c-command, which is apparently the fundamental relation of sentence grammar. Pending wider research, Local Binding, like Principle A, does not apply to any Z which is a pronoun or a variable. But Z may be a covert or overt phrase bound by a clitic.[60]

(6.74)   *Local Binding in LF. Let X, Y and Z be distinct nodes. If Y is a subject in ...X...Y...Z..., where X c-commands Y and Y asymmetrically c-commands Z, X may not be a local binder of Z.*

I first review five cases where this principle correctly has no effect, which include the paradigms indicated in (vi) above which are problematic for Kayne's approach.

(a) Free cliticization on V_x in *faire ... par*. Recall that all authors agree that cliticization onto V_x in the *faire ... par* construction is free. Burzio (1986, 273) exemplifies this with Italian reflexives in (6.75b-c).

(6.75)   a.   Marie les leur a fait distribuer par Anne.
                  Marie them-them made distribute by Anne
                  'Marie had them distributed to them by Ann.'
          b.   Maria$_i$ si$_i$ e fatta accusare da Giovanni.
                  Maria herself-had accuse by Giovanni
                  'Maria had herself accused by Giovanni.'
          c.   Maria$_i$ si$_i$ e fatta telefonare da Giovanni.
                  Maria herself-had telephone by Giovanni
                  'Maria had herself phoned by Giovanni.'

Since a clitic on V_x fails to c-command a *par*-phrase in adjunct position, the relation between X and Y in (6.74) fails, so that Local Binding in LF correctly has no effect in the *faire ... par* construction.

---

[60] By a stipulation, Chomsky (1981, Ch. 3) includes subject agreement on I among the "intervening subjects" Y which block lexical anaphors Z (i.e., as finite clause subjects). Clearly, Y doesn't asymmetrically c-command Z in this configuration but rather vice-versa; a lexical subject is higher than I. If we are to include this under a revised Principle A, we need to reformulate Local Binding in LF (6.74) to apply to any asymmetric c-command relation between Y and Z (either can asymmetrically c-command the other).

(b) Free cliticization on V_x of lower direct objects. Local Binding in LF *correctly permits cliticization of direct objects* of V_c onto V_x in the *faire ...* *à* construction, since a subject of V_c in a flat structure (6.56a) fails to asymmetrically c-command these objects; i.e. the relation between Y and Z in (6.74) fails. The initial examples of the Appendix (6.47), repeated here without glosses, illustrate such (italicized) clitics on V_x.

(6.47)   a. French causative *laisser* 'let': Marie *les* a laissés laver à Anne.
        b. Italian causative fare 'make': *La* ho fatta riparare a Giovanni.
        c. Spanish causative *dejar* 'let':
          Los hermanos *la* han dejado preparar a Ana.

This freely allowed cliticization of a direct object of V_c onto V_x in the *faire ... à* causative, which has forced bi-clausal accounts into postulating causative formation rules, ad hoc phrasal groupings, and/or clitic raising, is trivial and unproblematic within the flat structure analysis. The lower object DP must be a sister to V_c to be case-marked and is thereby high enough in the tree to escape Local Binding.

(c) Free cliticization on V_x of PP complements. The importance of *asymmetric* c-command between Y and Z in (6.74) is further underscored by the fact that PP complements in the flat structure (6.56a) are straightforward phrasal sisters of V_c. They are hence c-commanded by the lower subject but not *asymmetrically*, and so the invariant French PP clitics *y* and *en* on V_x can perfectly well replace them. (These facts are from Kayne, 1975, Ch. 4.)

(6.76)   a. Cela y fait   penser tout le monde.
        That there-makes think all the world
        'That makes everybody think about it.'
        b. On essaiera d'en faire   parler ton ami.
        On will-try to-thereof-make speak your friend
        'We will try to make your friend talk about it.'

Similarly, Rouverct and Vergnaud (1980, section 6) provide examples of invariant clitics on V_x which replace PP complements of transitive V_c.[61]

---

[61] In contrast to the examples in (6.76)–(6.77), some oblique complements alternatively realized by the French invariant clitic *y*, as in (i), are apparently *not* cliticizable on V_x in the *faire ... à* causative, as seen in (ii).

(6.77) a. Jean y fera   envoyer ces livres à Pierre.
            John thereto-will-make send those books to Peter
            'John will have Peter   send those books there.'
        b. Jean en fera   déduire cette conclusion à Lucie.
            John thereof-will-make deduce that conclusion to Lucy
            'John will make Lucy   deduce that conclusion from it.'

(d) Free cliticization on V_x of adjunct PPs. An adjunct of V_c in a flat structure may also cliticize onto V_x, since the lower subject DP of V_c fails to c-command adjuncts. Local Binding in LF therefore has no effect on adjuncts outside V'. The data in Rouveret and Vergnaud (1980, section 6) show that this prediction is correct: in the presence of a lexical subject for V_c, adjunct status as in (6.78) is a sufficient condition for replacing a PP with a French adverbial clitic *y* or *en* on V_x.

(6.78)   Marie y a laissé   lire ces romans à Paul. (Aoun, 1985, 128)
         Marie there-has-let read those novels to Paul
         'Marie let Paul read those novels there.'

(e) Free cliticization on V_x of lower subjects. Local Binding in LF also correctly allows any lower subject of V_c to itself be an (italicized) clitic on V_x, for (6.74) doesn't apply unless Y and Z are distinct.

(i)   Pièrre y a mis ce livre.   Paul y a comparé cette sonantine.
      Peter there-put that book   Paul thereto-compared this sonata
      'Peter put that book there.'   'Paul compared this sonata to it.'

(ii) *Jean y fera   mettre ce livre à Pierre.   Aoun (1985, 124)
      John there-will-make put that book to Peter
      'John will make Peter put that book there.'
      *Jean y fera comparer cette sonatine à Paul.   Rouveret and Vergnaud (1980, 178)
      John thereto-will-make compare that sonata to Paul
      'John will make Paul compare that sonata to it.'

It is difficult to characterize in any framework the distinction between the cliticizable complements in (6.76)–(6.77) and the excluded ones in (ii). Perhaps in (ii) the clitic would alternatively realize not a PP sister to V_c but rather an XP within a structure $[_{PP} [_P \varnothing] XP]$. If so, the lower subjects of V_c again asymmetrically c-command XP at LF; Local Binding in LF (but not the SSC) then succeeds in correctly predicting which complements *y* can alternatively realize on V_x.

(6.79) a. French: Marie les *lui* a laissés distribuer.
Marie them-her-has let distribute
'Marie has let her distribute them.'
b. Spanish: Los hermanos *se* la han dejado preparar.
The brothers her-it +[FEM]-have let prepare
'The brothers have let her prepare it.'

The revised limit on local binding (6.74) thus escapes many pitfalls in Kayne's use of the original SSC, essentially because the reformulation doesn't impose a clausal node @ over the blocking subject, and hence avoids all the problems such a node introduces.

Let us finally review the comparatively few cases where a lower subject DP_c in a flat structure (6.56a) actually does block cliticization onto a causative/ perception verb V_x. Since such a lower subject, Y in (6.74), asymmetrically c-commands an intransitive verb's indirect object, Z in (6.74), the latter cannot appear as a clitic.[62]

(6.80) a. French: *Marie leur a fait   parler Jean.
Marie them-has made   speak John
b. Italian: *Maria si e fatta telefonare Giovanni. (Burzio, 1986, 273)
Maria herself-had telephone Giovanni

In somewhat less obvious fashion, (6.74) also blocks cliticization of indirect objects of transitive V_c. Recall that postposed agent phrases in both passives and the *faire ... par* construction are true subjects, i.e., such DP c-command their predicates in LF (section A.2 and note 48). The PPs which house them at Spell Out for case-assigning purposes play no structural role in their final LF representations, in which the meaningless P marking the

---

[62] A complement verb V_c with a reflexive object in a French climbing structure generally acts like an intransitive (Kayne, 1975, Ch. 6); the lower subject is not marked with a P and *se* appears directly on V_c as in (i).

(i)   Marie (*y) a fait se comparer Pierre et Jean.   (Rouveret and Vergnaud, 1980, 179)
Marie (thereto-)made selves-compare Peter and John

Perhaps we might hypothesize that all reflexive objects are uniformly realized as structurally *oblique* in Romance; this would account for why all clitic forms of direct and indirect reflexive objects are "accidentally" identical in the languages considered here. At the same time, this permits lower subjects to occupy the accusative position and hence block the variant of (i) with *y* by virtue of Local Binding in LF.

agent phrase is ultimately deleted. Along the same lines, the [$_P$ *à*] providing case to the lower subject in the *faire ... à* construction is also deleted in LF prior to Local Binding. Thus, the italicized lower subjects in (6.81) end up asymmetrically c-commanding the oblique DP$_i$, which are the Z in (6.74), exactly as required in order for Local Binding to prevent them from being alternatively realized as clitics.[63]

(6.81)   a. Los hermanos (*se$_i$) la han dejado preparar [$_{PP}$ [$_P$ Ø] [$_{DP'}$ Ø]$_i$]
              a *Ana*.
              The brothers   (them)-it-have let prepare to Ana
              'The brothers have let Ana prepare it (for them).'
          b. Marie les (*leur$_i$) a laissés distribuer [$_{PP}$ [$_P$ Ø] [$_{DP'}$ Ø]$_i$] à *Anne*.
              Marie them-them-has let distribute to Anne
              Marie has let Anne distribute them (to them).'

In conclusion to this section, just as the Specified Subject Condition and its successor Principle A apply to a range of constructions, so does Local Binding in LF (6.74). As with the SSC and with Principle A, personal pronouns and traces of phrasal movements to A-bar positions are exempt. Local Binding is more general than Principle A because it again subsumes the SSC restrictions on clitics in climbing (flat) structures, which Principle A failed to account for. But the big advantage of Local Binding in LF over the SSC and Principle A is that it correctly *fails to apply* to the four constructions (a)–(d) above where the SSC has always proven to be too restrictive. Moreover, (6.74) has none of the drawbacks (i)–(vi) discussed in section A.4 that inevitably result from a dogmatic insistence that a clausal node @ must immediately dominate every subject.[64]

---

[63] The dative prepositions with the (italicized) lower subjects of the transitive V$_c$ in (6.81) are unmistakable indications of a clitic climbing or flat structure pattern.

[64] An advocate of these clausal nodes @ will occasionally bring out the difficulties they cause. Several of the arguments against them in section A.4 are in fact drawn from Kayne's own discussions. Burzio (1986, 261–262) summarizes problems raised by his embedded VP in clitic-climbing patterns (with an internal subject this serves as @): his analysis involves "government across VP boundaries, contrary to the general definition of government," and he observes that an embedded VP in clitic-climbing structures cannot account for its "near-obligatoriness."

In the analysis developed here, Romance cliticizations in both simple and climbing patterns have exactly the same status: they exemplify the Phrase Mate Hypothesis (6.9).

In summary, this chapter and its appendix have argued that grammatical V_x interpreted at LF (Romance restructuring verbs and causative/ perception verbs) may head flat structures only if they are inserted during a syntactic derivation rather than at deep structure. Only such grammatical verbs V_x have non-phrasal V_c complements, and only V_c in these flat configurations can have a postposed, VP-internal subject positioned either as a complement in (6.56a) or as an adjunct in (6.57a). These lower subjects, particularly those in complement position, are not only interpreted at LF as subjects of V_c; they also play a syntactic role as structural subjects in blocking certain cliticizations, as this last section has shown.

Unlike other mono-clausal or mono-stratal analyses of causative and restructuring sequences, the present analysis insists that *all the single clause structures for restructuring (6.44) and causatives (6.56a) and (6.57a) contain two separate LF predications* – exactly the same two predications as in a layered "separate VP" causative structure (6.55b). All these varied subject-predicate configurations are determined by a single definition, Generalized Subjects (1.15).

As an extended illustrative example of the role of empty heads in deep structure, one bi-clausal and two mono-clausal structures for Romance causatives have been derived from applying the lexical theory of Chapter 4 to grammatical verbs such as French *laisser* with a simple subcategorization. These three structures, the separate VP structure (6.55b), one flat structure (6.56a) for Kayne's *faire ... à* construction and another (6.57a) for his *faire ... par* construction, together with the Phrase Mate Hypothesis (6.9), Generalized Subjects (1.15) and Local Binding (6.74), succeed in predicting the extremely complex patterns of clitics and their verbal hosts in Romance causatives.

Chapter 7
Subcategorization across syntactic empty heads

7.1 A review of Revised Classical Subcategorization

Chapter 2 reviewed the classical subcategorization frames for phrasal sisters proposed in Chomsky (1965), and argued that lexical entries specify such frames in terms of the categories and features of the *heads* of those sisters.

(2.13) *Lexical Interface Principle. The lexicon uses only morpheme categories in its statements. It cannot mention phrases, nor distinguish between X and XP.*[1]

(2.18) *Extended Classical Subcategorization. @, Y, +___X is satisfied if and only if X is a cognitive syntactic feature of a lexical head of a complement in YP.*

The argumentation of Chapter 2 led to the conclusion that contextual subcategorizations, stated as a purely syntactic device, are *the only lexical devices which assemble heads and complements.* That is, that semantic aspects of head-complement relations (e.g. theta roles, various types of propositional force) are read off syntactic configurations by principles whose only interaction with lexical entries consists of access to their inherent syntactic and semantic features.

Chapters 3 and 6 have shown that such subcategorization frames Y, +___X, replaced now with the order-free notation +<X>, indeed sometimes select phrases XP but sometimes select only X^0 sisters, since Y and X being the same category can give rise to the flat structures of section 6.4. Nonetheless, outside of compounding, *the subcategorization frames +<X> of open class items Y do invariably project to phrases* even though, due to category-changing morphology such as -*ing*, these phrases are not always

---

[1] The Lexical Interface Principle (2.13) is not a primitive condition but is rather a consequence of (2.18). "Morpheme category" is a loose term for any category thought of as typically dominating only single morphemes. The second sentence of (2.13) constitutes its actual content.

of category XP. For example, the gerund complements of verbs projected from the frame +___V (section 4.7.1) are DPs.

Moreover, phrases which satisfy a frame Y, ___X are not invariably sisters of Y. The decoupling of the categories of head and phrase effected by (4.27) sometimes allows an XP sister of some other head Z^0 to satisfy a subcategorization frame of Y.

(4.27)   *Lexical Head/Projection. Let Y^0 be the highest lexically filled head in Z^j. Then Y^0 is the lexical head of Z^j, and Z^j is a lexical projection of Y^0.*

In particular, Chapter 6 has explored configurations where *a higher head Z which is empty at deep structure*, such as a light verb or a linking verb, has a complement of category Y which in turn takes its own complements.

(7.1) $[_{ZP} [_Z \emptyset (\Rightarrow \text{have in PF})] [_{YP} a [_Y \text{look}]] [_{XP} \text{at that}]]$

In such cases, a second structural sister XP of Z is an "extended sister" (but not a sister) of ZP's deep lexical head Y and can thus satisfy Y, +__X.

(4.28)   *Extended Sisterhood. If Z^0 and XP are sisters and if Z^1 is the smallest phrase (besides structural projections of Y) whose lexical head is Y^0, then Y^0 and XP are extended sisters.*

To accommodate *extended* sisters, (2.18) was minimally modified as (4.29), incorporating the "directionless" <X> notation.

(4.29)   *Revised Classical Subcategorization. @, Y, +<(___)X(___)> is satisfied if and only if X is a cognitive syntactic feature of the lexical head of an (extended) sister of $Y^0 = @$.*

To sum up, previous chapters have reviewed deep structure configurations $[_Z \emptyset]$-$[_{YP} Y]$-XP and $[_Z Y - [_Z \emptyset]]$-XP which satisfy Y, +__X; the former involve *higher* empty heads and the latter concern *inflectional* empty heads. This chapter now investigates instances where Z is an *intermediate* empty head in a structure Y- $[_{ZP} [_Z \emptyset] - XP]$ satisfying Y, +__X. Revised Classical Subcategorization handles, in fact predicts, such dependencies with no additional stipulation or modification.

7.2 The source of intermediate empty heads

7.2.1 Factors requiring extra structure

This section reviews constructions in which various grammatical principles conspire to prevent certain complements from being generated as sisters of the heads which select them. Such complements can then be realized only inside more complex "empty-headed" sisters. The kernel of the reasoning is that in each construction, some principle of grammar makes it impossible for a frame Y, +<X> to simply select an XP as Y's sister. Rather, some larger structure ZP *containing XP* must be the sister of Y. This larger structure is sanctioned provided that X is still the lexical head of ZP at the point of selection; in other words, if all heads in c-command relations lower than Y but higher than X are empty. In this way, principles of grammar can in effect require *extra but empty structure* ZP between an XP complement and the Y which selects it.

(i) Obligatory control. A first example of a construction with an intermediate empty head is furnished by infinitival complements of obligatory control. According to the analysis in Emonds (1985, Ch. 2), refined using this study's framework in section 10.1, obligatory control infinitives (but not finite clauses or optional control infinitives) are generated by a lexical frame +___V (equivalently +<V>) with verbs like *decide* and *force,* nouns like *decision* and *courage* and grammatical elements like *whether* and *so as*.[2]

An additional argument that obligatory control clauses are selected by +___V is based on the fact that in some of these complements, stative verbs are less than fully acceptable (Lakoff and Ross, 1966).

(7.2)   a. They { decided/ convinced us } to { change/ borrow/ discuss } bank cards.
?They { decided/ convinced us } to { possess/ need/ prefer } bank cards.

---

[2] Jackendoff (1985) establishes that obligatory control complements of certain classes of transitive verbs are semantically "Action arguments," while their *that*-clause counterparts are "State/ Event arguments." In present terms, complements projected from +___V or +___ACTIVITY are typically interpreted as Actions, while those projected from +___I have the sense of States/ Events, a natural enough correlation.

b. They { decided / convinced us } that they { possessed / needed / preferred } bank cards.

The contrast in (7.2a) suggests that these infinitives are selected not by +<V> but by +<ACTIVITY>, universally a canonical feature on V. By Revised Classical Subcategorization (4.29), ACTIVITY must be a feature on the *lexical head* of the complement, i.e. we can conclude that the lexical head of an obligatory control infinitive is V. As expected, violating a selection restriction leads to metaphorical interpretation rather than clear-cut unacceptability (note 13 of Ch. 2). The fact that finite complements (7.2b) of these or any other verbs never exhibit this restriction equally well suggests that the lexical head of finite clauses is *not* V.

An obligatorily controlled subject arises from tension between selecting a "bare VP" to satisfy +<V> and the requirement of the Extended Projection Principle (1.17) that each head verb in LF have a subject. A V selected by +<V> typically projects up to IP to satisfy the EPP. But this V must still remain the lexical head of IP, according to (4.27), which means that at the level of selecting, the I above V is empty in syntax. Finally, because an empty (non-finite) I does not assign case, the DP in SPEC(IP) is also empty, resulting in obligatory control.

(ii) Realizing DPs as complements of nouns. In addition to obligatory control complements, other structures selected to satisfy <X> are sometimes "forced" to be embedded in more than just XP. The bracketed DP complements of transitive and double object verbs as in (7.3a) do not carry over unmodified to corresponding nominalizations (7.3b).

(7.3)   a. They splashed [red paint] on the wall.
          They splashed [the wall] with red paint.
          We elected [Ann] [treasurer].
          The owner paid [Bill] [$100].
          The children respected [the new law].
        b. *The splash red paint on the wall was shocking.
          *The splash the wall with red paint was shocking.
          *People contested our election Ann treasurer.
          *Her payment Bill $100 was late.
          *The children's respect the new law surprised us.

Rather, appropriate grammatical prepositions in bold, often but not always *of*, must appear with complements inside nominalizations, as in (7.4).

(7.4)   The splash **of** red paint on the wall was shocking.
         The splash { **on/** *****of** } the wall was shocking.
         People contested our election **of** Ann { **as/** *****of** } treasurer.
         Her payment **of** $100 **to** Bill was late.
         Her payment { **to/** *****of** } Bill was late.
         The children's respect { **for/** *****of** } the new law was surprising.

A consensus of government and binding analyses is that a semantically empty, featureless P *of* is PF-inserted in such nominalizations to assign abstract case to an object DP (e.g. *red paint, Ann, $100*). This *of*-insertion is clearly part of *a more general pattern*; the data as in (7.3)–(7.4) show that *all* DP arguments of N require extra structure in order to be well-formed. Again, some principle of grammar, a generalization of Rouveret and Vergnaud's (1980) Case Filter to be discussed in section 7.3, requires extra but empty-headed structure between the nominalized heads and their selected complements prior to Spell Out.

(iii) Indirect objects. Second objects of verbs seem to reveal the same principle at work. We cannot say that the second object of a verb results from subcategorization for a PP complement, as seen from (7.5):

(7.5)   Susan { gave/ sold/ read/ taught/ handed/ recommended }
         Shakespeare { to/ *into/ *toward/ *at/ *from/ *on } Bill.

At the same time, the choice of *to* seems regular and not idiomatic, since hundreds of verbs follow the same pattern. That is, the indirect object DP appears in a PP only because it needs abstract case at Spell Out. The *to* is inserted during the derivation to legitimize the empty P needed for case-assignment; its PATH feature is apparently the cross-linguistically unmarked value for a (V'-internal) PP complement of activity verbs. In other words, some larger PP *containing* the second DP complement must be the sister of V. A generalized Case Filter thus seems to play a role in inducing extra structure not only for DPs inside noun phrases (7.4) but also for second or oblique objects in verb phrases (7.5).

Consequently, minimal lexical entries for typical verbs with double objects should not have to mention P at all. Rather, case theory alone should force a structure with an empty P. Their entries (7.6a) are then appropriately simpler than those (7.6b) for the smaller groups of verbs in (7.6c) whose indirect object DPs have more marked source or benefactive prepositions.

(ANIM is the animacy feature and LOC' is a feature distinguishing *to* from *for*).[3]

(7.6)   a.   read, V, +< (D), (ANIM) >
           teach, V, +< D, (ANIM) >
           hand, V, +< D, ANIM >
           recommend, V, +< D, (ANIM) >
     b.   ask, V, +< D, SOURCE^ANIM >, ...
           demand, V, +< D, (SOURCE^ANIM) >, ...
           paint, V, +< (D), (LOC'^ANIM) >
           buy, V, +< D, (SOURCE^ANIM), (LOC'^ANIM) >
     c.   Ann { asked/ begged/ demanded/ expected } cooperation { of/ from/ ?out of/ *off / *away (from)/ *through } him.
           Nobody { made/ bought/ prepared/ painted } a picture { for/ *to/ *at/ *onto/ *towards } Sally.
           Sally bought The Nightwatch from Sam for Bill.

There is no need for lexical frames as in (7.6b) to reflect the linear order in syntactic trees of the two features for the indirect objects, the D feature ANIM and the P feature SOURCE, since phrasal ordering is fixed independently of lexical entries. I thus replace the concatenation notation in (7.6) with (7.7), where e.g., ANIM and a PATH feature on P are written as a pair.[4]

(7.7)   a.   ask, V, +< D, [ANIM, SOURCE] >, ...
     b.   demand, V, +< D, ([ANIM, SOURCE]) >, ...
     c.   paint, V, +< (D), ([ANIM, LOC']) >
     d.   buy, V, +< D, ([ANIM, SOURCE]), ([ANIM, LOC']) >

---

[3]   Incidentally, the lexical frames for DPs in (7.6a-b) have to contrast with those for the verbs in (i) whose objects are modified by secondary predication.

(i)   We { called/ declared/ elected/ named } [DP Ann] [DP our treasurer].

Such secondary predicates manage to receive abstract case without a P, often via what traditional grammar calls agreement. An appropriate notation for predicate nominal frames is treated in section 8.1.2, and a corresponding second variant of case assignment will be the matter of section 8.3.

[4]   This still leaves open the possibilities of writing the pair in ordered or unordered notation. Ordering the Fs may well be needed to distinguish a feature of the lexical head from a feature of an (empty) intermediate head. Only the former, i.e. ANIM in (7.7), licenses a productive class of full XPs. Section 8.1.4 will introduce an appropriate notational convention to ensure this.

The fact that a complement frame for an indirect object can thus combine features of two different categories, the lexical head D and the empty structural head P, necessitates a final sharpening of subcategorization, since e.g., only ANIM but not SOURCE is actually a feature *on the lexical head* (4.27) of the verb's oblique complement.

(7.8)   *Generalized Subcategorization.* @, Y, +<(___)X(___)> *is satisfied if and only if X is a cognitive syntactic feature of an (extended) sister ß of Y **or of ß's lexical head.***

With this refinement, (7.8) is the most general statement of subcategorization proposed in this study as the basis of lexical co-occurrence.

The structure (7.9) illustrates how (7.8) operates, based on the lexical entry (7.7a). PP is the sister ß of the V *ask*. By percolation from the empty structural head of this PP, the feature SOURCE appears on the PP itself, while ANIM is a feature of the lexical head D of ß.

(7.9)

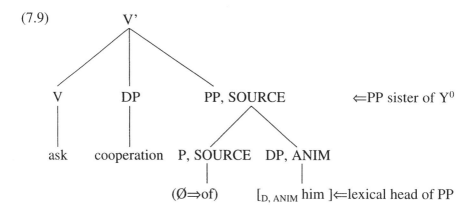

Let us summarize the framework of subcategorization-induced empty heads developed so far. Subcategorization frames of open class heads are sometimes satisfied not only by phrases that are "higher" in the tree, as with linking verbs (Section 6.2) and light verbs (Section 6.3), but also by phrases that are "lower," i.e., which are sisters of lower empty heads. These lower phrases with empty heads, which are IPs of obligatory control and case-producing PPs in the constructions reviewed so far, do not appear freely but only when principles of grammar (the Extended Projection Principle, the Case Filter) require their presence.

7.2.2 Factors limiting extra structure

In response to early questions about the Case Filter, N. Chomsky in class lectures responded that processes such as *of*-insertion should be considered as "last resorts," i.e. extra structure is permitted if needed for the satisfaction of certain grammatical principles, but not otherwise. Roughly, the sentences in (7.10a) have no variants such as (7.10b) because the former are well-formed without the extra phrasal structure needed to house the case-assigning *of*.

(7.10)   a.   The nurse examined the patient.
                 The patient was examined at the scene.
           b.   *The nurse examined of the patient. (Cf. the examining of the patient)
                 *There was examined of a patient at the scene.

This intuition I believe underlies Economy of Representation, which basically allows extra structure only if needed. In the preceding chapter, I formulated it as follows:

(6.23)   *Economy of Representation. Structural requirements such as sub-categorization frames are to be satisfied at a level of derivation with as few phrasal nodes as possible.*[5]

It is easy enough to see that (6.23) excludes examples like (7.10b) or (7.11).

(7.11)   *They supplied to the guerrillas with gas masks.
           *We elected of Ann as treasurer.
           *The owner paid to Bill of $100.

One might be apprehensive that Economy of Representation would rule out various structures that are actually grammatical. However, because the principle is a condition on executing particular requirements and not a global condition on derivations, it does not interfere with various structural options that derivations or choices among subcategorization frames provide.

---

[5]   In a derivational theory, structural requirements are in fact generally satisfied "at a level," so (6.23) in a more succinct (but perhaps easily misinterpreted) form is: Structural requirements are to be satisfied with as few phrasal nodes as possible.

For instance, since the examples in (7.12a) appear to have less structure than the corresponding synonymous examples in (7.12b), one might ask why Economy doesn't exclude those in (7.12b).

(7.12)   a.   The owner paid Bill $100.
             Hc forcsaw the city's dcstruction.
             That she was late seemed to be inevitable.
         b.   The owner paid $100 to Bill.
             He foresaw the destruction of the city.
             It seemed to be inevitable that she was late.

In these cases, the corresponding pairs are related *transformationally*, and so they satisfy subcategorizations of *pay, destruction* and *seem* at a level, as (6.23) requires, whatever happens in derived structure. Thus, Economy of Representation has no effect on derivations.[6]

A somewhat different lack of effect of (6.23) was seen in the analyses of the Romance causative structures in the Appendix to Chapter 6. More structure, namely a phrasal complement, results if a causative verb's subcategorization frame +<D, V> is satisfied at deep structure rather than later in the derivation, "in syntax," which gives rise to flat structures. But again, Economy of Representation is indifferent to what happens after the passage is made from lexicon to representation. Principle (6.23) then restricts the extra structure required by others such as the Case Filter and the Extended Projection Principle to the minimum needed *at a level.*

A second factor limiting the generation of extra structure was briefly introduced in section 5.4 as part of the account for why the passive/ past participle morpheme *-en* has such a limited distribution.

(5.47)   *Condition on Selection. If a frame* $+<[X, F_i]>$ *is satisfied by ZP, any features in ZP not licensed by its lexical head X must be stipulated among the* F_i.

This condition in fact sharply distinguishes the *intermediate* empty heads being examined in this section from the *higher* empty deep structure V of Chapter 6 which give rise to the flat structures studied there. While higher

---

[6] Concerning the first pair in (7.12), persuasive arguments for treating English dative alternations and related benefactive applicative alternations of other languages derivationally can be found in: Anderson (1971), Chung (1976) on Indonesian; Kimenyi (1980) on Kinyarwanda, Whitney (1983), Baker (1988), and Larson (1988, 1990). The transformational analysis in Emonds (1993) is also consistent with this study's framework.

empty heads can be freely specified for cognitive syntactic features F, the Condition on Selection permits marked features on empty heads between selecting and selected lexical heads *only if the selecting lexical entries stipulate them*. There are thus two cases of intermediate empty heads, those entirely lacking features and those whose features result from explicit lexical specifications as in (5.47).

The entries (7.7) have exemplified some typical (minimal) stipulations on an empty intermediate head; a (partial) frame +< [ANIM, SOURCE] >, in conjunction with the Case Filter, licenses a PP with an empty head P as the structure for indirect objects.

(7.7)   ask, V, +< D, [ANIM, SOURCE] >, ...   "ask something of John"
         demand, V, +< D, ([ANIM, SOURCE]) >, ...
                                                    "demand that (of John)"
         paint, V, +< (D), ([ANIM, LOC']) >   "paint (that) (for John)"
         buy, V, +< D, ([ANIM, SOURCE]), ([ANIM, LOC']) >
                                                    "buy it (from Sue) (for Ann)"

Any marked features such as SOURCE on the skipped P must be explicitly stipulated in the frame. Since features of other prepositions (*at, into, on, out of, towards,* etc.) are not present in (7.7), the Condition on Selection correctly predicts that these Ps cannot appear with these verbs, as seen in (7.6c). In the absence of any stipulated features in a lexical entry, empty heads between the selecting and the selected head cannot have any interpretable feature; that is by (4.21), they *must be PF-inserted*. This effect of (5.47) applies equally well to intermediate grammatical Ps and Is (*of,* infinitival *to,* etc.).

In contrast (5.47) simply does not affect higher empty heads. Consequently, while such heads must be empty in underlying structure, they need not be featureless. They may be specified for combinations of purely grammatical features F which lead to either syntactic or PF insertion. We saw ample evidence of this in Chapter 6; light verbs, linking verbs, restructuring verbs and causative verbs all exemplify higher interpreted heads which are empty at deep structure.

7.2.3 Why P is the favored intermediate category

The most usual factor forcing extra structures (and empty heads) which house subcategorized complements is the Case Filter, as discussed in section 7.2.1. According to a widely accepted view, this device requires that each argument DP must have exactly one among several abstract cases. DPs receive their case from an adjacent case-assigning category, namely, I ("nominative"), V ("accusative"), P ("oblique") or D ("genitive").

In this work, as in Emonds (1985, section 1.8), case features are not primitives but rather the case-assigning categories themselves, realized as indices on the DPs. That is, case-assignment is a device whereby the basic categories of language become "self-indexing."[7] Moreover, I maintain a very simple case typology: all cases are straightforwardly structural (direct reflections of appropriate structural configurations) or can be "quirky" (assigned to complement XPs by a lexical stipulation of a selecting head V or P). So-called inherent or adverbial cases do not constitute a third type of case; they should be analyzed as alternative realizations of empty Ps, as argued extensively in Emonds (1985, section 5.8, and 1987).[8]

Whether or not the status of the categories { V, P, I, D } as case-assigners is primitive or derived, assignment of these features to DP occurs under the same structural condition as Alternative Realization (4.20), the general principle used in this work to characterize inflection and clitics.

(4.20)   *Alternative Realization. A syntactic feature F canonically associated in UG with category B can be alternatively realized in a closed class grammatical morpheme under X^0, provided X^0 is the lexical head of a sister of B^j.*

Assuming that by definition B itself is a feature of all its projections B^j, abstract case is assigned when F = { V, P, I, D } is realized on a D^0 (as a case), where DP is a sister of $[B, F]^j = \{ V^0, P^0, I^1, D^1 \}$. This fit between AR and case assignment suggests a possible reformulation of the classical Case Filter:

---

[7]   Mathematically, an index is a mapping from a set (the indexed set) into another set (the indices), with the positive integers conventionally taken as the "simplest" set of indices. While this makes sense in mathematics, it is likely that counting integers are not primitive but derivative of natural language. Hence, prior to integers, the only set available for indexing (i.e. case-marking) syntactic categories must be the grammatical categories themselves, i.e. case-marking is a mapping from grammatical categories (various XP) into grammatical categories (the case-markers). Since case maps a subset of grammatical categories into another subset of grammatical categories, I term it "self-indexing." Viewed in any other way, the nature of case features is obscure and arbitrary.

[8]   So-called quirky case is plausibly part of complement selection, while structural case assignment is a last domain-internal step in processing an extended projection containing the case-assigner(s). That is, oblique cases are assigned when a complement PP is selected, while nominative and accusative are assigned only after processing of a containing IP. It follows that operations within IP such as passivization cannot modify quirky (or oblique) cases. There is no need to appeal to different types of case to explain this; it is due to bottom-up processing.

(7.13)   *The Case Filter as Alternative Realization. An overt DP$_i$ can occur only where a V, P, I or D exterior to DP$_i$ are potentially alternatively realized on D$_i$.*[9]

I digress here to discuss a perhaps unexpected implication of considering case as alternative realization of the case assigner. Since V is also a feature on V[1], accusative case is available for sisters of V[1] (i.e. adjuncts) as well as of V (complements). This accounts for why DP adjuncts to verb phrases can be accusative in several languages.[10] For example, Japanese exhibits a puzzling type of accusatively case-marked embedded clause perhaps misleadingly named head-internal relatives ("HIR"), bracketed in (7.14).

(7.14)   a.   Keikan-wa   [doroboo$_i$ -ga ginkoo-kara detekita-no]-o   pro$_i$
              policeman-TOP robber$_i$ -NOM bank-from exited-???-ACC pro$_i$
              tukamaeta.
              arrested
              'The policeman arrested the robber that came out from the bank.'
         b.   Keikan-wa   [doroboo$_i$-ga ginkoo-kara detekita-tokoro]-o
              policeman-TOP robber$_i$-NOM bank-from exited-scene-ACC
              pro$_i$ tukamaeta.
              pro$_i$ arrested
              'The policeman arrested the robber coming out from the bank.'

Murasugi (1991, 2000) argues convincingly "that the so-called head-internal relative clause in Japanese is not a relative clause, but is an adjunct pure complex NP." According to her analysis, *neither* of the bracketed clauses in (7.14) form direct object constituents headed by a null object pronoun pro$_i$; they are rather adverbial clauses outside V[1]. This status explains why they can contain antecedents of pro$_i$, since pro$_i$ does not then c-command these antecedents.

Moreover, an HIR cannot appear as an object of a lexical P; that is, it does not appear freely in DP positions, as would be expected if it were a relative

---

[9]   While I do not incorporate left to right order into case assignment, case assignment configurations might be a factor in some language-particular condition imposing left hand heads (cf. sections 3.1 and 3.2). As noted there, Chinese has right hand heads (as favored in UG) except when a head X^0 (V or P) assigns case; under these conditions, the head precedes the phrase.

[10]   Kim and Maling's (1993) study of certain accusative adverbials in Korean suggests that V assigns them case. Certain adverbials of Path are accusative in both Icelandic (Zaenen, Maling and Thrainsson, 1985) and in Japanese.

clause. At the same time, the clause still has DP status; its head is the "semantically null" nominal element *no* in (7.14a) or the somewhat more contentful grammatical noun *tokoro* 'place' in (7.14b).

We of course expect that such adverbial clause DPs must pass the Case Filter. It is then of some interest that these adjunct clauses in (7.14) typically exhibit the accusative marker *o* (less often the dative *ni*). This is precisely the type of accusative case-marking available for adjunct sisters of V¹ predicted by (7.13).

Let us return now to the Case Filter. Its formulation in (7.13) suffices for understanding why PPs are the favored mechanism for default case-assignment. The issue at hand is this: when extra structure is needed for assigning case to a DP satisfying +<D>, why is the familiar (7.15) chosen to house PF case-assigners over the imaginable alternatives (7.16)?

(7.15)   N'   (The election of Ann surprised us.)

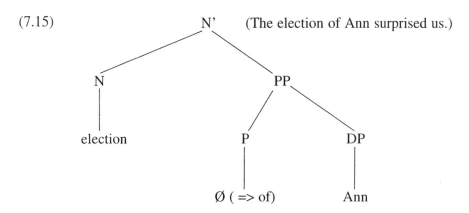

(7.16) a.   N'   (*The election have Ann surprised us.)

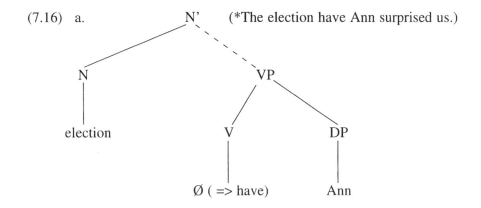

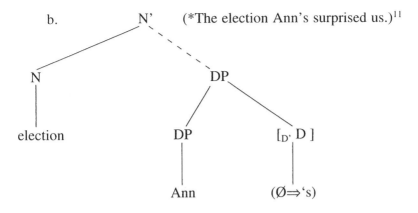

b. N' (*The election Ann's surprised us.)[11]

N — election

DP

DP — Ann

[D' D] (Ø⟹'s)

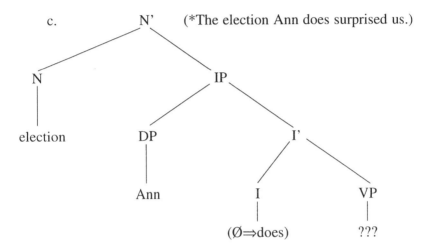

c. N' (*The election Ann does surprised us.)

N — election

IP

DP — Ann

I'

I (Ø⟹does)

VP ???

It doesn't suffice to say that the structures of (7.16) are "too complex" or "never found in natural language," unless these intuitions reflect some principle of grammar. And indeed, Economy of Representation (6.23) does rule out these alternatives.

(6.23) *Economy of Representation. Structural requirements such as sub-categorization frames are to be satisfied at a level of derivation with as few phrasal nodes as possible.*

---

[11] The possessive *'s* is widely thought to realize the functional head D. However, *'s* may be *alternatively realizing D* under SPEC(DP), a suggestion of note 16 in Ch. 1. Such a view would be consistent with the sense of Chapter 4 that inflections are typically alternative rather than canonical realizations.

(7.16a). A VP in fact must be housed in its extended projection IP (section 1.3.2), as represented by the broken line between N' and VP in the tree. Hence (7.16a) necessarily has more phrases than (7.15).

(7.16b). The Case Filter (7.13) also requires the higher DP shown to have case. Whatever phrase would contain a case assigner for the higher DP would force (7.16b) to have more phrases than (7.15).

(7.16c). Hankamer and Sag (1976) show that ellipted VPs always have a linguistic antecedent; that is, *Ann does* is not well-formed in linguistic isolation, no matter how rich the gestural and situational context. Thus, null VPs are necessarily interpreted in LF, which means that IP always structurally dominates VP.[12] Consequently, (7.16c) would always have more phrases than (7.15).

Economy of Representation therefore explains why PP is the favored category for providing any PF-inserted heads needed to satisfy the Case Filter.[13]

7.2.4 An empty V with *have* in I

We have just seen in section 7.2.1 several instances of Case Theory forcing the presence of empty Ps between a selecting head and its complement. Moreover, we have seen why P is the expected category for an intermediate empty head. Nonetheless, as shown by the way subcategorization forces an empty I and obligatory control in section 7.2.1, an intermediate empty head need not always be P.

The dual behavior of finite *have* in Modern Standard English as either an "auxiliary" or a main verb provides an interesting example of how the theory of extended projections can interact with a Syntacticon frame to induce a lower empty V.

---

[12] The main point of Chapters 9 and 10 is that interpreted unprojected arguments don't exist, i.e. any covert argument interpreted at LF is present in syntax (though of course its reference may not yet be determined). I extrapolate and conclude that any covert phrase interpreted at LF is present in syntax.

[13] The explanation of why (7.15) is preferred to (7.16) is lost in any theory of categories in which all types of XP have the same internal structure (i.e. if PP and VP have isomorphic extended projections). It is in fact curious that many linguistic analyses surround the different "atoms" of syntax (N, V, A, P) with identical projected structures. Physics, in contrast, postulates distinct atoms and elementary particles only if they occur in distinct configurations.

Let us first put aside any uses of *have* as an activity verb: *have Mary help you, have a good vacation, have a serious look*, etc. As indicated in Chapter 1, +ACTIVITY (= -STATIVE) is a lexically unmarked feature on verbs, perhaps the fundamental one, and *is* interpreted in LF. Therefore, any *have* associated with ACTIVITY must be present under V at s-structure. Such main verb uses of *have* never act like they are under I:

(7.17)   *Had Mary a serious look at the newspaper?
         *They have Mary help you often, haven't they?
         *John and Mary haven't good vacation plans at Christmas.
         *Bill had second thoughts before Mary had.

This section treats only uses of *have* which may appear under I and hence does not concern any uses with the unmarked value of [V, -STATIVE].

The use of *have* as a minimal stative verb which assigns case has been characterized in section 5.6 by the lexical entry (5.62); recall that active perfect participles were analyzed there as headed by a bound suffixal adjective -*en* which carries quirky accusative case. This entry yields examples as in (7.18); the lexical heads D and A of the complements are italicized.[14]

(5.62)   have, V, STATIVE, +__X_{ACC}

(7.18)   a. Bill may have *another* broken leg.
             My friends never have *any* chairs.
         b. Bill may have just brok*en* another leg.
             You will have grow*n* a lot.

Restricting ourselves momentarily to transitive *have* as in (7.18a), since its Syntacticon entry expresses only context and marked absence of LF content (STATIVE), the lexical insertion theory of Chapter 4 determines that *have* undergoes Phonological Lexicalization (4.21). If so, the following transitive s-structure (7.19) for (7.18a) must be interpretable independently of any PF realizations of I; intermediate projections are omitted.

---

[14] The Syntacticon entry (5.62) should be combined with an additional frame +__ [V, MODAL] for an obligatory control infinitive with the *have* of obligation: *Bill may have to leave early*. With respect to distribution, this use of *have* can appear under I only if followed by the dummy verb *got*, treated briefly below.

(7.19)

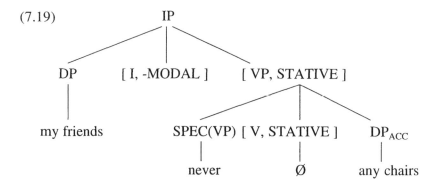

As with any English main verb either the auxiliary *do* will lexically realize I as in (7.20a), or inflected forms (*has, have* and *had*) will alternatively realize the features of I within the VP (7.20b).

(7.20)   a. Does Bill [vp have *another* broken leg]?
              My friends don't [vp ever have *any* chairs].
          b. Bill [vp has *another* broken leg], doesn't he?
              My friends [vp never have *any* chairs].

Now unless we modify (5.62), *have* will never appear under I, since English lacks finite verb raising (Cf. Emonds, 1994, for supporting arguments). But we know *have* can appear outside VP under [I, -MODAL]:

(7.21)   Has Bill [vp { got/ Ø } *another* broken leg]?
          My friends haven't [vp ever { got/ Ø } *any* chairs].

The following revision of (5.62) to (7.22) permits stative uses of *have* to appear (optionally) under I in the absence of a modal. That is, the category feature of *have* can be either V or I.

(7.22)   have, { V/ TENSE }, STATIVE, +__X_{ACC}

Now before we discuss the somewhat complex alternations of (7.21), let's go back to the lexicalization of perfect participles as in (7.18b), which will prove to be more straightforward. As in section 5.6, the perfect *-en* is analyzed here as an adjectival suffix with quirky accusative case. A counterpart to (7.19) for the frame +__A_{ACC} and the example *you have grown a lot* is (7.23):

(7.23)

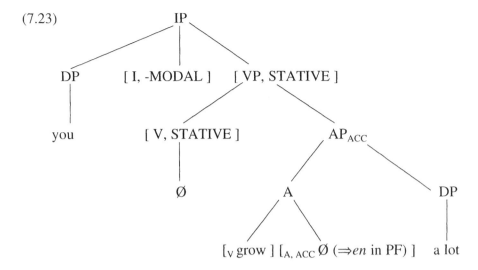

When *have* inserts under TENSE (= [I, -MODAL]) in (7.23) to yield the familiar English perfect tense (7.24), we need to know both (i) how its subcategorization +__A_{ACC} is satisfied and (ii) what licenses the empty V.

(7.24)   Has Bill [$_V$ Ø] just broken another leg?
         You haven't [$_V$ Ø] grown much, have you?
         Bill has [$_V$ Ø] had second thoughts but Mary hasn't.

As for question (i), *have* can be inserted under [I, -MODAL] at PF provided the lexical head of its sister is marked accusative. Since the theory of extended projections (section 1.3.2) forces the I node to have a sister VP, this VP must have a potentially case-marked lexical head X^0 such as A, which implies that the intervening V^0 is empty when *have* is PF-inserted.[15] Thus, principles of grammar again sanction an intermediate empty head in order to satisfy a subcategorization frame; in this case that head is a V rather than the more usual P.

The answer to question (ii) once more appeals to Alternative Realization (4.20). Wherever *have* is inserted, it carries the marked Absence of Content feature STATIVE. Under I, *have* alternatively realizes the marked feature

---

[15] As discussed in section 5.6, the head A -*en* in (7.23) is itself PF-inserted and contributes only the abstract property of "case-marked" to interpretation of the perfect participle, whose lexical head at LF is the lower V which is its host.

STATIVE on V in (7.23), and hence the Invisible Category Principle (4.35) licenses V as empty.

In addition, we wish to know what excludes inserting *have* (or *got*) under V in these contexts, as in (7.25).

(7.25) a. *Does Bill have just broken another leg?
            *You don't have grown much, do you?
            *Bill does have had second thoughts but Mary doesn't.
        b. *Has Bill just got broken another leg?
            *You haven't got grown much, have you?
            *Bill has got had second thoughts but Mary hasn't.

In fact, once the empty V is licensed in (7.23), Economy of Derivation then clearly prefers the strings (7.24) to their LF equivalents (7.25) with an extra word.

(4.36) *Economy of Derivation: Two deep structures which differ only by empty categories not interpretable at LF count as equivalent. Of equivalent deep structures, prefer the derivation with the fewest insertions of free morphemes.*

Let's return now to transitive *have* with the frame +__$D_{ACC,}$ which apparently fully exploits the two options in (7.22) of insertion under either V (7.20) or TENSE (7.21), repeated here for convenience.

(7.20) Does Bill [$_{VP}$ have *another* broken leg]?
        My friends don't [$_{VP}$ ever have *any* chairs].

(7.21) Has Bill [$_{VP}$ { got/ Ø } *another* broken leg]?
        My friends haven't [$_{VP}$ ever { got/ Ø } *any* chairs].

Clearly neither Economy of Representation or Economy of Derivation are relevant for choosing between these structurally identical variants of the tree (7.19) with *do* and *got*, and in empirical fact the two sets seem equally acceptable.[16] One might nonetheless be tempted to conclude that the latter principle should choose a variant with neither word, where V is Ø. In reality,

---

[16] If TENSE is alternatively realized in the V position (*John has another broken leg*), then Economy of Derivation should prefer this to the unstressed, uncontracted *?John has got another broken leg*. My own usage conforms to this.

however, this possibility, i.e. the currency of (7.21) without *got*, is dying out in English.[17]

What seems to me most plausible here is that a *lexical* null V, at one time needed for continuity with earlier versions of English, is competing with *got*. As noted in Chapter 3, the Syntacticon tolerates null morphemes, free as well as bound; see note 32 of Chapter 1 for more examples.[18] The facts of usage seem to suggest that null free morphemes count *against* Economy of Derivation, and indeed such is its formulation (4.36). Therefore, the variants of (7.21) with null V are neither more nor less economical than those with *got* or *have* under V; the increasing rarity of a null V is simply a question of a particular grammatical morpheme becoming less and less frequent, akin to e.g. *hither, shan't*, irregular *-en* (as opposed to *-ed*), *whom*, etc.[19]

We therefore only need to explain (separately) the well-formedness of the equally economical variants with *have* under V (7.20) and those with *have* under TENSE (7.21). In the first case, there is nothing to explain, since *have* is acting like a standard verb. For *have* under TENSE, we need to know both why *got* or, at least in earlier stages of English, a null V is even required, since the reasoning given above for *have* in the perfect construction might suggest that the subcategorization frame $+\_D_{ACC}$ is satisfied with *have* under I in (7.19), with V serving as a by now familiar intermediate empty head.

An answer to this perhaps requires that we again inspect the tree (7.19). Plausibly, LF can assign an independent theta role to a complement only if its selecting head is eventually lexicalized. From this point of view, transi-

---

[17] Over many years, university students presented with the variants in (7.21) without *got* typically attribute them to transatlantic usage; Americans say they never use them and assume they are British, while British students call them Americanisms. Probably they are rather easily processed archaisms, akin to *What think you? I kid you not; if that be the case,* etc.

[18] I note here some additional clear cases of empty free forms. The so-called present subjunctive in American English (*the demand that he Ø not be late*), which alternates with *should* in British English, is one. In formal French retaining the pre-verbal clitic *ne*, the least marked of the co-occurring negative free morphemes *pas* can be dropped after a small class of grammatical verbs such as *pouvoir* and *savoir*. Such free empty morphemes must be difficult to learn and naturally result in dialectal instabilities.

[19] Most candidates for null morphemes throughout this book are unmarked members of paradigms and alternate with grammatical morphemes such as *that* or the copula, whose feature specifications are really minimal. Earlier stages of English may have permitted a null V in (7.21) precisely because its principal marked feature STATIVE is alternatively realized under I by *have*.

tive *have* under I can satisfy its frame +__D_{ACC} in the syntax. The exceptional item *got* would then be PF-inserted in the context [$_{-PAST}$ *have*]__, yielding (7.21) above as possible realizations of the tree (7.19).[20] In contrast, the AP in the tree for the perfect construction (7.23) receives no theta role, so its V sister can economically remain empty throughout a derivation.

The unique and complex distribution of *have* in Modern Standard English has thus illustrated several points. First, its presence under I reveals how not only P but also V can serve as an empty intermediate head between a selecting and selected head in a subcategorization frame. Second, its dual positioning in transitive structures confirms that Economy of Representation takes into account only the *number* of phrases needed to satisfy subcategorization. Third, the paradigms with the perfect participle and with irregular *got* behave as expected under Economy of Derivation.

7.3 The Deep Case Filter: a basis for articulated structure and recursion

In section 7.2, we observed that all DP complements in nominalizations and second objects of verbs must appear inside PPs whose heads assign them case. For reasons I now go into, I propose to account for this by extending the classical Case Filter account of Rouveret and Vergnaud (1980). Retaining their name is perhaps misleading because (7.26) affects constituents which bear no case, but it recalls the source of the idea. As in Chapter 1, an IP is an extended projection of V and a DP is an extended projection of N.

My proposals for generalizing case theory incorporate certain conclusions of Emonds (1985, section 1.8):

(i) "Accusative" is just a name for the case index V on nominal projections, and "oblique" or "dative" are just names for the case index P. In terms of the DP-hypothesis, "genitive" is a name for the case index D.

(ii) Case assignment must be optional in order to allow DPs to move to higher case positions.

(iii) However, case must be assigned to a DP within the smallest extended lexical projection containing that DP; hence, oblique case is as-

---

[20] Usual American usage doesn't tolerate *got* with PAST:

  *Had Bill got another broken leg?
  *My friends hadn't got any chairs.
  *John had got to borrow chairs, hadn't he?

signed within a PP but accusative case is not assigned until IP is transformationally processed. This explains why objects of V but not of P can
passivize, and eliminates any need to differentiate some kind of special
"early" or "inherent" case from structural case.

With these preliminaries, (7.26)–(7.27) serve as a preliminary statement
of deep case theory:

(7.26)   *The Deep Case Filter (tentative). Arguments @ which are projec-*
         tions of N, V or A (including predicate attributes) must at some
         point in syntax (prior to s-structure) be a sister to a non-maximal
         lexical projection of β = V, P, I or D.

(7.27)   *Case Indices (tentative): If @ = DP, then β can be assigned to @*
         as its case index.[21]

As a first motivation for these principles, consider again the structure
needed for secondary predications inside nominalizations, as in some typical examples *our election of Ann *(as) treasurer* and *an appointment of Ann*
(as) our guardian. Apparently PPs are needed to house both DPs, not just
the DP counterpart to a direct object.

(7.28)

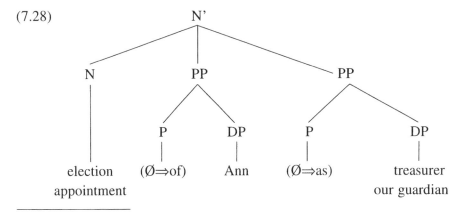

---

[21] For the six basic categories N, V, A, P, D and I, one marked feature F characterizes the
relational categories V and P (in Chomsky's terms this F is -N) and another marked feature
F' the extended projection heads I and D. Thus, the Deep Case Filter and Case Indices
assign either of these marked features to extended projections of the unmarked category N.

No case-markers are available for AP complements to V inside corresponding
nominalizations (Emonds, 1985, section 1.7), so (7.26) excludes them: **Mary's look*
worried about math; *John's appearance reluctant to leave; *Mary's sound flatter than
John.

The structure (7.28) is well motivated for English; Emonds (1985, Ch. 6) provides six arguments that the DP sister of non-comparative *as* is a predicate nominal and six more that *as* itself heads a PP.

It is a commonplace of traditional grammars of Indo-European languages with strong morphological case systems that the case of predicate nominals is not assigned by some counterpart of *as* (e.g., Czech *jako* or German *als*) but rather by the DPs they modify. In other words, predicate nominals such as *treasurer* and *our guardian* in (7.28) require PP housing but nonetheless typically receive a case not from this P but by agreement. (Section 8.3 provides examples and a formal mechanism for this "secondary case assignment" on predicate nominals.) This suggests then, that the second P in (7.28) is needed, not to actually assign case, but rather as the Deep Case Filter (7.26) implies, as a *potential* case assigner.[22]

In fact, the need for PP structure inside DPs is even less connected to actual case than this. More motivation for (7.26) is provided by two relevant paradigms of clausal complements to nominalizations (Emonds, 1985, section 1.7). First, while most French infinitival complements are introduced by grammatical P *de* 'of' or *à* 'to', a few French verbs such as *vouloir* 'want' and *préférer* 'prefer' take "bare infinitive" complements: *vouloir survivre* 'want to survive'. Yet their lexical nominalizations (*volonté, préférence*) conform to the general pattern and *de* must reappear: *la volonté *(de) survivre* 'the will to survive'.

Thus, even though French infinitives don't require actual case, they must be in a position to potentially receive case. The relevant descriptive generalization is a special case of the Deep Case Filter:

(7.29) a. All French infinitival complements of an N are introduced by P.

Second, the introductory *that* of finite complements to N in English is obligatory, although *that* is optional in most finite complements of V. Then if complementizers are a special case of grammatical P (Emonds, 1985, Ch. 7), this pattern reduces to a similar conclusion:

(7.29) b. All English (and French) finite complements of an N are introduced by P.

From these two statements (7.29), it is a short step to saying that all clausal complements to N in English and French must be introduced by a

---

[22] Gerunds show that the Deep Case Filter applies in syntax (i.e. prior to s-structure): a head N or A which is empty in syntax but spelled out as PF-inserted *-ing* (section 4.7.1) doesn't prevent its lexical head V and its extended XP sisters from satisfying (7.26).

PF-inserted P. The only apparent exceptions are English infinitives: *his tendency to lie, a decision by John to attend college*. Independently of the structure of NPs, I argue in Emonds (1987) that the infinitival English *to*, historically a GOAL preposition, in fact still alternatively realizes a prepositional feature and hence by the Invisible Category Principle (4.35) permits the GOAL Complementizer to be zero. With this final step, we reach the broad conclusion that subsumes (7.29a–b):

(7.30)   IP arguments of N must be introduced by Ps which are empty in syntax.[23]

Obviously, (7.30) still remains a special case of the Deep Case Filter (7.26). Economy of Representation is once again the factor forcing the potential case assigner of these IP to be an intervening P (i.e. C, assimilated here to P) rather than some other category.

The introductory P (including C) of predicate nominal and clausal complements of N demonstrate that the Deep Case Filter forces more embedding than subcategorization or case assignment alone. It requires PPs in a range of constructions where P does not actually assign case. This filter consequently plays a central role in limiting the "flatness" of structures at the precomputational lexical interface, and does so without benefit of small clause categories and/ or binary branching.

Government and Binding analyses practically take as axiomatic that any surface structures of complements larger than those specified in subcategorization must be due to the need for DPs to have abstract case. It is assumed that Ps can be inserted in some (but not all) positions in PF to provide this case (generally without asking why some other "case-assigner," e.g. a dummy INFL, could not do as well). No deeper explanation for abstract case has been deemed necessary. However, the structures just observed and others in the next section strongly suggest that the need for case on nominal projections, as reflected overtly by the morphological case of Indo-European languages, is not primitive. Case on DPs is rather a particular instance of a more general licensing condition on all phrasal recursion in language: the Deep Case Filter.[24]

---

[23] As shown in section 6.3, clausal complements of nouns in light verb constructions may be generated as sisters to V; hence they can lack an overt C.

[24] My earlier phrasing of this condition tried to relate abstract case to a more central architectural feature of human language, namely recursion:

An essential aspect of this Filter is its applicability to a broader range of categories than just DP. To highlight this point, I digress in the next section to focus on some generally unobserved properties of adjuncts, which I claim also finally reflect the pervasive influence of deep case.

7.4 The range and genesis of adjunct constructions

The term adjunct covers a really broad range of constructions: restrictive relative clauses and participles, noun-modifying adjective phrases, spatial and temporal expressions, manner adverbs, benefactives and "datives of interest," agent phrases, comparative clauses, conditional and causal phrases and clauses, absolute constructions (*with Mary in control*), etc., etc. In a head-initial language like English, they commonly appear as additional constituents on the right of projections headed by a lexical category N, V or A. Sometimes, as in (7.31), they seem to be added essentially freely.

(7.31)   The crowd seemed calm { in a dignified way / afterwards / near the stadium / for the next speaker / milling about aimlessly / due to the holiday / if no police were around / whatever issues you addressed / though the speaker got angry }.

In others cases, interpretation of a clausal adjunct requires some kind of structural link with an element in the containing clause, as indicated by the italicized pairs in (7.32a–e).

(7.32)   a. A result clause requires a *so* or *such* in the main clause:
             The crowd seemed **(so)* calm *that John was suspicious.*

         b. A degree clause needs certain SPEC(AP) and may contain a co-indexed gap:
             The crowd seemed **(too)* calm to me *for us to consider (it) interesting.*

(i)   Recursion Hypothesis. Outside of Specifiers, all "A-over-A" recursion in languages passes through the relational phrases VP and PP. (Emonds, 1985, 332)

In the framework used to formulate (i), Specifiers include subjects and measure phrases, which thereby include any constituents that pass the Deep Case Filter by virtue of being a sister to a D' or I'. Both the Recursion Hypothesis and the Deep Case Filter (7.26) require other arguments either to be sisters of V, V', P or P' or to themselves be a PP (i.e., not a projection of N, V or A). Thus, the Deep Case Filter, despite its different form, is essentially the same as an earlier version (i) of this idea.

c. A comparative clause must contain a co-indexed gap (Bresnan, 1973).
I saw *as few* men there as I ordinarily expect to see *(*few)* women.

d. A relative clause must contain a gap co-indexed with the modified NP:
The salesmen who I saw *(*them)* at the bar laughed nervously.

e. A participial adjunct must modify the main clause subject:
John found Ann { while/ by } *closeting { himself/ *herself } in the library.*

Whether a type of adjunct is free (7.31) or structurally linked by some type of co-indexing with the clause it is added to (7.32), they all enter a tree *independent of any item-specific subcategorization frames* of lexical heads.[25]

7.4.1 The PP form of adjuncts

Among all the various meanings of adjuncts (causes, conditions, benefactives, instruments, exceptions, etc.), spatial and temporal locational phrases and clauses having the form of PPs seem fundamental:

(7.33)   *LF Role of P. UG provides a category P, which is relational like V, whose basic LF role is to situate reference and events on an innate space-time grid.*[26]

---

[25] I appreciate discussion with M. Saito on this topic, who suggested the approach of this section, that any dependencies between adjuncts and lexical heads are pragmatic and not part of formal grammar. Any grammatical restrictions on adjuncts involve only functional heads (e.g., tense) or specifier morphemes, as in (7.32). Although adjuncts are thus syntactically free, it is easy enough to construct pragmatic oddities:

?Mary needed a house in a dignified way.
?One hundred was the square of ten afterwards.
?Troy was east of Athens, though I got angry.
?The book I hope to write weighs five pounds.
?The crowd seemed calm on John.   (Malefactive; John is disappointed.)
?The crowd seemed calm enough to find in ten minutes.

[26] The final sections of Emonds (1986) bring out grammatical implications of the innate psychological space-time grid discovered by Kant in his *Critique of Pure Reason.*

Almost all the *contentful* Ps of both the Syntacticon and the Dictionary express various types of spatial and temporal coordinates on this grid.

When adjuncts with other interpretations are used, we nonetheless find that they also appear to be housed in PP structures. That is, the *grammatical detail "at the top" of the adjunct typically involves some minimally specified introductory P or some type of phrase with PP characteristics*. The following list (i)–(vii) of adjunct types illustrates both the idiosyncracies and the way these idiosyncracies revolve around the category P.

(i) Adjuncts based on DP. English manner adverbial PPs are introduced by *in;* yet in not so syntactically distinct French, they are introduced by a different grammatical P *de* 'of'. Languages also differ according to which P marks passive agent phrases: English *by,* French *par* 'by' and *de* 'of', German *von* 'of, from', Japanese *ni* 'to'. English malefactive PPs use (stylistically stigmatized) *on*, while French malefactives appear only as indirect object clitics; no lexical P is available. But the overall generalization is clear enough: manner adverbials, agent phrases and datives of interest are realized in PPs, with the exact choice of P being highly variable.

(ii) Adjunct clauses inside AP. The particular choice of COMP introducing an adjunct clause in an English AP depends on the modifier of that A: *too* and *enough* are paired with *for*; *so* takes *that*; *as* requires *as*; and *more* and *less* take *than*. Typical examples are seen in (7.32a-c). Emonds (1985, Ch. 7) provides several arguments that these COMPs are PF-inserted Ps whose subcategorization frames are +___IP. Consequently, these clauses are PPs.

(iii) Participial adjuncts. Participles at clausal peripheries which modify the clause's subject seem at first glance to be overt bare VPs. However, they are inevitably introduced by particular choices of semantically empty morphemes. It turns out that one can usually argue that these are P; French *en* 'in' is a transparent example: *en parlant anglais* 'in speaking English'.

Spanish active participles in adjuncts are headed by the inflected form V+*ndo,* which is somewhat like the English participle V+*ing* in this function (cf. Emonds, 1991a):

(7.34)   La mujer rica   trató de retroceder, insultando a la gente del barrio.
          'The rich woman tried to back up,   insulting   the local people.'

Two properties of this inflectional head suggest that it actually alternatively realizes an empty introductory P: (a) V+*ndo* never exhibits the otherwise pervasive Spanish adjectival agreement (7.35a), and (b) the grammatical verbs which introduce V+*ndo* include those subcategorized to take spatial PPs: *andar* 'go' and the special copula for canonical spatial PPs *estar* (7.35b).[27]

(7.35)   a.   *La mujer rica trató de retroceder, insultanda a la gente del barrio.
      b.   Los alumnos { están/ *son } { insultando al profesor/ en el parque }.
          'The pupils   are   { insulting the teacher/ in the park }.'

French and Spanish participial adjuncts are thus arguably structural PPs.

(iv) Absolute constructions. The "absolute constructions" of many languages, consisting of an overt subject and a non-finite predicate (*with Mary so happy*), function only as adjuncts to clauses and never as complements. They are almost invariably introduced by a "semantically empty" preposition such as English *with* or an oblique case appropriate for PPs of location such as the Latin "ablative absolute" (G. Holland, 1984 University of California at Berkeley lecture).

Japanese participial absolutes are headed by V+*te,* and by head-final parameterization appear to the left of a finite main clause. They are widely used as substitutes for all but the last of a series of coordinate finite clauses. Kubo (1994) argues that this -*te* is a head-final grammatical P; for example, like the Spanish progressive *estar* + V+*ndo*, a Japanese progressive consists of a copula *iru* used with PPs of location and its complement headed by V+*te*.

Thus, in every case where argument seems available, the structural head of an absolute clause seems to be a grammatical P, again with variation as to its exact specification.

(v) Adverbial AP adjuncts. In Standard English, APs used as adverbial adjuncts must be accompanied by -*ly*.

(7.36)   Relatives of residents visit that nursing home very {frequently/ *frequent}.
        They worked more {carelessly/ *careless} than expected.

---

[27] This analysis of Spanish present participles ('gerundios' in some traditional Spanish grammars) as PPs is suggested by the several arguments in Artiagoitia (1992) that the Basque active participle V+*te* is structurally a PP.

These superficial APs share a number of distributional characteristics with PPs; for example, PPs of manner and *-ly* adverbs can coordinate and can satisfy obligatory subcategorizations for verbs such as *word* and *tread*: *Harry worded the response *({ carelessly / with a certain flair })*. The parallels suggest that *-ly* may alternatively realize a P feature under A, thereby rendering the PP structure of these adjuncts opaque.

(vi) Bare NP adverbials. Larson (1985) analyzes this intriguing type of adjunct, whose head Ns are a small set of grammatical nouns such as *place, time, day* and *way,* which lack purely semantic features *f*: *Mary did the work* **a new way**; *I won't visit* **this time**; *we live* **the same place** *you do.* Bresnan and Grimshaw (1978) claim that such adverbials are structurally complements of empty Ps, and Emonds (1987) argues that this "hidden P" better accounts for their case and distribution. The cognitive syntactic features of the head nouns, such as LOCATION, alternatively realize features of the structural P which introduces them and thus allow P to be empty, giving the impression that the adverbials are "bare" when in fact, as Larson admits, they are distributed like PPs.

(vii) Finite and *for-to* clause adjuncts. Another broad class of adjuncts includes restrictive relative clauses, conditionals, comparative clauses, result clauses, purpose clauses, etc. Emonds (1985, Ch. 7) argues that these (and all) CPs are best analyzed as [$_{PP}$ P - IP], with heads (English *that, if, for, than, as*) which are inserted in PF rather than in syntax. If this is correct, another large class of adjuncts in addition to the basic locational phrases of (7.33) is assimilated to PP structures.

Though the English COMP (i.e. P) *that* alternates with Ø in some untransformed structures *(The crowd seemed so calm (that) John was suspicious)*, most adjunct configurations require *that,* as can be seen by carefully inspecting the variants in (7.37). Thus, even bare finite result clauses turn out to instantiate a structure with an introductory P, in certain cases possibly null but always at least optionally realizable as *that*.

(7.37)   The person it seemed so calm to *(that) he was suspicious was John.
　　　　Mary did that in order *(that) we could save time.
　　　　We can both help, now *(that) Bill is here.
　　　　You are wrong in *(that) you have not reported the crime.
　　　　The boy *(that) came late apologized.[28]

---

[28] In English restrictive relatives, the P (COMP) *that* alternates with overt WH-phrases. In addition, a *pre-subject* WH relative pronoun in SPEC(CP) may be zeroed.

Although many details remain to be worked out, the cross-linguistic sample of grammatical patterns in (i)–(vii) establishes that PP not only provides arguments with "extra structure" for case-assignment, but also serves as the default means of syntactic expression in the realm of adjuncts. That is, phrasal modifiers not lexically selected by individual verbs, nouns and adjectives almost invariably have the deep properties (if not the superficial form) of PPs.[29]

It would be misleading to *identify* adjuncts (i.e., phrases not selected by subcategorization) with PP structures. The interesting *one-way implication* between the two concepts does not go in the direction many analysts assume. It is not that all PPs are adjuncts, but that *all adjuncts are PPs*. The only set of adjuncts which does not seem reducible to PP structure is the set of potentially agreeing APs, in both DPs and IPs (see the previous note). But even leaving aside a more general claim, the fact remains that PP structures are incontestably widely available for many different kinds of both adjuncts and complements.

The question now is, what allows all these PPs to get into trees? Since they are not licensed by subcategorization or as subjects or predicates, they must benefit from some other licensing mechanism. Moroever, this licensing is not limited to adjuncts – it also licenses complements to N and A – but it does encompass them. Such a schema replaces any distributional statements about adjuncts or undifferentiated "adverbs" in competing accounts, vague terms at best which linguistic theory would do well to dispense with. Thus, in addition to subcategorization for complements and the EPP for subjects, I propose that (7.38) is a kind of universal default licensing for syntactic structure:

(7.38)   *PP Licensing. A phrasal projection PP is freely licensed as a daughter of any phrasal projection Y^j of a lexical category.*[30]

Under this conception of free syntactic licensing, the distribution of PP adjuncts must be limited by their LF interpretations. The canonical interpre-

---

[29] I have left aside a range of adjectival AP adjuncts that modify DPs in both clause-final and DP-internal positions. Co-indexation with a subject (reflected by agreement) is characteristic of adjectival APs in Indo-European languages; such co-indexation may suffice to license an adjunct.

[30] Emonds (1985, section 1.4), building on Williams (1975), proposes a variant of (7.38). We can also express (7.38) in terms of merger as follows:

PP Merging. A phrasal projection PP can merge with any Y^j of a lexical category ($Y =$ N, V, A, P) to form a further phrasal projection Y^j

tation of PPs with lexical content heads is of course given by the LF Role of PP (7.33). But the actual constituents *which are interpreted in LF* in the various adjoined structures surveyed in (i)–(vii) above are typically *not* PPs. Rather, (7.31) and (7.36) have exemplifed *phrases of all types* which constitute the interpreted parts of the adjuncts.These examples are reproduced in (7.39) with italics for introductory Ps which have no role in LF; bold grammatical morphemes inside the adjuncts arguably alternatively realize empty introductory P.

(7.39)   DP: *in* [$_{DP}$ a dignified way]
                      for [$_{DP}$ the next speaker]
                      [$_P$ Ø] [$_{DP}$ the same **place**]
         AP: [$_P$ Ø] [$_{AP}$ more frequent-**ly**]
         NP: *as* [$_{DP}$ [$_D$ Ø] [$_{NP}$ head teacher]]
         IP: *if* [$_{IP}$ no police were around]
                      for [$_{IP}$ us to consider it interesting]
         VP: *en* [$_{VP}$ par**lant** anglais]   'in speaking English'
                                                            (French)
                      [$_P$ Ø] [$_{VP}$ hab**lando** ingles]   'in speaking English'
                                                            (Spanish)
         DP - XP: *with* [$_{DP}$ Mary] [$_{XP}$ { so happy / in a new house / helping
                      us }]
         CP (=PP): [$_{SPEC(PP)}$ what-**ever** issues] [$_{P, WH}$ Ø] [$_{IP}$ you
                      addressed][31]

The interpretation of these sentential adjuncts (*a dignified way, the next speaker, more frequent, no police were around, speak English, Mary so happy, you addressed any issues,* etc.) should thus be thought of as just "juxtaposition" with the main clause. The introductory Ps are playing no LF role, except perhaps to underscore Absence of Content. Similarly, the essential LF properties of the more complex result, relative, and comparative adjunct IPs in (7.32) are due to their link or co-indexed gap with the main clause, not to the empty grammatical formatives which introduce them.

---

[31] The suffix *-ever* satisfies AR (4.20) perfectly. The feature WH on C (=B) is alternatively realized as a closed class morpheme *-ever* under D^0, satisfying the proviso of AR that this D° is the lexical head of a sister (DP) of B^j (=C^1). It would be next to impossible to fit this grammatical dependency into any scheme of "head to head movement," since neither head c-commands the other.

7.4.2 The Deep Case and economy of adjunct phrases

Empirical patterns such as (7.39) strongly suggest that the only way to license an XP adjunct which is not itself a PP is for XP to be part of a PP. In other terms, adjunct XP need to be in a position to receive deep case. We should thus remove the restriction of the Deep Case Filter (7.26) to arguments; (7.40) encompasses adjuncts without stipulation.

(7.40)   *The Deep Case Filter. Extended and maximal projections of @ (= N, V, A) must, prior to s-structure, be a sister to a non-maximal lexical projection of β = V, P, I or D.*

As its wording implies, Economy of Representation (6.23) is not restricted to arguments; subcategorization is only the most familiar area where it operates. But this principle regulates the effects of *any* grammatical factors which give rise to "extra" phrasal structure. So by exactly the same reasoning used for complements of N in section 7.2.3, uninterpreted (i.e., late-inserted) grammatical Ps are the most economical means by which adjuncts can satisfy (7.40).

(6.23)   *Economy of Representation. Structural requirements such as subcategorization frames are to be satisfied at a level of derivation with as few phrasal nodes as possible.*

The scenario for a typical adjunct is thus as follows. Some XP other than a PP is to be juxtaposed with a main clause in LF. XP must receive deep case like any other XP. The most economical way for this to happen is by embedding XP in a simple phrase [$_{PP}$ P - XP], where P is PF-inserted and hence not present at LF.

Exactly which Ps are used to provide Deep Case to adjuncts depends on a language's Syntacticon. But as with all nodes in trees, an uninterpreted P inserted for providing deep case necessarily must be licensed in PF, either as a free lexical morpheme (e.g., in manner adverbial PPs, benefactive and agent phrases, conditional clauses, absolute constructions, comparative clauses, etc.) or via alternative realization, for example by oblique morphological case or participial or adverbial inflection in the adjunct itself. How P is lexicalized in various adjunct constructions is precisely the source of the language-particular grammatical detail "at the top" of adjuncts reviewed in the previous subsection. The Syntacticon entries for P of individual languages thus determine any language-particular properties in the form of adjuncts and indeed sometimes limit the types of adjuncts available.[32]

Finally, once the various adjunct constructions pass the Deep Case Filter in the most economical way, their PP housing must be licensed, i.e. allowed to enter a larger sentence as a constituent. This is effected by general PP Licensing (7.38). As a result, *any* phrasal category XP (sometimes subject to a linking or co-indexing condition) can serve as an interpreted adjunct in LF, as is indeed exemplified in (7.39).[33] Like any other XP, an adjunct satisfies a syntactic licensing condition, even when its LF link to the main clause is only juxtaposition. PP Licensing (7.38) alone or in conjunction with the Deep Case Filter (7.40) are the sole alternatives for getting adjuncts into trees.

7.5 Empty inflectional heads and economy of non-finite clauses

Let's now return to the main theme of this chapter, empty heads which intervene between a Y and X that satisfy a subcategorization frame Y, $+<X>$. We have treated empty heads lower than Y which are free forms (most often P but also some I and V). The final two sections will discuss how lower heads which are bound forms, namely category-changing inflections, conform to and thus further confirm the principles regulating the relation between syntax and subcategorization. As pointed out in section 4.4.4 the general motivation for all inflection is Economy, so it is not surprising that we will meet with it again here.

Chapter 6 discussed in detail flat structures generated by the frame V_x, $+<V_c>$ for the case where V_x is a closed class item.[34] This section will focus on more familiar configurations where V_x is an *open class item* with the frame $+<V_c>$ and so must be inserted pre-transformationally. As established

---

[32] E.g., Standard French has no lexical P for malefactives, which can then only surface as (dative) pronominal clitics.

[33] It is widely understood that adjuncts take on different forms depending on the category of the modified head. Thus, restrictive relative clauses and their paraphrases (so-called reduced relatives) modify only nominal projections; certain logical and causal complements appear to modify only verb-headed phrases, etc. Milner (1973) proposes formal mechanisms to reduce apparent category-particular asymmetries between comparative and relative clauses.

[34] English doesn't exercise this option, perhaps because flat structures use post-verbal subjects. As the ungrammatical glosses below show, English lacks post-verbal subjects even to the limited extent tolerated in French, the most similar Romance system.

in Chapter 6, V_c is then necessarily the lexical head of a (non-finite) complement *phrase*.[35] We will see in this section how empty intermediate heads and Economy of Representation play central roles in predicting whether these phrases take the form in English of infinitives, gerunds or participles.

According to the analysis of obligatory control in Emonds (1985, Ch.2) and section 7.2.1, complements of obligatory control as in (7.41) are generated by frames as in (7.42). ACTIVITY is a canonical feature for the large class of non-stative verbs.

(7.41) They managed (*for their children) to own two cars.
City experiences influenced us (*for the children) to live in the country.
They decided (*for their children) to buy two cars.
They forced us (*for our children) to visit the countryside.

(7.42) manage, V, +< V >, ...
influence, V, +< ANIMATE, (V) >, ...
decide, V, +< ACTIVITY >, ...
force, V, +< D, (ACTIVITY) >, ...

According to the Condition on Selection (5.47), if Y selects a complement whose lexical head is V, then all the heads between Y and V must be empty in the syntax. This insures that any intermediate I and C heads in the infinitives in (7.41) are Ø, except possibly in PF. An I which is Ø in syntax (*to* in PF) in turn leads to the non-case-marked and hence empty subject of obligatory control infinitives.

A question arises as to whether empty intermediate heads might have any role in some other type of obligatory control complement. In positions where case-marking for complements is available, English DP gerunds of obligatory control seem to compete with infinitives, often to the exclusion of the latter:

(i) C'est l'endroit vers lequel se précipite la foule.
*It is the place towards which is rushing the crowd.
(ii) Marie a laissé parler Jean longuement.
*Mary has let speak John for a long time.
(iii) Sont cruciaux à retenir les trois noms suivants: Marc, Sophie, et Luc.
*Are crucial to retain the three following names: Mark, Sophie, and Luke.

I have no theoretical proposal for this difference between English and French. Note that in most government and binding analyses, the limited post-verbal subjects of French are *not* related to a possible pro-drop of a subject.

[35] Finite complements are chosen by +<I> or +<C>, at least in languages with productive infinitives. Cf. section 8.1.3.

(7.43)   a. They avoided [(*their children's) owning two cars].
             *They avoided to own two cars.
         b. They { prevented / discouraged } me from [(*us) moving away].
             *They { prevented/ discouraged } me (from) to move away.
         c. John took up (*his assistant) re-organizing the library.
             *John took up to re-organize the library.
         d. The teacher might try [(*his department's) designing a new course].
             The teacher might try to design a new course.

So under what conditions do the frames +<V> or +<ACTIVITY> of an open class lexical item lead to *infinitives* with empty I, and when do such frames project instead to other structures such as gerunds?[36]

Let us compare the two obligatory control configurations, using an analysis of the English gerund justified in Emonds (1991a) and adopted in section 4.7.1. For concreteness, I compare the strings *avoid owning two cars* (7.44) and **avoid to own two cars* (7.45). These trees omit intermediate projections.

(7.44)

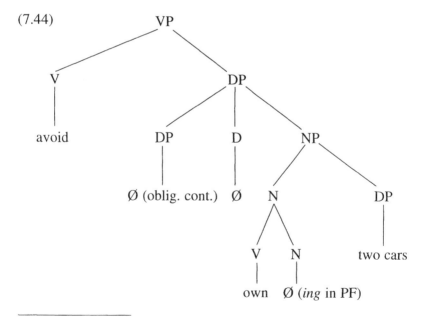

---

[36] It is widely thought that English DP gerunds are always based on the frame +___DP. It can be seen from (7.43b) that this is false: **They { prevented/ discouraged } our friends from { a vacation/ the purchase of a house }*.

(7.45)

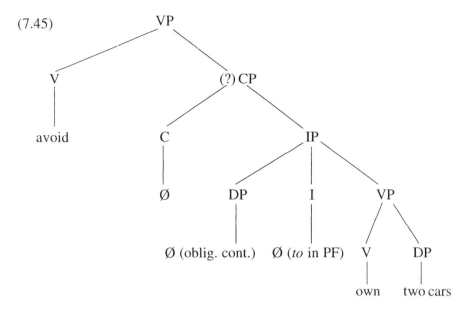

I wish to claim here a role for Economy, namely *that the NP gerund (7.44) is the more economical of these two structures* for satisfying the frame +<V> whenever the availability of case for DP presents a choice between the two. (If so, there must be further reasons for why the frame +<V> sometimes selects infinitives as in (7.41) and (7.43d); I return to these after considering the role of economy.)

If IPs of obligatory control are always housed in a CP, as in typical government and binding analyses (Chomsky, 1981), Economy of Representation (6.23) straightforwardly and correctly prefers the gerund (7.44) to the infinitive (7.45). But since I am not confident of this premise, for purposes of argument another possibility is that the infinitival complements are *not* CPs. If (7.45) lacks CP, Economy of Representation will treat it as equivalent to (7.44) and not explain why the former is preferred.

In this light, consider again Economy of Derivation from Chapter 4.

(4.36)   *Economy of Derivation: Two deep structures which differ only by empty categories not interpretable at LF count as equivalent. Of equivalent deep structures, prefer the derivation with the fewest insertions of free morphemes.*

It seems a fair enough interpretation of (4.36) to say that (7.44) and especially a *CP-less* (7.45) differ only by uninterpretable, PF-inserted empty heads. Hence the two trees are equivalent deep structures for (4.36), which then determines that the more economical option is (7.44), which has one less free morpheme (*owning* vs. *to own*). Thus, even though the exact nature of the more economical status of a gerund of obligatory control is not certain, some conclusion based on economy seems warranted.[37] For reasons of economy, a lexical frame +<V> prefers an English DP gerund to an infinitive, provided a case-assigner is available.

Let us now return to why the frames +<V> or +<ACTIVITY> nonetheless sometimes choose an infinitival IP as in (7.45), as with *manage, decide, force, try* (optionally), etc. There is a tendency for such complements to refer to unrealized events. There are in fact several other places listed below in (i)–(iv) where infinitives compete with -*ing* forms in English, and in all such situations, infinitival IP structures seem to reflect the MODAL or "irrealis" feature canonically associated with I.

(i) The infinitival counterparts to reduced relatives, infinitival relatives, are widely understood as indicating an unrealized predicate: *The man to fix the sink will soon be on his way.* Ordinary reduced relatives have no such implication: *The man fixing the sink will soon be on his way.*

(ii) Subject-modifying infinitives, adjoined outside V^1, are purpose clauses and thus also unrealized: *We brought the guest a book (in order) to thus introduce ourselves.* In contrast, participles in the same position introduced by V-*ing* again are realis: *We brought the guest a book thus introducing ourselves.*

(iii) Infinitival secondary predications modifying direct objects, so-called "lower purpose clauses" (discussed in detail in section 9.1.1), are similarly unrealized: *The landlord sent his son to pay the rent to.* A clausal complement introduced by V-*ing* in the same position reports a realized event: *The landlord watched his son paying the rent.*

(iv) Some temporal aspect verbs (*begin, start, continue,* but not *finish, keep, resume*) allow both infinitives and participles; the infinitives convey a sense of less actuality than the participles: *We started { to eat/ eating }, but were interrupted.* The first of these is easily compatible with 'no eating at all'; the second less so.

In all these structures (i)–(iv), infinitival IPs are apparently selected and interpreted by virtue of their head feature MODAL. We have argued just above that in the absence of stipulation, the unmarked and most economical realization of an English non-finite structure selected by +<V> is some version of V+*ing*. Consequently, and in accord with the Condition on Se-

---

[37] Emonds (1985, Ch. 3) claims that S (i.e. IP) has more internal structure than NP (i.e., DP). If so, Economy of Representation again prefers (7.44) to (7.45).

lection (5.47), at least the intransitive frames in (7.42) need to be revised as in (7.46) to include MODAL.

(7.46)   manage, V, +< [V, MODAL] >, ...
         decide, V, +< [ACTIVITY, MODAL] >, ...
         try, V, +< [ACTIVITY, (MODAL)] >, ...

The selection of this feature forces the V-headed complements to project to IP. A parenthesized MODAL indicates that a verb such as *try* can take *either* an infinitive IP with a distinctly irrealis sense *or* a gerund where this sense is not specified (but is still pragmatically possible).

Two points need to be retained from the discussion. (a) One of the Economy principles plays a crucial role in choosing gerunds over infinitives. (b) The favored phrasal structure (7.44) for satisfying the frame V, +<V> requires two intermediate empty heads, D and N, the latter realized in PF as the English inflection *-ing*. We have thus extended the class of intervening empty heads induced by subcategorization to include both D and also an inflectional word-internal right hand head N.

Let us now inspect this so far favored (7.44) and ask whether Economy of Representation might sometimes prefer even some third candidate to project from the frame +<V>. Developing arguments in Rosenbaum (1967), Emonds (1991a) argues that the participial AP in (7.47) rather than the gerund DP (7.44) correctly represents the complement structure of a temporal aspect verb (*start, begin, continue, be, resume, keep (on), go on, stop, finish,* etc.).

(7.47)

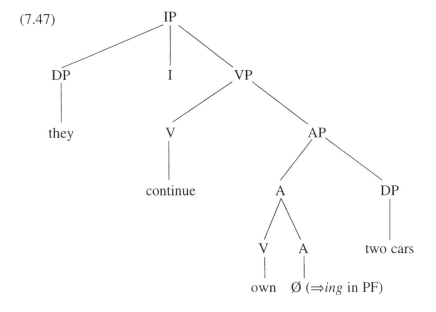

Several straightforward empirical differences confirm the structural contrast between DP gerunds in the (a) examples and AP participles in the (b) examples:[38]

(7.48)   a. It was owning two cars that they { avoided/ considered }.
       b. *It was owning two cars that they { continued/ kept on }.

(7.49)   a. Scheduling extra classes was { avoided/ taken on } by the registrar.
       b. *Scheduling extra classes was { continued/ kept on } by the registrar.

(7.50)   a. We took making double payments on.
         We put making double payments off.
       b. *We { went/ kept } making double payments on.
       c. We { took on/ put off/ went on/ kept on } making double payments.

Certainly a participial AP structure (7.47) contains fewer phrases and hence realizes a V-headed complement more economically than either a gerund (7.44) or an infinitive (7.45). This contrast therefore raises a question: why should the feature +<V> *ever* give rise to gerund or (in non-case marked positions) infinitive complements if "smaller" non-NP participles as in (7.47) can satisfy the same subcategorization? There must be some general grammatical principle which allows AP participles to realize the frame +<V> only under restricted conditions. Then, only when participles are possible in principle does Economy of Representation prefer them to infinitives and gerunds of obligatory control.[39]

---

[38] The surface subject of a temporal aspect verb is always the understood subject of its participial complement, and the verbs together report a single event. In contrast, a lower PRO_{arb} subject and separate time adverbials can occur only in gerunds, even if the governing verbs take both kinds of complements:

(i)   This afternoon, the police will { forbid/ ?stop/ *go on } demonstrating next month for higher pay.

(ii)   The city should { initiate/ ?begin/ *keep on } registering oneself for drug addiction.

As DPs, these gerunds can be focused in cleft sentences and passivized like the gerunds in (7.48)–(7.49).

[39] Approaches which claim that APs have the same internal phrasal structure as DPs (e.g., they are small clauses with internal subjects) cannot explain why AP participles are

7.6 Present participles and the Revised Theta Criterion

The key to the puzzle of when and why participles are the "favored" non-finite English construction is a proper interpretation of the Extended Projection Principle which we have been using throughout this study.

(1.17) *Extended Projection Principle. Every head verb present in LF must have a structural subject phrase to which a semantic role may be assigned.*

The definition of Generalized Subjects (1.15) is also repeated for reference (particularized to verbs for clarity).

(6.54) *Verbal Subjects: The subject of a V is the lowest DP which c-commands some phrasal projection of V within a minimal containing IP or DP.*

In the analysis of flat structures in Chapter 6, the EPP requires that *each verb* interpreted in LF must have its own *separate* subject phrase. Indeed, separate subjects were crucial in explaining in section 6.5.2 why Italian and Spanish but not Modern French tolerate restructuring. However, inspection of a participial structure (7.47) shows that while both LF verbs *continue* and *own* in the participial structure have a subject, by (6.54) they have the *same subject*. Some clarification of this discrepancy is therefore in order.

In other words, we need to determine a principled basis for when the EPP requires *separate* subjects. The empirical key for finding this principle can be gleaned from the following list of six English participial constructions.

---

preferred to identically sized DP gerunds. Such approaches must ultimately differentiate various non-finite structures with diacritics, which the language-learner must decipher even though English participles and gerunds have the same terminal strings.

Such analyses also fail to explain why small clauses with covert subjects can focus in pseudo-clefts like other XP (i), while those with overt subjects (ii) cannot:

(i)   Mary felt guilty.   What Mary felt was guilty.
(ii) Mary considered Bill honest.   *What Mary considered was Bill honest.

This asymmetry cannot be attributed to a failure of case-marking in focus position, since nothing prevents it in (iii):

(iii) Mary considered a small school.   What Mary considered was a small school.

Nor can it be attributed to the small clause node "protecting" its subject from case-marking, since the same putative AP is transparent for case-marking in the untransformed version. Whatever difference is invoked to distinguish (i) from (ii) thus comes down to a scholastic exercise to save the otherwise unsupported small clause premise.

Note that while every interpreted verb in them has an LF subject, all the dependent verbs in them (in italics) have *a subject which is in the position of an argument of a higher X^0.*

(7.51)   Participial complements of temporal aspect verbs:
They { kept on/ continued } *owning* two cars.

(7.52)   Secondary predicates on direct objects of certain perception verbs:
The parents { caught/ found } the baby *covering* itself with mud.

(7.53)   Participial complements to V whose DP sisters serve as their subjects:[40]
We could { hear/ smell } the oxygen *exploding.*

(7.54)   Subject-modifying participles, adjoined outside V^1:
We brought the guest a book thus *introducing* ourselves.

(7.55)   NP-internal reduced relatives:
The man *fixing* the sink will soon be on his way.

(7.56)   Sisters to a grammatical P whose object serves as their subjects (the "absolute construction"):
With Mary *typing* the report, there will be no problem.

The tree (7.57) illustrates the secondary participial predication in (7.52):

(7.57)

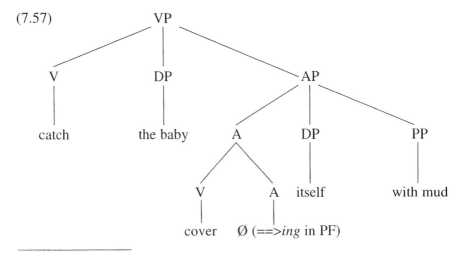

---

[40] As will be seen below, nothing here hinges on exactly determining whether a given complement sequence should be classed under (7.52) or (7.53).

As phrases, the italicized participles in (7.51)–(7.56) all occur in structural positions of APs, and by the now familiar definition of Lexical Projection (4.27), a V stem is the lexical head of these APs at all levels except PF. A striking confirmation that some single factor must unite the six structures where English uses present participles is that (traditionally termed) Spanish *gerundios* formed from V heads with the inflection *-ndo* have *exactly* the same structural distribution (Emonds, 1985, Ch. 2).[41]

What these six apparently heterogeneous constructions have in common is a certain type of "deficiency" in theta role assignments among their grammatically related heads of phrases. For instance, the very essence of a temporal aspect verb (7.51) is that unlike other verbs it assigns no independent semantic role to its own grammatical subject.[42] Along similar lines (still informally), the three types of adjuncts as in (7.54)–(7.56) receive no semantic roles as complements of the main verb.

To make all this precise, we first need a definition.

(7.58)   *Theta Relatedness. X^0 and Y^0 are theta-related if and only if one provides a theta role to a lexical projection of the other.*

For exposition, I am assuming that DPs rather than NPs receive theta roles and hence that a D which heads an argument is theta-related to V.

I will now use (7.58) to characterize the "deficient theta role assignment" which is always in evidence with participles. As just remarked, temporal aspect verbs as in (7.51) are not theta-related to their subject D^0. In (7.52) and (7.53), either a DP object or a clausal complement receives a theta role from the main V, however we partition individual verbs between the two structures. That is, perception verbs and verbs of "discovery" (*find, catch,* etc.) have one complement in LF, not two. So in these cases, either the lower V itself is not theta-related to the main verb (7.52) or else the lower V's subject is not (7.53).

From these three cases, we can extrapolate to a generalization which regulates the "density" of theta-role distribution (Emonds, 1985, Ch. 2); this formulation uses "anti-transitive" in the algebraic sense:

---

[41] These Spanish *gerundios* derive their name from Latin grammar but synchronically have no nominal properties or distribution whatever. They tend to be used as reduced relatives only in root contexts, as in picture titles: *Un hombre lavando su camisa* 'A man washing his shirt'.

[42] This semantic fact has led to "obligatory raising" analyses of these verbs in the grammatical literature.

(7.59)   *Revised Theta Criterion. Theta-relatedness is anti-transitive.*

In all six participial structures (7.51)–(7.56), the three lexical heads concerned are a lower V ("LV"), its subject D and a higher V ("HV"). By (7.59), a structure is well-formed only if some pair from among these is not theta-related. In (7.51) {D, HV} are not; in (7.52) {HV, LV} are not; in (7.53) again {D, HV} are not, where in this case D is the object rather than the subject of the higher verb.

In the two adjunct structures (7.54) and (7.55), HV and LV share a subject, *brought* and *introducing* in (7.54) and *fixing* and *be* in (7.55), but they are not themselves theta-related because main verbs never assign theta roles to adjuncts.[43] In (7.56), in the traditional conception of an "absolute construction" as a predication whose only relation to a main clause is pragmatic, the higher V is theta-related to *neither* the participial V nor the latter's subject. Thus, all the participial constructions in (7.51)–(7.56), and equally well all the *gerundio* constructions of Spanish, conform to the Revised Theta Criterion (7.59).

Once we look beyond the configurations where participles occur, the Revised Theta Criterion tells a different story. Let us form similar triplets of theta-related heads (the complement verb LV, its subject D and the higher verb HV) for obligatory control complements discussed earlier, repeated as (7.60).

(7.60)   They { avoided/ considered } *owning two cars.*
         John took on *re-organizing the library.*
         The teacher might try *designing a new course.*
         They { prevented/ discouraged } our friends from *moving away.*
         They forced us *to visit the countryside.*
         City experiences influenced us *to live in the country.*

If we pictured the lower verb LV in these sentences as not projecting to a DP or IP, but rather as simply sharing a DP argument with the higher verb HV, then *each configuration would violate the Revised Theta Criterion.* In every triplet {D, HV, LV}, namely {*they, avoid, own*}, {*John, take on, re-*

---

[43] Throughout this work, complements are defined by subcategorization and adjuncts by what is not subcategorized. As remarked in Chapter 2, other authors use the term adjunct in many different ways, sometimes even for obligatorily subcategorized PPs, DP "chômeurs," etc. My argument here naturally is based on my usage and not on the vacillating usage in the literature.

organize}, {*our friends, discourage, move away*}, {*us, force, visit*}, etc., each element would be theta-related to both of the others, contra (7.59).

Thus, the lower verbs selected by the subcategorization frames of the higher ones in (7.60) would all violate the Revised Theta Criterion *unless* they project up to a constituent @ whose subject DP is separate from any main clause DP. In this situation, any separate subject DP of V within that @ is *not* theta-related to the higher verb. This separateness correctly "unpacks" the theta-relatedness of these triplets and permits well-formed realizations of frames like +<V> and +<D, V> as the gerunds and infinitives exemplified in (7.60). The additional fact that these lower subject DPs must be empty (so-called obligatory PRO) is due to the lack of case assignment, as reviewed earlier in section 7.2. For more details, see Emonds (1991a).

We can now see why a V *must* project only to a participial AP rather than to an infinitival IP or gerundive DP if the Revised Theta Criterion permits all three. Economy of Representation (6.23) compares a DP (7.44) or an infinitive (7.45) with an AP participle (7.47) as candidates for satisfying the subcategorization +<V>, and must prefer the subjectless AP structure over either DP or IP.[44]

Exactly the same reasoning applies in adjunct structures. A little reflection on (7.54) and (7.55) reveals that infinitival IPs are permitted alternatives in most AP (participial) adjunct positions. In such situations, an infinitival (IP) structure seems to reflect the presence of the MODAL (irrealis) feature on I. When this content is absent, the participle is the favored, i.e., most economic structure for realizing a V-headed complement of an adjunct P.

A participle V+*ing* is thus a third realization in English of an overtly subjectless clause, generated either as an adjunct or by verbs with a frame +<V> or +<ACTIVITY>. A general principle, the Revised Theta Criterion (7.59), predicts when +<V> may project to a participial AP rather than to a DP or IP of obligatory control.[45] It is never necessary to stipulate separately

---

[44] *(6.23) Economy of Representation. Structural requirements such as subcategorization frames are to be satisfied at a level of derivation with as few phrasal nodes as possible.*
[45] There are apparent cases where two complements of a verb receive theta roles and where the first (direct object) is the subject of the other (a PP of location), as in *put the cat in the yard*. If this were the full story, it would violate the Revised Theta Criterion.

However, closer examination of relevant empirical paradigms (Section 8.2.3 here; Emonds, 1996) suggests that whenever two non-clausal complements receive theta roles (the text here deals with *clausal* complements), then the second theta role is assigned to a (sometimes covert) intermediate P of PATH (*to, from*), whose complement is in turn a PP of PLACE. This is seen in e.g. *We took the cat (from) [behind the barn]*. Within this

in the English lexicon or grammar that a participle, a gerund or an infinitive may or may not occur in some configuration. Principles of Universal Grammar, in particular the Economy Principles and the Revised Theta Criterion, entirely predict their distribution and properties.

---

sequence, it is the bracketed PP of PLACE, unrelated to V, which is predicated of the direct object. This independently supported constellation of four heads (V, an object D, a P of PATH and a P of PLACE) fully respects the Revised Theta Criterion.

Chapter 8
The restricted complement space of lexical frames

8.1 The range of single phrase complements

In setting out to defend subcategorization as the sole lexical device for stating combinatory restrictions, I stated at the beginning of Chapter 2 that Chomsky's original conceptions would need revision. And as we have seen, under certain conditions non-phrasal categories and sometimes non-sister categories satisfy frames of the form X, +___Y (subsequently in order-free notation X, +<Y>). Justifying these extensions and the constraints on them has been a principal focus of this book.

It should be kept in mind that these extensions concern only universal representational *interpretations* of the lexical formulae employed. The actual lexical formalisms imputed here to the ideal speaker-hearer (i.e. the formal grammar) are far more restricted than in any earlier framework – they are reduced to the ultra-simple format in (2.14). Later accretions in the generative lexicon (theta grids, linking devices, item-particular event structures and argument structures, etc.) have been eliminated entirely.

Even with the extensions on interpreting X, +___Y, the range of complement types and combinations does not much exceed those listed in Chomsky (1965, Ch. 2). What has in some cases changed is *only* the structural relation between the selecting head and the complement: in a few instances a complement Y^j can be realized as a Y^0 rather than a YP (the flat structures in Ch. 6), in others the head X can be inside an empty-headed Z^0 structure which branches (Ch. 4 and 5), and in still others Y^j is the sister of a higher (Ch. 6) or lower (Ch. 7) empty head rather than of X itself.

The fact that the complement types listed by Chomsky (plus a few familiar additions such as English double objects) are such common currency in syntactic analyses does not mean, however, that generative grammar has been operating with a model of why these types and combinations exist and not others. In fact, as argued in Chapter 1, since embracing "s-selection" around 1980 it has not in practice even included a device to formally describe them – running on empty, so to speak. Precisely for this reason, formal modeling would have been better served by at least maintaining classical subcategorization. This work not only maintains subcategorization but I hope has significantly expanded the areas where it provides descriptive generalizations and explanations.

The subcategorization device for stating lexical combinations exterior to a Z^0 which dominates a lexical item @ is then the frame in (2.14):

(2.14)   @, X, F_i, f_j, +___F_k

X is the category of @, the F_i are its inherent cognitive syntactic features, the f_j its inherent purely semantic features and the F_k are features in the subcategorization frame. An order-free notation replacing ___F_k with $<F_k>$ was justified in Chapter 3, but since this chapter will not discuss any Z^0-internal frames, I will often use the older, familiar notation of (2.14).

It is frames of this form that formally describe head complement combinations according to Generalized Subcategorization (7.8), which subsumes the Unified Classical Subcategorization (3.24) and Revised Classical Subcategorization (4.29) of earlier chapters.

(7.8)   *Generalized Subcategorization.* @, X, +<F> *is satisfied if and only if F is a cognitive syntactic feature of an (extended) sister β of* X^0=@ *or of β's lexical head.*

As just observed, the extensions of classical subcategorization do not increase the types of possible lexical frames, so a discussion of limitations on lexical entries will be more transparent by abstracting away from Z^0-internal frames.

 We will investigate in this section the range of possible sets of F_k for single complements and also in section 8.2 any combinations of multiple complements which (2.14) can generate. The goal is to propose a hypothesis for characterizing the notion "possible lexical entry" and *hence set limits on what kinds of frames a child can learn* – i.e. not to shift implications of the poverty of the stimulus argument for universal grammar to some other component but to explain them.

8.1.1 Variations on the frames ___D, ___A and ___P

The widest range of complement types occurs with verbs, so in setting an upper limit on lexical frames, I concentrate on when X is V in (2.14) and (7.8).[1] The most prosaic frames are +___D for simple transitivity and +___A

---

[1]   Since this chapter concerns upper limits on the kinds and combinations of complement types, it is not concerned with optionality (parenthesis notation) or choices among single alternatives (the brace notation {F/ G}) in lexical frames.

for predicate adjectives (*seem, become, get, remain,* etc.). Section 2.2 has illustrated subclasses of these complement types chosen by frames such as +___[D, ANIMATE] (*frighten*), +___[D, PLURAL] (*disperse*) and +___[A, INHERENT] (*become,* Spanish *ser* 'be').

The frame ___P calls for more comment. Section 2.2 brought out differences among various types of verbs which take single PP complements. Verbs such as *glance* and *reside* (from the list of prototypical frames in Chomsky, 1965, Ch. 2) and *go* thus plausibly have entries as in (8.1). For such entries, I assume there are some "underspecification" principles of lexical form which permit not listing (i) certain inherent features with unmarked values and (ii) certain features with less specificity in the presence of those with more. Exactly how many features can be deduced rather than stipulated is not a central concern here.

The feature value -STATIVE (= ACTIVITY) with V is unmarked, and LOCATION is less specific than PATH or PLACE; these features therefore need not appear in (8.1a-b). Several relevant examples of the broad distribution of *go* are repeated in (8.2):

(8.1)   a. glance, V, +*f*, +___[P, SPACE, PATH]
        b. reside, V, STATIVE, +*f*, +___[P, SPACE, PLACE]
        c. go, V, (STATIVE), +___[P, LOCATION][2]

(8.2)   a. This ugly machine goes { into the trunk, near the others, by the door, downstairs, outside, at the entrance, to the foreman, *of the director, *for another firm, *about the sale, *despite its usefulness, *instead of that }.
        b. The meeting { will go until seven/ has been going since seven/ goes on }.
        c. This suitcase goes { without postage/ with your hat/ by train/ off (soon) }.

Of course, verbs irrespective of their class can appear with PP *adjuncts* of static location; these unselected PPs are not at issue here (cf. section 7.4).

There are still redundancies in (8.1); stative verbs have PP complements of static location (PLACE) while activity verbs take complements of direction toward (PATH) or of source ([PATH, SOURCE]). It is thus likely that item-particular contextual specifications for PATH vs. PLACE comple-

---

[2] There are some intransitive idioms with *go* not of concern here: *This { car/ watch } still goes. Since we are cleaning, this junk should go. It's time to go.*

ments are unnecessary. The few verbs like *go* which are optional activity verbs, as illustrated in (8.2), can be listed as (STATIVE); hence their PP complements can be *either* of static location or of direction toward.

Another question for refining the lexical formalism is whether the frames +___P and +___[P, LOCATION] are distinct. At first glance no verb would seem to have a subcategorization that can be satisfied by *any* PP (headed by say *toward, at, for, by, of, without, despite,* etc.) irrespective of its cognitive content, so perhaps the simpler frame +___P should really be interpreted as +___[P, LOCATION]. Nonetheless, the discussion of the *spray/ load/ drain* classes of predicates in section 2.4 concluded that the best treatment of the second complement generalizes across the variation in ±LOCATION; i.e. the proposed frames were of the form +___D, (P) where P is *not* limited to +LOCATION.

However this question is resolved, predicted frames of form +___[P, F] are attested and remain well within the limits on lexical entries set by (2.14).

8.1.2 The predicate nominal frame +___N

The notation (2.14) also provides the frame +___N (i.e., +<N>) as a source of complements. Section 6.4.3 has examined Kubo's (1996) proposal that this frame explains the behavior of a particular class of grammatical nouns, the so-called "numeric classifiers" found in Japanese and many languages but rarely if at all in Indo-European. In her proposal, classifiers are lexically specified as N, +<N>, which generates flat or "mono-phrasal" structures inside DP.

The present framework predicts that lexical entries of the form V, +<N> (i.e. V, +___N) also exist. If so, the conjuncture of this frame with Abney's DP Hypothesis (section 1.3) makes some novel but I think correct predictions. According to the theory of extended lexical projections, any NP complement selected by V, +___N must further project to DP. But at the same time, the N must remain the lexical head of this DP, by the definition of lexical head (4.27), yielding (8.3) with an empty D as the internal structure of the complement at the point of lexical insertion of V.[3]

---

[3] Recall, only a *lexical* head satisfies subcategorization; higher empty heads such as the D in (8.3) are irrelevant. Again, for convenience:

(4.27) Lexical Head/Projection. Let X^0 be the highest lexically filled head in Z^i. Then X^0 is the lexical head of Z^i, and Z^i is a lexical projection of X^0.

(8.3)   Complement generated by V, +___N at the point of inserting V:

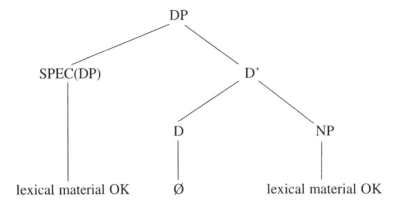

So the question is, does some complement type systematically exclude morphemes of a category D, with the possible exception of members of D inserted late at PF? Such complements can readily be generated by the frame +___N.[4]

As pointed out in section 1.3.3, Abney (1987) does not actually establish any argued link between his D category and some specific class of English modifiers. But according to Lobeck (1995, Ch. 3), who carefully integrates previous research on noun-modifying paradigms, the head D is best identified with Jackendoff's (1977, Ch. 4) leftmost pre-nominal morpheme class SPEC(N''): *some, any, no, every, each, which, what*, etc. Her evidence based on NP-ellipsis then confirms this choice. Lobeck thus establishes independently of our present concerns that D is precisely the category name of demonstratives, WH-determiners, and Jackendoff's non-adjectival quantifiers. It is therefore of interest that a certain type of verbal complement, namely predicate nominals, excludes exactly this class of quantifiers:

---

[4]   Kalluli (1999) convincingly analyzes non-specific "bare NP" objects in Albanian and Mainland Scandinavian, which alternate with *both* definite and indefinite DPs, as NPs which *don't* project to DP. If her analysis is correct, whether NP *must* project to DP or not is language-particular, requiring modifying the theory of extended projections of section 1.3. A reviewer points out that base-generated bare NPs would furnish a natural source for the transformationally derived N-incorporation structures of Baker (1988). They might also solve the mystery of the missing D in those presumably head-final Japanese noun phrases lacking numeral classifiers – such D may simply not exist.

(8.4)   a. *Mary's son(s) { became/ looked/ remained/ seemed/ will
be } { every local teacher/ each town clerk/ no success(es)/
some other friend(s) }.
*Which expert did she expect to { become/ feel/ remain }?
b. *{ I don't consider his son(s)/ Nobody could judge you/ We
hired you as } { any friend(s)/ each teacher/ some expert(s) }.

Nor do predicate nominals freely permit demonstratives or WH-determiners:

(8.5)   *Mary's daughter became this famous success.
*Her son looked that available bachelor.
*Her children still remain these friends of mine.
*{ What/ Which } expert did Sam seem?
*I don't consider his sons those good teachers.
*{ What/ which } teacher did they judge you?

The elements excluded in selected predicate nominals are thus of
Lobeck's category D. But since subcategorization theory predicts that some
type of verbal complement selected by +___N should exhibit exactly this
restriction, as indicated in (8.3), one naturally concludes that predicate
nominals result from the frames V, +<N> (for intransitives) and V, +<D, N>
(for transitives).

One could be led astray by focusing only on the form of the most frequently studied predicate nominals, those with the copula *be*. These can
indeed include demonstratives and WH-modifiers, particularly in those
predicate nominals with a specificational rather than a predicational sense
(cf. Heycock and Kroch, 1999), as well as somewhat contrived uses of
quantifiers:[5]

(8.6)   Mary's daughter is that famous actress.
His cousins are those good teachers.
Which expert could that person have been?
What teacher are you, the chemistry teacher?
His children were all the friends I had.
John has never been any help.

---

[5] The linking verb *become* also marginally tolerates demonstratives in its predicate
nominal complement; the marginality suggests to me that they are interpretable but not
grammatical. (Cf. section 1.1.2 on the grammatical status of marginal examples.)

?I'd like to become that famous actor.
?Will they become those good teachers?

But recall (section 4.5) that *be* is the otherwise unmarked stative verb inserted in PF via the very general frame +___X (= +<X>). This implies that *be* can have either a predicate nominal complement (8.3) like other linking verbs *or* a full DP complement as in (8.6). Hence the contrast between (8.4)–(8.5) and (8.6) is fully expected and in fact predicted by the differing subcategorizations of *be* and other linking verbs.

If one tried to simply generate English predicate nominals using a classical subcategorization frame +___NP and Abney's phrase structure, their internal possessives and articles as in (8.7)–(8.8) would falsify the proposal.

(8.7)   Mary's son { became/ looked/ remained/ seemed } { the teacher/ a (young woman's) ideal candidate }.
        She wanted to { become/ feel/ remain } { the/ an/ its } expert.

(8.8)   { I don't consider his son/ Nobody judges you/ We hired you as } { the best speaker/ a good speaker/ John's equal/ a small town's best hope }.

But these data actually *confirm* the present framework, because the theory of extended lexical projections of Chapter 1 requires that an NP appear *within a DP shell*. Consequently, predicate nominals (8.3) generated by +___N should tolerate both possessive DPs, which are under SPEC(DP), and definite articles, which are inserted in PF and hence not present under D when a verb selects a phrase with the structure (8.3).

Finally, it is well-known that verbs do not assign accusative case to predicate nominals cross-linguistically; predicate nominals either agree with the DP they modify at s-structure, receive some oblique case, or are morphologically caseless. Generating predicate nominals via the frame +___N can thus also explain why the verb which selects them fails to mark them for case. To this end I replace the potential case assigners in (7.27) with the more accurate (8.9).

(8.9)   *Case Indices. The case assigners (= potential case indices) are I, D and any V or P whose lexical realizations enter a tree by satisfying +___Y, where Y = I or D.*[6]

---

[6]   The lexical item which realizes a case-assigning category need not be present in a tree when its category assigns case. That is, syntactic structure not lexical items assigns (non-quirky) case. A number of PF-inserted prepositions (*by, for, of, to*) are not present in a tree when their P node assigns case in the syntax.

The point of (8.9) is to directly link case-assignment with subcategorization frames. Thus, if a DP as in (8.3) implied by a predicate nominal frame +___N or +___X is ensured not by +___D but only by the theory of extended projections, no case is assigned. A general restriction on case assigners thus blocks case on predicate nominals.

This restriction affects not only linking verbs but also grammatical P. As discussed in Emonds (1985, Ch. 6), a DP complement of the "copular P," non-comparative *as,* shares all predicate nominal properties, such as the exclusion of lexical choices for D seen in (8.4)–(8.5). Its Syntacticon frame is therefore +___N rather than +___D, and exactly as predicted by (8.9), its counterparts in Czech *jako* and German *als* fail to assign a morphological case. Case Indices (8.9) thus eliminates any stipulative features by which individual V or P can "fail to assign case," replacing this with a mechanism that expresses a general and eminently predictable cross-linguistic pattern.

Another function of Case Indices is to guarantee that any V or P (=C) whose lexical realizations are subcategorized for obligatory control via the feature +___V, such as French *à* or *de* or possibly English *whether*, will fail to assign case within IP. Since (8.9) requires Y to head a cyclic domain node, no X^0 whose only complement satisfies +___V can assign case. Thus, whether a given IP "blocks" or "allows" case to be assigned across it is predictable on the basis of the frame it satisfies; if IP results from +___I, case can be assigned, but if IP results from +___V, case cannot be.

8.1.3 Variations on the frames ___V and ___I

Perhaps the central conceptual difference between subcategorization in this work and Chomsky's classic proposals is that there is no longer a one-to-one (i.e. redundant) relation between the notations in the lexical frames +<Y^0> and the trees which they license: (i) The frames do not mention phrases (by the Lexical Interface Principle 2.13) even though they generally do license them. (ii) A frame such as +<D> projects not only to a DP but in many cases to a higher PP as well (section 7.2). (iii) An entry such as X^0, +<N> can generate a flat structure if X = N (e.g., the pseudo-partitive or numeric classifier constructions), but can also generate predicate nominal NP phrases, which are themselves further embedded in DPs required by the extended lexical projection theory of Chapter 1.

Such complex interactions between simple lexical frames and general category-independent principles are nowhere more evident than in the area of clausal complement selection by +___V and +___I. The core of Chapter 6 and last two sections of Chapter 7 have been devoted to how the simple and hence easily learnable frame +___V (= +<V>) interacts with principles of Universal Grammar to yield a stunning variety of different grammatical structures and behaviors.

(i) Selection by the frame +___V. To avoid repetition, I only briefly summarize general properties which are uniformly associated with +___V. First I review default cases where V projects to at least a phrase. In all such situations, the definition of Lexical Head (4.27) requires that the head of any higher projected phrase ZP such as an IP or a gerundive DP be empty. The Condition on Selection (5.47) guarantees that such empty I or D, induced by subcategorization, lack marked features. Assuming now that empty and featureless functional heads don't assign case, any subject DP inside ZP must be null, i.e., any higher ZP projected above +___V will exhibit obligatory control.[7] Moreover, at least for English, it seems that +___V is the principal and perhaps only source of obligatory control. I return to justifying this in section 10.1.[8]

A second type of realization of +___V as a "flat structure" results from a conjuncture of two conditions: occurring both (i) in a lexical entry of a closed class verb and (ii) in a language which freely allows co-indexing of a post-verbal subject with the position in SPEC(IP). Standard Italian and Spanish are two such languages, and so verbs in their Syntacticons with the frames +<V> (restructuring verbs) or +<V, D> (causative and perception verbs) may appear as sisters to V as well as with V-headed phrasal complements. These structures have been justified in detail in Chapter 6.

---

[7] I will not review here how UG chooses among the three types of obligatory control phrasal projections above V in English (participles, gerunds and infinitives). This has been presented succinctly in section 7.6, which cites more detailed versions in my earlier work.

[8] Hence, the easiest way for (C. Fillmore's) "working grammarian" (and perhaps the English language learner) to associate +__V with structures is to link the frame with non-finite complements of obligatory control. But the same working grammarian *should not* then wrongly fall back on the earlier one-to-one relation between lexical frames and their structural realization and imagine that my +__V is simply shorthand for the notoriously debated "bare VP complements" (VPs not immediately dominated by IP).

In fact, precisely because of the theory of extended phrase structure of Chapter 1, *neither +___V nor any other frame can ever give rise to a "bare VP."* Rather, this frame "looks for" the most economic realization available among several structures that are everything but a bare VP. It is precisely because there are no bare VPs that the working grammarian, who still lacks full access to UG, finds clausal complements so complicated.

(ii) Selection by the frame +___I. Let us turn next to how the lexical frame +___[I, (F)] generates certain finite clausal complements and certain English infinitives as well: essentially those types not discussed elsewhere in this book.[9] Two familiar classes of verbs exemplify such complements and are thus specified as +___I: so-called epistemic verbs such as *assume, believe, consider, declare, imagine, judge, suppose,* etc. (8.10) and verbs of the *(dis)like* type: *dislike, hate, like, love, prefer,* etc. (8.11) *Expect* apparently belongs to both classes.[10]

(8.10) a. Jim imagines that { this city/ he } is more important than his school.

b. Jim imagines { this city/ himself } to be more important than his school.

(8.11) a. Most men (dis)like (it) { that/ if } a woman drives fast.

b. Most men (dis)like a woman to drive fast.

Consider first the standard case where I is finite in (8.10a)–(8.11a). As with all embedded English finite clauses, an I with lexical content requires a lexical subject. In this case, a finite clause IP satisfies the frame +___I. However, such an IP cannot simply be a sister to the selecting V, due to a consequence of Economy of Reference derived in section 1.5 of Chapter 1:

(1.35) *Theorem of LF Economy. An IP may be embedded other than as a sister to C only if its I is Ø in LF, i.e. only if it is non-finite and hence without truth value.*

A *finite* IP which satisfies +___I must therefore be embedded in a CP, whose head is empty (i.e. inserted in PF) in accordance with (7.8) and (4.27):

---

[9] The tree categories used for French complement types in Rochette (1988) correlate with the categories in my lexical features for similar types of English complements. Her typology suggested to me certain of my lexical specifications, and although there are some incompatibilities of framework, the two works broadly support each other. Rochette analyzes obligatory control complements as bare VP, for which I use the frame ___V; she analyzes French subjunctives as IP, which (roughly) translate a range of optional control infinitives and finite clauses for which my frame is ___I. We of course agree that indicative clauses including indirect questions are CPs.

[10] We return just below to infinitives of optional control, which are another kind of complement available for the *(dis)like* class but not the class of epistemics.

(4.27) *Lexical Head / Projection. Let X^0 be the highest lexically filled head in Z^j. Then X^0 is the lexical head of Z^j, and Z^j is a lexical projection of X^0.*

The unmarked C *that* with no intrinsic features is inserted in PF. A finite IP sister to such a C can thus satisfy +___I and still not violate (1.35).[11]

(iii) Selection by the frame +___SUBJUN.

(8.10b) and (8.11b) exemplify so-called "exceptional case marking" (ECM) complements which these classes of English verbs (but no others) permit. Besides their case property, they have three other coinciding properties:

(a) ECM infinitives do not express tense like finite clauses.

(b) ECM infinitives must be lexically marked, since a language such as French with syntax not so different from English does not allow them (with lexical subjects).

(c) ECM infinitives do not freely occur with all verbs whose semantics is similar, as seen in (8.12). They thus seem "selected."

(8.12) *Jim { concluded/ confirmed/ denied/ feared/ hoped/ recalled }
{ this city/ himself } to be more important than his school.

The key to understanding the ECM infinitives requires appeal, I think, to a cross-linguistic feature on I, namely SUBJUN ("subjunctive"). Two salient facts about this feature are relevant. First, SUBJUN appears to be an *Absence of Content feature* on I (cf. section 1.2.2). As argued in Picallo (1984), although Catalan subjunctive morphemes realize finite agreements in PF, they are *not* tense morphemes with LF content. Therefore, using SUBJUN for English ECM complements can explain why their temporal sense is more neutral than their finite counterparts.[12]

---

[11] If this CP is in the position of a complement to V at s-structure, *that* alternates with a null allomorph; more details are provided in note 32 of Chapter 1.

Finite complements selected by adjectives can be optionally realized as sisters to a linking verb which governs them, as shown in section 6.2. This factor makes *that* appear optional: *John seemed sure (that) the girls liked the show.* When the AP is moved, the optionality of *that* predictably disappears: *How sure *(that) the girls liked the show did John seem? What John seems is relieved *(that) the girls liked the show.*

[12] There seem to be two kinds of subjunctive systems in Romance, the Catalan system which contains no real tense distinctions and the Spanish system which does (D. Stringer, pers. comm.). However, all subjunctives share a +MODAL (i.e. -REALIS) sense.

Second, the fact that individual verbs in Romance languages may or may not select a subjunctive complement demonstrates that +___SUBJUN is a marked as well as a plausible lexical frame.[13] My proposal is then simply to extend this frame to English epistemic verbs which permit ECM infinitives as in (8.10b), even though no morphemes in the current English Syntacticon express only this feature.[14] Precisely because of this latter fact, [I, SUBJUN] is empty in English at Spell Out and hence fails to assign nominative case.

If this analysis of ECM is correct, the cross-linguistic role of the frame +___SUBJUN must be to provide an interpretation for an otherwise contentless, syntactically empty I in LF. Nonetheless, legitimizing a contentless form in LF does not suffice to license an empty I in PF; this requires phonological realization, provided in English by the all purpose infinitival marker *to*.

Selecting ECM infinitives by the frame +___[I, SUBJUN] or +___[I, (SUBJUN)] thus explains all of (a)–(c) above.

A final property of ECM infinitives (8.10b)–(8.11b) is that their subjects apparently receive case from the verbs which select them. I have accounted for this by formulating the list of Case Assigners (8.9) not only to cover standard assignment of accusative (case index V) and dative (case index P) but also to extend them to V and P which select IPs. Thus, when nominative and / or genitive are for any reason not available to subjects, an adjacent case assigner exterior to IP or DP can provide case.

(8.13)   *Case Assignment Condition. A potential case assigner β can be a case index on DP if some β^j which c-commands DP is the closest non-maximal projection of any potential case assigner.*[15]

We have now covered obligatory control infinitives generated by +___V and ECM infinitives generated by +___[I, SUBJUN]. It remains to discuss *for-to* infinitives of optional control. In configurations where *for-to* infini-

---

[13] French *espérer* 'hope', whose complement must be indicative, and Spanish *esperar* 'hope', whose complement must be subjunctive, demonstrate such selection.

[14] Jespersen (1940) considers the English past subjunctive (*Were John here, …*) an archaism. The "present subjunctive" in American English (*Suggest that she be on time*) simply acts like a null allomorph of British English *should* and is not SUBJUN.

[15] The Case Assignment Condition accounts for why a *finite* I rather than C (=P) case-marks SPEC(IP): I' is closer to SPEC(IP) than C, since I' but not C is its sister. Thus, I case-marks a subject whenever it can. (Irrelevantly, C' contains but does not c-command the subject.) That is, a C or V with the frame +___I can assign case to SPEC(IP) if and only if I is non-finite.

tives are *not selected as complements*, such as adjuncts (section 7.4) or topicalized DPs in root declaratives, they exemplify freely generated IPs which must be sisters to a higher empty head P, as required by the Deep Case Filter (7.40).[16]

(8.14)

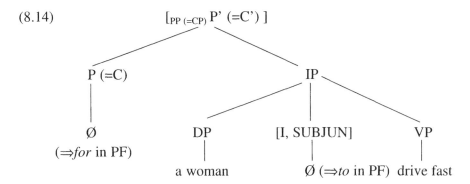

The English Syntacticon contains a P *for* whose characterizing feature is not always interpreted, i.e., *for* can be inserted in PF. Like ECM verbs, *for* has a subjunctive IP complement, i.e. an infinitive whose subject receives case in accord with (8.13). As is widely recognized, the IP in *for-to* clauses also has an irrealis sense and regularly paraphrases a finite IP with a modal.

The unified entry (8.15) expresses these properties of *for*. LOC' is some cognitive syntactic content feature which minimally distinguishes *for* from the PATH preposition *to*. As a first approximation, I parenthesize LOC' to express the fact that *for* can lack any specific sense in many uses with DPs as well (*This sells for $3; I mistook him for a woman; we have nothing for dessert*).

---

[16] A traditional idea based on examining only main clauses is that *that* clauses and *for-to* clauses freely serve as subjects. As shown in (Emonds (1976, Ch. 4) and Koster (1978b), many paradigms such as the following indicate the inadequacy of this conception:

> *Could { for John to buy a ticket now/ that it snowed} be possible?
> *My friends considered { for Sam to be late/ that we are cold } unlikely.

Such sentence-initial clauses pattern rather like *topicalized* subject PPs (Emonds, 1985, Ch. 7), in the sense that they are a root phenomenon.

> In the garden would be a bit warmer.
> *Could in the garden be a bit warmer?
> *My friends considered in the garden a bit warmer.

(8.15)   for, P, (LOC'), { +___D / +___[I, SUBJUN] }

In constituents which don't express space/ time and thus lack PATH, the feature LOC' is apparently uninterpretable and in these cases *for* is inserted in PF. The use of SUBJUN in (8.15) expresses a formal parallel with ECM verbs.

In contexts where *for-to* clauses are *selected* complements, *for* itself often seems to carry meaning in LF.[17] First, a wide range of predicates which select PP complements headed by *for* also select *for-to* clauses: *arrange, beg, hope, plan, prepare, pray, wait, anxious, eager, ready, chance, reason, time,* many manner of speaking verbs, etc. These predicates have an eminently simple lexical frame +___LOC'; the fact that both DPs and IPs alternate then follows from the entry (8.15). That is, these predicates do not themselves have the frame +___I (unless they are additionally in the ECM class), but they select *for,* which crucially uses this frame as in (8.15).[18]

This then completes the review of how a full range of finite and infinitival complements of the epistemic and *(dis)like* classes of verbs are generated; either directly or indirectly these complement structures involve the simple lexical frame +___[I, F], for some cognitive syntactic feature F.

Let's now review the basic frames available for single complements of predicates. The restricted syntactic category theory of Chapter 1 provides six basic head categories X: N, V, A, P, D and I. The theory of subcategorization developed in this study then expects different classes of predicates to realize all six frames of the form V, +___ X, and indeed we have seen that familiar and much studied classes of complements correspond to all the predicted classes. For English, (8.16) then constitutes a rough table

---

[17] *For-to* complements of verbs of the *(dis)like* type *(dislike, hate, like, love, prefer,* etc.) don't carry such meaning. However, such verbs allow freely generated PP as complements, sometimes with an additional overt expletive:

We really hate (it) in the park on Sundays.
We like (it) near the lake, though we prefer (it) out in the country.

Hence, it is not surprising that they allow the PP structure (8.14) as well:

Men often { (dis)like/ hate/ prefer } (it) for a woman to drive fast.

[18] If a predicate (e.g., *intend*) selecting *for-to* clauses actually excludes *for* + DP, it can be listed with a more marked frame ___[I, LOC']; the next subsection makes precise a formalism for this in (8.18).

of equivalents between the frames available in the category system and the structures they project.

(8.16)   Frame: Some instantiating complement structures:
    V, +<D>   Direct objects of transitive verbs
    V, +<A>   Predicate adjectives
    V, +<P>   Path PPs with activity verbs and Place PPs with statives
    V, +<N>   Predicate nominals
    V, +<V>   Participles, gerunds and infinitives of obligatory control
    V, +< I >   Clausal complements of epistemic and *(dis)like* class
        verbs

8.1.4 Extrinsic features in single frames

Throughout this work, we have seen scattered instances of subcategorization frames which require intermediate heads which are empty in the syntax, but are nonetheless specified for certain feature values. For example, marked indirect objects introduced by *of* rather than *to* require some kind of lexical stipulation.

(8.17)   She { asked/ demanded/ expected/ required } { of/ *to } Bill that he be early.

Similarly, while verbs such as *wonder* and *inquire* whose only clausal complements are indirect questions can be listed with the frame +___WH (section 2.3), other predicates (*explain, know*, etc.) which take either a *that*-clause or an indirect question require a slightly more complex frame, which was notated in Chapter 2 as (WH)^IP. However, our general subcat-egorization formalism (2.14) has eliminated the ad hoc concatenation sign from lexical frames, except perhaps to express truly idiomatic sequences.

We therefore need some notation to express features required on empty intermediate heads (i.e., those with PF insertion) such as the following:

(8.18)   *Subcategorized Features Convention. A feature complex in a lexical frame is written in an ordered sequence +___$[F_1, \ldots, F_i, \ldots]$, where at least F_1 is in its interpretable canonical position.*

Any F_i whose canonical position is not that of F_1 must be interpreted as a feature on a intermediate empty head permitted by Generalized Sub-categorization (7.8) and Economy of Representation. The formulation (8.18) has the probably correct consequence that subcategorization cannot select morphemes expressing *only* alternatively realized features, because no such feature satisfies the condition on F_1.[19]

With this clarification, we can now list in (8.19a) the extra feature needed for the (optional) marked indirect objects of source in (8.17), and in (8.19b) the (optional) indirect question feature for *explain*. These entries are of course partial, as I put aside alternative frames not being used to exemplify (8.18).

(8.19)   a. ask, V, +< D, ([ANIMATE, SOURCE]), . . . >, . . .
         b. explain, V, +< [I, (WH)], . . . >, . . .

In (8.19a), F_1 is ANIMATE, which must therefore be realized in its canonical position on the head of a DP. Since the canonical position of F_2 = SOURCE is not that of F_1 (that is, in this case, D), SOURCE must be a feature of a higher empty head, namely the PP required for assigning case to the second DP complement of *ask*.

Similarly, the node I is the F_1 for the complement of *explain* in (8.19b), which must be in its canonical position as head of an IP. If the optional WH is not chosen, a simple *that*-clause results, as explained in the previous subsection.[20] But if WH is chosen (i.e. when *explain* takes an indirect question), since its canonical position is not I, it must be a feature of an intermediate empty head, namely a C sister of IP.

We have already seen other constructions which require the Subcategorized Features Convention (8.18). Two have been mentioned in discussions of subcategorized clausal complements:

(i) Note 18 evokes the possibility of an English verb subcategorized for a *for-to* clause but not *for*+DP: such a verb would have the frame +___[I, LOC'], parallel to [I, (WH)].

---

[19] Recall that, according to (5.47), any features on empty heads higher than the actual selected lexical head must be explicitly mentioned in the lexical frame itself.
(5.47)   Condition on Selection. If a subcategorization frame +<[X, F_i]> is satisfied by ZP, any features in ZP not licensed by the lexical head X must be stipulated among the F_i.
That is, (5.47) allows a frame combining contextual features which are not all on the same node. Nonetheless, the convention (8.18) guarantees that the first such feature in a frame refers to a canonical position of the complement selected.
[20] The reader will recall that a CP must project above an embedded finite IP according to the Theorem of LF Economy (1.35).

(ii) The lexical entries (7.46) for certain obligatory control verbs can be revised to reflect the fact that obligatory control infinitives have more of an irrealis sense than participles or gerunds. E.g., *He should manage to leave* vs. *He should manage leaving*; further examples were furnished in section 7.5. In the revised entries (8.20), adding the feature MODAL to the frame +<V> forces a projection up to IP, whereby MODAL can furnish the irrealis part of the interpretation.

(8.20)   manage, V, +< [V, (MODAL)] >, ...
              decide, V, +< [ACTIVITY, MODAL] >, ...
              try, V, +< [ACTIVITY, (MODAL)] >, ...

These entries conform entirely to the convention (8.18) as well as to the Condition on Selection (5.47). The latter allows no feature on I other than the one(s) mentioned in the frame, and so the induced I cannot occur with any features of lexical modals; consequently, it is a "higher empty head" in the syntax (i.e., it must be realized as *to*).

8.2 Limitations on multiple complements

8.2.1 The puzzling descriptive generalizations

From the previous section, we can conclude that all subcategorization frames X, +<Y> for single complements are robustly exemplified in the English lexicon, for all expected values of Y. The question now arises, what combinations of complements can appear in a single frame? That is, how many lexical entries do we find of the form X, <Y, Z...> where Y, Z, ... each take on all the same potential values as earlier: N, A, V, P, D, I?

   Throughout this section, I will use the table (8.16) of complement types to exemplify various possible combinations.

(i) Direct objects with a second complement. There do indeed occur many structures containing two complements. To start with, *direct objects combine with all six values of Z*, instantiating the frames +<D, Z> and surveyed below in (8.21)–(8.26). As allowed by Generalized Subcategorization (7.8), a canonical cognitive syntactic feature of Z sometimes appears instead of Z, e.g., ANIMATE can replace D, PATH can replace P, etc. Any second subcategorized DP must be generated inside a PP in order to receive case from a grammatical P needed to satisfy the Case Filter (cf. section 7.2.1).

(8.21)   Z = D or P: direct objects with indirect objects or PPs
        give, V, +<D, D>   recommend, V, +<D, (ANIM)>
        ask, V, +<D, ([ANIM, SOURCE])> hand, V, +<D, { ANIM/ PATH }>
        put, V, +<D, PATH>   situate, V, +<D, (PLACE)>

Throughout this chapter, I assume that English prepositionless double object structures *(You {ask/ give/ hand} the contestant the answer)* do not reflect a basic lexical frame but rather derive from an underlying sequence with the objects in reverse order and the indirect object in a PP. Several arguments for this early "transformationalist" position, independent of various updated executions, are provided in Emonds (1993, sections 1 and 2). The rest of the article then develops a particular version of indirect object movement consistent with my present views.

(8.22)   Z = A or N: direct objects with secondary predication
        render a poison harmless   name an unknown person the winner
        consider John stupid   consider John a nuisance
        paint the house red   call them carbon copies of each other
        declare any addiction illegal declare any addiction a capital crime
        describe Mary as paranoid   describe Mary as an artist

(8.23)   Z = V, I or C: direct objects with clausal complements
        catch Mary studying in the library
        see Mary studying in the library
        persuade John { that it is raining/ to look for a job }
        remind John when { he has an appointment/ to leave the meeting }

As is well-known, not every DP position which alternates with clauses accepts a gerund (*John believed the box being open,* etc.). Less appreciated is the fact that DP gerunds can occur where lexically selected DPs cannot. The verbs in (8.24) illustrate the full independence of the features +<D> and +<V>.

(8.24)   prevent, V, +<D, [V, SOURCE]>
        discourage, V, +<D, ([V, SOURCE])>

Note that a DP-gerund generated by the obligatory control frame +<V> can be forced to appear (8.25a), even where DP itself is not lexically selected as in (8.25b), because V is followed by a feature of an intermediate empty head in accord with Conditions (5.47) and (8.18).

(8.25)   a.   That might { prevent/ discourage } Mary from studying in the library.
      b.   *Your reaction prevented Mary from serious work.
        *Let's not discourage Mary from a vacation.

Most possibilities for the frame V, +<D, Z> are realized with the verb *find*, whose lexical entry is (8.26a). Its direct object can accept secondary predication with all four lexical categories X (= N, A, V, P) as in (8.26b), and it also accepts indirect objects (8.26c) and clausal complements (8.26d).

(8.26)   a.   find, V, +<{ D, (X) / [I, (SUBJUN)] }>, where X is not I.
      b.   secondary predication, where X = N, A, V, P:[21]
        John found Mary { a pest/ very ill/ studying/ in the garden }.
        *I find my children$_i$ { some pests$_i$ / those spendthrifts$_i$ / that it's tiring }.
      c.   indirect objects, where X = D:
        John found good schools for his boy.
        John found his boy good schools.
      d.   clausal complements, where X = I including ECM subjunctive complements:
        John found that the lesson would be difficult.
        John found the lesson to be difficult.

Earlier or competing lexical frameworks using semantic selection would be hard pressed to succinctly express the complement range of this versatile verb.

(ii) Indirect objects with a second complement. The next examples in (8.27)–(8.28) show that (italicized) secondary predicates can also occur with *indirect* objects. Since the Case Filter in configurations without a direct object does not force oblique case, the lexical frame itself must be responsible for some feature such as LOC that induces a minimal case-assigning PP structure. In a frame +<Y, Z> indicating two such complements then, the indirect object Y is specified by e.g., [D, LOC] or [ANIMATE, LOC], in accord with (8.18). Moreover, predicate attributes generated in these double complement constructions modify the subject rather than the indirect object, a point to which we return in section 8.3.

---

[21] Recall from section 8.1.2 that predicate nominals are generated by +__N (not +__D) and from section 7.6 that the most economical English realization of +__V is a present participle.

(8.27) Z = A or N: indirect objects with secondary predication
Sue seems *quite confident* to me.
That cod tasted *too salty* to Mary.
Sam has always been *a brother* to me.
The famous horse Doctor Syntax appeared *the winner* to some.

Since the predicate adjectives and nominals in (8.27) do not themselves select *to*-phrase complements, the linking verbs themselves must be selecting the indirect objects as second complements.

(8.28) Z = V, I or C: indirect objects with clausal complements
promise (to) your parents to paint their house
whisper to that student { that it's late/ to close the door }
suggest to Mary when { she should leave/ to look for a house }
require of the students that they be more punctual

Finally, indirect objects can combine with other PPs whose heads are specified in lexical frames, as in (8.29).

(8.29) Some students spoke to her { about/ of } each other.
Mary has heard from her friends about the protests.
People argued with the salespeople over the new prices.

Surprisingly, however, combinations of apparent indirect objects with [PP, PATH] complements of motion verbs as in (8.30) do not seem to be separate complements of V despite their apparent semantic independence. The italicized sequences are rather single constituents, as shown by their fixed order in (8.31) and by classic diagnostics for PP constituency in (8.32) (cf. Jackendoff, 1973).

(8.30) The child ran *into the house to his mother*.
The tenants dashed *out of the house from the fire*.

(8.31) *The child ran to his mother into the house.
*The tenants dashed from the fire out of the house.

(8.32) a. Pseudo-cleft test:
*Where the child ran to his mother was into the house.
*Where the child ran into the house was to his mother.
*Where the tenants dashed from the fire was out of the house.
Where the child ran was into the house to his mother.
Where the tenants dashed was out of the house from the fire.

b. Cleft test:

*It was to his mother that the child ran into the house.

*It was from the fire that the tenants dashed out of the house.

*It was out of the house that the tenants dashed from the fire.

It was into the house to his mother that the child ran.

It was out of the house from the fire that the tenants dashed.

These diagnostics demonstrate that a *single* PP structure $[_{P'}$ P - DP $[\{ to/from \}$ - DP $]]$, analogous to that of a transitive VP containing both a direct and indirect object, is more appropriate for the italicized sequences in (8.30). That is, there seems to be something amiss with two PP complements both of whose heads are +PATH.

In fact, a puzzling restricted pattern of combined complements has begun to emerge. Internal subcategorized complements of a selecting head V may include: *a single direct object* typically marked accusative;[22] *a single "oblique" object* introduced by a grammatical P or morphologically marked as non-accusative (though some languages conflate morphological datives and accusatives); *and precisely one other phrase* chosen from among PPs with lexical heads, clausal structures and predicate attributes. Now the fact that predicate attributes don't receive case from the V which governs them (section 8.1.2) suggests that at some level they have no case at all. The observed pattern thus translates into what will be the main proposal of section 8.2.2; at some level of grammar other than PF:

(8.33)   *Subcategorized complements can specify at most one (abstract) accusative DP, one (abstract) oblique DP and one phrasal complement without abstract case.*

(iii) Excluded combinations of complements. In spite of all the double complements in (8.21)–(8.29), one needn't search too far to find that the many logically possible combinations of complements outside (8.33) simply don't occur. Moreover, the oddity of these constructs suggests that it is not a question of rarity but rather of some principled exclusion at work.

(a) No verbs combine two predicate attribute complements (+<A,A> (8.34), +<N,A> (8.35) or +<N,N> (8.36). In classical notation, while

---

[22] Certain Icelandic direct objects, i.e. DPs which can undergo passive movement into the SPEC(IP) position, are marked with quirky dative case; this is a highly unusual combination. Icelandic direct object DPs are never genitive, however. (Zaenen, Maling and Thrainsson, 1985).

+___DP^DP is possible and frequent, frames such as +___AP^AP are impossible.

(8.34) Exclusion of +___AP^AP:
        *They consider less expensive very chic.
        *John appeared sickly worrisome.
        *The guests changed irritated to cheerful.

(8.35) Exclusion of +___NP^AP:
        *Bill grew up [DP a Catholic] devout.
        *That university became [DP another Oxford] very famous.
        *He remains [DP the math teacher] stubborn.

(8.36) Exclusion of +___NP^NP:
        *Bill grew up [DP a Catholic] a small town boy.
        *That university became [DP another Oxford] my dream.
        *He remains [DP the math teacher] an example to youth.

Keep in mind that subject-modifying AP adjuncts exterior to V' or perhaps I' as in (8.37) are not structural complements and hence do not challenge the claim that no verbs take double predicate attributes.

(8.37) John [V' appeared sickly] drunk.
        Mary [V' felt mathematics too difficult] young.
        Sue [V' became a math teacher] young.

   (b) No verbs combine two clausal complements *unless at least one of them is a case-marked DP object of V or some P* (8.38). Since, as is well-known, gerunds and indirect questions are the only English clausal complements which appear freely in DP object positions (Emonds, 1976, Ch. 4), a non-DP clausal complement may combine with these (8.38a) but not others (8.38b).

(8.38) a. The strike forced [DP visiting Brooklyn] [IP to be postponed].
            He compared [DP how he fixed it] with [DP digging a tunnel].
            We limit [DP drinking a lot] to [DP how often I can afford it].
        b. *We prefer [CP to visit New York] [CP that you travel].
            *They prefer [IP Sue to be here] [CP to visit New York].
            *That prevented [CP that you were ill] [CP for us to be unhappy].

At the same time, since the direct object position is unique, two gerunds or a gerund and an indirect question together, without an additional P to assign case, are excluded (8.39).

(8.39)   *The workman compared [how he fixed it] [his digging a tunnel].
         *I couldn't prevent [selling used cars] [depressing me].

Again, participial adjuncts which modify the subject outside V' do not counterexemplify the restrictive pattern of limited complement combinations:

(8.40)   John [$_{V'}$ came running into the room] whistling Dixie.
         They [$_{V'}$ preferred to visit Greenwich Village] driving with locked doors.

(c) Predicate attributes and clausal complements never combine. In the examples (8.41), no verbs can be found which can select two such separate complements:

(8.41)   *We judged [that our kids visited New York] [too expensive].
         *The guests changed [to be irritated] [to cheerful].
         *They consider [for children to travel a lot] [an extravagance].
         *That book seemed [expensive] [to be in short supply].
         *Our friends felt [chilly] [that we couldn't afford more fuel].
         *Bill remained [a Communist] [that he needed a philosophy].

(d) With one (only apparent) exceptional pattern analyzed below in section 8.2.3, PP complements of direction or location cannot combine with either predicate attributes or clausal complements.

(8.42)   *Mary sounded proud onto the stage.
         *Sam became a salesman into the Prairie States.
         *The books looked very old { that/ like } they had been resold.
         *The child got ill what food to feed her.

With respect to the excluded patterns in (8.34)–(8.36), (8.38)–(8.39) and (8.41)–(8.42), I stress that the issue is not whether particular predicates appear in the exemplified frames. Rather, *such multiple frames are simply not available for any verbs,* in spite of the fact that many of the combinations are semantically plausible and often made acceptable with small morphological changes such as changing infinitival *to* to *-ing,* inserting a purely grammatical P, etc.

We therefore need a grammatical principle to explain why internal complements of verbs are restricted to three types: direct object DPs, oblique object DPs of grammatical prepositions (including those realized as oblique morphological case on their object), and non-DP arguments. Among the non-DP types of arguments (predicate attributes, finite and infinitival clauses, and PPs headed by lexical P), a given verb seems to take at most one. The proposal in the next section will attribute this pattern to a general principle of case theory.

Before formulating this proposal, one might ask whether a restriction to binary branching could correctly exclude some complement combinations. But purely formal restatements in terms of binary branching must then allow for multiple complements at different hierarchical levels, and the restrictions on combinations remain exactly as puzzling as before. Another binary branching alternative is to group any sequence of multiple complements into small clauses without any motivation based on predication. But then the italicized pairs of complements in (8.43), which lack any subject-predicate relation, can be so analyzed only at the cost of "constituent" becoming a non-predictive theory-internal notion postulated to save unmotivated constructs such as binary branching or Larson's (1988) "Sole Complement Condition."

(8.43) promise *Sam to shave myself*   require *higher fees of the students*
        rob *Bill of money*   speak *to a doctor about symptoms*
        strike *her as critical of each* suggest *to him how Mary did it*
                        other
        look *ill to { her / herself }*   prevent *Sue from getting depressed*

If the italicized sequences in (8.43) are small clauses (SC), then this term is just a name for "unexplained combinations of multiple complements," with an added stipulation that an extra constituent with this name but no otherwise attested phrasal properties be added to the set of syntactic categories.[23] Under this conception, the successful case-based restriction on com-

---

[23] Koster (1978a) was perhaps the first to observe that extraction from within the first DP of two complements is excluded. This pattern can easily be illustrated with the complement combinations in (8.43), whose italicized first elements are not subjects:

*Who did Mary promise *some friends of* { to buy wine / a free dinner }?
This is the cafe that they robbed *the manager of* (*of the payroll).
This is the room that you should strip *the door to* (*of its hardware).
Which councilman did your remarks impress *the wife of* (*as absurd)?
*Who did you suggest *to friends of* when to travel?
Cf. Who did you suggest that schedule to friends of?

bining complements of the next subsection would become a constitutive principle for small clauses or sole complements, replacing its definition in terms of subject and predicate (and hence any motivation for its name). I must admit that analyses moving in this direction strike me as unfruitful. A priori commitments to binary branching at best just displace the problem, which as we will now see can be better understood in terms of case theory.

8.2.2 The role of Abstract Case in Logical Form

Chapter 1 presented syntactic derivations as mediating between three interfaces, an interface with linguistic memory (e.g. the open class lexicon), LF and PF. In my view, two basic conditions operate at each interface, one of economy and one of case. I first review the economy principles and then turn to a final development of case theory.

As the economy conditions have been developed throughout this work, each has been formulated in terms of interface constructs. Perhaps the unity of the three conceptions of this study can best be grasped in terms of some aphorisms:[24]

(8.44)   a.   Economy of Representation at the lexical interface: begin a derivation with the fewest possible maximal syntactic units, or *"start with as few phrases as possible."*[25]

The reader can construct more examples on this pattern so as to be convinced that this restriction has nothing to do with extracting from "subjects," counter to what Kayne (1982) and others have so influentially argued in works on binary branching and extending the range of constructions construed as small clauses (e.g., [*SC the finances over*] as motivated by *A man we looked over the finances of* vs. **A man we looked the finances of over*).

As far as I can determine, the discovery of more and more "small clauses" motivated by this extraction property has spread out over time so that each extension has seemed only moderately implausible compared to the previous one; and conveniently, the thirty or so semantically different complement combinations in e.g. (8.22), (8.23), (8.26), (8.29), (8.38), (8.43) etc. have thus provided a rich yet reliable source of novel research topics.
[24] These formulations make clear the influence of some central ideas in Chomsky (1995). My execution of these ideas does not use covert movement, but it is not incompatible with it.
[25] Since the lexical theory laid out in Chapter 4 crucially uses insertion at different levels (or phases) of derivations, it naturally follows that lexical insertion is subject to Economy of Representation (6.23) *at any level*, as its formulation makes explicit. This use of "level" in (6.23) does not correspond to any traditional, essentially structuralist concept of level, but more to what in some recent discussions has been called a "phase" of a derivation.

b. Economy of Derivation at PF: arrive at PF by inserting the fewest possible maximal PF units, or "*insert as few words as possible.*"[26]

c. Economy of Reference at LF: arrive at LF with the fewest possible units of reference, that is, "*minimize separate references to a universe of discourse.*"

It seems to me that a similarly pleasing three-way symmetry emerges in the form of Case Theory. According to an intuitive notion which I believe was first suggested by J. Aoun, case may be understood as a means by which constituents are made "visible" for interpretation. Continuing the metaphor, objects are visible only if we can "distinguish" them from their surroundings, and objects are visibly different from each other only if some visible aspect *distinguishes them from each other.*

Extending this metaphor, then, syntax (i.e., a derivation prior to s-structure) makes visible the lexical interface units (phrases) by placing them in distinctive positions. I called this the Deep Case Filter in Chapter 7; it essentially guarantees that phrases must occur in defined structural positions, which is what "visibility" in syntax amounts to.

(7.40) *The Deep Case Filter. Extended and maximal projections of @ (= N, V, A) must, prior to s-structure, be a sister to a non-maximal lexical projection β = V, P, I or D.*

Precisely because this visibility marking is not fully achieved at one given "level" (e.g., in a bottom-up derivation, a direct object can either be accusative or remain caseless until it moves to subject position), a "check" at the end of the derivation is needed to ensure that case has actually been assigned. This is the function of the classical Case Filter, properly formulated as in the Government and Binding framework as a condition on PF. The reason it fails to apply to items such as PRO is then clear: for a PF condition, entirely covert units are simply not available for inspection. (Note that we are removing what was considered a conceptual anomaly in that framework: that a condition on visibility for *interpretation* apply at PF.)

---

[26] The formulation of Economy of Derivation used earlier throughout in the text ("Insert as few free morphemes as possible in the course of a derivation") sounds more technical but is exactly equivalent.

(8.45)　*Phonological Form Case Filter. At Phonological Form, any poten-*
　　　　tially phonological nominal projection (D^j, N^j and A^j) must have
　　　　Abstract Case.[27]

Some version of Stowell's (1981) adjacency condition on actual case-assignment should be adopted. The following somewhat less restrictive condition will suffice for the account of predicate attribute case in section 8.3.

(8.46)　*Proximity Condition on Case Assignment. A category X can be*
　　　　assigned as case index to @ only if the largest constituents sepa-
　　　　rating X and @ are not maximal YP.[28]

Bearing in mind that the main function of Abstract Case is to distinguish phrases (i.e. the interpreted units at LF) from each other, it makes sense that a central aspect of case theory must involve an LF condition requiring case *distinctions*. Now such a condition apparently focuses on internal arguments, since the previous section concluded: subcategorized complements include at most one accusative DP, one oblique DP and one phrasal complement without Abstract Case – where the latter perhaps surprisingly include predicate attributes.

(8.33)　*The Complement Space. Subcategorization frames can specify at*
　　　　most one (abstract) accusative DP, one (abstract) oblique DP and
　　　　one phrasal complement without abstract case.

Since V furnishes a case-index to a direct object and a P realized by a semantically empty item inserted at PF furnishes a case-index to a second object, these empirically justified patterns can be succinctly expressed as in (8.47).[29]

---

[27] PRO is not "potentially phonological." If nominal projections are generalized to movement chains of nominal projections along the lines of Chomsky (1981), the highest argument position in such a chain must have Abstract Case. Thus, the highest position in an "A chain" must receive case, while the highest non-A-bar position in an "A-bar chain" has case. The actual position in which case is assigned is thus often empty.

[28] The Deep Case Filter and the Proximity Condition together predict that a *non-adjacent DP sister* of a case assigner β can satisfy the former but fail to receive case because of the latter. Secondary predicates inside V' have precisely this status.

[29] As argued in some detail in Emonds (1985, sections 1.7, 5.7 and 5.8), any complement other than a direct object which carries morphological oblique case must be a sister of a P.

(8.47)   *Logical Form Case Filter. At Logical Form, internal arguments YP
of X^0 are each specified differently for Abstract Case, where "no
case" is one of the Case values.*[30]

The consequence of (8.47) is that internal arguments of an X^0 at LF may
include a single AP, DP, PP, CP or IP unspecified for case. This is correct,
provided that *predicate attributes count as unmarked for case in LF*, since
they readily co-occur as complements with both direct objects (8.22) and
indirect objects (8.27) and yet do *not* occur with the other caseless types of
complements. ➣ *point the former sect, consider left emission* ''

Nonetheless, predicate attributes marked with morphological case do
occur in many Indo-European languages, indeed frequently with the same
case as the DP they modify. Thus, translations of secondary predications as
in (8.22) in several languages would reveal that both structural complements of the V often *agree in case*; cf. the Czech examples of (8.50) below.
It is therefore crucial that a condition imposing distinct cases (8.47) holds
at LF and not at PF, and equally important that the very same predicate
attributes be forced to have PF case to satisfy (8.45).

There is no contradiction here, but only a proper and interesting theoretical tension that Chomsky and Lasnik's (1977) three-interface or "T model"
of derivations, as reviewed in Chapter 1, is quite able to handle.[31] If some
process between Spell Out and PF assigns case to predicate attribute APs
and predicate nominals (which are selected by +___N but realized as DPs),
then such YPs correctly count as "unspecified for case" for the LF side of
the Case Filter (8.47), while at the same time fully complying with the PF
side (8.45). I return to PF case-marking of predicate attributes in section 8.3.

Under this view of case, the complement space of lexical predicates
(8.33) realizes *all and only combinations of two complements predicted to*

---

[30] Actually, (8.47) must hold at Spell Out as well as at LF, since no case is assigned
between these two levels.

In section 7.2.3, I suggest that DP *adjuncts* to V can be accusative, which would result
from V^1 assigning case like V^0. In light of this, a reviewer asks whether (8.47) also holds
for adjuncts. More specifically, (s)he asks whether there might be only one "accusative
adverbial" per VP. If so, this would suggest that the LF Case Filter (8.47) holds separately
at both the levels of complements and adjuncts.

[31] As always, I find no need in this model for recourse to covert movement. Moreover,
a distinction between the case requirements at LF and PF does not entail that there are
separate LF movements not in the PF derivation; it only implies that the two levels are
derivationally distinct. Thus, the linear model of van Riemsdijk and Williams (1981) is
compatible with the Case Filter "split" proposed here.

exist by the "Two-sided" Case Filter – or perhaps better, the Three Interface Case Filter. This is the import of the grammatical patterns which the previous subsection extracted from the combinations of complements collected in (8.21)–(8.29) and the impossible combinations exemplified in (8.34)–(8.42).

8.2.3 Confirmation from triple complement structures

Since an internal argument of a verb can be specified for abstract case at s-structure in three ways, the LF Case Filter (8.47) should also tolerate lexical frames which combine up to three complements of a V, although such frames may be more marked and hence less frequent. At the same time, (8.47) sets a limit on what kinds of constituents may make up this "triple complementation." To repeat, any such VPs must contain a direct object, an obliquely case-marked indirect object introduced by a purely grammatical P (inserted in PF or otherwise licensed as empty), and one other XP which lacks case at s-structure: either a predicate attribute, a clausal complement, or a locational PP whose head is filled at s-structure (or alternatively realized by morphological case).

In fact, triple combinations with all and only the possible choices for the "caseless XP" are found in the data. This finding strongly confirms not only the possibility of multiple complements but also the role of the LF Case Filter.

(i) Double objects with predicate attributes. These combinations result from lexical entries which can be of the form V, +<D, D, { N/ A }> or V, +<D, [D, LOC'], { N/ A }>:

(8.48)   The staff keeps bringing the patients their meals cold.
         Many students handed examination books to the teacher blank.

In some combinations, the grammatical copular preposition *as* obligatorily introduces the predicate attributes:

(8.49)   a. *She described Clinton (to her friends) {a genius/ intolerant}.
             *She bought *War and Peace* (for John) a present.
         b. She described Clinton to her friends as {a genius/ intolerant}.
             She bought *War and Peace* for John as a present.

Translations into e.g. Czech or German indicate that this copular preposition, e.g. Czech *jako* 'as', does not assign a particular case (Cf. Emonds,

1985, Ch. 6). Rather, it introduces a predicate nominal (italicized) whose case varies according to that of the DP it modifies.[32]

(8.50) a. Cortéz   přijel do Ameriky jako *dobyvatel.*
        Cortez-NOM arrived to America as conqueror-NOM
        'Cortez arrived in America as a conqueror'

    b. Domorodci sledovali Cortéze (dlouhou dobu) jako *přitele.*
        Locals-NOM observed Cortez-ACC (long time) as friend-ACC
        'The locals observed Cortez (for a long time) as a friend'

    c. Cortéz   byl sledován (dlouhou dobu) jako *přitel.*
        Cortez-NOM was observed (long time)   as friend-NOM
        'Cortez was observed (for a long time) as a friend'

    d. Král   poslal guvernéra   kolonistům
        King-NOM sent governor-ACC colonists-DAT
        jako *poddaným.*
        as subjects-DAT
        'The king sent a governor to the colonists as royal subjects'

    e. Cortéz   se   neobešel   bez indiánů   jako *přátel.*
        Cortez-NOM refl. not-do without Indians-GEN as friends-GEN
        'Cortez could not do without Indians for friends'

The role of *as* in both Czech and English is thus not to assign case, but rather to circumvent potential violations of the Revised Theta Criterion of Chapter 7:

(7.58)   *Theta Relatedness. X^0 and Y^0 are theta-related if and only if one assigns a theta role to a lexical projection of the other.*

(7.59)   *Revised Theta Criterion. Theta-relatedness is anti-transitive.*

The problem with the English examples (8.49) is that each verb seems to assign theta roles to *each* of its complements, since the predicate attributes are integrally connected to the describing and the buying. At the same time, the predicate attributes assign a theta role to their own subjects

---

[32] I appreciate the efforts of L. Veselovská in constructing these and other Czech examples in this study so that the appropriate morphological contrasts are overt.

(that is, the direct objects of the main verbs). Consequently, the main verb, the direct object and the secondary predicate are all pairwise theta-related in the examples without *as* (8.49a), which violates (7.59). On the other hand, when *as* heads its own PP as in (8.49b), this P rather than its XP sister can be theta-related to the verb and thus the examples conform to (7.59). In contrast, the predicate attributes in (8.48) are irrelevant to the action of the main verb, and so *as* is not necessary.

In any case, the combination direct object – indirect object – predicate attribute occurs as predicted.

(ii) Double objects with clausal complements. So-called "lower purpose clauses" introduced by empty operators, which will be studied in some detail in section 9.1.1, exemplify triple complementation whose third element is a clause. The appropriate lexical frames are +<D, D, [V, MODAL]> or +<D, [D, LOC'], [V, MODAL]>:

(8.51)   We brought Hamlet to John to read on the train.
         We bought John Hamlet to read on the train.

(iii) Double objects with PPs. A third type of triple complementation includes a PP whose head has lexical content. These may also include idioms whose constituent parts satisfy the LF Case Filter (8.47). (It is sometimes unclear whether a given PP is a complement or an adjunct).

(8.52)   We pushed the salesman our form { through the slot / over the counter }.
         John painted Mary The Last Supper on rice paper.
         Sue traded her bicycle to Ann for a fur coat.
         That incident spoke volumes to me about their relationship.

There remains one combination of three complements which at first seems to undermine the LF Case Filter, because it includes both directional (PATH) PPs, italicized in (8.53), and either secondary predicates or additional PPs of PLACE in bold, none of which qualify as an indirect object.

(8.53)   The staff keeps putting main dishes *onto the tables* **cold**.
         Many students brought overdue books *into the library* **dirty**.
         Sue handed the purse *into the police* { **for a reward / through the slot** }.
         She sprinkled sage *over the soup* as **a seasoning**.
         The teacher brought a novel *to class* as **an experiment**.

The feel of these examples is that the directional PPs are simply alternating with indirect objects. The key to an analysis therefore lies in isolating what PATH PPs and indirect objects have formally in common. Now on grounds independent of this issue, the Revised Theta Criterion (7.59) requires that directional PP actually consist of a grammatical P of PATH whose own complement is a PP of PLACE, as in (8.54):

(8.54)

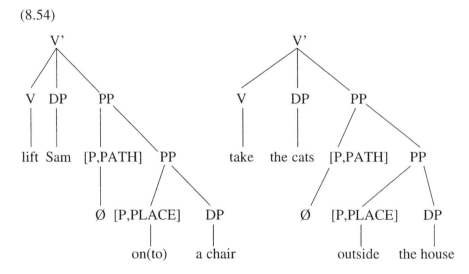

The proposed structure is overt in (8.55a), where a morpheme signals [P, SOURCE]. In some other languages such as Japanese and French (8.55b), even the PATH morpheme is overt. See note 45 of Chapter 7 and for more detail, consult Emonds (1996).

(8.55)   a. We had to remove the cats from behind the barn.
         b. Mets les chats en dehors de la maison.
             'Put the cats (to) outside the house.'

The only reason that (8.53) poses an apparent problem for the LF Case Filter (8.47) is that I have not yet fully specified what counts as an "indirect object" for the Filter or in fact for the LF component. The similarity of the structures in (8.54) to the structure of indirect objects suggests somewhat extending the usual limitation of the latter concept to obliquely case-marked DPs.

(8.56) *"Indirect Objects" or "Oblique Case" for the LF Case Filter. An XP in the LF structure [PATH - XP] counts as obliquely case-marked in LF.*[33]

The PATH prepositions which introduce indirect objects can be (a) PF-inserted free morphemes (e.g. *to* and *for*), (b) alternatively realized either as oblique case on the DP or as applicative morphemes on V, or (c) licensed as empty by dative clitics or indirect object movement (Emonds, 1993). All these PF realizations of indirect objects correspond to a locational P of PATH on the LF side, as required in (8.56). This definition now makes clear that the italicized directional PPs in (8.53) count as providing oblique case for purposes of the LF Case Filter (8.45) and hence satisfy it.

The formulation (8.56) also correctly entails that CPs, which never have an interpreted PATH feature, other non-locational PPs and even bare PPs of PLACE with interpretable lexical content all continue to count as having "no case" for the LF Case Filter, as throughout the preceding discussion.[34]

Although the definition of indirect object (8.56) is considerably broader than any envisaged in traditional grammar, it turns out that three additional paradigms confirm this formulation. If directional PPs count as indirect objects for the LF Case Filter, they should be compatible with frames which also select a clausal complement. And in fact paradigms involving intransitive (manner of speaking) verbs (8.57a) and transitive verbs (8.57b) satisfy such frames:

(8.57) a. Harry shouted [into the microphone] [(for everyone) to dance].
         Sue whispered [over my shoulder] [that Sam was watching].
        b. Mary brought John [into the aerobics class] [to exercise with].
         Take those magazines [up to your office] [to get ideas from].

In addition, the definition (8.56) explains why the strings *into the house to his mother* and *out of the house from the fire* in (8.30) are united into single PPs rather than being two separate PP sisters to a selecting verb. If both were

---

[33] The formulation in (8.56) deliberately omits a label for the outer brackets, as I don't exclude the possibility that languages with serial verbs have bare VPs which can house an indirect object if headed by a grammatical V with the feature PATH.

[34] The feature LOC', which has been defined as *distinguishing for* from *to,* is a value of PATH in constructions with a *for* dative. As the LF Case Filter (8.47) predicts, two distinct indirect objects, a *to* dative and a *for* dative, cannot co-exist: **She brought Jim a card to Bill.* (Adjunct *for*-phrases are of course irrelevant.)

sisters, each would contain obliquely marked complements introduced by PF-inserted directional P, and this would violate the LF Case Filter.

To my knowledge, the combinations in (8.48)–(8.53) exhaust the possibilities for triple complementation in English. On the basis of this language, we have thus arrived at a rather surprising and very strong hypothesis about the membership of the lexicon, in terms of the subcategorization frames of its predicates:

(8.58)   *Lexical Density. Predicates utilize all and only the subcategorization frames constructible by syntactic category theory (cf. Chapter 1) and the LF Case Filter.*

In light of (8.58), the lexicon seems to be much less the barely charted wilderness than studies which either abstract away from it or alternatively focus on semantics and conceptual structures would lead us to believe. In fact, the syntactic part of the lexical entries, which are the interface instructions for drawing out concepts from memory for use, now seems more understandable and transparent than either of their more "concrete" components, articulation and understanding.

8.3 The Case of predicate attributes

The combined implication of the PF part (8.45) and the LF part (8.47) of the Case Filter is that predicate attribute DPs and APs, italicized in (8.59), should all receive abstract case between Spell Out, where they are caseless, and PF, where at least all DPs must have case.

(8.59)   a. Mary became *a chiropractor.*
                 Sam has always been *a brother* to me.
                 Mary has become *obsessed* in recent months.
                 Sam always seemed *angry* to me.
           b. The florid judge declared the future mother *a criminal.*
                 Some call the economic reforms *a return to the jungle.*
                 Nobody wants to declare the elections *fraudulent.*
                 Many voters considered the system *undemocratic.*

In addition, assuming that the PF Case Filter is general, predicate attribute adjuncts exterior to X' which modify a subject as in (8.60) also need case at PF.

(8.60) a. Mary left the party *my friend*.
John worked in New York as *a clown*.
John's work in New York as *a clown* bothered his parents.
b. Mary left the party *thirsty*.
I found that book tedious *young*.
You will find the test a breeze *drunk*.

It should be kept in mind that no aspect of the "Three Interface Case Filter" has been motivated on the basis of morphology: the LF Case Filter is designed to account for the range of observed complement types in VPs, and the original Case Filter (at PF) has long been motivated at least for DPs in languages like English on syntactic rather than morphological grounds; for example, it plays an important role in the analysis of adjectival passives in Chapter 5 here.

It comes then as a massive independent confirmation of the Case Theory developed here that in Indo-European languages with rich morphological case-marking, both DP and AP predicate attributes overtly and robustly display exactly the case properties required by the split between the LF and PF aspects of the Case Filter. That is, predicate attributes in these languages are overtly and obligatorily case-marked in PF, and yet this case-marking appears to play no role whatever at LF.[35]

The Czech agreements in (8.61) exemplify this point. As in many similar case systems, the (italicized) predicate attribute agrees in case with its DP subject. (NOM = nominative; ACC = accusative; DAT = dative; MS = masculine singular.)[36]

(8.61) a. Kanibal   snědl turistu   { *syrového* / **-vý* }.
cannibal-MS-NOM ate   tourist-MS-ACC { raw-MS-ACC /
'The cannibal ate the tourist raw'   *MS-NOM }

b. Turista   byl sněden   { *syrový* /   **-vého* }.
tourist-MS-NOM was eat-en-MS { raw-MS-NOM / *MS-ACC }
'The tourist was eaten raw'

c. Únosci   vrátili chlapce   rodičům
kidnappers returned boy-MS-ACC parents-DAT
{ *živého* /   **-vý* }.
{ alive-MS-ACC / *MS-NOM }
'The kidnappers returned the boy to his parents alive'

---

[35] Chomsky (1995) also emphasizes the almost certain absence of PF agreement features at LF.

[36] Andrews (1971) provides Classical Greek paradigms of similar import.

    d. Chlapec   byl   vrácen   rodičům
       boy-MS-NOM   was return-en-MS parents-DAT
        { živý /   **-vého }.*
      { alive-MS-NOM / *MS-ACC }
      'The boy was returned to his parents alive'

As determined by Generalized Subjects (1.15), the subject of *raw* in (8.61a) is the accusative DP *the tourist*, while its subject in (8.61b) is the nominative chain consisting of *the tourist* and its trace in object position. As predicted, the PF case of the AP *raw* varies with no effect at or contribution to LF. (8.62c-d) are similar, with the added factor that the predicate adjective is separated from the object it modifies, probably due to Czech free word order.

More generally, both sorts of predicate attributes, DPs and APs, typically receive the abstract case of the DP they modify, often reflected in morphological agreement as in (8.61). Thus, the immediate source of abstract accusative case for secondary predicates modifying a direct object as in (8.22) and (8.59b) is not the governing verb, but the object DP itself. This "second chance" for receiving abstract and morphological case occurs after Spell Out but before PF.

The idea that case may be assigned at two levels conforms to a recurrent theme of this study: interpreted grammatical items are inserted prior to Spell Out, but those which don't contribute to meaning are inserted in PF. In particular, *the same elements can often be inserted in different components under nearly the same co-occurrence conditions* (e.g., those for *-en* and *-ing* studied in Chapters 4 and 5). Following this line of thought, abstract case indices whose only role is to satisfy the PF Case Filter (8.45) should be inserted subsequent to s-structure under (nearly) the same conditions as are those s-structure case indices which satisfy the LF Case Filter (8.47).[37]

In particular, the categories of the case assigners are the same before and after Spell Out (I, D and those V and P which select I or D), and Case Assignment, at least in languages without free word order, is again subject to the Proximity Condition (8.46):

(8.46)   *Proximity Condition on Case Assignment. A category X can be assigned as case index to @ only if the largest constituents separating X and @ are not maximal YP.*

---

[37] There is no need to stipulate a level at which a given structure receives case. For instance, if some direct object does not receive case prior to s-structure, it will be caseless at LF and fail to be interpretable as an argument.

Keeping in mind the goal of assigning case similarly in both syntax and PF, a near optimal solution for PF Case Assignment to predicate attributes is (8.62):

(8.62)   *PF Case. Apply the Case Assignment Condition (8.13) again in PF to all nominal XP.*[38]

Even though PF Case Assignment is formally like case assignment in syntax, its actual effects on predicate attributes are superficially dissimilar. To see its effects, let us inspect two s-structures (8.63)–(8.64) which each contain a predicate nominal in bold italics and a predicate adjective in simple italics. Although these attributes obviously lack overt morphological case in English, the following discussion should clarify the mechanics of how I assign case to attribute phrases which "agree" with the DPs they modify.[39] Case-indices already assigned to DPs at s-structure (prior to PF Case Assignment) are in bold, while attributes still needing PF case are marked "??". For clarity, these trees include prepositions and articles from the Syntacticon which are actually not inserted until PF.

(8.63)   You will find the test *a breeze drunk.*

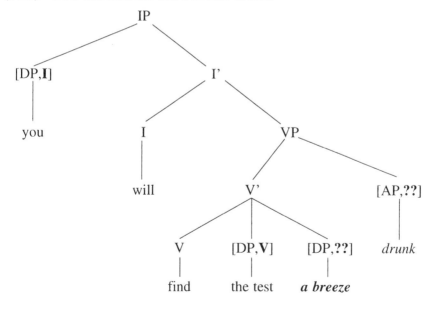

---

[38] (8.62) extends the syntactic Case Assignment Condition (8.13), which does not affect

(8.64)   John's work in N.Y. as ***a clown*** may seem *foolish* to you.

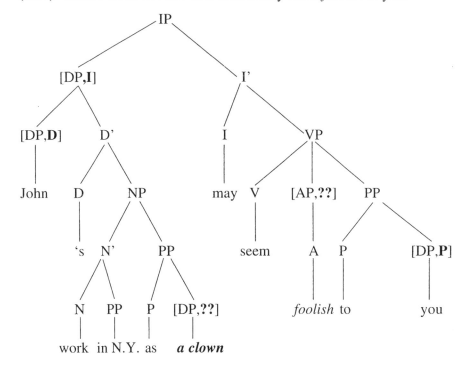

Let us examine in turn (i) the predicate nominal ***a breeze*** in (8.63), (ii) the predicate attribute adjuncts *drunk* and ***a clown*** in (8.63)–(8.64), and (iii) the predicate adjective complement *foolish* in (8.64).

(i) The predicate attribute *a breeze* in (8.63) needs case. The category V has been transferred as a case index to the direct object *the test* as a result of case assignment in the syntax, so this case index on the object itself

---

APs. I am unsure to what extent (8.62) or the Case Filter should be considered as applying to the bare NPs argued for in e.g. Kallulli (1999).

Case Assignment Condition. A potential case assigner β can be a case index on DP if some βʲ which c-commands DP is the closest non-maximal projection of any potential case assigner.

[39] Along with Mateos (1996), I take the pervasive number and gender agreement of Romance APs to reflect their abstract case.

This study does not examine *DP-internal* agreement, including in case, among N, D and numerals. Veselovská (2000) analyzes these agreements in Czech, using the differing patterns as evidence for which syntactic positions and levels of lexical insertion are most appropriate for the various classes of elements.

becomes a potential case-assigner. Since this V is moreover adjacent to the predicate nominal needing case, it can become the latter's PF case-index by (8.62). Accordingly, this predicate nominal is morphologically accusative in many Indo-European case systems.[40]

(ii) Predicate attributes in adjunct position, such as *drunk* in (8.63) and *a clown* in (8.64), also need case. The case-assigning categories I and D and also the corresponding case-indices I in (8.63) and D in (8.64) are respectively available for assigning them case according to the Proximity Condition (8.46), *because the intervening V' and N' are not maximal projections*.[41] Therefore, either instance of I and D may be available for assigning case to the predicate attributes they c-command.[42]

(iii) In (8.64) the intransitive linking verb *seem* cannot assign case to anything, since it does not enter the tree by satisfying a subcategorization frame +___D or +___I, the requirement imposed by Case Indices (8.9). However, both the node I and the case index I on the subject DP are again, by the Proximity Condition (8.46), "close enough" to assign as a case index to *foolish*; the largest constituents separating them are not maximal.

The empirical prediction that predicate attributes have case in PF is strongly confirmed by Indo-European morphological case systems which assign actual morphological case to predicate attributes along the lines just explained using English examples. The Czech system briefly exemplified in (8.61) is of this type.[43] Moreover, the mechanism for assigning PF case

---

[40] In the case theory I develop here, I continue to conflate traditional case names (e.g. accusative) with the category that assigns them (V). Only the latter have any status in linguistic theory, as argued in Emonds (1985, Ch. 1). If for some reason one granted terms like "accusative" a status different than V, then the generalizations of the present system which unite case assignment with case agreement would go unexpressed.

[41] The non-maximal nature of any projection which has an adjunct is one of the consequences of the bare phrase structure theory justified in Speas (1990, section 2.2).

[42] Alternatively, adjuncts might receive case *prior* to Spell Out, in as much as the LF Case Filter (8.47) does not affect adjuncts. Plausibly however, a case-assigner may be incapable of assigning case "in two directions at once," both leftward to the subject and rightward to a predicate attribute, or of assigning it "twice in one component." If either of these options is excluded, the categories I and D are first assigned in syntax as case-indices to their respective subjects (*you, John*) in (8.63)–(8.64), and then those case-indices in turn assign case by PF Case (8.62) to predicate attribute adjuncts: *drunk* in (8.63) and *a clown* in (8.64).

[43] Even though Czech has free word order related to discourse factors (the "functional sentence perspective" of the Prague School), which usually obscures the Proximity Condition (8.46), certain instances of secondary case assignment in PF still seem to require

(8.62) nicely mimics syntactic case assignment. Finally, the dual level Case Assignment system here provides accounts for several additional recalcitrant grammatical puzzles (a-f). These solutions in turn further strengthen the case for this model.

(a) Accusative secondary predicates. PF Case Assignment and the proposal in Emonds (1985, Ch. 1) that case assigning categories are actually themselves the case indices together explain how *secondary predicates not assigned case by V^0 are nonetheless accusative only when this V^0 assigns some accusative*, as seen in (8.61). It is the V assigned to the direct objects in syntax which serves a second time in PF as a case-assigner under adjacency. Such a unification of case assignment is impossible in frameworks which cling to the traditional case names as ad hoc constructs distinct from the assigners.

(b) Adjacency of direct objects and secondary predicates. Paradigms such as the following are often taken to support the existence of a small clause constituent uniting a direct object and a secondary predicate.

(8.65)   The judge (rashly) declared the future mother (*rashly) a criminal.
          Some have (prematurely) called the reforms (*prematurely) frauds.
          The manager (unfairly) judged the applicant (*unfairly) too short.

---

adjacency. Thus L. Veselovská points out that, while some reorderings (i) of the examples with *jako* 'as' in (8.50) are acceptable, others are excluded (ii).

(i)   Jako poddaným   poslal král   kolonistům   guvernéra.
       As   subjects-DAT   sent   king-NOM colonists-DAT governor-ACC
       'As subjects the king sent the colonists a governor'

       ?Jako bez   přátel   se Cortéz neobešel bez   indiánů.
       As without friends-GEN refl Cortez not-do without Indians-GEN
       'For friends Cortez could not do without Indians'

The oblique predicate nominal PPs with *jako* from (8.50d-e) are fronted in (i) probably to some kind of topic or focus position, as the examples reportedly sound pragmatically marked.

    However *within IP*, separating the italicized oblique predicate attribute from its bold subject leads to straightforward ungrammaticality:

(ii)   *Král poslal **kolonistům** guvernéra *jako poddaným*.
       *Cortéz se bez **indianů** neobešel *jako přátel*.

This suggests that the Proximity Condition on Case Assignment (8.46) has verifiable effects even within a free word order system.

When an English predicate attribute and a direct object are sisters, the object cannot be separated by an XP from its VP-initial V case-assigner. Thus, the predicate attribute XP must follow a direct object. Then, again by the Proximity Condition (8.46), an adverbial AP cannot intervene between this same object DP (marked with the case index V) and the secondary predicate to be marked for case in PF. Thus, Case Proximity accounts for the paradigm in (8.65) with no need for invoking small clause constituency.

(c) Absence of secondary predicates on indirect objects. When an English predicate attribute and an indirect object are sisters, the latter is in a PP and hence does not c-command the attribute. Consequently, according to Generalized Subjects (1.17) *an indirect object cannot be the subject of a predicate attribute.*

(8.66) *A country drive appealed to Bill fatigued.
 *He spoke to Mary pregnant.
 *We demanded some action of them irresponsible.

This restriction is reported in the literature as an ad hoc limitation on small clause distribution, i.e., small clauses cannot occur with obliquely case-marked subjects. In the framework developed here, it follows without stipulation.

(d) Word order of indirect objects and predicate nominals. The Proximity Condition (8.46) on case assignment *prohibits* an indirect object XP from intervening between the verb and an attribute which must receive nominative case from I. Thus, the system here also correctly predicts, on the basis of case assignment, that *a predicate nominal typically precedes an indirect object*:[44]

(8.67) John became { a brother to us / *to us a brother }.
 Mary appears { unstable to Sam / *to Sam unstable }.

(e) Simplification of the Binding Theory. It appears that principles of disjoint reference such as *Principles B and C of Chomsky's (1981, Ch. 3) Binding Theory should apply only to DPs which are case-marked at LF*; that is, to DP arguments with s-structure case. These principles have no effect

---

[44] Unsurprisingly, a complex or "heavy" predicate nominal can shift rightwards over a PP: *John became { to / for } us the brother we always wanted.*

on predicate nominal DPs. If both predication and co-reference are parsimoniously represented with indices of the same formal nature, and if moreover there were no difference in level between case-marking of predicate nominals and argument DPs, then predicate nominals need to be specially exempted from disjoint reference, as proposed in Safir (1985). (If not, simple examples such as *The best singer seemed to be him* and *His parents were an ideal couple* would violate Principles B and C respectively.) The case system of this section, which distinguishes Case Assignment in the syntax and PF, avoids this complication.

(f) Parameters of morphological realization. A final advantage to the split between PF and LF Case concerns succinct descriptions of morphological types of languages. It is well-known that some languages exhibit morphological case neither on DPs nor in PF agreements (Chinese and outside of pronouns, English), while many other languages (Classical Greek, Latin, most Slavic languages, etc.) exhibit both types of case morphology.

Certain other languages such as French and Spanish have no morphological case on DPs; case distinctions appear only among their clitics, which are bound morphemes on verbs. Thus, we might say that their phrasal morphology fails to exhibit syntactic (i.e. LF) case. At the same time, Romance languages have robust morphological gender and number agreement for predicate adjectives, which is operative exactly in the contexts where PF Case Assignment (8.62) imposes case agreement on adjectives. If this number and gender agreement on adjectives reflects PF case agreement (Mateos, 1996), then overall Romance morphologies exhibit PF case, but LF case only marginally, among their clitics.

These three typological configurations suggest that some languages could have morphology which exhibits syntactic case on DPs robustly but PF or agreement case only sparingly. And indeed Japanese and Korean morphologically mark syntactic case on DP arguments, but their predicate attributes exhibit very little morphological case and no agreement at all. The latter surface with either no case-marker (as with the Japanese copula) or in some non-agreeing oblique case. This latter point is not surprising, since some predicate attributes can surface with oblique case even in languages with robust predicate attribute agreement.

It appears then that Syntacticons of languages vary independently as to whether they house ample syntactic (LF) or PF realizations of morphological case. English and Chinese have neither; Romance languages exhibit PF case; Japanese and Korean exhibit syntactic case; and the Classical and Slavic Indo-European languages exhibit both. *The symmetry of these four*

*ting systems provides further conceptual support for a dual level
)f case assignment.*

e accounts (a)–(f) all result from a system of assigning syntactic and
according to the same principles but at two derivational levels.
r, they further support the "Three Interface" conception of the Case
his particular Case Theory in turn has played a key role earlier in
this chapter in showing that the notion of "possible lexical entry" developed
throughout this work dovetails exceedingly well with the observed range of
lexical complementation.

8.4 The restrictive Syntactic Lexicon confronts open-ended Conceptual Space

We have seen in this chapter that the system of lexical subcategorization
reviewed in its introductory paragraphs provides exactly the right range of
formal, simple subcategorization features for selecting complements to
verbs, the category which exhibits the widest diversity of complement types.
All six single frames provided by the extended projection category system
laid out in Chapter 1 are realized as in fact long familiar sub-classes of
predicates, as summarized in (8.16). Moreover, there are no construction
types unaccounted for or "left over," which might testify to some deficiency
in the system.

Perhaps even more surprisingly, with the aid of a plausible "LF Case
Filter" which states how complements must differ from each other at LF, we
have seen that the subcategorization framework formally predicts the existence of *all and only the combinations* of English complements which actually seem to exist. That is, the subcategorization formalism defines a "space"
of possible lexical entries, and this space is densely but evenly populated,
a property which I have called Lexical Density (8.58).

From the perspective of having completed this study, it appears that the
old shibboleths about the irregularity of the lexicon, about how its entries
shade off into unformalizable conditions of every sort, are just paraphrases
of a lack of knowledge about its structure. I hope that this study constitutes
a major step away from this attitude and toward achieving the goal an-
nounced in Chapter 1, "of working out some type of formalized lexicon to
actually generate the syntactic structures which then undergo the carefully
studied derivations." Finally, I hope that the proposals here for developing
syntactic theory also go a good part of the way toward explaining how such

minimally specified lexical frames manage to generate a complex variety of structures.

At least with regard to its syntactic structure then, I claim to have discovered a sharply divided lexicon (cf. again their differences summarized at the end of Chapter 4) which in both its parts, the Dictionary and the Syntacticon, is highly regular and amenable to predictive theoretical treatment. It is especially fortunate that the Syntacticon has this property, for young children quickly learn it without instruction. In fact, the hundreds of entries in the Syntacticon, which are largely unique in each language, and the ten thousand plus entries in the Dictionary, whose syntactic aspects are also far from entirely fixed, are learned almost without effort.

The principal device of (both parts of) the lexicon is a streamlined and yet more syntactically "active" version of the subcategorization mechanisms introduced in Chomsky (1965). But instead of being an incomplete set of statements drawn from a disparate inventory of categories, this work's subcategorization frames classify morphemes by means of a reduced and highly structured set of cognitive categories developed in the intervening decades, utilizing essentially all of the combinations available. Moreover, lexical entries here never mention phrases (the Lexical Interface Principle, 2.13), and possibly except for idioms (not investigated here), the syntactic frames stipulate neither concatenation nor any grammatical morphemes. The distribution of specific morphemes such as English *to, as, that, if, for,* etc. and of many bound morphemes in other languages is predictable from the effects of case theory and the Economy Principles of Representation and Derivation. Nor do the syntactic frames mention linear order, although such frames do combine with Lieber's (1980, 1983) ordered word-internal subcategorizations. In fact the subcategorization framework is finally the key that facilitates the merging of these two grammatical domains, morphology and syntax, too long segregated (Chapters 3 and 4).

Designing a simplified and predictive system of lexical frames has inevitably gone hand in hand with modifying various conceptions internal to syntax. The principal innovations, summarized and in part further developed in this chapter, concern case theory ("visibility theory") and the principles of economy. Both sub-theories operate in terms appropriate to the functions of the three interfaces with syntax: the lexical interface, LF and PF. I have called all three facets of case theory "filters": the Deep Case Filter (7.40), an extension of Rouveret and Vergnaud's (1980) classical Case Filter to the PF Case Filter (8.45), and the LF Case Filter (8.47). The economy principles are respectively of Representation (6.23) at the lexical interface, of Derivation (4.36) at PF, and of Reference (1.27) at LF.

In addition, a number of interpretive LF principles have been introduced to factor out what I have argued is redundant relational semantics from statements of individual lexical entries. Among these are the Revised Theta Criterion of section 7.6 and four principles of theta role assignment in Chapter 2: Full Interpretation (2.35) and Specifications of Agent (2.39), Ground (2.47) and Figure (2.48).[45]

It is true that this study has offered almost nothing in the way of semantics of individual lexical items – except to incorporate what is not individual into the just mentioned general interpretive principles. The remaining linkages of *particular lexical items* to conceptual space (= the psychological world which language tries to report on and modify) are, I feel, neither very amenable to formalization nor even particularly related to syntactic well-formedness.

I do not deny that particular meanings of morphemes are ultimately formalizable, but I do judge that we presently have no method for *reliably* accessing any aspects of those meanings. In practice, current linguistic semantics is either disguised syntax (i.e. using mnemonic terms which are actually justified on the basis of well-formedness, clear ambiguities, and intuitions of grammatical relatedness) or, especially when it treats concepts in isolation, without implications for natural language structure. Any approaches to lexical specifications recognizably labeled today as semantic seem to consist mainly of combining results from (non-verbal) psychology with "thinking hard" about how to represent meaning, and then trying to formalize these intuitions – usually by some analogy to syntactic structure, perhaps mediated by a dose of predicate calculus.

Overall, I judge this intuitive method to have been as unfruitful in explaining syntax as it has been persistent. Although it has produced a wealth of intelligent observations about what kinds of objects, events, situations or mental states words or classes of words can refer to, I fail to see an emerging systematic import for how words combine; the vast literature on presupposition, opacity and factivity is just one example. The problem is that there is no systematic "data check" on intuitions about concepts and relatedness of concepts other than whatever is afforded by syntax. But if at bottom syntax provides the only reliable data for checking on conceptual representations of words, then in fact the conceptual constructs are essentially guesses, usually question-begging guesses, about what governs syntactic well-formedness.

---

[45] Full Interpretation (2.35) is my application to theta role assignment of a general idea in Chomsky (1981); (2.39) is from Chomsky (1972); the disjointness of Figure and Ground built into (2.48) is from Talmy (1975, 1978).

They cannot be expected to be more successful than other attempts at informed philosophical speculation, clever as many of these have been.

In practice, no formal limits have been set on the lexical conceptual structures of individual words which are (pre)supposed to determine how they can combine. The representations that have been proposed, analogous to logical representations to be sure, arc taxonomic but otherwise open-ended. Restrictive systems of categories, either for separate concepts or systems of concepts, are entirely lacking. Moreover, couching shrewd intuitions in logical formulae only obscures the fact that modern logic itself, whose inventors were not even among the grammarians of the time, was just an early twentieth century guess about how to factor out what is "essential for proofs" from real language.

Even something as elegantly simple as L. Talmy's Figure-Ground dichotomy, certainly a central perceptual principle, seems to have import and predictive implications only when it interfaces with syntax and determines theta roles. Any conceptual semantic statements truly independent of syntax (we can't see colors at night, animate objects self-propel, we know the difference between up and down, etc.) come across as unrevealing truisms – unless we unexpectedly find syntactic verifications. But thinking hard about and reformulating truisms is a much slower road to syntactic confirmation than simply doing syntax. And the bonus of the syntactic method is its often interesting by-products for understanding semantics.[46]

I conclude that with methods and insights presently available, there is not nor can there be any reliable method for specifying lexical meanings in terms of concepts or conceptual space; the enterprise is too vague and too unsystematic. A fortiori, thinking about (classes of) concepts has not and doesn't show promise of shedding insight on the combinatory possibilities of language. The latter study, of syntax, is best undertaken autonomously: reference to meaning does not help us construct grammars. Rather, constructing grammars, which I take to be based on constructing a syntax of lexical combinations, sometimes – but not always – helps us understand meaning. This essential point of Chomsky (1957) remains as true as it was then.

This study has revealed a new and important justification for basing semantics on syntax. The fact that the range of lexical frames provided by

---

[46] The most interesting things we know about the semantic dichotomy between activity and stative predicates are by-products of early diagnostics which tried to make precise which verbs "take manner adverbials freely" (Lakoff and Ross, 1966). They involve compatibilities with imperatives, *do so* anaphora and progressive aspect.

syntactic theory seems to fit perfectly the range of actually occurring grammatical patterns suggests that whatever the semantics of head-complement combinations, this latter factor is not determining how the linguistic system works – or it if is, the semantic system is nearly isomorphic to its syntactic basis.[47] That is, the logical system of language is precisely the subcategorization system. Humans can say, not what they want to say, but what the frames of the lexicon allow them to say. The combinatorial aspects of the lexicon, to the extent that their elegance testifies to their truth, are fundamentally syntactic.

One might object that it is easy to turn this formulation around. I have even maintained throughout that all the Syntacticon's features and categories, which organize syntax (N, V, ACTIVITY, ANIMATE, INHERENT, NEGATIVE, PAST, PATH, etc.) and are notated F_i, are the *most central* cognitive features both in LF and in the open class dictionary. In fact, I have found no use whatever for purely formal or diacritic syntactic categories or features. We can well say that the only features available for syntax are the most central features of man's conceptual structures and open class Dictionary; in this sense syntax is entirely dependent on conceptual structure. That is, the syntactic feature inventory is a "perfect system" in the sense of Chomsky (1995): it is derived entirely from the LF interface with understanding and cognition.

But what remains constant in both formulations is *the method by which we arrive at this feature inventory* (the set of cognitive syntactic $\{F_i\}$) and the roles in grammar played by these features. The only *reliable* guide leading to specification of the feature inventory is syntactic behavior, and once a feature is in the inventory, we expect it to behave according to the principles of syntax; it becomes irrelevant whether it then conforms to any essentially intuitive semantic categories which might or might not conflict

---

[47] Once the theory embodied in chemistry's periodic table clearly started to successfully predict all and only the combinations of elements in observable compounds, chemistry lost interest in "deeper," less materialist principles which might or might not make the same predictions.

It has been another and deeper matter, of course, to investigate why the periodic table (e.g., the theory of valence, orbital size, nuclear charge, etc.) has exactly the internal structure that it does. Similarly in syntax, we would like to know why the extended projection category system of Chapter 1 is comprised of exactly six head categories, two of them closed and dependent on two of the others (I on V and D on N respectively), why each lexical category permits closed classes of grammatical modifiers, why N and V have parallel projections, why N and A don't assign case, etc. But present studies in lexical semantics seem as far from these concerns as alchemists were from the study of quarks.

with syntax. And in fact, whether researchers use a syntactic or semantic method, they seem to agree on labeling as syntactic any theory which privileges grammatical investigations as the high road to discovering the inventory of mental categories, whatever its ultimate claims are about semantics. In this sense, this book has developed an almost exclusively syntactic theory of the lexicon.

Chapter 9
Licensing and identification of null complements

9.1 Syntactic identification and subcategorization

Chapter 2 tried to establish that classical subcategorization features of the form (2.14), interpreted by (2.18), suffice to characterize the distribution of phrasal complements to verbs. (2.14) contains no theta grids or semantic co-occurrence statements; the semantic features f of the selecting head are intrinsic and non-contextual, while the F are the cognitive syntactic features of section 1.2.1. (These final chapters use the older notation +___F for phrasal subcategorization rather than the order-free notation +<F> of Ch. 4.)

(2.14) @, X, F_i, f_j, +___F_k

(2.18) *Extended Classical Subcategorization. @, X, +___Y is satisfied if and only if Y is a cognitive syntactic feature of a lexical head of a complement in XP.*

To establish the adequacy of subcategorization, Chapter 2 argued that the interaction of a few syntax-based interpretive principles with *inherent* verbal features (e.g., ±LOCATION, ±FACTIVE, or unlinked specification of a predicate's most salient semantic role) fully predicts both the propositional interpretations of CPs (as exclamatives, indirect questions, etc; cf. section 2.3) and the theta role interpretations of DPs (sections 2.4 through 2.6).

Throughout this study, various chapters have shown that features +___F_k in the form of (2.14) license a significantly wider class of structures than has been commonly thought. In Chomsky (1965), subcategorization features license only *overt phrasal sisters* of a head X^0. In Chapters 4 through 6 we have seen that complements *need not always be phrasal*, and in Chapters 6 and 7 that the licensed constituents, under certain circumstances, *need not be sisters* of X^0. In this chapter, we will see that phrasal complements *need not be overt.*

A central claim of this chapter is thus that subcategorization frames license null or "understood" internal arguments in a limited but interesting set of cases, in fact exactly those where very local *principles of sentence grammar* can technically "identify" the arguments in question. Identification

(9.1) depends crucially on syntactic proximity, though the exact nature of this proximity will be worked out only as we proceed.[1]

(9.1)   *Syntactic Identification. All and only empty DPs licensed by subcategorization must be locally rather than pragmatically identified.*

This conclusion has many interesting ramifications, but they probably can be appreciated only after reading this chapter's argumentation.[2] Section 9.1 establishes the correlation between subcategorization and local identification for sets of less controversial cases. Sections 9.2–9.4 extend this approach and also treat the issue of whether devices other than syntactic subcategorization ever license understood arguments.

My investigation of null arguments will conclude that they have but two sources: (i) subcategorization frames (sections 9.3 and 9.4) and (ii) the Extended Projection Principle for subjects formulated as (1.17) in Chapter 1. In both situations, empty DPs are actually present in trees. Consequently, I also reject the notion that a lexical item can contribute an "unprojected argument" as a grammatical construct interpreted in Logical Form. Chapter 10 additionally shows that null subjects licensed by the EPP do *not* require the local Syntactic Identification (9.1) of sentence grammar; discourse identification suffices.

A final section of this chapter analyzes a possible intellectual source of the persistent tendency to attribute generative power to lexical items, via theta grids and unprojected arguments. Briefly, I identify a perhaps laudable desire to "keep syntax pure" (i.e. elegant), but I claim that misguided use of this methodology has finally led lexical studies to a kind of "shadow syntax"

---

[1] This requirement that subcategorized DPs be identified in the sense of (9.1) may hold only of Huang's (1982) "hot languages" (e.g., English and French but not Chinese or Japanese, which are "cool"). Why should the former "need" identification? I speculate as follows: Universally, interpretation may require a simple algorithm for syntactically locating a verb's theme. In a cool language, it may suffice to look at a verb's subcategorization frames.

However, in a hot language, the syntactic location of the theme DP of a given verb also depends on whether a given clause has a (true) direct object. For example, the verb *open* / French *ouvrir* has a theme subject if the verb is intransitive (English) or its object is reflexive (French). Syntactic Identification is thus required to determine both whether an object is present and what its basic features are. In a hot language, this information is then a necessary supplement to the lexical entry for algorithmically locating a verb's theme.

[2] In terms of Government and Binding, (9.1) suggests that empty subcategorized DPs must be antecedent-governed, while in contrast, empty subjects are not subject to proper government.

which has avoided the challenge of how to make syntax answerable to lexical variation.

9.1.1 "Empty Operator" complement phrases

The examples (9.2)–(9.3) are a well-known type of infinitive licensed by modifiers of the category A. In addition to animate PRO subjects in certain of the examples, gaps in object positions and also inanimate gaps in subject position appear in this construction, indicated by O:

(9.2)   John is *(too) stubborn [$_{CP}$ PRO to speak (French)].
        John is too stubborn [$_{CP}$ PRO to speak (French) to O].
        *John is too stubborn [$_{CP}$ for us to speak (French)].
        John is too stubborn [$_{CP}$ for us to speak (French) to O].

(9.3)   More than enough movies [$_{CP}$ O to entertain him] await us in Paris.
        More than enough movies [$_{CP}$ PRO to critique O] await us in Paris.
        *More than enough movies [$_{CP}$ for us to entertain him] await us in Paris.
        More than enough movies [$_{CP}$ for us to critique O] await us in Paris.

According to arguments in Chomsky (1977), an "empty operator" DP is said to move to a clause-initial position in the internal CP in (9.2)–(9.3).[3] This empty category "O" can originate in any sentence-internal argument position, as the examples show. An O in a complement position must obviously satisfy subcategorization frames; in fact, these empty underlying phrases are postulated precisely because they conform to generalizations expressed by subcategorization (e.g. *to* and *critique* are transitive). Moreover, as the ungrammatical examples show, any putative O in complementizer position which fails to bind a trace in argument position is ill-formed. Thus, the paradigms (9.2)–(9.3) suffice to establish that subcategorization frames can license null arguments.

There are interesting distributional properties of O which have never been properly scrutinized. For instance, what is the most general distributional statement about O? An infinitival clause headed by a fronted O may be

---

[3]   Chomsky's (1986b, 109) later formulation: "The structure, then, must be (104), where O is an empty operator and e_k the variable that it binds:

John is too stubborn [O$_k$ [PRO$_j$ to talk to e_k]]   (104)"

He continues: O$_k$ "is the head of a chain formed by movement of O from its D-structure position to the position it occupies in (104)."

adjoined to a phrasal projection of "compared" A as in (9.2) or of compared N as in (9.3). Such an infinitive may also be adjoined to some projection of D or N like a restrictive relative (9.4). Finally, it can appear with a direct object DP sister as a lower, V^1-internal purpose clause complement (9.5).[4]

(9.4)   The best play [$_{CP}$ O to engross him on the train] might be Hamlet.
         The best play [$_{CP}$ to critique O on the train] might be Hamlet.
         *The best play [$_{CP}$ for us to converse on the train] might be Hamlet.
         The best play [$_{CP}$ for us to critique O on the train] might be Hamlet.

(9.5)   Mary bought John Hamlet [$_{CP}$ O to engross him on the train].
         Mary bought John Hamlet [$_{CP}$ to critique O on the train].
         *Mary bought John Hamlet [$_{CP}$ for us to converse on the train].
         Mary bought John Hamlet [$_{CP}$ for us to critique O on the train].

Overall then, clauses introduced by an empty operator apparently must satisfy condition (9.6) at Logical Form.

(9.6)   O is well formed only in X^j - [$_{CP}$ [$_{DP}$ O] - C - IP], where j > 0, X = +N (i.e. X^j is a "case-based" nominal projection), and X^j and CP are sisters.[5]

---

[4] These "lower" purpose clauses, incompatible with an introductory *in order*, pass the *do so* test for being complements rather than adjuncts:

  *Sue brought the professor a draft to comment on and Jim did so to proofread.

They are also idiosyncratically selected by verbs:

  *I asked John two questions to elaborate on.
  *My diet allows me an extra dessert to eat on Sunday.

Like complements and unlike adjuncts, they cannot be preposed with a comma:

  (In order) To flatter him on the train, Mary bought John Hamlet.
  *To critique on the train, Mary bought John Hamlet.

Since these complements are clausal, they often follow shorter adverbial adjuncts, as pointed out by a reviewer: *Mary bought John Hamlet yesterday to critique on the train*, parallel to *Mary persuaded John yesterday to improve his reading habits*.
[5] In prose, O must be the specifier in a CP sister to a phrasal projection of a +N category. This formulation clarifies a vague observation in Chomsky (1981, 329) that O is interpretable only if "coindexed with some argument of the matrix structure." This wrongly excludes *He's succeeded too many times for us to enumerate*, unless argument is taken to mean simply "phrase." But then Chomsky's condition only amounts to "co-indexed

In general empty categories must have their syntactic features identified in some local domain; since O is a D, the features to be identified are the phi-features of gender and number. Now, these are precisely the features that case-based but not verbal or prepositional projections carry. We can thus revise and simplify (9.6) as a principle of local identification (9.7):

(9.7)   *The phi-features of an empty operator O in SPEC(CP) must be identified within CP's phrasal sister.*[6]

I thus conclude that Extended Classical Subcategorization (2.18) licenses empty DPs (e.g., O) and that these DP are locally identified by sentence grammar, e.g., by (9.7).

The local requirement (9.7) accounts for the puzzling subject-object asymmetry that the only CP arguments of a V which can be introduced by O are a proper subset of sisters to direct objects as in (9.5). Cf:

(9.8)   *Another memo $_i$ managed [O$_i$ [to compose t $_i$ on the train]].
Another memo managed to take up my thoughts on the train.
*Hamlet $_i$ persuaded me [O $_i$ [to read t $_i$ again commuting]].
Hamlet persuaded me to read more Shakespeare commuting.
*[O $_i$ [to use t $_i$ on our salads]] would expose Bill to olive oil $_i$.
To use olive oil on our salads would expose Bill to better cuisine.

---

with XP in the matrix." This latter statement is incorrect in the other direction, since it vastly overgenerates:

> *Hamlet might be still in print to critique on the train.
> *Hamlet seemed very clever to Mary to critique on the train.
> *Mary compared another play to Hamlet to critique on the train.

The proper generalization is thus (9.6), where the +N phrase can be a direct object, a head of a relative clause in any position, or an Adjective or Noun Phrase modified by a degree phrase.

[6] I use "within" rather than "by" in (9.7), to accommodate a reviewer's example, in which identification of O is possibly by a measure phrase *inside* a sister of SPEC(CP):

> ?I think he put the treasure [too deep under the ground] O$_i$ for you to find t$_i$.

However, the judgment is not firm, so perhaps a more restrictive "by" should appear in (9.7).

The reviewer also asks how (9.7) permits an adverbial phrase to license a O in CP, since an adverbial presumably lacks phi-features needed for identification. However, it seems to me correct that (9.7) excludes identification of DPs by adverbials:

> *John reacted too stubbornly [O$_i$ to talk to t$_i$].
> *That movie depicted divorce too cleverly [O$_i$ for me to want to see t$_i$ again].

Note that the empty operators in English *finite* relative clauses also fall under (9.7) without stipulation.

When Chomsky (1977) first postulated empty operators, he assimilated them to the use of WH-operators. However, their entirely different distribution (9.7) suggests that this comparison was backwards. WH-operators include both adjectival and adverbial APs (*how clever, how soon, however long*, etc.), *whether, why,* "pied-piped" constituents, etc., and their uses in direct questions, indirect questions, conditionals and exclamations involve no feature identification. It is rather the other way around: the special use to which WH-operators are put in relative clauses is similar to empty operators, precisely because in this construction only, WH is subject to a feature identification condition reminiscent of (9.7).[7]

We now turn to a second type of locally identified empty phrase licensed by Extended Classical Subcategorization (2.18).

9.1.2 "Small pro" complement phrases

It is widely acknowledged that Romance verbal clitics are both necessary and sufficient for identifying empty phrases in a variety of both argument and adjunct positions (Kayne, 1975, Ch. 2; Borer, 1984, Ch. 5; Jaeggli, 1982).[8] In the obvious cases, the verbal host of a clitic governs an empty complement or adjunct phrase which agrees with the clitic's features, as in (9.9)–(9.10). Examples of these phrases are notated with*pro* in (9.9)–(9.10).

(9.9)   Marie veut [*vous$_i$ les$_j$* distribuer *pro$_j$ pro$_i$* pendant le week-end].
         Marie wants you-them-distribute   during the weekend
         'Marie wants to distribute them to you during the weekend.'

(9.10)   Jean *leur$_j$* semble intelligent *pro$_j$*.
         Jean them-seems intelligent
         'Jean seems intelligent to them.'

---

[7] The identification conditions of O and relative WH are different. As shown in Emonds (1979), WH-identification in relative clauses requires adjacency at some level but not sisterhood (e.g., in non-restrictive relatives, where O is excluded), permits pied-piping (but O does not), and requires a DP as a licenser. In contrast, O accepts*any* projection with phi-features (DP, NP or AP) as a licenser. Since WH requires a DP antecedent, traditional grammar correctly names these WH forms relative *pronouns.*

[8] Under a range of syntactic conditions, DPs and PPs corresponding to various Romance clitics need not be empty. When both the phrasal and the clitic position are overt, their syntactic feature values agree; this is said to constitute "clitic doubling."

Studies such as Jaeggli (1982), Borer (1984) and Rizzi (1986) argue that these *pro* are not traces of movement but rather are empty at deep structure, i.e. at the level where the verbal hosts of the clitics satisfy subcategorization.[9] If so, then subcategorization selects, in addition to overt phrases, not only the "empty operator" DPs of section 9.1.1 but also empty phrases as in (9.9)–(9.10) identified by clitic morphology.

Such empty phrases licensed by clitics which are DPs have roughly the same properties as unstressed definite pronouns in the corresponding phrasal positions in English; consequently, these empty base categories have been named "small pro." In essentially any variation of Chomsky's (1981) binding theory which utilizes pro, it then follows that a frame X, +___F can license empty pro phrases as well as overt phrasal complements of X, under some condition by means of which clitics identify the feature content of these empty phrases.

As we have seen in Chapters 6 and 7, the structural mechanism by which Romance clitics identify empty phrases must also include the italicized pairings in (9.11)–(9.13), which undermine any prima facie claim that clitics are invariably hosted by the verbs whose empty complements and/or adjuncts they license.[10]

(9.11) Elle [m_i'en_j paraît pro_i [capable pro_j]].
  She me-thereof-appears capable
  'She appears to me capable of it.'

(9.12) On y_i croit Jean [fidèle pro_i].
  One thereto-believes Jean faithful
  'People believe John faithful to it.'

(9.13) … bien qu'elle [ne $vous_i$ en_j ait lu pro_i que [la première partie pro_j]].
  … although she you-thereof-has read only the first part

---

[9] Haverkort (1989, 1993) and Sportiche (1992) again advocate versions of clitic movement for Romance. However, these analyses have serious inadequacies (Emonds, 1999, esp. sections 1.2 and 4.6).

[10] The condition for identifying features of pro has usually been formulated with some definition involving clitics in some kind of extension of government. My device of Alternative Realization, used throughout this study in a number of explanatory analyses, can be recast in terms of government, but it extends well beyond clitic systems.

In five Romance constructions ((9.11)–(9.13) exemplify adjectival complements and partitives) a verbal host such as *paraît* in (9.11) appears to govern the head rather than be the head (e.g., the adjective *capable*) whose complement is empty. Chapter 6 has discussed four paradigms exhibiting this discrepancy between the host of the clitic and the governor of the empty category, informally named "clitic-climbing." The analyses in that chapter, as well as the more detailed argumentation in Emonds (1999), show how the clitic-identified pro phrases are actually structural complements or adjuncts of the clitic's verbal host, even though they are not the semantic complements of that verb.[11] This conclusion was formulated in Chapter 6 as the Phrase Mate Hypothesis, repeated here as (9.14), and covers all cases of Romance clitic-climbing.

(9.14)   *Phrase Mate Hypothesis. Romance clitics on V_i are associated only with XP sisters to some V_i^k, where XP = DP, IP, PP, NP, AP, VP.*

---

[11] This study will not subsequently review a fifth case of climbing, of French *en* / Italian *ne* 'thereof, therefrom'. The analysis of Emonds (1999, section 2) showing how these clitics also conform to (9.14) differs from those for the other four cases of clitic-climbing discussed in preceding chapters. For completeness, I briefly and perhaps too densely summarize this argument concerning *en* / *ne*:

The main idea is that in terms of the DP-hypothesis (cf. section 1.1.3), French and Italian *de* / *di* 'of, from' can license a right-dislocated XP = PP, DP *or NP*, while right-dislocated Spanish *de* appears only in a PP. This freer French-Italian right dislocation of *de* / *di* + NP can occur even in constructions which exclude *en* / *ne*, showing that language-particular limits on right dislocation are independent of clitic properties (Kayne, 1975). Moreover, such raised, right-dislocated XP adjoin to VP in French and Italian and obey subjacency (Milner, 1978, Ch. 2), and hence result from movement.

Consider now any instance of *en* / *ne* which might be claimed to escape the V-sisterhood condition of (9.14), as in (i):

(i)   Elle n'*en* a   lu   que [la première partie *ec*]   à ses amis.
       She thereof-has read   only the first part   to her friends

But now, the empty category need not be construed as directly related to the clitic. Rather, it is a trace of a VP-adjoined right-dislocated XP, which may be overt or covert:

(ii)   Elle [n'*en* a lu que [la première partie ec_i] à ses amis, $[_{XPi}$ (de ce livre)]] .

This dislocated XP, overt or covert (i.e., doubling or not doubling the clitic), is a sister to a projection of the clitic host V, fully in accord with (9.14).

Since Spanish doesn't permit such free dislocation, this analysis correctly predicts that it can have no counterpart to *en*.

(iii)   *Ella a leido solamente el primero partido ec_i a sus amigos, $[_{XPi}$ de este libro].

The same condition applies trivially to the clitics which don't climb, i.e., which appear on the verb which governs the empty phrase which they replace.

The Phrase Mate Hypothesis is clearly the basis for some kind of local Syntactic Identification (9.1) of empty XP. However, as general as (9.14) is, any language-specific identification condition is unsatisfactory, especially since some properties of Romance clitics don't generalize across language families. We thus need to state (9.14) in some more general way.

To do this, we first observe that Romance clitics spell out under a V the features F person, number, gender and case (and ±SOURCE for the PP clitics *en* / *y*), which are features *not ordinarily associated with V*. Section 1.2.1 made precise the notion "F is ordinarily associated with B" as follows:

(9.15) =(1.5) *Canonical Realization. UG associates a few cognitive syntactic features F with each syntactic category B. These features F contribute to semantic interpretation (Logical Form) only in these "canonical positions" on B, and appear elsewhere only via language-particular lexical stipulation.*

In these terms, UG matches the features F of Romance clitics rather with DP and PP; hence, when these features appear on V, they are not canonically realized.

In the framework of this study, in particular of Chapters 4 and 5, features which are not canonically realized can be *alternatively realized*, provided they occur on closed class items, as defined in section 1.2.1:

(9.16) *A closed grammatical class is one whose members have no purely semantic features f, but only cognitive syntactic features F.*

(9.17) = (4.20) *Alternative Realization. A syntactic feature F canonically associated in UG with category B can be realized in a closed class grammatical morpheme under X^0, provided X^0 is the lexical head of a sister of B^j.*

As already argued in Chapter 6, (9.17) subsumes the Phrase Mate Hypothesis as a special case, and so AR is precisely a more general principle which can serve as the basis of local Syntactic Identification (9.1) of [$_{DP}$ pro]. To see how it applies to Romance clitics, let ∅F be the marked cognitive syntactic features of the clitics (which typically include +DEF), B the corresponding empty [$_{DP}$ pro] or PP, and X^0 the V which is host to the clitics. In accord with AR then, the clitic entries in a Romance Syntacticon specify realizations of D and P features under V.

This mechanism licenses the clitics themselves as alternatives to phrasal complements and adjuncts, but we have not yet specified why the latter may be empty in the presence of clitics, i.e., the actual identification condition for the pro phrases in (9.9)–(9.13). This is achieved by the following companion principle to Alternative Realization (Emonds, 1987).

(9.18)   *Invisible Category Principle ("ICP"). If all marked canonical features F on B are alternatively realized, except perhaps B itself, then B may be empty.*[12]

Thus, appropriate agreeing clitics on a verbal host suffice to locally identify empty phrasal sisters of some verbal projection. Such null "small pro" DP of Romance must of course satisfy the same lexical frames of V as do overt phrases. Thus these empty arguments, like the empty O of section 9.1.1, are both licensed by Extended Classical Subcategorization (2.18) and identified by a local principle of sentence grammar (9.18).[13]

9.1.3 Unifying small pro and the empty operator

One cannot but notice the similarity of these principles (9.17)–(9.18) which locally identify Romance small pro and the principle (9.7) which identifies an empty operator O, repeated for convenience.

(9.7)   *The phi-features of an empty operator O in SPEC(CP) must be identified within CP's phrasal sister.*

Both permit a grammatical (i.e. closed class) category @ to be empty if all its features are realized "nearby": under a lexical head of its sister as in (9.17)–(9.18), or on a phrase which minimally c-commands @ as in (9.7). In what follows, I try to further reduce the differences between (9.7) and (9.17)–(9.18).

---

[12] More precisely, the category features of an empty category licensed by (9.18), for example ±N and ±D, need not be alternatively realized.

[13] The ICP (9.18) permits grammatical categories to be empty, but doesn't require that they be empty. Emonds (1994) and Chapter 4 here propose that this latter step is guaranteed by a version of Economy of Derivation: the most economical of competing derivations (those with the same LF) is the one whose history has the fewest insertions of free morphemes.

To begin, (9.7) but not (9.17)–(9.18) explicitly refers to identification, i.e. co-indexing the operator O and its identifying [+N] phrase (= X^k). This distinction is easily removed by formally defining a constituent's index as one of its canonical features; this then makes Alternative Realization dependent on co-indexation. With respect to Romance this simply implies that clitics are co-indexed with their corresponding empty or doubled phrases, which is in any case commonly assumed.

A second difference is that the identifying phi-features in (9.7) aren't *alternatively realized*; they are rather agreement (9.2) or canonical (9.5) features of the italicized [+N] phrase:

(9.2)   John is *too stubborn* [O_i to talk French to t_i].

(9.5)   Mary bought John *Hamlet* [O_i to critique t_i on the train].

If we wish to subsume (9.7) under the ICP, the connection between closed classes and alternative realization should be retained in (9.17) but dropped in (9.18), which then takes the following form:

Generalized Invisible Category Principle (tentative). B may be empty if all its marked canonical syntactic features F, except perhaps B itself, are realized under X^0, where X^k is a sister of [B, F].

In one detail, this Generalized ICP still fails to identify the empty operator O. The formulation (9.7) reflects an assumption of most work on WH-movement that empty operators are in SPEC(CP) rather than in C.[14] If so and if a Generalized ICP is to subsume (9.7), then it must take the form (9.19):

(9.19)   *Generalized Invisible Category Principle. B or SPEC(BP) may be empty if all its marked canonical features F, except perhaps B itself, are realized under X^0, where X^k is a sister of B^j.*[15]

---

[14] The WH-fronting operation in Emonds (1985, Ch. 7) substitutes WH-phrases for the WH *head* of CP, thereby eliminating any need for a "doubly-filled COMP filter."

[15] Extending the ICP to configurations where a *base-generated* co-indexed constituent can effect zeroing naturally suggests the following objection: What prevents the bold XP in (i) from identifying and hence zeroing the adjacent co-indexed DPs in italics, thus wrongly yielding (ii) as their synonymous variants?

(i)   Sue considered *them* **too dark**.
      We showed **Mary** *her (own)* book.
(ii) *Sue considered too dark.
      *We showed Mary book.

The nature of the answer here seems clear. The italicized DP in (i) include in their LF

As I will not be analyzing zero specifiers in the rest of this work, I will continue citing the first formulation of the ICP (9.18), since its operation is perhaps more transparent. Nonetheless, the conflation of (9.7) and (9.18) in this subsection serves to demonstrate the no doubt unified nature of local identification, a general condition on empty subcategorized arguments (9.1).

The Generalized ICP (9.19) compares favorably to the use of "covert movement" between surface structure and LF. Some observers have informally suggested that many elements which alternatively realize some features F (e.g. a TENSE on V) can be analyzed as covertly moving to the canonical position of F (e.g. I for TENSE) in LF, an operation which they feel comes without cost by virtue of Chomsky's (1993) principle of "Procrastinate." The fact remains, however, that covert movement still must both characterize canonical positions (e.g. so that TENSE is not an LF feature of e.g. P or D or NUMERAL) *and* build the "permitted distance" expressed in (9.17) between a feature's canonical and alternative positions into the theory of LF movement; otherwise a D could move away from NP through P, V and I to C – or even to a higher D. Thus, even if LF movement is declared to be "costless," such a framework is simply concealing a need for constructs which express AR. But in addition, LF movement cannot be generalized to characterize relations between elements belonging to separate chains in LF, such as those related by (9.7); in this sense also, (9.19) is theoretically preferable to covert movement.

Returning from this somewhat heady issue to the main concerns of this chapter, it is hardly controversial to say that the empty operators O and non-subject small pro are *null DPs licensed by subcategorization, projected in the syntax and locally identified.* However, researchers have *not* agreed that *all* understood complements share such syntactic properties. So we now turn to some other elliptical constructions which have received quite different analyses.

9.2 Three hypotheses for understood complements

Classical and traditional grammarians have been intrigued by understood but unexpressed constituents, often treating them under the rubric of ellipsis. In accord with the topic of this chapter, I will focus on understood

---

interpretation some semantic role specification that counts as part of their feature content. Since these features are *not* realized by the bold phrases, the Generalized ICP or any other generalization of (9.7) does not apply. But in the case of empty operators O, this role specification is associated with the trace of O and hence doesn't block (9.19).

arguments. Generative research has proposed various ways of representing such constituents @; some representative examples occur in (9.20)–(9.22).

(9.20) Null (clausal) complement anaphora (examples from Grimshaw, 1979):
Has the Mayor resigned? John wouldn't tell me @.
@ = whether the Mayor resigned
John is telling lies again. Why didn't they say @?
@ = (that) John is telling lies again

(9.21) Understood direct objects (examples from Rizzi, 1986):
a. Italian
L'ambizione spesso spinge @ a commettere errori.
'Ambition often pushes to make mistakes'
Questa musica rende @ allegri.
'This music makes happy'
b. English
This sign cautions @ against avalanches.
I helped @ to solve the problem.

(9.22) Understood deep subjects in passives:
The meeting was started on time ({ by DP/ @ }) to please the host.
The chairs were moved around on purpose ({ by DP/ @ }).
This corn has been grown ({ by DP/ @ }) ({ voluntarily/ to stave off famine }).

The preceding subsection showed that lexical features V, +___F license null complements in Romance, provided that certain features of these phrases are realized on the verb as clitics. We can now ask, is subcategorization the basis for generating all null phrasal complements, or can some other, possibly purely semantic device sometimes provide null arguments in Logical Form?

According to the conception of Semantic Atomism in section 2.7, if some head X has a YP complement outside X, then no semantic device can supplant a simple syntactic frame X, ___F for generating X + YP. One might nonetheless postulate structurally represented understood (i.e., covert) arguments *within* X^0, thus circumventing Semantic Atomism almost trivially for this type of phenomenon.

But I wish to maintain a stronger position; namely, that subcategorization features +___F have a *monopoly* on lexically specifying understood com-

plements. In conjunction with Semantic Atomism, which requires that selection outside X is syntactic, this can be expressed as follows:

(9.23) *Any linguistically represented arguments of the head within X^0
       must be overt.*

It should be kept in mind, however, that a *head* may be lexically represented within X as null. This is exemplified in note 16 of Chapter 2 with the
denominal verbs *hammer, butter, box.* Walinska de Hackbeil (1986) develops many interesting consequences of this type of empty head analyses for
what is often termed English conversion (i.e., nouns used as verbs with no
extra morphology). So, while (9.23) excludes proposals to use theta grids or
lexical conceptual structures for representing "missing arguments" within
e.g. a verb, it does allow "abstract heads" within compound structures.[16]

Speaking now more generally of understood arguments, generative literature on this topic tends to produce one of three types of analysis:

Type (i). Some class of understood arguments is associated with some
characteristic syntactic behavior, and it is concluded that the understood
arguments are best represented as $[_{XP} \varnothing]$ in the syntax. Rizzi's analysis of
the Italian examples (9.21a) is of this type. While we need to know more
about what general principles of Universal Grammar license these empty
categories, successful analyses in terms of empty syntactic categories confirm the approach of this study.

Type (ii). Some class of understood arguments is associated with some
characteristic syntactic behavior, and it is concluded that the understood
arguments are best represented either within the semantic representation of
the lexical item or at Logical Form, but not in the syntax. Grimshaw's
analysis of the examples (9.20) is of this type. I will argue that such cases
are better treated as Type (i).

Type (iii). Some class of understood arguments exhibits no systematic
syntactic behavior, but gives rise to a range of intuitions about the meanings
of sentences in which they seemingly occur. Rizzi's examples (9.21b) are

---

[16] Besides conversion, another case of empty heads may be the productive Romance
compound pattern seen in French *vaut-rien* 'worth-nothing, good-for-nothing', *casse-
croûte* 'break-crust, snack', *garde-malade* 'watch-sick, nurse,' etc. If these nouns are
analyzed as $[[_N \varnothing] [_V [_V casse] [_N croûte]]]$, their internal structure suggestively
mimics a subject-verb-object pattern, which reflects their meaning. Since Romance compounds composed of free forms are left-headed, such an empty "subject" noun (whether
construed as animate or inanimate) inside the compound is then the head. This predicts
correctly the fact that these compounds refer to things or people which are characterized
by the predication given by the overt V-N combination in the compound.

of this type. I will argue that these intuitions are entirely insecure and misleading, and that at most various pragmatic inferences are at work. That is,
there are in fact no type (iii) understood arguments present in linguistic
structure at all.

The next two sections will discuss understood complements or "internal
arguments," as in (9.20) and (9.21). But understood subjects or "external
arguments" raise the same questions as to whether they should be represented in the syntax, only in LF, or only as part of a predicate's lexical entry.
Prime examples of such understood arguments are subjects of infinitives
("PRO") and the optionally ellipted deep or logical subjects in passive
clauses as in (9.22). Chapter 10 will treat these constructions, showing that
type (i) analyses are preferable, albeit in a way that interestingly and somewhat unexpectedly differentiates subjects from internal arguments.

9.3 Discourse identification: Grimshaw's null complement anaphora

Grimshaw (1979, section 2) discusses this phenomenon in detail. Predicates
of similar meanings differ as to whether they allow a null complement or
not:

(9.24)   Has the Mayor resigned? John wouldn't { tell me / *disclose } @.
         @ = whether the Mayor resigned
         John is telling lies again. Why didn't they { say / *announce } @?
         @ = (that) John is telling lies again
         When the game starts is a mystery. You should { find out / *figure
         out } @.
         @ = when the game starts

Grimshaw (1979, 291) comments:

> Apparently the difference between the two classes of verbs lies
> solely in whether or not they allow discourse-governed control of
> their complements; that is, whether or not they take complements
> which are *syntactically* [my emphasis, J.E.] and phonologically
> unrealized but in some sense semantically "filled".

She further shows that these understood complements illustrate certain
syntactic behavior, for instance, what she terms "lexical uniformity": "if a

predicate allows null complement anaphora at all, it allows it for the full range of complement types that it selects." Thus, these understood arguments exhibit characteristic syntactic behavior, as in analyses of types (i) or (ii) in the previous section.

Grimshaw opts for a type (ii) analysis, in which a rule of Logical Form interpretation, Williams's (1977) Null Complement Rule, "copies well-formed sentential formulae of logical form," according to phrasing for one particular example, "into the complement position for *know*."[17] At this point in her discussion (pp. 293–294), the reader might not understand exactly where this position is, but two pages later, we find that "Null complements can be analyzed as being literally null syntactically – having no syntactic realization at all." Thus, "the complement position" into which "well-formed sentential formulae of logical form" are copied exists in Logical Form and perhaps also in the lexical entries of null complement verbs, but not in syntax.

I fully agree with Grimshaw's decision that syntactic subcategorization distinguishes between predicates allowing and disallowing null complements, i.e., between *find out* and *figure out*. However, her execution of this decision is hampered by unwillingness to use *an empty syntactic phrase* for the null complement anaphora of verbs like *find out,* as the following observations show.

---

[17] For Grimshaw, copying "well-formed sentential formulae of logical form" here means that "wherever the rule copies an expression containing a variable, the operator which binds the variable must also be copied." (Grimshaw, 1979, 295) But other likely candidates for such interpretive rules, VP-ellipsis as in (i) and J. Ross's well-known sluicing rule as in (ii), fail to do this:

In VP-ellipsis (i), free variables are copied without copying the operator:

(i) What did Ann [$_{VP}$ buy in Paris], and what should we [$_{VP}$ (buy ec in Paris)]?
     You never [$_{VP}$ put the ones on sale] that you say you will [$_{VP}$(put ec on sale)].

If sluicing is done interpretively (if not, the null complement is of course syntactically represented), then the copying rule must supply a free variable in (ii), substitute a free variable for a disjunctive DP in (iii), and delete one of the free variables in (iv). In no case does the interpretation copy the operator binding the variable.

(ii) Shakespeare met John Harvard, but she didn't remember when [(S met JH ec)]
(iii) She will study S or JH, but she doesn't know which one [(she will study ec)]
(iv) She knew where and why S saw JH, but didn't know when [(S saw JH ec)]

Thus, the properties of Grimshaw's interpretive Null Complement Rule do not seem to be clearly worked out.

Other predicate classes besides those she discusses take clausal complements optionally. For example, consider manner-of-speaking verbs from Zwicky (1971).

(9.25) a. The switch flicked, and the man cried out.
        b. Unexpectedly, someone yelled.
        c. During the inspection, our son was whispering.
        d. But as we approached, the creature actually growled.

(9.26) a. The switch flicked, and the man cried out that he was guilty.
        b. Unexpectedly, someone yelled that the door had been locked.
        c. During the inspection, our son was whispering that we should leave.
        d. But as we approached, the creature actually growled that we were doomed.

This class of predicates is certainly an excellent candidate for being lexically specified as ___(CP), in present terms +___([C, -WH]). One would need an absolute a priori commitment to ellipted complements to find them in the Logical Forms of the intransitive examples, especially since intransitive uses of these manner of speaking verbs can initiate discourse.

Now, suppose that each sentence in (9.27) immediately precedes the corresponding examples of (9.25) and (9.26) in a discourse:

(9.27) a. Many felt the man was guilty. The switch flicked, ...
        b. I wasn't sure if the door had been locked. Unexpectedly, ...
        c. We thought we should leave. During the inspection, ...
        d. In our minds, we were doomed. But as we approached, ...

The corresponding sentences in *either* (9.25) or (9.26) can now serve as felicitous continuations of (9.27). However, they each mean entirely different things; that is, the examples of (9.25) cannot possibly be interpreted as anaphoric variants of those in (9.26).

Contrast this situation with Grimshaw's null complement anaphora predicates in (9.28) and (9.29). When these sentences are taken as continuations of (9.27), at least on one reading, *(9.28) are indeed anaphoric variants of those in (9.29):*

(9.28) a. The switch flicked, and it was obvious.
        b. Unexpectedly, someone found out.
        c. During the inspection, our son was sure.
        d. But as we approached, the captain didn't know.

(9.29) a. The switch flicked, and it was obvious that the man was guilty.
        b. Unexpectedly, someone found out if the door had been locked.
        c. During the inspection, our son was sure that we should leave.
        d. But as we approached, the captain didn't know we were doomed.

When Williams's Null Complement Rule applies to the sentences in (9.28) to (correctly) interpret them as (9.29), Grimshaw's framework requires only that it find predicates without a syntactic CP complement but compatible with a CP in Logical Form. Thus, it will equally well, but here entirely wrongly, also give the examples in (9.25) the readings of those in (9.26).

What has gone wrong? When treating overt clausal complements, Grimshaw posits too many possible semantic complement types, as discussed in. Ch. 2. Here semantic selection has the opposite problem. Her system has too few possibilities: a syntactic CP complement can only be overt or entirely absent. What is needed to account for (9.25)–(9.29) are two possibilities: overt presence vs. entire absence of a complement (appropriate for the manner-of-speaking verbs), or obligatory syntactic presence that can be either overt *or* covert (appropriate for her verbs allowing null complement anaphora). When such verb phrases include a null syntactic complement, it is this *syntactically represented position* which a Null Complement Rule uses to interpret as an IP or CP. This rule then has nothing to do with either manner-of-speaking verbs, which lack null complements, or with the verbs requiring overt complements, such as *disclose, figure out,* etc.

Abstracting away from particular C, the required lexical features are as follows:

(9.30)   yell, cry out, ...   V, +__(C)
         know, find out, ...   V, +__ C where C may be a null anaphor @.
         disclose, figure out, ... V, +__ C where C may not be a null anaphor.

A definitive treatment of the licensing of @ is beyond this study's scope, but without the three-way distinction in (9.30), a study of null clausal complement anaphora cannot attain even observational adequacy.[18] That is, a

---

[18] Other intransitive predicates closer in meaning to null complement verbs behave like manner-of-speaking verbs; that is, the first sentences below are not understood arguments of the second:

(i)   The Mayor actually resigned? His assistant didn't comment.
       The Mayor is telling lies again. Why don't the critics respond?
       It's a mystery as to when the game starts. So I think we can continue to debate.

semantically present but phonologically null complement cannot be equated with syntactic intransitivity. As just discussed, it can only be properly analyzed using a syntactic empty category, i.e. with a type (i) analysis.

I will now elaborate somewhat on the nature of @ in (9.30). As Grimshaw's term discourse anaphora implies, @ cannot be said to be locally identified in the syntax. So let us first clarify the use of "anaphor." Using indices to co-index constituents is a general convention in current formal grammar. The interpretation of co-indexing, however, depends on the constituents involved. Excluding traces, DP co-indexing usually indicates co-reference, while co-indexing of other constituents, including even NP sisters of D, indicates at most a Fregean-inspired identity of sense.[19] Moreover, the only *locally bound* anaphors (e.g., reflexives) are a subset of DPs with identity of reference, not of sense.

Summarizing, non-DP anaphors always involve identity of sense, and identity of sense anaphors are always discourse anaphors. Therefore, since the null anaphor @ in (9.30) is $[_C \varnothing]$ but not a DP, it is an identity of sense discourse anaphor.[20]

A certain few DPs are also limited to identity of sense rather than the expected identity of reference, i.e., their index may *not* be co-referential. Consequently, they should also be discourse anaphors. And, as illustrated in (9.31)–(9.32), unstressed (and hence necessarily non-ostensive) singular English demonstratives without an NP sister express only identity of sense and are discourse anaphors of this sort.

(9.31)   Bill bought a red wine and a white wine; he took one home (*and now I'll take that).

In (9.31), *that* can acquire reference only through contrastive stress and deixis; otherwise *that* is ill-formed when construed as identical in reference with either preceding DP, *a red wine* or *a white wine*.

Similarly, the unstressed anaphor *that* in (9.32) necessarily refers to the sense of *ridicule*, unlike the pronoun *it*, which can co-refer to the DP *military valor*.

---

[19] See Milner (1978, Ch. 1) for a related discussion in terms of virtual vs. actual reference.
[20] Appropriately then, the earlier restriction on local identification (9.1) does *not* apply to (discourse anaphoric) CP complements.

(9.1)   *Syntactic Identification. All and only empty DPs licensed by subcategorization must be locally rather than pragmatically identified.*

(9.32)   The speaker ridiculed military valor. Afterwards, Mary discussed {it/ that}.

These unstressed demonstratives as well as various non-DP anaphors are candidates for interpreted identity of sense through discourse principles of co-indexation. Only a few constituents (filled or empty) are potential discourse anaphors, just as only some Ds, namely personal pronouns and (most) demonstratives, are candidates for co-reference. Parsimony suggests that non-DP candidates for discourse anaphora carry the same feature as do definite D. Since using DEF for this unified feature might cause regrettable confusion, let me suggest DAF ("discourse anaphora feature"), which is then identical to the traditional DEF on a D with a co-referential index.

Among English identity of sense anaphors of rather general distribution specified as +DAF we find two groups. First, a group which are not lexically selected and hence occur freely, including some which are sisters to functional heads:[21]

(9.33)   one, N, +DAF, +COUNT: I sighted lions but he saw a bigger one.[22]
$\emptyset$, N, +DAF, -COUNT: She drank beer but didn't make any $\emptyset$.
$\emptyset$, V,+ DAF   She left early but he didn't $\emptyset$.
that, D, +DAF, -Index   See the examples (9.31)–(9.32).

Second, a group whose categories are those of lexically selected complements:

(9.34)   so, A, +DAF   Mary remained so for hours.
so, I, +DAF, -FACTIVE   We dared to hope so.
$\emptyset$, C, +DAF   You should find out $\emptyset$.
$\emptyset$, P, +DAF, +PATH   Mary will surely come $\emptyset$ tomorrow.[23]

---

[21] It appears that not only discourse anaphors but also bound anaphors (*each other, himself*) and pronouns pattern as maximal projections, not heads. That is, though their lexical entries contain a categorial specification X like those for any other morpheme, they don't permit other material inside XP.

[22] A reviewer observes that in addition to the English numeral *one*, I postulate an animate generic pronoun *one* in section 9.4.1 *and* this identity of sense noun anaphor (not necessarily animate). Though this might suggest that the N *one* can be raised into D, a difficulty would be that *one, someone* and *somebody* are +ANIMATE in the D position, while in the N position *one* and *body* are not +ANIMATE.

[23] There seem to be other item-particular selections of null discourse anaphors besides

Let us now focus on the null complement anaphor @ = [$_C \emptyset$] in (9.30). If Grimshaw has correctly surmised that it is a lexical property whether a CP predicate takes this null @ or not (her examples: *find* @ *out* vs. **figure* @ *out; say* @ vs. **disclose* @; *concur* @ vs. **affirm* @), then there can be no objection to predicate-specific listing of either +DAF or -DAF in lexical entries selecting C. Since further this null complement is allowed with only a minority of (frequently used) lexical items, which a language-learner can easily deduce from positive evidence, the lexical entries should list only the plus value, as in (9.35).

(9.35)　find out,　V, +___ [C, (WH), (DAF)], +___ D, …
　　　　figure out, V, +___ [C, (WH)], +___D, …
　　　　concur,　　V, +___ [C, (DAF)], +___ with^D, …
　　　　affirm,　　V, +___ [C], +___ D, …

Such null complements appear to be the only English discourse anaphors of category CP, since both the null anaphor in "sluicing" and the clausal anaphor *so* are arguably IPs, and the overt DPs *it* and *that* are the other anaphors which can refer to CPs. Consequently, the combination [C, DAF] can probably be licensed in English only by virtue of entries as in (9.35). These entries thus succeed in making those of (9.30) more explicit.

9.4 Rizzi's generic null objects

9.4.1 Null objects with the features of *one(s)*

Consider again the understood arguments @ in Rizzi's Italian examples (9.21a).

(9.21)　a.　L'ambizione spesso spinge @ a commettere errori.
　　　　　　'Ambition often pushes (one) to make mistakes'
　　　　　　Questa musica rende @ allegri.
　　　　　　'This music makes (one) happy'

---

those treated by Grimshaw. For example, *go* and *come* but not other motion verbs allow a null Goal PP:

(i)　Has Mary been into the office yet? No, but she is {going/ coming/ *driving/ *riding/ *getting (herself)/ *heading} tomorrow.

Rizzi (1986, 503–512) forcefully argues that these understood direct objects are syntactically present as null DPs with the features [HUMAN, GENERIC, ±PLURAL], i.e. in favor of a type (i) analysis of section 9.2. Additionally, he establishes that this "null generic pronoun" is an instance of small pro, with telling examples (his 25–26) demonstrating disjoint ref erence. His analysis thereby shows the existence of null object phrases (small pro) which (i) can satisfy subcategorization, and (ii) are not identified by an overt clitic.[24]

The English translation of this Italian null generic is *one,* not meaning 'one of them', but rather (roughly) 'people'. Its distribution as an object parallels that of the Italian null generic, most strikingly in several paradigms which Rizzi relates to a semantic, somewhat vague "affectedness constraint" (his section 5). To show these parallels, I reproduce Rizzi's contrasts in (9.36a-e) by replacing Italian null objects with the English pronominal DP *one.* These translations preserve his contrasts perfectly. As discussed in his note 38, longer introductory contexts (irrelevantly) ameliorate certain starred cases.

(9.36)   a. This exercise keeps one healthy.
             *Often the doctor considers one healthy.
         b. Certain decisions can make one more responsible.
             *Lately the government believes one more responsible.
         c. Sometimes Mario impresses one.
             *Often Gianni admires one.
         d. It is unlikely that the director can force one to work harder.
             A failure can deprive one of confidence.
             Before operating, a surgeon covers one with a white cloth.
             Gianni photographs one nude.
             *Gianni meets one angry.
             *Gianni meets one young.
         e. Gianni makes one happy.
             *Gianni sees one happy.
             *Gianni believes one happy.

These parallels reveal two things: (i) affectedness contrasts are *independent of licensing an empty category in Italian*; Rizzi's grammaticality

---

[24] An invisible DP identified by Alternative Realization (9.17) can be considered to define the binding theory concept "small pro." Clearly, AR is more general in scope than a binding theory statement covering only a particular subcase of DP.

judgments related to affectedness concern not empty categories but rather the distribution of the feature complex [HUMAN, GENERIC, ±PLURAL], which is Ø in Italian but overt in English. Both forms are grammatical under the same conditions. (ii) Therefore the closest English correlate to the Italian null DP object is generic *one*, and not some ephemeral unprojected arguments of a disparate collection of English intransitive sentences (cf. section 9.4.3 below).

Additionally, Rizzi's semantic condition that such sentences have a "generic time reference" equally well applies to the overt English generic object in translations of his examples:

(9.37)   a.   A general can force one to obey his orders.
             Good music reconciles one with oneself.
        b.   *At five, the general forced one to obey.
             *Yesterday's concert reconciled one with oneself.

Rizzi's arguments in favor of a null generic morpheme in direct object position in Italian seem incontrovertible and are in fact strengthened by the fact that exact translations of his examples reveal its overt counterpart *one* in English.

Let us now discuss briefly the feature composition of these generic objects. As Rizzi observes (his section 1.5), a so-called arbitrary interpretation on a D is nothing more than its features [HUMAN, GENERIC, ±PLURAL]. He further attributes +HUMAN, as well as appropriate person and gender specifications, to universal conditions on his feature GENERIC.

A question here is whether Rizzi's choice of GENERIC is a sufficiently general feature for his feature matrix. Later in his essay, he wishes to find a single device to encompass both null generic objects and certain Italian null expletive subjects "pro" of secondary predication, as in (9.38):

(9.38)   Gianni ritene [*pro* probabile che Mario venga].
         'Gianni believes likely that Mario comes'

What seems to me to unite these (null) expletives and generics and furthermore suffices to characterize them as a class is the more familiar feature -DEFINITE (-DEF). Rizzi hesitates to replace GENERIC with -DEF because he is concerned that null "quasi-argument" expletives referring to the weather and the time might also be -DEF; yet these are *not* allowed in secondary predication:

(9.39)   *Considero [*pro* presto]. *Ritengo [*pro* troppo tardi per tornare].
'I consider (it) early.'   'I believe (it) too late to come back.'

But suppose DEF means "already has a reference in the conceptual space of the speaker." From this point of view, since the weather and the time are permanently available to a speaker as fixed concepts, they should be analyzed as definite.[25]

In contrast, a D which is -DEF either (i) lacks marked phi-features and hence reference (e.g. it is a grammatical expletive as in (9.38)), or (ii) has reference but lacks previously fixed reference. When an indefinite D is additionally pronominal (i.e. without an NP sister), then it cannot actualize the virtual reference of a lexical N either (Milner, 1978, Ch. 1). Consequently, the only possible reference for an indefinite D without an NP sister must be generic. Thus, [D, -DEF] has both and only the generic and non-referential interpretations, as required. [26]

Moreover, this is the minimal feature set needed for null generic pronouns, since, according to Rizzi, generics are universally +HUMAN and "intrinsically plural in Italian" (his note 3).

His section 3.3 additionally argues that these null pro must be case-marked accusative rather than nominative. In an appendix, he observes that Italian dative objects can also be null generics, especially in causative sentences where a preposition case-marks an embedded overt subject. Rizzi summarizes (1986, 551): "Italian has an understood null dative with *arb* interpretation that has the same formal and interpretive properties of the null direct object; in particular, it can control and bind." I conclude then that the minimal feature matrix which predicts all the properties of Italian null objects is [D, -DEF, -NOMINATIVE], and that the same matrix serves to characterize the English generic object *one*.

Of course, a central argument for the syntactic presence of the Italian null generic object is that it satisfies subcategorization. I claim throughout this chapter that null subcategorized DPs always additionally conform to (9.1).

(9.1)   *Syntactic Identification. All and only empty DPs licensed by subcategorization must be locally rather than pragmatically identified.*

---

[25] Chomsky (1981, 324) first justifies such an interpretation of DEFINITE, using the cited phrase. But he then rejects it on the basis that the *it* of "weather" and "time", unlike other definites, can't be questioned. But if these concepts are permanently referenced as fixed concepts, it follows that a question as to their reference is senseless.

[26] The pronominal feature -___N is an unmarked property of D, according to a general convention of subcategorization.

According to this claim, the feature matrix [D, -DEF, -NOM] of the Italian null generic must be locally identified. Some relevant Romance – English contrasts suggest the nature of this identification:[27]

(9.40)

Syntactically projected arguments:	Italian	French	English
A. Null pronominal [+DEF] subjects, identified by nom. clitics or agreement	yes	yes	no, DP filled
B. Null pronominal [+DEF] objects, identified by accusative clitics	yes	yes	no, DP filled
C. Null pronominal generic [-DEF] subjects, identified by a nom. clitic	yes clitic=*si*	yes clitic=*on*	no, DP = *one*
D. Null pronominal generic [-DEF] objects, identified by ???	yes	yes	no, DP = *one*

Table (9.40) suggests two questions: first, why do only null generic objects lack identifiers, and second, could the Romance – English split in row D be reversed without loss of generality? According to Rizzi's analysis it could be, since a separate parameter is at work in the two systems *for only null objects.* A more restrictive hypothesis by far is that null subjects and objects in Romance are all similarly licensed; that is, Romance has (special) clitics on verbs and English does not. To make the above table reflect this (simultaneously answering the first question as well), we need only amend row D as follows:

(9.41)   *A Romance zero clitic identifies null subcategorized pronominal generic/ expletive objects i.e., [D, -DEF, -NOM].*

This zero clitic alternatively realizes the features [-DEF, -NOM] and licenses null DPs in object position by the Invisible Category Principle (9.18).

  Should one be apprehensive about postulating that a (relatively un-marked) member of a paradigm of bound clitics has a zero morph (9.42) alongside several overt clitics, e.g. Italian (9.43)?

(9.42)   ∅, -DEF, -NOMINATIVE, +<___V>[28]

---

[27] French and Italian diverge with respect to these generic pronouns only in that the French generic subject clitic *on* is not homonymous with its reflexive clitic (*se*).

[28] Recall that the subcategorization notation in Chapter 4 indicates prefixation on a host category X by +<___X>.

(9.43)   lo, +DEF, +ACCUSATIVE, +<___V>
         si, -DEF, +NOMINATIVE, +<___V>
         ...

Since zero morphs are quite common in paradigms of bound morphemes, I do not hesitate to propose that Italian null objects (generic and expletive) are simply null DPs (small pro) bound by clitics like other null objects in Romance. In fact, we now can better situate Rizzi's observation that null generic objects do not move; they fail to move for the same reason as Italian objects identified by overt accusative clitics undergo no NP-movement or movement to e.g., a focus position.

Under this view, the syntactically empty null generic object of Italian satisfies subcategorization entirely analogously to how its overt English counterpart *one* does so. The lack of syntactic null objects in English is a special case of English lacking special clitics, not the result of some separate "parameter." The indefinite accusative zero clitic of Italian locally identifies a null object phrase, just as do all other Italian object clitics. Moreover, the Italian null clitic itself results from an absolutely minimal lexical entry (9.42), necessitating no theoretical or conceptual complication of any sort.

We therefore have seen a third type of a null argument DP conforming to syntactic subcategorization (2.18) and local Syntactic Identification (9.1).

9.4.2 A note on zero morphs in the Syntacticon

The existence of a null object clitic in Italian (9.42) fails to surprise precisely because zero morphs are extremely common across languages in paradigms of bound morphemes. For example, the heavily inflected German indefinite and possessive determiners *ein* 'a(n)', *kein* 'no', *dein* 'your' etc. are unsuffixed for the matrix [+NOM, -FEM, -PLUR]; in many agglutinative languages with overt case paradigms, the nominative or absolutive case has a zero affix (e.g., Turkish); the third person singular present indicative of the otherwise notably inflected French verb is zero, etc.

Syntactic and distributional evidence moreover suggests that unmarked or "elsewhere" feature combinations of syntax zero morphs most frequently realize. To verify this match between "unmarked in syntax" and "phonologically unrealized," consider that both PAST and MODAL in English (and most languages) are phonologically overt, while present tense need not be. On the syntax side, an indication of the unmarked character of the values [-PAST, -MODAL] is the frequent observation that the present tense is really only "non-past," since it often expresses future time, general truth, or habit and repetition which need only include some non-pasts (*Sue smokes* vs. *Sue smoked*). That is, the present tense is a sort of elsewhere form for asserting (in a main clause declarative) that a proposition is "realis." [29] Moreover, when the distinction ±PAST is neutralized, as has occurred historically in the subjunctive mood in much of Romance, the present but not the past tense survives.

Benveniste (1966) establishes in more depth this cross-linguistic tendency of zero morphs to realize feature combinations which syntax itself reveals are unmarked. He focuses on showing that third person and singular for finite verbs are the grammatically unmarked values. Spanish verbal morphology furnishes an easily understood example of this correlation. A Spanish verbal root is followed by a mood vowel (*a, e, i*), then a tense marker (as in French, the syntactically unmarked present tense is also a zero) and then finite agreement with the subject. The present tense paradigm of this system in (9.44) contains the characteristic third singular zero morph:

(9.44)   VERB + MOOD + TENSE + AGREEMENT: SINGULAR or PLURAL

		SINGULAR	PLURAL
	1st:	u^{30}	mos
stem + mood vowel + $\emptyset$ +	2nd:	s	is
	3rd:	$\emptyset$	n

In other words, Spanish 3rd singular present tenses end in their mood vowel followed by two zero morphs for present tense and agreement.

In contrast, a full paradigm of say nominal case where only some random oblique case has a zero affix is actually quite rare. Although situations exist in which most of a paradigm consists of zero morphs (e.g. German case endings on N), such paradigms seem no more frequent than those with a nearly full range of overt realizations. Thus, acquisition of zero morphs should be privileged in unmarked syntactic configurations but not elsewhere.

A question thus arises as to whether the feature complex [-DEF, -NOM] of the Italian/ French indefinite null clitic is an unmarked combination within a paradigm of clitic forms. In fact, this seems likely: (i) Casa (1993) argues that definite DPs are unmarked in subject position in Romance (and

---

[29] +MODAL includes at least the class of features which can be realized as English modals and as Romance futures, conditionals and subjunctives, i.e., FUTURE, etc. O. Jespersen's more revealing terms are *realis* for -MODAL and *irrealis* for +MODAL.

[30] The first singular Spanish suffix *o* is plausibly a indicative mood vowel assimilated to an underlying final *u* derived from an Indo-European *-m* (that is, vowel + *u* $\Rightarrow$ *o*).

we note, often null) while indefinite DPs are unmarked in object positions. (ii) Karimi (1990) shows that DP specificity, no doubt akin to +DEF, is overtly marked in Persian in both direct and indirect object positions, while non-specific objects have no overt marker. If indefiniteness is thus unmarked on objects, the Romance null object clitic may require no learning at all; once a language learner sets up a clitic paradigm in the lexicon, acquisition of such a zero morph, in the absence of positive evidence, may be automatic.

Though it might seem at this point that a zero morph *can only* represent a syntactically unmarked feature matrix, English verb agreement reminds us that sometimes an unmarked feature matrix can be lexicalized while marked counterparts are not. That is, although Benveniste's correlation "syntactically unmarked ~ phonetic zero" holds widely, we are equally sure that a zero morph can also realize matrices with (few) marked features, because both PLURAL and 1st and 2nd Person agreement on an English present tense is zero. Thus, even if the matrix [-DEF, -NOM] (9.42) for the Italian null generic / expletive clitic should turn out to contain a marked feature, its existence is not thereby any less certain.

9.4.3 The asystematic "understood objects" of English

I return again to the issue of the understood arguments themselves. Rizzi (1986) contrasts Italian's null generic object not with its overt English counterpart but rather with a range of putative understood objects in English which, unlike in Italian, are "unprojected arguments," i.e. interpreted in LF even though not present in syntax. He proposes in particular that the examples in (9.45) contain syntactically unprojected ("lexically saturated") object arguments, which I notate x.[31]

(9.45)   a. John is always ready to [please x].
         b. This sign [cautions x] against avalanches.
            Yesterday, John [warned x] against this mistake.
         c. This [leads x] to the following conclusion.
         d. John [helped x] to solve the problem.
         e. John [ate x].

To my mind, the only common property in (9.45) is that these intransitive verbs all happen to have transitive usages, and that other arguments (sub-

---

[31] (9.45) contains all Rizzi's examples of unprojected direct objects in English except for one of the null complement anaphora discussed above in section 9.3. His understood indirect objects (of a somewhat different nature) are treated here in the next chapter.

jects and PPs) maintain their semantic roles across this variation. Otherwise, unlike the understood generic objects of Italian, the heterogeneous "understood arguments" of the English examples (9.45) fail to display any of the systematic linguistic properties (i)-(iv) of the former.

(i) Animacy and identification of the object. Recall that Italian understood generic objects are +HUMAN, and any pragmatically understood objects in (9.45a-b) are as well. But the predicates in (9.45c-d) are *not systematically* +HUMAN:

(9.46)   Buds lead to flowers.
         Inconceivable density led to the Big Bang.

In fact, it is hard to imagine any reference for objects in (9.46): *Inconceivable density led (?the universe) to the Big Bang. Buds lead (?plants) to flowers.*

   In *help to VP* (e.g. 9.45d), any understood participant intervening between the verbs is purely pragmatically deduced and again need not be animate. Suppose a family business is in trouble from bad location, loss of interest in the product, etc. On top of it all, cousin Sue, pressed into serving customers, alienates several of them. It can be said *Sue is helping to { ruin the business / bring on bankruptcy }.* Is there an understood lower agent here, perhaps fate? Or imagine a beach cottage whose lawn is slowly being covered with sand; one could comment *The storm helped to bury the lawn under the sand.* A paraphrase for *help to VP* is *contribute to VP,* in which a pragmatically deduced argument would certainly be inanimate.

   If the verbs in (9.45b) are understood transitively, perhaps the verb *speak* also always has a language as a direct object, i.e. if *Mary spoke to John,* Mary was no doubt speaking some language, or thought she was. This kind of thinking seems to trail off in speculation rather than clarify language structure.

(ii) A role in binding and control. Any putative object x of *help* in (9.45d) is syntactically inert and thereby contrasts with an overt object:

(9.47)   Mary came downtown quite distraught. I { helped her / *helped }
         to buy herself some good books.
         Sue's company is in big trouble. So I will { help her / *help } to
         work overtime to save the company.

These contrasts show it is linguistically misleading to propose an "unprojected argument" in *help to VP.*

(iii) Generic time reference. Rizzi (his note 12) observes that the "generic time reference" of his Italian paradigms carries over to English *only* in (9.45a), but not in (9.45b-c) and most certainly not in (9.45d-e). But generic time reference gives no more reason to speak of an object in these sentences than in their (stylistically unmarked) adjectival counterparts:

(9.48)   At parties, Bill's antics really amuse(*d).
          At parties, Bill's antics were very amusing.
          John is always as pleasing as one could want.

(iv) Interpretations of the understood object. Rizzi's ample observations (his note 6) about the non-equivalence of intransitive *eat* and *eat something* lead, if anywhere, to the conclusion that intransitive *eat* has no understood argument at all. Neither do, I imagine, similar optionally transitive verbs like *belch, breathe, stretch* or *vomit,* even though one physically belches something (?carbon dioxide) while a monster might belch hydrogen sulfide, etc.

This wealth of speculations about meanings and appropriateness in (9.45) have no *focus*; they suggest no pattern or paradigm beyond the vagaries of simple transitive / intransitive alternations. For these unprojected arguments we have thus what section 9.2 here calls a type (iii) analysis: a range of intuitions about meanings but no systematic behavior. *Thus, there is no reason to propose any argument x in (9.45) at any level of linguistic representation.*

I conclude that no linguistic representation of English sentences like (9.45) contains "unprojected" direct arguments. Any understood participants in the events described follow from pragmatic facts like only humans can read, so that signs caution only humans; a physical substance is involved in eating (for those not deranged), etc. Thus, a natural language predicate having a linguistic argument in a given sentence is equivalent to it having a syntactically represented one.

9.4.4 (Appendix) Licensing in the lexical labyrinth

Rizzi's theoretical analysis of the difference between Italian and English covert objects is as problematic as his English data in (9.45). This analysis, segregated in sections 1.6 (English) and 3 (Italian) from the richly empirical treatment of his Italian paradigms, presupposes intricately structured lexical argument structures, distorts any plausible notion of "reference," and utilizes sui generis "parameter setting" divorced from properties of lexical items. Superficially his parameter sounds elegant: broadly speaking, theta roles are assigned to covert direct objects in the syntax in Italian[32] but "in the lexicon" in English.

However, the problem is that direct objects don't exist "in the lexicon"; they exist rather in trees. Nor in Rizzi's lexicon are there even subcategorization frames corresponding to objects, since he espouses a vague and semi-formalized model of theta grids. Consequently, to construct a lexical parallel to an operation on direct objects, Rizzi must try to somehow reproduce the syntax of "projected arguments" in terms of lexical "unprojected arguments." And as in many lexical theorizations, auxiliary terms like saturation, absorption, direct theta role, theta role indexation, unprojected theta role and a variable range of theta role names are introduced to veil the complexity and/ or inadequacy of the actual ad hoc mechanisms.[33] The lexical shadow of direct object is "direct theta role," i.e. the role co-indexed with a projected syntactic direct object DP.

Rizzi's account then crucially depends on a contrast in how Italian and English index these "direct theta roles." Yet used independently of syntax this term is actually meaningless, since theta grids or argument structures often link *different* theta roles with direct objects: *John taught {math/ children}; John paid {bills/ Sam}; John asked {Sam/ questions}*. So if a certain English verb lacks a syntactic object (*John taught; John paid; John was afraid to ask*), direct theta role isn't even defined much less assigned, and is thus of no help in setting up a parallel with an Italian transitive verb.

This difficulty is only the first to be encountered. Putting it aside, the foundation on which a language-particular parameter will be stated is a proposed universal rule (Rizzi's 20). If we replace various lexicalist terms with their definitions, the principle has a quite ad hoc flavor:

(9.49) *Associate "arb", i.e., the D-features [HUMAN, GENERIC, $\pm PLU$-RAL], with whichever theta role within the theta grid inside a lexical entry for V is to be (or perhaps can be) assigned to V's direct object.*

---

[32] The first part of the formulation can hardly be faulted, since it is just a special case of Full Interpretation (2.35).

[33] The futility of theta role based discussion is particularly apparent in Rizzi's discussion of "affectedness" in section 3, where "theme" divides into "theme$_1$" and "theme$_2$", and "subjects of small clauses" must also be distinguished as "affected" or "not affected" by the verb of the higher clause. As indicated earlier in the text, these considerations relate to determining conditions for all generic objects, overt as well as covert.

Since this rule's "application amounts to saturating the internal theta role" (Rizzi, 1986, 509) and "a theta role is saturated when it is associated with some referential content" (508), *(9.49) associates referential content with a category within a subpart of a lexical entry for a verb.*

The idea that a verb (not even a sentence) contains reference, and moreover that of [HUMAN, GENERIC,±PLURAL] is in itself a second difficulty. But even if we could understand this, (9.49) introduces a third confusion between lexical entries and sentences. Lexical entries remain with us permanently and can never be said to "have reference." Rather, only certain constituents in particular sentences, presumably DPs in most cases, have reference, and particular sentences do not remain with us; they vanish in seconds, as does their "referential content."

As will be seen below, however, these last two problems concern only Rizzi's use of (9.49) as a lexical procedure for unprojected arguments. But since his evidence for unprojected English "direct theta role arguments" has just been rejected, I limit myself to very briefly critiquing how (9.49) could apply "in the lexicon," presumably to a V. Since its direct theta role, whichever one it is, must be "saturated," (9.49) actually assigns reference to the theta role itself, *inside* the lexical entry of V. What could this mean? (i) An English (but not Italian) speaker permanently associates not only sense but also reference with an entry for *warn*, but not with say the verb *address,* since the latter must license a syntactic object. Or (ii): Some as yet unformalized assignment of reference follows lexical selection but precedes syntax. Both alternatives would be unnecessary and murky complications of lexical theory.

Let us see now if Rizzi's analysis of Italian covert syntactic generic objects fares better. For them, Rizzi proposes (512) that *arb* is not a referential index after all, but simply the feature set [HUMAN, GENERIC, ±PLURAL]. So at this point (9.49) assigns only nominal features, not reference, to a category within a subpart of a lexical entry for a verb. The analysis of Italian is then that (9.49) "applies in the syntax." In more detail, lexical insertion first attaches all or part of a verb's (permanently stored) lexical entry, including its contextual features, to a V node in a tree. Moreover, some theta role name in this somehow structured entry gets co-indexed with a DP object. Then during a syntactic derivation, (9.49) attaches the *arb* feature set to whichever theta role name under V is co-indexed with that object. That is, applying in the syntactic component, (9.49) attaches a quite particular syntactic feature matrix to a purely semantic category inside a lexical entry associated with V.

Once these features are safely associated with a "direct theta role" (inside V), the features of a generic object DP, not too surprisingly, are also located on V (or rather, somewhere within V). This somewhat wearisome journey through the recesses of a verb's putative argument structure has thus finally allowed V to *identify* the features on Italian covert generic DP. Consequently, such a DP may be empty, by Rizzi's (41), his separate principle which licenses small pro essentially analogously to the ICP (9.18).

One may compare this complex method of identifying a subcategorized DP with that in section 9.4.1. The Italian lexical entry (9.42) stipulates a phonetically empty but syntactically unremarkable clitic, [-NOM, -DEF]. These are the only features that it need identify on the direct object in order to satisfy the Invisible Category Principle (9.18). This empty clitic entry is both simpler and more plausible than principle (9.49) and requires no series of highly questionable theoretical constructs and assumptions. Nor do (9.42) or the syntactic identification provided by the ICP (9.18) presuppose the existence of theta grids, which Chapter 2 has argued serve neither any semantic nor any syntactic purpose.

9.5 The impotence of the lexical item

In section 9.2, I observed that research on implicit arguments has variously proposed that those with characteristic syntactic behavior are sometimes represented syntactically (type i) and sometimes only lexically or in Logical Form (types ii and iii). By examining a number of respected analyses in the grammatical literature, I hope to have demonstrated that *systematically motivated* implicit arguments are all best and most parsimoniously analyzed as type (i), in syntax.

Nonetheless, previous research has rightly been cautious about freely postulating empty syntactic categories whenever some intriguing paradigm seems to suggest one. I endorse the caution, and have argued that features of any empty complement DPs in particular are subject to stringent Syntactic Identification (9.1). The following recapitulates these identification conditions and some empty phrases which exemplify them.

(i) A sisterhood condition (9.7) identifies empty operator DPs which move to certain clause-initial COMPs (section 9.1.1).[34]

(ii) A principle of Alternative Realization (9.17) of features by nearby closed class items (those characterized by cognitive syntactic features F) permits closed classes of bound (Romance) clitics on V to express and thus

---

[34] More needs to be said about the operators which bind parasitic gaps; they are apparently deleted prior to Logical Form, rather than identified.

identify the features of null DP and PP complements and adjuncts (Emonds, 1999).

(iii) For some relatively unmarked features, clitics themselves may be zero morphs in a clitic paradigm. A generic animate DP object identified in this way is indeed syntactically present in Italian, as Rizzi (1986) shows, though he doesn't relate this DP to a null clitic.

(iv) In Chapter 10, we will see that certain subject DPs without case (PRO) also require syntactic identification (so-called obligatory control): those in clauses selected by +___V. Other structurally present PRO subjects including subjects of imperatives and understood agents in verbal passives may be identified pragmatically.

Thus, in the framework developed in this study, *empty syntactic phrases are the only allowed notion of understood argument of X^0*; no additional formal devices permit "unprojected arguments" inside lexical entries of X^0 or projection of arguments only at Logical Form.[35] Moreover, the notion of operating on elements of a given sentence "in the lexicon" (e.g., saturating a theta role) is taken as senseless. The lexicon is a permanent inventory of information unaffected by use: any element in the lexicon is not in use, and any elements used in a sentence are by definition not in the lexicon.

Essays touching on the design of linguistic theory often broach the question of the trade-off in descriptive power between different components of the grammar. For example, the first expansion of the lexicon in Chomsky (1965) to include subcategorization accompanied a reduction in the expressive richness of the base component, and successive enrichments of the lexicon have inevitably been rhetorically motivated by the goal of "constraining syntax."[36] Consequently, the reader may feel that restricting formal lexical devices, as has been argued for here, to essentially what was current a quarter century ago must necessarily expand the expressive power of syntax.

But in fact, the present work restricts the lexicon not by increasing syntactic expressive power, but rather by clarifying it. Previously, no unified hypothesis has proposed exact conditions for identifying features of empty arguments, but now Syntactic Identification (9.1) and the Generalized ICP (9.19) are candidates. Previously, one accepted zero morphs in paradigms

---

[35] That is, within the extremely constrained format for lexical items adopted as (2.14), "unprojected argument" becomes synonymous with "unsatisfied subcategorization frame," i.e. ill-formedness if the frame is obligatory. Except for expletives, all and only syntactically present arguments are interpreted at LF.

[36] However, the use of syntactic data and argumentation in many efforts is so sparse as to occasion the suspicion that an unstated goal is rather its elimination.

of bound morphemes, and now an expected zero morph has taken its place in the paradigm of Romance object clitics. Previously, obligatory control has required a separate statement, but the next chapter will show that it follows from general subcategorization theory and the EPP (1.17). Chapter 10 will also show that null subjects of imperatives, long neglected within syntactic theory, actually exemplify expected properties of syntactically projected optional PRO. Similarly, ever since abandoning lowering transformations, grammatical theory has left aside the properties of postposed agents in passives; they also will be shown to have the properties of a syntactically projected case-less PRO.

In fact, the proposed drastic reduction in the expressive power of the lexicon to statements of the form (2.14) requires only one "trade-off," undertaken in the final chapter: the distribution of pragmatically identified caseless null DP must be generalized (simplified, but not really enriched). Previously, pragmatic identification of PRO_{arb} has applied only to subjects of infinitives; now it will extend to any caseless subjects of verbs, imperatives and passive participles as well as infinitives. So in fact a much impoverished view of the lexicon has been implemented without enriching the syntax or any other component.

Since both the data patterns and the theoretical tools used in this study to constrain the lexicon have been available through most of the generative era, one may wonder at the enthusiasm shown for elaborate and highly stipulative semantically based lexicons. I conjecture that the root of the competing richer conceptions of how lexical entries "work" – projecting and transferring theta roles and linking indices in various directions, externalizing and internalizing and incorporating arguments, absorbing and saturating cases and theta roles, etc. – is a fundamental lack of scientific confidence. Being unsure about the syntax of the simple clauses studied in traditional grammar, the field wants to keep the developing theory of "A-bar" and long-distance dependencies uncontaminated by potentially false steps in clause-internal syntax – and yet hopes to treat traditional grammatical issues in an interesting way.

Consequently, analysts mentally construct a kind of informal or play copy of clausal structure in something called "the lexical entry" of the proposition's head – in most cases studied, the verb.[37] Even as syntax is thus kept "pure" and "free of meaning," one is now at liberty to use proposition-

---

[37] Grimshaw (1990, Ch. 1) makes this explicit: her argument structures are not lexical constructs but a linguistic level distinguished from deep structure by virtue of operating in terms of semantically based principles.

like lexical entries to recycle all the semantics-based shibboleths that early generative grammar was at such pains to destroy. In the lexicon's "argument structures," the primitives are again semantic roles, all arguments are visible and nothing is inferred, each predicate and all its arguments are kept neatly segregated from the surrounding syntactic complexities; and in syntax, each lexical head with its family of arguments is conveniently housed in its private small clause. Everything irrelevant to the "core of meaning" is kept out, such as the many inconvenient and nearly meaningless grammatical morphemes that seem to clutter actual sentences.[38]

But in fact, there is just no evidence that any semantic or conceptual structures associated with say individual verbs have "argument slots" or are otherwise propositional in form. Beyond broadly classifying different predicates by means of a few primitive features (e.g. ±STATIVE, ±FACTIVE), who knows what verbs "mean"? Perhaps meanings associated with verbs contain little circles and sticks with oriented arrows; perhaps they are three dimensional in some irreducible way, etc. The entire enterprise of associating syntax-like propositional structures with lexical entries is at bottom only an arbitrary assumption.

It is better to admit that syntactic method and theory construction are the only formal disciplines which can constrain grammatical and lexical speculation, so they are the best point of departure. If we wish to study lexical properties, we should worry less about how findings might entail modifying accepted views of "pure" interclausal syntax. Rather than assuming that lexical items are like syntax, except more transparent and common-sensical, we should assume almost nothing about the structure of lexical items, beyond their actual co-occurrence properties for which we have concrete evidence: their contextual subcategorizations.

---

[38] Hand in glove with re-introducing common-sense "semantic syntax" in the form of propositional lexical entries there has again emerged a sense that syntax itself is not actually the basis of real or deep language. In this view, the wealth of syntactic data only obscures real organizing principles, which are in a different, more speculative realm.

A modified version of this conception, entirely compatible with much contemporary syntactic research, is that syntactic theory is useful principally for relations at a distance and logical notions such as quantification, co-reference, etc., while head-complement relations are projections from the (uninvestigated, unconstrained, or purely semantic) lexicon.

Under either view, a syntactically covert argument seems conceptually out of place, some kind of mixing of syntax with "deeper" semantic patterns of head-complement relations. Thus, the covert syntactic category is welcome perhaps in analyzing relations at a distance, but has become suspect if it is motivated mainly by clause-mate phenomena.

Chapter 10
Understood subjects: Generalizing Pro

10.1 Subcategorization and obligatory control

The previous chapter treated a range of null *internal* arguments: null complement anaphora (CPs) and three types of empty DPs: the base-generated empty operator O, the so-called "small pro" licensed by e.g. Romance clitics, and the Romance null generic object. These were all shown to be constituents in syntactic trees rather than "unprojected arguments." In addition, a feature identification condition (9.1) set stricter limits on the distribution of empty DPs (in English-type languages at least; cf. note 1 of Chapter 9) than on other, "identity of sense" anaphora.

(9.1)   *Syntactic Identification. All and only empty DPs licensed by subcategorization must be locally rather than pragmatically identified.*

The device proposed for enforcing (9.1) was a Generalized Invisible Category Principle (9.19).

This final chapter turns to understood *external* arguments in English, namely subjects. From one perspective, a chapter on subjects in a book on subcategorization could be judged as out of place, since subjects are generally taken to be licensed not by lexical selection but rather by a device such as the Extended Projection Principle (1.17). However, there are two good reasons for including them in the discussion. First, Chapter 9 claims that understood complements are syntactically present in trees and hence generated by subcategorization frames. If understood subjects are also shown to be systematically present in the syntax, my approach will support a more general claim: *the only understood arguments are syntactic ones.* Second, if some formal device such as (9.1) which licenses empty complements turns out to actually play a role in the distribution of null subjects, its full import can be appreciated only in terms of a theory of *all* types of empty arguments.

Except in a few root contexts, subjects of English finite verbs must be overt, so this chapter won't treat finite clauses.[1] To study null subjects in

---

[1] An English finite clause either has a morpheme realized in I or has a covert I which licenses a tense ending by AR (9.17). In both cases, SPEC(IP) is then available as a DP

English, one necessarily concentrates on non-finite forms: imperatives, passive participles and *to*-infinitives.[2] My claim is that if these subjects are not overt, they are still represented in trees as null DPs.

The English null subjects that have received by far the most attention are those of *to*-infinitives, which Chomsky (1981) has called PRO. According to arguments in Rosenbaum (1967) and Koster and May (1982), *to*-infinitive clauses are sentences (IP) and *to* is the non-finite realization of I. These IP like their finite cousins immediately dominate a subject DP, either understood (PRO) or expressed. Since the reasoning establishing that *to*-infinitives are IPs and contain PRO subjects is solid and widely-known, I will not summarize it further. I thus take the syntactic nature of null PRO as established; the task here is rather to explain what permits and requires PRO in various contexts.[3]

The most pertinent factor for answering this question is a bifurcation in the class of PRO, which seems related to the widely agreed property that PRO does not receive case like overt subjects do. Lobeck (1986) proposes that this lack of case results from *to* being inserted under I only in the PF component; in the syntax an infinitival I is then empty and incapable of assigning case.[4] But whatever the source of this defective case assignment, any overt subjects of *to*-infinitives can only receive case from outside of IP. Two subclasses of PRO are then those whose optional PRO subjects alternate with DPs case-marked from outside IP, and the non-alternating PRO, referred to as obligatory control.

Prior to offering an account of the difference, we can summarize the distributions of the two types of PRO. There are few restrictions on which kinds of positions accept optional PRO: it can be found in various sub-

---

subject and must receive nominative case from I. Since English does not permit null nominatives (it is not a "pro-drop" language), this subject must be overt. The pro-drop topic goes beyond this study's scope, but a subject pro in languages with verbal inflection is nonetheless easily explained by AR and the Invisible Category Principle (9.18); cf. Emonds (1994).

[2] English "bare infinitives" (*Mary made me finish it*) have been assimilated in the Appendix to Chapter 6 to one type of Romance causative, which are analyzed there in some detail. Understood subjects of English active participles and gerunds are analyzed in sections 7.5–7.6.

[3] Emonds (1985, Ch. 2) accepts and adds to what are there called "structure-based" arguments for concluding that *to*-infinitives are IPs, but distinguishes them from "subject-based" arguments, which can be accommodated in other ways.

[4] Lobeck (1986) shows that infinitival *to* (unlike finite verbs) doesn't always suffice to license VP deletion: **Someone should fix the drain, but a good man to is hard to find.*

categorized complements (10.1a) and in subject and adjunct infinitives as well (10.1b).

(10.1)   Optional Control PRO:
      a. Some customers have preferred *(for one of us) to fill out the forms.*
        People are hoping *(for someone) to help the children.*
        John is eager *(for his children) to leave now.*
        Any tendency *(for the students) to cheat* should be discouraged.
      b. Well, *(for an administrator) to finish this now* might { be necessary/ help us }.
        Mary worked extra in order *(for Ann) to have time to apply.*
        The outfit was too gaudy *(for a professor) to wear to class.*
        Bills *(for us) to pay* are piling up.

In fact, a subject of a *to*-infinitive in a subject or adjunct is never obligatorily PRO. As has been observed by Williams (1980) and Koster (1984), obligatory PRO, exemplified in (10.2), seems limited to subcategorized complements (10.3).

(10.2)   Obligatory Control PRO:
      John tried *(*for one of us) to fill out the forms.*
      Mary convinced me *(*for Ann) to apply for the job.*
      John is foolish *(*for his children) to leave now.*
      Any decision *(*for the students) to cheat* should be condemned.

(10.3)   Obligatory PRO subjects occur only in complement IPs.

Let us now seek a principled explanation for (10.3). Recall that according to (2.13), selecting frames like +___IP or +___VP are excluded in principle.

(2.13)   *Lexical Interface Principle. The lexicon uses only morpheme categories in its statements. It cannot mention phrases, nor distinguish between X and XP.*

Infinitives with either type of control must therefore be selected by features such as +___C, +___I or +___V.

(i) Optional control. Unsurprisingly, optional control occurs in essentially every kind of clausal context, as exemplified in (10.1). It arises whenever *for* is chosen as C, either by free generation in a subject or adjunct CP or as a complement via a frame +___[C, LOC'].[5] In turn, the complementizer *for* selects an infinitive via its own frame +___[I, SUBJUN] (8.15), as discussed earlier in section 8.1.3.

This latter frame allows the subject of IP either to be lexical (and case-marked by *for*) or empty, which is the definition of optional control. The surface sequence *for [$_{DP}$ Ø] to VP* is excluded in Standard English due to the fact that the goal feature (here LOC') of *for* is alternatively realized (4.20) on the *to* in I, as argued in Emonds (1987). Since *for* in this sequence does not assign case and Economy of Derivation minimizes insertions of free morphemes in a derivation, C = Ø is preferred to C = *for*. We return in section 10.2 to determining antecedents of optional PRO.

(ii) Obligatory control.[6] As described in (10.3), obligatory control clauses have a more restricted distribution, though possibly hundreds of selecting heads like those in (10.2) require them; cf. the lists in Rosenbaum (1967, Appendix). Indeed, (10.3) would follow if it can be shown that obligatory control results only from some type(s) of complement selection. We know however, that this selection cannot simply be for bare VPs; these are excluded by the theory of extended projections of section 1.3.

A central concept for complement selection is the definition of "lexical head X of ZP" (4.27), whereby the category X can differ from Z under limited conditions. In these terms, a ZP can satisfy a subcategorization feature +___X provided that X is "the highest lexically filled head in Z^j ." Thus, an IP whose head I is Ø in the syntax can satisfy a frame +___V because V qualifies as IP's lexical head. In terms of Lobeck's (1986) analysis just cited, infinitival IPs are precisely those clauses whose I is Ø in the syntax (and cannot assign case). Thus, a lexical item @ with a frame +___V can select an IP, and this IP must be infinitival.

There are then two possibilities for such an @: either (i) the infinitival IP is a sister of @, or (ii) the infinitival IP is embedded in a CP which is a sister of @.

---

[5] LOC' is the label that minimally distinguishes the goal feature of *for* from that of *to* (section 8.1.3).

Root clauses headed by *for* = [C, LOC'] seem excluded, unless they are to be identified with imperatives, as suggested by E. Klima (1967 class lectures). This idea would account for why imperatives are rendered in indirect speech by *for-to* clauses; cf. section 10.3 below.

[6] This account for determining when PRO is obligatory is based on Emonds (1985, Ch. 2), later refined using representational economy in Emonds (1991a).

(10.4)   (i)

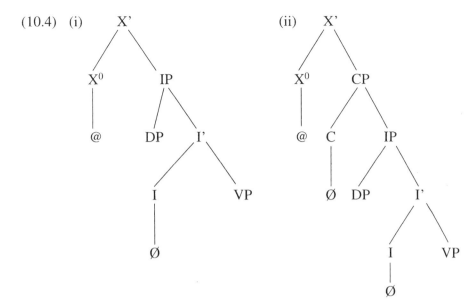

In (10.4i), @ cannot assign case to the subject of IP because of the final formulation of Case Indices (8.9): a lexical head @ can assign case only if is satisfies +___D or +___I, but by hypothesis here, @ satisfies rather +___V.[7] Therefore DP = Ø, which is the definition of obligatory control.

In (10.4ii), C must be empty just like I must be, again because of (4.27); if not V would not be the lexical head of a sister of @. Consequently the subject DP in (10.4ii) can again only be zero, since neither a filled I nor [c *for*] is available to assign case; i.e. obligatory control again results.

It thus follows that any IP selected by +___V is an infinitive and exhibits obligatory control, whatever the selecting element. Moreover, an infinitive with any C which doesn't assign case, such as e.g., *whether*, must also result in obligatory control. Assuming by parsimony that these are the only sources of obligatory control, we can sharpen the generalization (10.3) of Koster and Williams to (10.5).

(10.5)   Lexical Selection Corollary. Obligatory PRO subjects occur precisely in complements licensed by a subcategorization frame @, +___V and in indirect questions.

---

[7] *(8.9) Case Indices. The case assigners (= potential case indices) are I, D and any V or P whose lexical realizations enter a tree by satisfying +___Y, where Y = I or D.*

The subcategorization theory developed here thus predicts that a PRO subject is obligatory when *and only when* an element outside IP is either (i) a lexical head that selects a V or (ii) a non-case-marking [C, WH]. This contrasts with when a non-finite I (not a V) is either selected or freely generated in subject or adjunct positions; these latter possibilities result in optional PRO.

This subcategorization-based account of PRO answers two of Chomsky's (1981, 73–74) questions as to when (each type of) PRO may and must appear, with no need to refer to any distinction between governed and ungoverned categories. (Chomsky's third question, how the reference of PRO is determined, is independent of the other two.) Theorizing PRO in terms of subcategorization is conceptually advantageous because it eliminates theoretical constructs of highly skewed distribution, the ungoverned empty DP or its descendent in later work, "null case."[8]

In order to relate obligatory PRO to Syntactic Identification (9.1), another step is required. A link must be made between obligatory control and local syntactic identification. Fortunately previous research has established this link. In an early and insightful discussion of control, Jackendoff (1972, sections 5.8–5.12) concludes:

(10.6)   "… the generalization is that there is a unique identifiable controller position if and only if control is obligatory." (Jackendoff, 1972, 214)

---

[8]   An ungoverned empty category raises often ignored empirical issues. For example, since ungoverned PRO sometimes alternates with *for* - DP, the C *for* potentially case-marks and governs the PRO position; therefore, *PRO is ungoverned only if no potentially case-marking lexical item is inserted in C.*

But now consider the long noted fact that *for* as a P, which selects DP, and *for* as a C share distribution and must be closely related: they have a common role in both higher and lower purpose clauses / phrases and they are often lexically co-selected (*arrange, beg, hope, plan, pray, wait,* etc.) But then like C =*for,* why cannot the P *for,* or for that matter any P, fail to be inserted, resulting in a PRO object? In terms of Chomsky (1981, Ch. 3) such PROs should be ungoverned and hence licit wherever PPs are licensed – leading to empty PPs almost everywhere. The same general question could be posed for null case: what general principle stops it from having more general distribution?

Some additional distinction might be drawn between [$_P$ *for*] and [$_C$ *for*]: C can be left empty but P can't, CP is a barrier to government but PP isn't, government of a complement is obligatory but government of a lower SPEC(IP) position is optional, etc. But any such stipulation only supplements the ad hoc preliminary proposal that infinitival I doesn't govern. In contrast, accounting for distribution of PRO in terms of subcategorization doesn't use "ungoverned" (or "null case") and hence requires no additional theoretical statements to account for the extremely limited distribution of these constructs.

It is clear from Jackendoff's discussion that these unique controller positions are also *locally situated* with respect to PRO. In fact they usually satisfy the Minimal Distance Principle of Rosenbaum (1967).

His generalization (10.6) is, however, not quite accurate. Chomsky (1977) notes that the obligatorily controlled PRO in indirect questions (10.7a) does *not* have a unique identifiable controller position (10.7b):

(10.7) a. When (*for an administrator) to take care of this { is unclear/ puzzles me }.
Someone was asking whether (*for a customer) to fill out the forms.

 b. Bill, let's talk to Mary; when PRO best to take care of this is unclear.
Bill discussed how PRO to fill in the forms with { the applicants/ his boss }.
I was speaking to John about how PRO to play that piece most effectively.

That is, we must subtract indirect questions from the range of obligatory control structures (10.5) which have a unique identifier controller position. What remains is that in precisely those complements licensed by a subcategorization frame @, +___V, there is a unique local controller for PRO. I now wish to derive this descriptive generalization from (9.1).

(9.1) *Syntactic Identification. All and only empty DPs licensed by subcategorization must be locally rather than pragmatically identified.*

Suppose we construe the class of "empty XPs licensed by subcategorization" slightly liberally as "XPs which are empty due to satisfaction of a frame +___F." We have just concluded above that the subject DPs of clauses which satisfy +___V must be empty precisely because of how this frame interacts with the definition of lexical head (4.27). In other words, obligatory PROs are due to satisfaction of a frame +___V, i.e., are licensed by subcategorization. Consequently, Syntactic Identification (9.1) requires that precisely these PRO be locally identified, exactly as Jackendoff observes that they are. That is, his observation (10.6) turns out to be a special case of (9.1).

This principle devised for null complements in Chapter 9 thus turns out to make an interesting and correct prediction for empty subjects as well.

10.2 Pragmatic control

The only empty arguments that can escape Syntactic Identification are that subset of subject DPs not required to be empty by subcategorization. That is, empty DPs required only by the EPP (1.17), in particular those of optional control, need not be syntactically identified. Rather, their phi-features and reference can be determined by pragmatics or discourse principles.

Identification of such DPs by discourse principles groups them with other pragmatically identified null discourse anaphora, which in English are of categories NP, VP, CP and occasionally PP (cf. 9.33–9.34 in section 9.3). I thus formulate a somewhat limited role for pragmatic control, which may characterize Huang's (1984) "hot languages," those with less discourse control of null phrases.

(10.8)   *Pragmatic Control. Only non-DPs and DPs not licensed by sub-categorization (including optional PRO subjects) may be identified by pragmatics.*[9]

A moment's reflection shows that (9.1) and (10.8) are two sides of the same coin and could be subsumed under a single statement, possibly about identifying case-marked and caseless categories. However, for expository purposes, their content seems more salient when they are left uncombined.

In most cases, to claim that pragmatics determines reference of a PRO subject says little about actual reference. It is well-known that even first and second person pragmatic reference of optional PRO in various positions is permitted; for example, overt subjects in (10.9) do not change interpretation or acceptability:

(10.9)   [(For us) to hit ourselves] might be a bad idea.
          [(For you) to undress yourself in public] might shock the caretakers.

Structurally, a discourse antecedent of PRO can be almost anywhere; it can easily be lower than PRO and/ or exterior to the main clause, as in (10.10).

---

[9] Ultimately, one should indicate whether Pragmatic Control (10.8) holds at LF. In section 8.3, I have argued that predicate attributes are caseless at LF but have case at PF, so this would impinge on a more definitive formulation of (10.8). Note that the present formulation correctly allows null subjects of finite clauses to be pragmatically controlled, which seems to be appropriate in those languages that syntactically license pro-drop.

(10.10) When the sergeant saw the soldiers, he { yelled/ said } [PRO to take cover].

Still, pragmatic determination of reference for optional PRO often favors a "closer" antecedent; thus, without further information, *me* rather than *Mary* tends to be the reference of PRO in (10.11).

(10.11) I just saw Mary in court. But Bill told me that any decision [PRO to cancel the contract] would be unwise.

Since quite general (although poorly understood) pragmatic procedures determine the reference of PRO, allowing even first and second person reference, it would be strange to assume that these procedures somehow fail in embedded imperatives such as (10.12), in which overt subjects alternate with optional PRO in complements to communication verbs.

(10.12) Mary { shouted/ murmured/ said again } [(for the driver) to start the car].
   Next time you can yell back [(for people) to leave { you/ *yourself } alone].
   Ann$_i$ whispered [(for her friend) to not let { her$_i$ / *herself$_i$ } be insulted].

However, because the PRO alternatives to overt subjects in (10.12) are typically obligatorily *disjoint in reference* from the communication verb's own subject, Koster (1984) and Rizzi (1986) have concluded that the higher clauses must contain a closer null (and unidentified?) local DP antecedent for these PRO. Such a locally controlled but optional PRO would violate Syntactic Identification (9.1) and Jackendoff's generalization (10.6).

Thus, principles of pragmatics should be sharpened at least enough to account for the disjoint subjects in (10.12) without hypothesizing a null controller. Section 10.3 develops such an account without weakening the generalizations (9.1) and (10.8).

10.3 Imperatives, direct and embedded

The analysis of this section will reveal that the key to how pragmatics or discourse grammar determines the understood (optional) PRO subjects of the "unlike subject" infinitives of (10.12) is their status as embedded or "indirect" imperatives. As a preliminary, I spell out a few fairly controversial properties of imperative clauses in terms of some general discourse notions.

(10.13) *Discourse Participants. The speaker (first person reference) and the addressee (second person reference) of a given sentence are disjoint in reference.*

Grammarians have often remarked that languages may have (even morphologically distinct) root clause imperative forms for all persons and numbers except for first person singular, that is, the speaker.[10]

(10.14) a. First plural: Let's (us) get ourselves out of here.
      b. Third person: Each girl get herself a haircut.
                          All applicants be here at seven.

Nonetheless, it is obvious that any *null* subjects of imperatives are the addressee (10.15a) and that even their partially specified subjects can be covertly second person (10.15b):

(10.15) a. Get { yourself/ *herself } a haircut, could { you/ *she }?
              Be here at seven, won't { you/ *they }!
      b. Everybody get { yourself/ herself } here at seven.
              Somebody station { yourself/ himself } at the door.

---

[10] Like other languages, English lacks a "first singular imperative form" in root clauses. Apparently then, a speaker talking to himself must address himself other than in the first person singular:

(i)   *Get myself out of here.   *Let's get myself to work.
(ii)   Joe, get yourself out of here.   Joe, let's get ourselves to work.

On the other hand, a *to*-infinitive in a root clause seems to *require* a first singular "hortatively" interpreted PRO (iii) and to exclude an overt subject (iv):

(iii) Ah, to arrive on time for once!
      Just think, to find myself back in California again!

(iv) *Ah, for the longer days to arrive soon!
      *Just think, for her to be back with her husband!

Thus, the first-singular "gap" seems to be a syntactic constraint on the imperative mood; it is not a semantic or, given the lack of English endings, morphological constraint. The explanation for this gap appears just below in the text.

Parsimony suggests that we try to align these null subjects with PRO. If so they should lack nominative case, and happily there are independent reasons for this conclusion. First, Postal (1964) observes that English imperative main clauses can appear with tags containing *will, would, can* or *could,* as in (10.15a). The fact that the I in a tag regularly reproduces the main clause suggests that an imperative IP contains [$_I$ +MODAL], which in turn immediately explains the lack of agreement morphology on the third singular verb in (10.14b) and (10.15b). This imperative [I, +MODAL] is then empty, although it sometimes houses a modal-like uninflected *do (Do be here on time, would you? Don't anybody bring any flammable items please)*.

Next, an empty I is exactly a characteristic of PRO subjects, as seen in section 10.1. Moreover, whatever the case of the overt imperative subjects in (10.16) they are not nominative, since specifically nominative morphology is excluded.

(10.16) { Each girl/ *she } get herself a haircut.
         { All applicants/ *they } get themselves here on time.
         Let's { us (older guys) / *we (older guys) } get ourselves a beer.

Since English main clause imperatives thus have an empty I which fails to assign nominative case and their subject DPs can be empty, we can plausibly conclude that these empty subjects are PRO. Syntactic Identification (9.1) does not apply to these non-subcategorized root subjects. Like other PRO, they fall under (10.8):

(10.8) *Pragmatic Control. Only non-DPs and DPs not licensed by subcategorization (including optional PRO subjects) may be identified by pragmatics.*

In view of the fact that (10.8) has been motivated on the basis of embedded subjects, it seems reasonable to extend its scope and claim that the understood subjects of imperatives are also part of pragmatics:[11]

(10.17) *Imperative Subjects. A PRO subject of the imperative is the addressee.*

---

[11] Syntactic theory loses nothing by assigning the cross-linguistic generalization (10.17) to pragmatics. No principle of syntax has been able to relate this property to any other syntactic phenomenon besides those which Postal (1964) shows follow from it.

(10.18) *Theorem. By (10.17) and Discourse Participants (10.13), a PRO corresponding to the subject of an imperative clause is disjoint from that clause's speaker.*

(10.18) thus derives the syntactic "first singular gap" in root imperatives observed in note 10.

Having set out some principles for imperatives on the basis of main clauses, let us now take up indirect or embedded imperatives, such as those in (10.12) given earlier.

(10.12) Mary { shouted/ murmured/ said again } [(for the driver) to start the car].
Next time you can yell back [(for people) to leave { you/ *yourself } alone].
Ann$_i$ whispered [(for her friend) to not let { her$_i$ / *herself$_i$ } be insulted].

Such reported imperatives are special cases of the phenomenon traditionally termed *indirect speech*. A number of to some extent grammatical observations about this topic can shed light on the disjoint reference that often holds between the subject of a communication verb and the overt or PRO subject of its infinitival complement in e.g. (10.12). The same disjoint reference holds even when an overt or understood indirect object is co-referential with the subject, as evidenced in (10.19), thus showing that something is at stake other than "control" of PRO by this object:

(10.19) *Sam$_i$ wistfully mumbled [PRO$_i$ to get rich in spite of himself$_i$].
*Mary$_i$ was saying to herself$_i$ [PRO$_i$ to buy herself$_i$ a computer].
*The hikers$_i$ yelled (to each other$_j$) [PRO$_i$ to come back to each other$_i$].

Generative studies have contributed relatively little to elucidating indirect speech since the central issues concern what kinds of direct quotations are compatible with (i.e., felicitous paraphrases of) a given instance of indirect speech. For instance, suppose Jim uttered (10.20) yesterday:

(10.20) Sue { offended / offends / has offended } me.

It is then hard to say which answers today in (10.21) "accurately report" which statements in (10.20).

(10.21) Jim said that Sue (had) offended him.
   Jim said that Sue offends him.
   Jim says that Sue (has) offended him.

In other terms, traditional study of indirect speech is to a great extent a matter of appropriate paraphrase and language use, not language form, and hence has fallen outside the domain of generative grammar.[12]

But in any case, we at least need to say that appropriate indirect speech must faithfully reflect the content of quotations it paraphrases. At issue is "faithfully reflect"; paraphrases can be far from identical but not arbitrarily different. Thus, if Sam bitterly complains, *"My wife has wrongly been sent some parking tickets by the city,"* this can be felicitously reported as *Sam grumbled that the police mistakenly sent parking tickets to Mary,* assuming he is married to Mary. In this example at least, the passive voice, indirect object word order, the exact quantifier, and the definite description can all be changed in indirect discourse. (This fact about the passive voice will play a role in the argument just below.)

But the same quotation *cannot* be rendered by the almost identical *!Sam grumbled that his wife { **might** / **will** } wrongly be sent some parking tickets by the city*, because indirect speech cannot change the principal feature of I in the quote from -MODAL to +MODAL.

(10.22) *Preservation of ±REALIS. Accurate indirect speech retains the value of the feature MODAL.*

In the same vein, an embedded indirect report of an original declarative will keep the finite I. If the original is an imperative, the report will be infinitival, in both cases respecting (10.22). Thus an imperative containing [I, +MODAL] such as (10.23a) *Drop the toy!* can be felicitously reported by either an infinitive with [I, +MODAL] or equally well by a finite clause with a modal (10.23b); however, the report *cannot* introduce -MODAL, that is, "realis" (10.23c):

(10.23) a. Drop the toy!

---

[12] See Banfield (1982, Ch. 1) for a critique of early generative work which related indirect speech to direct quotation. Her own analysis focuses not on embedded indirect speech but on *free* (root clause) indirect speech, which is in the main in the domain of language form.

b.

$$\text{Sam } \{ \text{ shouted / said } \} \left\{ \begin{array}{l} \text{that she should drop the toy} \\ \text{that the toy must be dropped} \\ \text{(to the girl) to drop the toy} \\ \text{for the girl to drop the toy} \\ \text{for the toy to be dropped} \end{array} \right\}$$

c. !Sam { shouted / said } (to the girl) that she { is dropping / dropped } the toy.

However, it is not enough to say that an infinitive with a communication verb need only reflect a -REALIS direct quote. In addition, *a communication verb's infinitive complement with a PRO subject is always the indirect report of a command*. Thus, in spite of the pragmatic plausibility of all three continuations in (10.24a-b), the infinitives cannot render direct speech modals (i.e. declarative clauses) even though this would still respect (10.22).

(10.24) a. Bill was discussing his in-laws$_i$ with me.
  He grumbled, "they$_i$ may ruin my Sundays."
  He grumbled that they$_i$ might ruin his Sundays.
  *He grumbled [PRO$_i$ to ruin his Sundays].
 b. Bill was discussing the new neighbors$_j$ with Mary.
  He whispered, "they$_j$ will conceivably keep me awake."
  He whispered that they$_j$ would conceivably keep him awake.
  *He whispered [PRO$_j$ to conceivably keep him awake].

Moreover, the subject of a communication verb is of course the speaker of the reported clause; in particular if that complement is infinitival, the higher subject is the speaker of the reported imperative. By Discourse Participants (10.13) and Imperative Subjects (10.17), a PRO subject of an imperative, main or reported, must be disjoint in reference from the speaker of the clause. For example, PRO$_i$ in (10.24a) and PRO$_j$ in (10.24b) must be disjoint in reference from "Bill." Hence from discourse principles alone we have derived the result that subject PROs in infinitival complements of communication verbs, as in (10.12) and (10.19), must be disjoint in reference from the communication verb's own subject. There is no need to postulate some additional covert indirect object of the main verb which controls these optional PRO.

However, care is needed in interpreting exactly how this pragmatically determined disjoint reference of PRO is realized in syntax. An infinitive complement of a communication verb indeed corresponds to an imperative in a quotation. But by the pragmatic principle Discourse Participants (10.13), the subject *of that quoted imperative,* not the surface subject of the indirect speech infinitive itself, is disjoint in reference from the communication verb's subject (whose command is reported). As just seen with respect to (10.23), indirect speech need not retain the same voice, active or passive, of the quotation. Therefore, an infinitival indirect imperative can perfectly well be a passivized version of the reported imperative proposition.

In this way, passive infinitives of a type noted in Perlmutter (1971) can appropriately render the (bold) active imperative quotations (10.25) and still conform to the disjoint reference between i and j imposed by (10.18).

(10.25) a. **Please [PRO]**$_j$ **allow me to leave!**
 Sam$_i$ shouted [PRO$_i$ to be allowed (by PRO$_j$) to leave].
 b. **Now [PRO]**$_j$ **give me a pain-killer!**
 Sam$_i$ yelled to her$_j$ [PRO$_i$ to be given (by PRO$_j$) a pain-killer].

These sentences, in which the higher and lower subjects are co-referential, again show that neither any explicit nor any "understood" indirect objects of a communication verb need control a PRO subject of indirect impera-tives. Hence such indirect objects cannot have a systematic role in rendering any PRO disjoint in reference from a higher subject.[13]

---

[13] Perlmutter's (1971) proposal is that *deep* subjects of a communication verb and its infinitival complement have to be distinct. But his "unlike subject constraint" is a super-fluous special case of Theorem (10.18) if it is combined with analyzing such infinitives as indirect speech imperatives, as the analysis in the text shows. If it is not so combined, it is easily falsified in both directions:

(i) First, suppose the quoted command is a passive. E.g. a traveling bishop is in the hinterlands administering confirmation to a newly converted band of pagans, using as much tribal protocol as necessary to convince the skeptical. In Roman Catholic practice, only a bishop may confirm. Yet the following sentence is fine:

The bishop { signaled/ whispered } for the chief's son to be confirmed first.

In violation of Perlmutter's constraint, the deep subjects of both clauses are co-referential; nonetheless there is no inference that either Canon Law is to be violated or that a second bishop sequestered in the environs is about to appear.

(ii) In the other direction, suppose John complains, *"Pollution will soon force me to move"* or *"These little kids are exhausting me"* or voices hopes that *"A good education will prepare me for life"* or *"A vacation by the sea refreshes me."* The following are still excluded:

*John was grumbling to be forced to move by pollution.
*John shouted to be exhausted by those little kids.
*John sighed to be prepared for life by a good education.
*John says to be refreshed by a vacation by the sea.

Nonetheless, without raising the issue of disjoint subjects, Rizzi (1986, Appendix) claims that the examples in (10.26) contain not only a PRO subject of the embedded infinitive, but also an understood main clause argument, call it pro', which controls (i.e. is co-indexed with) this PRO. His numbering is at the right.

(10.26) John { shouted / said / gave the order } pro' [PRO to leave]. (104b)
John said pro' [PRO to speak about { oneself / ?themselves / ?each other }]. (108c)
Il sergente ha ordinato pro' [di PRO prepararsi/ci in cinque minuti]. (106b)
'The sergeant ordered to prepare oneself/ourselves in five minutes.'
Lo psichiatra ha detto pro' [di PRO parlare di se stessi / noi stessi]. (109)
'The psychiatrist said to speak about themselves / ourselves.'

Rizzi actually gives three arguments against his own position, but none for it, as far as I can discern. First, his data and discussion show that pro' is entirely distinct from the syntactically present null generic object of Italian discussed in the body of his article. Second, he provides examples (10.27) to show that the mystery argument pro' has no role in binding:

(10.27) *John said something pro'$_j$ about { themselves$_j$ / each other$_j$ / oneself$_j$ }. (108b)
Cf. John said something to the twins$_i$ about { themselves$_i$ / each other$_i$ }.

Third, he credits Mark Baker for pointing out "that the variants of (108c) with *themselves* and *each other*, impossible out of context, become quite acceptable if the null goal of *say* is salient in the discourse context." Paraphrasing, an antecedent of PRO must be found through discourse pragmatics; the supposed argument pro' and theta roles of the verb *say* are irrelevant.

Finally, the representational status of Rizzi's understood indirect object pro' is even more ephemeral than that of the understood direct objects of English discussed in section 9.4.3; at one point he suggests that pro' has a

---

Although these sentences satisfy Perlmutter's deep structure "unlike subject constraint" and should in his terms be grammatical, they are excluded because such infinitives cannot paraphrase imperatives.

"floating" theta role. "Contrary to a direct object theta role, an indirect object theta role can fail to be structurally projected even if it is not lexically saturated." (1986, 152)[14] Recall from section 9.4.4 that a theta role is saturated for Rizzi when associated with referential content. So in his terminology, since the higher controller pro' is neither lexically nor syntactically saturated, it has no referential content. Consequently, pro' shouldn't be able to control PRO, i.e. serve as its antecedent, whatever its visibility. Nor, since pro' is not in a syntactic argument position (but rather "floating" somewhere inside the lexical entry under V), can it play a role in any formal mechanism expressing disjoint reference, whether by Chomsky's (1981) Binding Theory Principle B or the Pragmatic Disjoint Reference (10.18).

Summarizing, the original idea behind pro' was control. But since Rizzi's third type of implicit argument pro' ends up without reference, it is unable either to control or to assure disjoint reference; hence, it serves no purpose whatever and must be discarded.[15]

Rizzi's unsatisfactory analysis, it seems to me, derives from a suspicion that some possibly covert higher indirect object (which could control PRO) is what actually effects disjoint reference with the higher subject in his examples in (10.26). While I am sympathetic to *syntactically projected* empty arguments, my doubt here, possibly shared by Rizzi, is that even though an internal argument's features should be *identified* (9.1), there is nothing in the syntactic context of examples like (10.12) to achieve this. This section has established that in fact no such empty internal argument exists, and that the disjoint reference of the two subjects in (10.12) has another source, namely the interaction of two principles of pragmatics: Discourse Participants (10.13) and Imperative Subjects (10.17).

The discussion has thus shown that any "implicit" indirect objects of communication verbs, in both Italian and English, are syntactically absent and at most pragmatically inferred. On the other hand, a PRO subject DP of their infinitival complements is indeed syntactically present, and finding principles for determining its reference has been an interesting and non-trivial problem of pragmatics and discourse analysis. The main claim of

---

[14] We might conclude from this and his section 1.6 that the indirect object theta role (or, the indirect object) is simply absent – but no: "Being lexically unsaturated, it is syntactically visible and can act as a controller." Thus, these indirect objects are syntactically somehow both absent (a reasonable synonym for "not structurally projected") and yet visible.

[15] This is fitting enough, since the only property of pro' (simultaneous absence and visibility in the same component) seems fairly close to a contradiction.

Chapter 9 has thus been maintained: a linguistically understood argument is always a syntactic argument. Furthermore, if it is a complement, (i) it satisfies a head's subcategorization feature and (ii) its own syntactic features are locally identified.

10.4 Understood agents in passive clauses

This chapter seeks to establish that null arguments with systematic linguistic behavior are always syntactically represented. Interestingly, we have also found that null *external* arguments, while robustly present in the syntax, are nonetheless typically identified by Pragmatic Control (10.8) rather than by Syntactic Identification (9.1).

The preceding sections have reviewed two quite distinct situations in which a null subject PRO of a non-finite V optionally alternates with an overt DP and is pragmatically identified. One case concerns main clause imperatives and the other concerns optional PRO in *for-to* clauses, i.e., embedded infinitival I selected by $[_{C,GOAL}$*for* / $\emptyset$]). As seen in the previous section, infinitival complements of communication verbs interestingly link these two instances of Pragmatic Control; optional control infinitives are used to represent an imperative in indirect speech. For both imperatives and optional control, my claim that their subject arguments are syntactically represented is consistent with most (but by no means all) generative syntactic treatments, which not only situate these understood subjects in syntactic trees but also locate them as daughters of IP.

10.4.1 The location of the agent phrase

There is less agreement about the syntactic status and location of a third type of unexpressed external argument connected to patterned syntactic behavior: the so-called "understood agent" which alternates with an adjunct *by* -phrase in passives. It is widely thought that a passive verb as in (10.28) – these include the examples (9.22) of Chapter 9 – is related to some constituent which represents its deep or logical subject, even when a *by*-phrase is not overt. This understood argument accounts for how verbal passives (10.28) contrast with middle verbs (10.29) and adjectival passives (10.30) (cf. Wasow, 1977), which have no understood agent.

(10.28) a. The meeting was started on time (by Susan) to please the host.
     b. The chairs were moved around on purpose (by the guests).
     c. This corn has been grown voluntarily ({by peasants / to stave off famine}).
     d. Our workers are better paid intentionally (by the new boss).
     e. Art classes are being restored (by the Board) in order to qualify for funding.

(10.29) a. *The meeting started on time (by Susan) to please the host.
     b. *The chairs moved around on purpose (by the guests).
     c. *This corn has grown voluntarily ({by peasants / to stave off famine}).

(10.30) a. That series of meetings sounds completed (*by the committee).
     b. Most of our furniture is still unmoved (*by the company).
     c. This corn looks fully grown (*voluntarily).
       We judge the corn fully grown (*to stave off famine).
     d. Our workers remain better paid (*intentionally).
     e. Some art classes seem restored (*in order to qualify for funding).

When a verbal passive has no overt *by*-phrase, a corresponding covertly represented logical subject can account for two properties: (i) A syntactically present animate subject seems to be a necessary condition for adverbs of intentionality, as in (10.28b,c,d), and for higher purpose clauses, optionally introduced by *in order,* as in (10.28a,c,e).[16] (ii) This logical subject may (not necessarily must) also control the optional PRO subject of a "higher" infinitive of purpose.

These paradigmatic regularities suggest a type (i) or (ii) analysis (section 9.2) of understood arguments, namely, that some means should be found to structurally represent an understood agent in at least those verbal passives which exhibit intentional adverbs or higher purpose clauses. Since no one has ever found any actual difference between verbal passives with overt *by*-phrases and those without (this regularity motivated an earlier "lowering"

---

[16] Unlike the "lower" purpose clauses of section 9.2.1, these "higher" purpose clauses are sisters of a phrasal projection of V rather than complements of V. Hence they cannot be sisters to a nominal projection such as a direct object. Because of their higher position, any empty operator fronted to their COMP will fail to be identified by condition (9.7) of Chapter 9, resulting in ill-formedness. (9.7) thus correctly predicts that higher purpose clauses contain no gaps other than their PRO subject.

transformation of agent postposing),[17] the most likely candidate for an understood agent is an empty, optionally controlled counterpart @ to the *by*-phrase itself, as in (10.31). Intermediate bar level projections are omitted.

(10.31)

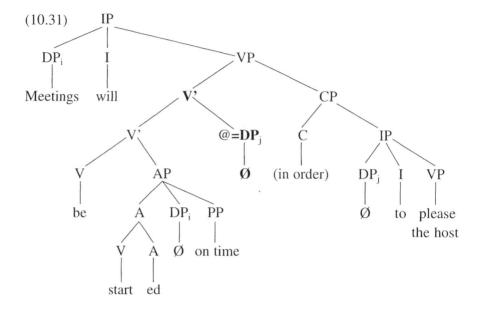

---

[17] Jaeggli (1986), crediting Chomsky (1986b), observes that an understood agent @ in a passive is sometimes disjoint in reference from a higher subject:

(i)   *They$_i$ expected [damaging testimony to be given @$_i$].

But as is well-known, definite pronouns are frequently infelicitous in *by*-phrases:

(ii)   *They$_i$ expected [damaging testimony to be given by them$_i$].

Thus, the ill-formed covert pronominal in (i) is more evidence for the parallel between covert and overt passive agents.

    In contrast to these examples, possible cases of co-reference are easily constructed; as expected, covert and overt agents again act alike:

(iii) The bishop$_i$ { expected/ persuaded} the chief to be confirmed { by him$_i$/ @$_i$ } first.
       The dentist$_i$ { forced/ wanted} her patient to be injected { by her$_i$/ @$_i$ } right away.

This type of parallel with overt pronouns is expected for optional PRO.

    Jaeggli seems to assume that a covert agent @ must be obligatory rather than optional PRO. But @ clearly has rather the properties of the latter: it alternates with an overt element, doesn't act like an internal argument, and can have an arbitrary interpretation.

The structure in (10.31) incorporates from Chapter 5 the analysis of a passive participle as an AP (based on selection, Romance and German agreement facts, etc.). The grammatical head of the AP in (10.31) is a PF-inserted morpheme *-en/ -ed*, which entails that, throughout the syntactic derivation, the verb *start* is the lexical head of AP, as per the definition of lexical head (4.27). The differentia specifica of passive constructions is the co-indexing of a DP object of a participle with its (most economical) structural subject position (cf. section 5.1.3).

One important consequence of this passive co-indexing of subject and object is that the lexical verb's external argument is thereby deprived of its most economical realization as the obligatory DP daughter of IP. Consequently, an external argument of the V must appear elsewhere, by the EPP (1.17): low enough to remain within the same IP and thus qualify as a subject of the lexical V, but high enough to not interfere with the subcategorization of the auxiliary V. The position of @ as a daughter to an additional phrasal projection of V, both bold in (10.31), satisfies both these requirements. If @ is overt and hence requires case, it appears in a PP (a *by*-phrase), but if it is covert as in (10.31), it is an optional PRO which needs no case or PP structure.[18]

To verify that DP_j in fact qualifies as the subject of the passive phrase *started t_i on time* in (10.31), let us re-examine the definition of subject from Chapter 1.

(1.15)   *Generalized Subjects: The subject or external argument of a head X is the lowest N-projection which c-commands a phrasal projection of X within its minimal cyclic domain.*

By inspection, while the subject of the highest VP in (10.31) headed by *be* can be DP_i, the subject of the lower AP, whose V head is *start,* must be DP_j. So it turns out that the postposed DP_j simply *is* the structural subject of the passive phrase *started t_i on time*. If covert, DP_j is an optionally controlled PRO and if overt, like other counterparts to optional PRO, DP_j requires a case-assigning PP structure.

---

[18] The sole role of passive *by* here is assigning oblique case to its sister DP. As is widely understood, this DP can carry a number of different theta roles (*No letters were received by Sue; social unrest is spawned by the horrors of war; the coast is inhabited by unwelcome newcomers; more services will be acquired by our neighborhood*). This compatibility of *by* with several theta roles independently suggests the conclusion in the text, that its sister is in fact a subject, and that *by* itself assigns no theta roles.

The definition (1.15) achieves this result without a lowering transformation and further without any of the dubious constructs invoked in Jaeggli (1986) such as agentive adjuncts, absorption, theta role assignments and transfers, or lexical rules. In a syntactic climate which liberally bestows subjecthood in other constructions, where neither predication, morphology, overt/ covert alternations, or in fact any evidence whatever suggests their presence, it is sort of amazing that *by*-phrases and their covert counterparts have not been analyzed as subjects.[19] But in fact they are well behaved optional PRO fully deserving this appellation.

10.4.2 The syntactic roles of the agent phrase

Let us now turn to what kind of empty category the understood logical subject @ in (10.31) is. It is certainly not a trace. Sections 9.1 and 9.4 argued that "small pro" results from Alternative Realization, not applicable in this structure. This suggests the conclusion that DP_j = PRO. Further, since case-marking is not necessary when DP_j is null, there is no reason for assuming that @ is a PP; case-marking would in any case be incompatible with PRO.[20]

---

[19] The chimerical subjects so widely distributed in recent work are invariably housed in small clauses, whose categorial status has never been made clear (in twenty years). Paradigms based on the "subject condition," which seem to be the most widespread syntactic argument for small clauses, are actually entirely unrelated to subject status, as can be seen in the original study of these paradigms (Koster, 1978a). Cf. note 23 of Chapter 8 here.

Generalized Subjects (1.15) succeeds empirically in picking out the right nominal projection as subject for adjectives in all but a few of the most recalcitrant cases. In the examples below, the bold nominal projection, N, NP or DP, serves as (lowest c-commanding) subject of the italicized AP. Unlabeled brackets indicate VPs in (i).

(i)   **Mary** [seemed to Bill [$_{AP}$ *as foolish as ever*]].
      Mary [[$_{V'}$ criticized Bill] (while) [$_{AP}$ *hungry*]].
      Mary [felt [$_{AP}$ *guilty*] near Sue].
      Mary [made **Bill** [$_{AP}$ *angry*]].
      Mary [regarded **Bill** as [$_{AP}$ *inconsiderate*]].

Unlabeled brackets indicate NPs in (ii).

(ii) Bill's [[$_{AP}$ *hungry*] [$_{N'}$ **look at the display**]]
      Bill's [[$_N$ **letter**] [$_{AP}$ *full of empty phrases*] to the landlord]
      Bill's [[$_{V'}$ reading the ads] *hungry*]

[20] Jaeggli's (1986) objects that a PRO as the covert agent in passives would be in a governed position. But all categories including PRO are governed in the present work (cf. note 8), so the objection vanishes. Moreover, *within* Jaeggli's framework, what if *by* is simply not selected, analogous to a *for* in an optional PRO context? What would result is precisely – in that framework – an ungoverned and hence legitimate PRO.

An optional PRO is widely considered to necessarily be +ANIMATE (e.g. the inferred animate subjects in *{ To explode like that / Exploding like that } does a lot of harm*), and yet understood agents in passives are not, as pointed out to me by K. Adachi. This suggests the following source in pragmatics for the animacy restriction on PRO, akin to the specification of PRO in imperatives as second person (10.17):

(10.32) *Animate PRO. A PRO in a SPEC position is +ANIMATE.*

Since an understood logical subject PRO in passives does not result from subcategorization, Pragmatic Control (10.8) determines its reference in verbal passives. Jaeggli (1986, 614–618) provides ample independent empirical support for this same conclusion.[21] This is a desirable result, because it has long been appreciated but never understood why understood agents in passives are discourse controlled – examples can be constructed where they can mean variously *anybody, everybody, somebody, him,* etc. Hence in escaping Syntactic Identification (9.1), the null DP_j in (10.31) is simply *acting like a subject.* In the phrasing of the previous sections, passive participles are now a third case where a subject PRO of a non-finite V is syntactically projected, optionally controlled and pragmatically identified. As in the other two cases (optional PRO infinitives and imperatives), PRO in verbal passives again occurs as a subject of a non-finite V which is itself unselected by a higher predicate.[22]

We can observe another optionally controlled PRO in the tree (10.31) as the subject of the adjunct purpose clause. As seen in section 10.1, optional PROs do not have controllers in a fixed syntactic position and are subject only to Pragmatic Control (10.8). Moreover, as illustrated there, pragmatic control often favors (without requiring) a proximately situated DP; accordingly, in the higher purpose clauses in (10.28a,c,e) the controller is the understood logical subject DP_j of the main clause. But the surface subjects of passive clauses can also serve as the antecedent for the PRO subject of a higher purpose clause:

---

[21] Terminological equivalents: Jaeggli's thematic control = my pragmatic control, and his argument control = my syntactic control or identification.

[22] The V stem of a passive is selected rather by the word-internal subcategorization +<V___> of the right hand head *-en*. The higher auxiliary V then selects *-en* by virtue of its frame +___A (that is, +<A>). For details on how various morphemes in the passive construction are selected, see Chapter 5.

(10.33) He$_j$ was vaccinated (by a nurse) before his trip PRO$_j$ to protect himself from typhoid.

Many politicians$_j$ are interviewed (by lowbrow magazines) in order PRO$_j$ to give themselves wider exposure.

One can moreover find verbs such as *arrest* and *examine* where *either* subject DP (an understood agent phrase or a surface subject) can be interpreted as controlling the PRO in the purpose clause:

(10.34) a. Were they arrested PRO$_j$ [just PRO$_j$ to legitimate the anti-drug campaign]?
            More children were examined free PRO$_j$ [PRO$_j$ to improve the image of the Health Department].
        b. Were [you]$_j$ arrested [just PRO$_j$ to make a point in front of your children]?
            [My sister and I]$_j$ were examined again [PRO$_j$ to reassure our parents].

Finally, one can construct contexts where the controller of the purpose clause DP$_j$ is *neither* of the two IP-internal subjects but is rather at least optionally exterior to IP, thus showing that the control of higher purpose clause PRO is squarely in the domain of discourse.

(10.35) [The Board]$_j$ finally made a decision. The banquet should be preceded by a cocktail party in order PRO$_j$ to woo the big shareholders into voting as a bloc.
        [The royal palace]$_j$ made its decision. More of the peasantry's sheep were to be impregnated in order PRO$_j$ to feed the growing population.

We are thus justified in concluding both that the subject of a higher purpose clause can be an optionally controlled PRO and that one of its possible antecedents is an understood agent PRO in a verb-headed passive structure, as in (10.28a,c,e) and (10.34a).

Jaeggli's (1986) proposals for passive agent phrases contrast fairly sharply with my analysis, in which these phrases are syntactic subjects essentially like other caseless PRO. Written like Rizzi (1986) in the heyday of enthusiasm over the promise of theta grids, Jaeggli's study contains a number of theoretical stipulations about theta role assignment, theta role absorption, positional indices of theta roles (these are indices *inside a verb's lexical entry* which can be "saturated" with DP co-reference – or lack of it), transmission of V-internal theta roles sometimes to affixes and sometimes from affixes to phrases, and linkages of theta roles with subcategorization features (both constructs being located inside the V). Certain of his proposals (e.g., that all theta roles must be assigned) are counterexemplified by middles and passive adjectives as in (10.29) and (10.30), which he leaves out of consideration. I claim that there is no need for any of these descriptive devices, nor indeed for the lexically listed item-particular theta grids without which these devices cannot be defined.

Baker, Johnson and Roberts (1989) develop further a key aspect of Jaeggli's analysis, his proposal that the passive participle morpheme *-en* is, in their terms, "an argument," or in Jaeggli's terms, "the recipient of the external theta role of the predicate." A question comes to mind immediately: what prevents other, almost fantastic analyses of the same inspiration? Could not some language treat its NEG, its disjunctive conjunction, its comparative suffix, its adjectival gender agreement or a modal as "an argument" which "receives an external theta role"? It's hard to evaluate such a proposal if it fails to specify conditions for when grammatical morphemes can receive theta roles, morphemes which lack any property, category or position resembling the DP arguments which ordinarily receive them.

In any case, the passive suffix *-en* is particularly ill-suited for expressing a theta role corresponding to an active verb's subject. Such an analysis cannot naturally distinguish verbal passives with understood agents (10.28) from adjectival passives without them (10.30), since both center around *-en*. Moreover, *-en* is a deep structure element in passive adjectives, and deep (pre-transformational) structure if anything more closely reflects argument structure. If *-en* carries a theta role, any distinction at deep structure between the two passives would then point toward adjectival rather than verbal passives containing understood agents, just the opposite of what holds empirically.[23] In light of these considerations, attributing the agent theta

---

[23] The Romance passive participle has the phi-features of the deep object of a passive verb, which, as Baker, Johnson and Roberts (1989) emphasize, is always disjoint in reference from the understood subject. In their account therefore, the Romance counterpart of "argument *en*" obligatorily agrees with a DP from which it must be disjoint in reference, a truly curious result.

A reviewer observes that their "argument *en*," which licenses a *by*-phrase by transmitting a theta role to it, is of course absent in "passive nominals" such as *the destruction of the city by the Romans*. This raises the question of what morpheme in these nominals can serve as an external argument, parallel to *-en*.

role in verbal passives to a pragmatically controlled subject PRO seems to be a superior analysis.

To summarize: two classic generative diagnostics for deep subjecthood, illustrated in (10.28)–(10.30), are licensing of intentionality adverbs and licensing and control of higher purpose clause subjects. Another diagnostic is of course the possibility of an agent theta role assigned by Chomsky's Agent Specification (2.39). Together these paradigms constitute systematic syntactic behavior of understood agents in English verbal passives, and all can be explained by representing the logical subjects of these passives as optional PRO within DP as in (10.31). Without additional stipulations, these covert agent phrases and their overt *by*-phrase counterparts occupy the exact position where the definition of Generalized Subjects (1.15) of Chapter 1 characterizes them as subjects of a passive V. As expected, these understood agent PROs, like the other optionally covert PRO subjects studied earlier, escape Syntactic Identification (9.1) and obey rather Pragmatic Control (10.8).

This analysis is then fully consistent with the analyses of other understood arguments in sections 10.1–10.3; these accounts all support the overriding generalization of the last two chapters: a linguistic argument is syntactically represented or not at all.

10.5 Nature's bottleneck

This quite syntactic conclusion about understood arguments is, in the light of some obvious facts about language use, perhaps not so surprising. Language use and lexical form are radically different in how they relate to human memory. It is by now a commonplace of psycholinguistic research that language users cannot accurately repeat or recall (outside of fixed expressions) the exact structure of a sentence just produced or understood, even after only a few seconds. They may retain its "meaning" or paraphrase it, but its form is irretrievably lost. That is, language use and the syntax which necessarily accompanies it are instantaneous – and instantaneously lost.

On the other hand the lexicon, both the Dictionary and the Syntacticon, are essentially *permanently stored* mental properties. As Saussure emphasized in his *Course*, although items can be slowly added to an adult Dictionary, the lexicon is otherwise inert; it does not significantly change from adolescence onward. Though items are constantly drawn from it for use in syntax, they are not and cannot be thereby modified in any way. Thus, no "lexical process" can affect an item selected for use; if it does, it is badly named. An item is selected for a certain sanctioned syntactic context or not; once selected, it is "in the syntax"; nothing in a syntactic derivation can "apply in the lexicon."

The main theme of Chapters 9 and 10, that understood arguments must be represented syntactically, is just a special case of this conclusion. For certainly, an "understood argument" is precisely one which is in use in a given sentence, i.e. it is not being used if its only locus is somewhere in the lexicon or in a lexical entry.

The sharp psychological dichotomy drawn here, between a permanently stored lexicon and the instantly created and lost representations of syntax, brings to light an I think little appreciated property of human language, considered as an amalgam of a lexicon and syntax. No one can deny, at least in light of our present understanding, that the constructs of both the lexicon and of syntax can be terribly complex. A proper syntactic representation of the first sentence of this paragraph, problematic as aspects of it may still be, could easily fill two pages. And the conceptual complexities of lexical items such as *game, flaw, Islam, advantage, machine*, etc. still defy analysis.

Yet, it appears to me, especially in the light of this study, that the complexities of each type of mental representation are largely inaccessible to those of the other. Most notably, lexical complexities seem to "get into syntax" (i.e., be used) only under very stringent conditions:

(i) **Many ideas, few categories.** Humans have huge lexicons of concepts differentiated by open class features f, but these are drastically constrained as to how they may combine. *They occur only on members of one of four lexical categories, N, V, A and P.* The concepts are arranged within these categories according to just a few further cognitive subdivisions by cognitive syntactic features F. Moreover, the number of categories which modify the lexical categories is few (Chapter 1).

(ii) **Syntactic opacity in the lexicon.** Dictionary items have very little access to the categories and principles of syntax. In particular, they have no access to phrasal structure, as seen in particular in Chapter 6. The limited combinatorial features of lexical items force them to be used with only certain (subclasses of) other categories, conforming to but a few sanctioned subcategorization frames of Universal Grammar (laid out in Chapter 8).

(iii) **Poverty of combination.** Once items combine according to lexical co-occurrence features and principles of Universal Grammar, a very few additional semantic principles (e.g. as in Chapter 2) impose conditions for globally understanding the resulting syntactic structures. In contrast, as argued there in detail, individual items make almost no systematic contributions to building up combinatorial interpretations.

Moreover, the syntax cannot "see back" into the lexicon:

(iv) Lexical opacity in the syntax. When one of a lexical item's perhaps multiple meanings is used in a permitted syntactic context, its other meanings and contextual features themselves are inaccessible.[24]

It is true enough that these conclusions imply that grammar very dramatically constrains rational thought. Many linguists and perhaps even a greater percentage of non-linguists feel such a conception as profoundly alienating: we cannot really say as much as we think we can. But in general scientific research always gives the initial impression of undermining human autonomy, while in fact the human's ability to reflect on its world is finally enhanced rather than limited by discoveries of our natural limits. In any case, this work has relentlessly pursued this view of impoverished lexical expressive power. While granting that the semantic treasure house of the human lexicon is conceptually very rich, it nonetheless appears that the four grammatical gates to the world of syntactic expression, named N, V, A and P, are narrow and unyielding.

---

[24] With the exception of Freudian free association. But free association as easily relates different items as different senses of the same item; there is no reason to assume that use of one sense of an item is any closer psychologically to its other senses than to other words.

It is a commonplace that in ordinary use, only one meaning is associated with a lexical item. Awareness of multiple meanings ("double-meaning") is a basis for humor, innuendo, literary turns, etc. But it would be verging on madness to claim that in ordinary use of e.g., *The last dish-washer cleaning up doesn't need to let any diners out,* a speaker / hearer *typically and simultaneously* thinks of the fact that dish-washers are also machines, that *clean up* can mean win at gambling, that *do* has an alternative main verb "activity" sense, that *need* can refer to poverty, that *let* often means rent, that *diners* may also refer to a type of restaurant, that *out* can mean 'unconscious', etc.

The Bifurcated Lexical Model

showing tri-level insertion of morphemes from the Lexicon; see also (4.9).

The following pages give groups of principles (italics) related to specific parts of the model. Double arrows are lexical insertions into derivations.

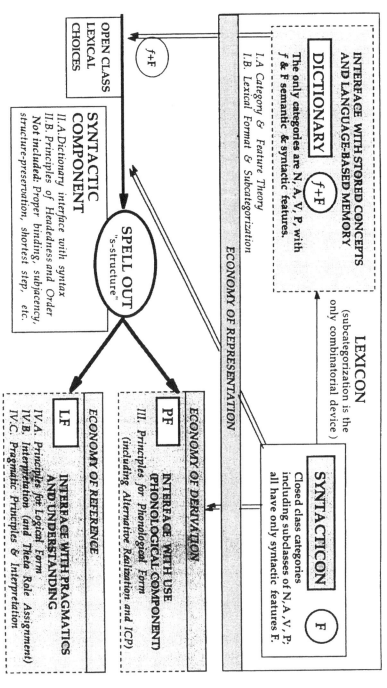

Summary of Principles[1]

I. Lexicon and Lexical Theory

I.A. Category and Feature Theory (Chapter 1)

Syntactic categories are subject to a **bar notation,** by which a small number of categories Y^0 combine with possible phrasal sisters to project (possibly recursively) only to phrases Y^1 of the same category. This is structural **endocentricity.** YP is a label for a Y^1 which does not further project.

a. Universal Grammar provides a restricted set of morpheme categories {B}: **lexical categories** X (= N, V, A and P), **specifiers** SPEC(XP), I, D and perhaps a few others.
b. UG matches a small range of **cognitive syntactic features F** with each B whose combinations [B, ±F] characterize up to a maximum of say twenty or so members of B.

(1.4)   **Some probable UG matches**

syntactic features F	associated categories B
tense and modal features	I
quantifier features	D or NUM
space-time co-ordinates	P
ACTIVITY	V
PERFECTIVE (aspect)	V
ANIMATE, COUNT	N
comparative features	SPEC(XP)

(1.5) **Canonical Realization.** UG matches a few cognitive syntactic features F to each syntactic category B. These features F contribute to semantic interpretation (Logical Form) only in these "canonical positions" on B. They appear elsewhere only via language-particular lexical stipulation.

Three classes of features:
i)   **Purely semantic features** *f* are present *only* on the head categories X = N, V, A and P. They are not used in syntax and are not present on closed subclasses of grammatical X.
ii) **Cognitive syntactic features F in canonical positions** occur with all syntactic categories. They play a central role in both syntax and at LF.
iii) **Purely syntactic features F** also occur with all syntactic categories. They are centrally used in syntax but play no role in LF. They indicate contexts, realize the features in (ii) in non-canonical positions, or stipulate a marked lack of content (e.g, +STATIVE on V).

(1.8) **Categorial Uniformity.** The categories defined in terms of the bar notation, X^j and SPEC(XP), do not differ from language to language, but their subcategories realized in each language's syntax may vary.

---

[1] These statements are reproduced from the text of the study, sometimes with minor changes in phrasing to allow understanding without reference to a surrounding text. In addition, many of these statements are keyed in the text to citations and/or explanatory footnotes, which are omitted here.

(1.9) **Hierarchical Universality**. The range of hierarchical combinations of syntactic categories does not vary from language to language at the level of deep structure.

(1.14) a. N and projections of N and D are "**N-projections**"; V and projections of V and I are "**V-projections**".
   b. DP and IP are "**extended projections**" of N and V respectively.
   c. DP and IP are "**cyclic domains**" of N and V respectively.

(1.19) **Functional Projections**. FP = (DP) - F - XP. When F is D, then X is N; when F is I, then X is V.

(1.20)
a. **Species-specific Lexicon**. The open class lexicon is plausibly the faculty of "human knowledge."
b. **The Lexicon as Knowledge**. The open class lexicon is the systematic shared part of human memory.
c. **Permanence of the Lexicon**. The entries of the lexicon remain basically unchanged and unaffected by use.

I.B. Lexical Format and Subcategorization (mainly Chapters 2 and 4)

(2.13) **Lexical Interface Principle**. The lexicon uses only morpheme categories. It cannot mention phrases, nor distinguish between X and XP.

(2.14) **General lexical format for free morphemes:** $@, X, F_i, f_j, +<F_k>$, where F_k "satisfies subcategorization." (There are no combinatorial statements in the lexicon which refer to purely semantic features.)

(4.8) **Multi-Level Lexical Insertion**. Lexical items from the Syntacticon, in accord with their feature content, can be inserted at different stages of a derivation: via the Dictionary ("at deep structure"), during a syntactic derivation and during a phonological derivation.

(7.8) **Generalized Subcategorization**. A frame $@, Y, +<X>, +<X\_\_\_>$ or $+<\_\_\_X>$ is satisfied if and only if X is a feature of an (extended) sister ß of Y or of ß's lexical head. (4.27) below defines "lexical head."[2]

(8.16) **Frames instantiating single complements**:

V, +<D>	Direct objects of transitive verbs
V, +<A>	Predicate adjectives
V, +<P>	Path PPs with Activity Verbs and Place PPs with Statives
V, +<N>	Predicate nominals
V, +<V>	Participles, gerunds and infinitives of obligatory control
V, +<I>	Clausal complements of epistemic and *(dis)like* class verbs

(8.58) **Lexical Density**. Lexical predicates utilize all and only the subcategorization frames constructable by syntactic category theory and the LF Case Filter (8.47) below. (Full discussion in Chapter 8.)

---

[2] In the rest of this summary of formal results, phrasal subcategorization is always notated by +<B>, while prefixes are +<__B> and suffixes are +<B__>, as in section 3.4.

(4.3)   **Language-particular syntax** resides entirely in lexical specifications, namely the inherent and contextual feature combinations associated with closed class items.

Successively more general statements extending subcategorization:

(2.18)   **Extended Classical Subcategorization.** @ , X , +___F is satisfied if and only if F is a cognitive syntactic feature of a lexical head of a complement in XP.

(3.22)   **Ordered subcategorization.** The entry "@, X, +< F___>" means that @ has a left-hand sister immediately dominated **by X^0** whose lexical head has a feature F. +<___F > means a right-hand sister of @ is +F.

(3.23)   **Order-free subcategorization.** The entry "@, X, +< F >" means that @ has a complement immediately dominated **by X^1** whose lexical head has a feature F.

(3.24)   **Unified Classical Subcategorization.** The frames +< F >, +< F___> or +<___F > in a lexical entry @, X are satisfied if and only if F is a feature of a lexical head of a sister to X^0.

(4.29)   **Revised Classical Subcategorization.** A frame @ , Y , +<F>, +<F___> or +<___F> is satisfied if and only if F is a feature of the lexical head of an (extended) sister of $Y^0 = $ @.

(4.28)   **Extended Sisterhood.** If Z^0 and XP are sisters and if Z^1 is the smallest phrase (besides structural projections of Y) whose lexical head is Y^0, then Y^0 and XP are extended sisters.

(5.47)   **Condition on Selection.** If a subcategorization frame +< [X, F_i] > is satisfied by ZP, any features in ZP not licensed by its lexical head X must be stipulated among the F_i.[3]

(8.18)   **Subcategorized Features Convention.** A feature complex in a lexical frame can be written in an ordered sequence +< [F_1, . . . , F_i, . . .] >, where at least F_1 is in its interpretable canonical position.

(4.75)   **Differences between the DICTIONARY and the SYNTACTICON**

	DICTIONARY	SYNTACTICON ↓
Items with both cognitive and purely syntactic features F	yes	yes
Cognitive features F canonically realized on UG-defined hosts	yes	yes
Insertion possible at the beginning of a syntactic derivation	yes	yes
Grammatical categories in the inventory	N, V, A, P	all
Items with purely semantic features *f*	YES	NO
Open classes; coining and neologisms for adult speakers	YES	NO
Bound forms have inherent stress and head true compounds	YES	NO
Interface with non-linguistic memory and culture	YES	NO
Full suppletion inside paradigms	NO	YES
Certain phonetically zero morphemes	NO	YES
Items must conform to core or primary vocabulary phonology	NO	YES
Items with alternatively realized features	NO	YES
Insertion also possible during syntax and at PF	NO	YES

---

[3] This explains (i) why heads intervening between selector and selectee must in general be empty, and (ii) why in particular open class verbs don't select V + *en*.

(4.12) **Types of insertion from the Syntacticon**

INSERTION LEVEL	FREE MORPHEMES	BOUND MORPHEMES
Prior to syntactic computation ("deep structure")	closed class X with specialized meanings, and parts of idioms	non-productive derivational morphology with specialized lexical meanings
During syntactic computation, prior to Spell Out	closed class grammatical words with LF syntactic features; cf. Chapter 6	productive derivational morphology; cf. sections 4.6, 4.7.2, 4.7.3 and Chapter 5
During PF computation, after Spell Out	closed class grammatical words which are "place-holders"; cf. Chapter 7	inflectional morphology; sections 4.4, 4.7.1 and Chapter 5

II. Syntactic Component

II.A. The Dictionary Interface with Syntax (mainly Chapters 4, 7, 8)

(6.23)   **Economy of Representation** (Economy at the Dictionary Interface). Structural requirements such as subcategorization frames are to be satisfied at a level of derivation with as few phrasal nodes as possible.

(4.7)   **Deep Lexicalization** (DL). Items associated with non-syntactic, purely semantic features f must satisfy lexical insertion conditions (just) before syntactic processing of the smallest cyclic domains containing them. Such f occur only on N, V, A and P.

(4.74)   **Cyclic Lexical Insertion.** A lexical head X imposes restrictions on its arguments only after the transformational cycle is terminated in all the cyclic domains properly contained inside X^{max}.

(7.38)   **PP Licensing.** A phrasal projection PP is freely licensed as a daughter of any phrasal projection Y^j of a lexical category.

(7.40)   **The Deep Case Filter.** Every extended and maximal projection of @ (= N, V, A) must, prior to s-structure, be a sister to a non-maximal lexical projection of ß = V, P, I or D.[4]

(8.9)   **Case Indices.** The case assigners (= potential case indices) are I, D and any V or P whose lexical realizations enter a tree by satisfying +___Y, where Y is a functional head D or I.

(8.13)   **Case Assignment Condition** ("Minimality"). A potential case assigner ß can be a case index on DP if some $ß^j$ ($ß^0$ or $ß^1$) is the closest non-maximal projection of any potential case assigner which c-commands DP.

(8.46)   **Proximity Condition on Case Assignment.** A category X can be assigned as case index to @ only if the largest constituents separating X and @ are not maximal YP.

(1.18)   **Number Filter** (Conjecture).[5] The functional heads (I and D) must have number ($\pm$PLURAL) at PF in certain languages, e.g., English but not Japanese. (This guarantees a DP under IP to furnish I with Number.)

II.B. Headedness and Left-Right Order (mainly Chapter 3)

(4.27)   **Lexical Head/Projection.** Let Y^0 be the highest **lexically filled** head in Z^j. Then Y^0 is the lexical head of Z^j, and Z^j is a lexical projection of Y^0. (An empty structural head Z^0 allows a $Y \neq Z$ to act as a head of Z^j.)

---

[4] The text in Chapter 7 fails to stress that this filter does not apply to some @ which are adjuncts (outside X^1), though this is mentioned in note 29.

[5] I mark as "conjectures" proposals for which I have presented quite scanty evidence.

(6.62)   **Phrasal Projection**. A phrasal projection of a lexical head X^0 consists of any of its lexical projections Z^1, as defined by (4.27). If X^0 is a daughter but not the head of Z^1, it counts as its own phrasal projection.

Compound constituents Y^0 are formed by sequences of lexical categories X^0. In regular cases, compounds are endocentric. **Words** consist of both simple and compound X^0, except for bound morphology as in (3.40).

(3.21)   **Unified headedness**. Headedness is transitive: heads of words which are in turn heads of phrases are also heads of those phrases.

(3.6)   **Universal Right Headedness**. In the absence of language-particular properties (of syntax or morphology), heads are always on the right.

(3.7)   **Complete Projection**. A maximal projection of a lexical or functional category which cannot be further extended is a complete projection. All other projections are termed incomplete.

(3.8)   **English Word Order**. In any incomplete phrasal projection X^1, the head precedes its phrasal Y^j sisters.

(3.17)   **French Word Order**. In any incomplete projection (either X^1 or X^0), a free head precedes its free Y^j sisters.

III. Principles for the PF Interface (mainly Chapters 3, 4, 8)

(4.36)   **Economy of Derivation** (Economy at the PF Interface): Of equivalent deep structures, prefer the derivation of PF containing the fewest insertions of free morphemes. (Two deep structures which differ only by empty categories not interpretable at LF count as equivalent.)

(4.21)   **Phonological Lexicalization** (PL). Items specified solely in terms of purely syntactic, uninterpreted features F (contextual, alternatively realized and "lack of content" features) are inserted subsequent to any operation contributing to LF.

(4.20)   **Alternative Realization** ("AR"). A syntactic feature F canonically realized in UG on category B can be alternatively realized in a closed class grammatical morpheme under X^0, provided X^0 is the lexical head of a sister of B^j.

(9.14)   **Phrase Mate Hypothesis for Romance clitics** (special case of 4.20). Romance clitics on V_i^0 are associated only with (features F of) YP sisters to some V_i^k, where YP = DP, IP, PP, NP, AP or VP.

(4.35)   **Invisible Category Principle** (ICP). If all marked canonical features F on B are alternatively realized by AR (4.20), except perhaps B itself, then B may be empty.

(4.42)   **Unmarked AR morphemes**. A bound morpheme alternatively realizing F_i with no marked notation in the Syntacticon appears only when it zeroes the canonical position of F_i.

(4.34)   **Free Riders** (Conjecture). If a morpheme @ alternatively realizes a feature F canonically associated with a category B, and some F' is also spelled out under B, then @ can also spell out F'.

(8.62)   **PF Case**. Apply the Case-assignment Condition (8.13) again in PF to all nominal [+N] projections.

(8.45)   **PF Case Filter**. At PF, any potentially phonological nominal {+N] projection (D^j, N^j and A^j) must have Abstract Case.

(3.47)   Morphology, in particular **affixation**, results from using a bound form in the Syntacticon in compounding.

(3.40)   **English Morphology**. If the head of a compound lacks purely semantic features f, then it contains at most one inherently stressless foot with a one-segment onset. (That is, it is not a free morpheme.)

Two conjectures for extending central principles

(5.16)   **Generalized Alternative Realization** (Conjecture for exceptional case marking on subjects of infinitives). A syntactic feature F canonically realized in UG on category B can be alternatively realized in a closed class grammatical morpheme under X^0, provided X^0 is the lexical head of an (**extended**) sister of B^j.

(9.19)   **Generalized Invisible Category Principle** (Conjecture for empty operators). B or SPEC(BP) may be empty if all its marked canonical features F, except perhaps B itself, are **realized** under X^0, where X^k is a sister of B^j.

IV. Principles for the LF Interface

IV.A. General Principles for LF (mainly Chapters 4, 6, 8)

Cognitive syntactic features F contribute centrally to meaning (Logical Form) in all syntactic classes. Finer distinctions of meaning in terms of **purely semantic features** *f* which play no role in syntax appear only in the four open lexical categories N, A, V and P.

(4.2) **Logical Form of a sentence.** Each (unambiguous) sentence has a universal representation formed by a syntactic derivation.

(4.10) **LF Visibility Condition.** A node is interpreted at LF if and only if it is either (canonically or alternatively) realized with a lexical morpheme or is co-indexed with an interpreted structure.

(1.27) **Economy of Reference** (Conjecture for Economy at the LF Interface). Among representations with the same LF interpretations, prefer the one with the fewest pragmatic references to the universe of discourse.

(8.47) **Logical Form Case Filter.** At Logical Form, internal arguments YP of X^0 are each specified differently for Abstract Case. In particular:

(8.33) **The Complement Space.** Subcategorization frames can specify at most one (abstract) accusative DP, one (abstract) oblique DP and one phrasal complement without case.

(8.56) **"Oblique Case" for the LF Case Filter.** An XP in [PATH - XP] counts as obliquely case-marked in LF.

(1.15) **Generalized Subjects.** The subject or external argument of a head X is the lowest N-projection which c-commands a phrasal projection of X within X's minimal cyclic domain.

(6.74) **Local Binding in LF (Revised Principle A).** Let X, Y and Z be distinct nodes. If Y is a subject in ...X...Y...Z..., where X c-commands Y and Y asymmetrically c-commands Z, X may not bind Z.

IV.B. Specific Principles and Theta Role Assignment (Chapters 2 and 7)

(2.35) **Full Interpretation.** Every DP argument of Y^0 is assigned at least one out of a universally specified list of semantic roles ("theta roles") *f*, unless its grammatical position is lexically specified by Y^0 as semantically empty. A given role can be assigned to at most one argument.

(1.17) **Extended Projection Principle.** Every head verb present in LF must have a structural subject phrase to which a theta role may be assigned.

(2.42) **Principal Argument Role.** A predicate @ of category V or A typically specifies in its lexical entry that some particular theta role *f* **must** be assigned to a subject or an object.

(2.39) **Agent Specification.** "Thus one rule (probably universal) will stipulate that for verbs of action, the animate subject may be interpreted as the agent." (Chomsky, 1972)

(7.33) **LF Role of P.** UG provides a category P, which is relational like V, whose basic LF role is to situate reference and events on an innate space-time grid.

(2.47)   **Ground Specification.** An object DP of Y^0 (Y = V, P, N, A) is a Ground if and only if Y^0 is +LOC. The features co-specified with +LOC determine subcases of Ground (Location, Goal, etc.).[6]

(2.48)   **Figure Specification.** Exactly one Figure DP, distinct from the Ground, may be present among the arguments of Y^0. (The Figure never appears in an adjunct unless with the Agent role.)

(7.58)   **Theta Relatedness.** X^0 and Y^0 are theta-related if and only if one assigns a theta role to a lexical projection of the other.

(7.59)   **Revised Theta Criterion.** Theta-relatedness is anti-transitive.

(4.48)   **Transparent Derivational Heads.** If a lexical suffix @ on X^0 at Spell Out selects no complements, then (i) the lowest DP argument c-commanding @ and (ii) any lower arguments may be interpreted as the corresponding arguments of X^0.

(1.31)   **Truth value** (English, French). Lexical items in I in LF carry reference, i.e. Frege's truth value.

(1.36)   **Truth value** (Conjecture for Japanese). Lexical items in I raised to C in LF carry reference, i.e. Frege's truth value.

(5.70)   **Perfect Tense in LF.** An AP whose lexical head is a V is taken as a property of the subject, i.e., it constitutes a V-headed phrase with "present relevance" (to the subject).

(9.41)   **Romance null generic objects**. A Romance zero accusative clitic identifies null subcategorized pronominal generic/ expletive objects i.e., [D, -DEF, -NOMINATIVE].

(10.32)   **Animate PRO.** A PRO in a SPEC position is +ANIMATE.

IV.C. Principles of Pragmatic Interpretation (Chapters 9 and 10)

(10.13)   **Discourse Participants.** The speaker (first person reference) and the addressee (second person reference) of a given sentence are disjoint in reference.

(10.17)   **Imperative Subjects.** A PRO subject of a (main or embedded) imperative clause is the addressee.

(10.22)   **Preservation of ±Realis.** Accurate indirect speech retains the feature value of MODAL.

(9.1)   **Syntactic Identification.** All and only empty DPs licensed by subcategorization must be locally rather than pragmatically identified.[7]

---

[6] Here are the special cases, as given by (2.46a):

DP, Static Location	= [P, +LOC, -PATH] ___
DP, Goal	= [P, +LOC, +PATH, +GOAL] ___
DP, Source	= [P, +LOC, +PATH, -GOAL] ___
DP, Experiencer	= [P, +LOC, +PATH, (GOAL)] ___,

where V has the feature f = PSYCHOLOGICAL

[7] This includes obligatory PRO subjects licensed by +<V>; cf. the discussion of (10.5) in Chapter 10.

(9.23)   **No "non-syntactic" arguments.** Any lexically represented arguments of the head within X^0 must be overt; i.e. the only null arguments are syntactically projected phrases outside X^0.

(2.30)   **Concealed Questions.** D ===> WH..., where DP is selected by V, +<{D / WH}>.

Some diverse theorems of interpretation:

(10.8)   **Pragmatic Control.** Only non-DPs and DPs not licensed by subcategorization (including optional PRO subjects) may be identified by pragmatics. **Reason:** Syntactic Identification (9.1).

(10.18)   **Theorem on Disjoint Reference.** A PRO corresponding to the subject of an imperative clause is disjoint from that clause's speaker. **Reason:** Discourse Participants (10.13) plus Imperative Subjects (10.17).

(6.59)   **Verbal Subjects** (special case of 1.15): The subject of a V is the lowest DP which c-commands some phrasal projection of V within a minimal containing IP.

(1.35)   **Theorem of LF Economy.** An English IP can fail to be a sister to C only if its I is $\varnothing$ in LF, i.e. only if it is non-finite (without truth value). **Reason:** (1.27), (1.31) and (1.34).

(5.68)   **Case Corollary of Alternative Realization.** Specific case features, whatever their provenance, do not contribute to interpretation at LF. **Reason:** (7.13) They are alternative realizations of case assigners.

Intuitive formulations	Economy Principles (8.44)	Case Principles
LEXICAL INTERFACE	**Economy of Representation:** Begin a derivation with the fewest possible maximal syntactic units, or **"start with as few phrases as possible."**	**Deep Case Filter** (7.40): XP other than PP must start as sisters or specifiers of case assigners.
INTERFACE WITH PF	**Economy of Derivation:** Arrive at PF by inserting the fewest possible maximal PF units, or **"insert as few words as possible."**	**PF Case Filter** (8.45): Phonological projections of [+N] must have case. (This is the classical Case Filter.)
INTERFACE WITH LF	**Economy of Reference:** Arrive at LF with the fewest units of reference possible, that is, **"minimize separate references to a universe of discourse."**	**LF Case Filter** (8.47): Internal arguments must each have a different abstract case, including no case.

Sample Lexicon

Final versions of entries in the text from the English Open Class Dictionary
(*f* often omitted)

(2.19)   Indirect question complements: wonder, V, +<WH>
exclaim, V, +<[I, (WH)]>

(8.1a-b) Selection by syntactic features F: glance, V, +< [SPACE, PATH] >
reside, V, +STATIVE, +< [SPACE, PLACE] >

(2.20)   Selection by syntactic features   amuse, V, +LOCATION, +PSYCH, +<ANIMATE>
disperse, V, +<PLURAL>
place, V, +<D, PLACE>

(2.38)   Principle Arguments (2.42) specified:
fill, V, *Ground,* +<(D)^(P)>
pack, V, *Agent,* +<(D)^(P)>

(3.26)   Combining morphology and syntax: free, A, +<[+N, -AD] (___)>

(5.33)   Basic Dictionary entry @ for V: attract, V, +f_i, +<D>, +(<to^D>)
Related derived entry: (un)+@+en, +<ANIM>, <to^D>

(5.34)   Basic Dictionary entry ß for V: tire, V, +LOCATION, +PSYCH, +f_i, +<ANIM>
Related derived entry: ß + en, +(<of^D>)

(5.38)   Basic Dictionary entry @ for V: strew, V, +f_i, +<D>, +<P>
Related derived entry: @ + en, +LOCATION

(7.42)   Obligatory control complements: influence, V, +< ANIMATE, (V) >, ...
force, V, +< D, (ACTIVITY) >, ...

(7.46)   Infinitives alternating with gerunds: manage, V, +< [V, (MODAL)] >, ...
decide, V, +< [ACTIVITY, MODAL] >, ...
try, V, +< [ACTIVITY, (MODAL)] >, ...

(8.21)   Direct objects with indirect objects or PPs:
ask, V, +<D, ([ANIM, SOURCE])>
recommend, V, +<D, (ANIM)>
hand, V, +<D, { ANIM/ PATH }>
situate, V, +<D, (PLACE)>
paint, V, +<(D), ([ANIM, LOC'])>

(8.24)   Gerunds not alternating with DPs: prevent, V, +<D, [V, SOURCE] >
discourage, V, +<D, ([V, SOURCE])>

(8.26a) Verb with multiple frames: find, V, +<{ D, (X) / [I, (SUBJUN)] }>, X ≠ I.

Some entries in the text from closed class Syntacticons[8]

(1.7) **Closed Classes**. A closed grammatical class X (including N, V, A, P) is one whose members have no purely semantic features *f*, but only cognitive syntactic features F.

(4.13) *Of*-insertion:	of, P, -LOCATION, +< [+N, -V] >
(4.14) *That*-insertion:	that, P, -WH, -LOCATION, +< I, FINITE >
(4.15) *Do so*:	do, V, { +< D > / +< so > } (< to^ANIM >)
Do-suppoort:	do, V, < ___ [I, -MODAL] >
(4.16) *There*-insertion:	there, D, -REFERENCE, -SPECIFIC
(8.1c) Motion verb:	go, V, (STATIVE), +< LOCATION >
(8.15) P with multiple frames:	for, P, (LOC'), { +<D> / +< [I, SUBJUN] > }
(4.23) Comparative inflection:	er, A, COMPARATIVE, +<A ___ >
(4.25) Past inflection:	ed, V, PAST, +<V__ >
(5.59) English plural:	(e) s, N, +<N__ >, + <u>PLUR</u>
(4.43) Copula under V:	be, V, STATIVE, +< X$_{-CASE}$ >
(4.45) Copulas in [I, -MODAL]:	were, I, PAST, PLUR, STATIVE, +< X$_{-CASE}$ > was, I, PAST, STATIVE, +< X$_{-CASE}$ > are, I, PLURAL, STATIVE, +< X$_{-CASE}$ > am, I, FIRST, STATIVE, +< X$_{-CASE}$ > is, I, STATIVE, +< X$_{-CASE}$ >
(7.22) Minimal case-assigner:	have, { V/ TENSE }, STATIVE, +<X$_{ACC}$ >
(2.22) Linking verbs:	get, V, +<-INHERENT> become, V, +<+INHERENT>
(4.55) Substantivization:	ing, [+N], +<V___>, ({+N = N: V = +ACTIVITY,...}) ({+N = A: V = +PSYCH, or ...})
(3.37) + (4.72) Agent nouns:	er, N, ANIMATE, +<[V, ACTIVITY]___, (D), (D) >
(3.27) A free form causative verb:	make, V, +CAUS, +< D, A >
A bound form causative verb:	ize, V, +CAUS, +< D, A___>

---

[8] Items from other than the English Syntacticon are so specified.

(5.22) In adjectival passives, the head [$_A$ -*en*] is present in LF and at all levels.
In verbal passives, -*en* is absent in the syntax and LF, being present only at PF.

(5.20) Passive participle entry: en, A, +<V___> , ØF, (-PROPERTY)

(5.67) Perfective participle entry: en, A, +<V___> , ACC, -PROPERTY

(5.71) Combined participle entry (Spanish and English have the same form):
en, A, +<V___> , { ØF/ -PROPERTY { ØF/ ACC } }

(5.60) Ukrainian passive: "en", A, +<V___> , (-PROPERTY), <u>ØF</u>

(5.61a) German passive: "en", A, +<V___> , (-PROPERTY), (ØF)

(5.61b) Norwegian passive: "en", A, +<V___> , (-PROPERTY), (<u>ØF</u>)

(3.31) Japanese passive bound verb: (r)are, V, +< V(___) >, +STATIVE

(4.11) **Null morphemes.** The Syntacticon (but not the Dictionary) tolerates phonetically zero morphemes, which tend to occur as least marked members of paradigms.

(9.42) Romance generic object clitic: Ø, -DEFINITE, -NOMINATIVE, +<___V>

(9,43) Certain overt Italian clitics: lo, +DEFINITE, +ACCUSATIVE, +<___V>
si, -DEFINITE, +NOMINATIVE, +<___V>

English discourse anaphors (DAF is a "discourse anaphora feature" generalizing DEF):

(9.33) So-called N-bar ellipsis: Ø, N, +DAF, -COUNT
VP-ellipsis: Ø, V,+ DAF
one, N, +DAF, +COUNT

(9.34) Null complement anaphora: Ø, C, +DAF (occurs if a higher V selects DAF)
so, A, +DAF (occurs if a higher V selects DAF)

(6.42) **Optional Clause Union.** Grammatical X^0, whose features F_i are interpretable at LF (unlike those of *be* and stative *have*), may be inserted either at the dictionary interface ("deep structure") or in the syntax.

(6.54a) French causative verb 'let':   laisser, V, +F_i, +<{ D, V }, ((PATH)^D)>

(6.54b) French perception verb 'hear': entendre, V, +F_i, +<{ D (V), V }>

References[1]

Abeillé, A., D. Godard and P. Miller (1997) "Les Causatives en Français: Un Cas de Compétition Syntaxique," *Langue Française* 115, 62-74.

Abney, S. (1987) *The English Noun Phrase in its Sentential Aspect*, MIT doctoral dissertation.

Åfarli, T. (1989) "Passive in Norwegian and in English," *Linguistic Inquiry* 20, 101-108.

Åfarli, T. (1992) *The Syntax of Norwegian Passive Constructions*, John Benjamins, Amsterdam.

Aissen, J. (1974) "Verb Raising," *Linguistic Inquiry* 5, 325-366.

Aissen, J. and D. Perlmutter (1976) "Clause Reduction in Spanish," *Proceedings of the Second Annual Meeting of the Berkeley Linguistic Society,* University of California, Berkeley.

Anderson, S. (1971) "On the Role of Deep Structure in Semantic Interpretation," *Foundations of Language* 7, 387-396.

Andrews, A. (1971) "Case Agreement of Predicate Modifiers in Ancient Greek," *Linguistic Inquiry* 2, 127-151.

Aoun, J. (1985) *A Grammar of Anaphora*, MIT Press, Cambridge.

Aoyagi, H. (1998) "Particles as Adjunct Clitics," in P. Tamanji and K. Kusumoto, eds., *Proceedings of the North East Linguistic Society*, University of Toronto, Toronto.

Aronoff, M. (1976) *Word Formation in Generative Grammar*, MIT Press, Cambridge.

Artiagoitia, X. (1992) *Verbal Projections in Basque and Minimal Structure,* University of Washington doctoral dissertation.

Authier, J.-M. and L. Reed (1992) "On the Syntactic Status of French Affected Datives," *The Linguistic Review* 9, 295-311.

Baker, M. (1985) "The Mirror Principle and Morphosyntactic Explanation," *Linguistic Inquiry* 16, 373-416.

Baker, M. (1988) *Incorporation: A Theory of Grammatical Function Changing*, University of Chicago Press, Chicago.

Baker, M., K. Johnson and I. Roberts (1989) "Passive Arguments Raised," *Linguistic Inquiry* 20, 219-252.

Baltin, M. (1987) "Heads and Projections," in M. Baltin and A. Kroch, eds., *Alternative Conceptions of Phrase Structure,* University of Chicago Press, Chicago.

Banfield, A. (1981) *Unspeakable Sentences,* Routledge and Kegan Paul, London.

Beermann, D. (1990), *Semantic and Syntactic Constraints on German Determiner Movement within the Prepositional Phrase*, University of Texas at El Paso master's thesis.

---

[1] These entries do not indicate countries. Cambridge University Press is in Cambridge, England, and MIT Press is in Cambridge, Massachusetts, and London.

Belletti, A. and L. Rizzi (1988) "Psych-verbs and Theta-theory," *Natural Language and Linguistic Theory* 6, 291-352.

Benveniste, E. (1966) *Problèmes de Linguistique Générale*, Gallimard, Paris.

Bloomfield, L. (1933) *Language*, Holt, Rinehart and Winston, New York.

Bok-Bennema, R. (1981) "Clitics and Binding in Spanish," in J. Koster and R. May, eds., *Levels of Syntactic Representation*, Foris, Dordrecht.

Borer, H. (1984) *Parametric Syntax*, Foris, Dordrecht.

Borer, H. (1989) "On the Morphological Parallelism between Compounds and Constructs," in G. Booij and J. van Marle, eds., *Yearbook of Morphology* 1, Foris, Dordrecht.

Borer, H. (1991) "The Causative-inchoative Alternation: A Case Study in Parallel Morphology," *The Linguistic Review* 8, 119-158.

Brame, M. (1984) "The Head-Selector Theory of Lexical Specifications and the Nonexistence of Coarse Categories," *Linguistic Analysis* 10, 321-325.

Bresnan, J. (1970) "On Complementizers: Toward a Syntactic Theory of Complement Types," *Foundations of Language* 6, 297-321.

Bresnan, J. (1973) "The Syntax of the Comparative Clause in English," *Linguistic Inquiry* 28, 119-164.

Bresnan, J. and J. Grimshaw (1978) "The Syntax of Free Relatives in English," *Linguistic Inquiry* 9, 331-391.

Brody, M. (1995) *Lexico-Logical Form: A Radically Minimalist Theory*, MIT Press, Cambridge.

Burzio, L. (1986) *Italian Syntax*, Reidel, Dordrecht.

Caink, A. (1998) *The Lexical Interface: Closed Class Items in South Slavic and English*, University of Durham doctoral dissertation.

Cardinaletti, A. and G. Giusti (1991) "Partitive *ne* and the QP-Hypothesis: a Case Study," *University of Venice Working Papers in Linguistics*, 1-19.

Cardinaletti, A. and M. Starke (1999) "The Typology of Structural Deficiency," in H. van Riemsdijk, ed., *Empirical Approaches to Language Typology: Clitics in the Languages of Europe*, Mouton de Gruyter, Berlin.

Casa, L. (1993) *Word Order in Italian, Romanian and Spanish*, University of Washington master's thesis.

Chomsky, N. (1957) *Syntactic Structures*, Mouton, The Hague.

Chomsky, N. (1964) *Current Issues in Linguistic Theory*, Mouton, The Hague.

Chomsky, N. (1965) *Aspects of the Theory of Syntax*, MIT Press, Cambridge.

Chomsky, N. (1970) "Remarks on Nominalizations," *Studies on Semantics in Generative Grammar*, Mouton, the Hague, 1-61.

Chomsky, N. (1972) "Deep Structure, Surface Structure and Semantic Interpretation," *Studies on Semantics in Generative Grammar*, Mouton, the Hague, 62-119.

Chomsky, N. (1973) "Conditions on Transformations," in S. Anderson and P. Kiparsky, eds., *A Festschrift for Morris Halle*, Holt, Rinehart and Winston, New York.

Chomsky, N. (1976) "Conditions on Rules of Grammar," *Linguistic Analysis* 2, 303-351.

Chomsky, N. (1977) "On Wh-movement," in P. Culicover, T. Wasow and A. Akmajian, eds., *Formal Syntax*, Academic Press, New York.

Chomsky, N. (1981) *Lectures on Government and Binding*, Foris, Dordrecht.

Chomsky, N. (1986a) *Barriers*, MIT Press, Cambridge.

Chomsky, N. (1986b) *Knowledge of Language: Its Nature, Origin, and Use*, Praeger, New York.

Chomsky, N. (1991) "Some Notes on Economy of Derivation and Representation," in R. Freidin, ed., *Principles and Parameters in Comparative Grammar*, MIT Press, Cambridge.

Chomsky, N. (1993) "A Minimalist Program for Linguistic Theory," in K. Hale and S. J. Keyser, eds., *The View from Building 20*, MIT Press, Cambridge.

Chomsky, N. (1995) *The Minimalist Program*, MIT Press, Cambridge.

Chomsky, N. and M. Halle (1968) *The Sound Pattern of English*, Harper and Row, New York.

Chomsky, N. and H. Lasnik (1977) "Filters and Control," *Linguistic Inquiry* 8, 425-504.

Contreras, H. (1979) "Clause Reduction, the Saturation Constraint and Clitic Promotion in Spanish," *Linguistic Analysis* 5, 161-181.

Corver, N. (1997) "The Internal Syntax of the Dutch Extended Adjectival Projection," *Natural Language and Linguistic Theory* 15, 289-368.

Chung, S. (1976) "An Object-Creating Rule in Bahasa Indonesia," *Linguistic Inquiry* 7, 41-88.

Di Sciullo, A.-M. and E. Williams (1987) *On the Definition of Word*, MIT Press, Cambridge.

Elliott, D. (1971) *The Grammar of Emotive and Exclamatory Sentences in English*, Ohio State University doctoral dissertation. [Reproduced in *Working Papers in Linguistics No. 8*, Computer and Information Science Research Center, Ohio State University, Columbus.]

Elliott, D. (1974) "Toward a Grammar of Exclamations," *Foundations of Language* 11, 231-246.

Emonds, J. (1974) "Arguments for Assigning Tense Meanings after Certain Syntactic Transformational Apply," in E. Keenan, ed., *Formal Semantics*, Cambridge University Press, Cambridge.

Emonds, J. (1976) *A Transformational Approach to English Syntax*, Academic Press, New York.

Emonds, J. (1978) "The Verbal Complex V'-V in French," *Linguistic Inquiry* 9, 151-175.

Emonds, J. (1979) "Appositive Relatives have no Properties," *Linguistic Inquiry* 10, 211-243.

Emonds, J. (1980) "Inversion Généralisée NP-Alpha: Marque Distinctive de l'Anglais," in A. Rouveret, ed., *Langages* 60, 1-65.

Emonds, J. (1985) *A Unified Theory of Syntactic Categories*, Foris, Dordrecht.

Emonds, J. (1986) "Parts of Speech in Generative Grammar," *Linguistic Analysis* 17, 3-42.

Emonds, J. (1987) "The Invisible Category Principle," *Linguistic Inquiry* 18, 613-631.

Emonds, J. (1991a) "The Autonomy of the (Syntactic) Lexicon and Syntax," in C. Georgopoulos and R. Ishihara, eds., *Interdisciplinary Approaches to Language: Essays in Honor of S.-Y. Kuroda*, Kluwer Academic Press, Dordrecht.

Emonds, J. (1991b) "Subcategorization and Syntax-Based Theta-Role Assignment," *Natural Language and Linguistic Theory* 9, 369-429.

Emonds, J. (1992a) "Complement Selection and the Syntactic Lexicon: Rereading *Syntactic Structures*," in L. Tasmowski and A. Zribi-Hertz, eds., *De la musique à la linguistique: Hommages à Nicolas Ruwet,* Communication and Cognition, Ghent.

Emonds, J. (1992b) "Economy of Representation: the Realizations of X, +__YP," in K. Hunt, T. Perry, and V. Samiian, eds., *Proceedings of the Western Conference on Linguistics 4,* California State University Linguistics Department, Fresno.

Emonds, J. (1993) "Projecting Indirect Objects," *The Linguistic Review* 10, 211-262.

Emonds, J. (1994) "Two Conditions of Economy," in G. Cinque et al., eds., *Paths toward Universal Grammar: Papers in Honor of Richard Kayne*, Georgetown University Press, Washington, D.C.

Emonds, J. (1995) "Deep Free and Surface Bound Pronouns," in H. Campos and P. Kempchinsky, eds., *Evolucion y Revolucion en Romance: Festschrift for Carlos Otero*, Georgetown University Press, Washington, D.C.

Emonds, J. (1996) "Secondary Predication, Stationary Particles and Silent Prepositions," in A. Baba et al., eds., *Essays in Linguistics and Philology Presented to Professor Kinsuke Hasegawa,* Kenkyusha Press, Tokyo.

Emonds, J. (1997) "Stating Syntactic Co-occurrence," in M. Ukaji et al., eds., *Studies in English Linguistics: A Festschrift for Professor Akira Ota*, Taishukan Press, Tokyo.

Emonds, J. (1999) "How Clitics License Null Phrases: a Theory of the Lexical Interface," in H. van Riemsdijk, ed., *Empirical Approaches to Language Typology: Clitics in the Languages of Europe,* Mouton de Gruyter, Berlin.

Emonds, J. (2000) "The Flat Structure Economy of Semi-lexical Heads," in N. Corver and H. van Riemsdijk, eds., *The Function of Content Words and the Content of Function Words,* Mouton de Gruyter, Berlin.

Fassi-Fehri, A. (1993) *Issues in the Structure of Arabic Clauses and Words*, Kluwer Academic Press, Dordrecht.

Foulet, L. (1930) *Petite Syntaxe de l'Ancien Français,* H. Champion, Paris.

Fraser, B. (1970) "Some Remarks on the Action Nominalization in English," in R. Jacobs and P. Rosenbaum, eds., *Readings in English Transformational Grammar,* Ginn, Waltham.

George, L. and J. Kornfilt (1981) "Finiteness and Boundedness in Turkish," in F. Heny, ed., *Binding and Filtering*, Croom Helm, London.

Giusti, G. (1991) "The Categorial Status of Quantified Nominals," *Linguistische Berichte* 136, 438-454.

Greenberg, J. (1963) "Some Universals of Grammar with Particular Reference to the Order of Meaningful Elements," in J. Greenberg, ed., *Universals of Language,* MIT Press, Cambridge.

Grimshaw, J. (1979) "Complement Selection and the Lexicon," *Linguistic Inquiry* 10, 279-326.

Grimshaw, J. (1990) *Argument Structure*, MIT Press, Cambridge.

Grimshaw, J. and A. Mester (1988) "Light Verbs and Theta Marking," *Linguistic Inquiry* 19, 205-232.

Gruber, J. (1976) *Lexical Structures in Syntax and Semantics,* North-Holland Publishing, Amsterdam.

Haegeman, L. (1992) *Theory and Description in Generative Syntax*, Cambridge University Press, Cambridge.

Hankamer, J. and I. Sag (1976) "Deep and Surface Anaphora," *Linguistic Inquiry* 7, 391-426.

Hannahs, S. J. (1995) *Prosodic structure and French morphophonology: Linguistische Arbeiten 337*, Niemeyer Verlag, Tuebingen.

Harada, K. and T. Furuta (1999) "On the Maturation of A-chains: A View from Japanese Passives," in K. Inoue, ed., *Researching and Verifying an Advanced Theory of Human Language, Report 3B,* Graduate School of Language Sciences of Kanda University, Chiba.

Hasegawa, N. (1988) "Passive, Verb Raising, and the Affectedness Condition," in *Proceedings of the Seventh West Coast Conference on Formal Linguistics*, University of California, Irvine.

Haverkort, M. (1989) "Clitic Climbing and Barrierhood of VP," *Current Approaches to African Linguistics* 7, 145-158.

Haverkort, M. (1993) "Clitics and Parameterization," *Eurotyp Working Papers* VIII, 2, European Science Foundation, Strasbourg.

Hendrick, R. (1978) "The Phrase Structure of Adjectives and Complements," *Linguistic Analysis* 4, 255-299.

Herschensohn, J. (1981) "French Causatives: Restructuring, Opacity, Filters and Construal," *Linguistic Analysis* 7, 217-280.

Heycock, C. and A. Kroch (1999) "Pseudocleft Connectedness: Implications for the LF Interface Level," *Linguistic Inquiry* 30, 365-397.

Hockett, C. (1960) "The Origin of Speech," *Scientific American* 203, 88-96.

Huang, C.-T. (1984) "On the Distribution and Reference of Empty Pronouns," *Linguistic Inquiry*, 531-574.

Huang, L.-Y. (1990) *The Deep Word Order and Some Propositional Constructions of Mandarin Chinese,* University of Washington doctoral dissertation.

Jackendoff, R. (1972) *Semantic Interpretation in Generative Grammar*, MIT Press, Cambridge.

Jackendoff, R. (1973) "The Base Rules for Prepositional Phrases," in S. Anderson and P. Kiparsky, eds.,*A Festschrift for Morris Halle*, Holt, Rinehart and Winston, New York.

Jackendoff, R. (1977) *X-bar Syntax*, MIT Press, Cambridge.

Jackendoff, R. (1983) *Semantics and Cognition,* MIT Press, Cambridge.

Jackendoff, R. (1985) "Believing and Intending: Two Sides of the Same Coin," *Linguistic Inquiry* 16, 445-459.

Jackendoff, R. (1987) "The Status of Thematic Relations in Linguistic Theory," *Linguistic Inquiry* 18, 369-411.

Jackendoff, R. (1990) *Semantic Structures,* MIT Press, Cambridge.

Jaeggli, O. (1982) *Topics in Romance Syntax,* Foris, Dordrecht.

Jaeggli, O. (1986) "Passive," *Linguistic Inquiry* 17, 587-621.

Jespersen, O. (1905) *Growth and Structure of the English Language,* Doubleday and Co., Garden City.

Jespersen, O. (1940) *A Modern English Grammar on Historical Principles,* Ejnaar Munksgaard, Copenhagen.

Jo, M.-J. (1996) "Morphosyntactic Roles of the Grammatical Verb *Ha*," *Korean Journal of Linguistics* 21, 1179-1204.

Kader, M. (1981) *The Syntax of Malay Interrogatives,* Dewan Bahasa Dan Pustaka, Kuala Lumpur.

Kajihara, S. (1991) *The Syntactic Nature of Argument Transfer with suru,* University of Washington master's thesis.

Kallulli, D. (1999) *The Comparative syntax of Albanian: on the Contribution of Syntactic Types to Propositional Interpretation,* University of Durham doctoral dissertation.

Karimi, S. (1990) "Obliqueness, Specificity, and Discourse Functions: *Ra* in Persian," *Linguistic Analysis* 20, 139-169.

Kato, Y. (1985) "Negative Sentences in Japanese," *Sophia Linguistica Working Papers in Japanese* 19, Sophia University Linguistic Institute for International Communication, Tokyo.

Kayne, R. (1975) *French Syntax,* MIT Press, Cambridge.

Kayne, R. (1982) "Unambiguous Paths," in R. May and J. Koster, eds., *Levels of Syntactic Representation,* Foris, Dordrecht.

Keenan, E. (1975) "The Logical Diversity of Natural Languages," *Annals of the New York Academy of Sciences.*

Keenan, E. (1976) "Towards a Universal Definition of 'Subject', in C. Li, ed., *Subject and Topic,* Academic Press, New York.

Keyser, S. J. and T. Roeper (1992) "Re: The Abstract Clitic Hypothesis," *Linguistic Inquiry* 23, 89-125.

Kim, S.-W. and J. Maling (1993) "Syntactic Case and Frequency Adverbials in Korean," *Harvard Studies in Korean Linguistics* 5, 368-378.

Kimball, J. (1973) "Get," in J. Kimball, ed., *Syntax and Semantics* 1, Seminar Press, New York.

Kimenyi, A. (1980) *A Relational Grammar of Kinyarwanda,* University of California Press, Berkeley.

Koopman, H. (1984) *Verb Phrase Syntax,* Foris, Dordrecht.

Koster, J. (1978a) "Conditions, Empty Nodes and Markedness," *Linguistic Inquiry* 9, 551-594.

Koster, J. (1978b) "Why Subject Sentences don't Exist," in S. J. Keyser, ed., *Recent Transformational Studies in European Languages*, MIT Press, Cambridge.

Koster, J. (1984) "On Binding and Control," *Linguistic Inquiry* 15, 417-459.

Koster, J. and R. May (1982) "On the Constituency of Infinitives," *Language* 58, 116-143.

Kubo, M. (1992) "Japanese Passives," *Hokkaido University Institute of Language and Culture Studies* 23, 231-301.

Kubo, M. (1993a) "Domain and Principles of Japanese Word Accent," *Hokkaido University Institute of Language and Culture Studies* 24, 131-178.

Kubo, M. (1993b) "Are Subject Small Clauses Really Small Clauses?" in Y. Otsu, ed., *MITA Working Papers in Psycholinguistics 3*, Keio University, Tokyo.

Kubo, M. (1994) *Japanese Syntactic Structures and their Constructional Meanings*, Hituzi Syobo, Tokyo.

Kubo, M. (1996) "Some Considerations on Noun Clauses and Numeral Classifiers: A Study of (Pseudo)partitives in Japanese and English," *Keio Studies in Theoretical Linguistics* 1, 89-124.

Kuroda, S.-Y. (1965) *Generative Grammatical Studies in the Japanese Language*, MIT doctoral dissertation. [Reprinted in 1979 by Garland Press, New York.]

Kuroda, S.-Y. (1992) "Whether We Agree or Not: A Comparative Syntax of English and Japanese," in *Japanese Syntax and Semantics, Collected Papers*, Kluwer Academic Press, Dordrecht.

Laka, M. I. (1990) *Negation in Syntax: on the Nature of Functional Categories and Projections*, MIT doctoral dissertation.

Lakatos, I. (1978) *The Methodology of Scientific Research Programmes*, Cambridge University Press, Cambridge.

Lakoff, G. and J. Ross (1966) "A Criterion for Verb Phrase Constituency," *National Science Foundation Report* 17, Harvard University Computation Laboratory, Cambridge.

Lapointe, S. (1980) *A Theory of Grammatical Agreement*, University of Massachusetts doctoral dissertation.

Lappin, S. (1991) "Concepts of Logical Form in Linguistics and Philosophy," in A. Kasher, ed., *The Chomskyan Turn*, 301-333, Basil Blackwell, Oxford.

Lappin, S. and U. Shlonsky (1993) "Impersonal Passives," *Linguistics* 31, 5-24.

Larson, R. (1985) "Bare-NP Adverbs," *Linguistic Inquiry* 16, 595-621.

Larson, R. (1988) "On the Double Object Construction," *Linguistic Inquiry* 19, 335-391.

Larson, R. (1990) "Double Objects Revisited (Reply to Jackendoff), *Linguistic Inquiry* 21, 589-632.

Lasnik, H. (1991) "Language Acquisition and Two Types of Constraints," *Behavioral and Brain Sciences* 14.

Lasnik, H. and M. Saito (1984) "On the Nature of Proper Government," *Linguistic Inquiry* 15, 235-289.

Lee, S.-H. (1993) "The Syntax of Serialization in Korean," in P. M. Clancy, ed., *Japanese and Korean Linguistics 2*, Stanford University, Stanford.

Lefebvre, C. (1988) "Past Participle Agreement in French: Agreement = Case," in D. Birdsong and J. P. Montreuil, eds., *Advances in Romance Linguistics: Publications in Language Sciences* 28, 233-251.

Levin, B. and M. Rappaport (1986) "The Formation of Adjectival Passives," *Linguistic Inquiry* 17, 623-661.

Lieber, R. (1980) *On the Organization of the Lexicon*, MIT doctoral dissertation.

Lieber, R. (1983) "Argument Linking and Compounds in English," *Linguistic Inquiry* 14, 251-286.

Lobeck, A. (1986) *Syntactic Constraints on VP Ellipsis*, University of Washington doctoral dissertation.

Lobeck, A. (1995) *Ellipsis: Functional Heads, Licensing, and Identification*, Oxford University Press, Oxford.

Longobardi, G. (1980) "Remarks on Infinitives: A Case for a Filter," *Journal of Italian Linguistics* 5, 101-155.

Longobardi, G. (1994) "Reference and Proper Names: A Theory of N-Movement in Syntax and Logical Form," *Linguistic Inquiry* 23, 609-665.

Manzini, R. and K. Wexler (1987) "Parameters, Binding Theory and Learnability," *Linguistic Inquiry* 18, 413-444.

Marantz, A. (1984) *On the Nature of Grammatical Relations,* MIT Press, Cambridge.

Mateos, A. (1996) *The Categorial Status of Locative Words in Spanish*, unpublished paper, University of Durham.

Maylor, R. (1999) *The Morphosyntax of the German Inseparable Prefixes in a Figure/ Ground Framework,* University of Durham doctoral dissertation.

McA'Nulty, J. (1983) "Moving Features of [e]," paper given at the Southern California Conference on Romance Linguistics. [Revised in A.-M. di Sciullo and A. Rochette, eds., *Binding in Romance*, Canadian Linguistic Association, Ottawa.]

Miller, P. (1992) *Clitics and Complements in Phrase Structure Grammar*, Garland Press, New York.

Milner, J.-C. (1973) *Arguments Linguistiques,* Editions Mame, Paris.

Milner, J.-C. (1978) *De la Syntaxe à l'Interprétation*, Le Seuil, Paris.

Milner, J.-C. (1982) *Ordres et Raisons de Langue,* Le Seuil, Paris.

Murasugi, K. (1991) *Noun Phrases in Japanese and English: a Study in Syntax, Learnability and Acquisition*, University of Connecticut doctoral dissertation.

Murasugi, K. (1994) "Head-Internal Relative Clauses as Adjunct Pure Complex NPs," *Synchronic and Diachronic Approaches to Language: a Festschrift for Toshio Nakao,* Kaitakusha, Tokyo.

Murasugi, K. (2000) "Japanese Complex Noun Phrases and the Antisymmetry Theory," in R. Martin, D. Michaels and J. Uriagereka, eds., *Step by Step*, MIT Press, Cambridge.

Napoli, D. J. (1981) "Semantic Interpretation vs. Lexical Governance," *Language* 57, 841-887.

Ouhalla, J. (1991) *Functional Categories and Parametric Variation,* Routledge and Kegan Paul, London.

Perlmutter, D. (1971) *Deep and Surface Structure Constraints in Syntax*, Holt, Rinehart and Winston, New York.

Pesetsky, D. (1982) *Paths and Categories*, MIT doctoral dissertation.

Picallo, M. C. (1984) "The Infl Node and the Null Subject Parameter," *Linguistic Inquiry* 15, 75-101.

Pinker, S. (1989) *Learnability and Cognition: The Acquisition of Argument Structure*, MIT Press, Cambridge.

Plann, S. (1981) "The Two *el* + infinitive Constructions in Spanish," *Linguistic Analysis* 7, 203-240.

Platzack, C. (1982) "Transitive Adjectives in Swedish: a Phenomenon with Implications for the Theory of Abstract Case," *The Linguistic Review* 2, 39-56.

Postal, P. (1964) "Underlying and Superficial Linguistic Structure," *Harvard Educational Review* 34, 246-266.

Quicoli, C. (1980) "Clitic Movement in French Causatives," *Linguistic Analysis* 6, 131-185.

Randall, J. (1988) "Inheritance," in W. Wilkins, ed., *Thematic Roles: Syntax and Semantics* 21, Academic Press, New York.

Reinhart, T. (1983) *Anaphora and Semantic Interpretation*, University of Chicago Press, Chicago.

Riemsdijk, H. van (1978) *A Case Study in Syntactic Markedness: the Binding Nature of Prepositional Phrases,* Foris, Dordrecht.

Riemsdijk, H. van (1982) "Locality Principles in Syntax and Phonology," in I.-S. Yang, ed., *Linguistics in the Morning Calm*, Hanshin, Seoul.

Riemsdijk, H. van (1998a) "Head Movement and Adjacency," *Natural Language and Linguistic Theory* 16, 633-678.

Riemsdijk, H. van (1998b) "Categorial Feature Magnetism: the Endocentricity and Distribution of Projections," *Journal of Comparative Germanic Linguistics* 2, 1-48.

Riemsdijk, H. van and R. Huijbregts (1999) "Interface in Space – How Natural Language Expresses Spatial Relations," paper presented at the Third International Symposium on Language, Logic and Computation, Batumi.

Riemsdijk, H. van and E. Williams (1981) "NP-structure," *The Linguistic Review* 1, 171-217.

Ritter, E. (1988) "A Head-Movement Approach to Construct-State Noun Phrases," *Linguistics* 26, 909-929.

Ritter, E. (1993) "Where's Gender?" *Linguistic Inquiry* 24, 795-803.

Rizzi, L. (1978) "A Restructuring Rule in Italian Syntax," in S. J. Keyser, ed., *Recent Transformational Studies in European Languages*, MIT Press, Cambridge.

Rizzi, L. (1986) "Null Objects in Italian and the Theory of pro," *Linguistic Inquiry* 17, 501-557.

Rochette, A. (1988) *Semantic and Syntactic Aspects of Romance Sentential Complementation*, MIT doctoral dissertation.

Rosenbaum, P. (1967) *The Grammar of English Predicate Complement Constructions,* MIT Press, Cambridge.

Ross, J. (1967) *Constraints on Variables in Syntax,* MIT doctoral dissertation. [Republished as *Infinite Syntax,* Garland Press, New York.]

Ross, J. (1973) "Act'" in D. Birdsong and G. Harman, eds., *Semantics of Natural Languages,* Kluwer Academic Press, Dordrecht.

Rouveret, A. and J.-R. Vergnaud (1980) "Specifying Reference to the Subject: French Causatives and Conditions on Representations," *Linguistic Inquiry* 11, 97-202.

Safir, K. (1985) *Syntactic Chains,* Cambridge University Press, Cambridge.

Sapir, E. (1921) *Language,* Harcourt, Brace and World, New York.

Saussure, F. de (1916) *Cours de Linguistique Générale,* Payot, Paris.

Selkirk, E. (1977) "Some Remarks on Noun Phrase Structure," in P. Culicover, T. Wasow and A. Akmajian, eds., *Formal Syntax,* Academic Press, New York.

Selkirk, E. (1982) *The Syntax of Words,* MIT Press, Cambridge.

Sells, P. (1996) "The Projection of Phrase Structure and Argument Structure in Japanese," in T. Gunji, ed., *Studies on the Universality of Constraint-Based Phrase Structure Grammars,* Osaka University Graduate School of Language and Culture, Osaka.

Siegel, D. (1973) "Nonsources of Unpassives," in J. Kimball, ed., *Syntax and Semantics* 2 Seminar Press, New York.

Siloni, T. (1997) *Noun Phrases and Nominalizations: the Syntax of DPs,* Kluwer Academic Press, Dordrecht.

Sobin, M. (1985) "Case Assignment in Ukrainian Morphological Passive Constructions," *Linguistic Inquiry* 16, 649-662.

Speas, M. (1990) *Phrase Structure in Natural Language,* Kluwer Academic Press, Dordrecht.

Sportiche, D. (1992) *Clitic Constructions,* unpublished paper, University of California at Los Angeles.

Stockwell, R., P. Schachter and B. Partee (1973) *The Major Syntactic Structures of English,* Holt, Rinehart and Winston, New York.

Stowell, T. (1981) *Origins of Phrase Structure,* MIT doctoral dissertation.

Szabolcsi, A. (1987) "Functional Categories in the Noun Phrase," in. I. Kenesei, ed., *Approaches to Hungarian* 2, 167-189.

Szabolcsi, A. (1989) "Noun Phrases and Clauses: is DP analogous to IP or to CP?" in J. Payne, ed., *The Structure of Noun Phrases,* Mouton, Amsterdam.

Talmy, L. (1975) "Semantics and Syntax of Motion," in J. Kimball, ed., *Syntax and Semantics,* Academic Press, New York.

Talmy, L. (1978) "Figure and Ground in Complex Sentences," in J. Greenberg, ed., *Universals of Human Language: Syntax,* vol. 4, Stanford University Press, Stanford.

Tsimpli, I.-M. and J. Ouhalla (1990) *Functional Categories, UG and Modularity,* unpublished paper, University College and Queen Mary and Westfield College, London.

Veselovská, L. (1998) "Possessive Movement in the Czech Nominal Phrase," *Journal of Slavic Linguistics* 6, 255-300.

Veselovská, L. (2000) "Agreement Patterns of Czech Group Nouns and Quantifiers," in N. Corver and H. van Riemsdijk, eds., *The Function of Content Words and the Content of Function Words,* Mouton de Gruyter, Berlin.

Vikner, S. (1995) *Verb Movement and Expletive Subjects in the Germanic Languages,* Oxford University Press, Oxford.

Walinska de Hackbeil, H. (1984) "On Two Types of Derived Nominals," in D. Testen, V. Mishra and J. Drogo, eds., *Papers from the Parasession on Lexical Semantics,* Chicago Linguistics Society, Chicago.

Walinska de Hackbeil, H. (1985) "*En-* Prefixation and the Syntactic Domain of Zero Derivation," *Proceedings of the 11th Annual Meeting of the Berkeley Linguistics Society,* Berkeley Linguistics Society, Berkeley.

Walinska de Hackbeil, H. (1986) *The Roots of Phrase Structure: the Syntactic Basis of English Morphology,* University of Washington doctoral dissertation.

Wasow, T. (1972) *Anaphoric Relations in English,* MIT doctoral dissertation.

Wasow, T. (1977) "Transformations and the Lexicon," in P. Culicover, T. Wasow and A. Akmajian, eds., *Formal Syntax,* Academic Press, New York.

Wasow, T. and T. Roeper (1972) "On the Subject of Gerunds," *Foundations of Language* 8, 44-61.

Whitney, R. (1983) "The Place of Dative Movement in Generative Theory," *Linguistic Analysis* 12, 315-322.

Williams, E. (1975) "Small Clauses in English," in J. Kimball, ed., *Syntax and Semantics* 4, Academic Press, New York.

Williams, E. (1977) "Discourse and Logical Form," *Linguistic Inquiry* 8, 103-139.

Williams, E. (1980) "Predication," *Linguistic Inquiry* 11, 203-238.

Williams, E. (1981) "Argument Structure and Morphology," *The Linguistic Review* 1, 81-114.

Zaenen, A., J. Maling and H. Thrainsson (1985) "Case and Grammatical Functions: the Icelandic Passive," *Natural Language and Linguistic Theory* 3, 441-483.

Zagona, K. (1982) *Government and Proper Government of Verbal Projections,* University of Washington doctoral dissertation.

Zagona, K. (1988) *Verb Phrase Syntax: A Parametric Study of English and Spanish,* Kluwer Academic Press, Dordrecht.

Zubizarreta, M.-L. (1987) *Levels of Representation in the Lexicon and in the Syntax,* Foris, Dordrecht.

Zwicky, A. (1971) "In a manner of speaking," *Linguistic Inquiry* 2, 223-233.

Subject Index

Bold page numbers indicate the most important references to the heading. Italic page references indicate the footnotes. Please also consult Table of Contents.